Collection Constitutional Law

Directed by
Domingo García Belaunde

Edited by
Carlos Antonio Agurto Gonzáles
Sonia Lidia Quequejana Mamani
María-Pía Guadalupe Díaz Díaz
Benigno Choque Cuenca

Allan R. Brewer-Carías
Emeritus Professor of Law, Central University of Venezuela
Adjunct Professor of Law, Columbia Law School, New York (2006-2008)
Vice President, International Academy of Comparative Law (1982-2010)

THE CIVIL RIGHTS INJUNCTION FOR THE PROTECTION OF FUNDAMENTAL RIGHTS THE LATIN AMERICAN «AMPARO» PROCEEDING

Course of lectures 2006-2008

editorial jurídica venezolana

Ediciones Olejnik

Title of a book:
THE CIVIL RIGHTS INJUNCTION FOR THE PROTECTION OF FUNDAMENTAL RIGHTS
THE LATIN AMERICAN «AMPARO» PROCEEDING
COURSE OF LECTURES 2006-2008

Huérfanos 611, Santiago - Chile
E-mail: contacto@edicionesolejnik.com
Web site: http://www.edicionesolejnik.com

ISBN: 978-956-392-972-0

Diseño de Carátula: Ena Zuñiga
Diagramación: Luis A. Sierra Cárdenas

La primera edición de Ediciones Olejnik fue impresa en Argentina, 2021

La reimpresión en coedición entre Ediciones Olejnik y Editorial Jurídica Venezolana fue impresa por Lightning Source, an Ingram Company, para Editorial Jurídica International Inc., 2021

ÍNDICE

PREFACE
WITH SOME COMMENTS ON THE AMPARO AS AN INSTRUMENT OF IUS CONSTITUTIONALE COMMUNE

I. THE INTERNATIONALIZATION OF THE AMPARO PROCEEDING 17
II. GENERAL FEATURES OF THE AMPARO PROCEEDING IN LATIN AMERICAN COMPARATIVE CONSTITUTIONAL LAW 23
1. The injured party 23
2. Justiciable constitutional rights 23
3. The extraordinary character of the amparo proceeding 24
4. The injury in the amparo proceeding 24
5. The injuring party 24
6. The injuring public actions or omissions 25
7. Adjudication in the amparo proceeding 26
III. THE ENFORCEMENT OF THE IUS COMMUNE PRINCIPLES OF THE AMPARO PROCEEDING BY THE INTER-AMERICAN COURT OF HUMAN RIGHTS 27
FINAL REFLECTIONS 31

INTRODUCTION 35

CHAPTER I
THE CONSTITUTIONAL DECLARATIONS OF HUMAN RIGHTS IN LATIN AMERICA

I. Rights: constitutional rights, human rights, civil rights, fundamental rights 39
II. The constitutional declarations of human rights 41
1. The North American and French Declarations 41
2. The Influence in Latin America 45
3. The Situation in France 47
III. The expansion of the constitutional declarations of rights beginning with the individual and civil rights 50
1. The Individual and Civil Rights 50
2. The social, economic and cultural rights 54
3. The collective rights 57
4. The problem of the relation between rights and obligation in the constitutional declarations 60
IV. Changes in the obliged party regarding constitutional rights and freedoms 63
V. The declarative nature of the constitutional Declarations of rights and the open constitutional clauses 64
VI. Absolute or limitative character of the Declarations 69

CHAPTER II
THE CONSTITUTIONALIZATION OF THE INTERNATIONALIZATION OF HUMAN RIGHTS

I. The constitutional and international regulations 71
II. The American internationalization of human rights 74
III. The constitutionalization of the internationalization of human rights 83
 1. The supra constitutional rank of international instruments of human rights 83
 2. The constitutional rank of international instruments of human rights 93
 3. The supra statutory rank of international treaties on human rights .. 99
 4. The statutory rank of international treaties on human rights 103
IV. The interpretative constitutional rules regarding the international instruments on human rights 106
 1. The constitutional general references to the universal declarations on human rights 108
 2. The enforcement of rights regardless of their statutory regulation ... 111
 3. The principle of progressive interpretation of constitutional rights .. 112

CHAPTER III
THE JUDICIAL MEANS FOR THE PROTECTION OF HUMAN RIGHTS

I. The constitutional guarantees to the Declarations of Rights 117
II. The Judicial guarantee of constitutional rights 120
 1. The right to have access to justice and the protection of rights 120
 2. Judicial means for the protection of constitutional rights 126
 3. The United States judicial means for the protection of rights (including constitutional rights) 126
 4. The protection of human rights in France and Italy through the general judicial means 131
III. THE SPECIFIC JUDICIAL MEANS FOR THE PROTECTION OF HUMAN RIGHTS 134
 1. Origins of the Latin American «amparo» suit 134
 2. The judicial review methods as means for the protection of human rights 138
 3. The European «amparo» actions 141

CHAPTER IV
THE LATIN AMERICAN «AMPARO» ACTION OR RECOURSE AND THE AMERICAN CONVENTION ON HUMAN RIGHTS

I. The «amparo» action, recourse or suit: a Latin American constitutional Institution 145
 1. Constitutions establishing the three protective judicial means: amparo, habeas corpus and habeas data 146
  A. «Amparo», habeas corpus and habeas data in Argentina 146
  B. «Mandado de segurança», «mandado de injunção», habeas corpus and habeas data in Brazil 147
  C. «Amparo», habeas corpus and habeas data in Ecuador 148
  D. «Amparo», habeas corpus and habeas data in Paraguay 151
  E. «Amparo», habeas corpus and habeas data in Perú 153

2. Constitutions establishing the two protective judicial means: amparo and habeas corpus 154
A. «Amparo» and habeas corpus in Bolivia 154
B. Recourse for «tutela» and habeas corpus in Colombia 156
C. «Amparo» and habeas corpus in Costa Rica 157
D. Recourses for protection and of habeas corpus in Chile 158
E. «Amparo» and habeas corpus in El Salvador 159
F. «Amparo» and habeas corpus in Honduras 160
G. «Amparo» and habeas corpus in Nicaragua 161
H. «Amparo» and habeas corpus in Panama 161
I. Habeas corpus in Uruguay 162
J. Habeas corpus in Dominican Republic 163
3. Constitutions Establishing the Amparo as the General Protective Judicial Means 164
A. «Amparo» in Guatemala 164
B. Suit for «amparo» in México 164
C. «Amparo» in Venezuela 166
II. The internationalization of the «amparo» in the Latin America 169
1. The «amparo» in the American Convention on Human Rights 171
2. The meaning of the regulation of the «amparo» in the American Convention 173
3. The «amparo» as a Human Right 174
4. The «amparo» as a judicial guarantee 175
5. The «amparo» as a simple, prompt and effective judicial guarantee .. 176
6. The «amparo» as a judicial guarantee for the protection of everyone's rights and guarantees 177
7. The «amparo» as a judicial guarantee for the protection of all constitutional rights and guarantees 178
8. The «amparo» as a judicial guarantee for the protection of all constitutional rights and guarantees, against any violation or harm from the State or individuals 180
9. The «amparo» as a judicial guarantee that can be filed at any time, including in situations of emergency 182

CHAPTER V

THE AMPARO AS A CONSTITUTIONAL REMEDY WITHIN THE LATIN AMERICAN DIFFUSE AND CONCENTRATED SYSTEMS OF JUDICIAL REVIEW OF LEGISLATION

I. The amparo as a specific judicial guarantee for the protection of constitutional rights and freedoms and the systems of judicial review of legislation 185
II. The amparo action in countries with only a diffuse system of judicial review: the case of Argentina 190
III. The amparo action in countries with only a concentra-ted system of judicial review 201
1. The amparo action exercised before one single tribunal: the Constitutional Chamber of the Supreme Court in Costa Rica and El Salvador 201
A. The recourse of amparo in Costa Rica 202
B. The recourse of amparo in El Salvador 204

2. The amparo action exercised before a universality of courts: the case of Bolivia, Chile, Honduras, Panama, Paraguay and Uruguay ... 205
A. The recourse of amparo in Bolivia ... 206
B. The «recourse of protection» in Chile ... 207
C. The action of amparo in Honduras ... 210
D. The action of amparo in Panamá ... 212
E. The petition for amparo in Paraguay ... 214
F. The action of amparo in Uruguay ... 215

CHAPTER VI
THE AMPARO AS A CONSTITUTIONAL REMEDY WITHIN THE LATIN AMERICAN MIXED SYSTEMS (DIFfUSE AND CONCENTRATED) OF JUDICIAL REVIEW OF LEGISLATION

I. The amparo action or recourse in mixed systems of judicial review, exercised before one single tribunal: the case of the Supreme Court of Nicaragua ... 220
II. The amparo action or recourse in mixed systems of judicial review exercised before a universality of courts: the case of México, Venezuela, Brazil, Colombia, Domini-can Republic, Ecuador, Guatemala and Perú .. 221
1. The «amparo» as a constitutional right ... 223
A. The Mexican suit of «amparo» ... 223
B. The right to «amparo» in Venezuela ... 230
2. The amparo action or recourse as a constitutional guarantee ... 251
A. The actions of constitutional protection in Brazil ... 251
B. The action of «tutela» in Colombia ... 256
C. The action of amparo in Dominican Republic ... 260
D. The action of amparo in Ecuador ... 261
E. The «amparo» in Guatemala ... 263
F. The recourse of amparo in Perú ... 266

CHAPTER VII
THE JUSTICIABLE CONSTITUTIONAL RIGHTS BY MEANS OF THE «AMPARO» AND HABEAS CORPUS ACTIONS

I. Constitutional rights and justiciability ... 269
II. Amparo for the justiciability of constitutional rights only in cases of constitutional violations ... 271
III. Amparo and habeas corpus for the protection of all constitutional rights .. 274
IV. Amparo and habeas corpus for the protection of only some constitutional rights ... 280
1. The European antecedents ... 280
2. The Chilean «acción de protección» for the protection of some constitutional rights ... 284
3. The Colombian «action de tutela» for the protection of fundamental rights ... 285
4. The mexican amparo suit for the protection of only the «individual guarantees» ... 287
V. The question of the protection of rights in situations of emergency ... 289

CHAPTER VIII
THE QUESTION OF THE JUSTICIABILITY OF SOCIAL CONSTITUTIONAL RIGHTS BY MEANS OF THE «AMPARO» ACTION

I. The question of the justiciability of social rights 295
II. The case of the right to health in Latin American Constitutions and the State's obligations 297
III. The justiciability of the right to health 301
1. The right to health and the State's financial resources 306
2. The rejection to protect the right to health in an abstract way 307

CHAPTER IX
TI IE EXTRAORDINARY CHARACTER OF THE AMPARO ACTION AND THE GENERAL PROCEDURAL RULES OF THE SUIT

I. The extraordinary character of the amparo 311
1. The question of the previous exhaustion of the ordinary judicial means 312
2. The question of the non availability of other adequate judicial or administrative means for protection 315
3. The question of the previous election of other remedies that are pending of decision, including amparo suits 320
II. The character of the amparo suit procedure 323
1. The brief character of the procedure 323
2. The brief and prompt nature of the procedure 324
III. The principles governing the preferred character of the procedure 325
1. General provisions regarding the filing of the petition 326
3. The decision regarding the admissibility of the petition 329
4. The defendant (the injurer or aggrieving party) pleading or answer 330
5. The hearing in the amparo suit 331

CHAPTER X
THE PROTECTED PERSONS: THE INJURED PARTY IN THE AMPARO SUIT INDIVIDUAL AND COLLECTIVE ACTIONS AND THE GENERAL STANDING CONDITIONS

I. The parties in the amparo suit 333
II. The injured party 335
1. Injured persons and standing 336
2. Natural persons: Standing ad causam and ad processum 338
3. Artificial persons: Standing at causam and ad processum 341
III. Standing and the protection of collective and iffuse constitutional rights 345
IV. The Peoples' Defendant standing on the amparo suit 354
V. The question of other public (State) institutions standing on the amparo suit 358
VI. The injured third party 360

CHAPTER XI
THE DAMAGING OR INJURING PARTY IN THE AMPARO SUIT, AND THE ACTS OR OMISSIONS CAUSING THE HARM OR THE THREATS TO CONSTITUTIONAL RIGHTS

I. The question of the individuation of the defendant 363
II. The defendant in the amparo suit: authorities and individuals 368

III. The amparo against public authorities: public entities and public officers 369
1. The Amparo against legislative actions ... 374
A. Amparo against parliamentary bodies' and their commissions' decisions ... 374
B. Amparo against laws (statutes) ... 375
2. Amparo against executive and administrative acts and actions ... 381
3. Amparo against judicial acts and decisions ... 385
4. Amparo against acts of other constitutional entities ... 387
5. The amparo action and the political questions ... 388
6. The amparo against executive and administrative omissions ... 390
IV. THE Amparo against individuals or private persons ... 392
V. The participation of third parties for the defendant in the amparo suit ... 395

CHAPTER XII
THE MOTIVES FOR THE AMPARO SUIT: THE INJURY OR THE THREAT OF VIOLATION TO THE PLAINTIFF'S CONSTITUTIONAL RIGHTS

I. The general personal and direct character of the injury ... 397
II. The arbitrary, illegal and illegitimate manifest injury ... 399
III. The actual and real character of the injury ... 400
IV. The restorative nature of amparo suit and the reparable character of the injury ... 403
V. The preventive nature of amparo suit and the imminent character of the threat ... 407
VI. The non consented character of the injury ... 414
VII. Exceptions to the tacit consent rule ... 416

CHAPTER XIII
JUDICIAL ADJUDICATIONS IN THE «AMPARO» SUIT: PRELIMINARY MEASURES AND DEFINITIVE RULINGS: PREVENTIVE AND RESTORATIVE DECISIONS

I. PRELIMINARY MEASURES IN THE AMPARO SUIT ... 422
1. The suspension of the effects of the challenged act ... 423
2. The order not to adopt innovative actions ... 426
3. The other preliminary protective measures ... 427
4. The conditions for the issuing of preliminary protective measures ... 427
5. The inaudita pars issuing of the preliminary protective measures ... 428
II. THE DEFINITIVE JUDICIAL ADJUDICATION IN THE AMPARO SUIT ... 429
1. The preventive and restorative nature of the amparo ... 430
2. The question of the annulling content of the amparo decision ... 432
3. The non compensatory character of the amparo decision ... 434
4. The effects of the definitive judicial ruling on the amparo suit ... 436
A. The inter partes effects and its exceptions ... 436
B. The question of the scope of the res judicata effects ... 438
III. THE OBLIGATORY CHARACTER OF THE AMPARO RULINGS AND THE PUNISHMENT FOR CONTEMPT ... 441
IV. THE REVISION OF THE AMPARO DECISIONS BY A CONSTITUTIONAL COURT OR THE SUPREME COURT ... 442

PREFACE

WITH SOME COMMENTS ON THE AMPARO AS AN INSTRUMENT OF *IUS CONSTITUTIONALE COMMUNE*

I

This book on *The Civil Rights Injunction for the protection of Fundamental Rights. The Latin American «Amparo» Proceeding*, is the original version of the text I wrote for the Couse of Lectures I gave, as Adjunct Professor of Law, on a Seminar on *Judicial Protection of Fundamental Rights in Latin America: the Amparo Proceeding*, at the Columbia Law School in New York, University of Columbia, during the years 2006-2008.* Thanks to the iniciative of Professor Geroge Bergman of the Columbia Law School, and President of the International Academy of Comparative Law, I was able to continue my teaching at a time when I was beginning my now long exile in New York.

The Seminar was intended to examine the most recent trends in the constitutional and legal regulations in all Latin American countries regarding the «amparo» suit, action or recourse- including the old *habeas corpus* writ and the new *habeas data* actions or recourses. By means of a comparative constitutional law approach, also with reference to the United States civil rights injunctions, the Course analyzed this Latin American institution departing from the regulation of the «amparo» guarantee established in Article 25 of the 1969 American Convention of Human Rights which entered into force in 1978 after being ratified by all Latin American States.

The amparo suit or proceeding is not only an effective judicial means for the restoration of the injured constitutional rights that has been harmed, similar to the reparative or restorative civil rights injunctions in the United States, but it is also the effective judicial means for the protection of such rights and guaranties when threatened to be violated or harmed. This latter amparo suit is then similar to the preventive civil rights injunctions in the United States; «preventive» in the

---

* This original version of the Course of Lecture was initially published by the Columbia Law School for the exclusive use of the students (New York, 2006, 383 pp.); and was included in my book: *Judicial Review. Comparative Constitucional Law Essays, Lectures and Courses (1985-2011)*, Fundación de Derecho Público, Editorial Jurídica Venezolana, Caracas 2014, pp. 435-847. An abridge and revised version of this Course of Lectures was published in 2009: *Constitutional Protection of Human Rights in Latin America. A Comparative Study of Amparo Proceedings*, Cambridge University Press, New York 2009, 432 pp.

sense of avoiding harm;[1] which, in this case, «seeks to prohibit some discrete act or series of acts from occurring in the future»[2], and is designed to avoid future harm to a party by prohibiting or mandating certain behavior to another party.

From that point of view, thus, in a constitutional comparative law approach, the Latin American amparo action or proceeding, is a judicial remedy similar to the civil rights injunctions (restorative or preventive) in the United States.

Although during the past years some changes have occurred in some of the Latin American countries on these matters of judicial protection of fundamental rights, I have decided to publish the lectures delivered fifteen years ago, in its integrality, as they were: the written work of a law professor made as a consequence of his research for the preparation of his lectures, not pretending to be anything else, but the academic testimony of the state of the subject of the amparo proceeding in Latin America in 2006-2008.

II

That is why, in this Preface, as a sort of specific update, I am including the following comments on the «Amparo as an instrument of *Ius Constitutionale Commune*»,[*] referring in general to this injunction against any kind of violation affecting fundamental rights, in particular, when committed by public officials,[3] which without doubts, is perhaps the most Latin American of all constitutional law institutions developed in the continent.

The amparo proceeding serves as the common judicial guarantee of rights. It is meant to protect, not only the rights established in national constitutional law, but also those found in the relevant applicable international law, those which are part of the «constitutional block' (*bloque de constitutionalidad*) of all Latin American

---

1 See William M. TABB and Eliane W. SHOBEN, *Remedies*, Thomson West, 2005, p. 22. The last sentence is very important from the terminological point of view when comparing the injunctions with the amparo suits: in Spanish the word «*preventivo*» is used in procedural law (*medidas preventivas o cautelares*) to refers to the «temporary»: or «preliminary» orders or restraints that in North America the judge can issue during the proceeding. So the preventive character of the amparo and of the injunctions cannot be confused with the «*medidas preventivas*» or temporary or preliminary measures that the courts can issue during the trial for the immediate protection of rights, facing the prospect of an irremediable harm that can be caused.

2 See Owen M. Fiss, *The Civil Rights Injunction*, Indiana University Press, 1978, p. 7.

* These comments are based on the paper I wrote on the «Amparo as an instrument of *ius constitutionale commune*» for the book edited by: Armin von Bogdandy, Eduardo Ferrer Mad-Gregor, Mariekla Morales Antoniazzi, Flávia Piovesan and Ximena Soley (Editrors), *Transformative Constitutionalism In Latin America. The Emergence of a New Ius Commune*, Oxford University Press 2017, pp. 171-190.

3 This remedy has received different denominations, always meaning the same: *Amparo* (Guatemala), *Acción de amparo* (Argentina, Ecuador, Honduras, Paraguay, Uruguay, Venezuela), *Acción de tutela* (Colombia), *Juicio de amparo* (México), *Proceso de amparo* (El Salvador, Perú), *Recurso de amparo* (Bolivia, Costa Rica, Dominican Republic, Nicaragua, Panama), *Recurso de protección* (Chile) or *Mandado de segurança* and *mandado de injunçao* (Brazil). See Allan R. Brewer-Carías, *Constitutional Protection of Human Rights in Latin America: A Comparative Stury of the Amparo Proceeding*, Cambridge University Press, New York, 2008); *El amparo a los derechos y garantías constitucionales. Una aproximación comparativa*, Editorial Jurídica Venezolana, Caracas, 1993; Eduardo Ferrer Mac-Gregor, «Breves notas sobre el amparo latinoamericano (desde el derecho procesal constitucional comparado)», in Héctor Fix-Zamudio and Ferrer Mac-Gregor, *El derecho de amparo en el mundo* (Porrúa, México City, 2006) 3-39.

countries, and which give common orientation to national legal orders. The long history of the amparo, which goes back to the early 19th century, has not made it lose its relevance. Today it connects national law with international law, thus allowing the development of a common comparative legal approach.

The trust placed by citizens on the judicial branch in Latin American countries varies from country to country and throughout history. Sometimes this level of trust is quite low but on other occasions, particularly during periods of democratic rule, the judiciary has enjoyed high levels of approval. Particularly at such times they have contributed substantively to updating and unfolding the potential of this legal institute, often jointly with the Inter-American system for the protection of human rights.

After the introduction of amparo proceedings in México, the institution spread across all Latin America. In the different countries where it was adopted it took on slightly different forms, becoming in many cases more protective than the original Mexican institution.[4] The amparo was introduced in the second half of the nineteenth century in the constitutions of Guatemala (1879), El Salvador (1886) and Honduras (1894); and during the twentieth century, in the constitutions of Nicaragua (1911), Brazil (*mandado de securança*, 1934), Panama (1941), Costa Rica (1949), Venezuela (1961), Bolivia, Paraguay, Ecuador (1967), Perú (1976), Chile (*recurso de protección*, 1976), Uruguay (1988), and Colombia (*acción de tutela*, 1991). In 1957, the writ of amparo was introduced in Argentina through court decisions; it was regulated in a special statute in 1966, and subsequently included in the 1994 Constitution. Since 2000, the Supreme Court of the Dominican Republic also admitted the writ of amparo, which in 2006 was regulated in a special statute, and incorporated in the 2010 Constitution.

As a consequence of various constitutional processes, all Latin American countries, with the exception of Cuba, have adopted the writs of habeas corpus and amparo as specific judicial mechanisms exclusively designed for the protection of constitutional rights. In all countries of the region, the writs are expressly enshrined in the constitution; and in all of them, except in Chile, the proceeding has been the object of statutory regulation.

These statutes are, in general, of a special nature, adopted for the specific purpose of regulating amparo proceedings (Argentina, Brazil, Colombia, Dominican Republic, México, Nicaragua, Uruguay, Venezuela); or else they refer, in general, to the constitutional jurisdiction or to constitutional procedures (Bolivia, Guatemala, Perú, Costa Rica, Ecuador, El Salvador, Honduras, Dominican Republic). Only in Panama and Paraguay is the amparo regulated in the general procedural codes. Chile is the only country that has not promulgated a statute regulating the amparo, the general procedural rules that govern it were established by the Chilean Supreme Court.

In some constitutions, for example in Guatemala, México and Venezuela, the writ of amparo is meant to protect all constitutional rights and freedoms, including personal liberty, in which case the habeas corpus is considered a type of amparo, and is referred to, for instance, as a writ for personal exhibition (Guatemala) or amparo for the protection of personal freedom (Venezuela). However, in general, in all other Latin American countries (Argentina, Bolivia, Brazil, Colombia, Costa

[4] See Joaquín Brage Camazano, *La Jurisdicción constitucional de la libertad: Teoría general, Argentina, México*, Corte Interamericana de Derechos Humanos (Porrúa, México City 2005, 156ff.

Rica, Chile, the Dominican Republic, Ecuador, El Salvador, Honduras, Nicaragua, Panama, Paraguay, Perú and Uruguay), in addition to the writ of amparo, a separate writ of habeas corpus has always been expressly established in the constitution for the specific protection of personal freedom and integrity. In recent times, in some countries (Argentina, Ecuador, Paraguay, Perú and Venezuela), in addition to the writs of amparo and habeas corpus, constitutions have also provided for a writ of habeas data (Argentina, Brazil, Ecuador, Paraguay, Perú, Venezuela), by which any person can file a suit requesting access to data which refers to them and is stored in public or private registries or data banks. If the information found is false, inaccurate or discriminatory, claimants may seek its suppression, rectification, confidentiality and update.

Today, there are three different scenarios in Latin America regarding available mechanisms for the protection of constitutional rights. Some countries offer three different remedies: the writs of amparo, habeas corpus and habeas data. This is the situation in Argentina, Brazil, Ecuador, Paraguay and Perú. Other countries offer two remedies: the amparo and the habeas corpus. This is the case in Bolivia, Colombia, Costa Rica, Chile, the Dominican Republic, El Salvador, Honduras, Nicaragua, Panama and Uruguay. Venezuela also has two remedies, but these are the writs of amparo and habeas data. And other countries like México and Guatemala, offer only one general writ of amparo, which also protects the right to personal freedom, exists.

In general terms, the rights protected by amparo proceedings are all those set forth in the constitution or those having constitutional rank. However, some constitutions reduce the protective scope of amparo protection to only some constitutional guarantees or fundamental rights, as is the case in Colombia and Chile. This model, where the only rights protected by the amparo are the rights to life, liberty and security, was also followed in Germany and Spain, and in the Philippines.

As mentioned before though, in Latin America, the writ of amparo is not only a remedy of national constitutional law, but also an international law institution. It was enshrined in the American Convention on Human Rights of 1969 (ACHR, the American Convention or the Convention) as the «right to judicial protection», that is, the right to «a simple and prompt recourse, or any other effective recourse, before a competent court or tribunal for protection against acts that violate his fundamental rights recognized by the constitution or laws of the state or by this Convention» (article 25). State parties to the Convention have the duty «to ensure that any person claiming such remedy shall have his rights determined by the competent authority provided for by the legal system of the state»; to develop «the possibilities of judicial remedy»; and «to ensure that the competent authorities shall enforce such remedies when granted».

In the words of the Inter-American Court of Human Rights (IACtHR, or the Inter-American Court), this article of the American Convention is a «general provision that gives expression to the procedural institution known as amparo».[5] The American Convention also foresees the writ of habeas corpus for the protection

[5] See IACtHR, Habeas Corpus in Emergency Situations (Arts. 27.2, 25.1 and 7.6 American Convention on Human Rights), Advisory Opinion OC-8/87, Series A No 8 (30 January 1987) para 32.

of the right to personal freedom and security (article 7). Examining both the writs of habeas corpus and amparo, the IACtHR has declared that the «amparo» comprises a whole series of remedies and that habeas corpus is but one of its components», so that in some instances «habeas corpus is considered either as the «amparo» of freedom or as an integral part of the «amparo».[6]

These provisions of the American Convention can be seen as the conclusion of a process of internationalization of the protection of human rights. In particular, article 25, on the right to judicial protection of rights, has become an institution of the *ius constitutionale commune*. After a long evolution, the IACtHR has interpreted the human right to «effective judicial protection» in the broadest sense, to include the right of access to justice. Thus, the Court has followed the lead of Judge Antonio Cançado Trindade in his dissenting opinion in the case of *Genie Lacayo v Nicaragua* of 29 January 1997, where he considered the provision not only as one of the «basic pillars of the Convention», but also «of the rule of law (État de Droit) itself in a democratic society (in the sense of the Convention)»;[7] an argument that was subsequently affirmed in the jurisprudence of the Inter-American Court in the judgment of *Castillo Páez v Perú* of November of that same year.[8] In this context, the right of amparo is only one of the pieces of the human right to judicial protection - a basic pillar of democracy - but it does not exhaust it. Access to justice, together with the guarantees of due process, (that is, article 25(1) in connection with article 8), make up this pillar.[9]

As stated by the IACtHR in *La Masacre de las Dos Erres v Guatemala*, the amparo is part of the «realm of article 25 of the American Convention, therefore it has to meet certain requirements, including suitability and effectiveness».[10] Thus, there are minimum parameters under which member states should fulfill their obligation to ensure all people not only of the existence but also the effectiveness of a simple and fast remedy to protect their rights. States must uphold these standards when adopting and regulating the amparo.

I. THE INTERNATIONALIZATION OF THE AMPARO PROCEEDING

The internationalization of the amparo proceeding in Latin America can be traced back to the 1948 American Declaration of the Rights and Duties of Man of the Organization of American States, the first international human rights declaration in the world. Article 18 of this declaration enshrined the «right to access to justice», in the following terms:

---

6 Ibid para 34.

7 IACtHR, *Case of Genie-Lacayo v Nicaragua* (13 September 1997), Application for Judicial Review of the Judgment of Merits, Reparations and Costs, Series C No 45, Dissenting opinion of judge Antônio A Cançado Trindade, para 18.

8 See IACtHR, *Case of Castillo Páez v Perú* (3 November 1997), Series C No 34, Merits, para 82.

9 That is why Anamari Garro Vargas believes that it «is not the same to state that the system of effective legal remedies is one of the pillars of the Convention and of the rule of law in a democratic system, than to argue that one of these pillars is a simple and effective remedy to protect the fundamental rights». See Anamari Garro Vargas, *La improcedencia del recurso de amparo contra las resoluciones y actuaciones jurisdiccionales del Poder Judicial a la luz de la Constitución costarricense y del artículo 25 de la Convención Americana sobre Derechos Humanos* (Doctoral dissertation), Universidad de los Andes, Santiago de Chile 2012, p. 213.

10 See decision in IACtHR, *Case of «Los Dos Erres Massacre» v Guatemala* (24 November 2009), Series C No 211, Preliminary Objections, Merits, Reparations and Costs, para 107.

«Article XVIII. Every person may resort to the courts to ensure respect for his legal rights. A simple and brief procedure should be available for the courts to protect every person (que lo ampare) against acts of authority that, to his prejudice, violate any of the fundamental rights constitutionally enshrined».

Article 8 of the Universal Declaration of Human Rights, adopted by the United Nations in December of the same year, is worded in similar terms. After these first two international declarations on human rights, the 1950 European Convention on Human Rights also regulated the «right to an effective remedy» (not necessarily of a judicial nature) before a national authority, even when the violation was committed by persons acting in an official capacity (article 13).

Subsequently, article 2(3) of the 1966 International Covenant on Civil and Political Rights of the United Nations, also included the right to an effective remedy (also not necessarily of a judicial nature) against human rights violations. This right could also be exercised against violations committed by persons acting in their official capacity.

Nonetheless, it was in the 1969 American Convention on Human Rights that the amparo proceeding was declared «the right to judicial protection», in the following terms:

«Article 25. Right to Judicial Protection

1. Everyone has the right to simple and prompt recourse, or any other effective recourse, before a competent court or tribunal for protection (que la ampare) against acts that violate his fundamental rights recognized by the constitution or laws of the state concerned or by this Convention, even though such violation may have been committed by persons acting in the course of their official duties».

To ensure this right, the Convention imposes the following obligations on states parties:

«a. to ensure that any person claiming such remedy shall have his rights determined by the competent authority provided for by the legal system of the state;

b. to develop the possibilities of judicial remedy; and

c. to ensure that the competent authorities shall enforce such remedies when granted».

The American Convention, in article 7 on the right to personal liberty and security, also provides for the writ of habeas corpus as follows:

6. Anyone who is deprived of his liberty shall be entitled to recourse to a competent court, in order that the court decides without delay on the lawfulness of his arrest or detention and order his release if the arrest or detention is unlawful...

Examining the habeas corpus and the amparo jointly, the IACtHR came to the following conclusion:

«The amparo comprises a whole series of remedies and that habeas corpus is but one of its components. An examination of the essential aspects of both guarantees, as embodied in the Convention and, in their different forms in the legal systems of the States parties, indicates that in some instances habeas corpus functions as an independent remedy. Here its primary purpose is to protect the personal freedom of those who are being detained or who have been threatened with detention. In other circumstances,

however, habeas corpus is viewed either as the amparo of freedom' or as an integral part of amparo».[11]

These provisions of the American Convention were the result of a process of internationalization in the protection of human rights - a process that began with the constitutionalization of the amparo proceeding. As a consequence of this process of internationalization, the right to a judicial guarantee of human rights (amparo and habeas corpus) has become an international obligation of state parties. A failure to regulate such remedies internally or to ensure their effective functioning constitutes a breach of the Convention.

This implies, according to the Inter-American Court on numerous decisions, that:

«The general obligation that the State should adapt its domestic laws to the provisions of the Convention to guarantee the rights it embodies, which is established in Article 2, includes the issuance of rules and the development of practices leading to effective enforcement of the rights and freedoms embodied in the Convention, and also the adoption of measures to derogate norms and practices of any kind that entail a violation of the guarantees established in the Convention. This general obligation of the State Party implies that the measures of domestic law must be effective (the principle of effet utile), and to this end the State must adapt its actions to the protection norms of the Convention».[12]

In effect, the most important consequence of the internationalization of the amparo, is that state parties are not only obligated «*to respect*» the right to amparo recognized in their constitutions, but also «*to ensure* to all persons subject to their jurisdiction the free and full exercise» of such right, without any discrimination (all this in accordance with article 1(1) ACHR). This «implies the duty of States Parties to organize the governmental apparatus and, in general, all the structures through which public power is exercised, so that they are capable of juridically ensuring the free and full enjoyment of human rights».[13]

To comply with this obligation, the actions of states parties may not be limited to formal measures. That is, the obligation is not fulfilled merely «by the existence of a legal system designed to make it possible» but rather it is also required that the government «conduct itself so as to effectively ensure the free and full exercise of human rights».[14] Referring to the amparo as a judicial guarantee of human rights, the IACtHR has held that «[...] for such a remedy to exist, it is not sufficient that it be provided for by the Constitution or by law or that it be formally recognized, but rather it must be truly effective in establishing whether there has been a violation of human rights and in providing redress»; «the absence of an effective remedy to

---

11 The Inter-American Court of Human Rights has considered «the writs of habeas corpus and of «amparo» among those judicial remedies that are essential for the protection of various rights whose derogation is prohibited by Article 27(2) and that serve, moreover, to preserve legality in a democratic society». Ibid para 42; IACtHR, Judicial Guarantees in States of Emergency (Arts. 27.2, 25 and 8 American Convention on Human Rights), Advisory Opinion OC-9/87, Series A No 9 (6 October 1987) para 33.

12 See decision in IACtHR, *Case of Yatama v Nicaragua* (23 June 2005), Series C No 127, para 170 (footnotes omitted).

13 IACtHR, Case of Velásquez Rodríguez v Honduras (29 July 1988), Series C No 4, Merits, para 166.

14 Ibid. para 167.

violations of the rights recognized by the Convention is itself a violation of the Convention by the State Party in which the remedy is lacking».[15]

Now, in accordance with article 25 ACHR, and considering in particular that the writ of amparo has been considered by the IACtHR, as «one of the fundamental pillars not only of the American Convention, but of the very rule of law in a democratic society in the terms of the Convention»;[16] the following four elements can be said to characterize the amparo in the Inter-American context:

First, the amparo is not only conceived as a specific judicial recourse or action, that is, as a judicial guaranty; but also as a fundamental human right in itself, that is to say, the right of citizens to be protected by the judiciary, as reaffirmed in the Mexican and Venezuelan legal systems. The wording of the ACHR confirms this. Article 25 provides for the «right to judicial protection», in the sense of individuals having at their disposal an effective, simple and prompt judicial means for the protection of their rights. Additionally, the right to judicial protection is considered one of the «fundamental» rights that cannot be suspended or restricted in a state of emergency (article 27).

This differentiates the provisions of the American Convention from those of the International Covenant on Civil and Political Rights (article 2(3)) and of the European Convention on Human Rights (article 13), which only provide for an effective remedy, without qualifying it as «judicial». Conversely, under the regime of the ACHR, protection can be obtained not only through a writ of amparo but also through other judicial means («any other effective remedy») for the protection of human rights. Accordingly, many Latin American lawmakers have determined that the writ of amparo has an extraordinary nature, in the sense that it is admitted only when there are no other effective judicial means to protect human rights (similar to Anglo-American injunctions).

However, despite the fact that the American Convention considers the amparo as a right in itself, in most Latin American countries, the amparo has been regulated as a specific adjective institution or remedy. Only in México and in Venezuela can it be said that the amparo is also conceived as a civil right in itself, one that can be exercised by multiple judicial recourses, in addition to the writ of amparo.

Second, the remedy is directed at protecting all the rights of every person. As mentioned before, the rights protected are not only those recognized in the constitution, and domestic statutes, but also those of the ACHR. This right belongs to everybody in the broadest sense, without distinction or discrimination of any kind: individuals, nationals, foreigners, legally capable or not, corporations or

---

[15] IACtHR, Judicial Guarantees in States of Emergency (n13), para 24. See in a similar sense IACtHR, Case of Mayagna (Sumo) Awas Tingni Community v Nicaragua (31 August 2001), Series C No 79, para 113; Case of Ivcher Bronstein v Perú (6 February 2001), Series C No 74, Merits, Reparations and Costs, para 136; Case of Cantoral Benavides v Perú (18 August 2000), Series C No 69, Merits, para 164; Case of Durand and Ugarte v Perú (16 August 2000), Series C No 68, Merits, para 102.

[16] See IACtHR, *Castillo Páez v Perú* (n8), para 82; Case of Suárez Rosero v Ecuador (12 November 1997), Series C No 35, Merits, para 65; and Case of Blake v Guatemala (24 January 1998), Series C No 36, Merits, para 102. See the references in Cecilia Medina Quiroga, *La Convención Americana: Teoría y jurisprudencia*, IIDH, San José, 2003, 358.

entities of public or private law;[17] including those acting in representation of diffuse or collective constitutional rights, the violation of which affects the community as a whole, as expressly established in the Argentinean, Brazilian, Colombian and Venezuelan constitutions.

Perhaps because of European influence, the Chilean and Colombian constitutions have limited the rights that can be protected by means of the *«recurso de protección»* and *«acción de tutela»*, respectively; a limitation that is eventually incompatible with the international obligations of these states under the ACHR.[18] Several Latin American constitutions expressly state that the rights protected through judicial means are not only those of the constitution, but also those recognized in international human rights law, as is the case in Argentina, Colombia, Costa Rica and Venezuela. Some constitutions also include within the protective scope of the writ of amparo human rights recognized in statutes (Argentina, Bolivia, Ecuador, Guatemala and Paraguay).

Third, the judicial remedy established must be simple, prompt and effective.[19] Regarding simplicity, it refers to a procedure that has none of the dilatory procedural formalities of ordinary judicial remedies. The special character of the protection sought, constitutional and not ordinary, necessitate this. Regarding the prompt character of the remedy, the IACtHR has considered that a remedy is not prompt, when there is an unreasonable delay in the decision; those resolved after «a long time».[20]

The effective character of the remedy refers to the fact that it must be capable of producing the results for which it has been created.[21] In the words of the Inter-American Court of Human Rights:

> *«[...] it must be truly effective in establishing whether there has been a violation of human rights and in providing redress. A remedy which proves illusory because of the general conditions prevailing in the country, or even in the particular circumstances of a given case, cannot be considered effective. That could be the case, for example, when practice has shown its ineffectiveness: when the Judicial Power lacks the necessary independence to render impartial decisions or the means to carry out its judgments; or in any other situation that constitutes a denial of justice, as there is an unjustified delay in the decision; or when, for any reason, the alleged victim is denied access to a judicial remedy».*[22]

Thus, in order to be effective, it is not enough that the remedy is regulated in internal law. The existence of other basic conditions is necessary in order for the

---

17 It is true that article 1(2) of the Convention provides that «for the purposes of this Convention, 'person' means every human being». Nonetheless, article 25 states that «everyone' should enjoy the judicial guarantee of rights. Thus, everyone, and not only natural persons, have the right to the writ of amparo for the protection of their rights.

18 However, it must be highlighted that fortunately the courts in Colombia have been gradually correcting this restriction through constitutional interpretation, in such a way that today, due to the interrelation, universality, indivisibility, connection and interdependence of rights, there are almost no constitutional rights that cannot be protected by means of the «acción de tutela».

19 See IACtHR, Suárez Romero v Ecuador (n18), para 66.

20 See IACtHR, Case of Ivcher Bronstein v Perú (n17), para 140.

21 See IACtHR, Case of Velásquez Rodríguez v Honduras (n15), para 66.

22 IACtHR, Judicial Guarantees in States of Emergency (n1310), para 24.

remedy to function and be applied with the expected results. In this regard, for a judicial remedy to be effective, above all, it is necessary for the judiciary to be truly independent and impartial. The IACtHR has had the opportunity to adjudicate on this matter. In the *Ivcher Bronstein* case (2000), it held that Perúvian courts at that time were not independent or impartial, so that the claim lodged by the plaintiff could not be effective.[23] The Inter-American Court has also considered that a remedy is not effective when the specific court - and not the court system as a whole - dealing with a claim or petition is not impartial.[24]

Fourth, the remedy should cover any act, omission, fact or action that violates human rights and, of course, which threatens to violate them, regardless of the origin or the author of the harm or threat (whether public authorities or private individuals and corporations). Thus, the writ of amparo against private individuals has been broadly admitted in Latin America, following a trend that began in Argentina in 1957. In some countries, this is expressly provided for in the text of the constitution (Argentina, Bolivia, Paraguay and Perú). In other constitutions, it is admitted only regarding certain individuals, such as those who exercise public functions, special prerogatives, or who are in a position of control, for example, concession holders that render public services. This is the case, for example, in Colombia, Ecuador and Honduras. In other countries, the amparo against private individuals has been introduced through statutes or case law (Chile, Costa Rica, Nicaragua, the Dominican Republic, Uruguay and Venezuela). Not all Latin American countries allow for a writ of amparo against individuals, a situation that is distant from the orientation of the American Convention. This is the case in Brazil, El Salvador, Guatemala, México and Panama.

The scope of the writ of amparo is further limited in some countries of the region, in the sense that some public acts cannot be reviewed by courts in the framework of amparo proceedings. This runs counter to the ACHR, pursuant to which there is not a single state act that could escape from its scope. If the amparo is a legal means for the protection of human rights, individuals should be able to file it against any public act or conduct that violates their rights. It is inconceivable that certain state acts cannot be challenged through the writ of amparo.

Nevertheless, a trend toward exclusion can be identified as follows. In some cases, the exclusion refers to acts of certain public authorities, such as the electoral authorities, whose acts are expressly excluded from the writ of amparo in Costa Rica, México, Nicaragua, Panama, Perú and Uruguay. In Perú, an exclusion from the scope of constitutional protection of the amparo is established with respect to the acts of the National Council of the Judiciary. Only a few countries, like Guatemala, Honduras, México and Venezuela, admit the possibility of filing a writ of amparo against statutes. This stands in stark contrast to the trend set forth by the American Convention.

In other countries, a writ of amparo cannot be filed against judicial decisions, notwithstanding that judges too can infringe constitutional rights when adjudicating. As a matter of principle, no judge should be empowered to violate constitutional rights in his decisions; therefore, the writ of amparo should also be admitted against

[23] See IACtHR, Case of Ivcher Bronstein v Perú (n17), para 139.

[24] See IACtHR, Case of the Constitutional Court v Perú (31 January 2001), Series C No 71, Merits, Reparations and Costs, para 96.

judicial decisions. Nonetheless, only some countries like Colombia, Honduras, Guatemala, México, Panama and Venezuela expressly admit the writ of amparo against judicial decisions. Other countries have expressly excluded it (Argentina, Uruguay, Costa Rica, the Dominican Republic, Panama, El Salvador, Honduras, Nicaragua and Paraguay).

The case of Colombia must be highlighted. Although it had express provisions allowing the «acción de tutela» against judicial decisions, in 1992, the Constitutional Court considered it contrary to the principle of res judicata, annulling the respective article of the statute.[25] Nonetheless, in spite of the aforementioned annulment, all the main courts and the Council of State have progressively admitted the «acción de tutela» against judicial decisions when these are considered arbitrary or the product of judicial voi de fait.[26] This is also the case in Perú, where the writ of amparo against judicial decisions is admitted when regular procedures are flaunted.

II. GENERAL FEATURES OF THE AMPARO PROCEEDING IN LATIN AMERICAN COMPARATIVE CONSTITUTIONAL LAW

1. *The injured party*

The general principle is that only the injured party can initiate proceedings, excluding ex officio amparo proceedings, except in some countries, on matters of habeas corpus (Guatemala). The injured party is the person whose constitutional rights have been violated (*action in personam*). A person does not need to be a natural person (national or foreign); but may also be a legal or artificial person (corporations, associations, etc). On matters of collective rights, the writ of amparo may also be filed by the group or association on behalf of its members, even if said group or association is not formally a legal entity (Paraguay). For these purposes, a collective amparo has been developed in many Latin American countries, for instance for the protection of environmental rights in Colombia. Such collective amparos are occasionally linked to the granting of standing to the ombudsperson.

2. *Justiciable constitutional rights*

As a matter of principle, the amparo proceeding (writs of habeas corpus or amparo) has been established exclusively for the protection those rights enshrined in the constitution or that have acquired constitutional rank and value. Thus, the writ of amparo cannot be based only on the violation of statutory provisions, showing the importance of constitutional recognition of rights.

Consequently, in Latin America, all constitutional or fundamental rights, including economic, cultural and social rights, are in principle justiciable. Chile and Colombia constitute exceptions. The scope of amparo protection has been reduced to only certain constitutional rights, those specifically qualified and listed as «fundamental rights». Nonetheless, in the case of Colombia, the Colombian Constitutional Court has recognized such character to other rights, extending protection based on their connection to others that are expressly considered fundamental rights, like the right to life.

[25] See Constitucional Court of Colombia, Sentence C-543 (24 September 1992), in Manuel J Cepeda, *Derecho Constitucional Jurisprudencial: Las grandes decisiones de la Corte Constitucional*, Legis, Bogotá 2001, pp. 1009ff.

[26] Ibid 1022ff; see also Constitucional Court of Colombia, Sentence T-231 (13 May 1994).

3. *The extraordinary character of the amparo proceeding*

Because the writ of amparo was specifically created as a judicial mechanism for the protection of constitutional rights, it is an extraordinary remedy and is not meant to substitute all other ordinary judicial remedies established for the protection of personal rights and interests. This principle led to two general rules of admissibility. First, the writ of amparo is only admissible when there are no other judicial means for granting constitutional protection, that is, when no other adequate judicial remedy is available in order to obtain the immediate protection of violated constitutional rights. Second, the writ of amparo is admissible when other legally available remedies are inadequate to obtain the immediate protection of the harmed or threatened constitutional rights.

Nonetheless, in some countries, the plaintiff must first exhaust existing ordinary judicial or administrative remedies in order to file a writ of amparo (Brazil, Colombia, Guatemala, México and Perú). Moreover, the general rule in Latin America is that if the plaintiff has chosen and filed a writ of amparo, he cannot activate additional proceedings, as established, for instance, in Chile, Perú, México, Argentina and in Venezuela.

The matter of the general rules governing procedure in amparo proceedings is also connected to its extraordinary character. In general terms, proceedings should be simple and brief. They should not be extended, suspended, nor interrupted, and they should not be excessively formal (substantive law should prevail over formal provisions). The need for immediate protection of the injured person justifies such procedural requirements.

4. *The injury in the amparo proceeding*

The injury in the amparo proceeding consists of damages or harm affecting or destroying the object of the right, or threats that, without destroying such object, put the enjoyment of the right at risk or diminish it. These injuries, harms or threats to constitutional rights must fulfill a series of conditions, commonly established in the laws of amparo, for the writ to be admissible.

In addition to these general conditions, specifically regarding harms, it is also necessary that they be reparable. Regarding threats, they must affect the rights in an imminent manner. Thus, the type of injury inflicted on constitutional rights conditions the purpose of the amparo proceeding. In the case of (reparable) harms, the amparo has a restorative effect; and in the case of (imminent) threats, the amparo has a preventive effect.

Harms, in addition, must have a personal and direct character, in the sense that they must personally affect the plaintiff. They must also be actual and real; manifestly or ostensibly arbitrary, illegal and illegitimate. Furthermore, they must not be consented to by the plaintiff, whether expressly or tacitly, the latter occurring when the plaintiff does not file the amparo within the respective legal term. Only in some countries, can the writ of amparo be filed at any moment (Ecuador and Colombia).

5. *The injuring party*

Since the final result of amparo proceedings is a judicial order addressed to some clearly identified individual, public official or public entity, the writ of amparo must always be filed against an individual, a public official or a public entity that must be individuated and identified in the complaint. Nonetheless, when it is impossible for the plaintiff or for the judge to clearly identify the defendant, the constitutional complaint can be filed and eventually protection can be granted, if the fact or action causing the harm can be clearly determined.

Historically, the amparo was created to protect individuals against the state, that is, against public officials or public entities. One of the main trends of the Latin American amparo today is the admission of the writ of amparo against private individuals, juridical persons, corporations or institutions. This development began in Argentina in the *Samuel Kot* case of 1958. The Supreme Court of the Nation ruled that «nothing in the letter and spirit of the Constitution can be interpreted as circumscribing the protection of constitutional rights to attacks by the state'. Admitting the writ of amparo against private individuals constitutes recognition that it is not only the origin of the injury to constitutional rights, but the rights themselves that are important.[27] Many Latin American countries followed suit: Bolivia, Chile, the Dominican Republic, Paraguay, Perú, Uruguay and Venezuela.

Other countries of the region, such as Guatemala, Colombia, Costa Rica, Ecuador, Honduras and México, restrict the admissibility of writs of amparo against private individuals. Only those individuals or corporations that are in a position of superiority regarding citizens or that in some way, exercise public functions or activities, or provide public services or public utilities, can be defendants in amparo proceedings.

Finally, the writ of amparo, is only admissible against public authorities in Brazil, El Salvador, Panama, and Nicaragua.

6. *The injuring public actions or omissions*

The universal character of the amparo proceeding means that any act, fact or omission of any public authority, entity or public officials causing an injury to constitutional rights can be challenged through this mechanism. In this sense, for instance, the Guatemalan Amparo Law provides that «no sphere of competence shall be excluded from the writ of amparo», it is admissible against «any act, resolution, disposition and statute of authority which could imply a threat, a restriction or a violation of the rights guaranteed in the constitution and in statutory law» (article 8). That is also why Venezuelan courts have held that «there is no state act that can be excluded from review in amparo proceedings, the purpose of which is not to annul state acts but to protect public freedoms and restore their enjoyment when violated or harmed», thereby admitting that the constitutional writ of amparo may be filed even against acts excluded from judicial review, when the harm or violation of constitutional rights or guarantees has been alleged.[28]

[27] See José L Lazzarini, *El juicio de amparo*, La Ley, Buenos Aires, 1987, p. 228; Brage Camanazo, *La Jurisdicción constitucional de la libertad: Teoría general, Argentina, México*, Corte Interamericana de Derechos Humanos (Porrúa, México City, 2005, p. 99; Néstor Pedro Sagüés, *Acción de amparo*, Astrea, Buenos Aires, 1988, pp. 13, 512, 527ff. Nonetheless, when the 1966 Law 16.986 was issued, it only referred to the writ of amparo against the state, that is «against every act or omission of the authorities» (article 1), the amparo against individuals was regulated in articles 321(2) and 498 of the Code of Civil and Commercial Procedure.

[28] See the former Supreme Court of Justice, Case of Anselmo Natale (31 January 1991), Case No 22, in *Revista de Derecho Público*, No. 45, Editorial Jurídica Venezolana, Caracas 1991, p. 118.

Notwithstanding this general principle of universality, which also finds expression in the ACHR, a series of exceptions can be identified in many Latin American amparo laws, regarding some particular and specific state acts or activities (of legislative, executive, administrative or judicial nature) that are expressly excluded from the scope of amparo proceedings.

In general, the writ of amparo is inadmissible against statutes (Bolivia, Brazil, Colombia, Chile, Costa Rica, the Dominican Republic, Ecuador, El Salvador, Panama, Perú, Paraguay, Nicaragua and Uruguay). Guatemala and Honduras are exceptions in this sense. In México and Venezuela, amparo proceedings are admissible only against self-executing statutes, those that can violate constitutional rights without the need for any further state act of execution or application.

Regarding administrative acts and actions, the general rule is the admissibility of the writ of amparo action against all acts, facts or omissions from public entities or bodies of the public administration at all its levels. This includes decentralized, autonomous, or independent bodies as well as acts issued by the head of the executive branch. In Argentina and Perú, an exception is established regarding political questions, or acts of government.

In contrast with the general admission of the writ of amparo against executive and administrative acts, including those administrative acts issued by courts and tribunals, the same cannot be said regarding judicial decisions issued on jurisdictional matters. In most countries of the region, judicial decisions are expressly excluded from the scope of amparo proceedings and considered inadmissible. There are some exceptions. In México, it has been the long-standing tradition to admit the writ of amparo against judicial decisions. Guatemala, Honduras, Panama, Perú and Venezuela also admit this remedy against judicial decisions.

Regarding the acts of other independent state organs, some exceptions have also been established regarding the electoral bodies of Costa Rica, México, Nicaragua, Panama, Perú, and Uruguay.

The writ of amparo can also be filed against omissions of authorities. That is, when the competent entities or public officials fail to comply with their general obligations, thereby causing harm or threat to constitutional rights. In such cases, the judicial order of mandamus will be a command directed at the concerned public authority to perform the constitutional duty which had been refused or neglected.

7. *Adjudication in the amparo proceeding*

The purpose of the amparo proceeding is for the plaintiff to obtain a judicial decision from the competent court granting immediate protection to harmed or threatened constitutional rights. For instance, the judicial decision may preserve the status quo, or command or prohibit actions. Two general types of decisions can be issued by courts for the protection of constitutional rights. First, preliminary or interlocutory measures («*medidas preventivas o cautelares*»), that can be ordered from the beginning of the procedure and whose effects are subject to the final court ruling. These are ordered to prevent the fulfillment of the threat to constitutional rights or guarantees, or to prevent the configuration of an irreparable situation that would make the amparo futile. The second type of decision, a definitive ruling, prevents the violation from occurring or restores the enjoyment of the threatened or harmed rights.

Definitive rulings may order different things. They may be prohibitory, that is, issued to restrain an action, to forbid certain acts or to command a person to refrain from doing specific acts. They may be of a mandatory character, in the sense that they require the undoing of an act, or the restoring of the status quo ante by compelling the execution of some act, or commanding a person to do a specific act. An amparo order can also be directed at a court, which normally happens when the writ of amparo is filed against judicial decisions. Lastly, definitive rulings may also be declaratory, when courts are called on to declare the constitutional right of the plaintiff regarding other parties.

Although the amparo is a remedy that is restorative in character, in general terms, the immediate effect of the decision is to suspend the effects of the challenged act regarding the plaintiff. Amparo proceedings are not directed at annulling state acts. In principle, this is a task for constitutional and administrative courts. On the contrary, when an amparo is filed against a judicial decision, the effects of the ruling granting amparo protection also consists in the annulment of the challenged judicial act or decision, as is the case in Venezuela.

Regarding appeals to amparo rulings, in some countries an appeal is not possible since it is the highest court in the country that rules on writs of amparo (Constitutional Chamber of the Supreme Court of Justice). This is the case in Costa Rica, Nicaragua and El Salvador. In other countries of the region, amparo decisions can be appealed before higher courts; and they can only reach the highest supreme or constitutional court, through the extraordinary channels established in almost all Latin American countries. Mostly, such appeals are aimed at ensuring the uniformity of constitutional interpretation and rights» enforcement.

Apex courts that receive appeals regarding writs of amparo may have the discretion to decide whether they will review the decision (Honduras, México and Venezuela). In Brazil, Guatemala and Perú, the review of an amparo decision on appeal is mandatory. The constitutional tribunals of Bolivia, Ecuador and Colombia must automatically, and not only at the behest of a party, review judicial decisions on matters of amparo.

III. THE ENFORCEMENT OF THE *IUS COMMUNE* PRINCIPLES OF THE AMPARO PROCEEDING BY THE INTER-AMERICAN COURT OF HUMAN RIGHTS

As mentioned before, article 25(1) of the American Convention establishes the framework for amparo proceedings, under which both the IACtHR and national courts and tribunals, must exercise the conventionality control[29] to ensure the right

[29] On the conventionality control see Ernesto Rey Cantor, *Control de convencionalidad de las leyes y derechos humanos,* Porrúa, Instituto Mexicano de Derecho Procesal Constitucional, México City, 2008; Juan C. Hitters, «Control de constitucionalidad y control de convencionalidad: Comparación», in *Estudios Constitucionales* No. 7, Centro de Estudios Constitucionales de Chile, Universidad de Talca, 2009, pp. 109-128; Susana Albanese (ed), *El control de convencionalidad,* Ediar, Buenos Aires, 2008; Eduardo Ferrer Mac-Gregor, «El control difuso de convencionalidad en el Estado constitucional», in Héctor Fix-Zamudio and Diego Valadés (eds), *Formación y perspectiva del Estado mexicano,* El Colegio Nacional-UNAM, México City, 2010, pp. 151-188; Allan R. Brewer-Carías, *Control de convencionalidad. Marco concpetual, antecedentes, derecho de amparo y derecho administrativo,* Biblioteca de Derecho Administrativo, Ediciones Olejnik, Buenos Aires, Santiago de Chile, Madrid 2019, 106

of amparo for the protection of human rights and to overcome the restrictions to the institution of amparo that still persist in many countries. In the IACtHR»s own words, «the sense of the protection afforded by Article 25 of the Convention», consists of:

> *«the real possibility of access to a judicial remedy so that the competent authority, with jurisdiction to issue a binding decision, determines whether there has been a violation of a right claimed by the person filing the action, and that in such case, the remedy is useful to restitute to the interested party the enjoyment of his right and to repair it».*[30]

Based on this, I have maintained that article 25 ACHR, embodying the «right of amparo», cannot be restricted. Thus, when regulating the writ of amparo domestically, the scope of protection should not exclude certain rights; state actions; or categories of persons. Something else entirely, is when the scope of the amparo is so broad that it becomes a procedural delaying technique that in practice prevents any effective, simple and fast protection of rights.

In this sense, the IACtHR noted in the *Case of «Los Dos Erres Massacre» v Guatemala* that even though it considered that in Guatemala the amparo remedy was an «adequate remedy to protect individuals» human rights»,[31] its «inadequate use», its «current structure» and «the provisions that regulated it», coupled with «the lack of due diligence and tolerance by the courts when processing them», have shown that it does not grant effective judicial protection. In addition, courts «have allowed the abusive use of the appeal as a delaying practice in the proceeding»,[32] so that «its inadequate use has impeded its true efficiency, as it is not capable of producing the result for which it was conceived».[33] It concluded by stating:

> *«Based on the foregoing, the Court considers that, within the framework of the current Guatemalan legislation, in the this case the recourse of amparo has been transformed into a means to delay and hinder the judicial process, and into a factor for impunity. Consequently, this Court believes that in this case the State violated the rights to a fair trial and right to judicial protection, which constitute the victims' access to justice, recognized in Articles 8(1) and 25(1) of the Convention, and also failed to comply with the provisions contained in Articles 1(1) and 2 thereof».*[34]

Regarding restrictions or limits to substantive aspects of the writ of amparo, I disagree with the IACtHR's decision in the *Case of Jorge Castañeda Gutman v México* of 6 August 2008, when it accepted that states can set limits on the admissibility of the writ of amparo, and considered that «it is not inherently incompatible with the Convention that a State limits the application for amparo to specific matters».[35]

---

pp.; Carlos M. Ayala Corao, *Del diálogo jurisprudencial al control de convencionalidad*, Editorial Jurídica Venezolana, Caracas, 2013, p. 123. See also Allan R. Brewer-Carías, Ernesto Jinesta Lobo, Víctor Hernández Mendible y Jaime Orlando Santofimio, *El control de convencionalidad y responsabilidad del Estado* (Prólogo de Luciano Parejo), Editorial Jurídica Venezolana, Colección Estudios Jurídicos No. 109, Caracas 2015, 434 pp.

30 See decision in IACtHR, *Case of Castañeda Gutman v México* (6 August 2008), Series C No 184, para 100.

31 See decision in the IACtHR, Case of « *Los Dos Erres Massacre» v Guatemala* (n10), para 121.

32 Ibid para 120.

33 Ibid para 121.

34 Ibid para 124.

35 See decision in the IACtHR, *Case of Castañeda Gutman v México* (n32), para 92.

First of all, it should be noted that to exclude the scope of amparo protection in «some areas» cannot be regarded as an issue of «admissibility», because it is not a procedural matter. The exclusion of certain rights or certain state actions from the protective scope of the writ of amparo constitutes a substantive matter that cannot be limited under article 25(1) ACHR. A different question is the capacity of states to establish procedural conditions of admissibility of legal proceedings. However, this can never mean a denial of the right to judicial protection of certain human rights, or against certain state acts that violate them.

The «clarification» that the Court itself made in *Castañeda Gutman*, indicating that restrictions by states to the amparo would not be incompatible with the Convention «provided that it [the State] offers another remedy of a similar nature and equal scope for those rights that cannot be heard by the courts using the amparo proceeding».[36] This confirms the fact that it is not possible to restrict the right to an amparo proceeding, because if a right is not guaranteed by the specific provisions regulating the «writ of amparo» it should be guaranteed by other judicial remedies of «similar nature and equal scope». In short, guaranteed by other legal means of amparo protection.

When faced with a restriction to formal amparo proceedings, the IACtHR and national courts have the obligation to analyze all judicial remedies available in order to determine if there is «another recourse of similar nature and equal scope» established for the protection of the right. That is, if another legal means for amparo has been established. That is precisely why in *Castañeda Gutman*, the IACtHR concluded - regarding the protection of the political right to be elected - that «since an amparo proceeding was not accepted in electoral matters», and the victim did not have other effective protective remedies, the state had not provided the victim «an appropriate remedy to claim the alleged violation of his political right to be elected, and therefore violated Article 25 of the Convention».[37]

In the case of the *Constitutional Court v Perú* of 31 January 2001, the IACtHR had the opportunity to render judgment regarding restrictions to the scope of amparo proceedings based on «political questions». It was a case brought by dismissed judges of the Constitutional Tribunal, removed by congress without the proper guarantees of judicial protection. When analyzing the decision of the Perúvian Constitutional Tribunal on the writ of amparo filed by the dismissed judges, the IACtHR considered that «[t]he exercise of the power of sanction, specifically that of the dismissal of senior officials, cannot be openly evaluated in a jurisdictional seat, because it constitutes an act that is exclusive to the Congress of the Republic, equivalent to what, in doctrine, is called non-actionable political questions»,[38] noting however, that the Court itself had established that:

> *«this power is not unlimited or absolutely discretionary, but is subject to certain parameters, one of which, and perhaps the principal one, is that it should be exercised according to the principle of reasonableness, because it would not be logical or fair to decide to impose a measure of sanction following a situation of total uncertainty or lack of substantiation. Accordingly, in cases where an act of a political nature, such as the one questioned in this application for amparo, manifests an evident infringement of this*

36 Ibid.
37 Ibid para 131.
38 Ibid para 95.

principle and, by extension, others such as that of the democratic rule of law or due material process, it is an unobjectionable fact that this body can evaluate its coherence in the light of the Political Constitution of the State».[39]

The Inter-American Court passed up the opportunity to perform a conventionality control with respect to the unconventional denial of amparo against judicial decisions in a case against Ecuador. Specifically the issue was raised in *Acosta Calderón v Ecuador* of 24 June 2005, where the representatives of the victims, alleged that even «with the constitutional amendments of 1996 and 1998, the exercise of the guarantee of legal protection is not regulated in accordance with the rule of [Article] 25 of the Convention, since it expressly prohibits that the amparo action be presented against judicial orders».[40] The IACtHR, however, instead of scrutinizing this important aspect, merely stated that it was not ruling on the allegations of the representatives because «these amendments are not within the conditions of the current case».[41]

The acts of electoral bodies are also sometimes excluded from the protective scope of the writ of amparo. This was the case in Perú where article 5(8) of the Procedural Code excluded the constitutional writ of amparo against the decisions of the National Electoral Court. The Constitutional Court of Perú annulled this provision by invoking the binding nature of the jurisprudence of the Inter-American Court, including its advisory opinions.[42]

The IACtHR also rendered a decision regarding the exclusion of amparo or effective legal protection against acts of electoral authorities in Nicaragua. In *Yatama v Nicaragua* of 23 June 2005, the Court first found that the Supreme Electoral Council of Nicaragua had not respected the guarantees of due process of Yatama's political party by rejecting the nomination of candidates for the 2000 elections, thus affecting the right to political participation of candidates (paragraphs 160-164). The IACtHR also considered that the state had violated the right to judicial protection or amparo, provided for in article 25(1) ACHR, because its domestic law excluded acts of the National Electoral Council from the scope of the writ of amparo. The Inter-American Court found, in essence, that «the inexistence of effective domestic remedies places the individual in a situation of defenselessness» so that «the absence of an effective remedy to violations of the rights recognized in the Convention is itself a violation of the Convention by the State Party».[43]

---

39 Ibid para 95.

40 See IACtHR, *Case of Acosta Calderón v Ecuador* (24 June 2005), Series C No 129, paras 87f.

41 Ibid para 98.

42 See the ruling of the Constitutional Court of Perú, *Colegio de Abogados del Callao v Congreso de la República* (19 June 2007), Tribunal Constitucional Pleno Jurisdiccional 00007-2007-PI/TC-19; mentioned in Carlos Ayala Corao, «El diálogo jurisprudencial entre los Tribunales internacionales de derechos humanos y los Tribunales constitucionales», in Boris Barrios González (ed), *Temas de Derecho Procesal Constitucional latinoamericano: Memorias I Congreso panameño de Derecho Procesal Constitucional y III Congreso Internacional Proceso y Constitución,* Universal Books, Panama City, 2012, p. 176. Before this law was annulled though, the amparo was admitted if the decision of the National Elections Board did not have a jurisdictional nature or, having it, when it violated effective judicial protection (due process). See Samuel B Abad Yupanqui, *El proceso constitucional de amparo,* Gaceta Jurídica, Lima, 2004, pp. 128, 421, 447.

43 See IACtHR, *Case of Yatama v Nicaragua* (n14), paras 167f.

The IACtHR continued by asserting that although the Nicaraguan Constitution had established that the resolutions of the Supreme Electoral Council on electoral matters were not subject to judicial review, that could not mean «that the Council should not be subject to judicial controls, as are the other branches of government», saying, correctly, that «the requirements arising from the principle of the independence of the powers of the State are not incompatible with the need to establish recourses or mechanisms to protect human rights».[44] The Court stated:

> *«irrespective of the regulations that each State establishes for its supreme electoral body, the latter must be subject to some form of jurisdictional control that allows it to be determined whether its acts have been adopted respecting the minimum guarantees and rights established in the American Convention, as well as those established in its own laws; which is not incompatible with regard for the functions inherent in this body concerning electoral matter"*[45]

As a remedy, the IACtHR ordered the state of Nicaragua to:

> *«adopt, within a reasonable time, the necessary legislative measures to establish a simple, prompt and effective judicial recourse that allow the decisions of the Supreme Electoral Council, which affect human rights, such as political rights, respecting the corresponding treaty-based and legal guarantees, and to abrogate the provisions that prevent the filing of such recourse».*[46]

FINAL REFLECTIONS

The amparo proceeding is a central institution of the Latin American *ius constititutionale commune*. It emerged from a two centuries long constitutional tradition, characterized by the insertion of very extensive declarations on human rights, and consequently, of the judicial means to assure their protection in the constitution. The protection of rights though is only possible when an independent and impartial judiciary exists, and courts can effectively fulfill their duties.

It should not be surprising then, that the writ of amparo has been a very effective means for the protection of constitutional rights, particularly in democratic regimes, where the judiciary functions as an independent branch of government. Unfortunately, in many Latin American countries, the judiciary has not always accomplished its fundamental duty, and all the constitutional declarations and provisions for amparo rights, are no match for the rather dismal situation regarding the effectiveness of the judiciary as a whole, and its standing as an efficient and just protector of fundamental rights.[47]

In order to achieve the aims of the state of justice, the most elemental institutional condition needed in any country is the existence of a truly impartial and independent judiciary. Courts must be out of the reach and control of the other branches of government, empowered to interpret and apply the law impartially and protect citizens, particularly regarding when it comes to the enforcement of rights against the state. The judiciary must be built upon the principle of separation

---

44 Ibid para 174.
45 Ibid para 175.
46 Ibid para 254.
47 On the judiciary, see the introduction to this volume.

of powers. If this principle is not enforced and the government controls courts and judges, no effective guaranty of constitutional rights will be available, particularly when the offending party is a governmental agency.[48]

This has been the unfortunate situation of Venezuela during the past years.[49] The existence of a very progressive constitution in force since 1999, which contains one of the most extensive declarations of constitutional rights in all Latin America, including a provision considering the writ of amparo as a constitutional right in itself[50], and provisions affirming the independence and impartiality of the judiciary, has been overpowered by facts. The authoritarianism that has developed since 2000,[51] where the executive has gained complete control of the judiciary,[52] has reduced the declaration of constitutional rights to dead letter and the writ of

---

48 See Allan R. Brewer-Carías, «El principio de la separación de poderes como elemento esencial de la democracia y de la libertad, y su demolición en Venezuela mediante la sujeción política del Tribunal Supremo de Justicia», in *Revista Iberoamericana de Derecho Administrativo - Homenaje a Luciano Parejo Alfonso,* No. 12, 2012, pp. 31-43.

49 See Allan R. Brewer-Carías, «La progresiva y sistemática demolición institucional de la autonomía e independencia del Poder Judicial en Venezuela 1999-2004», in *XXX Jornadas J.M. Domínguez Escovar: Estado de derecho, administración de justicia y derechos humanos,* Instituto de Estudios Jurídicos del Estado Lara, Barquisimeto, 2005, pp. 33-174; «La justicia sometida al poder (La ausencia de independencia y autonomía de los jueces en Venezuela por la interminable emergencia del Poder Judicial (1999-2006)», in *Cuestiones Internacionales: Anuario Jurídico Villanueva 2007,* Centro Universitario Villanueva, Marcial Pons, Madrid, 2007, pp. 25-57; «Sobre la ausencia de independencia y autonomía judicial en Venezuela, a los doce años de vigencia de la constitución de 1999 (O sobre la interminable transitoriedad que en fraude continuado a la voluntad popular y a las normas de la Constitución, ha impedido la vigencia de la garantía de la estabilidad de los jueces y el funcionamiento efectivo de una «jurisdicción disciplinaria judicial»)», in *Independencia Judicial,* Colección Estado de Derecho, vol 1, Acceso a la Justicia org., Editorial Jurídica Venezolana, Caracas, 2012, pp. 9-103; «La demolición de las instituciones judiciales y la destrucción de la democracia: La experiencia venezolana», in *Instituciones Judiciales y Democracia: Reflexiones con ocasión del Bicentenario de la Independencia y del Centenario del Acto Legislativo 3 de 1910,* Consejo de Estado, Sala de Consulta y Servicio Civil, Bogotá, 2012, pp. 230-254; and «The Government of Judges and Democracy. The Tragic Situation of the Venezuelan Judiciary», in Sophie Turenne (Editor.), *Fair Reflection of Society in Judicial Systems - A Comparative Study,* Ius Comparatum. Global Studies in Comparative Law, Vol 7, Springer 2015, pp. 205-231.

50 Véase Allan R. Brewer-Carías, *Derecho de amparo y acción de amparo constitucional,* Academia de Ciencias Políticas y Sociales, Instituto Iberoamericano de Derecho Procesal Constitucional, Editorial Jurídica Venezolana, Caracas 2021.

51 See Allan R. Brewer-Carías, *Dismantling Democracy: The Chávez Authoritarian Experiment,* Cambridge University Press, New York 2010); *Authoritarian Government v The Rule of Law: Lectures and Essays (1999-2014) on the Venezuelan Authoritarian Regime Established in Contempt of the Constitution,* Fundación de Derecho Público, Editorial Jurídica Venezolana, Caracas, 2014; *The Collapse of the Rule of Law in Venezuela,* Editorial Jurídica Venezolana International, 2020.

52 See Chavero Gazdik, *La justicia revolucionaria: Una década de restructuración (o involución) judicial en Venezuela,* Aequitas, Caracas, 2011; and Allan R. Brewer-Carías, *Estado Totalitario y Desprecio a la Ley: La desconstitucionalización, desjuridificación, desjudicialización y desdemocratización de Venezuela* (Fundación de Derecho Público, Editorial Jurídica Venezolana, Caracas, 2014; *La dictadura judicial y la perversión del Estado de derecho. El Juez Constitucional y la destrucción de la democracia en Venezuela* (Prólogo de Santiago Muñoz Machado), Ediciones El Cronista, Fundación Alfonso Martín Escudero, Editorial IUSTEL, Madrid

amparo to complete ineffectiveness.[53] In addition, not only can citizens not claim their constitutional rights before national courts, but the withdrawal of Venezuela in 2013 from the American Convention on Human Rights has also closed off the possibility of accessing the Inter-American Court of Human Rights - a dire situation indeed.[54]

New York, January 2021
ALLAN R. BREWER-CARÍAS

2017, 608 pp. *La consolidación de la tiranía judicial. El Juez Constitucional controlado por el Poder Ejecutivo, asumiendo el poder absoluto*, Colección Estudios Políticos, No. 15, Editorial Jurídica Venezolana International. Caracas / New York, 2017, 238 pp.

53 See Jorge C. Kariakidis Longhi, *El amparo constitucional venezolano: mitos y realidades*, Editorial Jurídica Venezolana, Caracas, 2012; Antonio Canova González and others, *El TSJ al servicio de la revolución: La toma, los números y los criterios del TSJ venezolano (2004-2013)*, Galipán, Caracas, 2014.

54 See Carlos Ayala Corao, «Inconstitucionalidad de la denuncia de la Convención Americana sobre Derechos Humanos por Venezuela», in *Revista Europea de Derechos Fundamentales*, No. 20, 2012, pp. 45-82; also, *Estudios Constitucionales*, No. 10, Centro de Estudios Constitucionales de Chile - Universidad de Talca, 2012, pp. 643-682; in *Revista de Derecho Público*, No, 131, Editrorial Jurídica Venezolana, Caracas 2012, pp. 39-73; and in *Anuario de Derecho Constitucional Latinoamericano 2013*,Konrad-Adenauer-Stiftung: Programa Estado de Derecho para Latinoamérica, Universidad del Rosario, Bogotá, 2013, pp. 43-79.

INTRODUCTION

Latin American countries have a longstanding tradition on extensive constitutional declarations of human rights. Since the beginning of republican constitutionalism in 1811, Latin American constitutions have enshrined a Bill of Rights and the authority of courts to adjudicate on constitutional violation.

Particularly during the second half of the XX Century, these declarations have been progressively enlarged, adding economic, social, cultural, environmental and indigenous rights to the traditional list of civil rights and political liberties; and have entrenched, in many cases, not only such rights and liberties, but also principles relating to the social goals of the State and of the political system.

However, Latin American Countries have also had a long history of human rights violations and disdain. That is why, in an effort to ensure for its effective guaranty and enforcement, another main trend in Latin America has been to formally insert all human rights, *expressis verbis,* in the texts of the Constitutions.

Additionally to the enlargement of the constitutional declarations, a new tendency among these countries has been to constitutionalize the rights enumerated in the dully ratified international treaties and conventions on human rights, therefore expanding the constitutional declarations and provisions with the ratification of such international instruments.

Moreover, regarding statutes, other Constitutions have granted pre-emptive status to duly ratified international treaties or conventions on human rights, whenever the treaty provides for more favourable provisions in the exercise of a human right. Some Constitutions even go as far as granting this pre-emption with respect to other constitutional provisions.

Together with this expansive and protective process of human rights declarations, Latin American constitutions have incorporated into their constitutional text, specific judicial remedies for the protection of constitutional rights; which in some constitutions, has been incorporated itself as a civil right, and not merely as a procedural or adjective device to guarantee human rights.

Accordingly, and in addition to the writ of *habeas corpus*, and *habeas data*, the individual's constitutional right to be protected on their fundamental rights has prompted the development of a peculiar Latin American institution known as: suit, judgment or writ of «amparo». The «amparo» was initially established in México in 1857 where it was developed as the «amparo suit» or judgment (*juicio de amparo*). Particularly during the last century (XX Century), the «amparo» spread all over Latin America but took a different shape to the Mexican «amparo».

The Mexican suit of «amparo» is a very complex institution -found exclusively in México- developed with the purpose of both protecting human rights and as a mean for judicial review of the constitutionality and legality of statutes, administrative actions, judicial decisions, as well as peasant's rights protection. On the contrary, in the rest of the Latin American countries, the «amparo» action or recourse was established as a specific judicial remedy with the exclusive purpose of protecting human rights and freedoms, so that it can be said that many of the «amparo» actions or recourses in these later countries became more effective as a means of protection of human rights than the original Mexican institution.[1]

This course is intended to examine the most recent trends in the constitutional and legal regulations in all Latin American countries regarding the «amparo» suit, action or recourse- including the old *habeas corpus* writ and the new *habeas data* actions or recourses. By means of a comparative constitutional law approach, also with reference to the United States civil rights injunctions, the course will analyze this Latin American institution departing from the regulation of the «amparo» guarantee established in Article 25 of the 1969 American Convention of Human Rights which entered into force in 1978 after being ratified by all Latin American States.

The main purpose of this course is to study the character of this judicial remedy both from the perspective of the constitutional right and the action or procedural recourse for protection; to identify the courts with jurisdiction to grant the protection; to examine the general procedural rules to bring an «amparo»; to determine the kind of constitutional rights worthy of protection by means of an «amparo» (whether all constitutional rights or only some of them, namely «fundamental rights», should be covered); to analyze the individuals or legal entities that may be entitled to the protection of an «amparo», that is, the aggrieved, affected or injured party (the plaintiff); to study the standing requirements to file the action; to analyze the potential proper defendants in the judicial process, namely, the party perpetrator of the nuisance, whether a State body, a public officer, individuals or private entities; to analyze the particular types of public or private actions or omissions that can cause the violation of constitutional rights, with particular reference to the various State acts which can be the object of the «amparo» action or recourse: statutes, administrative acts or judicial decisions, as well as State bodies' omissions; and finally, to study the purpose of the protection that may be awarded and the available remedies for the re-establishment of the individual or collective rights infringed, as well as the means for the enforcement of the judicial adjudication[2].

---

1 See Joaquín BRAGUE CAMAZANO, *La Jurisdicción constitucional de la libertad. Teoría general, Argentina, México, Corte Interamericana de Derechos Humanos*, Editorial Porrúa, México 2005, p. 156.

2 See in general Allar R. BREWER-CARÍAS, *El amparo a los derechos y libertades constitucionales. Una aproximación comparativa*, Cuadernos de la Cátedra Allan R. Brewer--Carías de Derecho Público, N° 1, Universidad Católica del Táchira, San Cristóbal 1993, 138 pp; also published by the Inter Americanl Institute on Human Rights, (Interdisciplinary Course), San José, Costa Rica, 1993, (mimeo), 120 pp. and in *La protección jurídica del ciudadano. Estudios en Homenaje al Profesor Jesús González Pérez*, Tomo 3, Editorial Civitas, Madrid 1993, pp. 2.695-2.74; and Allan R. BREWER-CARÍAS, *Mecanismos nacionales de protección de los derechos humanos (Garantías judiciales de los derechos humanos en el derecho constitucional comparado latinoamericano)*, Instituto Interamericano de Derechos Humanos, San José 2005.

One of the main aspects to be analyzed regarding the «amparo» suit in Latin America is the one referred to the special character of this judicial mean. This particularity comes from the fact that the «amparo» is not incorporated in the general judicial procedures law regulations, but specifically regulated in the Constitution, as a separate and specific mean for the protection of human rights. In this respect, it is also relevant to our analysis, the justification for such treatment, particularly when compared with other legal systems that also effectively protect human rights, but by means of the normal or common judicial actions, recourses or writs.

In other words, we will examine why Latin American countries have established a special judicial mean for human rights protection; considering that, in general terms, the most important duty of all the Judiciary as the Judicial Branch of Government, in any country, is to decide and resolve in specific cases, questions or controversies regarding individual rights and interests. That is, the reasons why the common and general judicial means established in the Civil Codes and Civil procedures Codes of Latin America are not the only devoted to guaranteeing the effective protection of human rights.

CHAPTER I

THE CONSTITUTIONAL DECLARATIONS OF HUMAN RIGHTS IN LATIN AMERICA

I. RIGHTS: CONSTITUTIONAL RIGHTS, HUMAN RIGHTS, CIVIL RIGHTS, FUNDAMENTAL RIGHTS

In general terms, the Judiciary is established in any country in order to decide cases and to make binding judgments which affect personal and proprietary rights. In this regard, the expression «rights» is used to describe that which is legally guaranteed and due to a person; or the power, privilege or immunity secured to a person by law. That is to say, rights are legal or constitutional situations that empower a person to act (freedom of expression) or not to act (conscience objection), usually being personal freedoms or liberties what oblige the State and other individuals not to interfere with or obstruct the exercise of rights of others.

But rights can also be considered as legal situations that entitle a person to request something or to receive goods or services form a public entity (right to health protection or right to education) in which case the State is obliged to furnish services or to accomplish certain activities. In both cases, the rights are recognized and protected, the violation of which is a wrong.

It can be said that in any society, from a legal point of view, all persons are in one way or another in one of two situations: either they are in a legal situation or condition of having power to do something or request something, or in a legal situation of having some duties or obligations to accomplish. In some cases, a person may have the right to act or not to act, or to make, to enjoy or to take advantage of something, or to dispose of determined possessions. In all these legal interpersonal relations, they are in a status or position of being empowered.

But in other cases, the same person can be in the legal situation of having a duty to accomplish; that is, they can be in a position of being obliged to respect, to refrain from, to abstain from or to render or give certain services or goods to others.

What is certain is that it is inconceivable that a society could exist without such personal interrelations of powers and duties. If one person for instance, has freedom of religion or speech as a constitutional right, that situation always implies that the State, the public officials and every other individual have the duty to respect, to abstain from embarrassing or to impede the freedom of others. In this case, the situation of the obliged person is a status of having the duty to abstain from interfering with the freedom of others.

In other cases, if the constitutional right is not conceived as a right to act or not to act, that is, as a freedom, but instead is conceived as a right to receive certain services or goods, for instance health care, education or cultural services, that situation implies that the State has the duty to render those services in the form of public utilities. In this situation, the status of the obliged person is to act or to provide something to others.

So rights are always attributed to persons, whether as freedoms to act or as rights to receive something; and in both situations, «persons» are not only human beings but also entities or corporations recognized by law as having rights and duties.

Now, among the «rights» attributed to a person, it is possible to distinguish those which are declared or recognized in the Constitution, that is to say, «constitutional rights». Those rights can not only be attributed to natural persons or human beings, but also to artificial persons like entities or corporations. This is the case, for instance, of property rights or the right to due process of law.

Other rights, conversely, such as the right to life or in general, the rights known as freedoms, like freedom of association, freedom of expression or freedom of speech are only attributed to human beings. Thus, the expression «human rights», in a strict sense, is referred to those attributed to human beings. Among these it is also possible to distinguish those called in North American law as «civil rights», or civil liberties, that is, the individual rights of personal liberty or freedom guaranteed in the Constitution, such as freedom of speech, press, assembly, or religion guaranteed by the First Amendment of the U.S. Constitution.

However, «civil rights» do not exhaust the list of constitutional rights, which nowadays also comprises social, economic, cultural and environmental rights. It may be true that civil rights were those first declared in the Constitutions, but at present time they are accompanied by a long list of other rights belonging to what has been called other «generations» of rights.

In other countries, mainly in Europe, as evidenced in the cases of Germany and Spain, the expression «fundamental rights» is also used in the Constitutions, in order to identify certain constitutional rights that can be protected by a special judicial mean of protection or «amparo», which in general terms are equivalent to the individual or civil rights. This expression of «fundamental rights» is also used in the Colombian Constitution, to identify a category of constitutional rights, mainly the individual rights, which are of immediate application and can be protected by the «acción de tutela».

These regulations, in particular, tend to distinguish among the constitutional rights, those that can be considered as «justiciable rights» particularly by means of the specific judicial action or recourse of «amparo», and constitutional rights not considered «fundamental rights». The latter group is left to be protected by means of the general or common judicial means. Constitutional rights can always be considered essentially justiciables, but their «justiciability» -as the quality or state of being appropriate or suitable for reviewing by a court-, will vary depending on the judicial means available in the legal system for such purpose. In some countries, all constitutional rights are justiciables by means of the general judicial means of protection, such as in the United States; in other countries all constitutional rights are justiciables by means of a specific judicial mean of protection like the *habeas corpus* or «amparo» action or recourse, such as in the case of Venezuela; and in other countries, the constitutional rights are protected by a special mean of protection if they are «fundamental rights», being the other constitutional rights justiciables through the common judicial means.

In the United States, regarding rights, the word «fundamental» is used when referring to civil rights that are protected in the Constitution, as «fundamental civil rights». As has been ruled by the Supreme Court in *United States v. Wong Kim Ark*, 169 U.S. 649; 18 S. Ct. 456; 42 L. Ed. 890; (1898) on March 28, 1898, referring to «fundamental civil rights for the security of which organized society was instituted, and which remain, with certain exceptions mentioned in the Federal Constitution...».

Thus, this expression «fundamental rights» is commonly used with various meanings: form a formal point of view, they can be considered as the rights embodied in the Constitution; from a substantive point of view, fundamental rights can also be considered as are the most important rights that according to their own principles and value are recognized in a society[1]; and from a judicial point of view, they are such when they can be judicially protected by special means as the «amparo».

Our intention is to analyze the process of constitutionalization of rights in modern constitutionalism, and for this purpose it is possible to consider all «constitutional rights» as «human rights», in spite of the fact that some of them are also attributed to artificial persons. This is why, for the purpose of this Course, the expressions «constitutional rights» and «human rights» are used in an equivalent sense.

II. THE CONSTITUTIONAL DECLARATIONS OF HUMAN RIGHTS

1. The North American and French Declarations

The declaration of rights in the text of the Constitutions began with constitutionalism itself, and with the very notion of Constitution as a superior law[2].

This happened with at the Convention of Virginia in 1776, at the beginning of the Independence process of the American Colonies, when the first Declaration of Rights in constitutional history was approved. Practice followed subsequently by the other Colonies.

This practice differed from the English precedents, mainly because in establishing entrenched rights, they did not refer to rights based on the common law and tradition, but rather to the rights derived from human nature and reason. Thus the rights declared in the Bill of Rights of those colonies were those natural

1 See Alfonso GAIRAUD BRENES, «Los Mecanismos de interpretación de los derechos humanos: especial referencia a la jurisprudencia Perúana» in José F. PALOMINO MANCHEGO, *El derecho procesal constitucional Perúano. Estudios en Homenaje a Domingo García Belaunde*, Editorial Jurídica Grijley, Lima, 2005, Tomo I, p. 124.

2 See in general Allan R. BREWER-CARÍAS, *Reflexiones sobre la Revolución Americana (1776) y la Revolución Francesa (1789) y sus aportes al constitucionalismo moderno,* Cuadernos de la Cátedra Allan R. Brewer-Carías de Derecho Administrativo, Universidad Católica Andrés Bello, N° 1, Editorial Jurídica Venezolana, Caracas, 1992.

rights which «do pertain to ... [the people] and their posterity, as the basis and foundation of government» as the Virginia Declaration of Rights stated.

In the brief preamble to that Declaration (which precedes the text of the Constitution or Form of Government of Virginia of June 29, 1776), the relation between natural rights and government was clearly established. Also evident is the direct influence of Locke's theories in the sense that political society forms itself upon those rights as the basis and foundation of government. That is why the Declaration was based on the fact of the existence of «inherent rights» to all men, which by nature were declared «equally free and independent» (I); enumerating as individual rights the following: the «enjoyment of life and liberty»; the right to «acquiring and possessing property» (I) so that no property could be taken from any person for public usage without his consent (VI); «the freedom of the press» (XII); and the freedom of religion «according to the dictates of conscience» (XVI).

The due process of law rights were also declared, by stating the right of all men in criminal prosecutions «to demand the cause and nature of his accusation, to be confronted with the accusers and witnesses, to call for evidence in his favor, and to a speedy trial by an impartial jury of his vicinage, without whose unanimous consent he cannot be found guilty, nor can he be compelled to give evidence against himself»; and also «that no man be deprived of his liberty except by the law of the land or the judgment of his peers» (VIII); «that excessive bail ought not to be required, nor excessive fines imposed; nor cruel and unusual punishments inflicted» (IX); and that no «general warrants... may be commanded to search suspected places without evidence of a fact committed, or to seize any person or persons not named, or whose offence is not particularly described and supported by evidence» (X).

The Virginia Declaration also guaranteed, as a political right, the right of suffrage and to have free elections of representatives (VI).

Finally, a collective right was also declared, a right appertaining to «a majority of the community» and considered as «an indubitable, unalienable, and indefeasible right» to «reform, alter or abolish» any government founded «inadequate or contrary» to the purposes set forth in the Declaration (III).

The same fundamental liberal principles of the Virginia Declaration can also be found in the Declaration of Independence of the United States of America, approved less than one month later (July 4, 1776), holding as a self evident truths «That all men are created equal; that they are endowed by their Creator with certain unalienable rights; that among these are life, liberty, and the pursuit of happiness»; and that, «to secure these rights, government is instituted among men, deriving their just powers from the consent of the governed»; «that, whenever any form of government becomes destructive of these ends, it is the right of the people to alter or to abolish it and to institute new government, laying its foundation on such principles and organizing its powers in such form, as to them shall seem most likely to effect their safety and happiness».

These declarations, undoubtedly, marked the beginning of the democratic and liberal era of the modern rule of law constitutionalism.

Although the 1787 Constitution of the United States did not contain a declaration of fundamental rights, such Declarations nevertheless constituted one of the main characteristics of American constitutionalism, influencing modern constitutional law.

The 1787 Constitution was criticized for the fact that it did not include a Bill of Rights, but this deficiency was solved two years later when ten first Amendments to the Constitution were drafted by the first Congress and approved on September 29, 1789 just one month after the approval on August 26, 1789 of the French Declaration of the Rights of Man and of the Citizen.

The Bill of Rights entered in force in 1791 after the last ratifications were approved by Vermont and Virginia, where «certain rights» were enumerated, but with the express statement that said enumeration, «shall not be construed to deny or disparage other [rights] retained by the people» (IX), thus, reinforcing the «declarative» character of the constitutional declaration of rights.

The following «certain rights» were the ones declared: the freedom of religion and of the exercise of cult; freedom of speech, or of the press; the right to peaceably assemble, the right to petition the Government (I); the right to keep and bear arms (II); the right to not accept quarters of soldiers in any house in time of peace, without the consent of the owner (III); and the right of the people to be secure in their persons, houses, papers, and effects, against unreasonable searches and seizures (IV).

The due process of law rights were also declared as follows: only to be condemned by the Judiciary; not to be subject twice to prosecution for the same offence; not to be witness against himself, nor be deprived of life, liberty, or property, without due process of law; nor shall private property be taken for public use without just compensation (V). In criminal prosecutions, the right of the accused to a speedy and public trial, by an impartial jury of the State and district wherein the crime shall have been committed, which district shall have been previously ascertained by law; and the rights to be informed of the nature and cause of the accusation; to be confronted with the witnesses against him; to have compulsory process for obtaining witnesses in his favor, and to have the assistance of counsel for his defence (VI). Additionally, in suits at common law, the right of trial by jury; and the right not to have re-examined the fact tried by a jury except according to the rules of the common law (VII). Finally, the right people have not to be asked for excessive bail, nor to be imposed of excessive fines, nor to be subjected to cruel and unusual punishments (VIII).

The Bill of Rights contained in the first Ten Amendments was complemented with the declaration of other rights in subsequent Amendments. In 1865, the prohibition of slavery and involuntary servitude (XIII); in 1868, 1970 and 1920, the right to elect representatives, to vote and to be elected, as political rights (XIV,2,3; XV; XIX); and in 1868, the right to citizenship; the right of persons not to be deprived of life, liberty, or property by any State, without due process of law; and the right to have equal protection of laws (XIV,1).

The general trend to declare human rights in the Constitutions, as superior laws, seeking their entrenchment, was immediately followed by the French Revolution, first adopting the Declaration of the Rights of Man and of the Citizen by the National Assembly on August 26, 1789 and second by embodying it at the beginning of the 1791 First French Constitution[3].

---

[3] See in general Allan R. BREWER-CARÍAS, *Reflexiones sobre la Revolución Americana (1776) y la Revolución Francesa (1789) y sus aportes al constitucionalismo moderno,* Cuadernos de la Cátedra Allan R. Brewer-Carías de Derecho Administrativo, Universidad Católica Andrés Bello, N° 1, Editorial Jurídica Venezolana, Caracas 1992.

In the drafting of the seventeen articles of the Declaration recognizing and proclaiming all the fundamental rights of man, the influence of the American Declarations was decisive, particularly in the principle itself of the need of a formal declaration of rights, and in its contents. The mutual influence that the continents had on each other at the time are well known: the French philosophers, including Montesquieu and Rousseau were studied in North America; French participation in the War of Independence was important; Lafayette was a member of the drafting committee of the Constituent Assembly which produced the French Declaration and submitted his own draft based on the Declaration of Independence and the Virginia Bill of Rights; the *repporteur* of the Constitutional Commission proposed «transplanting to France the noble idea conceived in North America»; and Jefferson himself was present in Paris in 1789, having succeeded Benjamin Franklin as American Minister to France[4].

The main objectives in both declarations were the same: to protect the citizen against arbitrary power and to establish the rule of law.

However, it is certain that the French Declaration was, of course, more directly influenced by the thoughts of Rousseau and Montesquieu. The drafters of the Declaration took from Rousseau the principles of considering the role of society as being related to the natural liberty of man, and the idea that the law, as the expression of the general will passed by the representatives of the nation, cannot be an instrument for oppression. They also took from Montesquieu his fundamental distrust of power, and therefore, the principle of separation of powers also embodied in the Virginia Declaration[5].

Of course, the rights proclaimed in the French Declaration were also natural rights of man, thus inalienable and universal; rights that was not granted by political society, but rights inherent to the nature of human beings.

This conception is clear in the justifying text of the Declaration issued «considering that the ignorance, forgetfulness or contempt of the rights of man is the sole causes of public misfortunes and of the corruption of government»; originating a perpetual reminder of the «natural inalienable and sacred rights of man».

The rights and freedoms were recognized and proclaimed forwarded by these declaration of principles: that «men are born and remain free and equal in rights» (1); that «liberty, property, security, and resistance to oppression» are «natural and inalienable rights of man» (2); that «liberty consists of the power to do whatever is not injurious to others; hence the enjoyment of the natural rights of every man has as its limits only those that assure to other members of society the enjoyment of those same rights; limits that can only be determined by law (4); that «nothing may be prevented which is not forbidden by law», and that «no one may be constrained to do what it is not provided for by law (5); that «all citizens have the right to concur personally, or through their representatives» in the formation of the law, as the «expression of the general will»; and that the law «must be the same for all, whether it protects or punishes» (6). There is express reference to the following civil rights: rights to free expression and to free communication of ideas and opinions, considered in the Declaration as «one of the most precious of the rights of

[4] J. RIVERO, *Les libertés publiques*, Dalloz, París, 1973, Vol. I, p. 45.

[5] J. RIVERO, *op. cit*, pp. 41-42.

man»; the right of every citizen to «speak, write, and print with freedom» (11); the right not to «be disquieted on account of his opinions, including his religious views» (10); and the right to property considered «sacred and inviolable», and the right to be «equitably indemnified» when someone is deprive of his property because of a legally determined public necessity, (17).

The rest of the Declaration refers to the due process of law rights: the right of all persons not to «be accused, arrested, or imprisoned except in the cases and according to the forms prescribed by law» (7); the right to be punished «only as are strictly and obviously necessary» and only when the punishment is «legally inflicted in virtue of a law passed and promulgated before the commission of the offence» (8); and the right of all persons to be «held innocent until they shall have been declared guilty» (9).

As for political rights, the Declarations recognized the right of all citizens to be «equally eligible to all dignities and to all public positions and occupations» (6); and the right to «require of every public agent an account of his administration» (15).

The whole process of the development of modern constitutionalism based on the rule of law or the *État de droit*, began with the products of the American and French revolutions and with the general principles they motivated: the idea of Constitution as a superior and fundamental law adopted by the people as sovereign; the democratic and republican principles, based on popular representation, the separation of powers, in the horizontal and the vertical systems; the role of the Judicial Branch, and the formal Declarations of Rights; principles that were subsequently incorporated into all written constitutions of the modern world.

2. The Influence in Latin America

These principles first had an immediate impact in Latin American constitutionalism, long before than in other European countries[6].

We must bear in mind that the process of independence of the Spanish Colonies in Latin America started in 1810, only twenty three years after the sanctioning of the American Constitution, and seven years after the Marbury v. Madison landmark judicial review case. This happens in a moment in which Spain was occupied by French troops after Napoleon had imposed to the invaded realm the Bayonne Constitution of 1808. Spain was fighting for independence from France, and the American Colonies, repudiating the French invasion, began to seek independence from Spain.

So the principles of modern constitutionalism were first adopted in Latin America, from 1811 on, before than in Spain. In Spain these principles were embodied with a monarchical framework a few months after -in the Cadiz 1812 Constitution- which remained in force only for two years, until the Monarchy was restored in 1814. The important aspect to be stressed out is that no Spanish constitutional influence can be found in the beginning of Latin American modern constitutionalism, which basically followed the North American trend.

6 See in general Allan R. BREWER-CARÍAS, *Los derechos humanos en Venezuela: casi 200 años de historia*, Biblioteca de la Academia de Ciencias Políticas y Sociales, Serie Estudios, N° 38, Caracas 1990.

It can be said that, in general, the American -North American and Latin-American- constitutional revolution process and its declarations of rights were very different to the French and even the Spanish ones.

In the French Revolution and Declaration, it was not a case of establishing a new state but of the continuation of a national state already in existence, within the monarchical principle. The same occurred in Spain. On the contrary, in the American Revolution and Declarations, new states were being built upon a new basis.

The purpose of the French Declaration, as stated in its introduction, was to solemnly remind all members of the community of their natural rights and duties. Hence the new principle of individual liberty appeared only as an important modification within the context of a political unity already in existence.

On the other hand, in the North American and Latin-American declarations, the enforcement of rights was an important factor in the independence process, and thus, in the building of the new states upon a new basis. Particularly relevant was the principle of the sovereignty of people with all its democratic content. Therefore, on the American Continent, the solemn Declaration of Fundamental Rights meant the establishment of principles on which the political unity of the nations was based, and the validity of which was recognized as the most important assumption in the emergence and formation of that unity.

Putting aside the Haiti Constitution of 1805, it can be said that the third formal declaration of rights by an independent state in constitutional history was the «Declaration of Rights of the People» adopted by the Supreme Congress of Venezuela in 1811 four days before the formal Venezuelan Independence Act of July 5th, 1811, was approved.

The content of that Declaration followed both the French and the American Declarations, but was much more detailed in the enumeration of rights, including new ones such as the right to industrial and commercial freedom and the freedom to work (20); and the right to consider peoples' home as an inviolable asylum (22). In the declaration of the rights of people, there is also a reference to a social right when it states that «instruction is necessary for all. The society must favor with all its power the progress of public reason to put instruction at the reach of all» (Ch. 4, 4).

The Declaration was also incorporated as a final Chapter of the first of all Latin-American constitutions, the Venezuelan Constitution of December 21, 1811[7], in 59 extensive articles, among which, as an example, articles 151 ff. can be pointed out. This set of articles follow what was established in the French and American declarations, stating that governments are established in order to guarantee the exercise of rights of man, namely «liberty, equality, property and security», defining such rights as follows:

> 153. Liberty (freedom) is the power to do whatever is not injurious to others or to society, which limits can only be establish by law.

[7] See in general Allan R. BREWER-CARÍAS, *Las Constituciones de Venezuela,* Universidad Católica del Táchira (Venezuela), Instituto de Estudios de Administración Local y del Centro de Estudios Constitucionales (España), Madrid 1985, 1.086 pp. A second edition was published by Academia de Ciencias Políticas y Sociales, Caracas, Biblioteca de la Academia de Ciencias Políticas y Sociales, Caracas 1997.

154. Equality consists in that the law must be the same for all citizens, whether it punishes or protects.

155. Property is the right of everybody to enjoy and dispose goods acquired with its work and industry.

156. Security exists within the guaranty and protection that the society gives to each of its members regarding the preservation of their person, their rights and properties.

These two Venezuelan Declarations of Rights of 1811 mark the beginning of a very long tradition of almost 200 hundred years of continuous, extensive and always enlarging Latin American Declarations of Rights; a tradition very different from the European one.

3. The Situation in France

For instance, we must remember that in France, after the Declaration of 1789, no other Declaration of Rights was adopted. After the 1875 Constitutional Laws[8] even its contents were excluded from the text of the Constitution, considering that their provisions were not directly applicable to individuals. That is why the 1958 French Constitution only refers to human rights in an indirect way when it states in its Preamble that «The French people, solemnly proclaim their subjection to the rights of Man and to the national sovereignty principles as have been defined by the Declaration of 1789, confirmed and completed by the Preamble to the constitution of 1946».

Moreover, this Preamble to the Constitution was initially considered by the Constitutional Council itself, only as a principle for the orientation of constitutional interpretation[9]; criteria that began to change after the Constitutional Council decision of July, 16, 1971 regarding the freedom of association, when it was decided that a proposed law establishing a particular judicial controls in order for an association acquiring legal capacity, was against the Constitution. The proposed statute was an amendment bill to a 1901 statute relating to non-profit associations, which the Council considered unconstitutional[10], using the following argument:

The 1958 Constitution through the Preamble to the 1946 Constitution referred to the «fundamental principles recognized by the laws of the Republic» among which the freedom of association must be listed.

In conformity with this principle, associations were to be constituted freely and could publicly develop their activities. The only condition to this association

---

8 J. RIVERO, *Les libertés publiques*, Vol. 1, París, 1973, p. 70.

9 L. HAMON, «Contrôle de Constitutionalité et protection des droits individuels. A propos de trois décisions récents du Conseil Constitutionnel», *Recueil Dalloz Sirey 1974*, Chronique XVI, p. 85.

10 See the Constitutional Council decision in L. FAVOREU, y J. PHILIP, *Les grandes décisions du Conseil Constitutionnel*, París 1984., p. 222. See the comments of the 16 July, 1971 decisions in J. RIVERO, «Note», *L'Actualité Juridique. Droit Administratif*, 1971, p. 537; J. Rivero, «Principes fondamentaux reconnus par les lois de la Republique; une nouvelle categorie constitutionnelle?», *Dalloz 1974*, Chroniques, p. 265; and J.E. BRADSLEY, «The Constitutional Council and Constitutional Liberties in France», *The American Journal of Comparative Law*, 20, (3), 1972, p. 43; B. NICHOLAS, «Fundamental Rights and Judicial Review in France», *Public Law*, 1978, p. 83.

was making a previous declaration, the validity of which was not to be submitted to a previous intervention by either administrative or judicial authorities.

Thus, the Constitutional Council determined that the limits imposed on associations by the proposed bill establishing a prior judicial control of said declaration, were unconstitutional. This decision allowed Professor Jean Rivero to say,

> «The liberty of association, which is not expressly established either in the Declaration or by the particularly needed principles of our times, but which is only recognized by a Statute of July 1st., 1901, has been recognized by the Constitutional Council decision, as having a constitutional character, not only as a principle, but in relation to the modalities of its exercise»[11].

This decision of 1971 is an example of the creative tendency regarding fundamental rights of the Constitutional Council, even though for that purpose its decision was based on the Preamble to the Constitution, and through it, in what the Preamble to the 1946 Constitution considered the «fundamental principles recognized by the laws of the Republic». In general, therefore, to establish a fundamental right or liberty as a «fundamental principle», the Constitutional Council based itself on a particular existing statute, as happened with the liberty of association which was recognized by the Statute of July 1st, 1901.

But in other cases[12], as has happened with the right to self defense, the Constitutional Council has not based itself in a particular Statute for deducing a right based on «the fundamental principles recognized by the laws of the Republic». In that decision dated January 19th-20th 1981[13], the Constitutional Council radically changed the previous approach regarding the right to one's own defense, which was considered by the *Conseil d'État* simply as a general principle of law[14]. Conversely, after the 1981 decision, the Constitutional Council recognized it as part of the «principles and rules of constitutional value», an expression used by the Constitutional Council to describe in a generic manner all the norms that, without being contained in the text of the constitution itself, have Constitutional status[15].

Therefore, in France, «conformity with the constitution» as a consequence of the principle of constitutionality, is not understood today strictly as conformity with an express disposition of the Constitution. Since the 1970's, the notion of constitutional norms that could serve as reference norms to control the constitutionality of legislation has been progressively understood in a wider sense, comprising dispositions or principles outside the constitutional text, and in particu-

---

11 J. RIVERO, «Les garanties constitutionnelles des droits de l'homme en droit français», *IX Journees Juridiques Franco-Latino Americaines*, Bayonne 21-23 mai 1976, (mimeo), p. 11.

12 Decisions of 8 Nov. 1976; 2 Dec. 1976; 20 July 77, 19 January 1981; 20 January 1981, *Cf.* the quotations in F. LUCHAIRE, «Procedures et techniques de protection des droits fondamentaux. Conseil Constitutionnel français», in L Favoreu (ed.), *Cours constitutionnelles européennes et droit fondamentaux*, Aix-en-Provence 1982, pp. 69, 70, 83.

13 L. FAVOREU and L. PHILIP, *Les grandes décisions..., cit.*, pp. 490, 517.

14 *Cf.* D.G. LAVROFF, «El Consejo Constitucional francés y la garantía de las libertades públicas», *Revista española de derecho constitucional*, 1 (3), 1981, pp. 54-55; L. FAVOREU and L. PHILIP, *Les grandes décisions..., cit.*, p. 213.

15 L. Favoreu, «Les décisions du Conseil Constitutionnel dans l'affaire des nationalisations», *Revue du droit public et de la science politique en France et à l'étranger*, T. XCVIII, N° 2, París, 1982, p. 401.

lar, the Declaration of 1789, the Preambles to the 1946 and 1958 Constitutions, the fundamental principles recognized by the laws of the Republic, and the general principles of constitutional value[16]. All these sources of the principle of constitutionality enjoy the same authority as the written articles of the Constitution.

This process of adaptation of the Constitution by the constitutional judge was also confirmed in France in the decision of the Constitutional Council in the *Nationalizations* case of 1982. In this case, the Council applied the article concerning property rights of the 1789 Declaration, thus declaring such right as having constitutional status. In the decision dated January 16 1982[17], the Council considered that even though the relevant article of the 1789 Declaration was obsolete, and that it ought to be interpreted in a completely different way from the sense it had in 1789[18], it:

> Considering that, after 1789 and up to date, the purposes and conditions of the exercise of property rights have evolved because of the expansion of its range of application regarding new individual domains and because of the limitations imposed by the general interest, the principles contained in the Declarations of Man's Rights have full constitutional value, regarding both the fundamental character of the right to property, being its preservation one of the objectives of political society, located in the same level as liberty, security and resistance to oppression, as well as the guaranties given to the holders of such right and the public bodies prerogatives...»[19].

Consequently, the Constitutional Council in this case, not only «created» a fundamental constitutional right when giving constitutional rank and value to the 1789 Declaration, but «adapted» the former «sacred» and absolute property right set forth 200 hundred years ago creating the limited and limitable right of our times. Its preservation led the Council to declare some articles of the Nationalization Law as unconstitutional.

Since these decisions of the Constitutional Council adopted in the seventies, the *block of constitutionality*[20] was enlarged precisely to include the Declaration of Rights of Man and Citizens of 1789 and the Preamble of the 1946 Constitution, by means of interpretation of the 1958 Constitution Preambles, and of the fundamental principles recognized by the laws of the Republic[21]. This also led Professor Rivero

---

16 L. FAVOREU, «L'application directe et l'effect indirect des normes constitutionnelles», *French Report to the XI International Congres of Comparative Law*, Caracas, 1982, (mineo), p. 4.

17 See L. FAVOREU y L. PHILIP, *Les grandes décisions..., cit.*, pp. 525-562.

18 L. FAVOREU, *Le contrôle juridictionnel des lois et sa légitimité. Développements récents en Europe Occidentale*, Association Internationale des Sciences Juridiques, Colloque d'Uppsala 1984, (mineo), p. 32; also published in L. FAVOREU and J.A. JOLOWICZ, *Le contrôle juridictionnel des lois. Légitimité, effectivité et developments récents*, París 1986, pp. 17-68.

19 L. FAVOREU y L. PHILIP, *Les grandes décisions..., cit.*, p. 526. *Cfr.* L. FAVOREU, «Les décisions du Conseil Constitutionnel dans l'affaire des nationalisations», *Revue du droit public et de la science politique en France et à l'étranger*, T. XCVIII, N° 2, París 1982, p. 406.

20 L. FAVOREU, «Le principe de constitutionalité. Essai de définition d'après la jurisprudence du Conseil constitutionnel», in *Recueil d'études en 1'honneur de Charles Eisenmann*, París, 1977, p. 33.

21 L. FAVOREU, *Le contrôle juridictionnel des lois et sa légitimité. Développements récents en Europe Occidentale*, Association Internationale des Sciences Juridiques, Colloque d'Uppsala, 1984, (mineo), p. 8; also published in L. FAVOREU and J.A. JOLOWICZ, *op. cit.*, pp. 17-68.

to assert, with respect to the activism of the Constitutional Council, that with those decisions -based on «the constitution and particularly on its Preamble»-, a revolution has taken place, stating that «In a single blow, the 1789 Declaration, the 1946 Preamble, the fundamental principles recognized by the laws of the Republic, have been integrated into the French Constitution, even if the Constituent did not want to do it. The French Constitution has doubled its volume through the single will of the Constitutional Council»[22]. The author concludes by saying that «Through the single will of the Constitutional Council the French Constitution has doubled its volume»[23].

This process of expansion of constitutional declarations of rights can be considered as one of the main characteristics of the recent evolution of modern constitutionalism, in which various «generations» of rights can be distinguished.

III. THE EXPANSION OF THE CONSTITUTIONAL DECLARATIONS OF RIGHTS BEGINNING WITH THE INDIVIDUAL AND CIVIL RIGHTS

1. The Individual and Civil Rights

In effect, the initial human rights set forth in the Constitutions, as was the case of the North American Bill of Rights or the French Declaration of Citizens and Man's Rights, or of the XIX Century Latin American constitutional declarations of human rights, have been considered the «First declaration» of human rights, containing those rights essential to human nature, or essential to the quality of the human being, and which are common to all human persons. These rights were precisely those referred to in the French declaration, when stating that «The aim of all political association is the preservation of the natural and imprescriptibly rights of man». At the end of the XVIII Century those rights were reduced to freedom, equality before the law, personal safety and safety of property. To these original human rights, the American Bill of Rights added the freedom of religion and cult, freedom of speech and of the press, the right to peaceably assemble, the right to petition, the due process of law guaranties, the right to move and the right to vote. During the XX Century the list of political rights was also enlarged, adding to the right to vote the right to public demonstration, the right to participate in political parties, the right to seek for asylum and in general terms, the right to participate in political life.

All those rights have configured what has been called the «First generation» of human rights[24], as civil or individual rights essential to all human beings, which were regulated in all of the XIX and XX Centuries' constitutions. This First generation of rights is still important, particularly regarding the justiciability of human rights. For instance, in the Spanish Constitution, they are equivalent to «fundamental rights» in order to be protected by means of the «amparo» recourse that can be brought before the Constitutional Tribunal.

---

22 J. RIVERO, «Rapport de Synthèse» in L. FAVOREU, (ed.), *Cours constitutionnelles europeenes et droit fondamentar,* Aix-en-Provence, 1982, p. 520.

23 *Idem,* p. 520.

24 The classification of human rights in «generations», only serves to more or less appreciate the chronological trends of the evolution process of their constitutionalization. See Antonio A. CANÇADO TRINDADE, «Derechos de solidaridad», in *Estudios Básicos de Derechos Humanos,* Vol. I, Instituto Interamericano de Derechos Humanos, San José, 1994, pp. 64 ff.

In effect, Article 53,2 of the Spanish Constitution empowered any citizen to ask for the protection («tutela») of the liberties and rights recognized in Article 14 and in the first Section of the Second Chapter of the Constitution. This protection is sought before the regular courts through a process based on the principles of preference and speed, and when appropriate, through the recourse of «amparo» before the Constitutional Court. This last recourse shall be applicable to objections of conscience recognized in Article 30. Accordingly, as mentioned before, the recourse of «amparo» is only reserved to protect certain constitutional rights equivalent in general contemporary terms to the First generation of Rights, called «fundamental rights», which are the following: The right to equality before the law, without any discrimination (Article 14); the right to life and to physical and moral integrity and not to be subjected to torture or inhuman or degrading punishment or treatment, and the right to the abolishment of death penalty (Article 15); the freedom of ideology, religion, and cult (Article 16); the right to personal liberty and security, particularly regarding detentions (Article 17); the right to honor, to personal and family privacy and to identity; the right to the inviolability of home; and the right to secrecy of communications (postal, telegraphic, and telephone communication) (Article 18); freedom to move (Article 19); the rights to freely express and disseminate thoughts, ideas and opinions through words, writing, or any other means of reproduction and the right to freely communicate or receive truthful information without any kind of censorship (Article 20); the right to peaceful and unarmed assembly and the right to demonstrate (Article 21); the right to association (article 22); the right to participate in public affairs, directly or through representatives freely elected in periodic elections and the right to accede, under conditions of equality, to public functions and positions (Article 23); the right to be effectively protected by judges and courts in the exercise of their rights; the right to self defense and the due process of law rights (no self-incrimination, the presumption of innocence) (Article 24); the *Nulla Poena Sine Lege* rights (Article 25); the right to personal and collective petition (Article 29); and the right oppose conscientious objection for exemption from compulsory military service (Article 30).

All these rights are the civil or political rights that for example, have also been declared in the United Nations International Covenant on Civil and Political Rights of 1966.

One recently enacted Constitution in which all these individual or civil rights are regulated in an extensive way is the 1999 Venezuelan Constitution. I want to highlight this example, not only because it is an illustration of contemporary tendency to constitutionalize human rights by means of very rich and progressive declarations, but also because it is an example that even with such impressive declarations, there is still an absence of an effective independent and autonomous Judiciary, that renders very difficult the justiciability of such rights.

In the Venezuelan Constitution above all one can find a group of very important regulations related to the constitutional guarantees of human rights, that is to say, to the instruments that allow the exercise of such rights.

In this regard, the following guarantees are largely regulated: general freedom in the sense of the right of every one to develop its own personality with only the limits connected to the other individuals rights and to the social and public interest (Article 20); the general principle of the non-retroactive effects of statutes (Article 24); the principle of the nullity of any State act that violates constitutional rights and the principle that all public officials that produced or executed them, are liable (Article 25); and the general principle of equality before the law forbidding any kind of discrimination (Article 21). The Constitution also regulates, following the Spanish Constitution provision, the right of any person to have access to the courts in order to demand enforcement of his rights and interests, including the collective or diffuse rights; the right to obtain effective protection of his rights and to obtain a promptly corresponding decision (Article 26).

The Constitution also regulates the persons' right to have the immediate guarantee or protection of his constitutional rights by means of effective actions or recourse such as the action of «amparo»; the action of protection of personal freedom or *habeas corpus*; and the action of *habeas data* devoted to protect personal data from public or private data bank institutions (Article 27).

On the other hand, the rights to due process of law are also expressly regulated, as well as the right to access to justice, which impose the duty to the Judiciary to only decide cases in accordance with the standards established in the Constitution and the law. The rights to the due process had been established in detail in Article 49, which requires that «due process be applied to all judicial and administrative actions», specifically regulating the following guarantees: the right to self defence; the presumption of innocence; the right to be heard; the right to be judged by the competent and pre-existing judge, that must be independent and impartial; the guarantees against self indictment; the principle of *nullum crimen nulla poena sine lege*; the principle of *non bis in idem* and the guarantee of the State's liability for errors or judicial delays.

Nevertheless, of all the constitutional guarantees of human rights, there can be no doubt that the most important is the guarantee of legality in the sense that only by means of statutes constitutional rights can be limited and restricted. Hence the reference in all constitutional articles on constitutional rights to the «law», is made to law in the sense of statutes (formal law), as acts emanating from the National Assembly acting as a legislative body (Article 202). Additionally, these are the only acts that can restrict or limit constitutional guarantees, as provided in Article 30 of the American Convention on Human Rights, pursuant to the interpretation of the Inter American Court for Human Rights (Advisory Opinion N° 6).

One aspect that we must mention is that even with these kind of constitutional guarantees, the same Constitution provides a formula for its bypassing and potential violation, when regulating the possibility for the Assembly to «delegate legislative powers» in the President of the Republic, by means of so-called «enabling laws» (Article 203), whereby he can dictate executive acts with the rank and value of statutes on any subject (Article 206, Ordinal 8). This provision contrasts with the previous 1961 Constitution which used to set forth that the President could only regulate, by means of enabling laws, matters related to the economy and finance (Article 190, Ordinal 8)[25].

The 1999 Constitution provision, instead, has unfortunately opened up a constitutional loophole that allows the National Assembly and the President, even

---

25 See Pedro NIKKEN, «Constitución Venezolana de 1999: La habilitación para dictar decretos ejecutivos con fuerza de ley restrictivos de los derechos humanos y su contradicción con el derecho internacional», in *Revista de Derecho Público*, N° 83, Editorial Jurídica Vvenezolana, Caracas, 2000, p. 5 ff.

with the impressive range of rights and guarantees embodied in the Constitution, to violate the guarantee of legality which, as stated above, is the most important guarantee for the effective enforcement and execution of human rights.

When referring to constitutional guarantees, it should finally be mentioned that under Article 29 of the Venezuelan Constitution, the State is expressly compelled to investigate and legally sanction any human rights violations committed by its authorities, and Article 30 establishes the State's obligation to wholly indemnify victims of human rights abuse attributable to the State, including the payment of damages. The State shall also protect victims of ordinary offences and endeavor to have the guilty parties repair the damage caused.

Title III, Chapter III of the Venezuelan Constitution is devoted to regulate civil or individual rights, beginning with the right to life, as inviolable thus banning the death penalty (Article 43). This right has also been reinforced by obliging the State to protect «the life of people when deprived of their freedom, rendering military or civil service, or in any other way are submitted to its authority».

The Constitution also expressly regulates the peoples right to a name (identification right) (Article 56); the right to the inviolability of personal freedom (Article. 44), establishing guarantees against arrest and detention, and the prohibition to be held incommunicado (Article 44), the prohibition of slavery or servitude (Article 54) and prohibition of forced disappearance of people.

It is also regulated in detail the right to personal safety (Article 46), with the following rights: the right to not be subjected to torture or degrading punishment; the right of those arrested to be treated with respect on their human dignity; the right to consent upon experiments or treatments; and the liability of public officials for infringements of such rights.

The text of the Constitution, in accordance with the tradition of previous texts, additionally enshrines the inviolability of the home (Article 47); the inviolability of private communications (Article 48); free passage or right to move (Article 50); the right to petition and to a timely response (Article 51); and the right of association (Article 52). This last right, however, has certain constitutional limitations first with respect to judges, who may not associate (Article 256); and second a very inconvenient one, referred to the intervention of the State in the internal elections of labor unions and professional associations, which must be organized by the National Electoral Council, as one of the five branches of government (Electoral Power) (Article 293, 6).

In relation to individual rights, the Constitution also guarantees the right to public or private unarmed assemble, without requiring any previous permits from authorities (Article 53); the right to the free expression of thought, ideas and opinion, by any means and without censorship (Article 57); and the right to «opportune, true and unbiased» information, as well as the right to response and correction when directly affected by incorrect or offensive information (Article 58). Express regulation also exists regarding the right to religious freedom and cult (Article 59); the right to protection of honor, privacy, self image, confidentiality and reputation (Article 60); the right to freedom of conscience (Article 61); and the right to be protected by the State (Article 55).

All these civil rights can be protected by means of the amparo and habeas corpus actions set fourth in article 27 of the Constitution.

2. The social, economic and cultural rights

But regarding the already mentioned «fundamental rights» listed in the Spanish Constitution in order to guaranty their protection by means of the «amparo» recourse -mainly referred to civil rights, it must be indicated that additionally to those civil and political rights, the Spanish Constitution has listed within the «fundamental rights», two social rights: the right to education, including the freedom to teach and to create educational institutions (Article 27); and the workers right to found unions and to strike in defense of their interest (Article 28). These rights are thus also protected by means of the recourse of «amparo».

These social rights can be considered as part of the so called Second Generation of human rights referred to the social, economic and cultural rights, which began to be incorporated in the constitutional declarations of Rights with the Mexican Constitution of 1917 and with the Weimar Constitution of Germany of 1919. All those rights were also the object of the United Nations International Covenant on Social, Economic and Cultural Rights of 1966.

But in fact, well before the adoption of the UN Covenant, after World War II, and due to the Welfare State model that spread all over the Occidental world, almost all Latin American Constitutions started to incorporate in their Declarations of rights, additionally to the civil and political rights, the social, economic, and cultural rights. In this sense, the right to education and the right to health care were constitutionalized, as well as the labor rights: the right to work, the right to membership of labor unions, the right to strike, the right to social security; and additionally, the right to equal treatment at work and the right to a salary. The rights to social benefits and to have stability at work and the right to bargain collectively for labor benefits.

Other rights that were progressively constitutionalized, were the right to have proper housing and the right to cultural heritage; as well as all the right to social protection or welfare, such as the right to have family, children protection, maternity and disabled persons protections.

Many of these social rights were incorporated in the Constitutions in order to set forth a constitutional duty or obligation for the State to provide social protection to the people or to render certain public services, as public utilities.

On the other hand, also as Second generation of rights, additionally to the property rights, the economic rights were also constitutionalized, particularly the economic freedom which implies the freedom of industry and trade and the freedom to work.

The 1999 Venezuelan Constitution can be mentioned not only regarding the regulation of these social, economic and cultural rights, but also as an example of extensive and complex policy declarations, regarding which is difficult to find the necessary relation between right and obligation[26]. On the other hand, the Constitution, in a highly paternalistic and State oriented trend, attributes innumerable social obligations to the State bodies, and in the compliance of which society's participation is expressly excluded. Thus, in the 1999 Constitution, the State is

---

[26] See in general Allan R. BREWER-CARÍAS, *Derecho Constitucional Venezolano. La Constitución de 1999*, Editorial jurídica Venezolana, Caracas 2004, 2 vols.

responsible for almost all social goals and welfare, a task impossible to be accomplished, even with the rich oil producing State that Venezuela is, where in the first six years of the enforcement of the Constitution (1999-2005), because the rising oil prices, State revenues rose to a level never dreamed before. The tragic result has been that in the same period of time, in parallel to the State populist distribution of money policy, poverty has risen.

Anyway, regarding constitutional regulations, the Constitution starts by regulating a group of social rights, referring to families (Article 75); maternity and paternity (Article 76); marriage «between a man and a woman» (Article 77); children and teenagers (Article 78); young people (Article 79); the elderly (Article 80); and to disabled (Article 81); with express regulation of the obligation of televised media to include subtitles and translation into sign language for people with hearing problems (Article 101).

The Constitution also expressly regulated, as a declaration, the people's right to a dwelling place, that must be «adequate, sure, comfortable, hygienic with the essential utilities, including an habitat that humanizes family, neighborhood and communal relations» (Article 82); and the right to health care (Article 83), imposing on the State the obligation to create, oversee and administer a «national public health system», that must be inter-sectorial, decentralized and participative, integrated with the social security system, governed by the principles of freeness, universality, integrity, fairness, social integration and solidarity (Article 84).

Hence, the health service is constitutionally conceived as being integrated with the social security system (as a sub-system), and also conceived as being free and universal, which bears no relationship whatsoever with the social security system established for the affiliates or the insured. It is also set forth with constitutional rank, that public health goods and services are considered as State ownership and shall not be privatized. Finally, it is set forth that the organized community shall have the right and duty to participate in decisions regarding the planning, execution and control of specific policies at the public health institutions (Article 84).

Article 85 of the Constitution establishes that the State shall be obliged to finance the public health system by means of tax income, the obligatory contributions to social security and any other source of financing determined by law. The State shall also guarantee a health budget that covers the objectives of the health policy. Finally, the above-mentioned Article 85 indicates that the State «shall regulate public and private health institutions»; this being the only ruling that names private health institutions, but merely as subjects to regulation.

In regard to the right to social security, Article 86 of the Constitution regulates it «as a non-lucrative public service that guarantees the health and assures protection in contingencies concerning maternity, paternity, sickness, invalidity, catastrophic illnesses, disability, special needs, labor risks, loss of employment, old-age, widowhood, orphanage, housing, costs derived from family life and any other circumstance of social welfare».

In the same Chapter relative to social and family rights, the 1999 Constitution, in a way similar to the 1961 Constitution, incorporated the group of labor rights into the text of the Constitution, but this time it broadened them and reinforced them even more, raising many rights to a constitutional rank. Thus, the right and duty to work was expressly regulated (Article 87); as well as the right to equality at work (Article 88); the State protection of work (Article 89); the workday and right to rest (Article 90); the right to a salary (Article 91); the right to social benefits (Article 92); the right to work stability (Article 93); responsibilities at the workplace (Article 94); the right to join a labor union (Article 95); the right to collective bargain (96); and the right to strike (Article 97).

In regard to the right to join labor unions, the very inconvenient State's influence over the unions' functions should be emphasized, by reason of Article 293.6 of the Constitution, which states that the National Electoral Council shall be the organ competent to «organize the elections of labor unions and professional associations». In Venezuela, therefore, the unions are not free to organize their own elections of their authorities and representatives, since such elections organization shall be carried out by the State.

On the other hand, Title III, Chapter VI of the Constitution enshrines a series of rights regarding culture, such as cultural freedom and creation, and intellectual property (Article 98); cultural values and the protection of cultural heritage (Article 99); the protection of popular culture (Article 100) and cultural information (Article 101), establishing that the State shall guarantee the broadcasting, reception and circulation of cultural information. To this end, the media is duty-bound to assist in the broadcasting of the values of popular tradition and the work of artists, composers, filmmakers, scientists and other such creators of culture.

With regards to education, Article 102 of the Constitution begins by establishing, in general terms, that «education is a human right and an essential social duty, democratic, free and obligatory». The consequence of this is the provision under Article 102 that imposes on the State the obligation to assume education as an «indeclinable function» and one of maximum interest at all its levels and types, and as an instrument of scientific, humanistic and technological knowledge at the service of society. Hence, constitutionally speaking, education is declared a public utility or service, emphasizing however that: «the State shall encourage and protect any private education that is rendered according to the principles provided in the Constitution and the Law».

The right to an integral education, the free nature of public education and the obligatory character of all levels of education from pre-school to diversified secondary level, are also regulated. Insofar as State school education is concerned, this shall be free up to pre-university level (Article 103). The teachers´ regime is also established (Article 104); as are the right to educate (Article 106), and the obligatory teaching of environmental and civic education; as well as the history and geography of Venezuela (Article 107). Article 108 also emphasizes that social communication media, both public and private, shall contribute to the citizens' education. Additionally, the 1999 Constitution formalizes the principle of the universities' autonomy (Article 109); regulates the regime of the liberal professions (Article 105); the regime of science and technology (Article 110); and the right to sporting activities (Article 111).

All these social rights imply State obligations and can also be enforced by means of the «amparo» action or recourse, as has been used mainly regarding social protection rights, like maternity rights, and right to education and health care.

The 1999 Constitution also incorporates in Chapter VII, with detail, the economic rights of people, as follows: on the one hand economic freedom (Article 112); and on the other the right to property and right to only be expropriated by means of due process and just compensation (Article 115). This form of regulation follows the orientation of Venezuelan constitutionalism, although certain variations with regard to its equivalent in the previous 1961 Constitution (Article 99), should be emphasized: *firstly*, it is not mentioned that private property shall perform a social function, as indicated in the 1961 Constitution; *secondly*, in the 1999 Constitution the attributes of the ownership of property (use, possession and disposal) are detailed, where such provision were previously a legal matter (dealt with under Article 545 of the Civil Code); and *thirdly*, in regard to expropriation, the new constitutional text provides that the payment of fair compensation be «timely». Thus the regulation guarantees more strongly the right to ownership of property. But in contrast to these guarantees, it can be said that never before the State has occupied more land without proper compensation as has occurred since the enactment of the Constitution in 2000, particularly in the country side.

The Constitution also forbids any kind of confiscation of goods, except in the cases allowed by the Constitution itself, by way of exception and due process, to the goods and property of national or foreign individuals or companies guilty of corruption crimes committed against public property, or those who have illicitly enriched themselves acting as public officials, or in cases of enrichment arising from commercial, financial or other activities associated with the illicit traffic of drugs and narcotics (Articles 116 and 271).

Additionally, Title VI of the 1999 Constitution is dedicated to the regulation of the socio-economic system. Amongst its regulations, Article 307 should be mentioned, since it declares the regime of large rural estates (*latifundio*) as being contrary to social interest, and encouraging the legislator to tax idle land and to establish the measures necessary to transform such land into productive economic units, also rescuing land being eminently agricultural land.

This same regulation establishes the right of peasants and other countryman to own land, pursuant to the methods and cases specified by the respective law. This implies the establishment of constitutional State obligations to protect and encourage associative and individual ownership mechanisms in order to guaranty farm production, and to control the sustainable organization of farm land in order to ensure food and agricultural potential.

The same article exceptionally provides that the legislator create taxlike contributions to facilitate the funding for the financing, research, technical assistance, technology transfer and other activities promoting productivity and competition in the agricultural sector.

3. The collective rights

More recently, in the past decades, a Third generation of rights has developed, related to collective rights, considered as human kind rights or solidarity rights, like the right to have a healthy environment; the right to development; the right to free competition; the consumer's rights to have products and services of quality; the right to have a certain standard of living; the right to human kind heritage, the rights of the indigenous communities and even the right to peace, as is set forth in the Colombian Constitution of 1991 (Article 22).

Many recent constitutions have incorporated such rights in their texts, as has happened with the right to have a healthy environment, to which Constitutions devote extensive articles. This is the case of the 1994 Argentinean Constitution, whose article 41 states that:

(1) All inhabitants are entitled to the right to a healthy and balanced environment fit for human development in order that productive activities shall meet present needs without endangering those of future generations; and shall have the duty to preserve it. As a first priority, environmental damage shall bring about the obligation to repair it according to law.

(2) The authorities shall provide for the protection of this right, the rational use of natural resources, the preservation of the natural and cultural heritage and of the biological diversity, and shall also provide for environmental information and education.

(3) The Nation shall regulate the minimum protection standards, and the provinces those necessary to reinforce them, without altering their local jurisdictions.

(4) The entry into the national territory of present or potential dangerous wastes, and of radioactive ones, is forbidden.

Before the Argentinean Constitution, the 1988 Constitution of Brazil initiated the constitutionalization process of the rights to healthy environment, with its article 255, in which it is also regulated the general policy of the State regarding environment, as follows:

«All persons are entitled to an ecologically balanced environment, which is an asset for the people's common use and is essential to healthy life, it being the duty of the Government and of the community to defend and preserve it for present and future generations.

(1) In order to ensure the effectiveness of this right, it is incumbent upon the Government to:

I. preserve and restore essential ecological processes and provide ecological handling of the species and ecosystems;

II. preserve the variety and integrity of Brazil's genetic wealth and supervise entities engaged in research and handling of genetic material;

III. determine, in all units of the Federation, territorial spaces and components which are to receive special protection, any alteration and suppression only being allowed by means of a law, and any use which adversely affects the integrity of the attributes which justify their protection being forbidden;

IV. demand, according to the law, for the installation of works or activities which may cause significant degradation of the environment, a prior environment impact study, which shall be made public;

V. control the production, marketing, and use of techniques, methods, and substances which represent a risk to life, to the quality of life, and to the environment;

VI. promote environmental education at all school levels and public awareness of the need to preserve the environment;

VII. protect the fauna and the flora, all practices which jeopardize their ecological function, cause the extinction of species or subject animals to cruelty being forbidden according to the law.

(2) Those who explore mineral resources shall be required to restore the degraded environment according to the technical solution required by the proper government agency, according to the law.

(3) Conduct and activities considered harmful to the environment shall subject the individual or corporate wrongdoers to penal and administrative sanctions, in addition to the obligation to repair the damages caused.

(4) The Brazilian Amazon Forest, the Atlantic Woodlands, the «Serra do Mar», the «Pantanal Mato Grossense» and the Coastline are part of the national wealth, and they shall be used, according to the law, under conditions which ensure preservation of the environment, including the use of natural resources.

(5) Vacant governmental lands or lands seized by the States through discriminatory actions, which are necessary to protect natural ecosystems, are inalienable.

(6) Power plants operated by nuclear reactor shall have their location defined in a federal law and may otherwise not be installed.

Following this general pattern, the right to the environment is also regulated in the Constitutions of Colombia (Article 79), Cuba (Article 27), Chile (Article 8), Ecuador (Articles 86-91); Guatemala (Articles 97-98), México (Article 4), Panamá (Article 114), Paraguay (article 7), Perú (Article 22) and Venezuela (Articles 127-129).

In the 1999 Venezuelan Constitution, which we have been commenting as a Latin American example of contemporary constitutional declarations of rights, and as an innovation is the regulation of rights relative to the environment -establishing standards for the right and duty to enjoy and maintain a healthy environment (Article 127); the territorial land planning policy (Article 128); environmental impact studies and the toxic substances régime; and the obligatory inclusion of environmental clauses in public contracts (Article 129).

Another constitutional innovation regarding economic matters, but as collective rights, is regulated by Article 117, referred to the right of everybody to possess quality goods and services, as well as adequate and non-deceptive information of the products and services they consume; to freedom of choice; and to a fair and dignified treatment. In this case, in fact, the Constitution has established a collective right of the Third generation, as well as in Article 113 referred to the prohibition of monopoly and to the abuse of dominion position in trade competitions relations.

Also regarding collective rights, the rights of the indigenous peoples have been regulated in a very extensive way in many recent Constitutions of Latin America, as has happened in the Constitutions of Colombia (Articles 171, 246, 329, 330), Ecuador (Articles 83-85), México (Article 2), Paraguay (Articles 62-67) and Venezuela (Articles 119-126).

In the latter, Chapter VIII contains a group of regulations of the rights of the indigenous people, in contrast with the previous Constitution of 1961 (Article 77) which contained only a brief protection regulation. In this regard, the 1999 Constitution recognizes «the existence of indigenous peoples and communities, their social, political and economic organization; their cultures, usages and customs, languages and religions; and their habitat and their original rights over their ancestral and traditional lands, necessary for developing and guaranteeing their lifestyles» (Article 119). The Constitution sought to neutralize the danger that might arise from this regulation in regard to the national territory integrity, by stating that «since they represent cultures with ancestral roots, the indigenous people are part of the Nation, the State and the sole, sovereign and indivisible Venezuelan people», where the term «people» should not be interpreted in the sense provided under international law (Article 126).

Apart from this, the Constitution provided a set of regulations relative to the development of natural resources to be found in indigenous habitats (Article 120); to the indigenous cultural values (Article 121); to the right of the indigenous people to integral health care (Article 122); and to indigenous people's rights to the collective intellectual property of their knowledge, technologies and innovations (Article 124). Finally, Article 125 of the Constitution enshrines the indigenous people's right to political participation, with Article 126 of the Constitution guaranteeing «indigenous representation in the National Assembly and the consultant bodies of the federal and local entities that have indigenous populations, pursuant to the law».

In all these cases, the Constitutions regulates these rights not as individual rights, but as collective rights, which are also different to the individual rights that can be collectively claimed, like the labor rights.

Some of these rights have been the object of international regulations, as is the case of the right to development incorporated in article 1 of the United Nations Declarations on the Right of Development (1986), as follows:

1. The right to development is an inalienable human right by virtue of which every human person and all peoples are entitled to participate in, contribute to, and enjoy economic, social, cultural and political development, in which all human rights and fundamental freedoms can be fully realized.

2. The human right to development also implies the full realization of the right of peoples to self-determination, which includes, subject to the relevant provisions of both International Covenants on Human Rights, the exercise of their inalienable right to full sovereignty over all their natural wealth and resources.

Finally, it must be mentioned that beside these collective rights, in the contemporary world, a Fourth generation of human rights is beginning to appear, yet in the process to be constructed, such as the human right to the protection of the human genome and the genetic identity and also the rights to the informatics technology progress.

4. The problem of the relation between rights and obligation in the constitutional declarations

As mentioned before, when analyzing the subject of rights and freedoms, as constitutional rights, they essentially are legal situations of power that individuals hold within a society, by which they have the right to do or not to do, to make, to act or to be protected. Being situations of power, they must always have a direct relationship with other legal situations of duty that are held by the State or by other individuals in the same society, in the sense that if somebody has the power to act, some other person has the duty to refrain from or to impede that action; or if somebody has the right to be protected for instance on his health, the State is obliged to developed institutions in order to care for the health of individuals.

Hence a society cannot be conceived without these direct relations among the subjects that act therein, between those situations of power that are correlative to situations of duty. That is to say, a society cannot be imagined without this interrelation between subjects that, on the one hand, hold the legal power to do, enjoy, use or have, and other subjects that, on the other hand, are in a legal situation of duty, respect, abstention, rendering or giving. In other words, there is always a relationship between a right and an obligation or, in general, between a power and a duty.

From a legal viewpoint, human rights are legal situations of power that are consubstantial with human nature or with the quality of being human, in fact, with the quality of man, and which all men have in equal measure, but in whose regime and declaration, of course, the principle of relation or correlatively with duties has to be always present. Thus, if there is an active subject that has a right, there always has to be someone with an obligation (a passive subject) towards that right, that is, someone who is obliged to abstain from or to perform certain activities to satisfy the enjoyment of those determined rights; therefore there can be no right without a correlative obligation.

In this sense, for instance, there cannot be a human right «to not to get ill». This is a wish, a political declaration, a general purpose of society, but not a right, because correlatively to that dream there is no a particular subject with the duty of ensuring that peoples will not get ill.

In the case of the Venezuelan Constitution, for example, one of the problems that arise when facing the most ample and excellent listing of human rights contained in it, is the confusion that can be found in the constitutional text between good intentions, declarations of public policy and constitutional rights. In some cases, illusion or frustration can derive from the impossibility of satisfying certain aims that have been formulated as social rights, that, because of conceptual impossibility, cannot originate obligations or obligated parties.

This happens with several social rights and guarantees established in the Constitution that are simply impossible to satisfy literally. They are excellent declarations of principle and intent of an unquestionably teleological nature, but it is difficult to conceive them as «rights», since there cannot exist a subject with the obligation to satisfy them.

Such is the case, for example, of the «right to health», enshrined as an «essential social right and obligation of the State, that it shall guarantee as part of the right to life» (Article 83). The fact is that it is impossible for anybody to guarantee somebody else's health, and therefore that constitutionally the «right to health» be established. This would be like, as mentioned before, establishing in the Constitution the right to not become ill, which is impossible since nobody can guarantee to another person that they are not going to become ill.

Constitutional formulas in these matters, however, are quite similar over Latin America. In some cases health is declared public property, as provided in the Constitution of El Salvador: «... the health of the inhabitants of the Republic is considered public property» (Article 65). The Constitution of Guatemala (Article 95) regulates health in a similar sense, and for this reason, both Constitutions establish that the State and the people are under the obligation to ensure its conservation and reestablishment. In this sense it can be said that the right to health is more conceived as a collective right, rather than an individual right.

Yet apart from these general declarations of a constitutional nature, in the majority of the Constitutions of Latin America, the «right to health» is expressly established within the fundamental or constitutional rights of the people (Bolivia, Article 7.a; Brasil, Articles 6 and 196; Ecuador, Article 42; Nicaragua, Article 59; Venezuela, Article 84). This fundamental right corresponds «equally» to all people, as declared in the Constitution of Nicaragua (Article 59); and the Constitution of Guatemala reaffirms this, providing that «the enjoyment of good health is a fundamental right of every human person, and there shall be no discrimination whatsoever in this regard» (Article 93).

Therefore, this constitutional formula of the «right to health», as mentioned above, in fact constitutes a declaration of principles relative to the State's commitment and that of society as a whole to the human person, which would be very difficult to identify «literally» as a real «constitutional right», except from the collective point of view, since such description or declaration lacks the principle of reciprocity.

Nevertheless, it can be said that what the Constitutions seeks to establish with this formula, from the individual rights point of view, is in fact the right of all people to have their health protected by the State, whose corresponding obligation is to ensure the care and recuperation of the health of the people.

For this reason, other Latin American Constitutions declare, more exactly, as an individual right, «the right to the protection of health» (Honduras, Article 145); or they refer more precisely to the right of all people to the protection of their health» (Chile, Article 19,9; México, Article 4; Perú, Article 7); or that «their health be cared for and protected» (Cuba, Article 50); or that «all people be guaranteed access to the promotion, protection and recuperation of health» (Colombia, Article 49). In Panama, Article 105 of the Constitution even provides that:

> «The individual, as part of society, is entitled to the promotion, protection, conservation, restitution and rehabilitation of his or her health and the obligation to maintain such health, this being understood to be complete physical, mental and social well-being».

In certain cases, as occurs in the above-mentioned Constitution of Venezuela, it could be said that both formulas are mixed together, when, for example, Article 83 provides that «health is an essential social right», moreover adding that «all people shall have the right to the protection of their health». A similar situation occurs in Article 68 of the Constitution of Paraguay, where, under the heading «right to health», it establishes that «the State shall protect and promote health as being a fundamental right of the individual and in the interest of society».

Another case that can be highlighted as an example of this relationship between constitutional declarations and the relation of rights with duties, is the right that the Venezuelan Constitution enshrines in favor of «all people to an adequate, safe, comfortable and healthy dwelling, with all the basic essential utilities and a habitat that humanizes family, neighborhood and community relationships» (Article 82). This «right», as written, is impossible to satisfy, and not even a rich State can be obliged to satisfy it. It is, rather, a declaration of principles or intent, beautifully structured, that cannot however lead to identifying a party that is obligated to satisfy it, and much less to the State. Here, good intentions and social declarations were confused with constitutional rights and obligations, which cause a different type of legal relationship that are even justifiable or entitled to constitutional protection. What in fact can and must be constructed from such «right to dwelling», in the obligation of the State to provide everyone with the means and conditions to have such a home.

IV. CHANGES IN THE OBLIGED PARTY REGARDING CONSTITUTIONAL RIGHTS AND FREEDOMS

In any case, according to the initial concept behind the formulation of the declaration of civil rights, the responsible party in the relation right/duty was the State. This means that the rights were originally formulated before the State, in order to be protected from State actions or intrusions, so the active subject was always man, a citizen, and the passive subject - the obligated party - was the State.

This initial concept of the formulation of constitutional rights, particularly regarding civil or individual rights, even led to their justiciability by means of the «amparo» action or recourse always conceived as a protection mechanisms against the State. So in its origin, the «amparo» action was not conceived to protect individuals from other individuals' offences.

This of course changed later on with the alteration of the way of conceiving the relationship between rights and duties (in the sense that the passive subject in the constitutional rights is not only the State). The latter continues to be so, but not exclusively, since the field of the passive subject has been progressively universalized, to the point where there now exist obligations -that is, situations of duty in the field of rights- that correspond, naturally, to individuals, to groups, to communities, and even to the international community. This is the case of the Third generation of rights like the right to development, a right which, moreover, is not only held by man as an individual but by peoples and communities and also the international community.

On the other hand, referring to the necessary relationship between situations of power and situations of duty, it can be found that the situations of duty, -those corresponding to the passive subject, are not always of the same nature.

Often the situations of duty are configured as situations of being obliged to provide or to give or render something, accomplishing a positive obligation, that is to say, as obligations to render, give or make. This is the common situation regarding social rights, such as the right to education or right to health care, in relation to which the State is obliged to carry out a positive activity, or to render a public service or utility, that the citizens have the right to received or enjoy, as the active subjects in the legal relation.

In other fields, constitutional rights instead of being rights to receive something as a service, are rather «freedoms», because the situation of the passive subject, for example of the State itself, does not correspond to any obligation to do or to give. In these cases, the obligation is basically an obligation to abstain from acting, to not disturb, to not harm, to not stop, to not deprive. Therefore, from the strictly legal viewpoint, these are more freedoms rather than rights. For example, the freedom of moving implies more a correlative situation of duty consisting in the obligation to restrict the free circulation of people; the freedom or the right to free expression of thoughts, to free speech or to free press implies the State's duty not to bother, not to censor, not to prevent or impede the exercise of such rights.

This relation between the various situations of power and duty leads to a clear distinction between freedoms and rights, when the situation of the obligated subject is not, in the case of freedoms, an obligation to give or to do, but rather not to do, to abstain. In contrast, in the rights as such, there is an obligation to render, as occurs, for example, in general, in public services and, particularly, in those of a social nature (health, education).

From this point of view, regarding the rights in strict sense, it can be said that in general, the obliged party is the State, that is the party with the duty to provide health care or education to the people; instead, regarding freedoms, not only the State is obliged not to restrict, or not to impede its exercise, but also other individuals have the duty to abstain or to refrain. That is why, in contemporary constitutional law, the action of «amparo» in many countries can also be exercised against individuals and not only against the State, as was the initial constitutional trend.

V. THE DECLARATIVE NATURE OF THE CONSTITUTIONAL DECLARATIONS OF RIGHTS AND THE OPEN CONSTITUTIONAL CLAUSES

From a legal point of view, and regarding all the «generations» of rights, it is important to note how the declarations are not «constitutive» of such rights, in the sense that they do not create such rights, but rather, as their name itself implies, are of a declaratory nature, that is, they only recognize the existence of rights. Therefore neither the Constitutions nor the International Conventions create or establish them, but rather admit them as being inherent to the human person, as natural rights.

From this angle, the most important aspect of the expansion process of the constitutional declarations of human rights in Latin America, has been the progressive and continuous incorporation in the Constitutions of the «open clauses» of a person's rights, which has also arisen through the influence of the United States IX (1791) in which it is stated that «the enumeration in the Constitution, of certain rights, shall not be constructed to deny or disparage others retained by the people».

The express enshrining of clauses of such sort in the Constitutions confirms that the list of constitutional rights does not end with those that are expressly listed in the constitutional declaration, but that all others rights which are inherent to the human person or those declared in international instruments are also considered as human rights.

In this respect it can even be said that all Latin American Constitutions, with only very few exceptions (Cuba, Chile, México and Panamá), contain open clauses of the rights, according to which it is expressly indicated that the declaration and enunciation of the rights that is made in the Constitution shall not be understood to be a denial of others not listed therein, that are inherent to the human person or to human dignity. Clauses of this type are to be found, for example, in the Constitutions of Argentina (Article 33), Bolivia (Article 33), Colombia (Article 94), Costa Rica (Article 74), Ecuador (Article 19), Guatemala (Article 44), Honduras (Article 63), Nicaragua (Article 46), Paraguay (Article 45), Perú (Article 3), Uruguay (Article 72) and Venezuela (Article 22).

In the Dominican Republic, the Constitution is less expressive, only indicating that the constitutional list (Articles 8 and 9) «is not limitative, and therefore does not exclude other rights and duties of a similar nature» (Article 10).

Regarding the rights inherent to human persons referred to in many of the open clauses, the former Supreme Court of Justice of Venezuela in a decision of January 31, 1991 (Case: *Anselmo Natale*), stated:

> «The inherent rights of a human person are natural, universal rights which find their origin and are direct consequence of the relationships of solidarity among men, of the need for the individual development of mankind and for the protection of the environment».

Therefore the same Court concluded by stating that

> «...such rights are commonly enshrined in Universal declarations and in national and supranational texts, and their nature and content as human rights shall leave no room for doubt, since they are the very essence of a human person and shall therefore be necessarily respected and protected»[27].

Accordingly, Article 22 of the Constitution of Venezuela, following the tradition of previous Constitutions, expressly establishes that «the enunciation of the rights and guarantees contained in this Constitution and in the international instruments on human rights shall not be understood to be a denial of others that being inherent to the human person, are not expressly set forth in those texts»; adding that «the absence of the regulating statute of such rights do not impede its exercise» (Article 22).

This article, like Article 94 of the 1991 Colombian Constitution and Article 44 of the Guatemalan Constitution, refers to the «inherent rights of a human person», thus incorporating notions of a natural right, in the sense that human rights precede the State and the Constitutions themselves. The Constitution of Paraguay, in the same sense, refers to «rights inherent to human personality» (Article 45).

But in the case of Colombia and Venezuela, the open clause allows for the identification of rights inherent to human persons, not only regarding those listed in the Constitution, but also in international human rights instruments, thus considerably broadening their scope. On the other hand the clause has allowed national Courts to identify human rights inherent to human beings not expressly regulated in the Constitutions, but set forth in international instruments. It was the case during the nineties of the former Supreme Court of Justice of Venezuela, which annulled statutes basing its rulings in the violation of rights set forth in the American Convention which were considered as rights inherent to human beings according to open clause incorporated in article 50 of the 1961 Constitution.

---

27 See the reference in Carlos AYALA CORAO, «La jerarquía de los instrumentos internacionales sobre derechos humanos», en *El nuevo derecho constitucional latinoamericano, IV Congreso venezolano de Derecho constitucional*, Vol. II, Caracas, 1996, and in *La jerarquía constitucional de los tratados sobre derechos humanos y sus consecuencias*, México, 2003.

In effect, in 1996, the Supreme Court of Justice, when deciding a judicial review action brought before the Court against the State of *Amazonas* legislation setting its territorial division, ruled that being the State mainly populated by indigenous people, the sanctioning of the statute without hearing the opinion of the indigenous communities, violated the constitutional right to political participation. Such right was not expressly regulated in the 1961 Constitution, so the Court founded its ruling in the open clause enshrined in Article 50 of the Constitution (equivalent to Article 22 of the 1999 Constitution), considering the right to political participation as inherent to human being, in particular, as a «general principle of constitutional rank in a democratic society», adding, regarding the case, that «because of being a minorities rights (indigenous peoples in the case), it must be judicially protected, according to Article 50 of the Constitution, to the great international treaties and conventions on human rights, and to the national and states legislation». In the December 5, 1996 ruling it was provided:

> In the case, there was no evidence of the accomplishment of the previsions regarding citizens participation, lacking the statute of its original legitimacy derived from the popular hearing. The defendants argued that the advice of public bodies such as the Ministry of the Environment and the Environment Autonomous Services of the Amazon States where asked, as well as the advice of some indigenous organization. The Court deems that such procedure does only constitute a timid and insignificant expression of the constitutional right to political participation in the process of elaborating statutes, which must be guarantied before and pending the legislative activity and not only when the legislation is promulgated... Regarding a statute referred to the political-territorial division of a State like the Amazonas State (mainly populated by indigenous communities), it is a statute that changes and modifies the economic and social conditions of the region, the vital environment of individuals, the municipal boundaries, the land ownership regime and the daily life of indigenous peoples. Thus their participation must be considered with special attention, due to the fact that indigenous peoples are one of the most exposed groups to human rights violations, due to their socio-economic and cultural conditions, in which habitat intervenes various interest some times contrary to the legitimate rights of autochthonous populations... It is in this context that the rights of indigenous peoples acquire more force, as it is expressly recognized by this Court[28].

According to the aforementioned, the Court's decision referred to the violation of constitutional rights of minorities set forth in the Constitution and in the international treaties and conventions on human rights, particularly the right to citizenship participation in the statute elaborating process, particularly because no public consultation was made in the case to the minority indigenous communities, as a consequence of which, the Court decided to annul the challenged statute.

The following year, in 1997, another important decision was issued by the former Supreme Court of Justice of Venezuela, this time annulling a national (federal) statute referred to wicked and crooked persons (Ley de vagos y maleantes) which was considered unconstitutional, based on the «constitutionalization of human rights process according to Article 50 of the Constitution», because such statute «violated

---

[28] Caso: *Antonio Guzmán, Lucas Omashi y otros,* in *Revista de Derecho Público,* N° 67-68, Editorial Jurídica Venezolana, Caracas, 1996, pp. 176 ff.

ipso jure the international conventions and treaties on human rights which had acquired constitutional rank». In its November 6, 1997 ruling, the Supreme Court considered the challenged statute which allowed executive detentions without due process to persons considered wicked or crooks, as infamous, supporting its decision on Article 5 of the Universal Declaration on Human Rights, and in the American Convention on Human Rights «which has been incorporated on internal law as self applicable regulation reinforced by courts decisions that has given the Convention constitutional force, which implies the incorporation to our internal legal order of the regime set forth in the international conventions». The Court considered that the challenged statute was unconstitutional because it omitted the guaranties for a fair trail set forth in Articles 7 and 8 of the American Convention and Articles 9 and 14 of the International Covenant on Human Rights, and because it was discriminatory violating Article 24 of the same American Convention, transcribing in the ruling text the entire text of those articles. The Court also referred in its annulling ruling, to the existence of «reports of human rights organization which openly condemn the Venezuelan legislation on wicked and crook persons, particularly on the grounds of promoting the sanction of a statute on citizen's security protection»[29].

More recently, and regarding the challenging of the proposed call for a consultative referendum for the convening of a National Constituent Assembly by the elected President of the Republic in December 1998, which was not regulated in the 1961 Constitution as a mean for constitutional review or reform, the Supreme Court in January 1999, issued two rulings deciding interpretative recourses, allowing the convening of such Constituent Assembly by means of a referendum based on the peoples right to political participation also founded in the open clause on human rights set forth in Article 50 of the Constitution, considering it as an implicit, constitutionally not enumerated right inherent in the human person.

Considering the referendum as a right inherent to the human person, the Court specifically indicated that:

> This is applicable, not only from a methodological point of view, but ontologically as well, since if the right to a constitutional referendum were considered to depend on a reform of the current Constitution, it would be subordinate to the will of the constituted power, which in turn would be placed above the sovereign power. The absence of such a right in the Fundamental Charter must be interpreted as a gap in the Constitution, since it could not be sustained that the sovereign power had renounced, *ab inicio*, the exercise of a power that is the work of its own political decision.[30]

The conclusion of the Court's decision was that it was not necessary to previously reform the Constitution in order to recognize the referendum or popular consultation on whether to convene a Constituent Assembly as being a constitutional right[31].

---

29 See in *Revista de Derecho Público* N° 71-72, Editorial Jurídica Venezolana, Caracas, 1997, pp. 177 ff.

30 See in *Revista de Derecho Público,* N° 77-80, Editorial Jurídica Venezolana, Caracas, 1999, p. 67.

31 See the comments in Allan R. Brewer-Carias, «La configuración judicial del proceso constituyente o de cómo el guardián de la Constitución abrió el camino para su violación y para su propia extinción», in *Revista de Derecho Público,* N° 77-80, Editorial Jurídica Venezolana, Caracas, 1999, pp. 453 ff.

Open clauses of human rights, of the same nature, which have served in Latin American countries to resolve important constitutional issues, are found in almost all their Constitutions, even with different contents. The Constitution of Ecuador, for instance, indicates that «the rights and guarantees provided in this Constitution and in international instruments do not exclude others derived from the nature of the human person and are necessary for his or her full moral and material development (Article 19). This provision is complemented by Article 18 in which it is stated that the rights and guaranties enshrined in the Constitution and in the international instruments, are directly and immediately applicable by and before any court or authority; and that the absence of regulatory statutes can not be alleged in order to justify the violation or the ignorance of the rights set forth in the Constitution, or to reject the action for its protection, or to deny the recognizance of such rights.

In Nicaragua, the Constitution is more detailed regarding the listing of international instruments and, as such, more limitative, when its Article 46 provides as follows:

> **Article 46.-** Every person in the land shall enjoy State protection and the recognition of the rights inherent to the human person, of the unrestricted respect, promotion and protection of human rights, and of the full enforcement of the rights consigned in the Universal Declaration of Human Rights; in the American Declaration of the Rights and Duties of Man; in the International Covenant on Economic, Social and Cultural Rights; in the United Nations' International Covenant on Civil and Political Rights; and in the American Convention on Human Rights of the Organization of American States.

In other cases, such as the Constitution of Brazil, the open clause, without referring to the inherent rights of human persons, indicates that the listing in the Constitution of right and guaranties, does not exclude others «derived form the regime and principles adopted by the Constitution or by international treaties to which the Federative Republic of Brazil is a party» (Article 5.2). However, pursuant to the majority of international instruments, the rights listed therein are considered human attributes, and therefore the effect when applying this enunciative clause is the same.

Other Latin American Constitutions also contain these open clauses allowing for the extension of the human rights listed in the text of the Constitution, even though perhaps with some lesser scope regarding the previous examples.

It is the case of the Constitution of Costa Rica when indicating that the enunciation of rights and benefits it contained does not exclude others «which derive from the Christian principle of social justice» (Article 74), expression that nonetheless must be interpreted in the sense of occidental notion of human dignity and social justice.

In other Constitutions, the open clauses on human rights refer to the sovereignty of the people and the republican form of government and therefore more emphasis is made on regarding political rights, than on the inherent rights of human persons, as occurs in Argentina, where Article 33 of the Constitution states that:

> «The declarations, rights and guaranties enumerated in the Constitution, can not be understood as to deny others rights and guaranties not enumerated, but that rose from the principle of the people's sovereignty and from the republican form of government».

An almost exact regulation is contained in article 35 of the Constitution of Bolivia. Also in similar way, other Constitutions make reference to the rights derived both from the republican form of government and from the representative nature of the government as well as from the dignity of man. This is the case of Uruguay where Article 72 of the Constitution states that «the enunciation of rights, duties and guaranties made by the Constitution does not exclude the others that are inherent to human personality or derive from the republican form of government». Also in Perú Article 3 of the Constitution refers to «others guaranteed by the Constitution, nor others of an analogous nature or that are based on the dignity of man, or on the sovereignty of the people, of the democratic rule of law and of the republican form of government».

Also in Honduras, Article 63 states that

> «The declarations, rights and guaranties enumerated in this Constitution, must not be understood as a denial of other unspecified declarations, rights and guarantees, rising from sovereignty, the republican, democratic and representative form of Government and from the dignity of man».

Naturally, in all these cases, the incorporation of open clauses in the Constitution regarding human rights, as mentioned before regarding the Venezuelan constitutional provision, implies that the absence of statutory regulation of such rights cannot be invoked to deny or undermine the exercise of these rights by the people, as is expressed in many Constitutions (Argentina, Bolivia, Paraguay, Venezuela, and Ecuador). This, of course responds to the principle of the direct applicability of the Constitution in human rights matters, which excludes the traditional concept of the so-called «programmatic clauses» which was constructed under the constitutionalism of some decades ago, particularly in the question of social rights, which impeded their being exercised until legally regulated, and also impeded their justiciability.

In this regard, as mentioned, the Constitution of Ecuador is careful to point out the following:

> *Article 18.* The rights and guarantees determined in this Constitution and in the international instruments in force, shall be directly and immediately enforceable by and before any judge, court or authority...
>
> ...The lack of statutes shall not be alleged in order to justify the violation or ignorance of the rights established in this Constitution; to dismiss actions by reason of these facts; or to deny the recognition of such rights.

VI. ABSOLUTE OR LIMITATIVE CHARACTER OF THE DECLARATIONS

It must also be noted, on the other hand, that the constitutional enunciation of rights, notwithstanding the increase of scope we have mentioned, and even including the enunciative character of their constitutional declarations, has been laid down in parallel with the establishment of a specific scope for the limitations to such rights.

It is true that there are absolute rights, as are all the rights considered and declared as inviolable and not limitable, such as the right to life, the right to not be tortured, and the right to not receive shameful sentences or the right self defense.

But beyond these, there exists the principle of the limitability of rights and freedoms, whose borderline is always marked by both the rights of others persons and public and social order, because, unquestionably, rights are exercised in society and they have many titleholders. This requires, therefore, the need to conciliate the exercising of rights by everyone, in order that it not bring about, in particular, the violation of other people's rights and, in general, of public and social general order.

Of course, this principle can lead to extreme dangerous situations such as the one which unfortunately still remains in the Constitutions of Cuba, which leaves open an «unlimited» possibility of limitations to human rights, founded on the conservation of principles that can only be determined by the established Power, thus rendering the rights futile. In this regard, Article 62 of the Cuban Constitution provides that: «None of the citizens' recognized freedoms may be exercised against the provisions of the Constitution and the laws, or against the existence and purposes of the socialist State, or against the Cuban people's decision to construct socialism and communism. Offences against such principle are punishable».

Generally speaking however, and leaving aside this fortunately isolated case, the limitation to rights allowed by the Constitutions are only linked to the demands for public and social general order and to the exercise of the same rights by others.

Legally speaking, this all leads to important matters that concern the exercise of rights. Firstly, that any limitation confronts a fundamental guarantee in the sense that is constitutionally required that they be imposed only by means of statutory regulations or by a formal law sanctioned by the elected legislative body.

In this regard and as we have mentioned before, in spite of the advances contained for instance in the 1999 Constitution, with its exhaustive list of rights and the constitutionalization of international treaties concerning human rights, a specific negative aspect of its regulations which signifies a serious and potential harm to the guarantee of the principle of legality, is the establishment of the broad legislative delegation in the President of the Republic (Article 302), that can lead to executive limitations of constitutional rights.

On the other hand, mention must be made of the progressive search for the balance that must exist between the different rights, which must be done in such a way that the exercise of one right does not imply the infringement of another. That is the reason for the principles of indivisibility and interdependence in the enjoyment and exercise of rights; a matter that cannot be completely resolved through the sole provision of the Constitution. It only can be achieved through the progressive application of such texts by an effective and efficient Judiciary, which is the only branch of government that can clarify when the exercise of one right shall outweigh that of another.

There have been many legal cases, for example in relation to freedom of speech, that have determined how far freedom of speech can signify, for instance, the infringement of a child's rights, or to what extent freedom of speech can affect the right to privacy. In these cases the judge is the one who has to decide which right shall prevail in a specific moment, or under what circumstances precedence shall be given to the rights of a child, for example, as has happened in court cases in Venezuela, in regard to the right to free expression of thought[32].

In this task of interpretation, the principles of progressiveness, interdependence, reasonableness, *favor libertatis* and the concept of the essential nucleus of rights, among others, are essential for guaranteeing for they exercise and enforceability.

---

[32] See for example, Allan R. Brewer-Carías *et a. Los derechos del niño vs. los abusos parlamentarios de la libertad de expresión*, Colección Opiniones y Alegatos Jurídicos, N° 4, Editorial Jurídica Venezolana, Caracas, 1994.

CHAPTER II

THE CONSTITUTIONALIZATION OF THE INTERNATIONALIZATION OF HUMAN RIGHTS

I. THE CONSTITUTIONAL AND INTERNATIONAL REGULATIONS

Human rights today are not solely a matter concerning constitutional law and constitutional regulations. Progressively, and particularly after the Second World War, they have been also a main and essential matter of international law. During the past decades both branches of law have mutually feedback one to the other in setting forth declarations and regulations regarding human rights.

Initially, and particularly until the Second World War, the human rights regulations were the process of a constitutionalization process, by mean of the expansion of the declarations of rights, freedoms and guarantees enshrined in the Constitutions. This was the case of the initial declarations of civil rights in the XVIII Century American and French Constitutions, and of the extensive subsequent chapter devoted to enumerate constitutional rights in all the Latin American Constitutions.

The first stage of the protection of human rights process was, then, a process of constitutionalization of the declarations of human rights.

That first stage was then followed by a second one, that of the internationalization of the constitutionalization of human rights, particularly after the Second World War, characterized not only by the general approval in the United States and in the Organization of American States in 1948 of general declarations on human rights, but also by the approval of multilateral treaties on the matter. It was, undoubtedly, the evil and most aberrant violations of human rights uncovered after the end of the War that provoked such international reaction seeking for the protection of human right as a matter of international and supranational law, not being considered enough for the effective protection and enforcement of rights, their sole national constitutional provisions.

For this purpose, a re-arrangement of the concept of sovereignty was needed, in order for the States to accept the imposition of international law over national regulations. International law began to play an important role in the establishing of limits to constitutional law itself, as a result of the new international principles and commitments that came about after the War to guarantee peace.

Therefore it is not surprising that precisely following the end of the War began the process of internationalization of human rights, with the adoption in 1948 of both the American Declaration of the Rights and Duties of Man by the Organization of American States, and the Universal Declaration of Human Rights by the United Nations Organization. Those declarations were followed only two years latter by the first multilateral treaty on the matter, the 1950 European Convention on Human Rights, which entered into force in 1953.

Regarding the American Declaration adopted in 1948, its contents referred basically to civil, social and political rights, as follows: right to life, liberty and personal security (I); right to equality before the law (II); right to religious freedom and cult (III); right to freely search information, to opinion, and expression (IV); right to protection of honor, personal reputation and privacy (V); right to family and to its protection (VI); rights to maternity and children protections (VII); right to residence and move (VIII); right to the inviolability of the home (IX); right to the inviolability and transmission of correspondence (X); right to the preservation of health (XI); right to education (XII); right to culture (XIII); right to work and to fair remuneration (XIV); right to leisure time (XV); right to social security (XVI); right to the recognition of personality (XVII); right to fair trial (due process) (XVIII); right to nationality (XIX); right to vote and to political participation (XX); right to assembly (XXI); right to association (XXII); right to property (XXIII); right to petition (XXIV); right to personal liberty and to protection from arbitrary arrests (XXV); and right to presumption of innocence, to impartial hearing (XXVI), to seek for asylum (XXVII).

The process of internationalization of human rights was consolidated in 1966, with the adoption of the United Nations International Covenant on Civil and Political Rights, and the International Covenant on Economic, Social and Cultural Rights, both in effect since 1976; and, in 1969, with the adoption of the American Convention on Human Rights, which also entered into force in 1976.

The International Covenant on Civil and Political Rights declared the following rights: the right to life and restrictions on death penalty (6); the right not to be subjected to torture or to cruel, inhuman or degrading treatment or punishment, and without his free consent to medical or scientific experimentation (7); the prohibition of slavery, servitude and compulsory labor (8); the right to liberty, to personal security, not to be subjected to arbitrary arrest or detention, and only to be deprived of his liberty by means of due process of law (9); the right of detainees to be treated with humanity and with respect for the inherent dignity of the human person (10); the right not to be imprisoned due to contractual obligations (11); the right to liberty of movement and freedom to choose residence (12); the right of aliens to be expelled only by means of due process (13); the rights and guaranties of due process of law, among them: to be equal before the courts; to have a fair and public hearing by a competent, independent and impartial tribunal established by law; to be presumed innocent; to be informed and to self defense; to not to be compelled to testify against himself or to confess guilt; to the reviewing of the convicting judicial decision; and the *non bis in idem* right (14); the *nulla pena sine lege* right (15); the right to be recognized as a person (16); the right to privacy, honor and reputation (17); the right to freedom of thought, conscience and religion (18); the right to hold opinions and to express them and the freedom to seek, receive and impart information and ideas (19), except in cases of propaganda for war and incitement to discrimination, hostility or violence (20); the right of peaceful assembly (21); right to freedom of association, including the right to form and join trade unions (22); the rights to protections of family, the right of men and women to marry and to found a family (23); the right of children to be protected, to have a name and a nationality (24); the citizens rights to take part in the conduct of public affairs, to vote and to be elected, and have access to public service (25); the right to be equal before the law and to the equal protection of the law 26); and the minority groups rights to enjoy their own culture, to profess and practice their own religion, or to use their own language (27).

Article 2 of the International Covenant expressly provides for the obligation of each State Party to respect and to ensure to all individuals within its territory and subject to its jurisdiction the rights recognized in the Covenant, without distinction of any kind, such as race, color, sex, language, religion, political or other opinion, national or social origin, property, birth or other status. Additionally, the State Parties are obliged to take the necessary steps, in accordance with its constitutional processes and with the provisions of the present Covenant, «to adopt such laws or other measures as may be necessary to give effect to the rights recognized in the present Covenant».

In particular, regarding the judicial guarantee for the protection of the rights declared in the Covenant, article 2,3 oblige each State Party:

> «(a) To ensure that any person whose rights or freedoms as herein recognized are violated shall have an effective remedy, notwithstanding that the violation has been committed by persons acting in an official capacity;
>
> (b) To ensure that any person claiming such a remedy shall have his right thereto determined by competent judicial, administrative or legislative authorities, or by any other competent authority provided for by the legal system of the State, and to develop the possibilities of judicial remedy;
>
> (c) To ensure that when granted, the competent authorities shall enforce such remedies».

Accordingly, the Covenant also establishes a general right of any person not only to have access to justice for the protections of their rights but to have at their disposition an effective remedy to seek protection to their rights not only against public official actions but also against individual actions.

Regarding the International Covenant on Economic, Social and Cultural Rights, it declares the following rights: the right to work (6); the right to the enjoyment of just and favorable conditions of work, in particular, remuneration with fair wages providing decent living; safe and healthy working conditions; equal opportunity, and rest, leisure and reasonable limitation of working hours (7); the right of everyone to form and join trade unions and the right of trade unions to function freely; and the right to strike (8); the right of everyone to social security, including social insurance (9); the right to family, marriage, maternity and children's protection (10); right of everyone to an adequate standard of living for himself and his family, including adequate food, clothing and housing, and to the continuous improvement of living conditions (11); the fundamental right of everyone to be free from hunger (12); the right of everyone to the enjoyment of the highest attainable standard of physical and mental health and to health care (13); the right of everyone to education, the liberty of parents to choose for their children schools, other than those established by the public authorities, and the liberty of individuals and bodies to establish and direct educational institutions (13) and the right of everyone to culture and to enjoy the benefits of scientific progress (14).

Article 2,2 of the Covenant obligated the States Parties to guarantee that the rights enunciated in it will be exercised without discrimination of any kind as to race, color, sex, language, religion, political or other opinion, national or social origin, property, birth or other status; and Article 3 obligated them to ensure the equal right of men and women to the enjoyment of all economic, social and cultural rights set forth in the Covenant. In Article 4 of the Covenant, the guarantee of legality concerning the social, economic and cultural rights was set forth by stating that the States Parties «recognize that, in the enjoyment of those rights provided by the State in conformity with the present Covenant, the State may subject such rights only to such limitations as are determined by law only in so far as this may be compatible with the nature of these rights and solely for the purpose of promoting the general welfare in a democratic society».

Nevertheless, in contrast with what was established in the International Covenant on Civil and Political Rights, in the International Covenant on Economic, Social and Cultural Rights, no justi-fiability rights for their enforcement were set forth.

II. THE AMERICAN INTERNATIONALIZATION OF HUMAN RIGHTS

The American Convention on Human Rights, as mentioned, was approved in the Organization of American States General Assembly in Costa Rica in 1969, and entered into force in 1979. It has been ratified by all Latin American Countries, all of which have recognized the jurisdiction of the Inter American Court on Human Rights. It must be noted that the only American country that has not signed the Convention is Canada, and the United States of America, even though has signed the Convention on June 1st, 1977 at the OAS General Secretariat, has not yet ratified it.

The American Convention has extreme importance in Latin America, being its content mainly referred to civil and political rights. Regarding economic and social rights, the Convention just limits its scope to declare that «the States Parties undertake to adopt measures, both internally and through international cooperation, especially those of an economic and technical nature, with a view to achieving progressively, by legislation or other appropriate means, the full realization of the rights implicit in the economic, social, educational, scientific, and cultural standards set forth in the Charter of the Organization of American States».

Now, regarding civil and political rights, the American Convention declares the following rights:

Article 3. Right to Juridical Personality:

Every person has the right to recognition as a person before the law.

Article 4. Right to Life:

1. Every person has the right to have his life respected. This right shall be protected by law and, in general, from the moment of conception. No one shall be arbitrarily deprived of his life.

2. In countries that have not abolished the death penalty, it may be imposed only for the most serious crimes and pursuant to a final judgment rendered by a competent court and in accordance with a law establishing such punishment, enacted prior to the commission of the crime. The application of such punishment shall not be extended to crimes to which it does not presently apply.
3. The death penalty shall not be reestablished in states that have abolished it.
4. In no case shall capital punishment be inflicted for political offenses or related common crimes.
5. Capital punishment shall not be imposed upon persons who, at the time the crime was committed, were under 18 years of age or over 70 years of age; nor shall it be applied to pregnant women.
6. Every person condemned to death shall have the right to apply for amnesty, pardon, or commutation of sentence, which may be granted in all cases. Capital punishment shall not be imposed while such a petition is pending decision by the competent authority.

Article 5. Right to Humane Treatment:

1. Every person has the right to have his physical, mental, and moral integrity respected.
2. No one shall be subjected to torture or to cruel, inhuman, or degrading punishment or treatment. All persons deprived of their liberty shall be treated with respect for the inherent dignity of the human person.
3. Punishment shall not be extended to any person other than the criminal.
4. Accused persons shall, save in exceptional circumstances, be segregated from convicted persons, and shall be subject to separate treatment appropriate to their status as unconvicted persons.
5. Minors while subject to criminal proceedings shall be separated from adults and brought before specialized tribunals, as speedily as possible, so that they may be treated in accordance with their status as minors.
6. Punishments consisting of deprivation of liberty shall have as an essential aim the reform and social readaptation of the prisoners.

Article 6. Freedom from Slavery

1. No one shall be subject to slavery or to involuntary servitude, which are prohibited in all their forms, as are the slave trade and traffic in women.
2. No one shall be required to perform forced or compulsory labor. This provision shall not be interpreted to mean that, in those countries in which the penalty established for certain crimes is deprivation of liberty at forced labor, the carrying out of such a sentence imposed by a competent court is prohibited. Forced labor shall not adversely affect the dignity or the physical or intellectual capacity of the prisoner.
3. For the purposes of this article, the following do not constitute forced or compulsory labor:

a. work or service normally required of a person imprisoned in execution of a sentence or formal decision passed by the competent judicial authority. Such work or service shall be carried out under the supervision and control of public authorities, and any persons performing such work or service shall not be placed at the disposal of any private party, company, or juridical person;

b. military service and, in countries in which conscientious objectors are recognized, national service that the law may provide for in lieu of military service;

c. service exacted in time of danger or calamity that threatens the existence or the well-being of the community; or

d. work or service that forms part of normal civic obligations.

Article 7. Right to Personal Liberty

1. Every person has the right to personal liberty and security.

2. No one shall be deprived of his physical liberty except for the reasons and under the conditions established beforehand by the constitution of the State Party concerned or by a law established pursuant thereto.

3. No one shall be subject to arbitrary arrest or imprisonment.

4. Anyone who is detained shall be informed of the reasons for his detention and shall be promptly notified of the charge or charges against him.

5. Any person detained shall be brought promptly before a judge or other officer authorized by law to exercise judicial power and shall be entitled to trial within a reasonable time or to be released without prejudice to the continuation of the proceedings. His release may be subject to guarantees to assure his appearance for trial.

6. Anyone who is deprived of his liberty shall be entitled to recourse to a competent court, in order that the court may decide without delay on the lawfulness of his arrest or detention and order his release if the arrest or detention is unlawful. In States Parties whose laws provide that anyone who believes himself to be threatened with deprivation of his liberty is entitled to recourse to a competent court in order that it may decide on the lawfulness of such threat, this remedy may not be restricted or abolished. The interested party or another person in his behalf is entitled to seek these remedies.

7. No one shall be detained for debt. This principle shall not limit the orders of a competent judicial authority issued for no fulfillment of duties of support.

Article 8. Right to a Fair Trial

1. Every person has the right to a hearing, with due guarantees and within a reasonable time, by a competent, independent, and impartial tribunal, previously established by law, in the substantiation of any accusation of a criminal nature made against him or for the determination of his rights and obligations of a civil, labor, fiscal, or any other nature.

2. Every person accused of a criminal offence has the right to be presumed innocent so long as his guilt has not been proven according to law. During the proceedings, every person is entitled, with full equality, to the following minimum guarantees:
   a. the right of the accused to be assisted without charge by a translator or interpreter, if he does not understand or does not speak the language of the tribunal or court;
   b. prior notification in detail to the accused of the charges against him;
   c. adequate time and means for the preparation of his defense;
   d. the right of the accused to defend himself personally or to be assisted by legal counsel of his own choosing, and to communicate freely and privately with his counsel;
   e. the inalienable right to be assisted by counsel provided by the state, paid or not as the domestic law provides, if the accused does not defend himself personally or engage his own counsel within the time period established by law;
   f. the right of the defense to examine witnesses present in the court and to obtain the appearance, as witnesses, of experts or other persons who may throw light on the facts;
   g. the right not to be compelled to be a witness against himself or to plead guilty; and
   h. the right to appeal the judgment to a higher court.
3. A confession of guilt by the accused shall be valid only if it is made without coercion of any kind.
4. An accused person acquitted by a nonappealable judgment shall not be subjected to a new trial for the same cause.
5. Criminal proceedings shall be public, except insofar as may be necessary to protect the interests of justice.

Article 9. Freedom from Ex Post Facto Laws

No one shall be convicted of any act or omission that did not constitute a criminal offense, under the applicable law, at the time it was committed. A heavier penalty shall not be imposed than the one that was applicable at the time the criminal offence was committed. If subsequent to the commission of the offence the law provides for the imposition of a lighter punishment, the guilty person shall benefit there from.

Article 10. Right to Compensation

Every person has the right to be compensated in accordance with the law in the event he has been sentenced by a final judgment through a miscarriage of justice.

Article 11. Right to Privacy

1. Everyone has the right to have his honor respected and his dignity recognized.

2. No one may be the object of arbitrary or abusive interference with his private life, his family, his home, or his correspondence, or of unlawful attacks on his honor or reputation.
3. Everyone has the right to the protection of the law against such interference or attacks.

Article 12. Freedom of Conscience and Religion

1. Everyone has the right to freedom of conscience and of religion. This right includes freedom to maintain or to change one's religion or beliefs, and freedom to profess or disseminate one's religion or beliefs, either individually or together with others, in public or in private.
2. No one shall be subject to restrictions that might impair his freedom to maintain or to change his religion or beliefs.
3. Freedom to manifest one's religion and beliefs may be subject only to the limitations prescribed by law that are necessary to protect public safety, order, health, or morals, or the rights or freedoms of others.
4. Parents or guardians, as the case may be, have the right to provide for the religious and moral education of their children or wards that is in accord with their own convictions.

Article 13. Freedom of Thought and Expression

1. Everyone has the right to freedom of thought and expression. This right includes freedom to seek, receive, and impart information and ideas of all kinds, regardless of frontiers, either orally, in writing, in print, in the form of art, or through any other medium of one's choice.
2. The exercise of the right provided for in the foregoing paragraph shall not be subject to prior censorship but shall be subject to subsequent imposition of liability, which shall be expressly established by law to the extent necessary to ensure:
   a. respect for the rights or reputations of others; or
   b. the protection of national security, public order, or public health or morals.
3. The right of expression may not be restricted by indirect methods or means, such as the abuse of government or private controls over newsprint, radio broadcasting frequencies, or equipment used in the dissemination of information, or by any other means tending to impede the communication and circulation of ideas and opinions.
4. Notwithstanding the provisions of paragraph 2 above, public entertainments may be subject by law to prior censorship for the sole purpose of regulating access to them for the moral protection of childhood and adolescence.
5. Any propaganda for war and any advocacy of national, racial, or religious hatred that constitute incitements to lawless violence or to any other similar action against any person or group of persons on any grounds including those of race, color, religion, language, or national origin shall be considered as offenses punishable by law.

Article 14. Right of Reply

1. Anyone injured by inaccurate or offensive statements or ideas disseminated to the public in general by a legally regulated medium of communication has the right to reply or to make a correction using the same communications outlet, under such conditions as the law may establish.
2. The correction or reply shall not in any case remit other legal liabilities that may have been incurred.
3. For the effective protection of honor and reputation, every publisher, and every newspaper, motion picture, radio, and Television Company, shall have a person responsible who is not protected by immunities or special privileges.

Article 15. Right of Assembly

The right of peaceful assembly, without arms, is recognized. No restrictions may be placed on the exercise of this right other than those imposed in conformity with the law and necessary in a democratic society in the interest of national security, public safety or public order, or to protect public health or morals or the rights or freedom of others.

Article 16. Freedom of Association

1. Everyone has the right to associate freely for ideological, religious, political, econo-mic, labor, social, cultural, sports, or other purposes.
2. The exercise of this right shall be subject only to such restrictions established by law as may be necessary in a democratic society, in the interest of national security, public safety or public order, or to protect public health or morals or the rights and freedoms of others.
3. The provisions of this article do not bar the imposition of legal restrictions, including even deprivation of the exercise of the right of association, on members of the armed forces and the police.

Article 17. Rights of the Family

1. The family is the natural and fundamental group unit of society and is entitled to protection by society and the state.
2. The right of men and women of marriageable age to marry and to raise a family shall be recognized, if they meet the conditions required by domestic laws, insofar as such conditions do not affect the principle of nondiscrimination established in this Convention.
3. No marriage shall be entered into without the free and full consent of the intending spouses.
4. The States Parties shall take appropriate steps to ensure the equality of rights and the adequate balancing of responsibilities of the spouses as to marriage, during marriage, and in the event of its dissolution. In case of dissolution, provision shall be made for the necessary protection of any children solely on the basis of their own best interests.
5. The law shall recognize equal rights for children born out of wedlock and those born in wedlock.

Article 18. Right to a Name

Every person has the right to a given name and to the surnames of his parents or that of one of them. The law shall regulate the manner in which this right shall be ensured for all, by the use of assumed names if necessary.

Article 19. Rights of the Child

Every minor child has the right to the measures of protection required by his condition as a minor on the part of his family, society, and the state.

Article 20. Right to Nationality

1. Every person has the right to a nationality.
2. Every person has the right to the nationality of the state in whose territory he was born if he does not have the right to any other nationality.
3. No one shall be arbitrarily deprived of his nationality or of the right to change it.

Article 21. Right to Property

1. Everyone has the right to the use and enjoyment of his property. The law may subordinate such use and enjoyment to the interest of society.
2. No one shall be deprived of his property except upon payment of just compensation, for reasons of public utility or social interest, and in the cases and according to the forms established by law.
3. Usury and any other form of exploitation of man by man shall be prohibited by law.

Article 22. Freedom of Movement and Residence

1. Every person lawfully in the territory of a State Party has the right to move about in it, and to reside in it subject to the provisions of the law.
2. Every person has the right lo leave any country freely, including his own.
3. The exercise of the foregoing rights may be restricted only pursuant to a law to the extent necessary in a democratic society to prevent crime or to protect national security, public safety, public order, public morals, public health, or the rights or freedoms of others.
4. The exercise of the rights recognized in paragraph 1 may also be restricted by law in designated zones for reasons of public interest.
5. No one can be expelled from the territory of the state of which he is a national or be deprived of the right to enter it.
6. An alien lawfully in the territory of a State Party to this Convention may be expelled from it only pursuant to a decision reached in accordance with law.
7. Every person has the right to seek and be granted asylum in a foreign territory, in accordance with the legislation of the state and international conventions, in the event he is being pursued for political offenses or related common crimes.

8. In no case may an alien be deported or returned to a country, regardless of whether or not it is his country of origin, if in that country his right to life or personal freedom is in danger of being violated because of his race, nationality, religion, social status, or political opinions.

9. The collective expulsion of aliens is prohibited.

Article 23. Right to Participate in Government

1. Every citizen shall enjoy the following rights and opportunities:

   a. to take part in The conduct of public affairs, directly or through freely chosen representatives;

   b. to vote and to be elected in genuine periodic elections, which shall be by universal and equal suffrage and by secret ballot that guarantees the free expression of the will of the voters; and

   c. to have access, under general conditions of equality, to the public service of his country.

2. The law may regulate the exercise of the rights and opportunities referred to in the preceding paragraph only on the basis of age, nationality, residence, language, education, civil and mental capacity, or sentencing by a competent court in criminal proceedings.

Article 24. Right to Equal Protection

All persons are equal before the law. Consequently, they are entitled, without discrimination, to equal protection of the law.

But additionally to all the previous rights, in these American Convention, and in a different way to what was established in the International Covenant on Civil and Political Rights, it was expressly set forth as the right of everyone to judicial protection of human rights, by means of the «amparo» action, recourse or suit, as follows:

Article 25. Right to Judicial Protection

1. Everyone has the right to simple and prompt recourse, or any other effective recourse, to a competent court or tribunal for protection («*que la ampare*») against acts that violate his fundamental rights recognized by the constitution or laws of the state concerned or by this Convention, even though such violation may have been committed by persons acting in the course of their official duties.

2. The States Parties undertake:

a. to ensure that any person claiming such remedy shall have his rights determined by the competent authority provided for by the legal system of the state;

b. to develop the possibilities of judicial remedy; and

c. to ensure that the competent authorities shall enforce such remedies when granted.

Finally, in order to ensure fulfillment of the commitments made by the States Parties to the Convention, the Inter-American Commission on Human Rights, and the Inter-American Court of Human Rights were created (33). For that purpose the Convention recognized the right of any person or group of persons, or any nongovernmental entity legally recognized in one or more member states of the Organization, to lodge petitions with the Commission containing denunciations or complaints of violation of the Convention by a State Party (44), as well as the power of the State Parties to allege before the Commission that another State Party has committed a violation of a human right set forth in the Convention (45). Following a very extensive regulated procedure, the Commission can bring before the Inter American Court on Human Rights cases of violation of the State Parties obligations and if the Court, following the procedure set forth in the Convention, finds that there has been a violation of a right or freedom protected by the Convention, the Court shall rule that the injured party be ensured the enjoyment of his right or freedom that was violated, and if appropriate, can also rule that the consequences of the measure or situation that constituted the breach of such right or freedom be remedied and that fair compensation be paid to the injured party (63).

The general rule of admissibility of the petition is that «the remedies under domestic law have been pursued and exhausted in accordance with generally recognized principles of international law»(Article 46,1,a); rule that has the following exceptions: when in the internal law of the State the due process for the protection for the violated rights is non existent; when the affected party has been impeded in his rights to access to the internal jurisdictional recourses, or when he has been impeded of exhausting them; or when a unjustified delay has occurred regarding such recourses (Article 77,2 of the Internal regulation of the Commission).

Even though the petition before the Inter-American Commission has been qualified as an «international amparo»[1], not being the Commission a jurisdictional body, the initial petition can not qualify as a judicial mean. Eventually, the Commission is the only body that can bring before the Inter American Court a request for protection on behalf individuals. On the contrary, in the European system, individuals can bring direct petitions against Member States before the European Tribunal on Human Rights regarding the protection of human rights.

Nevertheless, it must be mentioned that in some Latin American Constitutions, as is the case of the 1999 Venezuelan Constitution, the right to petition for the protection of human rights before international organizations has been regulated as an individual constitutional right. In this regard, Article 31 sets forth:

> Article 31. According to what is set forth in the treaties, covenants and conventions on human rights ratified by the Republic, everybody has the right to file petitions or complaints before the international organizations created for such purposes, in order to seek for the protection (amparo) of his human rights.

The Constitution also imposes the State the obligation, according to the procedures provided in the Constitution and the statutes, to adopt the necessary measures in order to comply with the decisions of the abovementioned international organizations.

---

1 See Carlos AYALA CORAO, «Del amparo constitucional al amparo interamericano como institutos para la protección de los derechos humanos» in *Memoria del VI Congreso Iberoamericano de derecho constitucional*, Tomo I, Bogotá, 1998.

Anyway, since the beginning of its activities in 1979, the Commission and the Court have been very active in the exercise of its functions, having decided in numerous cases against State parties for violations of human rights. The Courts consultative opinions and rulings now constitute the basic doctrine on human rights in Latin America.

Finally, regarding international treaties, mention must also be made to the African Charter of Human Rights, adopted in 1981. The fact, in any case, is that since the establishment of the United Nations, many other declarations and treaties referring to human rights -more than 70- have been adopted, creating various international organizations on human rights, including two International Courts - the European and the Inter American Courts–as international judicial organs with the purpose of assuring the accomplishment of State obligations regarding human rights and to protect them.

From all these international regulations on human rights, it can be clearly appreciated that following the initial process of constitutionalization of human rights by means of the progressively enlarged national constitutional declarations, which took place up to the Second World War, a second stage was developed, marked by the internationalization of such constitutionalization process, by means of the international declarations of rights.

III. THE CONSTITUTIONALIZATION OF THE INTERNATIONALIZATION OF HUMAN RIGHTS

But in recent times, we have witnessed a third stage on the process of protecting human rights, which can be characterized as a process now again of constitutionalization but of the internationalization of human rights, that has developed precisely, by the incorporation in the constitutional internal regulations, of the international systems of protection.

This process can be characterized, first of all by the process of giving internal constitutional or statutory rank to the international instruments on human rights, that is to say, by setting forth expressly in the Constitutions, the value to be given to both the international declarations and treaties on human rights regarding the internal constitutional norms and statutes concerning human rights, even determining which shall prevail in the event of there being a conflict among them.

This is a matter that of course must be regulated in the Constitutions themselves, whether by mean of enshrining the regulatory rank of international treaties in the constitutional texts, or by means of setting forth in the Constitutions for the rules for constitutional interpretation of human rights and of the international instruments referring to them.

1. The supra constitutional rank of international instruments of human rights

In many Latin American Constitutions the question of the internal normative value and rank of the international human rights instruments has been expressly resolved in four different ways: by granting the international instruments supra-constitutional rank, constitutional rank, supra-legal rank or statutory rank[2].

---

[2] For a general comment regarding this classification, see Rodolfo E. PIZA R., *Derecho internacional de los derechos humanos: La Convención Americana*, San José, 1989; Carlos AYALA CORAO,

Firstly, certain Constitutions have expressly set forth the supra-constitutional rank of human rights declared in international instruments. This has implied giving the international regulation a superior rank regarding the Constitution itself, therefore prevailing over their provisions.

Such is the case, for example, of the Constitution of Guatemala, whose Article 46 sets forth the general principle of pre-eminence of International law, by stating that in declaring that «in human rights matters, the treaties and conventions accepted and ratified by Guatemala shall have pre-eminence over internal law», in which it must be included other that the statutes, the Constitution itself. Based on this prevalence of international treaties, the Constitutional Court has decided cases applying the American Convention, as was the case of the decision issued on May 27, 1997 regarding freedom of expression and the rectification rights. In the case, by means of an «amparo» action, a person asks the constitutional protection of the Court regarding the news published in two news papers referring to his as forming part of a band of criminals, and asking before the Court to be respected in his right to seek for the rectification of the news by the news papers. Even tough the constitutional right to seek for rectification in cases of news published affecting the honor, reputation and privacy of any body is not expressly set forth in the Constitution, the Constitutional Court applied Articles 11, 13 and 14 of the American Convention which guarantee the right of any affected party by news papers information to «rectification and response that must be published in the same news paper», considering such provisions as forming part of the constitutional order of Guatemala[3].

Also in Honduras, Article 16 of the Constitution sets forth that the all treaties subscribed with other States (not only related to human rights), are part of internal law; and Article 18 establishes the pre-eminence of treaties over statutes in case of conflict between them. In addition, the Honduran Constitution admits the possibility of ratification of treaties contrary to what is set forth in the Constitution, in which case they must be approved according to the procedure set forth for constitutional revision (Article 17). A similar regulation is established in Article 53 of the Perúvian Constitution.

In Colombia, the Constitution has also established a similar provision, with Article 93 providing that: «international treaties and conventions ratified by Congress, which recognize human rights and forbid their limitation in states of emergency, shall prevail over internal law». In this case, also, internal law must be understood to comprise not only statutes but the Constitution itself.

The Constitutional Court of Colombia in a decision N° T-447/95 of October 23, 1995, recognized the right of everybody to have an identity as a right inherent

«La jerarquía de los instrumentos internacionales sobre derechos humanos», in *El nuevo derecho constitucional latinoamericano*, IV Congreso venezolano *de Derecho constitucional*, Vol. II, Caracas, 1996 and *La jerarquía constitucional de los tratados sobre derechos humanos y sus consecuencias*, México, 2003; and Humberto HENDERSON, «Los tratados internacionales de derechos humanos en el orden interno: la importancia del principio pro homine», en *Revista IIDH*, Instituto Interamericano de Derechos Humanos, N° 39, San José, 2004, pp. 71 y ss. See also, Allan R. BREWER-CARÍAS, *Mecanismos nacionales de protección de los derechos humanos*, Instituto Internacional de Derechos Humanos, San José, 2004, pp.62 y ss.

3 See in *Iudicum et Vita, Jurisprudencia nacional de América Latina en Derechos Humanos*, N° 5, Instituto Interamericano de Derechos Humanos, San José, Costa Rica, Diciembre 1997, pp. 45 ff.

to human being, basing its ruling in what is set forth in the international treaties and covenants, for which it was recognized supra constitutional and supra legal rank. The Court began by referring to previous ruling of the former Supreme Court of Justice which had determined their supra-legal value, by arguing:

> Since 1928 the Supreme Court of Justice has given prevalent value to international treaties regarding legislative internal order; due to the fact that such international norms, by will of the Colombian state, enter to form part of the legal order with supra legal rank, setting forth the coactive force of provisions the signing State has the obligation to enforce. The supra legal value has been expressly established in article 93 of the Constitution of Colombia, as has been recognized by the Supreme Court of Justice, arguing that it must be added that such superiority has been sustained as an invariable doctrine that «is a public law principle, that the Constitution and the international treaties are the superior law of the land and their dispositions prevail over the legal norms contrary to their provisions even if they are posterior laws»[4].

In the same decision, the Constitutional Court referred to the «supra constitutional» rank of international treaties, which implies the State's obligation to guarantee the effective enforcement of human rights, basing the constitutional provision on Article 2,2 of the International Covenant on Human Rights and in Article 2 of the American Convention on Human Rights. The Court stated:

> The American Convention and the United Nations International Covenants set forth that the obligation of the States is not only to respect civil and political rights but also to guarantee, without discrimination, its free and complete enjoyment by any person subjected to its jurisdiction (Article 1, American Convention; Article 2,1 International Covenant on civil and political rights). For that purpose, these covenants that have been ratified by Colombia, and consequently prevail in the internal order (Article 93 Constitution), set forth that the Member States have the obligation according to the constitutional proceedings, to adopt «the legislative or other character measures in order to make human rights effective» (Article. 2, American Convention; Article 2,2, International Covenant on Civil and Political Rights). According to this authorized doctrine, the Constitutional Court considers that the judicial decisions and particularly this Court's rulings must be among the «other character» measures abovementioned, due to the fact that the Judiciary is one of the Branches of the Colombian State, which has the duty to adopt the necessary measures in order to make effective the persons' rights»...Consequently it is legitimate for the judges and particular for the Constitutional Court, when deciding cases, to consider within the legal order the rights recognized in the Constitution and in the Covenants»[5].

Based in the abovementioned, and considering that Article 29,C of the American Convention forbids the interpretation of its provisions that preclude other rights or

---

4 See the text in *Derechos Fundamentales e interpretación Constitucional, (Ensayos-Jurisprudencia)*, Comisión Andina de Juristas, Lima, 1997; and in Carlos AYALA CORAO, «Recepción de la jurisprudencia internacional sobre derechos humanos por la jurisprudencia constitucional», *Revista del Tribunal Constitucional*, N° 6, Sucre, Bolivia, Nov. 2004, pp. 275 y ss.

5 *Idem*.

guarantees that are inherent in the human personality and that give a very wide sense to the interpretation of such rights, the Court concluded that being «the right to have an identity implicitly set forth in all the international covenants and conventions, and thus, legally protected» it is possible to affirm such right «as being inherent to human person fully guaranteed due to the obligatory force of the international covenant» which also set forth the right to dignity and to the free development of own personality»[6].

To a certain point, the case of the 1999 Constitution of Venezuela could also be placed under this first system of supra-constitutional hierarchy of human rights contained in treaties, with its Article 23, which provides that:

> «Treaties, covenants and conventions referring to human rights, signed and ratified by Venezuela, shall have constitutional hierarchy and will prevail over internal legal order, when they contain regulations regarding their enjoyment and exercise, more favorable than those established in this Constitution and the statutes of the Republic. Those treaties and conventions shall be immediately and directly applicable by the courts and all other official authorities.

By declaring that human rights enshrined in international instruments shall prevail over internal legal order, when containing more favorable conditions of enjoyment and exercise such rights, it is referring not only to what is declared on statutes, but also in the Constitution. This undoubtedly grants supra-constitutional rank to such rights.

This article of the 1999 Constitution, without doubt, is one of the most important ones in matters of human rights[7], not only because it sets forth the supra-constitutional rank of human rights treaties, but because it prescribes the direct and immediate applicability of such treaties by all courts and authorities of the country. Its inclusion in the new Constitution was a significant advancement in the completion of the protection framework of human rights.

But unfortunately, this very clear constitutional provision has been interpreted by the Constitutional Chamber of the Supreme Court in a way openly contrary to what it states, and to what was the intention of the proponents and of the Constituent. In effect, in a decision N°1942 of July 7th, 2003 when resolving a judicial review action on the constitutionality of some Penal Code articles regarding the freedom of expression that where challenged because they were contrary to international treaties, the Constitutional Chamber ruled as follows:

First, the Chamber stated that Article 23 of the Constitution contained two key elements: «1) It refers to human rights applicable to human beings; 2) It refers to norms setting forth rights and not to decisions or opinions of institutions, resolutions of bodies, etc, established in the treaties; thus it only refers to norms that created human rights».

The Constitutional Chamber was repetitive by stating that: «It is a matter of prevalence of norms which conform treaties, covenants or Agreements (synonym

---

6 *Idem.*

7 See the author's proposal of the draft of this article to the National Constituent Assembly, in Allan R. BREWER-CARÍAS, *Debate Constituyente, (Aportes a la Asamblea Nacional Constituyente)*, Fundación de Derecho Público, Caracas, 1999, pp. 88 y ss y 111 y ss.

expressions) referred to human rights, but not to reports or opinions of international bodies which pretend to interpret the scope of international instruments». The Chamber concluded that it is clear that according to Article 23, «the constitutional hierarchy of treaties, covenants or conventions refers to its norms which once integrated into the Constitution, the only institution capable of interpreting them vis-à-vis Venezuelan law, is the constitutional judge according to Article 335 of the Constitution, only the Constitutional Chamber»; insisting in the same proposition by stating that:

> «Once the human rights substantive norms contained in Conventions, covenants and treaties have been incorporated to the constitutional hierarchy, the maximum and last interpreter of them, vis-à-vis internal law, is the Constitutional Chamber, which determines the content and scope of the constitutional norms and principles (Article 335), among them are the treaties, covenants and conventions on human rights, duly subscribed and ratified by Venezuela»

From this proposition, the Constitutional Chamber concluded that «is the Constitutional Chamber the only one that determines which norms on human rights contained in treaties, covenants and conventions, prevail in the internal legal order; as well as which human rights not incorporated in such international instruments have effects in Venezuela»; concluding that:

> «This power of the Constitutional Chamber on the matter, derived from the Constitution, cannot be diminished by adjective norms contained in the treaties or in other international texts on human rights subscribed by the country, allowing the States parties to ask international institutions for the interpretation of rights referred to in the Convention or covenant, as established in Article 64 of the Approbatory statute of the American Convention of Human Rights, San José Covenant, because otherwise, the situation would be of a constitutional amendment, without following the constitutional procedures, diminishing the powers of the Constitutional Chamber, transferring it to international or transnational bodies, with the power to dictate obligatory interpretations» [8].

The Constitutional Chamber based its decision on sovereignty principles, arguing that decisions adopted by international courts cannot be enforced in Venezuela, but only when they are in accordance with the Constitution. Thus, the supra constitutional rank of treaties when establishing more favorable regulations regarding human rights was suddenly eliminated by the Constitutional Chamber, assuming an absolute monopoly of Constitution interpretation, which, according to the constitution, the Chamber does not have.

The main problem regarding this restrictive criterion on the interpretation of international instruments is that unfortunately the ruling was set forth as an obligatory interpretation of the Constitution limiting the general powers of any court to resolve by means of judicial review on the matter, directly applying and giving prevalence to the American Convention regarding constitutional provisions.

This restrictive interpretation was really issued in a ruling devoted to deny any constitutional value and rank to the recommendations of the Inter-

---

8 See the text in *Revista de Derecho Público,* N° 93-96, Editorial Jurídica Venezolana, Caracas, 2003, pp. 136 ff.

American Commission on Human Rights, thus refusing to consider unconstitutional some articles of the Penal Code regarding restrictions to the freedom of expression when referring to public officials that were contrary to the recommendations of the Commission which was argued were obligatory for the country.

The Constitutional Chamber argued that according to the American Convention, the Commission may formulate «recommendations» to the governments in order for them to adopt progressive measures in favor of human rights within their internal laws and constitutional prescriptions, as well as provisions to promote the respect of such rights (Article 41.b), adding:

> If what is recommended by the Commission must be adapted to the Constitution and statutes of the States it means they do not have obligatory force, because the internal laws or the Constitution could be contrary to the recommendations. Thus, the articles of the Convention do not refer to the obligatory character of the recommendations, in contrast, they refer to the powers assigned to the other organ: the Court, which according to Article 62 of the Convention, can give obligatory interpretations of the Convention when requested by the States, which means that they accept the opinion,
>
> If the Court has such power, and the Commission does not, it is compulsory to conclude that the recommendations of the latter do not have the character of the opinions of the former, and consequently, the Chamber declares that the recommendations of the Inter American Commission of Human Rights are non obligatory regarding internal law.
>
> The Chamber considers that the recommendations must be weigh up by the Member States. They must adapt their legislation to the recommendations if they do not collide with the constitutional provisions, but for such adaptation there is no timing set, and until it is done, the statutes in effect which do not collide with the Constitution, or according to the Venezuelan courts with the human rights enshrined in the international conventions, will remain in force until declared unconstitutional of repealed by other states»[9].

Eventually, the Chamber concluded stating that the recommendations of the Commission regarding what has been called the «*leyes de desacato*» (statute protecting public officials from public criticism), are only the Commission's point of view without any imperative effect, and an alert directed to the States in order for them, in the future, to repeal or to reform them adapting them to international laws. Unfortunately, the Constitutional Chamber forgot that what the States are obliged to do regarding the recommendations, is to adopt the necessary measures in order to adapt their internal law to the Convention, measures that do not exhaust themselves with only repealing or reforming statutes, being one of such measures, precisely, the judicial interpretation which could be adopted by the constitutional judge in accordance with the Commission's recommendations. Contrary to what was resolved by the Venezuelan Tribunal, in Argentina, once the Inter American Commission determined that the amnesty statutes (*Punto Final* and *Obediencia Debida*) and the pardon measures adopted regarding the crimes

9 See the text in *Revista de Derecho Público*, N° 93-96, Editorial Jurídica Venezolana, Caracas, 2003, pp. 136 ff.

committed by the military dictatorship were contrary to the American Convention, some courts began to consider such statutes as unconstitutional because they were in violation of international law[10].

The Venezuelan Constitutional Chamber, in any case, concluded its restrictive interpretation by stating: that: «A different interpretation means giving the Commission a supranational character which weakened the Member State's sovereignty, something that is prohibited by the Constitution»[11]. Anyway, after the Constitutional Chamber's ruling, the Penal Code was reformed but not in the relevant parts regarding the crimes referred to as «*leyes de desacato*». This decision was contrary to what was decided in 1995 by the Argentinean Congress regarding the same matters, by repealing the articles related to the same crimes in compliance with the Inter American Commission recommendation on the matter[12]

The restrictive approach of the Venezuelan Constitutional Chamber regarding the importance on internal law of the Inter American Commission on Human Rights recommendations was previously stated in a decision dated May 5th, 2000. In this decision the Constitutional Chamber objected the quasi-jurisdictional powers of the Inter American Commission on Human Rights. The case was as follows: after a magazine (*Revista Exceso*) filed an «amparo» action before the national jurisdictions seeking constitutional protection of its right to free expression and information, the plaintiff went before the Inter American Commission on Human Rights denouncing the mal functioning of internal jurisdiction regarding the amparo action filed, and seeking international protection against the Venezuelan State for violation of its rights to freedom of expression and due process and against judicial harassment practices against one of its journalist and the director of the magazine. In the case, the Inter American Commission issued provisional protective measures.

When the time arrived to decide the «amparo» action, the Constitutional Chamber considered that in the case, the plaintiff's due process rights had been effectively violated (independently of its right to freedom of expression), but regarding the provisional measures adopted by the Inter American Commission, qualifying it as «unacceptable», the Chamber stated that:

> [The Constitutional Chamber] also considers unacceptable the instance of the Inter American Commission on Human Rights of the Organization of American States in the sense that asking for the adoption of measures that imply a gross intrusion in the country's judicial organs, like the suspension of the judicial

10 Decision de 4-03-2001, Juzgado Federal N° 4, caso: *Pobrete Hlaczik. Cit.*, por Kathryn Sikkink, «The transnacional dimension of judicialization of politics in latin America», in Rachel Sieder et al (ed), *The Judicalization of Politics In Latin America,* Palgrave Macmillan, New York, 2005, pp. 274, 290.

11 Decision N° 1942 of July, 15, 2003, in *Revista de Derecho Público,* N° 93-96, Editorial Jurídica Venezolana, Caracas, 2003, pp. 136 ff. i.

12 Case: *Verbistky, Report of the Comisión* N° 22/94 of September 20, 1994, case: *11.012* (Argentina). See the comments by Antonio CANÇADO TRINDADE, «Libertad de expresión y derecho a la información en los planos internacional y nacional», in *Iudicum et Vita, Jurisprudencia nacional de América Latina en Derechos Humanos,* N° 5, Instituto Interamericano de Derechos Humanos, San José, Costa Rica, Diciembre 1997, pp. 194-195. See the «Informe sobre la compatibilidad entre las leyes de desacato y la Convención Americana sobre Derechos Humanos de 17 de febrero de 1995», in *Estudios Básicos de derechos Humanos,* Vol. X, Instituto Interamericano de Derechos Humanos, San José, 2000.

proceeding against the plaintiff, are measures that can only be adopted by the judges exercising their judicial attributions and independence, according to what is stated in the Constitution and the statutes of the Republic. Additionally, article 46,b of the American Convention on Human Rights set forth that the petition on denunciations or complaint for the violations of the Convention by a State, requires the presentation and exhaustion of the internal jurisdiction remedies according to the generally accepted principles of international law, which was allowed in this case, due to the fact that the judicial delay was not attributable to the Chamber» [13].

This unfortunate ruling can also be considered contrary to Article 31 of the Venezuelan Constitution which sets forth the individual rights of anybody to bring before the international organizations on human rights, as it is the Inter American Commission on Human Rights, petitions or complaints to seek protection (amparo) of their violated rights. How can this right be enforced if it is the same Constitutional Chamber the one that refuses to accept the jurisdiction of the Commission?

In contrast to this reaction of the Venezuelan Constitutional Chamber, the situation is different in other countries, as is the case of Costa Rica, in which the Constitutional Chamber of the Supreme Court, in its decision N° 2313-95, based the annulment of Article 22 of the Journalist College Organic Statute (imposing the obligatory membership of the Journalist College in order to exercise the profession), on what the Inter American Court decided in its Advisory Opinion N° OC-5 of 1985[14], stating that «if the Inter American Court on Human Rights is the natural organ for the interpretation of the American Convention on Human Rights, the force of its decision when interpreting the Convention and judging on the national statutes according to the Convention, have the value of an interpreted norm»[15]. Consequently, the Chamber concluded the case by arguing that because Costa Rica was the Member State which requested from the Inter American Court its Advisory Opinion:

> «When the Inter American Court on Human Rights, in its OC-O5-85 unanimously decided that the obligatory affiliation of journalists set forth in Statute N° 4420 is incompatible with article 13 of the American Convention on

13 Case: *Faitha M.Nahmens L. y Ben Ami Fihman Z.* (*Revista Exceso*), Exp. N° 00-0216, decisión N° 386 de 17-5-2000. See in *cit.*, en Carlos AYALA CORAO, «Recepción de la jurisprudencia internacional sobre derechos humanos por la jurisprudencia constitucional» en *Revista del Tribunal Constitucional*, N° 6, Sucre, Bolivia, Nov. 2004, pp. 275 y ss.

14 Opinión Consultiva OC-5/85 de 13 de noviembre de 1985. *La colegiación obligatoria de periodistas (arts. 13 y 29 Convención Americana sobre Derechos Humanos). In such Opinion the Inter American Court considered that «the compulsory affiliation of journalists is incompatible with article 13 of the American Convention, because it impedes any other person to the full use of the Medias as a mean to express or transmit his information»*; and also «that the Costa Rican Organic Statute on Journalists (Ley n° 4420 of September 22, 1969), which is the subject of this Opinion, because it impedes certain persons to be affiliated to the Journalists Collage, and consequently, it is incompatible because it impedes the full use of the Media as a vehicle to express and transmit information».

15 Decision N° 2312-05 of May, 9, 1995, in Rodolfo PIZA ESCALANTE, *La justicia constitucional en Costa Rica*, San José, 1995; and en Carlos Ayala Corao, «Recepción de la jurisprudencia internacional sobre derechos humanos por la jurisprudencia constitucional» en *Revista del Tribunal Constitucional*, N° 6, Sucre, Bolivia, Nov. 2004, pp. 275 y ss.

> Human Rights because it impedes persons the access to the Media, [such Opinion] cannot but oblige the country that started the complex and costly procedure of the Inter American system of protection of human rights»

On the other hand, and according to the case law decisions of the Constitutional Chamber of Costa Rica, the constitutional system of this country can also be classified within the category of those that give supra constitutional rank to the international treaties on human rights when they contain more favorable provisions on the matter. Accordingly, in the abovementioned decision 2313-95, the Constitutional Chamber considered that:

> Being international instruments in force in the country, Article 7 of the Constitution does not apply, due to the fact that Article 48 of the same Constitution contains a special provision regarding treaties on human rights, giving them a normative force of constitutional level. To the point, as has been recognized by this Chamber's jurisprudence, the international instruments on human rights in force in Costa Rica, have not only a similar value to the Political Constitution, but they prevail over the Constitution when giving to persons more rights or guaranties (vid. decisions N° 3435-92 and N° 5759-93)[16].

Consequently, in the same 2313-95 decision, the Constitutional Chamber when considering its own powers of judicial review of constitutionality stated that:

> The Constitutional Chamber not only declares violations of constitutional rights, but of all the universe of fundamental rights set forth in the international instruments on human rights in force in the country. From this point of view, the Constitutional Chamber's recognition of the normative contents of the American Convention on Human Rights, as was interpreted by the Inter American Court on Human Rights in its Consultative Opinion OC-05-85, is natural and absolutely according with its wide powers. So, without needing to duplicate rulings, based on the same arguments of that Opinion, the Chamber considers that it is clear for Costa Rica that the norms of Statute N°40... are illegitimate and contrary to the right to information in the wide sense which is developed in Article 13 of the San José of Costa Rica Covenant, as well in Articles 28 and 29 of the Political Constitution.

Now, back to the Venezuelan situation, mention must be made to the fact that before the abovementioned restrictive interpretation was issued, many Venezuelan courts, when dealing with other matters, did apply the American Convention on Human Rights, thus declaring its prevalence vis-à-vis the Constitution and statutory provisions.

This is the case of the constitutional right to appeal judicial decisions before a superior court. According to the 1976 general statute regulating the special jurisdiction for judicial review of administrative acts (*jurisdicción contencioso-administrativa*)[17], some administrative acts, such as those of independent Administrations,

---

[16] See also the text of the decisión in Alfonso GAIRAUD BRENES, «Los Mecanismos de interpretación de los derechos humanos: especial referencia a la jurisprudencia Perúana» en José F. Palomino Manchego, *El derecho procesal constitucional Perúano. Estudios en Homenaje a Domingo García Belaunde*, Editorial Jurídica Grijley, Lima, 2005, Tomo I, p. 133, note 21.

[17] See the comments in Allan R. BREWER-CARÍAS y Josefina CALCAÑO DE TEMELTAS, *Ley Orgánica de la Corte Suprema de Justicia*, Editorial Jurídica Venezolana, Caracas, 1978.

were to be challenged before the First Court on judicial review of administrative action, in a proceeding that had to be decided in a sole instance, without any appeal before the corresponding Chamber of the Supreme Court of Justice. The 1999 Constitution only set forth the right to appeal regarding criminal cases in which a person would be declared guilty (Article 49,1); thus, in other cases, like judicial review of administrative acts, no constitutional norm guarantees the right to appeal. In particular cases, the appeal was brought before the Administrative Review Chamber of the Supreme Court alleging the unconstitutionality of the statutorily limits to appeal, and a few judicial decisions were taken by means of judicial review (diffuse method), admitting the appeal, based on «the right to appeal the judgment to a higher court», that is set forth in Article 8,2,h of the American Convention on Human Rights, which was considered as forming part of internal constitutional law of the country.

The matter eventually also reached the Constitutional Chamber of the Supreme Tribunal of Justice, which in a decision N° 87 of March 13, 2000 stated:

> If this provision (Article 8,2,h of the American Convention) is compared to Article 49,1 of the Constitution in which the right to appeal only corresponds to those who have been declared guilty in criminal cases, including an authorization to set forth statutory exceptions, it must be interpreted that the norm of the Convention is more favorable to the exercise of such right, due to the fact that it guarantees the right of everybody to be heard not only regarding to criminal procedures, but also regarding rights and obligations in civil, labor, taxation or any other procedure, in which the right to appeal without any exception is established; assigning such right to the category of minimal guarantee of anybody, independently of its condition in the proceeding, and governed by the principle of equality».
>
> If this international provision of the American Convention is compared with the first paragraph of Article 185 of the Organic statute on the Supreme Court of Justice, it must be interpreted that the latter is incompatible with the former, because it denies in absolute terms, the right that the Convention guarantees»[18].

Based on the aforementioned, the Constitutional Chamber concluded its ruling by stating that it:

> «recognized and declared, based on what is set forth in Article 23 of the Constitution, that Article 8,1 and 2,h of the American Convention on Human Rights, is part of the Venezuelan constitutional order; that its dispositions regarding the right to appeal are more favorable regarding the exercise of such right in relation to what is set forth in Article 49,1 of the Constitution; and that such provisions are of direct and immediate application by courts and authorities»[19].

The Constitutional Chamber even resolved in its obligatory interpretation, to re-write the statute, stating:

---

[18] Case: *C.A. Electricidad del Centro (Elecentro) y otra vs. Superintendencia para la Promoción y Protección de la Libre Competencia. (Procompetencia)* en *Revista de Derecho Público*, N° 81, Editorial Jurídica Venezolana, Caracas, 2000, pp. 157 y ss.

[19] *Idem*.

Consequently, and taking into account that last first paragraph of Article 185 of the Organic Statute of the Supreme Court of Justice sets forth that: «Against the First Court decisions in the matter listed in numbers 1 to 4 of such provision, no recourse or appeal will be heard»; that such provision is incompatible with the one set forth in Article 8,1 and 2,h of the American Convention of Human Rights which have constitutional hierarchy and are of prevalent application; that Article 334 of the Constitution sets forth that «In case of incompatibility between this Constitution and a statute or other legal norm, the constitutional provisions will apply, being attributed such power to decide to all courts in any case, even in an ex officio manner»; this (Constitutional) Chamber leaves without application the aforementioned disposition contained in the first paragraph of Article 185 of the Organic Statute, applying instead, in the case (File 99-22167), the provision of second paragraph of the same Article 185 of the Statute, which states: «Against definitive decisions of the same (First) Court...an appeal can be brought before the Supreme Court of Justice (rectius: Supreme Tribunal of Justice)». So is decided»[20].

2. The constitutional rank of international instruments of human rights

Secondly, other Constitutions also attributed in an express way the constitutional rank to international treaties on human rights, thus acquiring the same normative hierarchy as those set forth in the Constitution.

Two types of constitutional regimes can be distinguished in this group: Constitutions that confer constitutional rank on all international instruments of human rights, and Constitutions that only grant such rank to a group of instruments that are expressly listed in the Constitution.

In the *first group*, for example, is to be found Perú's 1979 Constitution, repealed in 1994, which in its Article 105 established that «the precepts contained in treaties on human rights, shall have constitutional hierarchy..». and therefore «...cannot be modified except by the procedure in force for reforming the Constitution».

Among the *second type* is to be found the 1994 Constitution of Argentina which grants to a group of treaties and declarations in force at the time, specifically listed in Article 75.22 of the Constitution, a hierarchy superior to the laws, that is, constitutional rank, listing only the following: the American Declaration of the Rights and Duties of Man; the Universal Declaration of Human Rights; the American Convention on Human Rights; the International Covenant on Economic, Social and Cultural Rights; the International Covenant on Civil and Political Rights and its Facultative Protocol; the Convention on the Prevention and Punishment of the Crime of Genocide; the International Convention on the Elimination of All Forms of Racial Discrimination; the Convention on the Elimination of All Forms of Discrimination against Women; the Convention against Torture and Other Cruel, Inhuman or Degrading Treatment or Punishment; the Convention on the Rights of the Child.

These instruments as set forth in the Constitution, «pursuant to the conditions determining their validity, shall have constitutional hierarchy, shall not abrogate any article of the first part of this Constitution, and shall be understood to be

[20] *Idem.*

complementary to the rights and guarantees recognized by such Constitution». Apart from this, «they may only be denounced, if such were the case, by the Executive, with prior approval of two thirds of the total members of each Chamber».

In regard to other human rights treaties different to those listed in Article 75,22, the Constitution established that they could enjoy such constitutional hierarchy, provided that they were approved by a qualified majority of 2/3 of the total members of the Senate and the Chamber of Deputies.

According with these constitutional provisions, the Supreme Court of the Nation of Argentina, has applied the American Convention on Human Rights, giving prevalence to its provisions regarding internal statutes, as has happened regarding the Criminal Procedural Code. In contrast to what is set forth in the American Convention, the Criminal Procedural Code excluded from the right to appeal, some judicial decisions according to the amount of the punishment. The Supreme Court of the Nation declared the invalidity on the grounds of its unconstitutionality of such limits, applying the American Convention which in Article 8, 1,h guarantees «the right to appeal the judgment to a higher court»[21].

Additionally, in Argentina, the courts have also considered the decisions of the Inter American Commission and of the Inter American Court as obligatory, even before the international treaties on human rights were constitutionalized. In a decision dated July 7, 1992 the Supreme Court applied the Inter American Court Advisory Opinion OC-7/86[22], stating that «the interpretation of the Covenant, additionally, must be oriented by the decisions of the Inter American Court on Human Rights, one of its purposes being the interpretation of the San José Covenant»[23].

In 1995, the same Supreme Court considered that due to the recognition by the Argentinean State of the Inter American Court jurisdiction to resolve on cases referred to the interpretation and application of the American Convention, its decisions «must serve as a guide for the interpretation of constitutional provisions»[24]. In other decisions the Supreme Court has repealed lower court decisions when

---

21 Decision of April, 4, 1995, Giroldi, H.D. an others. See the references in Aida KEMELMAJER DE CARLUCCI and María Gabriela ABALOS DE MOSSO, «Grandes líneas directrices de la jurisprudencia argentina sobre material constitucional durante el año 1995», in *Anuario de Derecho Constitucional latinoamericano 1996*, Fundación Konrad Adenauer, Bogotá, 1996, pp. 517 ff.; and in Carlos AYALA CORAO, «Recepción de la jurisprudencia internacional sobre derechos humanos por la jurisprudencia constitucional» in *Revista del Tribunal Constitucional*, N° 6, Sucre, Bolivia, Nov. 2004, pp. 275 ff.

22 Advisory Opinion OC-7/86 August 29, 1986. *Exigibilidad del derecho de rectificación o respuesta (arts. 14.1, 1.1 y 2 de la Convención Americana sobre Derechos Humanos).*

23 Case *Miguel A. Ekmkdjiam, Gerardo Sofivic and others*, in Ariel E. DULITZKY, «La aplicación de los Tratados sobre Derechos Humanos por los tribunales locales: un estudio comparado» in *La aplicación de los tratados sobre derechos Humanos por los tribunales locales*, Centro de Estudios Legales y Sociales, Buenos Aires, 1997. See Carlos AYALA CORAO, «Recepción de la jurisprudencia internacional sobre derechos humanos por la jurisprudencia constitucional» en *Revista del Tribunal Constitucional*, N° 6, Sucre, Bolivia, Nov. 2004, pp. 275 ff.

24 Case H Giroldi/Cassation Recourse, April 7, 1995 in *Jurisprudencia Argentina*, Vol. 1995-III, p. 571. See Carlos AYALA CORAO, «Recepción de la jurisprudencia internacional sobre derechos humanos por la jurisprudencia constitucional» in *Revista del Tribunal Constitucional*, N° 6, Sucre, Bolivia, Nov. 2004, pp. 275 ff.

considering that their interpretation was made in an incompatible way regarding the decision's doctrine of the Inter American Commission on Human Rights[25]

Reference should also be made to the case of Panama, where even though the Constitution has no express provision regarding the normative rank of treaties, from the jurisprudence of the Supreme Court such rank can be deducted, when considering that any violation of an international treaty is considered as a violation of Article 4 of the Constitution.

In effect, Article 4 of the Panamanian Constitution only sets forth that «The Republic of Panama respects the norms of international law». Thus, such norm has allowed the Supreme Court of Justice to consider as a constitutional violation any violation to norms of international treaties. In a decision of March 12, 1990, the Supreme Court declared the unconstitutionality of an Executive Decree which established general arbitrary conditions for the exercise of the rights to free expression and press, and stated that:

> Such act violates article 4 of the Constitution that oblige the national authorities to respect the international law norms. In the case under examination, as stated by the plaintiff, it is a matter of violation of the International Covenant on Human Rights and of the American Convention on Human Rights approved through statutes 14-1976 and 15-1977, which rejects any prior censorship regarding the exercise of the freedoms of expression and press, as fundamental human rights»[26].

One of the consequences of giving constitutional rank to international treaties, for instance, to the American Convention, is that the rights declared in it are out of the reach of the legislative body, which cannot legislate diminishing in any way the enforcement or scope of such rights.

It is the case, for instance, of the due process of law rights enshrined in the American Convention on Human Rights, like the right to a fair trial. According to Article 8,1 of the Convention «every person has the right to a hearing, with due guarantees and within a reasonable time, *by a competent, independent, and impartial tribunal, previously established by law*, in the substantiation of any accusation of a criminal nature made against him or for the determination of his rights and obligations of a civil, labor, fiscal, or any other nature». And regarding the right to personal liberty, Article 7,2 and 7,5 set forth the right of every person not to « be deprived of his physical liberty except for the *reasons and under the conditions established beforehand by the constitution* of the State Party concerned or by a law established pursuant thereto»; and the right of «any person detained *shall be brought promptly before a judge or other officer authorized by law to exercise judicial power* and shall be entitled to trial within a reasonable time or to be released without prejudice to the continuation of the proceedings».

---

[25] Case: *Bramajo,* September 12, 1996, in *Jurisprudencia Argentina,* Nov. 20, 1996. See Carlos AYALA CORAO, «Recepción de la jurisprudencia internacional sobre derechos humanos por la jurisprudencia constitucional» en *Revista del Tribunal Constitucional,* N° 6, Sucre, Bolivia, Nov. 2004, pp. 275 y ss.

[26] *Véase* en *Iudicum et Vita, Jurisprudencia nacional de América Latina en Derechos Humanos,* N° 5, Instituto Interamericano de Derechos Humanos, San José, Costa Rica, Diciembre 1997 pp. 80-82.

These rights are also enshrined in the national Constitutions and due to their declaration in the Convention, have constitutional rank, therefore, they are protected by the amparo and habeas corpus recourses, the latter being regulated in Article 7,6 of the Convention which sets forth the right of anyone who is deprived of his liberty to «be entitled to recourse to a competent court, in order that the court may decide without delay on the lawfulness of his arrest or detention and order his release if the arrest or detention is unlawful»; right that cannot «be restricted or abolished».

These provisions prohibit, in Latin America, any possibility for the creation or special commissions to try any kind of offenses; and also prohibits for civilians to be tried by ordinary military courts and of course by military commissions. It also prohibits the creation of special courts to hear some criminal procedures after the offenses have been committed, in the sense that every person has the right to be heard only before courts existing prior to the offenses. For instance, in the Cantoral Benavides case, the Inter American Court on Human Rights decided that Perú violated Article 8,1 of the Convention because Mr. Cantoral Benavides had been prosecuted by a military judge, which was not the «competent independent and impartial judge» provided for in that provision. Consequently the Court considered that Perú had also violated Article 7.5 of the Convention because the victim had been brought before a criminal military court[27]. By ruling this way it can even be considered that the Court has ruled that not any judiciary body can examine the legality and reasonability of a detention, but only those that do not violate the principle of «natural judge»[28].

And this is in fact one of the cores of the due process of law rights according to the Convention, the right to be heard by a competent court set forth not only by statute but by a statute that must be sanctioned previously to the offense. This is a provision tending to proscribe ad hoc courts or commissions. The Inter American Court has referred to this due process of law right in the Ivcher Bronstein case. In such case, the Perúvian Executive Commission of the Judiciary, weeks before a Resolution depriving Mr. Bronstein of his Perúvian citizenship was issued, altered the composition of a Chamber of the Supreme Court and empowered such Chamber to create in a transitory way, specialized Superior chambers and Public Law specialized courts. The Supreme Court Chamber created one of such courts and appointed its judges, who heard the recourses filed by Mr. Bronstein. The Inter American Court ruled as follows:

---

27 Case *Cantoral Benavides*, Augst 18, 2000. Paragraph 75: Also, the Court considers that the trial of Mr. Luis Alberto Cantoral-Benavides in the military criminal court violated Article 8(1) of the American Convention, which refers to the right to a fair trial before a competent, independent and impartial judge (*infra* para. 115). Consequently, the fact that Cantoral-Benavides was brought before a military criminal judge does not meet the requirements of Article 7(5) of the Convention. Also, the continuation of his detention by order of the military judges constituted arbitrary arrest, in violation of Article 7(3) of the Convention. Paragraph 76: The legal principle set forth in Article 7(5) of the Convention was not respected in this case until the accused was brought before a judge in the regular jurisdiction. In the file, there is no evidence of the date on which this occurred, but it can be reasonably concluded that it took place in early October 1993, since on October 8, 1993, the 43rd Criminal Court of Lima ordered that the investigation stage of a trial be opened against Cantoral-Benavides.

28 See Cecilia MEDINA QUIROGA, *La Convención Americana: Teoría y Jurisprudencia*, Universidad de Chile, Santiago 2003, p. 231.

> 114. The Court considers that, by creating temporary public law chambers and courts and appointing judges to them at the time that the facts of the case sub judice occurred, the State did not guarantee to Mr. Ivcher Bronstein the right to be heard by judges or courts «previously established by law», as stipulated in Article 8(1) of the American Convention[29].

The Inter American Court also ruled on these matters in the Castillo Petruzzi and others Case, where it decided that:

> 129. A basic principle of the independence of the judiciary is that every person has the right to be heard by regular courts, following procedures previously established by law. States are not to create «[t]ribunals that do not use the duly established procedures of the legal process [...] to displace the jurisdiction belonging to the ordinary courts or judicial tribu-nals»[30].

Particularly regarding the need of a competent court, and referring to the military courts, the Inter American Commission on Human Rights has considered that «to prosecute ordinary crimes as though they were military crimes simply because they had been committed by members of the military breached the guarantee of an independent and impartial tribunal» [31]; and the Inter American Court ruled in the Castillo Petruzzi et al. case that due process of law rights were violated when ordinary common offenses are transferred to the military jurisdiction; that judging civilians for treason in such courts imply to exclude their «natural judge» to hear those proceedings; and that because military jurisdiction is set forth for the purpose of maintaining order and discipline within the Armed Forces, civilians cannot incur in conducts contrary to such military duties. The Courts ruled as follows:

> 128. The Court notes that several pieces of legislation give the military courts jurisdiction for the purpose of maintaining order and discipline within the ranks of the armed forces. Application of this functional jurisdiction is confined to military personnel who have committed some crime or were derelict in performing their duties, and then, only under certain circumstances. This was the definition in Perú's own law (Article 282 of the 1979 Constitution). Transferring jurisdiction from civilian courts to military courts, thus allowing military courts to try civilians accused of treason, means that the competent, independent and impartial tribunal previously established by law is precluded from hearing these cases. In effect, military tribunals are not the tribunals previously established by law for civilians. Having no military functions or duties, civilians cannot engage in behaviors that violate military duties. When a military court takes jurisdiction over a matter that regular courts should hear, the individual's right to a hearing by a competent, independent and impartial tribunal previously established by law and, a fortiori, his right to due process is violated. That right to due process, in turn, is intimately linked to the very right of access to the courts».[32]

---

29 Case *Ivcher Bronstein*, February 6, 2001. Paragraphs 113-114.

30 Case *Castillo Petruzzi* el al., May 30, 1999, paragraph 129. The quotation correspond to *Basic Principles on the Independence of the Judiciary*, adopted by the Seventh United Nations Conference on the Prevention of Crime and Treatment of Offenders, held in Milan August 26 to September 6, 1985, and confirmed by the General Assembly in its resolutions 40/32 of 29 November 1985 and 40/146 of 13 December 1985.

31 Case *Genie Lacayo*, January 29, 1997. Paragraph 53.

32 Case *Castillo Petruzzi* et al, May 30, 1999, Paragraph 128 and 132.

Finally, in the Durand and *Ugarte Case*, the Inter American Court ruled that:

> 117. In a democratic Government of Laws, the penal military jurisdiction shall have a restrictive and exceptional scope and shall lead to the protection of special juridical interests, related to the functions assigned by law to the military forces. Consequently, civilians must be excluded from the military jurisdiction scope and only the military shall be judged by commission of crime or offenses that by its own nature attempt against legally protected interests of military order[33].

This excludes not only the processing of civilians by military courts, but additionally the possibility to assign to military courts to hear cases of common felonies committed by military, even in the exercise of its functions. As was ruled by the same Inter American Court:

> 118. In this case, the military in charge of subduing the riots that took place in El Frontón prison resorted to a disproportionate use of force, which surpassed the limits of their functions thus also causing a high number of inmate death toll. Thus, the actions which brought about this situation cannot be considered as military felonies, but common crimes, so investigation and punishment must be placed on the ordinary justice, apart from the fact that the alleged active parties had been military or not[34].

In contrast with the aforementioned, the absence of similar constitutional provisions in the United States allows those discussions to continue regarding the validity of military commissions set up by a military order of Nov. 13, 2001, to try non-citizens for «acts of international terrorism», after the September 11 terrorist attacks. This discussion was reported on March 26, 2006, in The New York Times[35] showing the struggle for supremacy between the courts and the Government, which can be briefed as follows:

According to the Detainee Treatment Act sanctioned on December 2005, the federal courts jurisdiction has been excluded over cases brought by detainees at the United States naval base at Guantánamo Bay, Cuba. In the case, *Hamdan v. Rumsfeld*, referred to a person held since 2002, the court must decide whether it retains the right to proceed with this case; a matter that has not being discussed since the immediate aftermath of the Civil War, in which the Supreme Court permitted Congress to divest the Court of jurisdiction over a case it has already agreed to decide. In the Ex Parte McCardle case, after arguments had been heard in an appeal brought by William H. McCardle, a Mississippi newspaper editor who was taken into custody and charged by the military government with fomenting insurrection; Congress, fearing that a Supreme Court ruling in favor of the editor could result in invalidating military control of the former Confederate state, enacted a law to deprive the court of jurisdiction. The court then dismissed the appeal, rejecting the argument that with the new statute it was permitting Congress to usurp the judicial function.

In the new case Hamdan v. Rumpfel N° 05-184, the administration also filed a motion with the court in January 2006, just days after the Detainee Treatment Act

---

33 Case *Durand and Ugarte*, August 16, 2000, paragraph 117.

34 *Idem*, Paragraph 118.

35 See Linda GREENHOUSE «Detainee case Will Pose delicate Question for Courts. A White House Challenge to Jurisdiction», *The New York Times* March 27, 2006, p. A12.

was signed into law, urging immediate dismissal of Mr. Hamdan's appeal. On February 21, the court declined to act on the motion, announcing instead that it would take up the jurisdictional question as part of the argument on the merits of the case. Contrary to the McCardle case in which the Congress spoke clearly in the court-stripping amendment, the Detainee Treatment Act seems to be ambiguous on its application to pending, as opposed to future, cases.

According to the Detainee Treatment Act, Guantánamo detainees are tried by a military commission and will have only a circumscribed right to a subsequent appeal in federal court, in which they can not raise the basic challenge to the commission's operation that Mr. Hamdan is presenting in his Supreme Court case. Military commissions are not new in the United States; they were first used during the war with México in the 1840's. But there have been none since the World War II era.

The main point to be resolved is if any Congressional enactment or inherent power authorized the administration to set up a special tribunal without the procedural protections offered by American military law and required by the Geneva Conventions; and if conspiracy, is or is not a war crime, and if it is or not subject to trial by military commissions. In the end, the question at hand is if the Geneva Conventions apply in the cases related to the Guantanamo detainees, and if their protections can or cannot be invoked by individual detainees[36].

The reference to the case is made in order to highlight what happens in cases such as the United States where there is no express constitutional rank with the right to be tried by judicial competent independent and impartial courts established before the offenses were committed, as set forth in the American Convention on Human Rights; and if the discussions regarding the struggle on the supremacy between the courts and the Government can still be developed as above mentioned; as well as the exclusion of any injunctive protection of rights in such cases. In Latin America, after so many cases and stories of ad hoc commissions or special courts to try people with no due process of law rights, the provisions of the American Convention and those set forth in the Constitutions, do not allow even the discussion to be sustained. The due process of law, with all its content, is a constitutional right, and its enforcement is out of the reach of Congress and no legislation can be passed to restrict the courts jurisdiction. And being it a constitutional right, the amparo and habeas corpus protection can always be sought by the affected party, and eventually reach the American Court on Human Rights for the protection, as shown in the aforementioned ca-ses.

3. The supra statutory rank of international treaties on human rights

Thirdly, other Latin American Constitutions have expressly established the supra-legal rank of international treaties and conventions in general, including those relative to human rights. In these systems, the treaties are subject to the Constitution, but prevail over the statutes.

This was the solution followed in the Constitutions of Germany (Article 25), Italy (Article 10) and France (Article 55), and in Latin America is the solution followed in the Constitution of Costa Rica, which provides that: «Public treaties, international agreements and covenants duly approved by the Legislative

---

36 *Idem.*

Assembly shall, as of their enactment or the day they themselves set forth, have superior authority to that of the laws» (Article 7). Nevertheless, as mentioned above, the jurisprudence of the Constitutional Chamber has given constitutional rank to international treaties on human rights, and even supra constitutional rank in cases in which they contain more favorable provisions regarding the exercise of such rights.

In this respect, the Constitutional Chamber has for instance, directly applied the American Convention on Human Rights, as prevailing regarding statutes, arguing that the legal «norms which contradict [a treaty] must be considered simply as repealed, by virtue precisely of the superior rank of the treaty (decision 282-90, case of violation of Article 8.2 of the American Convention on Human Rights by the repealed Article 472 of the Criminal Procedures Code). Thus, when considering that Article 8.2 of the American Convention «recognizes as a fundamental right of everybody who has been criminally indicted, to appeal the judicial decision»; the Chamber considered that Article 472 of the Criminal Procedure Code which limits the exercise of the cassation recourse, had to be considered as «not set forth» and understand «that the cassation recourse is a mean legally given to any condemned person regarding whatever sanction imposed in a criminal procedure». The Constitutional Chamber in a subsequent decision N° 719-90 accepted a judicial review action declaring the unconstitutionality of said Article 474 of the Criminal procedure Code, deciding its annulment and considering that the limits set forth in such article to the right to appeal in cassation in favor of any criminally condemned person, as «not being set forth».

It must be noted, that in another Constitutional Chamber decision (N° 1054-94), the challenging of Article 426 of the Criminal Procedures Code which denies appeal regarding decisions on other non criminal contraventions, was rejected according to the jurisprudence set by the Chamber, based on the fact that what the Chamber has clearly decided is that «what is established in the said American Convention is the fundamental right to appeal given to anybody condemned in a criminal procedures, and not indistinctively in other matters».

Now, regarding the supra legal rank of treaties and their prevalence over internal statutes in case of conflict, in a similar sense, Article 144 of the Constitution of El Salvador provides the legal status of treaties and their prevalence with respect to the statutes in the event of conflict, when stating that: «International treaties executed by El Salvador with other States or with international organisms, shall constitute laws of the Republic upon entering into force, pursuant to the provisions of the treaty itself and of this Constitution», adding the regulation that: «The statute shall not modify or abrogate that which is agreed upon in the treaty for El Salvador» and that: «In the event of conflicts between the treaty and the statute, the treaty shall prevail».

In accordance with these provisions, the Constitutional Chamber of the Supreme Court of Justice of El Salvador has also applied International treaties on human rights, on deciding cases on which the international regulations are considered to prevail. It was the case of a November 17, 1994 decision issued regarding a provisional detention of a former commander of the irregular armed forces, ordered in a defamatory criminal trial brought against him. The Chamber stated that «For the adequate comprehension of the provisional detention institution in our system, we must additionally bear in mind -according to Article 144 of the Constitution, what is set forth in the international treaties ratified by El Salvador»[37]. So the Court analyzed Articles 11,1 of the Universal Declaration on Human Rights, and Article 9,3 of the International Covenant on Civil and Political Rights, which refers to the presumption of innocence and to the exceptional character of the preventive detention, which must not be considered as a general rule. The Court also analyzed Article XXVI of the American Declarations of Human Rights, referred as well to the presumption of innocence; and Articles 7,2 and 8,2 of the American Convention on Human Rights, which refer to the rights of persons regarding detentions, particularly the principle *nulla pena sine lege*. From the aforementioned the Court concluded by stating that «It is within this -constitutional and international- context where the analysis of the provisional detention must be framed, because such provisions, due to their superior place in the normative hierarchy, are obligatory»[38].

Consequently and based on the international regulations, regarding the preventive detention the Chamber concluded that «It must never be considered as a general rule in criminal proceedings -as expressly forbidden in Article 9,3 of the International Covenant on Civil and Political Rights-, so that it cannot be automatically decided», because it cannot be understood as an anticipated sanction. On the contrary, in order to be decided, it needs in each case the judge's evaluation of the circumstances regarding its need and convenience for the protection of fundamental public interest.

Based in the aforementioned, the Chamber concluded regarding the case, that «when the provisional detention was decided, the judge did not base its decision in any justification at all, thus being unconstitutional»[39].

In another decision of the Constitutional Chamber of the Supreme Court of El Salvador issued on June 13, 1995, the Chamber declared the unconstitutionality of a local government regulation (*Ordenanza municipal*) setting forth restrictions to the exercise of the political rights to meeting and demonstration, basing its decision in Article 15 of the American Convention on Human Rights and in Article 21 of the International Covenant on Civil and Political Rights, according to which limitations to such rights can only be regulated by means of statutes. The Chamber argued as follows: «The international treaties in force in our country, having supremacy regarding secondary regulations, and among them, the Municipal Code, recognized the freedom of meeting and public demonstration and established that such rights can only be subjected to limitations or restrictions as are necessary in a democratic society and are provided in statutes», which «must be sanctions by the Legislative Assembly following the formalities set forth in the Constitution». The Chamber also ruled that such statute, according to Article XXVIII of the American Declaration on Human Rights, can only set forth limitations subjected to the «principle of reasonability», which means that they must be «intrinsically just, that is to say, that they must be in accordance to certain rules of enough value in order to give the sense to the substantive notion of justice enshrined in the Constitution». In this regard, the Chamber concluded its decision regarding the case, declaring the unconstitutionality of the challenged municipal regulation, stating:

---

37 See in *Iudicum et Vita, Jurisprudencia nacional de América Latina en Derechos Humanos*, Nº 5, Instituto Interamericano de Derechos Humanos, San José, Costa Rica, Diciembre 1997, p. 157.

38 *Idem*, p. 157.

39 *Idem*, p. 158.

> Non of these elements are found in the challenged instrument on grounds of unconstitutionality, that is to say, it is a typical case of authority abuse, not only because without any authorization it regulated a constitutional right, but because it usurped a function reserved to the Legislative body

The Constitution of México, when referring to international treaties is the one among the Latin American countries which more closely resembles the North American constitutional provision, stating:

> Article 133. This Constitution, the laws (statutes) of Congress of the Union and all the treaties that have been made and shall be made in accordance therewith by the President with the approval of the Senate according to the Constitution, shall be the supreme law of the Union. The judges of each state shall conform to the Constitution, laws and treaties, in spite of any disposition in contrary to them that could be contained in the Constitutions and statutes of the States.

According to this traditional supremacy clause, treaties were also traditionally considered as having the same rank as statutes. This was decided by the Supreme Court of the Nation by the ruling C/92, June 30, 1992, in which it stated that because the statutes have the same rank that treaties have, «immediately below the Constitution in the hierarchy of norms of the Mexican legal order», and:

> «international treaties cannot be the criteria in order to determine the unconstitutionality of a statute, nor vice versa. Thus, the Commerce and Industrial Associations Statute cannot be considered unconstitutional because it is contrary to what is regulated in an international treaty»[40]

But this criteria has been abandoned by the same Supreme Court in a ruling of revision of an amparo decision N° 1475/98, in which the Court, interpreting Article 133 of the Constitution according to the 1969 Vienna Convention on Treaties determined that because «the international compromises are assumed by the Mexican State as a whole and obliged all its authorities regarding international community», the international treaties are located in a second level immediately under the Constitution and above the federal and local statutes[41].

Among this group of countries that gives international treaties on human rights a superior rank regarding statutes, it can also be mentioned the case of Paraguay. The Constitution has a supremacy clause similar to the North American and Mexican one, with the following text:

> Article 137. On the supremacy of the Constitution. The supreme law of the Republic is the Constitution. The latter, the international treaties, covenants and agreements approved and ratified, the statutes sanctioned by Congress and the other legal hierarchical inferior regulations accordingly issued, integrate the positive national law in the enunciated preference order.

---

40 Tesis P. C/92, in *Gaceta del Semanario Judicial de la Federación*, N° 60, diciembre de 1992, p. 27.

41 *Véase* Guadalupe BARRENA y Carlos MONTEMAYOR «Incorporación del derecho internacional en la Constitución mexicana», *Derechos Humanos. Memoria del IV Congreso Nacional de Derecho Constitucional*, Vol. III, Instituto de Investigaciones Jurídicas, UNAM, México, 2001, *cit.*, por Humberto HENDERSON, «Los tratados internacionales de derechos humanos en el orden interno: la importancia del principio *pro homine*», en *Revista IIDH*, Instituto Interamericano de Derechos Humanos, N° 39, San José, 2004, p. 82, nota 15.

Nonetheless, this constitutional clause has a peculiarity regarding other similar clause, since it enunciates the order of preference given to the legal regulations; thus, the treaties being located under the Constitution but above the statutes. Additionally, the Article is complemented by Article 141 of the same Constitution which provides that «international treatises approved by the National Congress and which are duly ratified, are part of the internal legal order with the hierarchy established in Article 137»

According to these provisions, the Court of Appeal in criminal cases, First Chamber, in a decision dated June 10, 1996, revoked a judicial decision of an inferior court which had sentenced a person for a defamation offence regarding a public politician person. The argument of the Court was that in a «democratic society, the politicians are exposed to citizens criticism» and that in «no way individual interest can prevail over public interest», invoking for the revocation not only constitutional articles, but also Article 13 of the American Convention on Human Rights[42]

4. The statutory rank of international treaties on human rights

In *fourth* place, regarding the legal hierarchy of international instruments of human rights, it can be said that in general, constitutional systems have attributes to international treaties the same hierarchy as of statutes. It can be considered as the most widespread system in contemporary constitutional law, following the orientation begun by the Constitution of the United States of America, in which Article VI. 2, states:

> This Constitution, and the laws of the United States which shall be made in pursuance thereof; and all treaties made, or which shall be made, under the authority of the United States, shall be the supreme law of the land; and the judges in every state shall be bound thereby, anything in the Constitution or laws of any State to the contrary notwithstanding.

In such systems, therefore, «international law is part of the law of the land», the treaties having the same legal rank as the statutes. They are subject to the Constitution, and in their application regarding statutes, they are governed by the principles of subsequent law and special law in regard to the derogatory effects they may have.

Is the case of Uruguay, Article 6 of the Constitution only provides that in all treaties a clause must be incorporated regulating that «the differences between the parties must be decided by mean of arbitration or other peaceful means». In the article, no reference is made regarding the hierarchy of treaties in the legal order or human rights.

Nonetheless, for instance, the Supreme Court of Justice on a decision of October 23, 1996, directly applied international treaties in order to reject the question of unconstitutionality raised in the case by the Public Prosecutor regarding the Press Statute, whose regulations guarantied the right of the defendant to the be prosecuted while in freedom. The case referred to a press offence trial for critics to the President of Paraguay, in which the plaintiff was the Paraguayan Ambassador to Uruguay. In

[42] See in *Iudicum et Vita, Jurisprudencia nacional de América Latina en Derechos Humanos*, N° 5, Instituto Interamericano de Derechos Humanos, San José, Costa Rica, Diciembre 1997 pp. 82-86.

the case, the Public Prosecutor raised the question of unconstitutionality arguing that the Press Statute, when allowing only to certain persons to be tried while in freedom, violates the equality principle set forth in Article 7 of the American Declaration of Human Rights, and Article 24 of the American Convention on Human Rights. In order to decide the question, rejecting the Public prosecutor's argument, the Supreme Court carefully analyzed the human right of free expression, making reference to Article 19 of the International Covenant of Civil and Political Rights; to Article 13.1 of the American Convention on Human Rights; to the Consultative Opinion OC-O5 of the Inter American Court on Human Rights referred to the incompatibility of the freedom of expression with the obligatory affiliation of journalists to the Journalist's College in Costa Rica; and to the presumption of innocence right «expressly set forth in the international Declarations and Conventions to which the country has adhered or that in one way or another oblige it (Universal Declaration on Man's Rights, art. 11; International Covenant on Human Rights, art 14.4; and Inter American Convention on Human Rights, art. 8.2)», all allowing the defendant to be trial in freedom[43].

The Dominican Republic constitutional system can also be classified in this group of countries in which their Constitutions give treaties the same legal rank as statutes. Precisely due to that fact, being the Dominican Republic one of the very few Latin American Countries that do not have in its Constitution expressly regulated the «amparo» action or recourse as a special judicial mean for the protection of human rights; the Supreme Court did apply the American Convention of Human Rights in order to admit the «amparo» recourse.

In effect, Article 3 of the Dominican Republic Constitutions states that «The Dominican Republic recognizes and applies international law regulations, general and American ones, when they have been approved by the State organs», and accordingly, in 1977 the Congress approved the American Convention on Human Rights, whose Article 8 and 25,1 as abovementioned, regulate the general due process of law rules and the «amparo» action or recourse for the judicial protections of human rights. Thus, according to these regulations, if it is true that the Constitution does not set forth the «amparo» action, it is regulated in the American Convention and then it can be exercised by anybody seeking protection of his human rights. But the problem was the absence of procedure rules, comprising the absence of formal attribution to specific courts of the power to decide upon «amparo» suits. That explains why actions or recourses of «amparo» were never brought before courts, until 1999, when a private company, the Avon enterprise, did so before the Supreme Court of Justice, against a judicial decision on labor matters, alleging violations of constitutional rights.

The Supreme Court, in a decision of February 24, 1999 admitted the «amparo» suit brought before the Court by *Productos Avon S.A.*, an enterprise, declared the «amparo» as a «public law institution» and prescribed in the decision the basic rules of procedure for such actions[44]. The case developed as follows:

---

[43] See in *Iudicum et Vita, Jurisprudencia nacional de América Latina en Derechos Humanos*, N° 5, Instituto Interamericano de Derechos Humanos, San José, Costa Rica, Diciembre 1997 pp. 72-79.

[44] See in *Iudicum et Vita, Jurisprudencia nacional de América Latina en Derechos Humanos*, N° 7, Tomo I, Instituto Interamericano de Derechos Humanos, San José, Costa Rica, Diciembre, 2000 p. 329 ff. See the comments regarding the decisión in Allan R. BREWER-CARÍAS, «La admisión jurisprudencial de la acción de amparo en ausencia de regulación constitucional o legal en la República Dominicana», *Idem*, pp. 334 ff.

1. The plaintiff company claimed that a judicial decision on labor matters, issued by a lower court, violated its rights to be judged by the competent court of justice, asking the Supreme Court: First: To declare in its ruling that the «amparo» recourse be considered as a Dominican is a public law institution; and second, that the Supreme Court, according to the provisions of the Organic Judicial statute which attributed to the Supreme Court the power to resolve on adjective matters when a specific procedure does not have a statutory regulation, to set forth the procedure to be followed regarding the «amparo» recourses. Additionally, the plaintiff asked the Court to issue a preliminary order suspending the effects of the challenged judicial labor decisions, pending the course of the trial.

2. The Supreme Court, in order to decide, fixed the criteria that the international treaties invoked by the plaintiff, particularly Articles 8 and 25,1 of the American Convention on Human Rights, as internal Dominican law, have the purpose to guarantee the judicial protection of fundamental rights recognized in the Constitution, the law and the said Convention, against acts which violate such rights, committed by any person acting or not in their public functions thus also against individuals actions. In this regard, the Supreme Court decided that:

> «Contrary to what has been decided in the sense that the offending acts must be issued by judicial officials or persons acting in such functions, the «amparo» recourse, it is considered that as a protection mechanism of individual freedom in its various aspects, the «amparo» must not be excluded as a judicial remedy in order to resolve situations originated by persons accomplishing judicial functions. Article 25,1 of the Convention, provide that the «amparo» recourse is open in favor of anybody against acts which violate his fundamental rights «even when the violation is committed by individuals not acting exercise of public functions»; evidently including the judicial functions; ... as well as against any action or omission from individuals or public administration officials, including omissions or non jurisdictional administrative acts from the courts, if they affect a constitutional protected right»[45].

In this regard, the Dominican Republic Supreme Court decision is considered a very important ruling, clearly stating that the «amparo» recourse can be filed against individuals, following the broad conception of the «amparo» action initiated in Argentina, and followed in Uruguay, Chile, Perú, Bolivia and Venezuela. The narrow conception excluding the «amparo» recourse against individuals is followed in México, Brazil, Panama, El Salvador and Nicaragua. The Dominican Supreme Court also followed the broad conception of «amparo» admitting the action against judicial decisions, as it is accepted in the American Convention, contrary to the tendency observed in other Latin American countries that excluded judicial decisions from the «amparo» recourse, as is the case of Argentina, Uruguay, Costa Rica, Panama, El Salvador, Honduras and Nicaragua.

In Colombia, the 1991 statute regulating the action of «tutela» also admitted the amparo against judicial rulings, but the Constitutional Court annulled the corresponding article, considering that it violated the right to *res judicata* effects of

---

[45] *Idem*. p. 332.

definitive judicial decisions[46]. Nonetheless, the «tutela» against judicial decisions has indirectly been admitted when arbitrariness is alleged against judicial decisions[47]

3. Regarding the Dominican Republic Supreme Court decision, it additionally decided that even in the absence of procedural rules for the «amparo» recourse, contrary to what happens regarding habeas corpus recourses (where there is a statute establishing the competent court and the procedure); and because the amparo recourse is a simple, speedy and effective judicial mean for the protection of all constitutional rights other than those protected by means of habeas corpus, no judge can refuse to admit it adducing the absence of statutory regulation. For that purpose, the Supreme Court invoked its power according to Article 29,2 of the Judicial organization Statute, to establish the procedural rules in order to avoid the confusion that can cause the absence of such rules. Consequently, the Supreme Court decided «to declare that the recourse set forth in Article 25,1 of the November 22, 1969 San José, Costa Rica American Convention on Human Rights, is an institution of Dominican positive law, due to its approval by the National Congress through resolution N° 739 of December 1977, according to Article 3 of the Constitution».

On the other hand, the Supreme Court resolved the practical problems derived from the acceptance of the «amparo» suit, by setting forth the procedural rules, as follows: First, by determining that the competent courts to decide on the matter are the courts of first instance in the place in which the challenged act or omission has been produced; and second, by stating adjective rules of procedure, similar to those established in Articles 101 and following of the Statute N° 834 of 1978, adding references to the delay to bring the action before the court, to the hearing that has to take place, the delay for the decision and the delay for the appeal. The Supreme Court finally remembered, in order to avoid abuses in the use of the action, that the «amparo» recourse must not be understood as the introduction of a third instance in the judicial process[48].

This Dominican Republic Supreme Court 1999 decision, taken in absence of constitutional and statutory regulations regarding the «amparo» action, admitting this judicial means for protection of all human rights according to what is set forth in the American Convention on Human Rights, is without doubt a very important one, not only regarding the «amparo» recourse or action as a specific judicial means for human rights protection, but also regarding the enforcement within internal law of the American Convention on Human Rights.

IV. THE INTERPRETATIVE CONSTITUTIONAL RULES REGARDING THE INTERNATIONAL INSTRUMENTS ON HUMAN RIGHTS

Now, in absence of express constitutional regulations regarding the hierarchy of international treaties on human rights in the internal legal system, -whether

---

[46] Decision C.543 of September 24, 1992. See in Manuel José CEPEDA ESPINOSA, *Derecho Constitucional Jurisprudencia*, Legis, Bogotá, 2001, p. 1009 ff.

[47] Decision T-213 of May 13, 1994. See in Manuel José CEPEDA ESPINOSA, *Derecho Constitucional Jurisprudencia, Legis*, Bogotá, 2001, p. 1022 ff.

[48] See the text *Iudicum et Vita, Jurisprudencia nacional de América Latina en Derechos Humanos*, N° 7, Tomo I, Instituto Interamericano de Derechos Humanos, San José, Costa Rica, Diciembre 2000 p. 329 y ss. See the comments in Allan R. BREWER-CARÍAS, «La admisión jurisprudencial de la acción de amparo en ausencia de regulación constitucional o legal en la República Dominicana», *Idem*, pp. 334 ff.

constitutional, supra statutory or statutory rank-, such instruments can also acquire constitutional value and rank by means of different constitutional interpretation rules. In other words, the rights declared in international treaties can also be considered as constitutional rights, by means of other constitutional regulations or techniques: first, by referring the interpretation of constitutional rights to what is set forth in the international treaties; second, by enshrining in the Preambles or general declarations of the Constitutions references to the universal declarations on human rights.

In the first place, some Constitutions expressly set forth a guiding rule for interpreting human rights declared in their text, requiring that such interpretation must be made in accordance to what is set forth in the international treaties on human rights. This is the technique found in the Spanish Constitution, where article 10,2, states:

> The norms concerning fundamental rights or freedom recognized in the Constitution, must be interpreted in accordance to the Universal Declaration of Human Rights and the international treaties and conventions referred to the same matter ratified by Spain.

In similar way, the Portuguese Constitution also sets forth, that:

> Article 16,2. The provisions of the Constitution and laws relating to fundamental rights are to be read and interpreted in harmony with the Universal Declaration of Human Rights.

These two constitutional provisions, without doubt, influenced the drafting of the 1991 Colombian Constitution, where Article 93 establishes:

> Article 93. The rights and duties enshrined in this Charter shall be interpreted pursuant to the international treaties on human rights ratified by Colombia.

Following this constitutional provision, all State bodies, not just the courts, have to interpret the constitutional regulations regarding human rights pursuant to the provisions of the international treaties on the matter. The result of this constitutional principle of interpretation is the recognition of an equal rank and constitutional value for those constitutional rights declared in international treaties, which are the ones that will guide the interpretation of the rights enshrined in the Constitution.

This interpretative technique has been frequently used by the Constitutional Court in Colombia when interpreting the extent of constitutional rights, as was the case in a decision of February 22, 1996 issued when deciding a judicial review action filed on the grounds of unconstitutionality against the statute which regulates Television networks, considered by the plaintiff as being contrary to the constitutional right to inform.

The Constitutional Court began its decision by arguing that:

> «the internal validity of a statute is not only subjected to the conformity of its regulations to what is set forth in the Constitution, but also to what is prescribed in the international treaties approved by Congress and ratified by the President of the Republic».
>
> As clearly set forth in Article 93 of the Constitution, the conformity of the internal legislation to international treaties and obligations of the Colombian

State regarding other States and supranational entities, is imposed more severely by the Constitution when the matter relates to the application and exercise of fundamental rights. According to such article of the Constitution, the international treaties and covenants approved by Congress and ratified by the Executive in which human rights are recognized and its limitations are prohibited in states of exception, prevail regarding the internal legal order.

The constitutional article declares in a straightforward manner that the rights and duties enshrined in the Constitution must be interpreted in accordance to the international treaties on human rights ratified by Colombia»[49].

Based on the abovementioned, the Constitutional Chamber then referred in its decision to the constitutional right to freedom of expression of thoughts and of information, following what is set forth in Article 19,3 of the International Covenant on Human Rights and in Article 13,2 of the American Convention on Human Rights, particularly regarding the universality of the exercise of such rights «without any considerations of frontiers»; concluding by ruling that:

> To forbid in the national territory the installation or functioning of land stations devoted to receive and later to diffuse, transmit or distribute television signals coming from satellites, whether national or international, is a flagrant violation of the right to be informed which everybody has pursuant to Article 20 of the Constitution[50].

The interpretative technique of human rights according to what is established in international instruments on the matter has also been established, for instance, in the Perúvian Constitutional Procedure Code, by article V that sets forth:

> Article V. *Interpretation of constitutional rights*. The content and the scope of constitutional rights protected by means of the constitutional process established in this Code (including habeas corpus and amparo) must be interpreted according to the Universal Declaration on Human Rights, the treaties on human rights, as well as to the decisions issued by the international courts on human rights established according to treaties in which Perú is a Party».

1. The constitutional general references to the universal declarations on human rights

The second interpretative technique through which international declarations on human rights acquired constitutional rank and value, results from the general declarations enshrined in the Preambles or the constitutional text precisely referring to those international declarations on human rights.

Regarding the Preambles of the Constitution, many of the Post War Constitutions contain general declarations regarding human rights, with particular reference to universal declarations. The classic example is the 1958 French Constitution in which, without containing in its text a Bill of Rights, the following general declaration is contained in its Preamble:

---

49 See in *Iudicum et Vita, Jurisprudencia nacional de América Latina en Derechos Humanos*, N° 5, Instituto Interamericano de Derechos Humanos, San José, Costa Rica, Diciembre 1997 pp. 34-35.

50 *Idem*, p. 37.

> The French people hereby solemnly proclaim their dedication to the Rights of Man and the principle of national sovereignty as defined by the Declaration of 1789, reaffirmed and complemented by the Preamble to the 1946 Constitution.

By means of this general declaration the Constitutional Council has enlarged the constitutionality block, attributing constitutional value and rank to all the fundamental rights contained in the 1789 Declaration of Rights of Citizens and Man[51].

In other Constitutions, the Preambles contain general declarations in order to define a general purpose of the Constitution and to give a general orientation to State and society actions seeking the respect and full enforcement of human rights. For instance, the Preamble of the 1999 Venezuelan Constitution declares that the Constitution itself was sanctioned in order to «assure the rights to life, to work, to cultural heritage, to education, to social justice and to equality without any kind of discrimination», promoting «the universal and indivisible guarantee of human rights».

The Constitution of Guatemala also expressly declares in its Preamble that its text shall «encourage full enforcement of human rights within a stable, permanent and popular institutional order, where governed and governors shall proceed in strict observance of the law».

Being in those cases the general purpose of the countries' Constitution to guarantee, promote and encourage the full enjoyment and enforcement of human rights referred to their universal context, the rights enshrined in the international declarations and treaties can be considered or interpreted as having the same value and rank to those expressly declared in the Constitution's texts themselves.

Other Constitutions contain similar general declarations, not in their Preambles, but within their texts, when regulating specific aspects of the State bodies functioning and setting forth, for instance, the need for the effective guaranty that must be given to anybody to enjoy and exercise constitutional rights. In these cases, upon constituting as a State obligation the respect of human rights or to assure that they are properly enforced, it has been interpreted that such rights generally acquire constitutional rank and value even if not expressly listed in the constitutional declarations.

Such is the case of the Constitution of Chile, whose 1989 reform included a declaration pursuant to which it was expressly recognized that the exercise of sovereignty is limited by «respect for the essential rights to be found in human nature», also prescribing as a «duty of State bodies to respect and promote such rights guaranteed by this Constitution, as well as by international treaties ratified by Chile and currently in force» (Art. 5,II). Hence, if it is the State's duty to respect and promote human rights that are guaranteed by international treaties, such rights acquire the same rank and value as the constitutional rights expressly listed in the constitutional text itself. Moreover, the reference to «essential rights to be found in human nature» permits and requires that not only those expressly listed in the Constitution be identified as such, but also those established in international treaties and, what is more, those not expressly declared but that are part of human nature itself.

---

[51] See the references in Allan R. BREWER-CARÍAS, *Judicial Review in Comparative Law*, Cambridge, 1989.

The Constitution of Ecuador also prescribes the State's obligation «... to respect and have respected the human rights guaranteed by this Constitution» (Article 16); assuring to «all its citizens, with no discrimination whatsoever, the free and effective exercise and enjoyment of the human rights established in this Constitution and in the declarations, covenants, agreements and other current international instruments in force».

Therefore, in these cases, the State's obligation refers not only to its guaranteeing the exercise and enjoyment of the rights listed in the Constitution, but all those named in international instruments too, which therefore can be considered as acquiring the same rank and value of constitutional rights.

In this regard, special reference should be made to the Constitution of Nicaragua which establishes the general declaration that all people shall not only «enjoy State protection and the recognition of rights inherent to the human person and the unrestricted respect, promotion and protection of their human rights», but also the protection of the State for the «full enforcement of the rights enshrined in the Universal Declaration of Human Rights; in the American Declaration of the Rights and Duties of Man; in the United Nations' International Covenant on Civil and Political Rights; and in the American Convention on Human Rights of the Organization of American States».

In this case, the Constitution's reference to certain international instruments, due to the international dynamic on these matters, can only be interpreted as a non-exhaustive statement, given the preceding declarations referred in general to human rights and to those inherent to the human person.

Based on Article 46 of the Nicaraguan Constitution, statutes have been challenged on the grounds of unconstitutionally because they violate rights declared in international treaties. It was the case of the judicial review process of the 1989 General statute on Medias (*Ley General sobre los medios de la Comunicación Social (Ley Nº 57*), in which the Supreme Court, in its decision of August 22, 1989, even if it rejected the «amparo of unconstitutionality» recourse filed against the statute, in order to decide, the Court extensively considered the denounced violations not only regarding Article 46 of the Constitution but, through it, also considered articles of the Human Rights Declaration, the International Covenant on Civil and Political Rights and the American Convention on Human Rights[52].

Finally, the Constitution of Brazil proclaims that the State in its international relations, is ruled by the principle of the prevalence of human rights (Article 4,III); and that being constituted as a democratic rule of law State, it has as one of its foundations the dignity of human person (Article I, III). Regarding in particular human rights, Article 5,2 of the Constitutions declares, that:

> The rights and guarantees set forth in the Constitution do not exclude others which can result from the regime and principles therein set forth or from the international treaties on which the Federative Republic of Brazil may be part.

[52] See the text in *Iudicum et Vita, Jurisprudencia nacional de América Latina en Derechos Humanos*, Nº 5, Instituto Interamericano de Derechos Humanos, San José, Costa Rica, Diciembre 1997, pp. 128-140. See the comments of Antonio CANÇADO TRINDADE, «Libertad de expresión y derecho a la información en los planos internacional y nacional», *Idem*, p. 194.

This article has been interpreted as a mean for inserting the Constitution in the general trend of Latin American constitutionalism that gives a special treatment in internal law to the rights and guarantees internationally guarantied.

2. The enforcement of rights regardless of their statutory regulation

In addition to the abovementioned, regarding the process of constitutionalization of the internationalization of human rights, special reference must be made to constitutional clauses which prescribe the right to the enforcement of constitutional rights regardless of the existence or not of statutory regulations.

In these sense, for instance, the Venezuela Constitution since 1961 established that «The lack of statutory regulations of rights (inherent to human beings) does not impede their exercise» (Article 50), in the sense that there is no need for a statute to be enacted in order for the exercise of the constitutional rights. This is the same regulation that can be found for instance in the Ecuadorian Constitution in which Article 18 states: «The absence of statute cannot be alleged in order to justify or ignore rights set forth in this Constitution, or to not admit actions for their protections, or to deny the acknowledgment of such rights».

Regarding the Venezuelan regulation, now enshrined in Article 22 of the Constitution, it must be indicated that it has serve for the acknowledgment and enforcement of very important constitutional rights, like precisely, the enforcement of the right to «amparo».

In effect, the right to «amparo» was originally set forth in the 1961 Constitution, as follows:

> Article 49. The courts shall protect («ampararán») all inhabitants of the Republic in the exercise of their rights and guarantees set forth in the Constitution, according to the law (statute). The procedure shall be brief and speedy and the competent judge will have the power to immediately restore the infringed legal situation.

The wording of this article was interpreted by the courts in the sense that the acceptability of the amparo suit was conditioned to the previous enactment of the statute regulations on the matter, particularly because the same Constitution expressly regulated in a transitory way the procedure for the habeas corpus action, pending the sanctioning of such statute, «in order to not leave (its applicability) suspended». From this regulation the courts then understood that the intention of Article 49 was to condition the admissibility of the amparo action to the previous sanctioning of the statute on the matter, providing only in an exceptional way for the immediate acceptability of the habeas corpus action[53].

In this sense, the Supreme Court of Justice in 1970 regarding the amparo suit, considered Article 49 to be a «programmatic» one, thus not directly applicable, being necessary the previous enactment of the statute on the matter, in order to bring before a court an action of amparo. The Court said:

---

53 See Allan R. BREWER-CARÍAS, *Instituciones Políticas y Constitucionales*, Tomo V, *Derecho y Acción de Amparo*, Universidad Católica del Táchira, Editorial Jurídica Venezolana, Caracas, 1998, pp. 111 ff.

> The article is not a direct and immediately applicable stipulation by the courts, but only a programmatic one directed to Congress that is the competent body to regulate for constitutional guarantees; interpretation reinforced by the transitive constitutional regulation on habeas corpus[54].

This constitutional judicial approach regarding the acceptability of the amparo action began to change after the approval by Congress in 1977, of the 1969 American Convention on Human Rights and in 1978, of the International Covenant on Civil and Political Rights; treaties that regulated the specific need for a simple and speedy judicial mean for the protection of human rights. Consequently, contrary to the Supreme Court initial interpretation -which at the time had no *stare decisis* effects- the lower courts began in 1982 to accept amparo suits, funding directly their rulings in the American Convention[55]; situation that finally lead the Supreme Court to change its criteria by applying the open clause on human rights inherent to persons, and particularly the provision that states that the absence of a regulatory statute regarding human rights cannot affect the exercise of the rights declared in the Constitution. In a decision of October 20, 1983 the Supreme Court thus admitted the possibility of the filling of the constitutional protective amparo action regarding any constitutional right. Notwithstanding the Court said in its ruling that:

> «By admitting the possibility of the exercise of the amparo recourse, the Court must draw the attention of the lower courts, to be prudent and rational when using the powers granted in the Constitution (for the immediate constitutional protection of human rights), in order to fill the gap produced by the absence of the regulatory statute»[56].

The Organic Amparo statute for the protection of constitutional rights and guarantees was finally sanctioned in 1988[57], giving way to the massive use of this judicial mean for protection of human rights, particularly because of the unsuitability of the common judicial mean for that purpose. Nonetheless, it was by mean of the application of the open clause regarding human rights that the amparo suit was previously accepted.

3. The principle of progressive interpretation of constitutional rights

Finally, mention must be made to the principle of progressive interpretation of human rights, which implies that as a matter of principle, no interpretation of statutes related to human rights can be admitted if the result is the diminishing of the effective enjoyment, exercise or guarantee of constitutional rights; and also that in case involving various provisions, the one that should prevail is the one that contains the more favorable regulation[58]. As stated by the former Supreme Court of

---

54 See in *Gaceta Forense*, N° 70, Caracas, 1970, pp. 179 y ss; and in Allan R. BREWER-CARÍAS, «La reciente evolución jurisprudencial en relación a la admisibilidad del recurso de amparo», in *Revista de Derecho Público,* N° 19, Editorial Jurídica Venezolana, Caracas, 1984, pp. 207 ff.

55 See the references in A. R. BREWER-CARÍAS, «La reciente evolución jurisprudencial en relación con la admisibilidad del recurso de amparo», *Revista de Derecho Público*, N° 19, Editorial Jurídica Venezolana, Caracas, 1984, pp. 211 ff.

56 See in *Revista de Derecho Público,* N° 11, Editorial Jurídica Venezolana, Caracas, 1983, pp. 167-170.

57 *Gaceta Oficial* N° 33.891 de 22-01-1988. See Allan R. BREWER-CARÍAS y Carlos AYALA CORAO, *Ley Orgánica de Amparo sobre derechos y garantías constitucionales*, Caracas, 1988.

58 See in general, Pedro NIKKEN, *La protección internacional de los derechos humanos. Su desarrollo progresivo,* Instituto Interamericano de Derechos Humanos, Ed. Civitas, Madrid, 1987.

Justice of Venezuela, the principle of progressiveness in human rights implies the need to preferably apply the most favorable provision to human rights, whether of constitutional law, international law or ordinary law»[59]. Consequently, the interpretation of statutes must always be guided by the principle of progressiveness, in the sense that it must always result in more protection regarding rights.

The principle of progressiveness is expressly regulated, for example, in the 1999 Constitution of Venezuela, where Article 19 provides that the enjoyment and exercise of human rights shall be guaranteed to everybody by the State, «... pursuant to the principle of progressiveness and without any discrimination».

Other Constitutions also expressly establish it as a principle of interpretation, as may be seen in Article 18 of the Ecuadorian Constitution which provides that «... in matters of constitutional rights and guarantees, the interpretation that most favors its effective enforcement shall be the one upheld».

This principle of the progressive interpretation of human rights regulations is equivalent to the *pro homines* principle of interpretation, which has been defined as «the hermeneutical criteria that conditions all the human rights law, according to which the widest and most protective provision must be applied in the sense that one must always prefer the provision that is in favor of man (*pro homine*)»[60]. The principle has been incorporated in the Ecuadorian Constitution when specifying the method of interpretation that must be applied in matters of rights and guaranties established in the Constitution, in the sense that the interpretation must be done in the way «that most favors its effective enforcement» (article 18)[61]. It also has been deducted as incorporated in other Constitutions, as is the case of Chile and Perú, when they provide as one of the essential purposes of the State the protection of human rights. It was the case of the 1993 Perúvian Constitution which stated that «the defense of human beings and the respect of their dignity are society and State goal» (Article 1); and is the case of the Chilean Constitution when it provides that it is «the duty of the State to respect and promote human rights guaranteed in the Constitution, as well as in the international treaties in force ratified by Chile» (art. 5)[62]. In Perú, the Constitutional Tribunal, when choosing the most favorable interpretation for the protection of human rights, has defined «the *pro homine* principle as the one according to which

---

[59] Decision of July, 30, 1996, in *Revista de Derecho Público*, N° 67-68, Editorial Jurídica Venezolana, Caracas, 1996, p. 170.

[60] See Mónica PINTO, «El principio *pro homine*. Criterio hermenéutico y pautas para la regulación de los derechos humanos», in *La aplicación de los tratados sobre derechos Humanos por los tribunales locales*, Centro de Estudios Legales y Sociales, Buenos Aires, 1997, p. 163. Also see, Humberto HENDERSON, «Los tratados internacionales de derechos humanos en el orden interno: la importancia del principio *pro homine*», in *Revista IIDH, Instituto Interamericano de Derechos Humanos*, N° 39, San José, 2004, p. 92.

[61] See Hernán SALGADO PESANTES, *Manual de Justicia Constitucional Ecuatoriana*, Corporación Editora Nacional, Quito, 2004, p. 92.

[62] See Iván BAZÁN CHACÓN, «Aplicación del derecho internacional en la judicialización de violaciones de derechos humanos» in *Para hacer justicia. Reflexiones en torno a la judicialización de casos de violaciones de derechos humanos*, Coordinadora Nacional de Derechos Humanos, Lima, 2004, p. 27; Humberto HENDERSON, «Los tratados internacionales de derechos humanos en el orden interno: la importancia del principio *pro homine*», en *Revista IIDH, Instituto Interamericano de Derechos Humanos*, N° 39, San José, 2004, p. 89, nota 27.

a rule referred to human rights must be interpreted 'in the most favorable way for the person, that is, for the beneficiary of the interpretation'».[63]

As it has been indicated by Henderson, the *pro homine* principle has various application forms: first, when various provisions on human rights can be applied in the case, the one to be chosen is the one with the best and must favorable provisions regarding the individual; second, in cases rulings succession, it must be understood that the last provision does not repeal the previous one if this has better and more favorable provisions which must be preserved; and third, when it is a matter of application of just one legal provision on human rights, the same must be interpreted in the way resulting more favorable to the protection of the person[64].

In a certain way this *pro homine* interpretation was the one that guided *Chief Justice Warren* of the United States Supreme Court in its 1954 opinion in *Brown vs Board of Education of Topeka, Kansas*, 347 U.S. 483 (1954). in which, when referring to the XIV Amendment, he said that:

> In approaching this problem, we cannot turn the clock back to 1868 when the Amendment was adopted, or even to 1896 when *Plessy v. Fersugon* was written. We must consider public education in the light of its full development and its present place in American life throughout the Nation. Only in this way can it be determined if segregation in public schools deprives these plaintiffs of the equal protection of the laws.

From this, he concluded saying:

> We conclude that in the field of public education the doctrine of «separate but equal» has no place. Separate educational facilities are inherently unequal. Therefore, we hold that the plaintiffs and others similarly situated for whom the actions have been brought are, by reason of the segregation complained of, deprived of the equal protection of the laws guaranteed by the Fourteenth Amendment. This disposition makes unnecessary any discussion whether such segregation also violates the Due Process Clause of the Fourteenth Amendment».

This principle of progressivism, regarding the interpretation of constitutional rights, has also been incorporated in the American Convention on Human Rights in which Article 29 provides the following rules regarding «restrictions regarding interpretation», in the sense that «no provision of this Convention shall be interpreted as»:

a. permitting any State Party, group, or person to suppress the enjoyment or exercise of the rights and freedoms recognized in this Convention or to restrict them to a greater extent than is provided for herein;

b. restricting the enjoyment or exercise of any right or freedom recognized by virtue of the laws of any State Party or by virtue of another convention to which one of the said states is a party;

---

[63] See decisión 1049-2003-AA/TC of January 30, 2004 in Alfonso GAIRAUD BRENES, «Los Mecanismos de interpretación de los derechos humanos: especial referencia a la jurisprudencia Perúana» en José F. PALOMINO MANCHEGO, *El derecho procesal constitucional Perúano. Estudios en Homenaje a Domingo García Belaunde*, Editorial Jurídica Grijley, Lima, 2005, Tomo I, p. 138.

[64] See Humberto HENDERSON, «Los tratados internacionales de derechos humanos en el orden interno: la importancia del principio *pro homine*», in *Revista IIDH, Instituto Interamericano de Derechos Humanos*, no. 39, San José, 2004, pp. 92-96.

c. precluding other rights or guarantees that are inherent in the human personality or derived from representative democracy as a form of government; or

d. excluding or limiting the effect that the American Declaration of the Rights and Duties of Man and other international acts of the same nature may have.

Regarding the specific principle of progressiveness set forth in the Venezuelan Constitution, it also has implied that if a constitutional right is regulated with different contexts in the Constitution and in international treaties, then the most favorable provision must prevail and be applicable to the interested party.

In an «amparo» decision issued by the former Supreme Court of Justice on December 3, 1990, the Court applied the principle regarding the rights of a pregnant public official not to be unjustifiably dismissed of her job during pregnancy. At that time, the Organic Statute on Labor did not regulate such right, and it was only set forth in the Covenant N° 103 of the Labor International Organization and in the Convention eliminating all forms of discrimination against women. Regarding the constitutional provisions, Article 74 only provided for the general right to maternity protection. Notwithstanding the Supreme Court in the concrete case, after analyzing the protection asked by the employee whose dismissal impede her to enjoy the pre and post natal rest, admitted the «amparo» and declared the requested protection. In its decision, the Supreme Court ruled as followed:

> «The right not to be dismissed when pregnancy and the right to enjoy a pre and post natal rest are rights inherent to human beings that are constitutionalized due to Article 50 of the Constitution which stated that «the enunciation of rights and guarantees contained in the Constitution must not be understood to deny others not expressly within regulated. The lack of regulatory statute regarding such rights does not impede its exercise...».

Consequently, from all these supranational regulations and particularly due to the protection set forth in article 74 of the Constitution, which guaranties the protection of maternity and of the pregnant women, such protection being materialized through the right of the pregnant working women not to be dismissed and the right to enjoy the pre and post natal rest...

Based in such clear and conclusive dispositions, this Court considers that any attempt from the employer to diminish the right of the pregnant women not to be dismissed without justification or disciplinary reasons, and the consequent effect of denying the right to pre and post natal rest, constitute an evident and flagrant violation of the constitutional principle set forth in Articles 74 and 93 of the Constitution...»[65].

[65] See in *Revista de Derecho Público*, N° 45, Editorial Jurídica Venezolana, Caracas, 1991, pp. 84-85. See the references in decisión sentenciaos July 30, 1996 in *Revista de Derecho Público*, N° 97-98, Editorial Jurídica Venezolana, Caracas, 1996, p. 170.

CHAPTER III

THE JUDICIAL MEANS FOR THE PROTECTION OF HUMAN RIGHTS

I. THE CONSTITUTIONAL GUARANTEES TO THE DECLARATIONS OF RIGHTS

Constitutional declarations of rights, in the Constitutions or in international treaties and covenants, would be of no use at all, unless supported by a set of constitutional guarantees of the exercise of such rights.

The first of all constitutional guaranties is the guaranty of the supremacy of the Constitution and of entrenched declarations of human rights therein contained; the second is the judicial guaranty, that is to say, the set of judicial means established in benefit of persons in order to assure the effective exercise of such rights, and the effective protection of them.

In other words, the insertion of Declarations of rights in the Constitutions would be of no use to the citizen unless there is a fundamental right that establishes their supremacy, which can be enforced in court.

In fact, the idea of Rule of Law is indissolubly bound to the idea of the Constitution as an essential and supreme rule, which shall prevail over any state rule or action. This was the great and principal contribution of the American Revolution to modern constitutionalism, and its progressive development has provided the basis for the constitutional systems of justice in the modern world, particularly those aimed at protecting and defending the rights and freedoms enshrined in the Constitutions.

It can be said that this idea of constitutional supremacy, that is, of the Constitution as a fundamental and supreme law, was first developed in America in 1788 by Alexander Hamilton in *The Federalist*[1] when referring to the role of judges as interpreters of the law, stating:

> «A constitution is, in fact, and must be regarded by the judges, as a fundamental law. It therefore, belongs to them to ascertain its meaning, as well as the meaning of any particular act proceeding from the legislative body. If there should happen to be an irreconcilable variance between the two, that which has the superior obligation and validity ought, of course, to be preferred; or,

---

1 *The Federalist* (edited by B.F. Wright), Cambridge, Mass. 1961, pp. 491-493.

in other words, the constitution ought to be preferred to the Statute, the intention of the people to the intention of their agents».

He added in response to the assertion that «the rights of the courts to pronounce legislative acts void, because contrary to the constitution» would «imply a superiority of the judiciary to the legislative powers», the following:

«Nor does this conclusion -that the Courts must prefer the constitution over statutes- by any means supposes a superiority of the judicial to the legislative body. It only supposes that the power of the people is superior to both; and that where the will of the legislature, declared in its Statutes stands in opposition to that of the people declared in the constitution, the judges ought to be governed by the latter rather than the former. They ought to regulate their decisions by the fundamental laws, rather than by those which are not fundamental».

Thus, his conclusive assertion that:

«No legislative act, therefore, contrary to the constitution, can be valid. To deny this, would be to affirm, that the deputy is greater than his principal; that the servant is above his master; that the representative of the people are superior to the peoples themselves; that men acting by virtue of powers, may do not only what their powers do not authorize, but what they forbid'.

Thus, in *The Federalist*, Hamilton not only developed the doctrine of the supremacy of the constitution, but most importantly the doctrine of «the judges as guardians of the constitution», as the title of letter N° 78 reads, where Hamilton said, considering the constitution as a limit to state powers and particularly to the Legislative authority, that,

«Limitations of this kind can be preserved in practice no other way than through the medium of courts of justice, whose duty it must be, to declare all acts contrary to the manifest tenor of the constitution, void. Without this, all the reservations of particular rights or privileges would amount to nothing».[2]

But among Hamilton's proposals, I would like to place more emphasis on the idea itself that since the Constitution is the expression of the will of the people, the principal constitutional right the people can have, is the right to that supremacy, that is to say, the right to the respect for and preservation of their own will as expressed in the Constitution. The consequence of this principle is the other derived and fundamental principle, that the Judiciary shall have the power to declare null and void any state or federal law that is contrary to the Constitution[3]. It is clear, that nothing would be gained by stating that the Constitution, being the expression of the will of the people, shall prevail over that of the State entities and over individual actions, if the people do not have the right to demand the respect of the Constitution.

For this precise reason, one of the most recent Latin American Constitutions, that of Colombia (1991), expressly enshrines the principle of constitutional supremacy as follows:

---

2 *The Federalist* (ed. by B.F. Wright), Cambridge, Mass 1961, p. 491 -493.

3 See referentes to the cases *Vanhorne's Lessee v. Dorrance, 1776* and *Masbury v. Madison,* 1803 in Allan R. BREWER-CARÍAS in *Judicial Review in Comparative Law,* Cambridge University Press, Cambridge, 1989.

«**Article 4**. The Constitution is the rule of rules. Whenever a case of incompatibility between the Constitution and a statute or another legal norms, arises the constitutional provisions shall be applied ...»

The 1999 Constitution of Venezuela similarly establishes that: «... the Constitution is the supreme rule and basis of the legal system» (Article 7) and that «in case of incompatibility between this constitution and a statute or other legal norm, the constitutional provisions shall be applied, being the courts empowered to decide, even ex officio» (Article 334).

In both countries this implies that the custody of the basic constitutional right of the citizen to the protection of such supremacy, is assured by means of: first, the judicial review powers regarding statutes attributed to all court and judges (Article 4, Colombia; Article 334, Venezuela); second, the popular action that can be brought before the Constitutional Court (Colombia, Article 214) or Constitutional Chamber of the Supreme Tribunal (Venezuela, Article 336) in order to seek the concentrated judicial review of constitutionality of statutes; third, by means of the exercise of specific actions for protection of constitutional rights, as is the case of the actions of *habeas corpus*, of «amparo» or of habeas data (Articles 30 and 86, Colombia; Article 27, Venezuela).

Therefore, modern constitutionalism is founded not only on the principle of constitutional supremacy, but also on the principle that the *citizens have a constitutional right to such supremacy*, that in fact, pursuant to the principle of separation of powers, becomes *a fundamental right to the judicial protection of such constitutional supremacy*, both regarding the organic part of the Constitution (separation of powers, territorial distribution of powers), as well as regarding the dogmatic part of the Constitution (human rights), for the preservation of which a set of guarantees are established.

Among these guarantees it can be mentioned, the «objective guarantee» which declares that any acts contrary to the Constitution shall be considered null and void. The principle, explained in the twenties by Hans Kelsen[4], has been incorporated in the Latin American Constitutions since the beginning of the XIX Century, as occurred with the Venezuelan Constitution of 1811.

This principle implies that any State body decision that is contrary to the fundamental rights established in the Constitution is null and void, as has been set fourth in the 1999 Venezuelan Constitution:

«**Article 25**: Any State authority act that violates or lessens the rights guaranteed in this Constitution and the law, is null; and the public officials which orders or execute them shall be criminally, civil and administratively liable, without any possible excuses based on superior orders».

In the particular case of Perú, Article 31 lists the right of citizens to participate in public affairs through: a referendum; legislative initiative; removal or revocation of authorities and the demand for accounting; the right to be elected and freely choose their representatives; the right of the local population to participate in the municipal government of its jurisdiction; and the right to vote; adding that «any act that forbids or limits the citizen's exercise of his or her rights is null and punishable».

---

4 See Hans KELSEN: «La garantie jurisdictionnelle de la Constitution (La justice constitutionnelle)», *Revue du droit public et de la science politique en France et à l'étranger*, París, 1928, p. 250.

Other constitutional guaranty of the declarations of human rights, perhaps the most important, is the legislative privilege to set fourth restrictions or limitations to constitutional rights, which can only by established by statutes, that is to say, by the laws passed by the legislative body and not by executive regulations.

There is also, of course, the guarantee of liability, or the guarantee that the public officials or individuals responsible for the injury or nuisance are legally obligated or accountable under civil, criminal and administrative law.

Apart from all the above-mentioned guarantees, the other basic guarantee of constitutional rights is of course, precisely, the possibility of bringing claims before the courts in order to assure that such rights are protected, preventing its violation or restoring the aggrieved party in its exercise. Hence, the fundamental guarantee of constitutional rights is definitely the judicial guarantee.

II. THE JUDICIAL GUARANTEE OF CONSTITUTIONAL RIGHTS

1. The right to have access to justice and the protection of rights

In any country subjected to the rule of law, the judicial branch of government is established not only to guarantee the enforcement of the law, but in particular, to hear and decide cases or questions of rights affecting personal and proprietary interests, making the necessary binding judgments on them. Of course, among those rights to be protected and enforced by the Judiciary, are the constitutional rights.

In effect, in all constitutional judicial systems, the most classical of citizens' rights is to have access to justice. This is the right to obtain judicial protection and enforcement of one's rights and interests. This is the essential reason for the organization of the Judiciary, to assure the judicial guarantee of personal and proprietary rights.

However, the Judiciary not always accomplishes its fundamental duty, as has occurred in Latin America, where in spite of the constitutional declarations, many countries still are facing a rather dismal situation regarding the effectiveness of the Judiciary as a whole, as an efficient and just protector of fundamental rights.

In Venezuela, for example, the 1999 Constitution declares that the State is a «... democratic and social State of law *and justice*», emphasizing justice as being among the uppermost values of the legal system and of the State's actions (Article 2). To this end, it is expressly stated that «... the State shall guarantee free, accessible, impartial, ideal, transparent, autonomous, independent, liable, fair and timely justice, without undue delay, and without senseless formalities or reversals» (Article 26).

It is really very difficult to find in any Constitutions in the contemporary world, similar sort of magnificent declarations about justice and the Judiciary, to which, the Supreme Tribunal of Venezuela, has referred to very eloquently, by stating:

> Consequently, when the Constitution qualified the State as a State of law and justice and set fourth Justice and preeminence of fundamental rights as a superior value of the legal order, it is only stressing that all public entities -and specially the Judiciary- must inexorably privilege a notion of justice above formalities and technicalities that belongs to a formal legality which certainly

has give way to a new State conception. And this notion of Justice has a special meaning in the fertile field of the judicial proceeding in which the right to self defense and the due process of law rights (article 49), the search for the truth as an consubstantial element of justice, in which the former must not be scarified due to the omission of non essential formalities (article 257); bearing in mind that access to justice is set forth in order to allow citizens to ask for the enforcement of their rights and could obtain their effective and expedite judicial protection, without undue delays and without useless formalities and procedural reviews (article 26); all of which conform a Cosmo vision of a Lawful State, of the parties as element of democracy, and of the inescapable duty of the Judiciary and judges to maintain processes and judgments within the constitutional values and principles[5].

But in spite of these marvelous declarations, in order to achieve these aims of the State of Justice, the most elemental institutional condition needed, in any Country, is the existence of really autonomous and independent judges, empowered to interpret and apply the law, achieving justice in an impartial way; and that can effectively protect citizens, particularly when referring to the enforcement of rights against State actions.

For that purpose, an effective Judiciary has to be built upon the principle of separation of powers. On the contrary, if the Government controls the courts and judges, no effective guarantee exists regarding constitutional rights, particularly when the offender party is a governmental agency. In this case, and in spite of all constitutional declarations, it is impossible to speak of rule of law.

The braking news in the December 28, 2005 edition of *The New York Times* (front page left), was the title: «When Chinese Sue the State, cases are Often Smothered»; referring to the fact that if it is true that «the number of people wanting to sue the government is large and growing», the truth is that « the number of people who succeed in filing cases against the government is minuscule», concluding by stating that: «So you could say there is a gap between theory and practice». The article referred to the impossibility for peasants to even file complaints seeking compensation for the take over of farmed land converted for the construction of roads and commercial, noting that «the case would not even be registered and there would be no rejection notice, either», and adding: «They met Kafkaesque obstacles at every turn. The only party that used the courts successfully was the state-linked construction company. It won an injunction in March declaring peasants' protest illegal»; judicial decision that -in this case-, was massively published in the village and even «the party boss read the text of the decision over the village's loudspeakers». The «villagers said -points out the article- that they were outraged that the court acted so quickly after suppressing their own suit» adding that they «discovered that the law is what they say», «What they practice is power»[6]

This reportage sounds familiar when authoritarian governments take control of States, as has so frequently happened in Latin American history, and for instance, as it has been occurring since 1999 in Venezuela. There, the «gap between theory

---

[5] See decision N° 949 Politico Administrative Chamber of the Suporeme Court of Justice (SPA-CSJ) of April 26, 2000, in *Revista de Derecho Público*, N° 82, (abril-junio), Editorial Jurídica Venezolana, Caracas, 2000, pp. 163 ff.

[6] Article by Joseph Kahn, *The New York Times*, December 28, 2005, pp. A1 and A10.

and practice» is abysmal; the «State of Justice» being in the hands of a government controlled Judiciary. Just one example can enlighten the situation:

Since 1976, and for 25 years, Special Courts for judicial review of administrative action, acting within a democratic regime, developed a very important jurisdiction in order to control the legality of Public Administration activities.

In July 17, the Venezuelan Federation of Doctors or Physicians, brought before the Judicial Review of Administrative Actions First Court in Caracas, a nullity claim against the Mayor of Caracas and the Ministry of Health act taken in conjunction with the Caracas metropolitan College of Doctors, by which these bodies, regulated the hiring of Cuban doctors for a health program called «*Barrio Adentro*» (Inside the Slums); which the Federation of doctors considered discriminatory against the rights of Venezuelan doctors to exercise medicine, allowing foreign doctors to exercise the profession without complying with the Medicine Profession Statute regulations for the exercise of such profession. So the Federation also filed an «amparo» action seeking the collective protection of the Venezuelan doctor's constitutional rights»[7].

In August 21, 2003, the Court issued a preliminary injunction considering that there were sufficient elements to consider the equality before the law right violated. The Court ordered the suspension of the Cuban doctor's hiring and ordered the Collage of Doctors to substitute the Cuban doctors already hired by Venezuelan or foreign doctors who had fulfilled the Statute regulations in order to exercise the medical profession.

The preliminary injunction could not be executed; was rejected and ignored by the Ministry of Health and by the Mayor, and even the President of the Republic in his weekly TV program said that the judicial decision would not be executed[8]. In the mean time, the offender parties, on September 5th, 2003 also brought an «amparo» action before the Constitutional Chamber of the Supreme Tribunal, demanding the Supreme Court to take over the case; which decided on September 25, 2003, based on jurisdictional arguments. The result was the Supreme Tribunal, assuming the case, annulling the lower Court decision and intervening its attributions to ensure the non execution of the preliminary injunctions initially issued. Three years latter, no other decision was taken on the case.

But in the meantime, other governmental decisions were taken: days after the Supreme Tribunal's decision, in September 2005, Secret Service officials seized the lower Court, after detaining a clerk on futile motives; the President of the Republic publicly called the President of the lower Court a bandit[9]; and a few weeks later, the Special Commission of intervention of the Judiciary, dismissed all the five judges of the Lower Fist Court, basing its decision in a supposedly «inexcusable

---

7 See Claudia NIKKEN, «El caso «Barrio Adentro»: La Corte Primera de lo Contencioso Administrativo ante la Sala Constitucional del Tribunal Supremo de Justicia o el avocamiento como medio de amparo de derechos e intereses colectivos y difusos» in *Revista de Derecho Público*, N° 93-96, Editorial Jurídica Venezolana, Caracas, 2003, pp. 5 y ss.

8 «*Váyanse con su decisión no sé para donde, la cumplirán ustedes en su casa si quieren…*» (You can go with your decision, I don't know where; you Hill enforced in your house, if you want…) Talk in the TV programme *Aló Presidente*, N° 161, August 24, 2004.

9 Public declaration, September 20, 2004.

error» they had incurred in when deciding a case in 2002[10]. The decision was protected by the Bar Associations of all States[11] and also by the International Jurist Commission[12]; but in fact the lower First Court remained suspended and closed[13] for more than ten months[14], during which no judicial review of administrative action could be sought. This was the governmental response to a judicial decision which affected a very sensitive governmental populist program; response which was expressed trough the government controlled Judiciary administration[15]. It must be borne in mind that the same Commission for the intervention of the Judiciary, has dismissed without due process almost all judges. As a result of these massive dismissals the Judiciary ended up being composed by the end of 2005 by more that 90% of provisionally appointed judges, thus dependent of the ruling power[16].

One of the main political critics to the party-democratic system that functioned in Venezuela from 1961 up to 1998, was the exclusively political appointment process of the Supreme Court Justices by the National Congress. That is why in the 1999 Constitution a parliamentary proceeding was set forth, in order to limit the discretionary power of the National Assembly, assigning to a Proposing Committee integrated exclusively by representatives of civic society, the task to choose and postulate before the Assembly the candidates to be appointed Justices. Unfortunately, the Statute sanctioned for that purpose turned the independent Committee into traditional parliamentary commission, politically controlled, which was challenged by the Peoples Defender before the Constitutional Chamber on grounds of unconstitutionality, but the suit was never decided. Additionally, in the case, the Constitutional Chamber resolved that the Constitution did not apply for the appointment of the same Justices by ratification.

Thus, since 2000, the result has been a more partisan governmental controlled Supreme Tribunal, with the aggravating circumstance of the power the Constitution vested in the National Assembly to dismiss the Supreme Tribunal Justices by vote of two thirds of its members, which the Statute concerning the Tribunal has unconstitutionally modified, adding a procedure for «the annulment of the appointment act» just by the absolute majority voting, which was used in 2004[17].

Thus, with Justices of the Supreme Tribunal politically appointed and politically dismissible, the independence and autonomy of the Judiciary in Venezuela is simply an illusion; and without such independence and autonomy, it is difficult to think on effective guarantees of constitutional rights.

10 See the information in *El Nacional*, Caracas, November 5, 2004, p. A2. In the same page, the dismissed President of the First Court said: «La justicia venezolana vive un momento tenebroso, pues el tribunal que constituye un último resquicio de esperanza ha sido clausurado» (Venezuenal Judiciary lives a tenebrous moment, due to the Fac. that the last resort of espoir Court has been shout down»).

11 See the Communiqué of the Asociación Venezolana de Derecho Administrativo, in *El Nacional*, Caracas, October 12, 2003, A-5.

12 See in *El Nacional*, Caracas, November 18,-2004, p. A-6.

13 See in *El Nacional*, Caracas, October 24, 2003, p. A-2.

14 See in en *El Nacional*, Caracas, July 16,2004, p. A-6.

15 See Allan R. BREWER-CARÍAS, «La progresiva y sistemática demolición institucional de la autonomía e independencia del Poder Judicial en Venezuela 1999-2004», in *XXX Jornadas J.M Dominguez Escovar, Estado de derecho, Administración de justicia y derechos humanos*, Instituto de Estudios Jurídicos del Estado Lara, Barquisimeto, 2005, pp. 33-174.

16 *Idem*.

17 *Idem*.

Unfortunately, after more than 40 years of democratic ruling the time has come for Venezuela to have an authoritarian regime, showing that the historical pendulum movement between democracy and authoritarian regimes continues to be a general pattern in Latin America constitutional history, as has occurred in other countries and in other times.

Anyway, the lesson to be learned is that judicial guarantee of constitutional rights requires an independent and autonomous Judiciary, conducted out of reach of the government.

Other question is that even in democratic regimes; some times the Judiciary appears to be incapable of guaranteeing the effective resolution of disputes, thus respecting individual rights and protecting constitutional rights. Justice has not always been swift and efficient; on the contrary, it has proved to be slow; and slowness in judicial matters leads to the opposite, that is, injustice.

Thus the first and main problem of the Rule of Law in Latin America, even in democratic regimes, is the functioning of the judicial systems; which has provoked that almost all Latin American countries have taken on the challenge of restructuring the Judiciary, seeking to make it truly independent and giving truth to the provision of all the Constitutions. This is the cornerstone of the Rule of Law, in the sense that judges shall act only pursuant to the law, without being influenced by outside the law factors, whether they are exercised by other public bodies or by political pressures.

But beyond their substantive independence, Judge must also be personally independent to act, which has to do with their appointment stability. In this regard, again, for example, the Venezuelan 1999 Constitution has established, in general terms, the regime for entering the judicial career and promotion only «through public competition that assures suitability and excellence», guaranteeing «citizen's participation in the procedure of selection and appointment of the judges». The consequence is that they may not be removed or suspended from their positions except through a legal proceeding before a disciplinary jurisdiction (Article 255). This, again, unfortunately is just a theoretical aim, because all contests for judge's appointment have been suspended since 2002. Almost all judges are being provisionally appointed without citizen participation, and there is no disciplinary jurisdiction for their dismissal. Furthermore, the suspension and dismissal of all judges corresponds to a Commission for the intervention of the Judiciary that is not regulated in the Constitution[18]

On the other hand, and beyond achieving independence, the other challenge in all our countries, is to assure the effective administration of justice, that is to say, that the judicial cases be decided surpassing the trend of slow and unjust administration of justice. This is why reforms such as the ones being carried out in many countries on matters of procedure are so essential, since many of the procedures were conceived in other times and now only serve to delay, obstruct, slow down and, finally, not resolve cases.

These reforms had even led many countries to seek other mechanisms for solving disputes and conflicts, like conciliation and arbitration systems. The «privatization of justice» -as it has been called- has been developed in order to

[18] *Idem.*

guarantee the individual's right to recur to means of arbitration or conciliation without having to resort to the ordinary courts of justice. This approach is not new at all: in the 1824 Stature of the Regime of Administration of Justice of the Republic of Colombia (Colombia, Venezuela and Ecuador) it was stated that all citizens had the constitutional and fundamental right to be able to resolve their conflicts by means of arbitration, and even established the obligation to attempt to resolve disputes through arbitration or conciliation, before resorting to an ordinary legal procedure. In this regard, the 1999 Constitution of Venezuela also states that the law «... shall promote arbitration, conciliation, mediation and any other alternative means to resolve dispute» (Article 258).

Finally, regarding the administration of justice, another aspect that has to be mentioned is the matter of access to justice, which is another of the major problems surrounding the constitutional protection of constitutional rights in Latin America. The access to justice and the right to have effective judicial protection are enshrined in the Constitutions, as can be found in the 1999 Constitution of Venezuela in which it is expressly provided that «Everybody shall have the right of access to the institutions of administration of justice to assert their rights and interests, including collective and diffuse rights and interests; the right to the effective protection of such rights, and the right to obtain a prompt corresponding decision» (Article 26). For that purpose, adds the Constitution, that «the procedure is a fundamental instrument in achieving justice», and therefore «procedural laws shall establish the simplification, uniformity and effectiveness of the proceedings and shall adopt a brief, oral and public procedure» in order to ensure that «justice not be sacrificed because of the omission of non essential formalities» (Article 257).

The formula provided in Spain's 1978 Constitution is far more precise:

> **Article 24.1**. All persons have the right to obtain effective protection from the judges and the courts in the exercise of their rights and legitimate interests, and in no case may there be a lack of defense.

However, even when not expressly enshrined in the constitutional texts, this right to have access to justice for the protection of people's rights and interests - including the constitutional rights - is an essential element of all contemporary constitutional systems, and in many cases it is what guarantees the right to protection («amparo») of constitutional rights and freedoms even when the legal system has not established specific procedural means or special courts that are designed to guarantee such protection.

Nonetheless, in practice, access to justice has not always been guaranteed to everybody, and huge portions of the population simply know nothing about judicial protection mechanisms, since they have no possibility of accessing to justice to resolve disputes because of the costs and complications involved. Moreover, the Latin American State has not been able to establish the appropriate legal assistance mechanisms that for decades have been recognized and have been developed in European countries, as judicial assistance, but which we have been unable to be established in our countries to offer everyone the possibility of access to the judicial institutions.

In any case, the deterioration of the Judiciary in our countries is not a recent event, it has been occurring over several decades, with many generations involved. That is why the Judiciary reform program, while being one of the most important elements in achieving effective internal protection of constitutional rights, is something that has to be carried out over a lengthy period. The systematic change of the Judiciary and of the way justice is administered is not even a task of one generation, but rather of several generations, provided there is a consciousness of the need to establish such mechanisms and to initiate reform.

Any way, as I have noted, the Judiciary and the judicial system is established in any country in order to protect peoples' rights, and to resolve controversies between parties.

2. Judicial means for the protection of constitutional rights

Legal or constitutional rights are both to be protected and enforced by the courts by means of the judicial proceedings set forth for that purpose in procedural law, without being necessary or indispensable the establishment of specific judicial means only devoted to assure that protection. But of course, this is not excluded, and its existence depends on how the Judiciary accomplished its protective role regarding human rights.

That is why, in contemporary world, especially regarding constitutional rights and freedoms (those embodied in the constitutional Declarations of Rights), their judicial protection and guarantee can be achieved in two ways: first, by means of the general established (ordinary or extraordinary) suits, actions, recourses or writs set fourth in procedural law in order to have a right or duty judicially enforced; or second, in addition to the general means, by means of specific judicial suits, actions or recourses seeking remedies particularly established in order to protect and enforce constitutional rights and freedoms and to prevent and redress wrongs regarding those rights.

That is, the judicial guarantee of constitutional rights can be achieved through the general procedural regulations in order to enforce any kind of personal or proprietary rights and interest, as is the general trend in the United States and in Europe. It can also be achieved by means of specific judicial proceeding established only and particularly for the protection of the rights declared in the Constitution, being the latter the general trend in Latin America, mainly because the general judicial means have been insufficient for granting effective protection to the latter.

Our purpose in this Course of Lectures is to analyze this specific judicial means for protection of human rights in Latin America, generally called the «amparo» suit, action or recourse, but bearing in mind that such protection can also be achieved by the general judicial means, including the procedures set forth in case of urgency. This is the situation in Europe and in the United States, to which I want to refer first.

3. The United States judicial means for the protection of rights (including constitutional rights)

In the United States, following the British procedural law tradition, the protection of human rights, civil rights or constitutional rights (those embodied in the Bill of Eights), has always been achieved through the general ordinary or extraordinary judicial means, and particularly, be means of the remedies established in Law or in Equity.

This distinction between Law and Equity in order to construct two judicial system of courts, traditionally inherent to the Anglo-American legal system, has also penetrated the civil law countries, where the judges can also decide cases based on «*equidad*», term also used in procedural law. For example, in the Venezuelan Civil Code, article 12 impose the judges the duty to decide cases in conformity with the rules of law (*normas de derecho*), unless a statute authorize them to decide accordingly to «*equidad*»; and article 13 the indicates that the courts will decide the merits of the case based on to «*equidad*» only when asked to do so by the agreed consent of the parties and the rights involved in the controversy are rights that can be renounced or transferred, such as property rights. Only regarding arbitration the Code distinguishes between «law arbiters» (*árbitros de derecho*) and arbitrators. The former must always decide according to the legal procedure and to the law; the latter will proceed with complete liberty, according to their most convenient view in the parties' interest, particularly according to «equidad» (article 618).

The Venezuelan Constitution, when referring to the State as rule of law and Justice, also uses the expression «*justicia equitativa*» (equitable justice), which has lead the Supreme Court to consider the possibility of the existence of two sorts of jurisdictions: law and equity jurisdiction, identifying within the latter, the «peace judges» (*jueces de paz*), which in the local neighborhoods must try to decide controversies by means of conciliation and when resulting impossible, according to equity except when a law solution is imposed by a statute (art. 3, Peace Justice Statute). Peace judges must also decide according to equity when expressly asked by the parties. Regarding this concept of «*equidad*», the Constitutional Chamber of the Supreme Court has indicated that the concept:

> Of difficult comprehension, refers to a value judgment, related to the idea of justice when applied to a concrete case, view that is not based on the law, but in the conscience, the moral, the natural reason and other values. Due to the personal and subjective character of these values, the treatment of decisions based upon them ought to be different to the decisions issued based on legal norms»[19].

But with exceptions (such as the «peace judges» jurisdictions), in general, it can be said that in civil law countries the law jurisdiction prevails, and no general distinction can be found between law and equity courts. In the United Stated, on the contrary, it is fundamental to distinguish between trial or causes at law and actions in equity; as well as legal remedies as opposed to equitable ones. The latter being the ones in which the judicial resolution «does not come from established principles but simply derives from common sense and socially acceptable notions of fair play»[20].

Both are used for the protection of rights, to the point that the most common definition of remedy is «the means by which rights are enforced or the violation of rights is prevented, redressed or compensated»[21]. Of course they are not judicial means only conceived for the protection of constitutional rights, because remedies can and are also commonly used for the protections of rights based upon statutes and also derived from common law.

The most important procedural rule regarding remedies is that equitable remedies are always subordinated to the legal ones, in the sense that they proceed

---

19 Decision N° 1139 of October, 10, 2000 (Amparo case: *Héctor L. Quiroga*), in *Revista de Derecho Público*, N° 84, Editorial Jurídica Venezolana, Caracas, 2000, p. 351.

20 See William TABB and Elaine W. SHOBEN, *Remedies*, Thomson West, 2005, p. 13.

21 See William TABB and Elaine W. SHOBEN, *Remedies*, Thomson West, 2005, p. 1.

when the remedy at law is inadequate; in other words, the legal remedies are preferred in any individual case if they are adequate. As it was stated in *In re Debs case*, 158 U.S. 564, 15 S.Ct 900, 39 L Ed. 1092 (1895): «As a rule, injunctions are denied to those who have adequate remedy at law. Where the choice is between the ordinary and the extraordinary process of law, and the former are sufficient, the rule will not permit the use of the latter»[22]

The most common legal remedies are the damage remedies, the restitution remedies and the declaratory remedies.

The damage or compensatory remedies allow the injured party or the plaintiffs to seek compensation for losses sustained in violations of his rights. It is the main instrument to resolve disputes in contract law and regarding torts cases. These compensatory remedies find their equivalent in the actions for damages and prejudices in civil law countries.

On the other hand, restitution remedies are intended to restore property to its rightful owner or to obtain from the plaintiff any illegal profits or unjust enrichment he obtained as a consequence of the wrong made to the plaintiff property. The judicial ordinary writ or order commanding the offender party to do or to refrain from doing something that can be issued in these cases of restitution remedies, are the writ of detinue, issued to recover personal property; the writ of ejectment, for the recovery of land; the writ of entry, which allows a person wrongfully dispossessed of real property to enter and retake the property; and the writ of possession, issued to recover the possession of a land. In civil law countries, the equivalent remedies are the property restitution action («*acción reivindicatoria*») or the action for enrichment without cause. It can also be identified as an equivalent the actions to restore possession of land or to prevent its invasions («*interdictos*»).

The declaratory remedies are intended to obtain from a court a declaration of the rights or legal relations between parties, being commonly used in cases or controversy, to determine the constitutionality of a statute. It is also used to construct a private instrument between parties so that the interested party may obtain a resolution of the dispute. The latter is equivalent to the declaratory actions on civil law countries, and the former, to the petition to declare in a case or controversy, the non applicability of a statute on the grounds of its unconstitutionality, requesting the prevalent application of the Constitution. .

The equitable remedies they are the coercive ones, particularly injunctions, by means of which a court of equity can decide that the plaintiff or aggrieved party is entitled to an extraordinary relief consisting of an order issued by a court commanding the defendant or the offender party to do something or not to do something, that is to say, to refrain from doing specific acts. They are called coercive remedies because they are backed by the contempt power, that is to say, the power of the court to directly sanction the disobedient defendant.

Particularly regarding the protection of civil or constitutional rights, in the United States the coercive remedies that has been used, as extraordinary ones, are the following: first, the writ of injunction, in its four types: preventive, structural, restorative and prophylactic; and second, the writ of habeas corpus.

---

22 See in Owen M. FISS, *Injunctions*, The Foundation Press, 1984, p. 8.

In civil law countries, where «equitable» courts do not exist, the most common equivalent legal action to all these extraordinary coercive or equitable remedies or writs, are precisely the actions of «amparo» and of habeas corpus, for the protection of constitutional rights.

Regarding injunctions, and following what William M. Tabb and Elaine W. Shoben had explained[23], the four mentioned types of injunctions can be characterized as follows:

The preventive injunction, -preventive in the sense of avoiding harm- is a court order designed to avoid future harm to a party by prohibiting or mandating certain behavior by another party. In other words, to prevent the defendant from inflicting future injury to the plaintiff. These preventive injunctions can be mandatory, prohibitory or quia-timed injunctions.

The mandatory injunction consists in orders issued to the defendant to do an affirmative act or to mandates a specific course of conduct. Regarding the violations of rights made by public authorities, within the mandatory injunction it must be mentioned the writ of mandamus, issued by a court to compel a government officer to perform certain duties or to execute actions which is obliged to do.

Regarding the prohibitory injunction, they are the ones issued in order to forbid or restrain an act. Among these prohibitory remedies it can be also mentioned the writ of prohibition, when used as an instrument to correct judicial actions by preventing lower judicial courts from acting in certain way.

It can also be distinguished the quia-timet injunction, consisting of an order granted to prevent an action that has been threatened but has not yet violated the plaintiff rights. All these injunctions can be permanent injunctions that affect the legal relationship of the parties until subsequently modified or dissolved

All the above mentioned preventive injunctions, are «preventive» in the sense that they tend to avoid harm, and therefore are not equivalent to the preliminary injunctions. This is important to be stressed in order to avoid wrongs, particularly when comparing with the civil law countries institutions. In Spanish language, the expression «preventive measures» is used to identify what would be «preliminary or interlocutory injunctions» and not preventive injunctions. Thus, regarding the interlocutory injunctions (preliminary injunctions and temporary restraining orders), the general equivalent procedural decision in the civil law counties would be what has been called the «unlisted preventive measures» («*medidas cautelares innominadas*») that can be issued in order to preserve the status quo or to restore the factual situation during the specific trial development.

On the other hand, the structural injunction, were developed by the courts after the *Brown v. Board of Education* case (347 U.S. 483 (1954); 349 U.S. 294 (1955), in which the court declared the dual school system discriminatory, using injunction as an instrument of reform, by means of which the courts in certain cases, have undertaken the supervision over institutional State policies and practices where constitutional exists in those institutions. As described by Owen S. Fiss:

> «Brown gave the injunction a special prominence. School desegregation became one of prime litigative chores of courts in the period of 1954-1955, and in

[23] See William M. TABB and Elaine W. SHOBEN, *Remedies*, Thomson West, 2005, pp. 86 ff.

these cases the typical remedy was the injunction. School desegregation not only gave the injunction a greater currency, it also presented the injunction with new challenges, in terms of both the enormity and the kinds of tasks it was assigned. The injunction was to be used to restructure the educational systems throughout the nation.

The impact of Brown on our remedial jurisprudence -giving primacy to the injunction- was not confined to schools desegregation. It also extended to civil rights cases in general, and beyond civil rights to litigation involving electoral reappointments, mental hospitals, prisons, trade practices, and the environment. Having desegregated the schools of Alabama, it was only natural to Judge Johnson to try to reform the mental hospitals and then the prisons of the state in name of human rights -the right to treatment or to be free from cruel and unusual punishment- and to attempt this Herculean feat through injunction. And he was not alone. The same logic was manifest in actions of other judges, North and South»[24].

Thus, structural injunctions can be considered a modern constitutional law instrument specifically developed for the protection of human rights, particularly in State institutions; instrument that has been considered to « become an implicit part of the Constitutional guarantee of protecting individual rights from inappropriate government action»[25].

In the third place, the restorative injunctions must be mentioned, also called reparative injunctions, devoted to correct a past wrong situation. In these cases, the court order is devoted to require the defendant to restore the plaintiff to the position it occupied before the defendant committed the wrong. In order to protect a constitutional right, as for instance the right to be elected, the court order can also consist in the repetition of the election process itself.

Among these restorative remedies, it can also be mentioned the writ of error, consisting in an order for the revision by reasons of unconstitutionality, of a judicial decision of a lower court.

Finally, there are also the so called prophylactic injunctions, issued also to safeguard the plaintiff's rights, preventing future harm, by ordering certain behaviors from the defendant, other than the direct prohibition of future actions. These prophylactic injunctions refer to behavior indirectly related to the prohibited conduct, for instance devoted to ask the defendant to develop positive actions in order to minimize the risk of the repetition of the wrong in the future.

But other than by means of injunctions in order to protect freedom as a constitutional right particularly against government actions, the other extraordinary remedy in the United States -following the long British tradition-, is the writ of habeas corpus, the oldest judicial mean for the protections of life and personal integrity. It has also been employed to bring a person before a court in order to proof or certify that he is alive and in good health, or to determine that his imprisonment is not illegal. It has also been used to obtain review of the regularity of the extradition or the deportation process, of the right to bail or its amount.

---

24 See Owen M. FISS, *The Civil Rights Injunctions*, Indiana University Press, 1978 pp. 4-5; and in Owen M. FISS and Doug RENDELMAN, *Injunctions*, The Foundation Press, 1984, pp. 33-34.

25 See William M. TABB and Eliane W. SHOBEN, *Remedies*, pp. 87-88.

In conclusion, as seen in the brief analysis of the remedies in United States law, the protection of constitutional rights is assured by these general (ordinary or extraordinary) judicial means known as remedies, particularly the injunctions and the writs, most of which can also be used to protect legal (non constitutional) rights. So the Constitution in the United States does not provide for a specific judicial means for the protection of human rights, contrary to what happens in Latin America.

4. The protection of human rights in France and Italy through the general judicial means

The situation in Europe, in general terms, with the exception of Germany and Spain -where the Constitutions provide an «amparo» recourse, is similar to the one of the United States: the protection of human rights is assured by general judicial means, and in particular by the extraordinary preliminary and urgent proceedings devoted to prevent an irreparable injury from occurring, issued before or during a trail and before the court has the chance to decide the case, but also with the particular procedural development that in many cases, they have become permanent orders.

This is the case in France with the institution known as the *référé,* the case or Italy with the extraordinary urgent measures and the case of Spain with the precautionary measures (*«medidas cautelares»*).

In France, the Civil Procedural Code sets forth the distinction between proceedings regarding the decision of the substance and proceedings refers to decisions that must be taken before setting on legal grounds (*«avant dire droit»*); these are the writs of *référé,* which are judicial decisions issued in case of urgency, after a party request in order that the court adopt the necessary measures to immediately protect a right.

There are to types of *référés*[26]: first, the provisional one consisting in orders issued to prevent imminent damages or to order the cessation of an evidently illicit action. They are devoted to protect rights in a preliminary and interlocutory way pending the trial, that is, pending the judicial decision of the merits. The *référé* can be issued (art. 809 CPC). This *référés* are equivalent to the preliminary injunctions in the North American system, both designated to preserve the status quo in order to prevent irreparable damages before the court decides the substantive merits of the dispute[27].

Second, the other *référérs* are the ones issues in cases of urgency, based in the existence of an evidently illicit conduct that affects an unquestionable right, for its protection. The defendant, of course, must furnish the appropriate proof of the existence of the rights and of the manifest illegality of the defendant actions. These *référés* can also consist in conservatory or restitution measures to prevent imminent damages or to stop illicit actions, and also, orders issued to the plaintiff to accomplish particular duties if the obligations is proved. In this case, the principal procedural element is the need for the court to summon the defendant in order to hear his

[26] See R. LINDON, «Le juge des référés et la presse», *Dalloz 1985*, Chroniques, 61. See the comments by Enrique PAILLAS, *El recurso de protección ante el derecho comparado,* Santiago de Chile, 1990, pp. 19-26.

[27] See William M. TABB and Eliane W. SHOBEN, *Remedies,* Thomson West, 2005, p. 4.

argument in an oral hearing (art. 811 CPC). These *référé* are equivalent to the preventive or structural injunctions in the North American system, in the sense that they are not only devoted to protect constitutional or human rights but any legal right, and because their permanent injunctions. In France they are qualified as «provisional» judicial decisions but only in the sense that they do not produce substantive *res judicata* effects, that is, a definitive judicial decision regarding the merits which could prevent the principal lawsuit that can be brought before the courts. On the contrary, as it happened with the «amparo» decisions in almost all Latin American countries, the *référé* only produces formal *res judicata* effects in the sense that no other *référé* can be issued in the same matter, and between the same parties.

Thus, in the latter case, the *référé* is a judicial decision that is taken independently of the resolution of the controversy on the merits in the principal lawsuit that eventually can be brought before the courts. Consequently, the principal consequence of this «provisional» character of the decision is that if there is no principal lawsuit regarding the substantive merits of the case brought before the courts, the *référé* decisions becomes permanent.

As mentioned, and as it happened in the United States, the *référés* in France are a general procedural mean to seek judicial protection of any rights, and not only constitutional or human rights; but regarding the latter, they have been used successfully to protect them.

For instance, it has been used in controversies between individuals, for the protection of the constitutional right to privacy, and particularly to the individual right to each one's owns image. In 1980, the *Reader's Digest* magazine published in the front cover of one of its issues, the photo of a doctor showing him practicing medicine, in circumstance regarding which he did not give the magazine any consent for the publication. Consequently, he asked the Court of Great Instance of Paris the due protection, which on November 1980 decided on *référé* as follows: The Court took into account that in the cover of the issue N° 405 of the magazine, Dr. Antoine Chapman's photography was published in support of an article referring to Hospital patients rights regarding the medical treatment they can receive; that the photography of Dr. Chapman that was published has no relation to his work and life as a physician; and that according to deontological rules of the medical profession, physicians can avoid any kind of advertisement. Then the Court concluded considering that Dr. Chapman has an individual right to his own image, before his own patients and his colleagues, and that consequently, that the publication of his photo, without his consent, in the cover of a non professional magazine of great diffusion, and in a moment in which he was exercising his medical profession produced an evidently illicit overturn. The consequence was the judicial order directed to the magazine to publish in the following issue, a notice indicating that D. Chapman never gave his consent for the publication of his photograph in the previous issue[28].

In a similar case in 1981, a photo of a practicing lawyer was published in the weekly magazine *Le Nouvel Observateur*, showing her acting with her gown in courts; the photograph was published in order to support an article regarding the

[28] See the references in Enrique PAILLAS, *El recurso de protección ante el derecho comparado*, Santiago de Chile 1990, pp. 22-23.

legal practice by women and also was published without her consent. In order to grant the *référé* protection, the same argument of absence of consent of the lawyer to publish her photo in a non professional magazine prevail, considering the courts also, in the case, that the deontological rules of the legal profession allow to avoid any kind of advertisement. The court also considerer the right of the lawyer to give of her self the image she wanted to her clients and colleagues. The publication of the photo was also considered an illicit overture of her rights that had to be stopped. Thus the judicial order directed to the weekly magazine to publish in the following issue, the notice that the defendant never gave authorization for the publication[29].

The *référé* protection to constitutional rights has also been used to protect rights against public official actions. For instance, regarding the constitutional right to free enterprise, a case was decided in 1983, as follows: In the town Saint Cry-sur-Mer, Mr. Decurgis was the owner of a bar located near a public square, having next to the bar, a stand in which he used to sell fruits and legumes to the passing people. The Mayor of the town ordered the closing of the square passage, impeding the customers to have access to Mr. Decurigs stand, who could then not sell his merchandise. He asked judicial protection via *référé*, not for his supposedly property rights which he did not have, but for his right to develop economic and commercial activities, which has not been forbidden by any formal administrative act. The Court considered the right to develop commercial and industrial activities, as a fundamental public freedom of persons which cannot be limited by the *de facto* activities (*voi de fait*), expressed without any previous formal administrative act issue as a consequence of an administrative procedure, which was non existent in the case. Consequently the *référé* decision ordered the mayor to restore the situation Mr. Decurigs had before the arbitrary municipal action was taken[30].

The *référé* has also been used in France for the protection of property rights, regarding industrial factories against illegal occupation of its premises by the workers. In such cases, the Courts, even though recognizing the workers constitutional right to strike, in protection of the property rights of the owners of the factory and their rights to have access to their property, considered illegal the *de facto* occupation of the premises by the workers (*voi de fait illegal*), contrary to the owners rights, that prevented the continuation of work and impede the free entrance to the buildings. The ruling was an order directed to the workers to leave the premises, and if the order was not to be voluntarily carried out then it authorized the use of the police to do so.

In similar situations, injunction has been issued in the United States, even brought before the courts by the Attorney General asking for the protection of property rights of the United States regarding mail, and the protection of freedom of interstate commerce and of transportation of the mail, against striking workers members of the American Railway Union who in 1894 had sit in the railroad premises paralyzing the traffic in Chicago. Without challenging the workers right to quit work and without interfering with the organization of labor, the court considered that the strike interfered with the operation of trains carrying mail and with interstate commerce, and ordered the end of the sit in. In the well known *In Re Debs* case 158

29 See in Enrique PAILLAS, *El recurso de protección ante el derecho comparado,* Santiago de Chile 1990, pp 23-24.

30 See in Enrique PAILLAS, *El recurso de protección ante el derecho comparado,* Santiago de Chile 1990, p. 26.

U.S. 564, 15 S.ct. 900,39 L. Ed. 1092 (1895), the Supreme Court set forth the basic principles of injunctions, particularly regarding the power the courts have to punish the disobedience of its injunctive rulings by imposing fines and ordering imprisonment for contempt[31].

In Italy, the judicial mean equivalent to the French *référé* is the proceeding in case of urgency set forth in the Civil Procedural Code within the precautionary measures. According to article 700 of such Code those who have fundamental motives to fear that during the period in an ordinary process to enforce its rights, they can be threatened by an imminent and irreparable prejudice, may go before the court asking for the necessary urgent decisions that, according to the circumstances, could be suitable in order to provisionally assure the effects of the decision on the merits. Even though it is a precautionary power that can be used to protect any right, it has been used for the protection of constitutional rights such as the right to protection of health, environmental rights, rights to have a name and right to one owns' image.[32]

Mention has also to be made to the same institution of the in nominate precautionary judicial power established in the Latin American Procedural Code, which have also been used for the protection of human rights when asked for in ordinary procedures. In this regard, for instance, the reform of the Civil Procedure Code sanctioned in the eighties set forth in Articles 585 and 588, that when there is an evident risk that the execution of the decision be illusory and provided there is accompanying evidence which constitutes a serious presumption of such circumstance and of the right claimed, the court may adopt the precautionary decisions it considers appropriate, when there exists a well-founded fear that one of the parties may cause to the rights of the other party serious or difficult to repair harms. In these cases, to avoid the damage, the court may authorize or prohibit the execution of determined acts, and adopt the decisions that are intended to stop the damage from continuing. With a provision of this nature, the ordinary judge has very broad powers when protecting constitutional rights.

But in fact, these in nominated precautionary judicial powers have only been set forth in recent times in the Latin American civil procedure codes. Thus, in absence of those emergency judicial powers, including the injunction powers attributed to ordinary judges, and because the inefficiency of the general available judicial means in order to obtain an effective and quick protection of constitutional rights, the general trend in almost all of Latin America since the XIX Century has been the progressive regulation of special judicial means exclusively set forth for the protection of constitutional rights, as is the institution named the suit, action or recourse of «amparo», protection or tutelage.

III. THE SPECIFIC JUDICIAL MEANS FOR THE PROTECTION OF HUMAN RIGHTS

1. Origins of the Latin American «amparo» suit

The origin of this specific Latin American judicial mean for the protection of constitutional rights and guaranties can be found in México. In what was called the

---

31 See Owen M. FISS and Doug RENDELMAN, *Injunctions*, The Foundation Press, Mineola New York 1984, p. 13.

32 See Enrique PAILLAS, *El recurso de protección ante el derecho comparado*, Santiago de Chile, 1990, p. 46.

Constitutional «Reforms Act» of 1848, a special provision devoted to guarantee the fundamental rights declared in the Constitution, was incorporated (article 5), setting forth that in order to assure the human rights recognized in the Constitution, a statute had to regulate the guaranties of freedom, security, property and equality of all inhabitants of the Republic, and also had to establish the means for its enforcement. No statute was sanctioned but this disposition has always been considered as the remote antecedent of the «amparo» trial or law suit.

The «*Acta de Reformas*» provision was followed by the so called «*formula Otero*», a draft proposal made by one of the members of the Constitutional Commission, embodied in Article 25 of the 1848 Constitution, with the following text:

> **Article 25**. The courts of the federation will protect (*ampararán*) any inhabitant of the Republic in the exercise and conservation of the rights granted to him in the constitution and the constitutional statutes, against any offensive action by the Legislative or Executive powers, whether of the Federation or of the states; the said courts being limited to give protection in the particular case to which the process refers, without making any general statement regarding the statute or the act provoking the decision.[33]

From this «formula» the main characteristics of the «amparo» suit have always been that it only precedes against public entities actions (Legislative or Executive) and that the judicial decision adopted cannot have general effects, but rather, only effects regarding the concrete controversy and the parties involved, following in the latter case, the general trends of the effects decision of judicial review ruling in the United States.

Based on this Article 25 of the Constitution and even without a regulatory statute, the first judicial judgment of amparo was issued on August 13, 1848, impeding the exile of a citizen without due process.

The 1857 Constitution developed further the amparo institution, setting forth that any controversy derived from a statute or any other authority act which violates the individual guaranties, or from statutes or acts of the Federation which violate or restrict the sovereignty of the States, will be resolved by the Federal courts as a result of the aggrieved party petition, by means of a judicial decision issued after following a formal proceeding; decision that cannot refer but only to the particular individuals, only in order to protect and «*ampararlos*» in the special case to which the process refers to, without making any general statement regarding the statute or the challenged act (arts. 101 and 102).

The unanimous opinion regarding the origin of the amparo suit in México in the XIX Century, before its subsequent development, coincides in affirming that its antecedents are to be found in the North American system of judicial review of the constitutionality of statutes, which was known in México through the readings of

[33] See the text in J. CARPIZO, *La Constitución Mexicana de 1917*, México 1979, p. 271; Robert D. BAKER, *Judicial Review in México. A Study of the Amparo Suit*, Texas University Press, Austin, 1971, p. 23; and H. FIX-ZAMUDIO, «Algunos aspectos comparativos del derecho de amparo en México y Venezuela», *Libro Homenaje a la Memoria de Lorenzo Herrera Mendoza*, Caracas, 1970, Vol. II, p. 336. See also H. FIX-ZAMUDIO «A Brief Introduction to the Mexican Writ of Amparo», *California Western International Law Journal*, San Diego 1977, p. 313.

the book by Alexis de Tocqueville, *Democracy in America* (1835), in which he refers to the role of the Judiciary on matters of judicial review once the *Marbury v. Madison* Supreme Court decision of 1803 was issued[34].

When Alexis De Tocqueville visited America almost two hundred years ago, and described the political system of the United States, he stressed, in particular, the way Americans had organized their judicial power, which he considered unique in the world.[35] His observations about the powers of the courts, which he believed, «the most important power» of the country,[36] were directly referred to the powers for judicial review, whose basic trends can still be elaborated from them. He specifically pointed out that «that immense political power»[37] of the American courts, «lies in this one fact» -he said- «The Americans have given their judges the right to base their decisions on the constitution rather than on the laws. In other words, they allow them not to apply laws which they consider unconstitutional[38], adding that «If anyone invokes in an American Court a statute which the judge considers contrary to the constitution, he can refuse to apply it.[39] This power of American judges, De Tocqueville stressed, was «the only power peculiar to an American judge»[40], which at the time was correct. Today, it must be said, it is the power common to all judges in legal systems with a diffuse system of judicial review.

The influence of that American judicial review powers can be clearly appreciated regarding the original Mexican amparo regulation, particularly regarding the cases and controversy requirement, a basic element for judicial review and the amparo suit as well as the common exclusively the inter partes effects of the judicial decision.

But the original Mexican amparo institution devoted in the beginning to protect constitutional rights against authority acts, subsequently evolved into a unique and very complex judicial institution, that is not to be found in any other Latin American country, not only designed to guarantee judicial protection of constitutional rights against the State acts or actions, but as a multipurpose institution that additionally is used for the protection of personal freedom, equivalent to the habeas corpus writ (called «*amparo libertad*»); for judicial review of constitutionally of statutes (called «*amparo contra leyes*»), with trends similar to the North American diffuse system of judicial review; for judicial review of constitutionality and legality of judicial decisions (called «*amparo casación*») similar to the cassation recourse that existed in almost all civil law countries; for judicial review of administrative actions (called «*amparo administrativo*»), equivalent to the judicial review of administrative acts

---

34 See Roberet D. BAKER, *Judicial Review in México. A Study of the Amparo Suit*, University of Texas Press, Austin1971, pp. 15, 33; Eduardo FERRER MAC-GREGOR, *La acción constitucional de* amparo *en México y España, Estudio de Derecho Comparado*, 2nd Edition, Edit. Porrúa, México D.F. 2000; Héctor FIX-ZAMUDIO, *Ensayos sobre el derecho de amparo*, Universidad Nacional Autónoma de México, Editorial Porrúa, México 2003.

35 Alexis DE TOCQUEVILLE, *Democracy in America* (ed. by J.P. Mayer and M. Lerner), The Fontana Library, London, 1968, Vol. 1, p. 120.

36 *Idem*, p. 122.

37 *Ibid*, pp. 122, 124.

38 *Ibid*, p. 122.

39 *Ibid*, p. 124.

40 *Ibid*, p. 124.

jurisdictions developed in almost all civil law countries, following the influence of the French contentieux- administrative jurisdiction; and for the protection of peasants rights derived from the agrarian reform process (called «*amparo agrario*») equivalent to the agrarian jurisdictions that can be found in almost all Latin American countries.

All those jurisdictions and judicial means in México are all under the same «amparo» name and umbrella; which as mentioned, is a unique case in comparative law. No other country in the world follows the Mexican «amparo» omni comprehensive approach, by mean of which the original «amparo» judicial mean for the protection of constitutional rights was deformed in the sense that what in almost all civil law countries are separate actions, recourses or jurisdictions, with very different objectives, in México all are called «amparo». On the other hand, this omni comprehensive trend of the Mexican amparo resulting form the effort to expand its protection, in the end paradoxically has provoke that the effective protection of constitutional rights in practice has been weakened[41]. Thus, it can be said that what really spread in almost all the other Lain American countries from the Mexican «amparo» institution, was only the name given to the special judicial means for the protection of constitutional rights (amparo), but not at all of its complex content, as mentioned, unique to the Mexican system.

In other Latin American countries, also since the beginning of the XIX Century antecedents of the «amparo» can be found. In Venezuela, for instance, in the 1811 Declaration of Rights of the people, it was specifically provided the right to petition in order to protect such rights, as follows: «The citizens freedom of petition before public authorities in order to ask for the protection of his rights, in any way can be impeded or limited» (Article 22). This declaration was followed by the 1830 Constitution declaration regarding the need to a special protective means of the constitutional rights, in which was stated that: «Every person must find a prompt and safe remedy according to the law, regarding the injuries and damages suffered in their persons, properties, honor and esteem» (Article 189).

And according to this constitutional provision, it was the Organic Statute on the Judiciary of 1950 that attributed to the Superior Courts powers: «To decide recourses of force, «amparo» and protection against written and oral orders or prescription, given by authorities of the Republic» (Article 9), using for the first time the word «amparo» to identify a judicial mean; as well as the person's right to ask for «amparo» to freedom rights (habeas corpus), as follows:

> **10.** In case in which any public official were forming criminal cause against any person or had issued a detention order, the interested party or anybody acting in his name, can bring before the Superior Court by means of «amparo» or protection; and the latter, ordering the suspension of the procedure, will ask the files and the presence of the party (en vida), and if it finds the petition according to justice, will level the oppressive order».

Nevertheless, and inspite of these provisions, in Venezuela the «amparo» action was only developed after the enactment of the Constitution of 1961. Yet, in the XIX Century, in the Venezuelan 1897 Civil Procedure Code, judicial review as a

41 See the coments in this regard in Joaquín BRAGE CAMAZANO, *La Jurisdiccoión Constitucional de la Libertad (Teoría general, Argentina, México, Corte Interamericana de Derechos Humanos)*, Editorial Porrúa, Instituto Mexicano de Derecho Procesal Constitucional, México, 2005, p. 156.

power of all judges to consider null and void legal provisions contrary to the Constitution -in the North American legal tradition- was formally inserted in positive law, allowing judicial protection of constitutional rights. Article 20 of such Code provides: «When the law whose application is requested is contrary to any provision of the Constitution, the judges will give preference to the latter[42].

In other Latin American countries the amparo action or recourse as well as the habeas corpus recourse were introduced in positive law since the XIX century, as follows: regarding habeas corpus in Brasil (1830), El Salvador (1841), Argentina (1863) and Perú (1897), and regarding the amparo action or recourse in Guatemala (1879), El Salvador (1886), Honduras (1894), Nicaragua (1911), Brasil (*mandado de securança* 1934), Panama (1941), Costa Rica (1946), Venezuela (1961), Bolivia, Paraguay, Ecuador (1967), Panama (1972), Perú (1976), Chile (*recurso de protección* 1976) and Colombia (*acción de tutela* 1991). In Argentina, since 1957, the amparo action was admitted through court decisions and regulated in positive law in 1966; and in the Dominican Republic, since 2000 the Supreme Court has admitted the amparo action.

Currently (2006), in all Latin American countries, exception made of Cuba, the habeas corpus and amparo suits, actions or recourses (*«acción de protección»* in Chile and *«acción de tutela* in Colombia) it exists as a specific judicial means exclusively designed for the protection of constitutional rights; in all of them, exception made of the Dominican Republic, the provision for the action is embodied in the Constitutions and in all of them, exception made of Chile and Panamá, the ations of amparo have been expressly regulated in special statutes.

2. The judicial review methods as means for the protection of human rights

In the other hand, the regulation of the «amparo» actions in Latin America, must also be considered as a particular means for the protection of Constitution and of its supremacy regarding specifically the declarations of rights; a method of judicial review that complements the general systems of judicial review of the constitutionality of statutes developed in Latin America, also since the XIX century: the diffuse and the concentrated methods of judicial review.

According to the so called «American model», the diffuse method of judicial review empowers all the judges and courts of a given country to act as a constitutional judge, in the sense that when applying the law, they are allowed to judge its constitutionality and therefore, not to apply it in the concrete process when they consider it unconstitutional and void, giving priority to the Constitution[43]. This diffuse system of judicial review of constitutionality of legislation is not a system peculiar to the common law system of law and is perfectly compatible with the civil or Roman law tradition. It has existed since the XIX Century in most Latin

---

[42] The text of the norm in Spanish is as follows: «Cuando la ley vigente, cuya aplicación se pida, colidiere con alguna disposición constitucional, los jueces aplicarán ésta con preferencia». The text was originally adopted in the 1897 Code (Art. 10), followed by the 1904 Code (Art. 10) and the 1916 Code (Art. 7). In the 1985 Code the only change introduced in relation to the previous text, is the word «judges» which substituted the word «Tribunals». See the text of the 1897, 1904 and 1916 Codes in *Leyes y Decretos Reglamentarios de los Estados Unidos de Venezuela*, Caracas, 1943, Vol. V.

[43] See Allan R. BREWER CARÍAS, *Judicial Review in Comparative Law*, Cambridge University Press, Cambridge 1989.

American countries, as is the case of Dominican Republic (1844) [44], México (1857), Colombia (1850), Argentina (1860), Brazil (1890) and Venezuela (1897). In México, Argentina and Brazil, the method strictly follows the American model; and in Colombia, Venezuela and Perú, it exists in a mixed system with the concentrated method of judicial review. The diffuse method is also applied in some European countries with a civil law tradition, like Switzerland, Greece and Portugal.

The duty of the courts on the diffuse model of judicial review can only be accomplished *incidenter tantum*, through a particular process (cases and controversies) that have been brought before them, and where the unconstitutionality of a particular statute is neither «the issue» nor the principal issue in the process. Therefore, a process must be initiated before a court on any matter or subject whatsoever, the diffuse system of judicial review of constitutionality being, consequently, always an incidental system of review. In these cases, the decision adopted by the Supreme Court has *in casu et inter partes* effects, that is, effects related to the concrete case and exclusively to the parties who have participated in the process, and therefore, it cannot be applied to other individuals. The judicial decision has also declarative effect in the sense that it only declares the *ab initio* nullity of the challenged statute. Thus, when declaring the statute unconstitutional and inapplicable, in fact, the decision has *ex-tunc*, and *pro pretaerito* effects in the sense that they are retroactive to the moment of the enactment of the statute, considered as not having produced any effect regarding the concrete process and parties.

Finally, it must be said that in order to avoid the uncertainty of the legal order and contradictions due to the multiple decisions that can refers to constitutional issues, corrections have been made to these *inter partes* effects through the *stare decisis* doctrine or through positive law, when the decision is adopted by the Supreme Court of a given country[45].

But Latin American countries have also followed the so called «Austrian» or European model of judicial review, established well before it was invented in Europe, as a concentrated method, by Hans Kelsen in 1920[46]. In Latin America, since the XIX century some countries have adopted it as the only method of judicial review and others, mixed with the diffuse method of judicial review.

The concentrated method of judicial review, contrary to the diffuse system, is basically characterized by the fact that the constitutional system empowers one single state organ of a given country to act as a constitutional judge, in the sense of being the only State organ called to decide upon constitutional matters regarding legislative acts and other State acts with similar rank or value, in a jurisdictional way.

---

[44] The 1844 constitution, as well as the 1966 constitution (Art. 46) established that 'are null and void all Laws, Decrees, Resolutions, Regulations or Acts contrary to the constitution. Consequently all the Courts can declare an act unconstitutional and not applicable to the concrete case. *Cf.* M. BERGES CHUPANI, «Report» in *Memoria de la Reunión de Cortes Superiores de Justicia de Ibero-América, El Caribe, España y Portugal*, Caracas, 1983, p. 380.

[45] *Idem*.

[46] See H. KELSEN, «La garantie juridictionnelle de la Constitution (La Justice constitutionnelle), *Revue du droit public et de la science politique en France et à l'étranger*, París 1928, pp. 197-257; Allan R. BREWER CARÍAS, *Judicial Review in Comparative Law*, Cambridge University Press, Cambridge 1989.

This state body with the monopoly of acting as a constitutional judge can either be the Supreme Court of Justice of the country, in its character as the highest court in the judicial hierarchy or it can also be a special Constitutional Court, Council or Tribunal, specially created by the Constitution.

Therefore, the concentrated system of judicial review of the constitutionality of legislation, even though generally identified with the «European model» of special constitutional courts,[47] does not necessarily imply its existence. It only implies the assignment to a single state organ, which exercises jurisdictional activity, of the duty and power to act as a constitutional judge, with powers to declare the nullity of state acts, which has to be established and regulated expressly in the Constitution.

Contrary to the diffuse system of judicial review, which is always of an incidental character, the concentrated system of judicial review can have either a principal or incidental character, in the sense that constitutional questions regarding statutes may reach the supreme court or the constitutional court, by virtue of a direct action, some times a popular action, or request brought before the court or by reference of the question to the court, from a lower court, where the constitutional question has been raised in a concrete proceeding, either *ex-officio* or through the initiative of a party.

The decision adopted by the constitutional court or the supreme court acting as a constitutional judge in the concentrated method, has general effects, thus it applies *erga omnes*. Additionally the decision has a *constitutive* effect in the sense that: it declares the nullity of a statute which produces effects up to the moment in which its nullity is established. That is why it is said that the decision of the court, as it is a constitutive one, has *ex-nunc, pro futuro* or prospective effects, in the sense that, in principle, they do not go back to the moment of the enactment of the statute considered thereon unconstitutional, the effects produced by the annulled statute until that annulment are still considered valid.

In Latin America, since the middle of the XIX Century many countries have adopted a concentrated method of judicial review by assigning the supreme court of the country with the power to declare the nullity of legislation. This was the case in Colombia and Venezuela in which an authentic concentrated method of judicial review has existed since 1850 and in which the supreme courts have the monopoly of annulling statutes. It is also the case of Panamá, Uruguay and Paraguay.

Subsequently, in many countries the system moved to a mixed one, in which the diffuse and the concentrated systems of judicial review coexist, as is the case of Brazil, Colombia, Perú, Venezuela, Perú and Guatemala.

Also, in Latin America, some countries have established Constitutional Courts or Tribunal in order to perform the concentrated method of judicial review, as is the case of Guatemala, Chile, Perú, Ecuador and Colombia.

Therefore, the judicial protection of constitutional rights in Latin America, additionally to the amparo actions or recourses, can be achieved by means of the diffuse and concentrated methods of judicial review.

---

[47] M. Cappelletti, *Judicial Review in the Contemporary World*, Indianapolis, 1971, pp. 50-53.

3. The European «amparo» actions

Finally, we must mention that as a result of the regulation of the concentrated method of judicial review, in Austria, Germany and Spain, a specific judicial means for the protection of some constitutional rights was also established.

In effect, the «Austrian method» of judicial review was originated in Europe after the First World War under the influence of the ideas and direct work of Hans Kelsen, particularly regarding the concept of the supremacy of the constitution and the need for a jurisdictional guarantee of that supremacy;[48] but it was also a direct result of the absence of a diffuse system of judicial review of the constitutionality of legislation whose exclusion was expressly or indirectly established in the Constitution; and of the traditional European distrust regarding the judiciary to control the constitutionality or legislation. Thus, in order to accomplish such task it was necessary to establish an independent State body.

Accordingly, the first constitutional tribunals were established in Czechoslovakia and Austria, in their respective Constitutions of February 29 and October 1st 1920. Due to its permanence and its reestablishment in 1945, the Austrian Constitutional Tribunal, created in the 1920 Constitution, was to be the leading institution of the «European» concentrated system of judicial review. Hans Kelsen, a member himself of the Constitutional Tribunal until 1929, formulated the original general trends of the institution, very similar to the Czechoslovakian one, regulated in the 1945 Constitution[49] and in the Federal Law of the Constitutional Tribunal of 1953, modified on various occasions[50].

But in Austria, the Constitutional Tribunal not only has the power to act as a constitutional judge controlling the constitutionality of statutes, executive regulations and Treaties, but also to grant constitutional protection against the violation of fundamental rights. For this purpose, any individual has the right to bring before the Constitutional Tribunal, recourses or complaints against administrative acts when the claimant alleges that they infringe a right guaranteed in the constitution (art. 144).

This was the origin of the development of a special judicial means for the protection of fundamental rights in Europe, although in a concentrated way which establishes the difference with Latin American «amparo» recourses.

The Austrian model influenced the establishment of the a concentrated system of judicial review in the Second Spanish Republic, in accordance with the Constitution of December 9 1931, by which a Tribunal of Constitutional Guarantees was created[51].

---

48 H. KELSEN, «La garantie juridictionnelle de la Constitution (La Justice constitutionnelle), *Revue du droit public et de la science politique en France et à l'étranger*, París, 1928, pp. 197-257.

49 Arts.137-148, Constitution of I May 1945. See a Spanish version of the Constitution in I. MÉNDEZ DE VIGO, «El Verfassungsgerichthof (Tribunal Constitucional Austríaco)», *Boletín de Jurisprudencia Constitucional*, Cortes Generales, 7, Madrid, 1981, pp. 555-560.

50 Law N° 85, 1953. See in T. OHLINGER, *Legge sulla Corte Costituzionale Austriaca*, Firenze, 1982.

51 J.L. MELIÁN GIL, *El Tribunal de Garantías Constitucionales de la Segunda República Española*, Madrid, 1971, pp. 16-17, 53; P. Cruz VILLALÓN, «Dos modos de regulación del control de constitucionalidad: Checoslovaquia (1920-1938) y España (1931-1936), *Revista española de derecho constitucional*, 5, 1982, p. 118.

The system was also conceived as a concentrated one, in which the Tribunal of Constitutional Guarantees had exclusive powers to judge upon the constitutionality of statutes, and additionally, the power to protect fundamental rights by means of a recourse of constitutional protection called «*recurso de amparo*», regarding which some authors have also found some influence of the Mexican «amparo»[52].

After the Second World War, also following the Austrian model, the 1949 Constitution of Germany created a Federal Constitutional Tribunal as the «supreme guardian of the Constitution»[53] having «the last word on the construction of the Federal Constitution».[54] The Tribunal is empowered to decide in a concentrated way, upon petitions for the abstract control of norms and constitutional complaints against laws that can be brought before it in a direct way, or by the referrals made before it by any lower court to seek a concrete control of statutes. Additional to these means for judicial review, it was also established a constitutional complaint for the protection of a fundamental right that can be brought before the Federal Constitutional Tribunal against a judicial decision which is considered to have violated the rights and freedoms of a person because it applied a statute which is alleged to have been unconstitutional (Art. 93, 1, 4,a) FCT Law).

Finally, regarding an «amparo» action, we must mention the current Spanish regulations established in the 1978 Constitution with the creation of the Constitutional Tribunal, later regulated in the «Organic Law of the Constitutional Tribunal» of 3 October 1979[55], which had establish a concentrated method of judicial review, considered as an illustrative example of the concentrated European model[56]. In accordance with the Constitution, the Constitutional Tribunal is conceived as a constitutional organ, thus independent and separate from the Judicial Power, but with jurisdictional functions as the guarantor of the constitutionality of state action.[57]

Additionally to its functions to decide the «recourse of unconstitutionality against laws and normative acts with force of law» (art. 161, 1,1 Constitution), through which «the Constitutional Tribunal guarantees the primacy of the Constitution and judges the conformity or inconformity» of the laws and normative acts with force of law with it (art. 27, 1, Organic Law 2/79), the Constitutional Tribunal is empowered to decide the *recursos de amparo* (recourse for constitutional protection), that can be directly brought by individuals before the Constitutional Tribunal, when they deem their constitutional rights and liberties violated by

---

52 See Eduardo FERRER MAC-GREGOR, *La acción constitucional de* amparo *en México y España, Estudio de Derecho Comparado*, 2nd Edition, Edit. Porrúa, México D.F. 2000.

53 See G. MÜLLER, «El Tribunal Constitucional federal de la República Federal de Alemania», in *Revista de la Comisión Internacional de Juristas*, Vol VI, Ginebra 1965, p. 216; F. SAINZ MORENO, «Tribunal Constitucional federal alemán», *Boletín de Jurisprudencia Constitucional*, Cortes Generales, 8, Madrid 1981, p. 606.

54 See H. G. RUPP, «The Federal Constitutional Court and the Constitution of the Federal Republic of Germany», *Saint Louis University Law Journal*, Vol XVI, 1971-1972, p. 359.

55 Organic Law 2/1979. See the text in *Boletín Oficial del Estado*, N° 239, 5 October, 1979.

56 See P. BON, F. MODERNE and Y. RODRÍGUEZ, *La justice constitutionnelle en Espagne*, París 1982, p. 41.

57 M. GARCÍA PELAYO, «E1 Status del Tribunal Constitucional», *Revista española de derecho constitucional*, 1, 1981, pp. 11-34; F. Rubio Llorente, «Sobre la relación entre Tribunal Constitucional y poder judicial en el ejercicio de la jurisdicción constitucional», *Revista española de derecho constitucional*, 4, 1982, pp. 35-67, As an independent organ it also has autoregulatory powers: Art. 2,2 Organic Law 2/1979.

dispositions, juridical acts or simple factual actions of the public bodies, the Autonomous Communities and other public territorial entities or by their officials (Art. 161, 1, b) Constitution; Art. 41, 2 Organic Law 2/1979). This recourse for the protection of fundamental rights cannot be exercised directly against statutes, which violate fundamental rights in a direct way,[58] as in the West German system. Therefore, it can only be exercised against administrative or judicial acts and acts without force of law produced by the legislative authorities (Art. 42 Organic Law 2/1979), and only when the ordinary judicial means for the protection of fundamental rights have been exhausted (Art. 43, 1 Organic Law 2/1979.). Consequently, the recourse for *amparo* in general results in a direct action against judicial acts[59] and can only indirectly lead to judicial review of legislation when the particular state act challenged by it is based on a statute considered unconstitutional (Art. 55,2 Organic Law 2/1979).

The general trend of the European «amparo» recourse, in contrast to the Latin American institution, is that it is conceived as a concentrated judicial mean for the protection of fundamental rights against State actions, by assigning the power to decide them to a single Constitutional Tribunal; and only to protect certain constitutional rights listed in the Constitutions as «fundamental» rights, more or less equivalent to civil or individual rights. In contrast, in Latin American countries, the «amparo» action or recourse, exception made of Costa Rica and Panamá, can be exercised before all courts; exception made, at least formally, of Chile and Colombia, always for the protection of all constitutional rights, including social and economic ones; and in many countries can be exercised not only against State acts but also against individuals.

---

58 *Cf.*, Eduardo GARCÍA DE ENTERRÍA, *La Constitución como norma y el Tribunal Constitucional*, Madrid 1985, p. 151.

59 *Cf.* FAVOREU, «Actualité et légitimité du Contrôle juridictionnel des lois en Europe occidentale». *Revue du droit public et de la science politique en France et à 1'étranger*, París 1984 (5), pp. 1155-1156.

CHAPTER IV

THE LATIN AMERICAN «AMPARO» ACTION OR RECOURSE AND THE AMERICAN CONVENTION ON HUMAN RIGHTS

I. THE «AMPARO» ACTION, RECOURSE OR SUIT: A LATIN AMERICAN CONSTITUTIONAL INSTITUTION

Section 9, clause 2 of the Constitution of the United States regulates -although in an indirect way- the writ of habeas corpus, when it states that «The Privilege of the Writ of Habeas Corpus shall not be suspended, unless when in Cases of Rebellion or Invasion the public Safety may require it».

In contrast, as has been mentioned before, since the XIX Century, additionally to the common and general judicial guarantees of constitutional and other rights - and sometimes in parallel to the habeas corpus recourse-, a group of specific judicial remedies for the guarantee of constitutional rights has been developed in Latin America, expressly intended to protect those constitutional rights. Those are the action, recourse or suit of «amparo», also known as action of «tutela» (Colombia), recourse for «protección» (Chile), or in Brazil, the «*mandado de segurança*»[1].

In all of its versions, it is always a specific judicial guarantee set forth in order to protect constitutional rights, and is generally enshrined in the Constitutions, although it has also been developed without express constitutional or statutory provisions, as is case of the «amparo» recourse in the Dominican Republic.[2]

At present, the «amparo» action or recourse is expressly regulated in the Constitutions of Argentina, Bolivia, Brasil, Chile, Colombia, Costa Rica, Ecuador, El Salvador, Guatemala, Honduras, México, Nicaragua, Panamá, Paraguay, Perú, and Venezuela. Sometimes the provision also includes the protection of personal

---

1 See, in general, Allan R. BREWER-CARÍAS, *El «amparo» a los derechos y garantías constitucionales (una aproximación comparativa)*, Editorial Jurídica venezolana, Caracas, 1993.

2 As is the case of the Dominican Republic. See Juan DE LA ROSA, *El recurso de «amparo». Estudio Comparativo. Su aplicación en la República Dominicana*, Santo Domingo, 2001; Allan R. BREWER-CARÍAS, «La admisión jurisprudencial de la acción de «amparo», en ausencia de regulación constitucional o legal en la República Dominicana» in *Revista IIDH*, Instituto Interamericano de Derechos Humanos, N° 29, San José, January-June 1999, pp. 95-102; and in *Iudicium et vita, Jurisprudencia en Derechos Humanos*, N° 7, Edición Especial, Tomo I, Instituto Interamericano de Derechos Humanos, San José, 2000, pp. 334-341.

liberty, although most countries have set forth a different recourse of habeas corpus for the specific protection of personal freedom and integrity and even an habeas data recourse, of more recent creation, for the protection of personal data.

My purpose now is to make a general and brief reference to the constitutional regulations on the amparo process, action or recourse in the Latin American Constitution, which I will referred according to the way they establishes the amparo action: together with the habeas corpus and habeas data; only together with the habeas corpus, or comprising the protection of personal freedom.

1. Constitutions establishing the three protective judicial means: amparo, habeas corpus and habeas data

A. *«Amparo», habeas corpus and habeas data in Argentina*

In effect, in Article 43 of the Constitution of Argentina, introduced in the reform of 1994, these three specific actions for human rights protection («amparo», habeas data and habeas corpus actions), are expressly regulated. Regarding the «amparo» action, the Constitution provides[3]:

> **Article 43.-** Any person shall file a prompt and summary proceeding regarding constitutional guarantees, provided there is no other legal remedy, against any act or omission of the public authorities or individuals which currently or imminently may damage, limit, modify or threaten rights and guarantees recognized by this Constitution, treaties or laws, with open arbitrariness or illegality. In such case, the judge may declare that the act or omission is based on an unconstitutional rule.

Therefore, the «amparo» action can only be brought before a court if there is no other more suitable judicial mean. It proceeds not only against public official acts or omissions, but also against private individuals acts or omissions, for the protection of all constitutional rights and guaranties, not only the ones set forth in

---

3 **Article 43.** Toda persona puede interponer acción expedita y rápida de «amparo», siempre que no exista otro medio judicial mas idóneo, contra todo acto u omisión de autoridades publicas o de particulares, que en forma actual o inminente lesione, restrinja, altere o amenace, con arbitrariedad o ilegalidad manifiesta, derechos y garantías reconocidos por esta Constitución, un tratado o una ley. En el caso, el juez podrá declarar la inconstitucionalidad de la norma en que se funde el acto u omisión lesiva.
Podrán interponer esta acción contra cualquier forma de discriminación y en lo relativo a los derechos que protegen al ambiente, a la competencia, al usuario y al consumidor, así como a los derechos de incidencia colectiva en general, el afectado, el defensor del pueblo y las asociaciones que propendan a esos fines, registradas conforme a la ley, la que determinará los requisitos y formas de su organización.
Toda persona podrá interponer esta acción para tomar conocimiento de los datos a ella referidos y de su finalidad, que consten en registros o bancos de datos públicos, o privados destinados a proveer informes, y en caso de falsedad o discriminación, para exigir la supresión, rectificación, confidencialidad o actualización de aquellos. No podrá afectarse el secreto de las fuentes de información periodística.
Cuando el derecho lesionado, restringido, alterado o amenazado fuera la libertad física, o, en caso de agravamiento ilegitimo en la forma o condiciones de detención, o en el de desaparición forzada de personas, la acción de habeas corpus podrá ser interpuesta por el afectado o por cualquiera en su favor y el juez resolverá de inmediato, aun durante la vigencia del estado de sitio.

the Constitutions but also in international treaties and in statutes. Thus, the «amparo» action directly proceeds for the protections of all rights declared in international treaties ratified by Argentina.

The Constitution also provides a collective action of «amparo» that can be filed by the affected party, the people's defendant and Associations that seek general purposes, in order to protect collective rights. The rights protected are particularly the environment, free competition, user and consumer rights as well as rights of general collective incidence.

Additionally to the «amparo» action, the Argentinean Constitution also sets forth what in Latin America has been called the action of habeas data. This Constitution provides that any person can file a suit in order to acquire knowledge about data with reference to himself, contained in public or private registry or data banks set for preparing reports and about the purpose of this data. In case of falsity or discrimination, the plaintiff can also seek for its suppression, rectification, confidentiality and actualization. Nonetheless, the Constitution provides that the filing of this action must not affect the secrecy of journalistic information sources.

The Constitution also regulates the habeas corpus action, stating that:

> When the right affected, restrained, altered or threatened is that of physical freedom, or in case of an illegitimate worsening of procedure or conditions of detention, or in case of forced disappearance of persons, the action of habeas corpus can be filed by the affected party or by any other person on his behalf. In such cases, the judge will resolve immediately, even in state of siege

Therefore, in Argentina, by means of the three above mentioned specific remedies, any person can seek for the protection of all human rights declared in the Constitution, international treaties and statutes that could be violated by public officials and by individuals.

The three actions have been regulated in three separate statutes: the «amparo» Action Statute (*Ley de acción de «amparo», Ley 16986/1966*), the Habeas Corpus statute (*Ley 23098/1984*) and the Personal Data Protection Statute (*Ley 25366/2000*).

B. *«Mandado de segurança», «mandado de injunção», habeas corpus and habeas data in Brazil*

In Brazil, Article 5 of the Constitution, after enumerating all the constitutional rights and guarantees, provides the actions for protection (the habeas corpus, the *mandado de segurança* the *mandado de injunção* and the habeas-data), as follows[4]:

---

[4] **Article 5°**- Todos são iguais perante a lei, sem distinção de qualquer natureza, garantindo-se aos brasileiros e aos estrangeiros residentes no País a inviolabilidade do direito à vida, à liberdade, à igualdade, à segurança e a propriedade, nos termos seguintes:
-conceder-se-á habeas corpus sempre que alguém sofrer ou se achar ameaçado de sofrer violência ou coação em sua liberdade de locomoção, por ilegalidade ou abuso de poder;
-conceder-se-á mandado de segurança para proteger direito líquido e certo, não amparado por habeas-corpus ou habeas-data, quando o responsável pela ilegalidade ou abuso de poder for autoridade pública ou agente de pessoa jurídica no exercício de atribuições do poder público;
-o mandado de segurança coletivo pode ser impetrado por:
partido político com representação no Congresso Nacional;

«The habeas corpus to anybody who suffers o there is a threaten to suffer violence or coactions on his moving freedom because of illegality or authority abuse;

The *mandado de segurança* in order to protect any true and enforceable right not protected by means of habeas-corpus or habeas-data, when a public authority or an agent of a legal person acting exercising public functions is responsible for the illegality or the abuse.

It must be noted that the *mandado de segurança* is excluded regarding individual's acts or omissions; and that the Constitution also provides a *mandado de segurança coletivo* that can be excersised by political parties with Congressional representation, labor unions, class entities or associations legally established and with one year of activities in defense of their members or associates.

Additionally, the Constitution sets forth the *mandado de injunção* in cases that due to the absence of regulatory statutes, the exercise of constitutional rights and freedoms and the prerogatives inherent to nationality, sovereignty and citizenship, would become unviable».

The Constitution also regulates:

The habeas data in order to ensure the knowledge of information referred to the plaintiff, contained in registries or databanks of governmental or public bodies; or to rectify the data when the petitioner decides not to do so through a confidential process, either administrative or judicial.

The procedural rules regarding the mandado de segurança are set forth in Lei N° 1.533, of December 31,1951.

C. *«Amparo», habeas corpus and habeas data in Ecuador*

The Constitution of Ecuador also provides for the three fundamental means developed for the protection of human rights: the habeas corpus, habeas data and «amparo»; but not all as judicial remedies, contrary to the general trend of Latin America.

Article 95 of the Constitution[5] provides a detailed set of rules regarding the habeas corpus, as a right of «any person who thinks that he has been illegally deprived of his freedom»; but not as a right to a judicial remedy.

---

organização sindical, entidade de classe, ou associação legalmente constituída e em funcionamento há pelo menos um a no, em defesa dos interesses de seus membros ou associados;
-conceder-se-á mandado de injunção sempre que a falta de norma regulamentadora torne inviável o exercício dos direitos e liberdades constitucionais e das prerrogativas inerentes à nacionalidade, à soberania e à cidadania;
-conceder-se-á habeas-data:
para assegurar o conhecimento de informações relativas à pessoa do impetrante, constantes de registros ou bancos de dados de entidades governamentais ou de caráter público; para a retificação de dados, quando não se prefira fazê-lo por processo sigiloso, judicial ou administrativo;

[5] **Artículo 93.-** Toda persona que crea estar ilegalmente privada de su libertad, podrá acogerse al hábeas corpus. Ejercerá este derecho por sí o por interpuesta persona, sin necesidad de mandato escrito, ante el alcalde bajo cuya jurisdicción se encuentre, o ante

In the Constitution such right to habeas corpus is conceived as an a administrative request, in the sense that it must be filed not before a judge, but only before the corresponding local government authority or mayor (alcalde), being possible that the request be filed directly by the affected person or through another person, even without the need of a written power of attorney. Within 24 hours from the filing of the request, the local government authority must order that the aggrieved person be immediately brought before him, and that the order of detention be shown. The administrative order, according to the Constitution, «must be obeyed without any comment or excuse by the persons in charge of the center of detention».

It is also the «alcalde» who must issue the decision of the case in a 24 hour delay, deciding the immediate freedom of the claimant if the detainee were not brought before it, or the detention order were not shown, or such order does not fulfill the legal conditions, if the detention was irregular, or if the claim was justified.

The public official who disobeys the order will be immediately dismissed of his position by the mayor, without any other proceeding; decision that must be informed to the General Comptroller's Office and to the authority that must appoint his substitute.

Regarding the habeas data, Article 94 of the Constitution also conceives it as a right that all persons have, to access to the documents, data bank of reports referring to the person, or his properties, that are in public or private entities, as well as to know what is their use and purpose.

The person can request before the respective official for the data to be actualized or rectified, removed or annulled, when erroneous or when it illegitimately affects the claimant's rights.

In the Ecuadorian Constitution only the «amparo» action is directly conceived as a judicial remedy, for which, Article 95[6] sets forth extensive regulations:

---

quien haga sus veces. La autoridad municipal, en el plazo de veinticuatro horas contadas a partir de la recepción de la solicitud, ordenará que el recurrente sea conducido inmediatamente a su presencia, y se exhiba la orden de privación de libertad. Su mandato será obedecido sin observación ni excusa, por los encargados del centro de rehabilitación o del lugar de detención.

El alcalde dictará su resolución dentro de las veinticuatro horas siguientes. Dispondrá la inmediata libertad del reclamante si el detenido no fuere presentado, si no se exhibiere la orden, si ésta no cumpliere los requisitos legales, si se hubiere incurrido en vicios de procedimiento en la detención o, si se hubiere justificado el fundamento del recurso.

Si el alcalde no tramitare el recurso, será civil y penalmente responsable, de conformidad con la ley.

El funcionario o empleado que no acate la orden o la resolución será inmediatamente destituido de su cargo o empleo sin más trámite, por el alcalde, quien comunicará tal decisión a la Contraloría General del Estado y a la autoridad que deba nombrar su reemplazo.

El funcionario o empleado destituido, luego de haber puesto en libertad al detenido, podrá reclamar por su destitución ante los órganos competentes de la Función Judicial, dentro de los ocho días siguientes a aquel en que fue notificado.

[6] **Artículo 95.-** Cualquier persona, por sus propios derechos o como representante legitimado de una colectividad, podrá proponer una acción de «amparo» ante el órgano de la Función Judicial designado por la ley. Mediante esta acción, que se tramitará en forma preferente y sumaria, se requerirá la adopción de medidas urgentes destinadas a cesar,

Article 95. Any person, by his own rights or as representative of a collectivity, can file an action of «amparo» before the judicial organ indicated by statute. By means of this action that must be carried out in a preferred and summary way, it will be necessary to adopt urgent measures in order to stop, prevent or immediately remedy the consequences of an illegitimate act or omission of a public authority, which violates or could violate any right enshrined in the Constitution or in an international treaty or convention in force, and that in an imminent way threatens to cause a grave harm. The «amparo» action can also be filed if the act or the omission is executed by persons rendering public services or that act by delegation or concession from a public authority.

Judicial decisions issued in a procedure cannot be challenged by means of the «amparo» action.

The «amparo» action can also be filed against individuals, when its conduct affects grave and directly a communitarian or collective interest or a diffuse right.

In the «amparo» action there will be no inhibition from the judge that must decide it, and all days will be court day.

The judge must immediately convene the parties, to hear them within the next 24 hours in a public hearing, and in the same decision, if reasons exists, will order the suspension of any act which could signified a violation to a right.

Within the next 48 hours, the judge must issue a decision, which must be immediately executed, even though such decision can be appealed before the Constitutional Tribunal for its confirmation or repeal.

---

evitar la comisión o remediar inmediatamente las consecuencias de un acto u omisión ilegítimos de una autoridad pública, que viole o pueda violar cualquier derecho consagrado en la Constitución o en un tratado o convenio internacional vigente, y que, de modo inminente, amenace con causar un daño grave. También podrá interponerse la acción si el acto o la omisión hubieren sido realizados por personas que presten servicios públicos o actúen por delegación o concesión de una autoridad pública.
No serán susceptibles de acción de «amparo» las decisiones judiciales adoptadas en un proceso.
También se podrá presentar acción de «amparo» contra los particulares, cuando su conducta afecte grave y directamente un interés comunitario, colectivo o un derecho difuso.
Para la acción de «amparo» no habrá inhibición del juez que deba conocerla y todos los días serán hábiles.
El juez convocará de inmediato a las partes, para oírlas en audiencia pública dentro de las veinticuatro horas subsiguientes y, en la misma providencia, de existir fundamento, ordenará la suspensión de cualquier acto que pueda traducirse en violación de un derecho.
Dentro de las cuarenta y ocho horas siguientes, el juez dictará la resolución, la cual se cumplirá de inmediato, sin perjuicio de que tal resolución pueda ser apelada para su confirmación o revocatoria, para ante el Tribunal Constitucional.
La ley determinará las sanciones aplicables a las autoridades o personas que incumplan las resoluciones dictadas por el juez; y a los jueces y magistrados que violen el procedimiento de «amparo», independientemente de las acciones legales a que hubiere lugar.
Para asegurar el cumplimiento del «amparo», el juez podrá adoptar las medidas que considere pertinentes, e incluso acudir a la ayuda de la fuerza pública.
No serán aplicables las normas procesales que se opongan a la acción de «amparo», ni las disposiciones que tiendan a retardar su ágil despacho.

The statute must determine the sanctions applicable to the authorities or persons who disobey the judicial resolutions and the judges who violated the «amparo» procedures. In order to assure the accomplishment of the «amparo» decisions, the judges can adopt any pertinent measures; even ask the police for help.

All procedural norms contrary to the «amparo» action will not be applicable, nor the dispositions that could delay its quick application.

The habeas corpus, habeas data and the «amparo» -the last two ones as judicial remedies, are regulated in the Constitutional Judicial Review Statute (*Ley de Control Constitucional*, Ley N° 000. RO/99) of July 2nd, 1997.

D. *«Amparo», habeas corpus and habeas data in Paraguay*

Since the Constitution of Paraguay is a more recent one, not only has it regulated in a very extended way the «amparo» and habeas corpus recourses as constitutional guaranties regarding the rights declared in the Constitution (art. 131), but has also expressly regulated the habeas data recourse.

Regarding the habeas corpus, Article 133 of the Constitution[7] sets forth that this guaranty can be filed before any First Instance judge of the corresponding circuit, by he affected person or by someone on his behalf, without needing power of attorney, and distinguishes three types of habeas corpus: preventive, restorative and generic.

The preventive habeas corpus can be filed by any person in the situation of imminent deprivation of his physical freedom, in order to seek for the examination

[7] **Artículo 133.- Del Habeas Corpus.** Esta garantía podrá ser interpuesto por el afectado, por sí o por interpósita persona, sin necesidad de poder por cualquier medio fehaciente, y ante cualquier Juez de Primera Instancia de la circunscripción judicial respectiva.
El Hábeas Corpus podrá ser:
Preventivo: en virtud del cual toda persona, en trance inminente de ser privada ilegalmente de su libertad física, podrá recabar el examen de la legitimidad de las circunstancias que, a criterio del afectado, amenacen su libertad, así como una orden de cesación de dichas restricciones.
Reparador: en virtud del cual toda persona que se hallase ilegalmente privada de su libertad puede recabar la rectificación de las circunstancias del caso. El magistrado ordenará la comparecencia del detenido, con un informe del agente público o privado que lo detuvo, dentro de las veinticuatro horas de radicada la petición. Si el requerido no lo hiciese así, el Juez se constituirá en el sitio en el que se halle recluida la persona, y en dicho lugar hará juicio de méritos y dispondrá su inmediata libertad, igual que si se hubiere cumplido con la presentación del detenido y se haya radicado el informe. Si no existiesen motivos legales que autoricen la privación de su libertad, la dispondrá de inmediato; si hubiese orden escrita de autoridad judicial, remitirá los antecedentes a quien dispuso la detención.
Genérico: en virtud del cual se podrán demandar rectificación de circunstancias que, no estando contempladas en los dos casos anteriores, restrinjan la libertad o amenacen la seguridad personal. Asimismo, esta garantía podrá interponerse en casos de violencia física, psíquica o moral que agraven las condiciones de personas legalmente privadas de su libertad.
La ley reglamentará las diversas modalidades del hábeas corpus, las cuales procederán incluso, durante el Estado de excepción. El procedimiento será breve, sumario y gratuito, pudiendo ser iniciado de oficio.

of the legitimacy of the circumstances that, according to the affected party, could threaten his freedom, as well as for an order to stop such restrictions.

The restorative habeas corpus can be filed by any person that is in the situation illegal deprivation of his freedom in order seek for the rectification of the circumstances of the case. In this case, the judge will order the appearance of the detainee within the following 24 hours, with a report from the public or private agent who detained him. When the summoned party doesn't accomplish the order, the judge must go to the site where the person is confined, and in such place make a judgment on the merits and arrange his immediate freedom, similarly as if the appearance of the detainee would have been accomplished, and the requested report filed. If there were no legal motives to authorize the deprivation of freedom, it will dispose the immediate release; and in case of existence of a written order from a judicial authority, will envoy the back grounds to whom ordered the detention.

Finally, the generic habeas corpus recourse is intended to seek rectification of circumstances that are not comprised in the two above mentioned cases, restrict freedom or threatened personal safety. Also, this guaranty could be filed in cases of physical, psychical or moral violence which aggravates the conditions of persons already legally deprived from freedom.

The Constitution refers to a statute for the regulation of the habeas corpus guaranty, by means of a procedure that must be brief, succinct and without cost; clarifying that it is admissible in states of emergency situations and that it can be initiated *ex officio*.

Regarding the «amparo» recourse, Article 134 of the Constitution[8] states that it can be filed before the competent judge by any person that considers himself gravely damaged in his rights of guaranties set forth in the Constitution or in statutes or in imminent danger of being, by means of an authority or individual obviously illegitimate act or an omission, provided that because of the urgency of the case, the situation cannot be resolved through the ordinary judicial means. The procedure will be brief, succinct and without cost, and a popular action will be accepted in the cases allowed by the statute.

The judge will have the power to safeguard the right or guaranty or to immediately restore the infringed legal situation.

In electoral matters or related to political organizations, the jurisdiction will correspond to the electoral judiciary.

---

[8] **Artículo 134.- Del «amparo».** Toda persona que por un acto u omisión, manifestamente ilegítimo, de una autoridad o de un particular, se considere lesionada gravemente, o en peligro inminente de serlo en derechos o garantías consagradas en esta Constitución o en la ley, y que debido a la urgencia del caso no pudiera remediarse por la vía ordinaria, puede promover «amparo» ante el magistrado competente. El procedimiento será breve, sumario, gratuito, y de acción popular para los casos previstos en la ley.
El magistrado tendrá facultad para salvaguardar el derecho o garantía, o para restablecer inmediatamente la situación jurídica infringida.
Si se tratara de una cuestión electoral, o relativa a organizaciones políticas, será competente la justicia electoral.
El «amparo» no podrá promoverse en la tramitación de causas judiciales, ni contra actos de órganos judiciales, ni en el proceso de formación, sanción y promulgación de las leyes.
La ley reglamentará el respectivo procedimiento. Las sentencias recaídas en el «amparo» no causarán estado.

The Constitution sets forth that the «amparo» will not be admissible in judicial proceedings, nor against judicial decisions, nor in the procedure of formation, sanction and promulgation of statutes.

Finally, regarding the habeas data recourse, Article 135 of the Constitution[9], declares that any person may have access to the information and data referring to himself or to his properties that are in official or private public registries, and to know about the use and purpose of such information. The interested party can also ask from the competent judge, the update, the rectification or the destruction of the registries if they are erroneous or when they illegitimately affected his rights.

The statutory regulations regarding «amparo» are set forth in the «amparo» Statute (*Ley 341/71 reglamentaria del «amparo»)* de 1971.

E. *«Amparo», habeas corpus and habeas data in Perú*

The Constitution of Perú enumerates the constitutional guaranties in its Article 200, and among them, in particular, the actions of habeas corpus, «amparo» and habeas data[10].

The action of habeas corpus is admissible regarding any fact or omission of any authority, public official or person that harms or threatens the individual freedom or the related constitutional rights.

The action of «amparo» is admissible against any fact or omission of any authority, public official or person, which harms or threatens the other rights recognized in the Constitution. Nonetheless, according to the Constitution, the action of «amparo» is not admissible against legal norms or against judicial decisions adopted in a regular proceeding.

Regarding the habeas data action, the same Article 200 of the Constitution regulates its admissibility against the fact or omission of any authority, public official or person, which harms or threatens the following rights declared in Article 2, sections 5,6 and 7 of the Constitution:

First, the right to request without expressing motives, and to receive required information from any public entity, in the legal delay, with the due cost implied; exception is made regarding the information referred to the personal privacy and those expressly excluded by statute or because of national security reasons.

---

9 **Artículo 135.- Del habeas data.** Toda persona puede acceder a la información y a los datos que sobre si misma, o sobre sus bienes, obren en registros oficiales o privados de carácter público, así como conocer el uso que se haga de los mismos y de su finalidad. Podrá solicitar ante el magistrado competente la actualización, la rectificación o la destrucción de aquellos, si fuesen erróneos o afectaran ilegítimamente sus derechos.

10 **Artículo 200.-** Son garantías constitucionales:
La Acción de *Hábeas Corpus*, que procede ante el hecho u omisión, por parte de cualquier autoridad, funcionario o persona, que vulnera o amenaza la libertad individual o los derechos constitucionales conexos.
La Acción de *«amparo»*, que procede contra e hecho u omisión, por parte de cualquier autoridad, funcionario o persona, que vulnera o amenaza los demás derechos reconocidos por la Constitución. No procede contra normas legales ni contra resoluciones judiciales, emanadas de procedimiento regular.
La Acción de *Hábeas Data*, que procede contra el hecho u omisión, por parte de cualquier autoridad, funcionario o persona, que vulnera o amenaza los derechos a que se refiere el artículo 2°, incisos 5, 6, y 7 de la Constitución... .

Second, to secure that the information services, computerized or not, public or private, do not provide information affecting the personal and familiar intimacy.

Third, to honor and good reputation, to personal and familiar intimacy and to one's own voice and image.

The Constitution expressly states that the habeas corpus and «amparo» actions would not be suspended during exception constitutional regimes (art. 137). In such cases, when these actions are filed regarding restricted or suspended rights, the competent court will examine the reasonability and proportionality of the restrictive act, but is not allowed to challenge the state of emergency or of site declaration.

All the constitutional guaranties, including the habeas corpus, «amparo» and habeas data actions have been regulated in the Constitutional Procedure Code (*Código Procesal Constitucional*) of 2005.

2. Constitutions establishing the two protective judicial means: amparo and habeas corpus

A. *«Amparo» and habeas corpus in Bolivia*

In Bolivia, the Constitution regulates both, the «amparo» and the habeas corpus recourses, as follows[11]:

---

[11] **Artículo 18.-** Toda persona que creyere estar indebida o ilegalmente perseguida, detenida, procesada o presa podrá ocurrir, por sí o por cualquiera a su nombre, con poder notariado o sin él, ante la Corte Superior del Distrito o ante cualquier Juez de Partido, a elección suya, en demanda de que se guarden las formalidades legales. En los lugares donde no hubiere Juez de Partido la demanda podrá interponerse ante un Juez Instructor. La autoridad judicial señalará de inmediato día y hora de audiencia pública, disponiendo que el actor sea conducido a su presencia. Con dicha orden se practicará citación personal o por cédula en la oficina de la autoridad demandada, orden que será obedecida sin observación ni excusa, tanto por aquella cuanto por los encargados de las cárceles o lugares de detención sin que éstos, una vez citados, puedan desobedecer arguyendo orden superior.
En ninguna caso podrá suspenderse la audiencia. Instruida de los antecedentes, la autoridad judicial dictará sentencia en la misma audiencia ordenando la libertad, haciendo que se reparen los defectos legales o poniendo al demandante a disposición del juez competente. El fallo deberá ejecutarse en el acto. La decisión que se pronuncie se elevará en revisión, de oficio, ante el fallo.
Si el demandado después de asistir a la audiencia la abandona antes de escuchar la sentencia, ésta será notificada validamente en estrados. Si no concurriere, la audiencia se llevará a efecto en su rebeldía y oída la exposición del actor o su representante, se dictará sentencia.
Artículo 19.- Fuera del recurso de «habeas corpus» a que se refiere el artículo anterior, se establece el recurso de «amparo» contra los actos ilegales o las omisiones indebidas de los funcionarios o particulares que restrinjan, supriman o amenacen restringir o suprimir los derechos y garantías de la persona reconocidos por esta Constitución y las leyes.
El recurso de «amparo» se interpondrá por la persona que se creyere agraviada o por otra a su nombre con poder suficiente de esta Constitución, ante las Cortes Superiores en las capitales de Departamento y ante los Jueces de Partido en las provincias, tramitándose en forma sumarísima. El Ministerio Público podrá también interponer de oficio este recurso cuando no lo hubiere o no pudiere hacerlo la persona afectada.
La autoridad o la persona demandada será citada en la forma prevista por el artículo anterior a objeto de que preste información y presente, en su caso, los actuados concernien-

First, Article 18 refers to the habeas corpus recourse by stating that any person who thinks is being undue or illegally persecuted, detained, prosecuted or held, can, by himself or through any other person acting on his behalf, with or without power of attorney, file a suit before the District Superior Court or before any local judge, in order to ask for the respect of the legal formalities. In such cases, the judicial authority must immediately fix a day and hour for a public hearing ordering the appearance of the plaintiff before his presence; order which must be obeyed without excuse, not being a valid argument the obedience of superior orders. In no case the hearing can be suspended, and in it, once knowing about the antecedents, the judicial authority must decide ordering the freedom of the plaintiff, which must be sent before the competent judge, and must amend the legal wrongs.

Regarding the «amparo» recourse, Article 19 of the Constitution states as follows:

> **Article 19.-** Besides the recourse of habeas corpus, the recourse of «amparo» is set forth against the illegal acts or the undue omissions of public officials or of individuals, which restrict, suspend or threaten to restrict or to suspend the person's rights and guarantees recognized in the Constitution and in statutes.
>
> The recourse must be filed by the aggrieved person or by another on his behalf, before the Superior Courts of the Department's capitals or before the local judges of the provinces, and decided in a speedy procedure. The Public Prosecutor can also file the recourse on behalf of the affected person if he has not or could not file it.

Therefore, the «amparo» action is set forth for the protection of all constitutional rights declared in the Constitution and statutes. Additionally, about the Bolivian constitutional regulation, it must also be noted the possibility to file the «amparo» action against individuals, and not only against public officials; and the provision that the «amparo» judicial protection will only be issued «if there is no other mean or legal recourse for the immediate protection of the restricted, suspended or threatened rights or guarantees». Another important procedural regulation refers to the need to send *ex officio* the judicial decision to the Constitutional Tribunal for its revision before this court.

The «amparo» and the habeas corpus actions are regulated in the Constitutional Tribunal Statute (*Ley Nº 1836 del Tribunal Constitucional*) enacted in 1998, even though the Constitutional Tribunal of Bolivia only has reviewing powers over judicial decisions on the matter.

---

tes al hecho denunciado, en el plazo máximo de cuarenta y ocho horas. La resolución final se pronunciará en audiencia pública inmediatamente de recibida la información del denunciado y, a falta de ella, lo hará sobre la base de la prueba que ofrezca el recurrente.
La autoridad judicial examinará la competencia del funcionario o los actos del particular y, encontrando cierta y efectiva la denuncia, concederá el «amparo» solicitado siempre que no hubiere otro medio o recurso legal para la protección inmediata de los derechos y garantías restringidos, suprimidos o amenazados, elevando de oficio su resolución ante el Tribunal Constitucional para su revisión, en el plazo de veinticuatro horas.
Las determinaciones previas de la autoridad judicial y la decisión final que conceda el «amparo» serán ejecutadas inmediatamente y sin observación, aplicándose, en caso de resistencia, lo dispuesto en el artículo anterior.

B. *Recourse for «tutela» and habeas corpus in Colombia*

In Colombia, in addition to the habeas corpus recourse, the 1992 Constitution sets forth the «amparo» recourse but naming it «recurso de tutela», using a word that in Spanish has the same general meaning as «amparo» and as «protección».

In this regard, referring to the habeas corpus, Article 30 of the Constitution states[12]:

> **Article 30.**- Anyone who is deprived of his freedom, or who thinks has been illegally deprived of it, has the right to claim before any judicial authority for Habeas Corpus, personally of through any other person, which must be decided in 36 hours.

Regarding the action of «tutela» or «amparo», Article 86 of the Constitution provides[13]

> **Article 86.**- Everyone has the action of «tutela» in order to claim before the courts, by himself or by any other person acting on his behalf, at any moment and lieu, by means of a preferred and summary proceeding, the immediate protection of their constitutional fundamental rights, whenever they are violated of threatened by actions or omissions of any public authority.
>
> The protection will consist in an order directed to who is sued in tutela, in order for him to act or to abstain from acting. The decision will be of immediate accomplishment, but it can be challenged before the competent judge, who in this case, must send the case to the Constitutional Court for its possible revision.
>
> This action can only be filed when the aggrieved party has no other means for its judicial defense, unless it is used as a transitory mechanism to prevent an irremediable prejudice.

---

12 **Artículo 30.**- Quien estuviere privado de su libertad, y creyere estarlo ilegalmente, tiene derecho a invocar ante cualquier autoridad judicial, en todo tiempo, por sí o por interpuesta persona, el Habeas Corpus, el cual debe resolverse en el término de treinta y seis horas.

13 **Artículo 86.**- Toda persona tendrá acción de tutela para reclamar ante los jueces, en todo momento y lugar, mediante un procedimiento preferente y sumario, por sí misma o por quien actúe en su nombre, la protección inmediata de sus derechos constitucionales fundamentales, cuando quiera que éstos resultaren vulnerados o amenazados por la acción o la omisión de cualquier autoridad pública.
La protección consistirá en una orden para que aquel respecto de quien se solicita tutela, actúe o se abstenga de hacerlo. El fallo, que será de inmediato cumplimiento, podrá impugnarse ante el juez competente y, en todo caso, éste lo remitirá a la Corte Constitucional para su eventual revisión.
Esta acción sólo procederá cuando el afectado no disponga de otro medio de defensa judicial, salvo que aquella se utilice como mecanismo transitorio para evitar un perjuicio irremediable.
En ningún caso podrán transcurrir más de diez días entre la solicitud de tutela y su resolución.
La ley establecerá los casos en los que la acción de tutela procede contra particulares encargados de la prestación de un servicio público o cuya conducta afectare grave y directamente el interés colectivo, o respecto de quienes el solicitante se halle en estado de subordinación o indefensión.

In no case more that 10 days can elapse from the request of tutela and its resolution.

The statute will provide the cases in which the tutela will proceed against individuals that are in charge of providing public services or those whose conduct may affect collective interests in a grave and direct manner, or those to whom the claimant is in a situation of subordination or is defenseless.

Thus, the «tutela» action was constitutionally regulated to protect only certain constitutional rights, those listed in the Constitution as «fundamental» or considered as such because their conexity with the latter, in general, against public official violations, but also against only certain individual damaging actions. It must be said that notwithstanding the limitations regarding the protected rights, by means of judicial interpretation, the list of protected rights through the «tutela» has been progressively enlarged.

In Colombia, the incorporation of the tutela action in the 1991 Constitution with the additional creation of the Constitutional Court, triggered a very important and drastic change regarding the effective judicial protection of constitutional rights, allowing the access to justice to peoples that where previously excluded.

The tutela action has been regulated in the statute-decree N° 2591 of November 19th, 1991 which has been developed by decree N° 306 of February 19th 1992 and decree N° 382 of July 12, 2000.

C. *«Amparo» and habeas corpus in Costa Rica*

The Constitution of Costa Rica has expressly regulated the right of persons to file recourses of habeas corpus and «amparo» in order to seek for the protection of constitutional rights.

In this regard, Article 48 of the Constitution states that «every person has the right to the habeas corpus recourse in order to guarantee his personal freedom and integrity, and to the «amparo» recourse in order to maintain and reestablish the enjoyment of the rights enshrined in this Constitution, as well as those fundamental rights set forth in international instruments on human rights applicable in the republic»; assigning to the Constitutional Chamber of the Supreme Court the legal authority to decide them[14].

Since the creation of the IV Chamber (Constitutional Chamber) of the Supreme Court, Costa Rica has also experienced a very important change regarding the access to justice and the effective protection of human rights.

Both the habeas corpus and the «amparo» recourses are regulated in the Constitutional Judicial Review statute (*Ley de la Jurisdicción Constitucional, Ley N° 7135*) of October 11th, 1989.

---

[14] **Artículo 48.-** Toda persona tiene derecho al recurso de hábeas corpus para garantizar su libertad e integridad personales, y al recurso de «amparo» para mantener o restablecer el goce de los otros derechos consagrados en esta Constitución, así como de los de carácter fundamental establecidos en los instrumentos internacionales sobre derechos humanos, aplicables en la República. Ambos recursos serán de competencia de la Sala indicada en el artículo 10.

D. *Recourses for protection and of habeas corpus in Chile*

In Chile, Articles 20 and 21 of the Constitution regulate the recourse of protection (*recurso de protección*) but directing it only to a precise list of constitutional rights, and additionally, the habeas corpus recourse, as follows[15]:

> **Article 20.**- Anyone who, as a result of arbitrary or illegal acts or omissions suffers privation, perturbation or threat in the legitimate exercise of the rights and guaranties set forth in Article 19, numbers 1., 2., 3. clause fourth, 4., 5., 6., 9. final clause, 11., 12., 13., 15., 16., with respect to freedom to work and the right to freedom of contracting, and clause fourth, 19., 21., 22., 23., 24. and 25. by his own or anyone on his behalf, may file a complaint before the respective Appellate Courts, which shall immediately adopt the necessary measures in order to reestablish the rule of law and assure due protection to the affected party without prejudice to the other rights that it may allege before the respective authority or court.

The recourse of protection will also be admitted in case of number 8 of Article 19, when the right to live in a pollution-free environment would be affected by an arbitrary or illegal act attributed to a public official or to an individual

The Chilean regulation, as the Colombian one, is exceptional in Latin America, because it limits the protected rights only to a list expressly set forth in the Constitution, mainly referred to civil rights. The consequence is that all other constitutional rights not enumerated as protected by the recourse of protection, must be enforced by means of the ordinary judicial procedures. In this regard, the Chilean and Colombian Constitutions followed the pattern set by the German and Spanish constitutional regulations regarding the «amparo» recourse.

---

[15] **Artículo 20.**- El que por causa de actos u omisiones arbitrarios o ilegales, sufra privación, perturbación o amenaza en el legítimo ejercicio de los derechos y garantías establecidos en el artículo 19, números 1., 2., 3. inciso cuarto, 4., 5., 6., 9. inciso final, 11., 12., 13., 15., 16. en lo relativo a la libertad de trabajo y al derecho a su libre elección y libre contratación, y a lo establecido en el inciso cuarto, 19., 21., 22., 23., 24. y 25. podrá ocurrir por sí o por cualquiera a su nombre, a la Corte de Apelaciones respectiva, la que adoptará de inmediato las providencias que juzgue necesarias para restablecer el imperio del derecho y asegurar la debida protección del afectado, sin perjuicio de los demás derechos que pueda hacer valer ante la autoridad o los tribunales correspondientes.
Procederá también, el recurso de protección en el caso del N° 8. del artículo 19, cuando el derecho a vivir en un medio ambiente libre de contaminación sea afectado por un acto arbitrario e ilegal imputable a una autoridad o persona determinada.
Artículo 21.- Todo individuo que se hallare arrestado, detenido o preso con infracción de lo dispuesto en la Constitución o en las leyes, podrá ocurrir por sí, o por cualquiera a su nombre, a la magistratura que señale la ley, a fin de que ésta ordene se guarden las formalidades legales y adopte de inmediato las providencias que juzgue necesarias para restablecer el imperio del derecho y asegurar la debida protección del afectado.
Esa magistratura podrá ordenar que el individuo sea traído a su presencia y su decreto será precisamente obedecido por todos los encargados de las cárceles o lugares de detención. Instruida de los antecedentes, decretará su libertad inmediata o hará que se reparen los defectos legales o pondrá al individuo a disposición del juez competente, procediendo en todo breve y sumariamente, y corrigiendo por sí esos defectos o dando cuenta a quien corresponda para que los corrija.
El mismo recurso, y en igual forma, podrá ser deducido en favor de toda persona que ilegalmente sufra cualquiera otra privación, perturbación o amenaza en su derecho a la libertad personal y seguridad individual. La respectiva magistratura dictará en tal caso las medidas indicadas en los incisos anteriores que estime conducentes para restablecer el imperio del derecho y asegurar la debida protección del afectado.

In Chile, the Constitution also provides for the habeas corpus recourse, as follows:

> **Article 21.** Anybody being under arrest, detained or held-up in violation of what is set forth in the Constitution or in the statutes, can file before the court indicated by statute, by himself of by anyone on his behalf, a request for an order granting the protection of legal formalities, and the immediate adoption of the measures necessary in order to reestablish the rule of law and assure the due protection of the affected party.
>
> The court can order the person be brought before his presence and his orders must be precisely accomplished by all those in charge of prisons or detentions sites. Once the history of antecedents is known, the court will order the immediate release of the plaintiff, that the legal defects be repaired or to send the plaintiff before the competent judge. The court must always act by means of a brief and summary proceeding, correcting ex officio such defects or informing to whom it might concern in order for its correction.
>
> The same recourse can be filed in favor of any person that may illegally suffer any privation, perturbation or threatening of his personal freedom and individual safety. In such cases, the judge will order the measures previously indicated, in order to reestablish the rule of law and assure the due protection of the affected party.

The chilean «recurso de protección» has not yet been statutorily regulated, being only regulated in the constitution and by a supreme court regulation: *auto acordado de la corte suprema de justicia sobre tramitación del recurso de protección de garantías constitucionales, 1977.*

E. *«Amparo» and habeas corpus in El Salvador*

In El Salvador, Article 247 of the Constitution also sets forth two different specific judicial means for the protection of all constitutional right: the «amparo» action and the habeas corpus action, the latter for the protection of personal freedom[16].

Regarding the violation of the rights granted in the Constitution, every person has the right to request «protection («amparo») before the Constitutional Chamber of the Supreme Court of Justice.

Regarding the protection of personal freedom, the habeas corpus can be requested before the same Constitutional Chamber of the Supreme Court of Justice or before the Second Instance courts not located in the capital city. In the latter case, the decisions of such courts, when denying the freedom of the plaintiff, could be subjected to revision by the Constitutional Chamber of the Supreme Court of Justice., when requested by the interested party

---

16 **Art. 247.-** Toda persona puede pedir «amparo» ante la Sala de lo Constitucional de la Corte Suprema de Justicia por violación de los derechos que otorga la presente Constitución. El habeas corpus puede pedirse ante la Sala de lo Constitucional de la Corte Suprema de Justicia o ante las Cámaras de Segunda Instancia que no residen en la capital. La resolución de la Cámara que denegare la libertad del favorecido podrá ser objeto de revisión, a solicitud del interesado por la Sala de lo Constitucional de la Corte Suprema de Justicia.

The regulation of the «amparo» and habeas corpus action is set forth in the 1960 Statute on Constitutional proceedings (*Ley de Procedimientos Constitucionales*) of 1960, as amended in 1997.

F. *«Amparo» and habeas corpus in Honduras*

In the case of Honduras, the Constitution provides for two separate actions for the protection of human rights: «amparo» and habeas corpus[17].

Regarding habeas corpus, Article 182 of the Constitution states that

> «the State recognizes the guaranty of habeas corpus or personal exhibition»; thus, any aggrieved person or any other in his name has the right to file [the action], when illegally detained or in any way restrained in the enjoyment of his individual freedom; and when in his illegal detention or imprisonment; torments, tortures, abuses, illegal exaction and any repression, restriction or unnecessary annoyance regarding his individual safety or for the order of prison applied to the detainee».

The same article adds that the habeas corpus action may be filed without power of attorney or formality of any kind, orally or in writing, by means of any sort of communication, in any day and without costs. In no case shall the judges reject the action of habeas corpus, and they shall have the ineludible duty to immediately proceed in order to put an end to the violations to personal freedom or safety.

The courts that fail to admit these actions will become criminally and administratively liable. The authority that orders or the agent that executes the concealing or that in any way harm this guaranty, will incur in the illegal detention offence.

Regarding the recourse of «amparo», Article 183 of the Constitution also states that «the State recognizes the guaranty of '«amparo»'[18], thus any aggrieved person

---

17 **Artículo 182.-** El Estado reconoce la garantía de habeas corpus o de exhibición personal. En consecuencia, toda persona agraviada o cualquiera otra en nombre de ésta tiene derecho a promoverla:
Cuando se encuentre ilegalmente presa, detenida o cohibida de cualquier modo en el goce de su libertad individual; y,
Cuando en su detención o prisión legal, se apliquen al detenido o preso, tormentos, torturas, vejámenes, exacción ilegal y toda coacción, restricción o molestia innecesaria para su seguridad individual o para el orden de la prisión.
La acción de habeas corpus se ejercerá sin necesidad de poder ni de formalidad alguna, verbalmente o por escrito, utilizando cualquier medio de comunicación, en horas o días hábiles o inhábiles y libres de costas.
Los jueces o magistrados no podrán desechar la acción de habeas corpus y tienen la obligación ineludible de proceder de inmediato para hacer cesar la violación a la libertad o a la seguridad personal.
Los tribunales que dejaren de admitir estas acciones incurrirán en responsabilidad penal y administrativa. Las autoridades que ordenaren y los agentes que ejecutaren el ocultamiento del detenido o que en cualquier forma quebranten esta garantía incurrirán en el delito de detención ilegal.

18 **Artículo 183.-** El Estado reconoce la garantía de «amparo». En consecuencia toda persona agraviada o cualquiera otra en nombre de ésta, tiene derecho a interponer recurso de «amparo»:

or any other on his behalf has the right to file the recourse, in order to be maintained or to be restored in the enjoyment of the rights and guaranties set forth in the Constitution; and in order to have a declaration made that a statute or an authority resolution, act or fact does not oblige the plaintiff and is not applicable because it contravened, diminished or distorted any of the rights recognized in this Constitution»

The Constitution adds that the «amparo» recourse must be filed according to the statute; which in the particular case, is the Constitutional Judicial Review statute (*Ley sobre la Justicia Constitucional*) of 2004.

According to these regulations, the «amparo» action is conceived for the protection of all rights declared or recognized in the Constitution, against public authority actions or facts, and regarding individuals, is only admissible when they act with authority delegated powers.

G. *«Amparo» and habeas corpus in Nicaragua*

Regarding the «amparo» action, in Nicaragua[19], the Constitution only provides that «the persons whose constitutional rights have been violated or are in peril of being violated, can file according to the case the recourse of personal exhibition or [the recourse] of «amparo», in accordance with the «amparo» statute». No constitutional precision exists regarding the origin of the violation, so that if it is true that the recourse could then be brought against violations provoked by public officials and individuals, there are no provisions admitting it in the latter case

Thus, in the Constitution, for the protection of all constitutional rights, two specific judicial actions are regulated: personal exhibition (habeas corpus) and «amparo»; both regulated in the «amparo» statute (*Ley de «amparo»*) of 1988.

H. *«Amparo» and habeas corpus in Panama*

Following the general trend of Latin American Constitution, the Constitution of Panama also distinguishes two specific judicial means for the protection of constitutional rights, habeas corpus and «amparo».

Regarding habeas corpus, according to Article 23 of the Constitution[20], «any individual detained in cases not prescribed in or without fulfilling the formalities

---

Para que se le mantenga o restituya en el goce o disfrute de los derechos o garantías que la Constitución establece; y,
Para que se declare en casos concretos que una ley, resolución, acto o hecho de autoridad, no obliga al recurrente ni es aplicable por contravenir, disminuir o tergiversar cualesquiera de los derechos reconocidos por esta Constitución. el recurso de «amparo» se interpondrá de conformidad con la ley.

19 **Artículo 45.-** Las personas cuyos derechos constitucionales hayan sido violados o estén en peligro de serlo, pueden interponer el recurso de exhibición personal o de «amparo», según el caso y de acuerdo con la Ley de «amparo».

20 **Artículo 23.-** todo individuo detenido fuera de los casos y a la forma que prescriben esta Constitución y la Ley, será puesto en libertad a petición suya o de otra persona, mediante el recurso de habeas corpus que podrá ser interpuesto inmediatamente después de la detención y sin consideración a la pena aplicable. El recurso se tramitará con prelación a otros casos pendientes mediante procedimiento sumarísimo, sin que el trámite pueda ser suspendido por razón de horas o días inhábiles.

prescribed in the Constitution and statutes, by means of the habeas corpus recourse will be freed at his request or at the request of other person. The recourse can be filed immediately after the detention and without consideration regarding the applicable punishment».

The habeas corpus recourse must be treated with prevalence to other pending cases, by means of a very brief procedure, which cannot be suspended because of the hours or non working days.

The Constitution of Panama, in its Article 50[21], also regulates the recourse of «amparo», setting forth the right of any person to have revoked any order to do or not to do, issue by any public servant which violates the rights and guaranties set forth in the Constitution. For that purpose, the recourse of «amparo» regarding constitutional guaranties can be filed before the competent court at his request of by any other person; being subject to a brief procedure.

Thus, the «amparo» is also conceived in Panamá for the protection of constitutional rights against authority actions, not being admitted against individual unconstitutional actions.

The statutory regulation regarding habeas corpus and «amparo» are set forth in the Judicial Code (*Código Judicial, Libro IV Instituciones de garantía*), Articles 2574-2614 (habeas corpus) and 2615-2632 (*«amparo» de garantía constitucionales*).

I. *Habeas corpus in Uruguay*

The Constitution of Uruguay, even if it is true that it does not provide expressly for the action or recourse of «amparo», it can be deducted from its Article 7 when it declares the right of all inhabitants of the Republic «to be protected in the enjoyment of their life, honor, freedom, safety, work and property»[22].

Nonetheless, similarly to the Dominican Republic Constitution, the Uruguayan Constitution only regulated the action of habeas corpus, in Article 17[23], which states:

> **Article 17.**- In case of undue imprisonment, the interested party or any person can file before the competent judge the habeas corpus recourse in order to have the authority that has ordered the apprehension to immediately explain and justify its legal motive, being subjected to what the judge decides.

Notwithstanding, the «amparo» recourse has been regulated in the 1988 «Amparo» Law N° 16011 (*Ley de «amparo»*).

---

21 **Artículo 50.**- Toda persona contra la cual se expida o se ejecute, por cualquier servidor público, una orden de hacer o no hacer, que viole los derechos y garantías que está constitución consagra, tendrá derecho a que la orden sea revocada a petición suya o de cualquiera persona.
El recurso de «amparo» de garantías constitucionales a que este artículo se refiere, se tramitará mediante procedimiento sumario y será de competencia de los tribunales judiciales.

22 **Artículo 7°.**-Los habitantes de la República tienen derecho a ser protegidos en el goce de su vida, honor, libertad, seguridad, trabajo y propiedad. Nadie puede ser privado de estos derechos sino conforme a las leyes que se establecen por razones de interés general.

23 **Artículo 17.**- En caso de prisión indebida el interesado o cualquier persona podrá interponer ante el Juez competente el recurso de «habeas corpus», a fin de que la autoridad aprehensora explique y justifique de inmediato el motivo legal de la aprehensión, estándose a lo que decida el Juez indicado.

J. *Habeas corpus in Dominican Republic*

The Constitution of the Dominican Republic is one of the very few Latin American Constitution which does not expressly regulate the «amparo» action as a specific judicial mean for the protection of constitutional rights. Nonetheless, as mentioned above, this omission did not impede the Supreme Court of Justice from admitting and regulating the «amparo» action, applying for that purpose the Inter American Convention on Human Rights.

The basis procedure rules for amparo where established by the Supreme Court in its 1999 decision declaring the amparo recourse as a public positive law institution.

Regarding constitutional guaranties, the Constitution only sets forth the judicial guaranties for the protection of personal safety, by means of the action of habeas corpus. In this respect, Article 8 of the Constitution[24] provides that being «the effective protection of human rights the principal purpose of the State», the habeas Corpus statute will provide the way to proceed in a succinct way in order to secure, among others, with the compliance of the following individual safety rights: a. Not to be subject to corporal constraint because of debts not originated in violation of criminal statutes; b. Not to be imprisoned or to have restricted his freedom without motivated written judicial order, except in cases of flagrant crime; c. To be immediately freed at ones request or by any other person on one's behalf when deprived from one's freedom without due cause or without the legal formalities, on cases not set forth in the statutes; d. In case of detention, to be brought before a judicial authority within a 48 hour delay or to be freed; e. To be freed or to be

---

[24] **Artículo 8.-** Se reconoce como finalidad principal del Estado la protección efectiva de los derechos de la persona humana y el mantenimiento de los medios que le permitan perfeccionarse progresivamente dentro de un orden de libertad individual y de justicia social, compatible con el orden público, el bienestar general y los derechos de todos. Para garantizar la realización de esos fines se fijan las siguientes normas:
1. La inviolabilidad de la vida. En consecuencia no podrá establecerse, pronunciarse ni aplicarse en ningún caso la pena de muerte, ni las torturas, ni ninguna otra pena o procedimiento vejatorio o que implique la pérdida o la disminución de la integridad física o de la salud del individuo;
2. La seguridad individual. En consecuencia:
a) No se establecerá al apremio corporal por deuda que no proviniere de infracción a las leyes penales;
b) Nadie podrá ser reducido a prisión ni cohibido en su libertad sin orden motivada y escrita de funcionario judicial competente, salvo el caso de flagrante delito;
c) Toda persona privada de su libertad sin causa o sin las formalidades legales, o fuera de los casos previstos por las leyes, será puesta inmediatamente en libertad a requerimiento suyo o de cualquier persona;
d) Toda persona privada de su libertad será sometida a la autoridad judicial competente dentro de las cuarenta y ocho horas de su detención o puesta en libertad;
e) Todo arresto se dejará sin efecto o se elevará a prisión dentro de las cuarenta y ocho horas de haber sido sometido el arrestado a la autoridad judicial competente, debiendo notificarse al interesado dentro del mismo plazo, la providencia que al efecto se dictare;
f) Queda terminantemente prohibido el traslado de cualquier detenido de un establecimiento carcelario a otro lugar sin orden escrita y motivada de la autoridad judicial competente;
g) Toda persona que tenga bajo su guarda a un detenido estará obligada a presentarlo tan pronto como se lo requiera la autoridad competente. La Ley de Hábeas Corpus, determinará la manera de proceder sumariamente para el cumplimiento de las prescripciones contenidas en las letras a), b), c), d), e), f) y g) y establecerá las sanciones que proceda; ...

subjected to prison within a delay of 48 hours after the detainee is brought before the judicial authority; f. Not to be transported from one prison to another without written and motivated judicial order.

The habeas was initially regulated by the 1978 Habeas Corpus statute (*Ley de habeas corpus*), and since 2002 it is regulated in the Procedural Criminal Code (Ley 76-02) (articles 381-392).

3. Constitutions Establishing the Amparo as the General Protective Judicial Means

A. *«Amparo» in Guatemala*

In the case of Guatemala, as is the case of México, the Constitution provides only one specific judicial mean for the protection of all constitutional rights, the «amparo» action, comprising the protection of personal freedom.

In this regard, Article 265 of the Constitution sets forth the «amparo»[25], with the purpose of protecting the people against the threats of violations to their rights to restore their effectiveness in case of violations. The Constitution emphatically states that «There is no scope that is not susceptible of «amparo», and that [«amparo»] «will proceed whenever the authority acts, resolutions, dispositions or statutes imply a threat, restriction or violation of the rights guaranteed by the Constitution and the statutes».

The constitutional provision only refers to authorities, but nonetheless, the amparo has been admitted for the protection of all rights declared in the Constitution and also in statutes, also against individual actions.

The regulation of the action of «amparo» is set forth in the 1986 «Amparo», Personal Exhibition and Constitutionality Statute (*Ley de «amparo», exhibición personal y de constitucionalidad*).

B. *Suit for «amparo» in México*

As was already mentioned, the specific judicial means for the protection of human rights, named «amparo» in Latin America, has its origin in México, where it has been regulated in the Constitution since the XIX Century.

But from a remedy originally inspired in the North American injunctions, the Mexican institution of «amparo», was conceived as a suit, not only for the protection of constitutional rights and guaranties, but also to resolve what in other Countries is the object of different actions and procedures, in particular, judicial review of constitutionality of statutes, judicial review of administrative action and judicial review of judicial decisions (cassation).

But in particular, regarding the protection of constitutional rights and guaranties, in the Mexican Constitution the «amparo» is conceived as a general trail

---

25 **Artículo 265.-** Procedencia del «amparo». Se instituye el «amparo» con el fin de proteger a las personas contra las amenazas de violaciones a sus derechos o para restaurar el imperio de los mismos cuando la violación hubiere ocurrido. No hay ámbito que no sea susceptible de «amparo», y procederá siempre que los actos, resoluciones, disposiciones o leyes de autoridad lleven implícitos una amenaza, restricción o violación a los derechos que la Constitución y las leyes garantizan.

initiated be means of an action that can be brought before the courts for the protection of all individual guarantees declared in the Constitution, but only against actions of authorities such as statutes, judicial decisions or administrative acts, and not against private individual actions.

Article 107 of the Constitution regulates in a very extensive and detailed way the procedural rules for the exercise of the «amparo» action, as well as the competent courts. In its basic regulations[26], this article provides that all controversies that could arise «out of statutes or acts of the authorities that violate individual guarantees» (art. 103,I), as set forth in Article 107, shall be subject to the legal forms and procedure prescribed by the statute, on the following bases:

I. The trial in «amparo» shall always be held at the instance of the injured party.

---

[26] **Artículo 107.**- Todas las controversias de que habla el Artículo 103 se sujetaran a los procedimientos y formas del orden jurídico que determine la ley, de acuerdo a las bases siguientes:
I. El juicio de «amparo» se seguirá siempre a instancia de parte agraviada;
II. La sentencia será siempre tal, que solo se ocupe de individuos particulares, limitándose a ampararlos y protegerlos en el caso especial sobre el que verse la queja, sin hacer una declaración general respecto de la ley o acto que la motivare....
III. Cuando se reclamen actos de tribunales judiciales, administrativos o del trabajo, el «amparo» solo procederá en los casos siguientes:
a) Contra sentencias definitivas o laudos y resoluciones que pongan fin al juicio, respecto de las cuales no proceda ningún recurso ordinario por el que puedan ser modificados o reformados, ya sea que la violación se cometa en ellos o que, cometida durante el procedimiento, afecte a las defensas del quejoso, trascendiendo al resultado del fallo; siempre que en materia civil haya sido impugnada la violación en el curso del procedimiento mediante el recurso ordinario establecido por la ley e invocada como agravio en la segunda instancia, si se cometió en la primera. Estos requisitos no serán exigibles en el «amparo» contra sentencias dictadas en controversias sobre acciones del estado civil o que afecten al orden y a la estabilidad de la familia.
b) Contra actos en juicio cuya ejecución sea de imposible reparación, fuera del juicio o después de concluido, una vez agotados los recursos que en su caso procedan, y
c) Contra actos que afecten a personas extrañas al juicio;
IV. En materia administrativa el «amparo» procede, además, contra resoluciones que causen agravio no reparable mediante algún recurso, juicio o medio de defensa legal. No será necesario agotar estos cuando la ley que los establezca exija, para otorgar la suspensión del acto reclamado, mayores requisitos que los que la ley reglamentaria del juicio de «amparo» requiera como condición para decretar esa suspensión; ....
VIII. Contra las sentencias que pronuncien en «amparo» los jueces de distrito o los tribunales unitarios de circuito procede revisión. de ella conocerá la Suprema Corte de Justicia:
a) Cuando habiéndose impugnado en la demanda de «amparo», por estimarlos directamente violatorios de esta constitución, leyes federales o locales, tratados internacionales, reglamentos expedidos por el Presidente de la República de acuerdo con la Fracción I del Artículo 89 de esta constitución y reglamentos de leyes locales expedidos por los gobernadores de los estados o por el jefe del Distrito Federal, subsista en el recurso el problema de constitucionalidad;
b) Cuando se trate de los casos comprendidos en las fracciones II y III del Artículo 103 de esta constitución. La Suprema Corte de Justicia, de oficio o a petición fundada del correspondiente tribunal colegiado de circuito, o del procurador general de la República, podrá conocer de los «amparos» en revisión, que por su interés y trascendencia así lo ameriten. En los casos no previstos en los párrafos anteriores, conocerán de la revisión los tribunales colegiados de circuito y sus sentencias no admitirán recurso alguno;

II. The judgment shall always be such that it affects only private individuals and it is limited to the preserving (ampararlos) and protecting them in the special case to which the complaint refers, without making any general declaration as to the statute or act on which the complaint is based.

In particular, in the case of «amparo» against judicial decisions on civil, criminal, or labor matters, the writ of *«amparo»* shall be granted only:

1. Against final judgments or awards against which no ordinary recourse is available by virtue of which these judgments can be modified or amended, whether the violation [of the individual guarantees] is committed in the judgments or awards, or whether, if committed during the course of the trial, the violation prejudices the petitioner's defense by going beyond the outcome of the judgment; provided that in civil or criminal judicial matters timely objection and protest were made against it by means of the ordinary appeal, or if it occurred in the first instance, were raised in the second instance. None of these conditions are required in cases of «amparo» against judicial decisions referring to controversies related to personal statute and that affect the family stability and order.

2. Against acts at the trial, the execution of which would be irreparable out of court, or at the conclusion of the trial, once all available recourses have been exhausted.

3. Against acts that affect persons who are strangers to the trial.

In administrative matters, *«amparo»* may be filed against decisions which cause an injury that cannot be remedied through any legal recourse, trial, or defense. It shall not be necessary to exhaust these remedies when the statute that established them, in order to allow the suspension of the contested act, demands greater requirements than the regulatory statute for trials in *«amparo»* as a condition for ordering such suspension.

All the judgments in *«amparo»* rendered by district courts when a statute is impugned as unconstitutional or in cases of violation of individual guaranties, are subject to review by the Supreme Court of Justice (107, VIII). The Supreme Court, ex officio or when asked by the lower court or by the public prosecutor, may resolve the revision of «amparo» whose revision have been sought, if it considers it of interest or importance (art. 107, VIII).

The «amparo» suit has been regulated in the «amparo» statute developing Articles 103 and 107 of the Constitution (*Ley de «amparo» reglamentaria de los artículos 103 y 107 de la Constitución Política)* of 1935, which has been amended many times.

C. *«Amparo» in Venezuela*

The Venezuelan Constitution since 1961 has regulated the «amparo» not as a specific judicial means for the protection of constitutional right, but as a constitutional right in itself, of all persons to be judicially protected in the enjoyment of all human rights. This tradition has been followed in the 1999 Constitution, which guaranties the right of every person to have access to the Judiciary in order to have enforced his rights and interest, including the collective or diffuse ones, and to have the effective protection of the same, and to obtain in a speedy way the corresponding decision. For such purpose, «the State must guarantee a free justice, accessible, impartial, suitable, transparent, autonomous, independent, responsible, equitable, expeditious, without delay, without formalisms and useless repositions» (art. 26).

But in particular, regarding «amparo», Article 27 of the Constitution[27] sets forth the right to legal protection as follows:

> **Article 27.** Everyone has the right to be protected by the courts in the enjoyment and exercise of constitutional rights and guarantees, including even those inherent to persons not expressly mentioned in this Constitution or in international instruments on human rights.
>
> Proceedings on the action of constitutional «amparo» shall be oral, public, brief, free of charge and unencumbered by formalities, and the competent judge shall have the power to immediately restore the infringed legal situation infringed or the closest possible equivalent thereto.
>
> All time shall be available for the holding of such proceedings, and the court shall give priority to constitutional claims over any other matter. The action of «amparo» regarding freedom or safety, may be exercised by any person and the detainee shall be immediately transferred to the court, without delay. The exercise of this right shall not be affected in any way by the declaration of a state of exception or restriction of constitutional guarantees.

From this regulation, the «amparo» in conceived in Venezuela, as a constitutional right that all individuals have, to be protected on their human rights, even on those not expressly declared in the Constitution or in international treaties, but that are inherent to human beings, against any harm or threat from public officials or individuals. The action of «amparo» is thus expressly regulated, comprising the protection of individual freedom and safety.

But additionally, the Venezuelan Constitution has also set forth the habeas data recourse, by stating in its Article 28[28]:

---

[27] **Artículo 27.-** Toda persona tiene derecho a ser amparada por los tribunales en el goce y ejercicio de los derechos y garantías constitucionales, aun de aquellos inherentes a la persona que no figuren expresamente en esta Constitución o en los instrumentos internacionales sobre derechos humanos.
El procedimiento de la acción de «amparo» constitucional será oral, público, breve, gratuito y no sujeto a formalidad, y la autoridad judicial competente tendrá potestad para restablecer inmediatamente la situación jurídica infringida o la situación que más se asemeje a ella. Todo tiempo será hábil y el tribunal lo tramitará con preferencia a cualquier otro asunto. La acción de «amparo» a la libertad o seguridad podrá ser interpuesta por cualquier persona, y el detenido o detenida será puesto bajo la custodia del tribunal de manera inmediata, sin dilación alguna. El ejercicio de este derecho no puede ser afectado, en modo alguno, por la declaración del estado de excepción o de la restricción de garantías constitucionales.

[28] **Artículo 28.-** Toda persona tiene derecho de acceder a la información y a los datos que sobre sí misma o sobre sus bienes consten en registros oficiales o privados, con las excepciones que establezca la ley, así como de conocer el uso que se haga de los mismos y su finalidad, y a solicitar ante el tribunal competente la actualización, la rectificación o la destrucción de aquellos, si fuesen erróneos o afectasen ilegítimamente sus derechos. Igualmente, podrá acceder a documentos de cualquier naturaleza que contengan información cuyo conocimiento sea de interés para comunidades o grupos de personas. Queda a salvo el secreto de las fuentes de información periodística y de otras profesiones que determine la ley.

Article 28. Anyone has the right of access to the information and data concerning him or his goods which are contained in official or private registries, with the exceptions that may be established by statute, as well as to know what use is being made of the same and the purpose thereof, and to petition the competent court for the updating, rectification or destruction of erroneous records and those that unlawfully affect the petitioner's right. The petitioner may also have access to documents of any nature containing information whose knowledge could be of interest to communities or groups of persons. The foregoing is without prejudice to the confidentiality of sources from which information is received by journalists, or secrecy in other professions as may be determined by statute.

According to these constitutional provisions, the «*amparo*» has been consequently regulated *as a constitutional right* of the people, to require the protection of courts to ensure the enjoyment and exercise of *all the rights and guarantees* established by the Constitution or being inherent to the human being, against any distress, whether by public authorities or individuals, by means of proceedings that should be brief and summary, and that allow the judge to immediately restore the infringed legal situation[29].

Hence, the Constitution does not establish only «one» action or writ of protection as a particular remedy, but rather a «right to protection» as a fundamental right which can, and in fact is, exercised through a variety of legal actions and recourses, including a direct «action for protection» of a subsidiary nature.

Thus, the Constitution does not establish just a particular constitutional *adjective* «guarantee» of constitutional rank to protect constitutional rights, but moreover, what it has established is a true «constitutional right», the right of everyone to be protected by the courts in the enjoyment and exercise of their constitutional rights and guarantees. This character of the *amparo*, as a «constitutional right» is the basic element that identifies the Venezuelan institution[30] and that leads to its consideration not as a single action or complaint, but as a right. This criterion was the one that in our opinion, as abovementioned, led the Supreme Court in 1983, to change its criterion established in 1970, regarding the possibility of the exercise of the action for protection, even in the absence of the law regulating and developing the constitutional dispositions on the matter.[31]

The question could be stated as follows: If the norm of Article 49 were to establish an «action or recourse» for protection, then Article 50 of the Constitution which lays down that the absence of laws regulating the exercise of «constitutional rights» would not impede their exercise, would not be applicable[32] on the contrary, if Article 49 of the Constitution was to establish a «fundamental right», as it is

[29] The right of protection (Art. 27 Constitution) is thus different to the broader right to access to justice specifically regulated in Articles 26 and 48 of the Constitution

[30] See Allan R. BREWER-CARÍAS, «El derecho de *amparo* y la acción de *amparo*», in *Revista de derecho público,* N° 22, Editorial Jurídica Venezolana, Caracas, 1985, pp. 51-61.

[31] See Supreme Court of Justice in Político-Administrative Chamber, October 20, 1983, in *Revista de derecho público,* N° 16, Editorial Jurídica Venezolana, Caracas, 1983, p. 169.

[32] See the opinion stated by the Attorney's General Office in *Doctrina de la Procuraduría General de la República 1970,* Caracas, 1971, p. 35.

done, then Article 50 of the Constitution would be applicable,[33] and even without the law of the right of *amparo*, this right could be constitutionally exercised. The latter is the predominant criterion followed by the courts, and in our opinion is the most distinguishable feature of the *amparo* institution in Venezuela.

II. THE INTERNATIONALIZATION OF THE «AMPARO» IN THE LATIN AMERICA

As can be deducted from the constitutional regulations of the «amparo» right, action or recourse in all Latin American Countries, additional to the regulations of the habeas corpus and habeas data recourses, the existence of special judicial means for the protection of human rights can be considered as a general feature of Latin American constitutionalism; with Latin American origin and without real precedents in the historical European regimes.

That is why this characteristic institution of Latin American constitutionalism, was originally regulated in the American Declaration of the Rights and Duties of Man approved by the Ninth International Conference of American States, held in Bogotá, Colombia, in April 1948, in which Article 18 set forth:

> **Article XVIII.** Every person may resort to the courts to ensure respect for his legal rights. There should likewise be available to him a simple, brief procedure whereby the courts will protect him (*lo ampare*) from acts of authority that, to his prejudice, violate any fundamental constitutional rights[34].
>
> A similar regulation was later incorporated in Article 8 of the Universal Declaration of Human Rights adopted by United Nations in December the same year 1948. In the English version of the Declaration, Article 8 just states that: «Everyone has the right to an effective remedy by the competent national tribunals for acts violating the fundamental rights granted to him by the constitution or by law». Nonetheless, in the Spanish version, the wording is nearest to the American Declaration wording:
>
> **Article 8,** Toda persona tiene derecho a un recurso efectivo, ante los tribunales nacionales competentes, *que la ampare* contra actos que violen sus derechos fundamentales reconocidos por la constitución o por la ley.

A free English translation of this text will show not only a right to an effective remedy but a right to an effective remedy for the protection of human rights: «Every person has the right to an effective recourse before the national competent courts, for his protection (*que la ampare*) against acts that violate his fundamental rights recognized in the Constitution and in statutes».

---

[33] See J.R. QUINTERO «Recurso de *amparo*. La cuestión central en dos sentencias y un Voto Salvado» in *Revista de la Facultad de Derecho*, N° 9, Universidad Católica Andrés Bello, Caracas, 1969-1970, pp. 161-162-166. See the judicial decision and its dissident opinion in pp. 180-206. See the text also in O. MARÍN GÓMEZ, *Protección procesal de las garantías constitucionales de Venezuela. Amparo y Habeas Corpus*, Caracas, 1983, pp. 229-250.

[34] The Spanish vesion of article 18 is as follow: Derecho de justicia: Artículo XVIII: Toda persona puede ocurrir a los tribunales para hacer valer sus derechos. Asimismo debe disponer de un procedimiento sencillo y breve por el cual la justicia *lo ampare* contra actos de la autoridad que violen, en perjuicio suyo, alguno de los derechos fundamentales consagrados constitucionalmente.

After this first International Declarations, in 1950 the European Convention on Human Rights, which was the first international convention on human rights, also regulated the right to effective recourses in cases of violations of human rights, as follows:

> **Article 13.** Everyone whose rights and freedoms as set forth in this Convention are violated shall have an effective remedy before a national authority notwithstanding that the violation has been committed by persons acting in an official capacity[35].

The 1966 International Covenant on Civil and Political Rights of the United Nations, Article 2,3 also regulated the right to an effective remedy in case of violations of human rights, as follows, by obligating the Stats parties to undertake:

a) To ensure that any person whose rights or freedoms as herein recognized are violated shall have an effective remedy, notwithstanding that the violation has been committed by persons acting in an official capacity;

b) To ensure that any person claiming such a remedy shall have his right thereto determined by competent judicial, administrative or legislative authorities, or by any other competent authority provided for by the legal system of the State, and to develop the possibilities of judicial remedy;

c) To ensure that the competent authorities shall enforce such remedies when granted[36].

Finally, the 1969 American Convention on Human Rights declared the right to judicial protection, or more precisely, to the «amparo» recourse, as follows:

> **Article 25.** Right to Judicial Protection
>
> 1. Everyone has the right to simple and prompt recourse, or any other effective recourse, to a competent court or tribunal for protection (que la ampare) against acts that violate his fundamental rights recognized by the constitution or laws of the state concerned or by this Convention, even though such violation may have been committed by persons acting in the course of their official duties.

---

35 The Spanish version of article 13 is: **Artículo 13. Derecho a un recurso efectivo**. Toda persona cuyos derechos y libertades reconocidos en el presente Convenio hayan sido violados tiene derecho a la concesión de un recurso efectivo ante una instancia nacional, incluso cuando la violación haya sido cometida por personas que actúen en el ejercicio de sus funciones oficiales.

36 The Spanish version is: Article 2,3. Cada uno de los Estados Partes en el presente Pacto se compromete a garantizar que:
a) Toda persona cuyos derechos o libertades reconocidos en el presente Pacto hayan sido violados podrá interponer un recurso efectivo, aun cuando tal violación hubiera sido cometida por personas que actuaban en ejercicio de sus funciones oficiales;
b) La autoridad competente, judicial, administrativa o legislativa, o cualquiera otra autoridad competente prevista por el sistema legal del Esta do, decidirá sobre los derechos de toda persona que interponga tal recurso, y desarrollará las posibilidades de recurso judicial;
c) Las autoridades competentes cumplirán toda decisión en que se haya estimado procedente el recurso.

2. The States Parties undertake:

   a. to ensure that any person claiming such remedy shall have his rights determined by the competent authority provided for by the legal system of the state;

   b. to develop the possibilities of judicial remedy; and

   c. to ensure that the competent authorities shall enforce such remedies when gran-ted[37].

1. The «amparo» in the American Convention on Human Rights

This article of the American Convention regulates the «amparo» recourse for the protection of human rights, as their judicial guarantee *par excellence*, both those regulated in the Constitutions and other internal legal regulations of the Party States, as well as those listed in international declarations. That is why the Inter American Court on Human Rights has considered this Article 25 as a «general provision that gives expression to the procedural institution known as «amparo», which is a simple and prompt remedy designated for the protection of all of the rights recognized in the Constitution and laws of the States parties and by the Convention»; thus, that «can be applied to all rights»[38].

But the American Convention, in Article 7 regarding the right to personal liberty and security, also provides for the recourse of habeas corpus as follows:

> 6. Anyone who is deprived of his liberty shall be entitled to recourse to a competent court, in order that the court decides without delay on the lawfulness of his arrest or detention and order his release if the arrest or detention is unlawful. In States Parties whose laws provide that anyone who believes himself to be threatened with deprivation of his liberty is entitled to recourse to a competent court in order that it decides on the lawfulness of such threat, this remedy may not be restricted or abolished. The interested party or another person on his behalf is entitled to seek these remedies.

Examining the habeas corpus and the «amparo» together, it is possible to conclude, as asserted by the Inter American Court on Human Rights,

> «that '«amparo»' comprises a whole series of remedies and that habeas corpus is but one of its components. An examination of the essentials aspects of both

[37] The Spanish version is as follows: **Artículo 25. Protección Judicial.** Toda persona tiene derecho a un recurso sencillo y rápido o a cualquier otro recurso efectivo ante los jueces o tribunales competentes, *que la ampare* contra actos que violen sus derechos fundamentales reconocidos por la Constitución, la ley o la presente Convención, aun cuando tal violación sea cometida por personas que actúen en ejercicio de sus funciones oficiales.
Los Estados partes se comprometen:
a) a garantizar que la autoridad competente prevista por el sistema legal del Estado decidirá sobre los derechos de toda persona que interponga tal recurso;
b) a desarrollar las posibilidades de recurso judicial, y
c) a garantizar el cumplimiento, por las autoridades competentes, de toda decisión en que se haya estimado procedente el recurso.

[38] See Advisory Opinion OC-8/8 Habeas corpus in emergency situations), paragraph 32. (El artículo 25,1 de la Convención es una disposición de carácter general que recoge la institución procesal del «amparo», como procedimiento sencillo y breve que tiene por objeto la tutela de los derechos fundamentales»).

guarantees, as embodied in the Convention and, in their different forms, in the legal systems of the States parties, indicates that in some instances habeas corpus functions are an independent remedy. Here its primary purpose is to protect the personal freedom of those who are being detained or who have been threatened with detention. In other circumstances, however, habeas corpus is viewed either as the «»amparo» of freedom» or as an integral part of «amparo»[39].

These regulations can be considered the culmination of the process of internationalization of the constitutionalization of human rights, in particular regarding the provision of specific judicial means for their protection. So, if it is true that since the XIX Century, the «amparo» and habeas corpus recourses or actions, were initially regulated in many Latin American Constitutions; since the seventies, they have now passed to be regulated in a general way in an International Convention that has been ratified by all Latin American Countries, where, in general terms -as has been previously analyzed, it has been recognized as having constitutional o supra statutorily rank. Regarding both guarantees the Inter American Court of Human Rigts, has considered «the writs of habeas corpus and of «amparo» among those judicial remedies that are essential for the protection of various rights whose derogation is prohibited by Article 27 (2) and that serve, moreover, to preserve legality in a democratic society»[40].

After its ratification, it has been the Convention the one that has pushed for the subsequent process of constitucionalization of the internationalization of the «amparo», being the inspiration for many of the new Latin America constitutionals reforms or regulations, sanctioned during the last two decades, particularly regarding the «amparo» recourse.

Nowadays, therefore, the right to a judicial guaranty of human rights («amparo» and habeas corpus) set forth in the American Convention is also an international obligation imposed on the States Parties to guarantee their peoples these effective protective remedies of their human rights. This goes so far as to the point that lack of internal regulations and effective function, constitutes a breach of the Convention.

Referring in particular to the «amparo», from what it is set forth in Article 25 of the American Convention, as well as from the regulations of the other international instruments on human rights, the internationalization of the «amparo» recourse has concluded in the design of a specific remedy for the protection of human rights, considered by the Inter American Court on Human Rights, as «one of the basic pillars not only of the American Convention, but of the rule of Law in a democratic society»[41]; which can be characterized by the following elements:

First, in the American Convention the «amparo» is conceived as a specific judicial recourse or action, that is, as a judicial guaranty; but it is also conceived as

---

39 Advisory Opinion OC-8//87 of January 30, 1987 (Habeas Corpus in Emergency Situations), paragraph 34.

40 Advisory Opinion OC-8/87 of January 30, 1987 (Habeas Corpus in Emergency Situation), paragraph 42; Advisory Opinion OC-9/87 of October 6, 1987 (Judicial Guarantees in Status of Emergency), paragraph 33.

41 See Case: *Castillo Páez*, p. 83; Caso: *Suárez Roseo*, p. 65 and caso: *Blake*, p. 102. See the referentes in Cecilia MEDINA QUIROGA, *La Convención Americana: teoría y jurisprudencia*, IIDH, San José, 2003, p. 358.

a fundamental human right in itself, that is to say, the right of citizens to be protected by the Judiciary;

Second, the remedy is conceived to protect all human rights recognized in the Constitutions, in the statutes or in the international instruments;

Third, the recourse in order to seek the judicial protection must be simple, brief and effective;

Fourth, the recourse can be brought before the competent courts, which must be independent and autonomous according to the general terms of the international instruments;

Fifth, the protection refers to any kind of violations of human rights, thus produced by acts issued by private individuals as well as by public officials, even when acting in the course of their official duties;

Sixth, the effectiveness of the recourse is related to the effective repair of the offence by means of the enforcement of the judicial decision by the competent authorities.

The most important consequence of the internationalization of the «amparo», is that according to Article 1,1 of the Convention, the States Parties are obligated not only «*to respect*» the right to «amparo» recognized herein, but also «*to ensure* to all persons subject to their jurisdiction the free and full exercise» of such right, without any discrimination. This «implies the duty of States parties to organize the governmental apparatus and, in general, all the structures through which public power is exercised, so that they are capable of ensuring the free and full enjoyment of human rights»[42].

The actions of the State Parties in order to comply with this obligation are not only formal ones, in the sense that it «is not fulfilled by the existence of a legal system designed to make it possible to comply with this obligation, it also requires the government to conduct itself so as to effectively ensure the free and full exercise of human rights»[43]. On the contrary, as stressed by the Inter American Court on Human Rights, referring to the «amparo» as a judicial guaranty of human rights,

> «for such a remedy to exist, it is not sufficient that it be provided for by the Constitution or by law or that it be formally recognized, but rather it must be truly effective in establishing whether there has been a violation of human rights and in providing redress»[44].

2. The meaning of the regulation of the «amparo» in the American Convention

As mentioned before, Article 25 of the Convention provides that everyone has the right to simple and prompt recourse, or any other effective recourse, to a competent court or tribunal for protection (*que la ampare*) against acts that violate his fundamental rights recognized by the Constitution or laws of the state concerned and by the American Convention itself.

---

42 Case: *Velásquez Rodríguez,* Judgement July, 29, 1988, Paragraph 166.

43 *Idem,* paragrapf 167.

44 Advisory Opinión OC-9/87 of October 6, 1987 (Judicial Guarantees in Status of Emergency), paragraph 24. See in similar sense, Case: *Comunidad Mayagna (Sumo) Awas Tingni,* paragraph 113; Caso: *Ivcher Bronstein,* paragraph 136; Caso: *Cantoral benavides,* paragraph 164; caso: *Durand y Ugarte,* paragraph 102.

From this precise provision derives the framework that this action for the protection of fundamental rights should have in internal law[45] and which demands constitutionalization strategies for different countries in which Constitutions establish what could be considered restrictions to the exercise of the right to «amparo».

3. The «amparo» as a Human Right

Firstly, the American Convention conceives the «amparo» as a human right in itself, when providing that everybody «has the right» to a recourse. This does not mean that people only have a specific adjective law instrument for the protection of other rights, but that everyone has a human right in itself to obtain constitutional protection or «amparo» regarding all human rights.

Thus, we are in fact in the presence of a human right of the people to have at their disposal an effective, simple and prompt judicial means for the protection of their rights; which additionally, is considered in the Convention as one of the «fundamental» rights that cannot be suspended or restricted in cases of state of emergency.

Article 27 of the Convention allows that in time of war, public danger, or other emergency that threatens the independence or security of a State Party, certain measures to be taken derogating its obligations under the Convention to the extent and for the period of time strictly required by the exigencies of the situation, provided that such measures are not inconsistent with its other obligations under international law and do not involve discrimination on the ground of race, color, sex, language, religion, or social origin. In paragraph 2 of the same article, it set forth that

> «The foregoing provision does not authorize any suspension of the following articles: Article 3 (Right to juridical personality), Article 4 (Right to life), Article 5 (Right to humane treatment), Article 6 (Freedom from slavery), Article 9 (Freedom from ex post facto laws), Article 12 (Freedom of conscience and religion), Article 17 (Rights of the family), Article 18 (Right to a name), Article 19 (Rights of the child), Article 20 (Right to nationality), and Article 23 (Right to participate in Government), or of the judicial guarantees essential for the protection of such rights».

The Inter American Court on Human Rights has issued two Advisory Opinions on the matter regarding the possibility of the suspension of the «amparo» and habeas corpus provisions, having concluded that «the suspension of the legal remedies of habeas corpus or of «amparo» in emergency situations cannot be deemed to be compatible with the international obligations imposed on these States by the Convention»[46], being incompatible with «legality in a democratic society» which must be preserved[47].

---

[45] *Véase* Allan R. BREWER-CARÍAS, «El «*amparo*» en América Latina: La universalización del régimen de la Convención Americana sobre Derechos Humanos y la necesidad de superar las restricciones nacionales» in *Ética y Jurisprudencia,* 1/2003, Enero-Diciembre, Universidad Valle del Momboy, Facultad de Ciencias Jurídicas y Políticas, Centro de Estudios Jurídicos «Cristóbal Mendoza», Valera, Estado Trujillo, 2004, pp. 9-34.

[46] Advisory Opinion OC-8//87 of January 30, 1987 (Habeas Corpus in Emergency Situations), paragraph 43.

[47] *Idem,* paragraph 42.

But in spite of the American Convention provision considering the «amparo» as a human right, it is true that in the majority of internal legislation of Latin American Countries, the «amparo» has not been provided as a constitutional right in itself and it has taken the form of, rather, been regulated as an specific adjective action. In other words, the «amparo» has been regulated as a specific remedy or judicial means of protection, either a recourse of «amparo», «tutela» or protection, or as an action of *habeas corpus* or *habeas data*.

Instead, the American Convention sets forth the judicial protection of human rights, by mean of a prompt, simple and effective remedy that could be not only the specific action of «amparo» or habeas corpus, but another judicial mean, such as it occurs in countries where an «action of «amparo»» is not specifically regulated, as it is the case in the United States, England, France or Italy; but where although no legal means called «action of «amparo»» exist, there are nevertheless adequate mechanisms for the effective protection of human rights by means of ordinary judicial remedies. Nonetheless, it can be said that in some Latin American countries, following the orientation of the American Convention and, moreover, in advance of the adoption of such Convention, the «amparo» was conceived as a constitutional right in itself, and it has been developed with those characteristics, such as in the case of México and Venezuela and also in the case of Colombia.

4. The «amparo» as a judicial guarantee

Secondly, the recourse of «amparo» enshrined in Article 25 of the Convention devoted to regulate the «Right to judicial protection», must of course always be a judicial mean of protection. This feature differentiates the provisions of the American Convention from those of the International Covenant on Civil and Political Rights (Article 2,3) and of the European Convention on Human Rights, which only provides for an effective recourse, without qualifying it as «judicial».

The judicial protection mechanisms referred to such article of the American Convention is undoubtedly inspired in the Latin American action of «amparo», but it can be said that its scope may be wider. It comprises of course the Colombian action of tutela and the Chilean action of protection, but it also comprises all other judicial remedies that in an effective, simple and prompt way can protect human rights. The Convention speaks of an effective, prompt and simple means that may be of any type. Therefore, in fact, it can be any effective judicial means, and not necessarily a single and unique action of «amparo». In other words, the Convention not necessarily refers to an only and single judicial remedy, but rather that there can and must be a collection also effective, of ordinary legal means for the protection of human rights. That is why, regarding «amparo», in general terms most of the Latin American legislations set forth that this specific means has a subordinate nature, in the sense that it proceeds only when there are no other effective judicial means that can protect human rights; in similar sense than the subordinate character the Anglo-American injunction has.

On the other hand, referring to the judicial character of the action or recourse, the Convention also set forth that they can be brought before the «competent courts», thus being the intention of the Convention to set forth an essential function of the Judiciary, as also happens, for instance, under the Anglo-American systems, where the «amparo» exists in the various writs of injunctions, but without being named as such. In these systems judges routinely issue *mandamus*, *injunction* and *prohibition* orders or decisions, equivalent to the «»amparos» in Latin America. However, this is part of the routine actions of the Judiciary, without it being a specific judicial mean.

On the other hand, when the American Convention refers to the «competent courts» in order to decide «amparo» remedies, it is not referring to only one specific court, but to all the Judiciary. That is why, pursuant to the Convention and Latin American tradition, competence in «amparo» matters are in general essentially belonging to the Judiciary, in the sense that such competence shall belong to «the tribunals» - to all of them and not just one of them-, which is in fact a characteristic of the European model, in particular that of Germany and Spain, where competence in «amparo» matters is held by one single Tribunal, the Constitutional Tribunal.

Unfortunately, however, this reduction of the judicial competence to constitutionally protect through an «amparo» has occurred in some Latin American countries, upon assigning it to one single tribunal, particularly the Supreme Court. This is the case of the Constitutional Chamber of the Supreme Courts of Costa Rica, El Salvador and Nicaragua, where such courts are the exclusively competent to hear the recourse of «amparo».

Whatever the case, and apart from the examples mentioned, in all other countries of Latin America, judicial competence in matters of «amparo» is diffused, in the sense that it is a power that is attributed, generally speaking, to the courts of first instance or circumscription courts, but it is not concentrated in one single institution. What the concentration of the hearing of the «amparo» in one single judicial institution finally does is to restrict access to justice for the effective protection of rights.

5. The «amparo» as a simple, prompt and effective judicial guarantee

Thirdly, in any case, the judicial recourse that the Convention guarantees, as set forth in Article 25 and as has been stressed by the Inter American Court on Human Rights, must be all together «simple, prompt and effective»[48].

Regarding the simplicity, it refers to a procedure that must lack the dilatory procedural formalities of ordinary judicial means, imposed by the need to grant a constitutional -not ordinary- protection; and regarding the prompt character of the recourse, the Inter American court has argued about the need for a reasonable delay for the decision, not considering «prompt» recourses which were resolved after «a long time»[49].

The effective character of the recourse refers to the fact that it will be capable to produce the results for which it has been created[50]; in words of the Inter American Court on Human Rigths,

> «it must be truly effective in establishing whether there has been a violation of human rights and in providing redress. A remedy which proves illusory because of the general conditions prevailing in the country, or even in the particular circumstances of a given case, cannot be considered effective. That

[48] Case: *Suárez Romero,* Paragraph 66.
[49] Case: *Ivcher Bronstein,* paragraph 140.
[50] Inter American Court on Human Rights, case: *Velásquez Rodríguez,* paragraph 66.

could be the case, for example, when practice has shown its ineffectiveness: when the Judicial Power lacks the necessary independence to render impartial decisions or the means to carry out its judgments; or in any other situation that constitutes a denial of justice, as there is an unjustified delay in the decision; or when, for any reason, the alleged victim is denied access to a judicial remedy» [51].

Thus, it is not enough for being effective that a recourse be regulated in internal law for the purpose of protecting human rights, being necessary the existence of basic conditions to function and be applied with the expected results. In this regard, for a judicial recourse to be effective, above all is necessary for the Judiciary to be really independent and autonomous, so for instance in the case Ivcher Bronstein, the Inter American Court decided that in Perú at the time, the conditions of independence and autonomy of the court were not satisfied in the national proceeding, so the recourses that the plaintiff had had not been effective»[52]. The Inter American Court has also considered that a recourse is not effective when impartiality lacks in the corresponding court[53].

6. The «amparo» as a judicial guarantee for the protection of everyone's rights and guarantees

Fourthly, it should be emphasized that the Convention regulates a right that is guaranteed to «everyone», that is to say, everybody in the very broadest sense, without distinction or discrimination of any kind: individuals, nationals, foreigners, legally able or not, corporations or entities of public or private law.

It is true that Article 1,2 of the Convention sets forth that «for the purposes of this Convention, «person» means every human being». Nonetheless, Article 25 when guaranteeing the judicial protection right refers to such rights as corresponding to everyone and not to every person, so that regarding internal national law, artificial persons or legal entities have the right to the «amparo» recourse for the protection of their rights, like for instance, the due process of law and non discrimination rights.

But setting forth the «amparo» as a judicial remedy for the protection of any person or entity, that is to say, as a personal remedy, its results in principle, benefit the plaintiff, so that the effects of the «amparo» do not extend to third parties.

This feature gives rise, firstly, to the problem of the protection of collective rights, an initiative attributed in some legislation to the Ombudsmen or Defenders of Human Rights. But the fact is that it has been progressively admitted in much internal statutes, the possibility for the communities to exercise the action of «amparo», when collective constitutional rights are being violated. Additionally, as a consequence of reforms tending to increase citizens access to justice, some statutes have set forth remedies for the protection of diffuse or widespread interests, particularly in regard to third generation rights, such as the protection of the environment or consumers rights.

---

51 Advisory Opinión OC-9/87 of October 6, 1987 (Judicial Guarantees in Status of Emergency), paragraph 24.

52 Case: *Ivcher Bronstein*, paragraph 139.

53 Case: *Tribunal Constitucional* paragraph 96.

In this sense, the standing to bring the action before the courts has being gradually constructed to allow interested parties to act in representation of diffuse or collective interests, when dealing with constitutional rights, the violation of which affects the community as a whole. In certain Constitutions, such as the Venezuelan Constitution of 1999, there is already no question regarding the possibility of exercising the recourse of «amparo» to protect collective and diffuse rights, already widely developed by case law. Some statutes have even expressly provided such protection, as occurs with the Organic statute for the Protection of the Child and the Teenagers, where a «recourse of protection» is regulated. This recourse may be brought before the Tribunal for the Protection of the Child and the Teenagers «against facts, acts or omissions of individuals, public and private entities and institutions that threaten or violate collective or diffuse (widespread) rights of the children and teenagers» (Article 177,5 and 318).

Another aspect related to the standing to file the action of «amparo», as previously mentioned, related to the assertion of the American Conventions that the right to «amparo» is held by everyone, is the question of whether the public entities can be plaintiff on matters of «amparo». Public entities also have constitutional rights, such as the right to non discrimination, right to due process or right to own defense. Therefore, public entities are perfectly entitled to bring actions, so that the action of «amparo» is not only conceived as actions against the State.

In some countries it may even be considered that there is a constitutional «amparo» set forth in benefit of political entities, as the States and Municipal government in a Federation, when the respective Constitution guarantees their autonomy. In these cases, the constitutional guarantee set forth in the constitutional texts with respect to territorial autonomy, can also be the object of an action for protection, as has been admitted in México and Germany.

But in other countries, as has been the case in Venezuela, even if the constitutional guarantee of municipal autonomy has been judicially discussed at the Supreme Court, the Constitutional Chamber in a restrictive interpretation has rejected the admissibility of the «amparo» action for such purposes, adopting a restrictive scope rule confining «amparo» only to constitutional rights and not to constitutional territorial guaranties[54].

7. The «amparo» as a judicial guarantee for the protection of all constitutional rights and guarantees

Fifthly, pursuant to the Convention this right to an effective judicial means of protection before the courts, is established for the protection of all the constitutional rights contained in the Convention, the Constitution and statutes or those that are inherent to the human person. Therefore all rights established in international instruments are also entitled to protection. Thus the open clauses of the constitutional rights acquires here all their value, protecting them even when they are not listed in the texts, but which are subject to constitutional protection since they are inherent to the human person and human dignity.

---

[54] See Decision N° 1395 of November 11, 2000 (Case: *Gobernación del Estado Mérida y otros vs. Ministerio de Finanzas*), in *Revista de Derecho Público*, N° 84, Editorial Jurídica Venezolana, Caracas, 2000, pp. 317 ff.

Consequently, according to the American Convention, all rights can be protected by means of «amparo» actions. As mentioned, those declared in the texts of the Constitutions, of the statutes, of the American Convention, as well as those that are inherent to the human person. As has been stated by the Inter-American Court of Human Rights in its *Advisory Opinion* (OC-8/87) analyzing Article 25,1 of the Convention: «The above text is a general provision that gives expression to the procedural institution known as «»amparo»», which is a simple and prompt remedy designed for the protection *of all of the rights* recognized by the constitutions and laws of the States Parties and by the Convention».[55]

Therefore, pursuant to the Inter-American system, there is a complete and unlimited catalogue of the rights to be protected. However, in some cases, perhaps because of the influence of the European model of «amparo» recourse, particularly the one regulated by Germany and Spain, the rights protected by mean of «amparo» have been reduced to some of the rights listed in the constitutional text. Is the case, for example, of the German Constitution, which only admits the action of «amparo» for what it calls «fundamental rights», which constitutes only one species of the constitutional rights. In Spain too, the rights that may be protected by an «amparo» recourse are those expressly listed as «fundamental».

None of the above can be derived from the American Convention or from the majority of Latin American Constitutions, wherein all constitutional rights are subject to «amparo». Therefore it may be said that the Constitutions that establish a determined array of rights that are to be protected by means of a recourse to «amparo», are incompatible with the international obligations that are imposed on such States by the Convention. The American Convention does not allow the exclusion of constitutional protection by means of the «amparo» of determined constitutional rights, or in other words, it does not allow that the «amparo» be reduced to a protection only in respect of determined rights declared in a Constitution.

Consequently, systems such as those regulated by the constitutional texts of Chile and Colombia may be considered to be incompatible with the American Convention. In fact, in the case of Chile, the Constitution lists the rights that may be the object of recourse to protection (Article 20), and in the case of Colombia, the Constitution also includes a list of the «fundamental rights» that may be the object of protection. However, the courts in Colombia have fortunately been gradually correcting this restriction through constitutional interpretation, in such a way that today, due to the interrelation, universality, indivisibility and interdependence of rights, there are almost no constitutional rights that can not be protected by means of the action of «tutela».

In contrast to such cases of restrictive constitutional provisions on constitutional rights that may be the object of protection by means of a recourse to «amparo», «tutela» or protection, there are other Constitutions that expressly set forth as being within the scope of protected rights not only all constitutional rights, but also those that are declared in the international system of protection of human rights. This is the case, for example, of the Constitution of Costa Rica, which lists among the rights subject to protection by recourse of «amparo» those rights «of a fundamental nature established in the international instruments on human rights, applicable to the Republic» (Article 48).

---

[55] Advisory Opinion OC-8/87 (Habeas Corpus in Emergency Situations), paragraph 32.

In an even broader sense, the 1999 Constitution of Venezuela expressly states that the right to «amparo» includes protection of «constitutional rights and guarantees, even those that are inherent to the human person and which do not expressly figure in this Constitution or in the international instruments of human rights» (Article 27), which must be interpreted to mean that not only the constitutional rights and guarantees and those listed in international instruments are subject to protection, but also all those inherent to the human person, even when they are not expressly listed in the Constitution itself or in international instruments.

8. The «amparo» as a judicial guarantee for the protection of all constitutional rights and guarantees, against any violation or harm from the State or individuals

Sixthly, the protection that the Convention regulates is against any act, omission, fact or action that violates human rights and, of course, which threatens to violate them too, because it is not necessary to wait for the violation before being able to have recourse to the means of protection. This implies that this means of protection has to be able to exist before the violation occurs, when there is a real threat of such violation and, of course, before any violation or threat of violation, no matter who is the author. This is to say that no action or omission that could imply a violation of rights, shall be excluded from the «amparo», whether it emanates from individuals or from the authorities under any guise whatsoever, be it a statute, an administrative act, a judicial decision, a *fait accompli*, an action or an omission, or just a fact.

All this implies that the recourse of «amparo» can be brought before the courts against any persons. It must be remembered that the recourse of «amparo» was always originally conceived as a judicial means of protection against the State, precisely because human rights were initially conceived regarding the State, and as a limit to the actions of public entities. However, the progressive universalization of human rights as inherent to the human person, independently of who must respect them, the scope of protection has been widening, to the point of admitting that the «amparo» can also be a recourse against private individuals. Thus, pursuant to the American Convention, which makes no distinction in this regard, the «amparo» proceeds not only against impairment of human rights originated by a public entity, but also by a private individual.

In this regard, it may be said that the action of «amparo» against individuals in Latin America is broadly admitted, following a trend that began in Latin America, more precisely in Argentina in the 50s, when the possibility of exercising a recourse of «amparo» against individuals was admitted. This situation is in sharp contrast with what occurs in Europe where the «amparo» is essentially only exercised against the public authorities.

Nevertheless, certain restriction of this principle of universality of «amparo» that is a characteristic of Latin America can be found in some Constitutions that set forth that «amparo» can only proceed regarding certain individuals, such as those who act as agents exercising public functions, or who exercise some kind of prerogative, or who are in a position of control, for example, when rendering public services, by mean of a concession. This is the case, for example, in Costa Rica, Guatemala and Colombia.

Other countries following the European model as is the case of México, Brazil, Panama, El Salvador and Nicaragua simply excluded any possibility of filing a recourse of «amparo» against private individuals; a situation distant itself from the orientation of the American Convention.

But regarding the constitutional protection against actions of the State, another scope of reduction of «amparo» that contrasts with the universality deriving from the American Convention, refers to the acts of the authorities that may be challenged by means of a recourse of «amparo». Pursuant to the American Convention and the universal shaping of the recourse of «amparo», there cannot and must not exist a single State act that escapes its scope. If the «amparo» is a legal means for the protection of human rights, it is and has to be against any public action that violates them, and therefore it cannot be conceived that there can be certain acts of the State that are excluded from the possibility to be challenged by amparo.

Nevertheless, a tendency towards exclusions can be identified in Latin America in different aspects:

In some cases, the exclusion refers to actions of certain public authorities, such as the electoral authorities, whose actions, in some countries like Perú, Costa Rica and Uruguay, are expressly excluded from the recourse of «amparo».

In other cases, Perú also as an example, exclusion from the scope of constitutional protection of the «amparo» is provided with respect to the acts of the National Council of the Judiciary.

On the other hand, the exclusion from the scope of protection of the recourse of «amparo» can refer to certain State actions, as happened with regard to the statutes and judicial decisions. Some countries, for example, Colombia, Brazil and Uruguay, exclude the possibility of filing the recourse of «amparo» against statutes, that is, in general terms against regulations. In contrast, in other countries «amparo» against statutes is admitted as is the case of México, where the «amparo» against statutes began, even if in certain cases this requires self-application of the statute. In Venezuela, even though according to the Organic Statute of «amparo» the recourse is widely admitted against statutes, the Supreme Court has also developed the need for the statute to be self-applicable, in order to admit the «amparo» remedy.

In other cases, the restriction of «amparo» refers to judicial decisions. In principle, when judges decide particular cases, they too can infringe constitutional rights; and no judge is empowered to violate a constitutional right in his decisions. Therefore the recourse of «amparo», must also be admitted against judicial decisions. Nonetheless, in some countries the recourse of «amparo» against judicial decisions is expressly excluded, as is the case of Argentina, Uruguay, Costa Rica, Panama, El Salvador and Nicaragua. Yet, in other countries, like Colombia, although it is expressly regulated the admission of «amparo» against judicial decisions, in 1992, an unfortunate decision considered its admissibility as contrary to the principle of *res judicata*, so the Constitutional Court annulled the respective article of the statute[56]. But in spite of the annulment, progressively, all the main courts and the Council of State have admitted the action of «amparo» against judicial decisions, on the grounds of their arbitrary content (judicial *voi de fait*)[57].

---

[56] See Decision C-543, September 24, 1992 in Manuel José CEPEDA, *Derecho Constitucional Jurisprudencial. Las grandes decisiones de la Corte Constitucional*, Legis, Bogotá, 2001, pp. 1009 ff.

[57] See Decision T-231, May 13, 1994 in Manuel José CEPEDA, *Derecho Constitucional Jurisprudencial. Las grandes decisiones de la Corte Constitucional*, Legis, Bogotá, 2001, pp. 1022 ff.

9. The «amparo» as a judicial guarantee that can be filed at any time, including in situations of emergency

Seventhly and finally, the «amparo» recourse as well as the habeas corpus, are judicial means of protection that can be filed by the interested party at any time, without exception. Particularly, the right cannot be limited because of exceptional situations or states of emergency.

In particular, it must be mentioned that Article 27,1 of the American Convention allows that in time of war, public danger, or other emergency that threatens the independence or security of a State Party, «it may take measures derogating from its obligations under the present Convention to the extent and for the period of time strictly required by the exigencies of the situation, provided that such measures are not inconsistent with its other obligations under international law and do not involve discrimination on the ground of race, color, sex, language, religion, or social origin».

Nonetheless, in Article 27,2 it is expressly provided that no suspension at all is allowed regarding the following rights: right to juridical personality (Article 3); right to life (Article 4); right to humane treatment (Article 5); freedom from slavery (Article 6); freedom from ex post facto laws (Article 9); freedom of conscience and religion (Article 12); rights of the family (Article 17); right to a name (Article 18); rights of the child (Article 19); right to nationality (Article 20): and right to participate in Government (Article 23), «or of the judicial guarantees essential for the protection of such rights». Thus, the right to judicial protection of all those rights by means of «amparo» and habeas corpus cannot be suspended in situations of emergency.

The Inter-American Court of Human Rights in its *Advisory Opinion* (OC-8/87) of January 30, 1987 (Habeas Corpus in Emergency Situations) has referred to the question of whether habeas corpus as a judicial remedy «may remain in effect as a means of ensuring individual liberty even during states of emergency, despite the fact that Article 7 is not listed among the provisions that may not be suspended in exceptional circumstances». The Court concluded that if the exercise of State powers even in states of emergency has limits, «it follows that writs of habeas corpus and of «amparo» are among those judicial remedies that are essential for the protection of various rights whose derogation is prohibited by Article 27(2) and that serve, moreover, to preserve legality in a democratic society». Therefore, the Court ruled that «the Constitutions and legal systems of the States Parties that authorize, expressly or by implication, the suspension of the legal remedies of habeas corpus or of «amparo» in emergency situations cannot be deemed to be compatible with the international obligations imposed on these States by the Convention»[58].

Afterwards, the Inter-American Court of Human Rights in its Advisory Opinion (OC-9/87) of October 6, 1987 (Judicial Guarantees in States of Emergency) emphasizes its ruling, holding that «the judicial guarantees essential for the protection of the human rights not subject to derogation, according to Article 27(2) of the Convention, are those to which the Convention expressly refers in Articles 7(6) and 25(1), considered within the framework and the principles of Article 8, and also those necessary to the preservation of the rule of law, even during the state of

[58] Advisory Opinion oc-8/87 of January 30, 1987 (Habeas corpus in emergency situations), Paragraph 37, 42 and 43.

exception that results from the suspension of guarantees»[59]. Thus, the final Opinion of the Court was:

1. That the «essential» judicial guarantees which are not subject to derogation, according to Article 27(2) of the Convention, include habeas corpus (Art. 7(6)), «amparo», and any other effective remedy before judges or competent tribunals (Art. 25(1)), which is designed to guarantee the respect of the rights and freedoms whose suspension is not authorized by the Convention.
2. That the «essential» judicial guarantees which are not subject to suspension, include those judicial procedures, inherent to representative democracy as a form of government (Art. 29(c)), provided for in the laws of the States Parties as suitable for guaranteeing the full exercise of the rights referred to in Article 27(2) of the Convention and whose suppression or restriction entails the lack of protection of such rights.
3. That the above judicial guarantees should be exercised within the framework and the principles of due process of law, expressed in Article 8 of the Convention[60].

In general terms, the foregoing is the parameter that the American Convention establishes for the «amparo», and this is precisely what should prevail in the internal legal systems, where a huge effort has to be made from the constitutional perspective in order to adapt the internal regulations to such international system of protection of human rights.

[59] Advisory Opinion oc-9/87 of October 6, 1987 (Judicial Guarantees in States of Emergency), Paragraph 38.

[60] *Idem*, paragraph 41.

CHAPTER V

THE AMPARO AS A CONSTITUTIONAL REMEDY WITHIN THE LATIN AMERICAN DIFFUSE AND CONCENTRATED SYSTEMS OF JUDICIAL REVIEW OF LEGISLATION

I. THE AMPARO AS A SPECIFIC JUDICIAL GUARANTEE FOR THE PROTECTION OF CONSTITUTIONAL RIGHTS AND FREEDOMS AND THE SYSTEMS OF JUDICIAL REVIEW OF LEGISLATION

In contrast to the Mexican and Venezuelan systems of amparo, which comprises the protection of personal freedom (habeas corpus), in the rest of Latin American countries, the amparo and the habeas corpus have been constitutionally regulated as judicial guarantees for the protection of constitutional rights and freedoms, by establishing in both cases a specific recourse or an action for such purpose. These specific means of judicial protection some times are only exercised before one single court; but in the majority of cases, they are exercised before the universe of courts of first instance.

Of course, such specific actions for the protection of constitutional rights and guarantees, are a substantial part of the judicial review systems of legislation that have been developed in Latin America since the XIX century, where it is possible to distinguish tree systems: the ones that apply the diffuse method («American Model») of judicial review; and the ones that apply the concentrated method («Austrian Model») of judicial review; and a last one, typically Latin American, that conforms a mixed system of judicial review in which the diffuse method of judicial review is combined with the concentrated one.

Judicial review of constitutionality[1] is the power of the courts to control the conformity of acts of the state with the Constitution, particularly of legislative acts, issued in direct application of the Constitution. Therefore, in principle, judicial review can only exist in legal systems in which there is a written Constitution, imposing limits on the state organs' activities and within such organs, on Parliament in particular. As a result, the power of the courts to control the constitutionality of state acts is not necessarily a consequence of the sole judicial power, but of the legal

---

1 See Allan R. BREWER-CARÍAS, *Judicial Review in Comparative Law*, Cambridge University Press, Cambridge, 1989.

limitations imposed on state organs, particularly on Parliament and on the government, in a constitution established as a supreme law.

In this sense, judicial review of the constitutionality of state acts is the ultimate consequence of the consolidation of the *rule of law (État de Droit)* where the state organs are not sovereign, are subject to limits imposed by a constitution having the force of a superior law, and in particular, when the legislator is limited in his legislative action and there is judicial control over the «legality of laws».[2]

Therefore, acts of Parliament or Congress must always be submitted to the law, and cannot be contrary to the law. Consequently, the spirit of legality imposes the existence and functioning not only of a control of legality of administrative acts, but also of a control of the legality of laws as acts of Parliament. Only in countries where this control exists, are there truly organized democracies and *État de Droit*.

Therefore, this judicial control of the «legality of laws» is, precisely, the judicial control of the constitutionality of legislation and of other state acts issued in direct execution of the constitution, in relation to which legality means «constitutionality». Thus, there is the existence of judicial review of constitutionality that we are now going to study.

This judicial review of constitutionality is normally possible, of course, not only in those legal systems that have a *written* constitution as a supreme rule embodying the fundamental values of society, but when that superior rule is established in a rigid or entrenched way, in the sense that it cannot be modified by ordinary legislation. In principle, it is in a system of this kind that all the organs of the state are limited by and subject to the constitution and must therefore pursue their activities according to this supreme law.

This implies therefore, that not only are the traditional state organs for executing the law -the administration and the judges- subject to the law (Constitution and «legislation»), but that the organs which create the «legislation», particularly the legislative bodies, are also subject to the constitution.

Of course, a written and rigid constitution, situated at the apex of a legal system, not only demands that all the acts issued by state organs in direct execution thereof should not violate the constitution, but must also provide a guarantee to prevent or sanction such violations.[3] Thus, the judicial review of constitutionality as the power of the judiciary to control the submission of state organs to the superior rule of the country.

Different criteria can be adopted for classifying the various systems of constitutional justice or judicial review of the constitutionality of state acts, particularly of legislation.[4] However, all of them are related to a basic criteria referring to the state organs that can carry out constitutional justice functions.

---

2 *Ibid.* p. 215.

3 *Cf.* H. KELSEN, «La garantie juridictionnelle de la Constitution (La Justice constitutionnelle)» *Revue du droit public et de la science politique en France et à l'étranger*, T. XLV, 1928, pp. 197-257.

4 See in general M. CAPPELLETTI, *Judicial Review in the Contemporary World*, Indianapolis 1971, p. 45 and M. CAPPELLETI and J.C. ADAMS, «Judicial Review of Legislation: European Antecedents and Adaptations», *Harvard Law Review*, 79, 6, April 1966, p. 1207.

In effect, judicial review of constitutionality can be exercised by all the courts of a given country or only by the Supreme Court of the country or by a court specially created for that purpose.

In the first case, all the courts of a given country are empowered to judge the constitutionality of laws. This is the case in the United States of America, thus this system has been identified as the «American model», because it was first adopted in the United States particularly after the famous *Marbury* v. *Madison* case decided by the Supreme Court in 1803. This system is followed in many countries with or without a common law tradition. This is the case, for example, in Argentina, México, Greece, Australia, Canada, India, Japan, Sweden, Norway and Denmark. This system is also qualified as a diffuse system of judicial review of constitutionality,[5] because judicial control belongs to all the courts from the lowest level up to the Supreme Court of the country.

By contrast, there is the concentrated system of judicial review, in which the power to control the constitutionality of legislation and other state organs issued in direct execution of the Constitution is assigned to a single organ of the state, whether to its Supreme Court or to a special court created for that particular purpose. In the latter case, it is also called the Austrian system because it was first established in Austria, in 1920. This system is also called the «European model» and is followed, for instance, in Germany, Italy, and Spain. It is a concentrated system of judicial review, as opposed to the diffuse system, because the power of control over the constitutionality of state acts is given only to one single constitutional body that can be the Supreme Court of a given country or as in the Austrian or European model, to a specially created constitutional court or tribunal, that even though it exercises judicial functions, in general, it is created by the constitution outside ordinary judicial power, as a constitutional organ different to the Supreme Court of the country.

In regard to the judicial organs that can exercise the power of controlling the constitutionality of laws, other countries have adopted a mixture of the above mentioned diffuse and concentrate systems, in the sense that they allow for both types of control at the same time. Such is the case in Colombia and Venezuela where all courts are entitled to judge the constitutionality of laws and therefore decide autonomously upon their inapplicability in a given process, and the Supreme Court has the power to declare the unconstitutionality of laws in an objective process. One can say that these countries have a diffuse and concentrated parallel system of judicial review at one and the same time, perhaps the most complete in comparative law.

But regarding the so-called concentrated systems of judicial review, in which the power of control is given to the Supreme Court or to a constitutional court, other distinctions can be observed.

In the first place, in relation to the moment at which control of the constitutionality of laws is performed, it may be prior to the formal enactment of the particular law, as is the case in France, or the judicial control of the constitutionality of laws which can be exercised by the court after the law has come into effect, as is the case in Germany and Italy.

---

5 M. CAPPELLETTI, «El control judicial de la constitucionalidad de las leyes en el derecho comparado», *Revista de la Facultad de Derecho de México*, 61, 1966, p. 28.

In this respect, other countries have established both possibilities as is the case Spain, Portugal and Venezuela. In the latter, a law sanctioned by Congress prior to its enactment, can be placed by the President of the Republic before the Supreme Court to obtain a decision regarding its constitutionality, and the Supreme Court can also judge the constitutionality of the law after it has been published and has come into legal effect.

Moreover, in relation to the concentrated systems of judicial review, two other types of control can be distinguished regarding the manner in which review is required either incidentally or through an objective action. In the first place, the constitutional question is not considered justiciable unless it is closely and directly related to a particular process, in which the constitutionality of the concrete law is not normally necessary to the unique issue in the process. In this case, judicial control is incidental, and the Supreme Court or constitutional tribunal can only decide when it is required to do so by the ordinary court that has to decide the case. In this situation, it is basically the function of the ordinary courts, upon hearing a concrete case, to place the constitutional issue before the constitutional court.

Of course, the incidental nature of judicial review is essential to diffuse control systems and, therefore, to all legal systems that follow the American model.

But in the field of the concentrated system of judicial review, the control granted to the constitutional court can also be exercised through direct action where the constitutionality of the particular law is the only issue in the process, without reference or relation to a particular process.

In this latter case, another distinction can be made, in relation to the *locus standing* to exercise the direct action of unconstitutionality: in most countries with a concentrated system of judicial review, only other organs of the state can place the direct action of constitutionality before the constitutional court, for instance, the head of government, or a number of representatives in Parliament.

Other systems of concentrated judicial review grant the action of constitutionality to individuals, whether requiring that the particular law affect a fundamental right of the individual, or by means of a popular action, in which any citizen can request the constitutional court or Supreme Court to decide upon his claim concerning the constitutionality of a given law, without particular requirement regarding his standing.

As we have seen, the basic division we can establish regarding the various systems of judicial review, depends in our opinion, upon the concentrated or centralized or diffuse or decentralized character of judicial control of constitutionality, that is to say, when the power of control is given to all the courts of a given country or to one special constitutional court or to the Supreme Court of that country. We have also said that some countries have even adopted both systems of judicial review that developed in parallel. Related to this main classification, as we said, other criteria can be adopted to identify the various systems of judicial control of the constitutionality of laws: the incidental and the principal or objective action systems.

But in relation to the main distinction between the diffuse and concentrated systems of judicial review, we can also distinguish other criteria for classifying the various systems, according to the legal effects given to the particular judicial decision of review.

Within this scope, we can distinguish decisions with *in casu et inter partes* or *erga omnes* effects, that is to say, when the judicial decision has effects only within the parties in a concrete process, or when it has general effects applicable to everyone.

For instance, in the diffused systems of judicial review, according to the American system, the decision of the courts in principle, only has effect relating to the parties of the process; effects that are closely related to the incidental character of judicial review.

Whereas in the concentrated system of judicial review, following the Austrian model, when the judicial decision is a consequence of the exercise of an objective action, the effects of such a decision are general, with *erga omnes* validity.

Thus, in the diffuse systems of judicial review a law declared unconstitutional with *inter partes* effects, is in principle considered null and void, with no effect whatsoever. Therefore, in this case the decision in principle is retroactive in the sense that it has *ex tunc*, or *pro pretaerito* consequences; that is to say, the law declared unconstitutional is considered never to have existed or never to have been valid. Thus, this decision, in principle, has «declarative» effects, in the sense that it declares the pre-existing nullity of the unconstitutional law.

In the concentrated systems of judicial review, on the contrary, a law declared unconstitutional, with *erga omnes* effect, is in principle considered annullable. Therefore, in this case, the decision is prospective, in the sense that has *ex nunc, pro futuro* consequences, that is to say, the law declared unconstitutional is considered as having produced its effect until its annulment by the court, or until the moment determined by the court subsequent to the decision. In this case, therefore the decision has «constitutive» effects, in the sense that the law will become unconstitutional only after the decision has been made.

Nevertheless, this distinction related to the effects of the judicial decision regarding the unconstitutionality of a law is not absolute. On the one hand, if it is true that in the diffuse systems of judicial review, the decision has *inter partes* effects, when the decision is adopted by the Supreme Court, as a consequence of the *stare decisis* doctrine, the practical effects of the decision, in fact, are general, in the sense that it binds all the lower courts of the country. Therefore, as soon as the Supreme Court has declared a law unconstitutional, no other court can apply it.

On the other hand, in concentrated systems of judicial review, when a judicial decision is adopted on an incidental issue of constitutionality, some constitutional systems have established that the effects of that decision are only related in principle, to the particular process in which the constitutionality question was raised, and between the parties of that process, even though this is not the general rule.

In relation to the declarative or constitutive effects of the decision, or its retroactive or prospective effects, the absolute parallelism with the diffuse and concentrated systems has also disappeared.

In the diffuse systems of judicial review, even though the effects of the declarative decisions of unconstitutionality of the law, are *ex tunc, pro pretaerito*, in practice, exceptions have been made in civil cases to allow for the invalidity of the law not to be retroactive. In the same manner, in the concentrated systems of judicial review, even though the effects of the constitutive judicial decisions of unconstitutionality of the law are *ex nunc, pro futuro*, in practice, exceptions were needed to be made in criminal cases to allow for the invalidity of the law to be retroactive, and benefit the accused.

Our purpose in the following parts of the course is to study all these systems of judicial review of constitutionality of state acts, and particularly of legislation in comparative law. To that end we will analyze the most important legal systems in contemporary constitutional law, classifying them in accordance with the main distinctions we have made between the diffuse and the concentrated systems of judicial review.

Following the main distinction of methods of judicial review, and since also the specific actions for protection of constitutional rights and guaranties are means that can serve for judicial review of legislation, we will analyze the regulation of the amparo and habeas corpus actions or recourses in Latin America, classifying the Countries in accordance to the method of judicial review that exists in each of them, as follows:

a) The amparo action in countries with only a diffuse system of judicial review: the case of Argentina.

b) The amparo action in countries with only a concentrated system of judicial review: the case of Costa Rica, El Salvador, Bolivia, Chile, Honduras, Panama, Paraguay and Uruguay.

c) The amparo action in countries with mixed systems (diffuse and concentrated) of judicial review: in addition to México and Venezuela, the case of Nicaragua, Brazil, Colombia, Dominican Republic, Ecuador, Guatemala and Perú.

II. THE AMPARO ACTION IN COUNTRIES WITH ONLY A DIFFUSE SYSTEM OF JUDICIAL REVIEW: THE CASE OF ARGENTINA

Argentina is the only Latin American country where the diffuse method of judicial review remains as the only one established to control the constitutionality of legislation. The other Latin American Countries that have the diffuse method of judicial review, have it mixed with the concentrated method, as is the case of México and Venezuela, already studied, and of Brazil, Colombia, Dominican Republic, Ecuador, Guatemala and Perú.

Thus the amparo and habeas corpus actions in Argentina are essential adjective tools for judicial review, at present fully regulated by the Argentinean Constitution through the constitutional reform of 1994 (Article 43), following the guidelines of the American Convention on Human Rights, and having, moreover, developed the action of *habeas data*[6].

As above mentioned, the recourse of amparo was developed in Argentina as was the judicial review itself, as a result of a judicial doctrine[7] set forth by the

6 See: Juan F. ARMAGNAGUE *et al.*, *Derecho a la información, hábeas data e Internet*, Ediciones La Roca, Buenos Aires 2002; Miguel Ángel EKMEKDJIAN *et al.*, *Hábeas Data. El derecho a la intimidad frente a la revolución informática*, Edic. Depalma, Buenos Aires, 1998; Osvaldo Alfredo GOZAÍNI, *Derecho Procesal Constitucional, Hábeas Data. Protección de datos personales. Ley 25.326 y reglamentación (decreto 1558/2001)*, Rubinzal-Culzoni Editores, Santa Fe, Argentina, 2002

7 *Cf.* G. R. CARRIO, *Algunos aspectos del recurso de amparo*, Buenos Aires, 1959, p. 9; J. R. Vanossi, *Teoría constitucional*, *cit.*, Vol. II, p. 277.

Supreme Court in the Angel Siri Case of 27 December 1957,[8] in which the competence of ordinary courts to protect the fundamental rights of citizens, against violation from public authorities actions or from individuals was definitively accepted[9]. Prior to that date, in 1984, when interpreting Article 18 of the Constitution, which set forth the guarantee of all persons not to be arrested except by virtue of a written warrant of the competent authority, Congress, through Law 23.098, regulated the *habeas corpus* for the protection of physical and personal freedom against illegal or arbitrary detentions[10].

Insofar as other constitutional rights are concerned, they were protected through the ordinary judicial means, considering the courts that the habeas corpus could not be used for such purpose. Thus, in the absence of a legal provision, the Supreme Court of the Nation rejected the application of *habeas corpus* to obtain judicial protection to other constitutional rights. That is why in the Case *Bartolo* in 1959 the Supreme Court ruled that «nor in the text, or in the spirit, or in the constitutional tradition of the habeas corpus institution, can be found any basis for its application to the right of property, the freedom of commerce and industry ...; against the abuses or infringements of individuals or public officers regarding rights, the statutes and court decisions set forth administrative and judicial remedies»[11].

This situation radically changed in 1957, as a result of the resolution of the case of *Angel* Siri, who was director of the Newspaper (Mercedes) in the Province of Buenos Aires. After the Government closure of the Newspaper, Mr Siri brought before a criminal court a petition requesting amparo of the freedom of press and his right to work declared in the Constitution. The court rejected the claim arguing that the petition filed was a habeas corpus, which only protected physical and personal freedom. Once the judicial decision was confirmed by a superior court, an extraordinary recourse was filled against the decision before the Supreme Court, which in a decision of December 27, 1957 admitted the action of amparo. The argument of the Supreme Courts was that in the case, it was alleged the violation of the constitutional guarantee of freedom of press and the right to work; and that the arbitrary governmental decision violated those rights being proved, they have to be protected by the courts and so the absence of a statutory regulation on the amparo recourse is not a valid argument to reject the judicial protection,. In brief, the Supreme Court argued that the constitutional rights and guaranties of peoples, once embodied in the Constitution, must always be judicially protected regardless of the existence of a regulatory statute on the matter[12].

The second important decision of the Argentinean Supreme Court was issued the next year in the *Case Kot*, of October 5th, 1958. In this case, the action of amparo

[8] See G. R. CARRIO, *op. cit.*, p. 10.

[9] See the Samuel KOT Ltd. case of 5 September, 1958, S.V. Linares Quintana, *Acción de amparo*, Buenos Aires, 1960, p. 25.

[10] See: Néstor Pedro SAGÜES, *Derecho Procesal Constitucional. Hábeas Corpus*, Volumen 4, 2nd Edition, Editorial Astrea, Buenos Aires, 1988.

[11] See the referente in Joaquín BRAGE CAMAZANO, *La jurisdicción constitucional de la libertad (Teoría general, Argentina, México, Corte Interamericana de Derechos Humanos)*, Editorial Porrúa, Instituto Mexicano de Derecho Procesal Constitucional, México, 2005, p. 66.

[12] See the reference in José Luis LAZZARINI, *El juicio de amparo*, La Ley, Buenos Aires, 1987, pp. 26 ff y 373 ff.; Alí Joaquín SALGADO, *Juicio de amparo y acción de inconstitucionalidad*, Ed. Astrea, Buenos Aires, 1987, pp. 5.

was brought before a court by Samuel Kot, the owner of a factory whose premises had been occupied by its workers on strike. Having been initially rejected, eventually the action of amparo was admitted by the Supreme Court ordering the restitution of the factory to his owner. The Court decided that in any case in which it appears clear and in a manifest way the illegitimacy of a restriction to any of the essential constitutional rights, and also the grave and irreparable damages that can be caused if the question is referred to be resolved by the judicial ordinary means; the courts must immediately re-establish the restricted right, applying the habeas corpus procedure, by means of the prompt amparo recourse.

Nonetheless, in the case, the Court warned the whole Judiciary that in these cases of constitutional protection, the judicial power had to be exercised in a prudent way in order to avoid the complete substitution of the ordinary judicial means; that is to say, that by means of the prompt amparo guarantee, all the ordinary controversies where contradictory rights must be discussed, resulted being resolved. The Supreme Court resolved in the case, precisely that it was not wise to compel the plaintiff, whose property was taken, to seek for its restitution by mean of the ordinary judicial proceedings.

The other very important issue decided by the Supreme Court in the *Kot Case*, was that the amparo not only protected against acts of authorities but also against private individuals illegitimate actions based on the principle that in spite of the existence of an ordinary procedure, it was nevertheless admissible if the processing of the latter could cause serious and irreparable harm[13].

The judicial creation of the amparo lead to the approval of the 1966 Law 16.986[14] on the action of amparo, which nevertheless only regulates the action of amparo against acts of the State; so the amparo action against private parties is filed by means of the provisions of the Code of Civil and Commercial Procedure of the Nation (Article 32,1, Sub-sections 2 and 498)[15].

Thus, pursuant to Article 1st of Law 16.986, the action of amparo can be brought before a court against any act or omission of a public authority which in an overtly arbitrary or illegal manner, currently or imminently harms, restricts, alters or threatens, the rights or guarantees that are explicitly or implicitly recognized by the National Constitution, with the exception of individual freedom protected by *habeas corpus*.

Therefore, this is an action that can be brought before any judge of First Instance with jurisdiction over the place where the act takes place or where it has or could have effect, following the rules of jurisdiction attached to the concerned matter

---

13 See the reference in José Luis LAZZARINI, *El juicio de amparo*, La Ley, Buenos Aires, 1987, pp. 243 ff; Alí Joaquín SALGADO, *Juicio de amparo y acción de inconstitucionalidad*, Ed. Astrea, Buenos Aires, 1987, pp. 6.; Susana ALBANESE, *Garantías Judiciales. Algunos requisitos del debido proceso legal en el derecho internacional de los derechos humanos*, Ediar S.A. Editora, Comercial, Industrial y Financiera, Buenos Aires, 2000; Augusto M. MORILLO *et al.*, *El amparo. Régimen procesal*, 3rd Edition, Librería Editora Platense SRL, La Plata, 1998, 430 pp.; Néstor Pedro SAGÜES, *Derecho Procesal Constitucional. Acción de Amparo*, Volumen 3, 2nd Edition, Editorial Astrea, Buenos Aires, 1988.

14 See José Luis LAZZARINI, *El juicio de amparo*, Buenos Aires, 1987; Néstor Pedro SAGÜÉS, *Derecho Procesal Constitucional. Acción de Amparo*, Buenos Aires, 1988.

15 J. L. LAZZARINI, *op. cit.*, p. 229.

(Article 4, Amparo Law), for the protection of all constitutional rights and freedoms (even those implicitly recognized in the Constitution) against acts or omissions of the public authorities, except for those decisions or acts emanating from the Judiciary or against statutes. On the other hand, it is an action that is admissible only when no other judicial or administrative recourses or remedies exist to assure the protection. Thus, in order to bring the action of amparo, all judicial or administrative recourses or remedies that may assure the constitutional protection of the right or guarantee in question must be exhausted, since if they in fact exist, then the amparo is inadmissible, unless they are incapable of redressing the damage and their processing can lead to serious and irreparable harm. Thus the amparo is considered an exceptional proceeding.

The same regulatory trend is set forth in Article 321 of the Civil Procedure Code regarding the amparo against private damaging actions, in which it is also stressed that the action is only admissible in cases in which the urgent reparation of the damages or the immediate end of the challenged actions are needed, and always if the controversy, because of its nature, cannot be resolved by means of the ordinary judicial procedure.

On the other hand it must be stressed that even thought the actions of amparo are in general exercised before the judges of first instance, the cases can reach the Supreme Court of the Nation, by means of an extraordinary recourse when in the judicial decision a matter of judicial review of constitutionality is resolved[16].

This leads us to make a few comments regarding the judicial review system in Argentina[17], which follows very closely the North American model, also founded in the supremacy clause of the 1860 Constitution which set forth:

> **Article 31.** This constitution, the laws of the Nation that the Congress consequently approves and the treaties with foreign powers, are the supreme law of the Nation, and the authorities of each Province are obliged to conform to it, notwithstanding any contrary disposition which the provincial laws or Constitutions might contain.

On the other hand, Article 100 referring to judicial power, set forth:

> The Supreme Court and the inferior Courts of the Nation, are competent to try and decide all cases related to aspects ruled by the constitution, by the laws of the Nation and by the Treaties with foreign nations.

Therefore, in terms similar to the American constitution, the Argentinean Constitution does not expressly confer any judicial review power upon the Supreme Court or the other courts; being also judicial review a creation of the Supreme Court, based on the principles of supremacy of the Constitution and judicial duty when applying the law.

---

16 See Elias GUASTAVINO, *Recurso extraordinario de inconstitucionalidad,* Ed. La Roca, Buenos Aires, Argentina, 1992.

17 See in general Néstor Pedro SAGÜÉS, *Derecho procesal Constitucional,* Tomo I, Cuarta edición, 2002; Ricardo HARO, *El control de constitucionalidad,* Editorial Zavalia, Buenos Aires, Argentina, 2003; Juan Carlos HITTERS, «La jurisdicción constitucional en Argentina» en Domingo GARCÍA BELAUNDE, y Francisco FERNÁNDEZ SEGADO, (Coordinadores), *La jurisdicción constitucional en Iberoamérica,* Ed. Dykinson, Madrid, España, 1997; Maximiliano Toricelli, *El sistema de control constitucional argentino,* Editorial Lexis Nexis Depalma, Buenos Aires, Argentina, 2002.

The first case in which judicial review power was exercised regarding a federal statute was the *Sojo* case, (1887), also concerning the unconstitutionality of a law that tried to enlarge the original jurisdiction of the Supreme Court[18] as was the *Marbury* v. *Madison* case.

Nevertheless, the question of the powers of the judiciary to control the constitutionality of legislation was a matter of discussion in the Parana Constitutional Convention in 1857-1858, where the predominant opinion on the subject was: first, the character of the Constitution as a supreme law and the power of the courts to maintain its supremacy over the statutes which infringed it; second, the limits imposed over the constituted powers by popular sovereignty, so that statutes contrary to the principles embodied in the Constitution, could not be binding on the courts; and third, that the Judiciary was precisely the branch of government which ought to have enough power to interpret the Constitution regarding the other of the State.[19]

Therefore, through the work of the courts, the Argentinean system of judicial review was developed over more than a century ago as a diffuse system[20] in which all the courts have the power to declare the unconstitutionality of legislative acts, treaties,[21] executive and administrative acts and judicial decisions, whether at national or provincial levels.[22] This power of judicial review is, of course, reserved to the courts and the executive cannot decide not to apply a statute on unconstitutional grounds.

Therefore, in Argentina, the power to control the constitutionality of state acts is not reserved to one single judicial body or a group of them; it concerns all courts, of course, within the scope of the jurisdiction that each of them has.

Argentina, being a federal state, has two court systems established from their origin following the American model in the organization of the judiciary:[23] National and provincial courts. The provincial courts have jurisdiction over all matters of «ordinary law», (*derecho común*) like civil, commercial, criminal, labor, social security,

---

18 *Cf.* A.E. GHIGLIANI *Del control jurisdiccional de constitucionalidad*, Buenos Aires, 1952., p. 5; R. BIELSA, *La protección constitucional y el recurso extraordinario. Jurisdicción de la Corte Suprema*, Buenos Aires, 1958. pp. 41, 43, 179 who speaks about a «pretorian creation» of judicial review by the Supreme Court, *op. cit.*, p. 179. *Cf.* J.R. Vanossi and P.F. Ubertone, *Instituciones de defensa de la Constitución en la Argentina*, UNAM, Congreso Internacional sobre la Constitución y su defensa, México, 1982, (mimeo), p. 4 (also Publisher as «Control jurisdiccional de constitucionalidad». en *Desafíos del control de constitucionalidad*, Ediciones Ciudad Argentina, Buenos Aires, Argentina, 1996), H. QUIROGA LAVIE, *Derecho constitucional*, Buenos Aires, 1978, p. 481. Previously in 1863 the firsts Supreme Court decisions where adopted in constitutional matters but refered to provincial and executive acts. *Cf.* A. E. GHIGLIANI, *op. cit.*, p. 58.

19 *Cf.* A.E. GHIGLIANI, *op. cit.*, p. 58.

20 N.P. SAGÜES, *Recurso Extraordinario*, Buenos Aires, 1984, Vol. I, p. 91. J.R. Vanossi and P.F. UBERTONE, *op. cit.* p. 2, 14. See also J.R. VANOSSI, *Teoría constitucional*, Buenos Aires, Vol. II, *Supremacía y control de constitucionalidad*, Buenos Aires, 1976, p. 155.

21 In particular, regarding the unconstitutionality of Treaties and the posibility of the Courts to control them, A.G. GHIGLIANI, *op. cit.*, p. 62; J.R. VANOSSI, *Aspectos del recurso extraordinario de inconstitucionalidad*, Buenos Aires, 1966, p. 91, and *Teoría constitucional, op. cit.*, Vol. II, p. 277.

22 *Cf.* R. BIELSA, *op. cit.*, pp. 120-148. J.R. VANOSSI and P.F. UBERTONE, *doc. cit.*, p. 6.

23 *Cf.* R. BIELSA, *op. cit.*, p. 57; A.E. GHIGLIANI, *op. cit.*, p. 55.

and mining law and public provincial law (constitutional and administrative provincial law). In each Province there are courts of first and second instances, and at their apex a Superior Provincial Court.

At the national level, the national courts have jurisdiction over all matters regulated by «federal law»; particularly concerning constitutional and administrative law cases and in all cases in which the Nation is a party or foreign diplomatic agents are involved. The organization of the national courts is as follows: National courts with territorial jurisdiction in the first instance; national chambers of appeals, in the second instance, and at the apex the Supreme Court of Justice, that also acts as a third instance.[24]

The Supreme Court of Justice, the only judicial body created in the Constitution, considers itself «final interpreter of the Constitution» or «the defendant of the Constitution»,[25] and has two sorts of jurisdiction: original and appellate. The original jurisdiction is established in the Constitution and, therefore, is not extendible by statute, and concerns all matters related to ambassadors, ministers and foreign consuls and to which the Provinces are party (art. 101).

In its appellate jurisdiction, the Supreme Court has jurisdiction through two sorts of appeals: ordinary and extraordinary. In its appellate jurisdiction through ordinary appeals, the Supreme Court has the power of reviewing the decisions of the national chambers of appeal in the following cases: 1. Cases in which the Nation is a party according to an amount fixed periodically; 2. Cases concerning extradition of criminals sought by foreign countries; and 3. Cases concerning the seizure of ships in time of war and other cases concerning maritime law.[26]

In these cases of appellate jurisdiction through ordinary appeal, the Supreme Court acts as a court of third instance and last resort reviewing the whole case decided by the national chambers of appeals.

However, as we have said, the appellate jurisdiction of the Supreme Court of Justice can also be exercised through what has been called an «extraordinary recourse» that the party in a case decided by the national Chambers of appeals and by the Superior Courts of the Provinces can bring before the Supreme Court, in particular cases related to constitutional issues and with special conditions. This is, undoubtedly, the judicial mean through which the Supreme Court normally decides upon the final interpretation of the Constitution when reviewing the constitutionality of state acts, and consequently it is the most important mean for judicial review.

Before analyzing this «extraordinary recourse», reference has to be made to the general trends of the incidental character of the Argentinean diffuse system and its consequences.

In effect, as a diffuse system of judicial review, the Argentinean system is essentially an incidental one, in which the question of constitutionality is not the principal object of a process; thus the constitutional issue can be at any moment and at any stage of any proceeding. This incidental character has led to considering the

---

24 *Cf.* J.R. VANOSSI and P.F. UBERTONE, *doc. cit.*, pp. 14-18; A.E. GHIGLIANI, *op. cit.*, p. 76.

25 R. BIELSA, *op. cit.*, p. 270; J.R. VANOSSI and P.F. UBERTONE, *doc. cit.*, p. 18.

26 *Cf.* R. BIELSA, *op. cit.*, pp. 60-61; J.R. VANOSSI and P.F. UBERTONE, *doc. cit.*, p. 19.

Argentinean system of judicial review, as an «indirect» control system,[27] because the constitutional issue can only be raised in a judicial controversy, case or process, normally through an exception, at any moment before the decision is adopted by the court, and therefore not necessarily in the *litis contestatio* of the proceeding.[28]

The principal condition for raising constitutional questions is that they can only be raised in a «judicial case» or litigation between parties;[29] therefore, they cannot be raised as an abstract question before a court, and the courts cannot render declarative decisions upon unconstitutional matters.[30]

Nevertheless, the existence of a case or controversy in which the constitutional question could be raised is not only necessary, it is also indispensable that the question be raised by a party in the process with due interest in the matter, that is to say, which alleges a particular injury in his own right caused by the statute considered invalid.[31]

Consequently, the court on its own cannot raise constitutional issues in the Argentinean system. Thus, even if the court is convinced of the unconstitutionality of a statute, if a party has not raised the question, the Court is bound to apply the Statute to the decision of the case.[32] In this respect, it must be stressed that even though this has been the judicial doctrine invariably applied by courts, some authors have considered that the constitutional questions can be decided by courts without being raised by a party, based on the principle of constitutional supremacy and the notion of «public order».[33]

Nevertheless, an exemption to the need for party intervention when raising the constitutional issue has been established by the Supreme Court, allowing the court to consider constitutional questions on its own, only in matters concerning the jurisdiction of the courts themselves and their functional autonomy. Consequently, the Supreme Court decided upon the unconstitutionality of a statute that enlarged its original jurisdiction of the Supreme Court of Justice established in the Constitution, although not being raised by a party.[34]

Furthermore and related to the incidental or indirect character of judicial review in the Argentinean system, the constitutional question raised in a case particularly due to the presumption of constitutionality of all statutes,[35] must be of an un avoiding character, in the sense that its decision must be essential to the resolution of the case which depends on it.[36] Moreover, the constitutional question

27 A.E. GHIGLIANI, *op. cit.*, p. 75.

28 A.E. GHIGLIANI, *op. cit.*, p. 76.

29 Art. 100 of the constitution; *Cf.* R. Bielsa, *op. cit.*, pp. 213, 214; A.E. GHIGLIANI, *op. cit.*, p. 75; J.R. VANOSSI and P.F. UBERTONE, *doc. cit.*, p. 23.

30 *Cf.* R. BIELSA, *op. cit.*, pp. 213, 214; A.E. GHIGLIANI, *op. cit.*, p. 80; S.M. LOZADA, *Derecho Constitucional Argentino*, Buenos Aires, 1972, Vol. I, p. 342.

31 S.M. LOZADA, *op. cit.*, p. 342; A.E. GHIGLIANI, *op.cit.*, p. 82; J.R. VANOSSI and P.E. UBERTONE, *doc. cit.*, p. 23.

32 R. BIELSA, *op. cit.*, pp. 198, 214; H. QUIROGA LAVIE, *op. cit.*, p. 479.

33 G. BIDART CAMPOS, *El derecho constitucional del poder*, Vol. II, Chap. XXIX; J.R. VANOSSI, *Teoría constitucional*, *op. cit.*, Vol. II, pp. 318, 319.

34 *Cf.* J.R. VANOSSI and P.E. UBERTONE, *doc. cit.*, 25; .R. Bielsa, *op. cit.*, 255; H. QUIROGA LAVIE, *op. cit.*, p. 479.

35 A.E. GHIGLIANI, *op. cit.*, pp. 89, 90.

36 A.E. GHIGLIANI, *op. cit.*, p. 89; S.M. LOSADA, *op. cit*, p. 341.

must be clear and undoubted. Therefore, the declaration of unconstitutionality being considered an act of extreme gravity and the last ratio of the legal order, the court must abstain its consideration when there are doubts about the issue.[37] Thus when an interpretation of the statute avoiding the consideration of the constitutional question is possible the court must follow this path.[38]

Finally, it must be said that in the Argentinean system, the Supreme Court of the Nation has developed the same exception to judicial review established in the North American system, concerning political questions, even though the Constitution does not expressly establish anything on the matter.[39] These political questions are related to the «acts of government» or «political acts» doctrine developed in continental European law, and within which we can mention the following: the declaration of state of siege; the declaration of federal intervention in the provinces; the declaration of «public use» for means of expropriation; the declaration of war; the declaration of emergency to approve certain direct tax contributions; acts concerning foreign relations; the recognition of new foreign states or new foreign state governments; the expulsion of aliens, etc., In general, within these political questions there are acts exercised by the political powers of the state in accordance with powers exclusively and directly attributed to them in the Constitution,[40] which can be considered the key element for their identification.

The Supreme Court of the Nation is vested in the Argentinean system, like it is in the United States, with two sorts of jurisdiction: original and appellate jurisdiction, and in the latter two other sorts can be distinguished: ordinary appellate jurisdiction and «extraordinary appellate jurisdiction» that can be exercised by the Supreme Court through the so called «extraordinary recourse», which accomplishes a similar result to the request for writ of *certiorari* in the United States Supreme Court.

But of course, the «extraordinary recourse» is quite different to the American request for writ of *certiorari*, in the sense that the Supreme Court of the Nation does not have discretionary powers in accepting extraordinary recourses. Thus, in the Argentinean system, the appellate jurisdiction of the Supreme Court, whether ordinary or extraordinary, is a mandatory jurisdiction, exercised as a consequence of a right the parties have, whether to appeal or to introduce the extraordinary recourse.

When the extraordinary recourse is filed, the Supreme Court does not act as a mere third instance court,[41] particularly because the Court does not review the motives of the judicial decision under consideration, regarding the facts; its power of review being concentrated only in aspects of law regarding constitutional questions. That is why it has been said that the Supreme Court, as a consequence of an extraordinary recourse, «does not act *jure litigatoris*» but *jure constitutionis*, does not judge a *questio facti*, but a *questio juris*».[42]

---

37 H. QUIROGA LAVIE, *op. cit.*, p. 480.
38 A.E. GHIGLIANI, *op. cit.*, p. 91.
39 J.R. VANOSSI and P.E. UBERTONE, *doc. cit.*, p. 11.
40 *Cf.* A.E. GHIGLIANI, *op. cit.*, p. 85; H. QUIROGA LAVIE, *op. cit.*, p. 482; S.M. LOSADA, *op. cit.*, p. 343; J.R. VANOSSI and P.E. UBERTONE, *doc. cit.*, pp. 11, 12.
41 *Cf.* N. P. SAGÜES, *op. cit.*, p. 270; pp. 185, 221, 228, 275.
42 R. BIELSA, *op. cit.*, p. 222.

This substantive difference between the function of the Supreme Court as a consequence of the exercise of an appeal or an extraordinary recourse is followed by another formal difference, particularly, that contrary to the appeal, the extraordinary recourse must be motivated and founded on constitutional reasons.[43]

Even though it is called «extraordinary» it must be said that the ordinary appeal being reduced to the review of very few decisions of the National Chambers of Appeals, the «extraordinary recourse» is the judicial means through which the parties can most commonly reach the Supreme Court of Justice in order to obtain judicial review of constitutionality of state acts.[44] Particularly because, as we have mentioned, not only the definitive decisions of the National Chambers of Appeals can be the object of an extraordinary recourse but also the definitive decisions of the Superior Courts of the Provinces where the generality of ordinary law cases reach.

Now, the exercise of this extraordinary recourse is submitted to various particular rules, which must be stressed:

First of all, the extraordinary recourse can only be exercised in connection with constitutional matters, thus its importance regarding judicial review. In this respect, the extraordinary recourse can be exercised in three cases:

a. When in a case the question of validity of a treaty, an act of Congress or of another authority exercised in the Nation's name has been raised, and the judicial decision has been against the validity of the particular act;

b. When the validity of an act or decree of the Provincial authorities has been questioned on the grounds of its repugnance to the Constitution, treaties or acts of Congress, and the judicial decision has been in favor of the validity of the particular act.

c. When the interpretation of a clause of the Constitution, of a treaty or of an act of Congress or another national act has been questioned, and the judicial decision has been against the validity of a title, right, privilege or exemption founded in said clause which has been a matter of the case.[45]

As a creation of the Supreme Court of the Nation doctrine, the extraordinary recourse against «arbitrary judicial decisions» has also been accepted. Arbitrary judicial decisions are considered those in which the right to defend one self in a proceeding is said to have been violated. It has also been accepted in cases of so called «institutional gravity», when the Supreme Court can be reached even though the extraordinary recourse would be normally inadmissible; and in cases when an «effective deprivation of justice» has been committed.[46]

The second rule referred to the admissibility of the extraordinary recourse states that the constitutional question must have been discussed in the proceeding in the lower courts, and considered in its decision, before it can be brought before the Supreme Court through the extraordinary recourse.[47] Therefore, the Supreme

---

43 *Cf.* R. BIELSA, *op. cit.*, pp. 245, 252.

44 *Cf.* J.R. VANOSSI and P.E. UBERTONE, *doc. cit.*, p. 19.

45 Statute 48, Art. 14. *Cf.* J.R. VANOSSI and P.E. UBERTONE, *cit.* p. 20; R. BIELSA, *op. cit.*, pp. 210, 211; N.P. SAGÜES, *op. cit.*, p. 272.

46 *Cf.* J.R. VANOSSI and P.E. UBERTONE, *doc. cit.*, p. 20.

47 *Cf.* R. BIELSA, *op. cit.*, pp. 190, 202, 203, 205, 209.

Court has rejected the recourse when the constitutional issue has not been discussed in the lower courts and has not been considered in the decision.[48] Furthermore, the constitutional issue must have been maintained in the various judicial instances in the lower courts and not abandoned by the interested party. On the contrary, the Supreme Court would reject the extraordinary recourse.[49]

In third place, all the other aspects of the incidental character of judicial review already mentioned apply, of course, to the admissibility of the extraordinary recourse, and particularly the fact that it must be exercised by a party with direct interests in the matter, whose rights are affected by the decision regarding the invalidity of a statute, and that the solution of the constitutional question must be unavoidable and indispensable for the decision of the case. Regarding standing, it must be pointed out that in the Argentinean system, it is expressly accepted that public bodies whose acts have been questioned on the grounds of unconstitutionality and also the Public Prosecutor, are considered party regarding the exercise of the extraordinary recourse.[50]

Finally, in the Argentinean system of judicial review, as a pure diffuse system, we must refer to the effects of the decision adopted by the courts when exercising their powers of judicial review of constitutionality.

First of all, it must be said that judicial decisions adopted on matters of constitutionality, when they consider a statute to be unconstitutional, whether adopted by inferior courts or by the Supreme Court, they simply do not apply the invalid statute by giving preference to the Constitution, but there is no annulment. The courts in Argentina do not have the power to annul or repeal a law. That power is reserved to the legislator, and the only thing they can do is to refuse its application in the concrete case when they consider it unconstitutional.[51] The statute, therefore, when considered unconstitutional and non-applicable by the judge, is considered null and void, with no effect whatsoever[52] in the particular case. This leads to the consideration of the retroactive effect of the decision, bearing in mind its declarative character, thus *ex tunc, pro praeterito.* We insist, however, that the statute remains valid and generally applicable and even the same court can change its criteria about its unconstitutionality and apply it in the future.[53]

That is why these effects of the judicial decision on constitutional matters, in the Argentinean system are strictly *inter partes* effect, a consequence of the diffuse character of the system. Thus the decision considering the nullity of a statute has effect only in connection with the particular process where the question has been raised and between the parties which have intervened in it and, therefore, has no *erga omnes* effects at all.[54]

On the other hand, in the Argentinean system, the decision on judicial review, even the decisions of the Supreme Court on constitutional issues are not obligatory

48 *Cf.* R. BIELSA, *op. cit.*, p. 204.
49 *Cf.* R. BIELSA, *op. cit.*, p. 260.
50 *Cf.* R. BIELSA, *op. cit.*, pp. 237, 238.
51 *Cf.* R. BIELSA, *op. cit.*, pp. 197, 198, 345; N.P. Sagües, *op. cit.*, p. 156.
52 *Cf.* A.E. GHIGLIANI, *op. cit.*, p. 95.
53 *Cf.* R. BIELSA, *op. cit.*, p. 196; A.E. Ghigliani, *op. cit.*, pp. 92, 97; N. P. SAGÜES, *op. cit.*, p. 177.
54 *Cf.* H. QUIROGA LAVIE, *op. cit.*, p. 479.

for the other courts or the inferior courts.[55] Moreover, even though in the 1949 constitutional reform it was expressly established that the interpretation adopted by the Supreme Court of Justice upon the articles of the Constitution would be considered binding on the national and provincial courts,[56] this article of the constitution was later repealed and the situation today is the absolute power of all courts to render their judgment autonomously with their own constitutional interpretation.

Nevertheless, it is certain that the Supreme Court of Justice, because it is the highest court in the country with wide appellate jurisdiction, particularly through the extraordinary recourse, its decisions have a definitive influence upon all the inferior courts particularly when a doctrine has been clearly and reiterated established by the Court.

Finally, regarding the Argentinean system, discussions have arisen concerning the possibility of the exercise of the diffuse system of judicial review, by the courts, when deciding recourse for *amparo* brought before them for the protection of fundamental rights.

Now since its acceptance and despite the diffuse system of judicial review followed in Argentina, the Supreme Court established the criteria of the incompetence of the *amparo* judge to review the constitutionality of legislation, reducing the powers of the judge of *amparo* to decide only on acts or facts that could violate fundamental rights. Thus it was established that the *amparo* could not be granted when the complaint contained the allegation of unconstitutionality of a law on which the relevant acts or facts were based. Thus, the Supreme Court considered that the judicial decision in cases of recourse for *amparo* could not have declarative effects regarding the unconstitutionality of statutes, due to the summary nature of its proceeding.[57] This doctrine was followed later by law 16.986 of 18 October 1966 about the recourse for *amparo,* in which it was expressly established that the «action for *amparo* will not be admissible when the decision upon the invalidity of the act will require.... the declaration of the unconstitutionality of statutes, decrees or ordinances».(art. 2,d).

Nevertheless, in 1967, the Supreme Court, without declaring the unconstitutionality of the above mentioned disposition of law 16.986 in the *Outon* case,[58] in an implicit way, decided its inapplicability and accepted the criteria that when considering *amparo* cases, the courts have the power to review the unconstitutionality of legislation, which has been supported by the leading constitutional law authors of the country.[59]

---

[55] *Cf.* R. BIELSA, *op. cit.*, pp. 49, 198, 267; A.E. GHIGLIANI, *op. cit.*, pp. 97, 98.

[56] Art. 95 of the 1949 Constitution. *Cf.* C.A. Ayanagaray, *Efectos de la declaración de inconstitucionalidad*, Buenos Aires, 1955, p. 11; R. Bielsa, *op. cit.*, p. 268.

[57] See the *Aserradero Clipper SRL* case (1961), J. R. VANOSSI *Teoría constitucional, cit.*, Vol. II, p. 286.

[58] Outon case of 29 March 1967. J. R. VANOSSI, *Teoría constitucional, cit.*, Vol. II, p. 288.

[59] G. J. BIDART CAMPOS, *Régimen legal del amparo,* 1969; G. J. BIDART CAMPOS, «El control de constitucionalidad en el juicio de amparo y la arbitrariedad o ilegalidad del acto lesivo», *Jurisprudencia argentina*, 23-4-1969; N. P. Sagües, «El juicio de amparo y el planteo de inconstitucionalidad», *Jurisprudencia argentina*, 20-7-1973; J. R. J. R. VANOSSI, *Teoría constitucional, cit.*, Vol. II, pp. 288-292; José Luis LAZZARINI, *El juicio de amparo,* La Ley, Buenos Aires, 1987, pp. 80, 86; Alí Joaquín SALGADO, *Juicio de amparo y acción de inconstitucionalidad,*

Anyway, the acceptance of this means of judicial review of legislation, through the action for *amparo*, could lead to a direct action of unconstitutionality, although of a diffuse character, which differs from the incidental normal character of the constitutional review system, which is commonly exercised as a consequence of an exception raised by a party in a concrete process, whose main objective is not the constitutional question.

On the contrary, in the action of *amparo*, when founded on reasons of unconstitutionality of a statute on which the concrete act that violates the fundamental right that the petitioners seek to be protected is based, the unconstitutionality of the laws becomes a direct issue of the action itself. That is why it has been said that by accepting this feature of the action for protection, the Supreme Court has opened the way to a new direct means of judicial review of constitutionality of legislation.[60]

III. THE AMPARO ACTION IN COUNTRIES WITH ONLY A CONCENTRATED SYSTEM OF JUDICIAL REVIEW

Argentina is the only Latin American country that has kept the diffuse method of judicial review as the only one in order to control the constitutionality of legislation.

Others Latin American countries have also followed the trend of adopting only one system of judicial review, but on the opposite side, attached only to the concentrated method. It is the case of Bolivia, Chile, Costa Rica, El Salvador, Honduras, Panama, Paraguay and Uruguay, countries that have the concentrated method of judicial review as the only existing one in the country by reserving to the Supreme Court or to a Constitutional Tribunal the monopoly to control the constitutionality of legislation.

Notwithstanding, regarding the amparo and habeas corpus actions, the exclusive attribution of the Supreme Court or Constitutional Tribunal are not always empowered with judicial review, and on the contrary, in the majority of the countries with concentrated method of judicial review, the amparo jurisdiction corresponds to a universality of courts and judges.

Thus, regarding amparo in countries with concentrated method of judicial review, the systems can be classified distinguishing those where amparo is also attributed to the judicial review concentrated organ or is attributed to the whole judiciary.

1. The amparo action exercised before one single tribunal: the Constitutional Chamber of the Supreme Court in Costa Rica and El Salvador

Perhaps the most common trend of the amparo in Europe, existing only in countries with a concentrated system of judicial review as a means of judicial protection of constitutional rights and guarantees, is to consider it as a single action

Ed. Astrea, Buenos Aires, 1987, p. 58; Joaquín BRAGE CAMAZANO, *La jurisdicción constitucional de la libertad (Teoría general, Argentina, México, Corte Interamericana de Derechos Humanos)*, Editorial Porrúa, Instituto Mexicano de Derecho Procesal Constitucional, México, 2005, pp. 71, 117.

[60] J. R. VANOSSI, *Teoría constitucional*, *cit.*, Vol. II, p. 291.

or recourse that can only be brought before one single Tribunal specialized in constitutional matters. This is the case of the actions or recourses of amparo established in Germany[61], Austria[62] and Spain[63].

This system is also followed in some Latin American countries with concentrated systems of judicial review, when setting forth a sole and exclusive court to hear the actions of amparo and habeas corpus, as is the case of the Constitutional Chamber of the Supreme Court of Costa Rica and El Salvador.

This is also the case of the Supreme Court of Justice of Nicaragua, but with the basic distinction that in this country there is a mixed system of judicial review.

A. *The recourse of amparo in Costa Rica*

In Costa Rica, as mentioned above, every person has a right the file the recourse of *habeas corpus* in order to guarantee his personal freedom and safety, and the recourse of amparo to maintain or reestablish the enjoyment of the other rights set forth in the Constitution, as well as the fundamental rights established in international instruments on human rights that are applicable to the Republic (Article 48, Constitution).

According to the 1989 Constitutional Jurisdiction Law, both recourses can only be brought before the Constitutional Chamber of the Supreme Court of Justice[64]. Articles 2,a and 4 of such statute provide the specific attribution of that Constitutional Chamber to «guarantee by means of the recourses of habeas corpus and amparo, the rights and freedoms set forth in the Constitution and the human rights recognized by international law applicable in Costa Rica».

Regarding the habeas corpus recourse, Article 15 of the Law set forth that its purpose is to guaranty personal freedom and integrity, against acts or omissions from an authority of any kind, including judicial, against that freedom's threats and against the unduly disturbance and restrictions to such freedom adopted by authorities, as well as against illegitimate restrictions regarding the right to move from one place to another within the Republic, or the right to stay, to leave and to come back to its territory (Art. 15).

Pursuant to this same Law, and regarding the recourse of amparo, it is stated that it proceeds against any provision, agreement or resolution and, in general, against any action, omission or simple material action that is not founded on an effective administrative act, of the services or public institutions that have violated,

---

61 See I. V. MUNCH. «El recurso de amparo constitucional como instrumento jurídico y político en la República Federal de Alemania», *Revista de Estudios Políticos*, N° 7, Madrid, 1979, pp. 269-289; Klaus SCHLAICH, «El Tribunal constitucional alemán», in L. Favoreu *et al.*, *Tribunales Constitucionales Europeos Derechos Fundamentales*, Madrid, 1984, pp. 133-232.

62 See F. ERMACORA, «El Tribunal Constitucional Austríaco» in the *Tribunal Constitucional*, Dirección General de lo Contencioso del Estado, Instituto de Estudios Fiscales, Madrid, 1981, Volumen I, pp. 409-459.

63 See Joan Oliver ARAUJO, *El recurso de amparo*, Palma de Mallorca, 1986; Antonio MOYA GARRIDO, *El recurso de amparo según la doctrina del Tribunal Constitucional*, Barcelona, 1983; José L. CASCAJO CASTRO and Vicente GIMENO SENDRA, *El recurso de amparo*, Madrid, 1985; Antonio CANO MATA, *El recurso de amparo*, Madrid, 1983.

64 See, in general, Rubén HERNÁNDEZ VALLE, *La tutela de los derechos fundamentales*, Editorial Juricentro, San José, 1990.

violate or threatens to violate any of such rights (Article 29). The amparo not only proceeds against arbitrary acts, but also against actions or omissions founded on norms which are arbitrarily interpreted or unduly applied.

However, the Law excludes the amparo action against statutes or other regulatory provisions, unless they are challenged together with the individual acts that apply them or when the contents of the norms are automatically applicable, in the sense that their provisions become immediately obligatory simply upon their passing. It also excludes the amparo against the judicial resolutions and actions of the Judiciary, against acts carried out by the authorities upon executing judicial decisions, and against the acts or provisions of the Supreme Tribunal of Elections in electoral matters (Article 30).

Costa Rica's Law also regulates the action of amparo against actions or omissions of those private law subjects, but in a way similar to the Colombian regulation, only when they act or should act in exercise of public functions or powers or are by law or by fact in a position of power against which ordinary judicial remedies are clearly insufficient and tardy in guaranteeing the fundamental rights and freedoms established in the Constitution and the human rights recognized by International Law in force in Costa Rica (Article 57).

In particular, the same Law of Constitutional Jurisdiction specifically regulates the recourse of amparo to guarantee the right of correction or response to any person affected by incorrect or harmful report issued against him or her by the mass media, in order that it be rectified or responded by the same broadcaster. The Law regulates a specific procedure for such purpose (Articles 66 *et seq.*).

The recourse of amparo of Costa Rica, therefore, is conceived as a judicial means of constitutional protection against actions of the Public Administration, against individual's actions when exercising Public Authority, and against self-applicable laws or regulatory acts, which is brought directly before the Constitutional Chamber of the Supreme Court of Justice against the agent or titleholder of the institution or representative of the entity that appears to be the author of the offence, without it being necessary to exercise any administrative recourse prior to bringing the action.

On the other hand, the Constitutional Chamber of the Supreme Court of Costa Rica before which are filed the amparo recourses, was created as a result of the constitutional reform of 1989, with additional powers to declare the unconstitutionality of statutes and other State acts, with annulatory effects (Art. 10). Accordingly, in Costa Rica and following a long legislative tradition of absence of diffuse method of judicial review, a concentrated system of judicial review was established attributing exclusively to the Constitutional Chamber by mean of different judicial instruments like the action of unconstitutionality and the judicial referrals[65].

Article 73 of the Constitutional Jurisdiction Law sets forth the action of unconstitutionality that can be brought before the Chamber against any statute or regulation, when in their drafting it violates any essential constitutional formality, when a constitutional amendment has been approved in violation of the

[65] *Véase* en general Rubén HERNÁNDEZ VALLE, *El Control de la Constitucionalidad de las Leyes*, San José, 1990.

constitutional procedure, when a statute is contrary to the Constitution because opposing an international treaty or agreement, when an international convention or agreement is signed, approved or ratified in a contrary way to the Constitution provisions or when an international convention or agreement in its contents and effects infringe the Constitution or a constitutional principle. The decisions of the Chamber when declaring the unconstitutionality of the challenged statute have annulatory and *erga omnes* effects. The decisions also have declarative and retroactive ex tunc effects, except regarding bona fide acquired rights or consolidated legal situations by means of prescription, caducity of a judicial decision (Article 92).

This action can be exercise in an incidental or principal way. The incidental way may be brought before the Constitutional Chamber by any party in a judicial procedure, even in cases of habeas corpus and amparo, and in administrative procedures before Public Administration in which case the constitutional question must be raised as a reasonable mean for the protection of the rights and interest of the affected parties (Article 75).

The principal unconstitutionality action can only be brought before the Constitutional Chamber by the General Comptroller, the Attorney General, the Public Prosecutor an the Peoples' Defendant (Article 75). Nonetheless, the action can also be brought before the Chamber in cases of absence of individual harm or in cases devoted to the defense of diffuse or collective interests, in which cases, the action is brought against regulation or auto applicable statutes which do not require additional State actions for its enforcement. In these cases, no individual interest must be raised being then the constitutional action similar to a popular action.[66]

In addition to the action of unconstitutionality, the other important mean for judicial review is the judicial referrals on constitutionality matters that the courts can raise before the Constitutional Chamber when there are doubts regarding the constitutionality of the regulation or the statute that they must apply for the resolution of the case (Article 120). In these cases, the court must prepare a resolution where it must raise the constitutional questions to be sent to the Constitutional Chamber. The judicial procedure must be suspended until the Chamber decision is taken, which has obligatory character and res judicata effects (articles 104 and 117).

B. *The recourse of amparo in El Salvador*

In a similar way to the Costa Rican regulations, also in El Salvador, the Constitutional Chamber of the Supreme Court of Justice is the judicial body with the exclusive power to decide recourses of amparo for the protection against all the violations of the rights granted by the Constitution (Article 247). Also, regarding the *habeas corpus* recourses to protect personal freedom, the power to decide them is likewise attributed to the Constitutional Chamber of the Supreme Court of Justice.

Nonetheless, when the aggressive action takes place outside the capital, the habeas corpus recourse can be filed before the Chambers of Second Instance (article 42). In such cases, the decision of the Chambers that denies the liberty of the aggrieved party may be subject to review, at the request of the interested party, by the Constitutional Chamber of the Supreme Court of Justice.

---

66 See Rubén HERNÁNDEZ VALLE, *El Control de la Constitucionalidad de las Leyes*, San José, 1990.

Both actions, amparo and habeas corpus, have been regulated in the 1960 Law N° 2996 of Constitutional Proceedings, amended in multiple occasions up to 1997, setting forth that the action of amparo proceeds against any kind of actions or omissions of any authority, public official or decentralized bodies or of the judicial definitive decisions issued by the Judicial review of administrative action Chambers which violate the rights guaranteed in the Constitution or impede its exercise. When the State is the aggrieved party, the Constitutional Chamber must order the suspension of the challenged act (Article 12).

The Law disposed that the action of amparo can only be filed when the act against which it is formulated, cannot be reparable within the procedure by means of other remedies.

In cases in which the amparo is funded in the illegal detention or undue restriction of personal freedom, the protection must be sought through the habeas corpus recourse. In this regard, Article 38 of the same Law set forth the right of everyone to dispose of himself, considering that such right is harmed, when the person is detained against his will, due to threats, to fear to injury, constraint or other material obstacles, in which cases it is understood that the person is reduced to prison and in custody of authority or of the private persons that made the detention (Art. 38).

In all these cases of non-legally authorized prison, confinement, custody or restriction, or which is exercised in a way not legally authorized, the aggrieved party has the right to be protected by writ of personal exhibition (article 40).

In El Salvador, also a concentrated system of judicial review has been set forth in the Constitution, resulting from the creation of the Constitutional Chamber of the Supreme Court by means of the constitutional reforms of 1991-1992. The Constitution attributed to the Chamber the general and exclusive power not only to resolve the amparo and habeas corpus recourses but to declare the unconstitutionality of statutes, decrees and regulations, also with *erga omnes* effects. The unconstitutionality action is conceived in the Constitutional Proceeding Law as a popular action that can be brought before the Chamber by any citizen (Articles 2 and 10).

2. The amparo action exercised before a universality of courts: the case of Bolivia, Chile, Honduras, Panama, Paraguay and Uruguay

With the exception of the tree abovementioned cases of Costa Rica, El Salvador and Nicaragua, where the judicial protection of constitutional rights is concentrated in the Supreme Court, in all the other Latin American countries the actions or recourses of amparo and habeas corpus, as a specific judicial guarantees of constitutional rights and freedoms, are regulated in a diffuse way in the sense that it can be filled before a wide universe of courts instead of being concentrated in one sole Tribunal. This is the case of all other Latin American countries. In addition to the Mexican and Venezuelan systems already analyzed of the amparo as a constitutional right and as a remedy, it is also the case of Argentina, Bolivia, Brazil, Colombia, Chile, Dominican Republic, Ecuador, Guatemala, Honduras, Panama, Paraguay, Perú and Uruguay.

But regarding the countries where a concentrated system of judicial review exists as the only method to control the constitutionality of legislation, like Bolivia,

Chile, Honduras, panama, Paraguay and Uruguay, the jurisdiction to decide amparo and habeas corpus actions is attributed to multiple courts.

A. *The recourse of amparo in Bolivia*

According to the Constitution of Bolivia, the recourse of constitutional amparo can be brought before the High Courts in the Department capitals or before the District Judges in the Provinces, against any illegal act or unlawful omission of officials or private individuals that restrict, suppress or threaten to restrict or withhold personal rights and guarantees recognized by the Constitution and the statutes (Art. 19).

The recourse of amparo must be brought by the person who believes to have been wronged or by another sufficiently authorized person in his name, being extremely summarily processed. The Public Prosecutor may also bring, *ex officio*, this recourse when the affected party does not or is unable to do so. In these cases the amparo can only be conceded, provided there is no other means or legal recourse for the immediate protection of the restricted, suppressed and threatened rights and guarantees.

The Constitution also set forth the habeas corpus that can be filed by any person who believes to be illegitimately prosecuted, detained, or imprisoned or by another in his name, with or without power of attorney, Superior Courts of District or any Local judge, asking that the formalities be observed (Article. 18).

Regarding the recourse of habeas data it can also be brought before Superior Courts of District or any Local judge, by any person who believes himself to be illegitimately impeded from knowing, or to object or obtain the removal or rectification of data registered in any physical, electronic, magnetic or computerized in public or private files or data banks, that could affect his fundamental right to personal or familiar intimacy and privacy, self image, honor or reputation recognized in the Constitution (Article 23)

The tree recourses had been developed by Law 1.836 of 1998 on the Law of the Constitutional Tribunal, which states that the constitutional amparo shall be admitted «against any unlawful resolution, act or omission of an authority or official, provided there is no other procedure or recourse available to immediately protect the rights and guarantees, and also against any unlawful act or omission of a person or group of private individuals that restricts, suppresses or threatens the rights or guarantees recognized by the Political Constitution of the State and the Laws» (Article 94).

In Bolivia, according to the Constitution (Article 120,7), and the Law of the Constitutional Tribunal (Article 7,8), all the judicial decisions issued on amparo or habeas corpus must be sent to the Constitutional Tribunal in order to be reviewed. According to Articles 93 and 102,V of the Law on the Constitutional Tribunal, the decisions on amparo and habeas corpus must be sent ex officio to the Constitutional Tribunal in a 24 hours delay for their revision, without causing any suspension on its enforcement.

The revision, in the case of Bolivia, different to the Argentinean, Brazilian, Colombian and Venezuelan extraordinary recourses for revision, is not a recourse, but an obligatory revision that the Constitutional Tribunal must do, to which the decisions must be sent by the courts.

Even though the 1861 Constitution introduced in Bolivia the diffuse system of judicial review following the North American model, by means of the 1994 constitutional reform, the judicial review system in Bolivia was transformed into an exclusively concentrated one[67], corresponding to the Constitutional Tribunal, which began its functioning in 1999, the exclusive power to declare the nullity of statutes declared unconstitutional, with *erga omnes* effects[68].

Therefore, the Constitutional Tribunal has the attribution to control the constitutionality and to guaranty the supremacy of the Constitution, the respect and enforcement of fundamental rights and guarantees as well as the constitutionality of conventions and treaties (Art. 1 of the Law). Thus the courts, except by means of amparo, habeas corpus and habeas data, cannot rule on constitutional matters, and can only refer the control of constitutionality of statutes to the Constitutional Tribunal.

In such character of the Constitutional Tribunal as having the monopoly of judicial review, it also has the power to review the judicial decisions on amparo and habeas corpus, and consequently to seek for the uniform interpretation of the Constitution.

B. *The «recourse of protection» in Chile*

Chile's 1980 Constitution, with antecedents in Constitutional Act N° 3 (Decree-Law 1.552) of 1976, sets forth the recourse of protection of certain constitutional rights and freedoms that may be brought before the competent Courts of Appeals to immediately adopt the rulings they consider appropriate for re-establishing the rule of law and assuring the due protection of the affected party, without prejudice to the other rights that may be enforced before the corresponding authority or tribunals (Article 20)[69].

According to the Constitution, as we have analyzed, this recourse of protection is only set forth to protect the specific rights enshrined in «Article 19, Numbers 1; 2; 3 Subsection 4; 4; 5; 6; 9 Final Subsection; 11; 12; 13; 15; 16 related to the freedom to

---

67 See in general José Antonio RIVERA SANTIVAÑEZ, «La jurisdicción constitucional en Bolivia. Cinco años en defensa del orden constitucional y democrático» en *Revista Iberoamericana de Derecho Procesal Constitucional* N° 1, enero, junio 2004, Ed. Porrúa, 2004; José Antonio RIVERA SANTIVAÑEZ, «El control constitucional en Bolivia» en *Anuario Iberoamericano de Justicia Constitucional*. Centro de Estudios Políticos y Constitucionales N° 3, 1999, pp. 205-237; José Antonio RIVERA SANTIVAÑEZ, «Los valores supremos y principios fundamentales en la jurisprudencia constitucional» in *La Justicia Constitucional en Bolivia 1998-2003*, Ed. Tribunal Constitucional-AECI, Bolivia, 2003. pp. 347 y ss.; Benjamín Miguel HARB, «La jurisdicción constitucional en Bolivia» en *La Jurisdicción Constitucional en Iberoamérica,* Ed. Dykinson, Madrid, España, 1997, pp. 337 y ss, p. 131.

68 Jorge ASBÚN ROJAS, «Control constitucional en Bolivia, evolución y perspectivas» en *Jurisdicción Constitucional,* Academia Boliviana de Estudios Constitucionales. Editora El País, Santa Cruz, Bolivia, 2000, p. 86.

69 See (in general): Pedro ABERASTURY *et al., Acciones constitucionales de* amparo *y protección: realidad y prospectiva en Chile y América Latina*, Editorial Universidad de Talca, Talca 2000, Chile; Juan Manuel ERRAZURIZ GATICA *et al., Aspectos procesales del recurso de protección,* Editorial Jurídica de Chile, Santiago de Chile, 1989; Sergio LIRA HERRERA, *El recurso de protección. Naturaleza Jurídica, Doctrina, Jurisprudencia, Derecho Comparado,* Editorial Jurídica de Chile, Santiago de Chile, 1990; Enrique PAILLAS, *El recurso de protección ante el derecho comparado,* Editorial Jurídica de Chile, Santiago de Chile, 1990.

work and the freedom of free choice and free contracting, and the terms established in Subsection 4; 19; 21; 22; 23; 24 and 25». The recourse of protection is also admitted in the case of Article 19, Number 8, when the right to live in an environment free of contamination is affected by an arbitrary and illegal act attributable to a determined authority or person.

Pursuant to Article 21 of the Constitution, also in matters of constitutional rights protection, specifically regarding to personal freedom and safety, any individual who is under arrest, detained or imprisoned with infringement of the provisions of the Constitution or the statutes, by himself or by any one in his name, may request from the competent court, to order that legal formalities be observed and to immediately adopt the necessary provisions for the re-establishment of the rule of law and to assure the due protection of the affected party.

The court may order that the person be brought before it and its decree shall be precisely obeyed by those in charge of the prisons or places of detention. Once instructed of the antecedents, it shall order the immediate release or the correction of any legal defects, or order that the person be placed at the disposal of the competent judge, proceeding summarily and promptly, and correcting itself such defects or instructing whoever it corresponds to correct them.

The same recourse, in likewise, may be brought in favor of any person who illegally suffers any other deprival, disturbance or threat to the right to personal freedom and individual safety. In such cases, the respective court shall pronounce the above-mentioned measures it deems appropriate for re-establishing the rule of law and ensuring due protection of the affected party.

It must be noted that Chile is one of the few Latin American countries where the recourse of amparo or protection has not been regulated by a special statute. This lack of special statute does not impede its exercise in an efficient way, not only against public authorities harmful's actions but against individuals too. Some cases decided during the eighties', reported by Paillas[70] may illustrate this fact.

For instance, in a case, a farmer brought before a court an action for protection against a neighbor that had demolished the fence dividing their land, and by rebuilding it in another place it affected the plaintiff property rights. The court ordered the re-establishing of the fence to its original place, considering that the arbitrary action of the defendant threatened the property rights of the plaintiff. The decision sought to maintain the existing legal factual situation, in the sense that the recourse of protection was not set forth to resolve property controversies and to establish the real land division, for which the ordinary judicial means are regulated.

In other case, protection was granted to a physician and Medicine professor whose incorporation to the National Health Service was banned, because violation of the non discrimination constitutional guaranty. In other case, a protection was granted against a factory, ordering to halt the production of human consuming products until a ventilation system was set in the premises, in order to expel the gases produced. In the case, the plaintiffs were the neighbors who alleged violation to their rights to a healthy environment. A recourse of protection was filed by the Universidad Austral because of the occupation of its buildings by students, in which

[70] See in Enrique PAILLAS, *El recurso de protección ante el derecho comparado*, Santiago de Chile, 1990, pp. 80 ff.

case the protection was granted because a violation to the University's rights to teach and to use its own property was found. In all these cases, no decision was issued in order to resolve in a definitive way the legal controversy between parties regarding their respective rights. The decision of the recourse for protection was adopted just in order to resolve a factual problem and to preserve the situation affected by arbitrary actions, re-establishing the existing situation, in order for the interested parties to resolve their rights dispute by the ordinary judicial means.

Nevertheless, in other cases, the recourse for protection were brought before the courts in order to resolve controversies in a definitive way, for which no ordinary judicial mean were available for the resolution of the problem in a prompt an effective way. It is the case, for instance, of ignoring indubitable rights. It was the case of the owner of a land who sought protection to his property right against a railway Company authorized by the state to extract materials from the land for the building of a railway. The court granted the protection because the violation of property rights, not only by the Railway Company but also by the public body which authorized the seizure of the materials.

In all the cases, it can be said that the common denominator is always the urgency needed for the protection.

One aspect that must be highlighted is that in Chile, even though the judicial decisions regarding the recourses of protection are constitutional matters, when deciding the case, the courts cannot adopt any decision on judicial review of legislation. Since 1970 a Constitutional Tribunal was created in Chile, in charge of exercising a concentrated judicial review of statutes[71]; but since the 2005 constitutional reform, all sort of decisions on judicial review of legislation, even in concrete cases, have been concentrated in the Tribunal. Thus, when deciding a recourse of protection, if the court considers that the applicable statute is unconstitutional, it cannot decide on the matter, but has to refer the case to the Constitutional Tribunal for its decision.

In this regard, Article 82, 6 of the Constitution assigns the Constitutional Tribunal the power to resolve the inapplicability of statutory provisions in any case before any ordinary or special court, when contrary to the Constitution. Thus, the Constitutional Tribunal has the monopoly of judicial review. In these cases, according to the same Article 82 of the Constitution, the question of unconstitutionality of a statute can be raised by any of the party to the case or by the court that is hearing the case. The Constitutional Tribunal through any of its Chambers may declare without any possibility to be challenged, the admissibility of the question as long as it verifies that a judicial action is pending before an ordinary or special court, that the application of the challenged statutory provision can be decisive to resolve the case and that the challenge is reasonably founded. The same Chamber can decide the suspension of the proceedings where the action of inapplicability on grounds of unconstitutionality has been raised.

---

[71] See in general Raúl BERTELSEN REPETTO, *Control de constitucionalidad de la ley*, Editorial Jurídica de Chile, Santiago, Chile, 1969; Francisco Zúñiga Urbina, *Jurisdicción constitucional en Chile*, Tomo II, Ed. Universidad Central de Chile, Santiago, 2002; Humberto NOGUEIRA ALCALÁ, «El Tribunal Constitucional chileno» en *Lecturas Constitucionales Andinas* N° 1, Ed. Comisión Andina de Juristas, Lima, Perú, 1991; Lautaro RÍOS ÁLVAREZ, «La Justicia Constitucional en Chile» en *La Revista de Derecho* N° 1, Ed. Facultad de Derecho, Universidad Central, Santiago, Chile, 1988; Teodoro RIVERA, «El Tribunal Constitucional» en *Revista Chilena de Derecho*, Volumen 11, N° 23, Santiago, Chile, 1984.

When the Constitutional Tribunal has decided in a concrete case the inapplicability of a statutory provision, the decision has only *inter partes* effects. Following, by means of a public action, the question of the unconstitutionality of the provision can be brought before the same Constitutional Tribunal, seeking a ruling in order to annul the statute with general *erga omnes* effects (article 82,7).

C. *The action of amparo in Honduras*

Pursuant to Article 183 of its Constitution, in Honduras the State recognizes the guarantee of amparo; therefore, any offended party, or another in his or her name, shall be entitled to bring a recourse of amparo to uphold or reinstate the enjoyment or benefit of the rights or guarantees established by the Constitution; and in order that he or she declares in specific cases that a law, resolution, act or fact of authority does not apply to the petitioner, nor is it applicable, since it contravenes, diminishes or distorts one or other of the rights recognized by this Constitution. Also pursuant to Article 182 of the Constitution, the State recognizes the guarantee of *habeas corpus* (*exhibición personal*), consequently, any affected party or any other person in his or her name is entitled to bring such action when illegally imprisoned, detained or in any way deprived of the individual's right to enjoy freedom; and when in the course of the legal detention or imprisonment, torment, torture, humiliation, illegal extortion and any unnecessary force, restriction or molestation is applied for his or her individual safety or by order of the jail.

These actions were regulated by the 1936 Act of Amparo, until it was repeal by the 2004 Law of Constitutional Justice, in which the follow regulations should be highlighted[72]:

Regarding the purpose of the action of amparo and pursuant to the orientation of the American Convention on Human Rights (Article 25), its exercise is admitted against facts, acts, omissions or threats by any State Authority, including decentralized and de-concentrated entities, municipal corporations and autonomous institutes; those maintained by public funds and those that act through delegation of a State entity by reason of a concession, contract or other valid resolution (Article 42).

The power to hear the action of amparo is attributed to all levels of courts as follows:

According to Article 9 of the Law on Constitutional Justice, all actions of habeas data and the amparo recourses in cases of violation of fundamental rights perpetrated by the President of the Republic, the Appellate Courts, the Accounting Superior Tribunal, the General Attorney of the Republic, the Electoral Supreme Tribunal and by other officials with national jurisdiction, must be brought before the Constitutional Chamber of the Supreme Court of Justice which was created in the 2000 constitutional reform.

---

72 See Allan R. BREWER-CARÍAS, «La reforma del sistema de justicia constitucional en Honduras», en *Revista Iberoamericana de Derecho Procesal Constitucional. Proceso y Constitución* (Directores Eduardo FERRER MAC-GREGOR y Aníbal QUIROGA LEÓN), N° 4, 2005, Editorial Porrúa, México, pp. 57-77; and «El sistema de justicia constitucional en Honduras» in *El sistema de Justicia Constitucional en Honduras (Comentarios a la Ley sobre Justicia Constitucional)*, Instituto Interamericano de Derechos Humanos, Corte Suprema de Justicia. República de Honduras, San José, 2004, pp. 1-148

The Courts of Appeals are the competent courts to hear the amparo in cases of violation of fundamental rights perpetrated by the Departmental courts and sectional, executor judges and justices of peace, as well as by all political, administrative or military department or section employees (Article 10).

Finally, in the lower level of the Judiciary, the ordinary courts (Jueces de Letras) are competent to hear the amparo recourses in any other cases of violations of fundamental rights and particularly those perpetrated by lower level public officials, by municipal corporations or its members, comprising the police judges and auxiliary mayors (Article 11).

On the other hand, all the above mentioned courts have the power to hear and decide the habeas corpus or personal appearance recourse for the rights of personal freedom and safety (Article 13).

In matters concerning amparo, the most important characteristics of the Law's regulations are as follows:

The rights protected, pursuant to the guidelines of the American Convention, are those recognized in the Constitution and in the Treaties, covenants and other international instruments of human rights (Article 41,1).

Respecting the standing to sue, the action of amparo may be brought by any person without distinction, whether an individual or a legal entity, and it may also be brought by any person in representation of the aggrieved party (Article 44).

With respect to the defendant party, as has been said, the amparo shall be admitted against acts of any authority, such as norms, judicial decisions or administrative acts and also against omissions or threats of violation (Articles 13 and 41). The amparo shall also be admitted against private parties, although to a limited extent, in respect of institutions maintained by public funds and those acting by delegation of a State entity by virtue of a concession, contract or other valid resolution (Article 42).

The processing of the amparo, on the other hand, shall take preference over any other matter, except for cases of *habeas corpus* (Article 51).

A procedure of two instances is established in the Law and in all cases an obligatory consultation of the decisions is set forth. Regarding the decisions issued by the department courts, they must be sent in consultation before the Appellate Courts. The decision issued by these Appellate Courts can be subject to review by the Constitutional Chamber of the Supreme Court by means of the parties' request for study. In such cases the Constitutional Chamber has discretionary power to resolve the admissibility of the request (article 68). Regarding the decisions adopted in first instance by the Appeals Courts in questions of amparo, they must also be sent for consultation before the Constitutional Chamber of the Supreme Court (Article 69).

Thus, the Constitutional Chamber can always be the last resort to decide upon the matters of amparo. According to the Constitution, it can be said that the Honduran system of judicial review is conceived as a mixed one, combining the diffuse and the concentrated ones, the latter in the hands of the Constitutional Chamber. Regarding the diffuse method of judicial review of legislation, Article 320 of the Constitution set forth that «In cases of incompatibility between a constitutional norm and an ordinary statutory one, the courts must apply the former». A constitutional provision regarding the diffuse method of judicial review cannot be clearer[73]. Notwithstanding, and following the legislative practice of the past, the final version of the Law on Constitutional Justice of 2004, failed to regulate such method, setting forth a one and only concentrated method of judicial review of legislation by attributing to the Constitutional Chamber the power to annul statutes on the grounds of their unconstitutionality. Nevertheless, the diffuse method always persists by means of the amparo recourse, because in it, precisely, the court decision can be can be a judicial declaration that in the specific cases, a law is not to be enforced against the claimant nor is it applicable, since it contravenes, diminishes or distorts a right recognized by this Constitution» (183,2 Constitution).

Regarding the concentrated method of judicial review, the Constitution sets forth that «The statutes can be declared unconstitutional on grounds of form or in its contents» (Article 184), corresponding to the Constitutional Chamber of the Supreme Court the exclusive hearing and resolution on the matter (Article 315,5). The most important aspects of this concentrated method of judicial review are the followings:

Regarding the object of judicial review, the actions of unconstitutionality that can be brought before the Constitutional Chamber are about the statutes and general applicable norms, except regulations, that must be challenged before the administrative action judicial review courts; constitutional amendments approved contrary to the formalities set forth in the Constitution; approbatory statutes of international treaties sanctioned without following the constitutional formalities (Article 17); and against statutes that contravene the provisions of an international treaty or convention in force in Honduras (article 76).

The action of unconstitutionality can be brought before the Constitutional Chamber in a limited standing rule, set forth in the Law on Constitutional Justice following the Constitution, reduced to those persons having a personal, direct and legitimate interest (Article 77).

The concentrated method of judicial review can also be exercised in an incidental manner, as an exception of unconstitutionality of a statute that can be raised in any process (Article 82), or by the referral of the case that any court can make to the Constitutional Chamber of the Supreme Court before deciding the case (Article 87). In such cases, the proceeding must continue in the lower court up to the stage of deciding the case, in which it must be suspended waiting for the Constitutional Chambers decision on the constitutional question (Article 77).

In both cases, whether through the action of unconstitutionality or by means of the incidental constitutional question, the decision of the Constitutional Chamber has *erga omnes* effects, with repealing character (Article 94).

D. *The action of amparo in Panamá*

The amparo action of constitutional guaranties is set forth in Article 50 of Panama's 1972 Constitution, reformed in 1978, 1983 and 1994, for the benefit of any

[73] See Allan R. BREWER-CARÍAS, «El sistema de justicia constitucional en Honduras» in *El sistema de Justicia Constitucional en Honduras (Comentarios a la Ley sobre Justicia Constitucional)*, Instituto Interamericano de Derechos Humanos, Corte Suprema de Justicia. República de Honduras, San José, 2004, pp. 27 ff.

person against whom an order to do or not to do is issued or enforced by any public servant, which violates the rights and guarantees enshrined in this Constitution. In such cases the person has the right to have the order revoked at his request or that of any other person on his behalf». According to the same article, «the recourse of amparo of constitutional guarantees shall be brought by means of a summary procedure and shall be the competence of the judicial tribunals»[74].

Article 23 of the Constitution also sets forth the habeas corpus recourse in favor of any individual arrested in a manner or in cases other than those prescribed by the Constitution and the statute. In such cases, the person shall be released at his request or that of another person, by means of the recourse of *habeas corpus*, which may be brought immediately following the arrest and irrespective of the applicable punishment.

The regulation related to the amparo action and to the habeas corpus recourse is set forth in the Judicial Code of Panama. Regarding the amparo of constitutional guaranties, according to Article 2615 of the Code, it can be brought against any kind of acts that harm or injure the fundamental rights and guaranties set forth in the Constitution, having the form of an order to do or not no do, when the seriousness and imminence of the damage they cause requires an immediate repeal. It can also be brought against judicial decisions when all the existing judicial means to impugn it have been exhausted; but cannot refer to judicial decisions adopted by the Electoral Tribunal, the Supreme Court of Justice or any of its Chambers.

Pursuant to Article 2.616 of the Legal Code, the following are the competent courts to hear claims of amparo:

1. The Supreme Court of Justice, for acts issued by authorities or officials with rule and jurisdiction in the whole Republic or in two or more provinces.
2. The District High Courts, for acts issued by public servants with rule and jurisdiction in one Province; and
3. The Circuit Judges for acts issued by public servants with rule and jurisdiction in one district or part of such district.

The distribution of the judicial power to resolve in matters of amparo and habeas corpus among all levels of the Judiciary contrast with the judicial review system of Panama, conceived as a concentrated one, by attributing to the Supreme Court of Justice the exclusive power to decide upon the constitutionality of legislation.

Article 203,1 of the Panamanian Constitution gives the Supreme Court the exclusive role to protect the integrity of the Constitution and to control the constitutionality of legislation by means of two different methods: a direct popular action or by mean of a question of constitutionality that can be raised as an incident before a lower court.

Regarding the action of unconstitutionality, in similar terms as the Colombian and Venezuelan regulations, it is conceived as a popular action that can be brought

---

[74] See: Lao SANTIZO P., *Acotaciones al* amparo *de garantías constitucionales panameño,* Editorial Jurídica Sanvas, San José, Costa Rica, 1987.

before the Supreme Court by anybody in order to denounce the unconstitutionality of statutes, decrees, decisions or acts, founded in substantive or formal questions (Article 2556).

On the other hand, the question of the unconstitutionality of legal or executive norms applicable to a case can be raised by the parties to the case or ex officio by the respective court, in which case the incidental question must be sent to the Supreme Court for its decision. The procedure must be suspended at the stage previous to the decision that can only be issued once the Supreme Court has adopted its decision on the constitutional matters (Article 2557 Judicial Code).

In both cases, the Supreme Court decision is final, definitive, obligatory and with non retroactive effects, and must be published in the Official Gazette (article 2573 Judicial Code).

E. *The petition for amparo in Paraguay*

The 1992 Constitution of Paraguay also expressly regulates as constitutional guarantees, the petition for amparo, the action of *habeas corpus* (Article 133)[75] and the action of *habeas data* (Article 135).

Regarding the petition for amparo, according to Article 134 of the Constitution, it can be filed by anyone who considers himself seriously affected by a clearly illegitimate act or omission, either by governmental authorities or individuals, or who may be in imminent danger that the rights and guarantees set forth in the Constitution or the statutes may be curtailed, and whom, in light of the urgency of the matter cannot seek remedy through regular legal means. In such case, the affected person may file a petition for amparo before a competent judge. Proceedings will be brief, summary, and free of charge, and of popular action in the cases set forth by legislation.

The judge is empowered to safeguard rights, guarantee, or immediately restore the legal situation that existed prior to the violation.

The amparo petition which has been regulated in the 1971 Law 341 of Amparo, is not admissible against judicial decisions and resolutions and when the matter refers to the individual freedom protected by the recourse of habeas corpus (Article 2).

According to Article 3 of the Law of Amparo, the petition for amparo can be filed before any first instance court with jurisdiction in the place where the act or omission could have effect. Nonetheless, the Constitution provides that, regarding electoral questions and matters related to political organization, the competent court will be that of the electoral jurisdiction (Article 134).

The recourses of habeas data and habeas corpus must also be filed before the judges of first instance (Article 133); and in some cases the habeas corpus recourse before the Supreme Court (Article 259,5).

Except for the resolutions of the amparo petition, habeas corpus recourse or habeas data action, which in general corresponds to all courts of first instance, all

75 See: Evelio FERNÁNDEZ ARÉVALOS, *Habeas Corpus Régimen Constitucional y legal en el Paraguay*, Intercontinental Editora, Asunción, Paraguay 2000.

other constitutional matters dealing with judicial review of legislation are the exclusive attribution of the Constitutional Chamber of the Supreme Court of Justice. Therefore, in Paraguay, since the 1992 Constitution, a concentrated system of judicial review[76] has existed, by attributing the Supreme Court of Justice the power to decide actions and exceptions seeking to declare the unconstitutionality and inapplicability of statutes contrary to the Constitution. Article 260 of the Constitution, assigns the Constitutional Chamber created in 1995, the power to hear and resolve upon the unconstitutionality of statutes and other normative instruments, declaring in the concrete case, the inapplicability of their dispositions that are contrary to the Constitutions. The decision, thus, only has effects for the concrete case.[77]

The Constitutional Chamber also has the power to decide upon the unconstitutionality of judicial definitive or interlocutory decisions, declaring their nullity when contrary to the Constitution. In all these cases, the procedure can be initiated by means of an action before the Constitutional Chamber of the Supreme Court or through an exception raised in any instance, in which case the files must be sent to the Constitutional Chamber.

This is confirmed by Article 18,a) of the Civil Procedure Code which set forth that the when a judge hearing a concrete case considers the applicable statute contrary to the Constitution, even ex officio, he may send the files to the Supreme Court of Justice, in order for the Court to decide the question of unconstitutionality.

In particular, regarding actions of amparo, Article 582 of the same Civil Procedure Code (Law N° 600, 1995), set forth that when in order to decide an action for amparo, the competent court must determine the constitutionally or unconstitutionality of a statute, decree or regulation, the court must send the files to the Constitutional Chamber of the Supreme Court of Justice, who as soon as possible, must declare the unconstitutionality when evident.

F. *The action of amparo in Uruguay*

Notwithstanding the general declarations contained in Articles 7,72 and 332 of the 1966 Constitution, the action of amparo in Uruguay was expressly regulated by Law 16.011 of 1988, which establishes that any person, human or artificial, public or private, may bring an action of amparo against any act, omission or fact of the state or public sector authorities, as well as of private individuals that in a illegitimate evident way, currently or imminently impair, restrict, alter or threaten unlawfully any of the rights and freedoms expressly or implicitly recognized by the Constitution (Article 72), except in those cases where an action of *habeas corpus* is admitted.

This action of amparo for the protection of all constitutional rights and freedoms may be brought before the judges of First Instance in the matter

---

76 See in general, Norbert LÖSING, «La justicia constitucional en Paraguay y Uruguay» en *Anuario de Derecho Constitucional Latinoamericano 2002*. Ed. KAS, Montevideo, Uruguay, 2002; Luis LEZCANO CLAUDE, *El control de constitucionalidad en el Paraguay*, Ed. La Ley Paraguaya S.A. Asunción, Paraguay, 2000.

77 L.M. ARGAÑA, «Control de la Constitucionalidad de las Leyes en Paraguay», *Memoria de la Reunión de Presidentes de Cortes Supremas de Justicia en Iberoamérica, el Caribe, España y Portugal*, Caracas, 1982, pp. 550, 551, 669, 671.

corresponding to the act, fact or omission under dispute and of the place where they produce effect (Article 3)[78].

However, Law 16.011 excludes from action of amparo, all judicial acts issued in judicial controversies, no matter their nature and irrespective of the court that issues them; also acts of the Electoral Court, whatever their nature; as well as the statutes and decrees of departmental governments that have force of statute in their jurisdiction (Article 1).

This action of amparo in the Uruguayan system is only admitted when there are no other judicial or administrative means available for obtaining the same result of protection or amparo, or when, if they were to exist, are clearly ineffective for protecting the right Article 2).

In the process of amparo, constitutional questions may arise regarding the unconstitutionality of statutes, but the ordinary court cannot resolve them, and a referral to the Supreme Court must be made. This is the consequence of the concentrated method of judicial review of legislation that exists in Uruguay[79].

Article 256 of the Uruguayan Constitution, since 1934[80], assigns to the Supreme Court of Justice the exclusive and original power to declare the unconstitutionality of statutes and other State acts with force of statutes, whether founded on formal or substantive reasons.

This declaration of unconstitutionality of a statute and its inapplicability can be requested be means of an action of unconstitutionality that can be filed before the Supreme Court by all those who deem that their personal and legitimate interests have been harmed (Article 258)[81]. Thus, regarding standing, the Uruguayan regulation has similarities with the Honduran one.

The constitutional question can also be submitted to the Supreme Court in an incidental way by a referral made ex officio or as a consequence of an exception of

---

78 See (in general): Luis Alberto VIERA *et al.*, *Ley de Amparo. Comentarios, Texto Legal y Antecedentes legislativos a su sanción. Jurisprudencia sobre el* amparo, 2nd Edition, Ediciones IDEA, Montevideo, 1993; Miguel Ángel SEMINO, «Comentarios sobre la acción de amparo en el Derecha uruguayo», en *Boletín de la Comisión Andina de Jurista,* N° 27, Lima, 1986.

79 See in general José KORSENIAK, «La Justicia constitucional en Uruguay» en *La Revista de Derecho,* año III, enero-junio 1989, Facultad de Derecho, Universidad Central, 1989; Héctor GROS ESPIELL, «La jurisdicción constitucional en el Uruguay» en *La Jurisdicción Constitucional en Iberoamérica,* Ed. Universidad Externado de Colombia, Bogotá, Colombia, 1984; Eduardo ESTEVA G. «La jurisdicción constitucional en Uruguay» en Domingo GARCÍA BELAUNDE, y Francisco FERNÁNDEZ SEGADO, (Coord.), *La Jurisdicción Constitucional en Iberoamérica.* Ed. Dykinson, Madrid, España, 1997; Norbert Lösing, «La justicia constitucional en Paraguay y Uruguay» en *Anuario de Derecho Constitucional Latinoamericano 2002.* Ed. KAS, Montevideo, Uruguay, 2002.

80 Originally, the system was established in 1934, and latter in 1951. See H. GROSS ESPIELL, *La Constitución y su Defensa,* Congreso, «*La Constitución y su Defensa*», UNAM, 1982 (policopiado), pp. 7,11. The siystem remained in the 1966 Constitution, in the «Acta Institucional N° 8 de 1977» and in the «Acta Institucional N° 12 de 1981». *Idem,* pp. 16, 20.

81 Artículo 258. See H. GROSS ESPIELL, *op. cit.,* pp. 28, 29; J.P. GATTO DE SOUZA, «Control de la Constitucionalidad de los Actos del Poder público en Uruguay», *Memoria de la Reunión de Presidentes de Cortes Supremas de Justicia en Iberoamérica, el Caribe, España y Portugal,* Caracas, 1982, pp. 661, 662.

unconstitutionality raised by a party to a concrete process, by an inferior court (art. 258). In such cases, the inferior court must send to the Supreme Court an abstract of the question, the case having to be suspended at the stage of deciding it. Once the Supreme Court has decided, the inferior court must then decide according to what the Supreme Court has ruled (Articles 258, 259).

In all cases, the decisions of the Supreme Court on matters of constitutionality only refer to the concrete case in which the question is raised (Article 259). This principle is clear regarding the incidental mean of judicial review where the question of constitutionality is raised in a concrete case, but originates doubts regarding the action of unconstitutionality. According to the Law N° 13747 of 1969[82], which regulates the procedures in matters of judicial review, the decision of the Supreme Court impede the application of the challenged norms declared unconstitutional regarding the plaintiff, authorize its use as an exception in all other judicial proceedings, including the judicial review of Public administration activities[83].

---

82 See H. GROSS ESPIELL, *op. cit.*, p. 29.

83 *Idem.*

CHAPTER VI

THE AMPARO AS A CONSTITUTIONAL REMEDY WITHIN THE LATIN AMERICAN MIXED SYSTEMS (DIFFUSE AND CONCENTRATED) OF JUDICIAL REVIEW OF LEGISLATION

In the middle of the XIX Century, the North American system of judicial review influenced some Latin American countries which also adopted the diffuse system of judicial review. Alexis De Tocqueville's influential book, *Democracy in America,*[1] is considered to have played a fundamental role in this process, particularly regarding the Latin American countries with a federal form of state, all of whom adopted a form of constitutional justice, as was the case in Argentina (1860), México (1857), Venezuela (1858) and Brazil (1890). The system was also adopted in other countries with a brief federal experience like Colombia (1850) and even without connection with the federal form of state in the Dominican Republic (1844), where it is still in force.

But all the Latin American diffuse systems of judicial review, except for Argentina which remained the most similar to the American model[2], moved from the original diffuse system towards a mixed system, by adding the concentrated method of judicial review, or by adopting the mixed system from the beginning with its own natural characteristics. Even the Mexican system with the peculiarities of the *juicio de amparo* also moved from the original diffuse system to the current mixed system.

---

1 The first edition in Spanish of the book was issued in 1836, one year after the French and English edition. On the influence of the De Tocqueville book on the matter, see J. CARPIZO and H. FIX-ZAMUDIO, «La necesidad y la legitimidad de la revisión judicial en América Latina. Desarrollo reciente», in *Boletín Mexicano de Derecho Comparado*, 52, 1985, p. 33; R.D. Baker, *Judicial Review in México. A Study of the Amparo Suit*, Austin 1971, pp. 15, 33.

2 A. E. GHIGLIANI, *Del control jurisdiccional de constitucionalidad*, Buenos Aires 1952, who speaks about «Northamerican filiation» of the judicial control of constitutionality in Argentinian law, p. 6, 55, 115. *Cf.* R. BIELSA, *La protección constitucional y el recurso extraordinario. Jurisdicción de la Corte Suprema*, Buenos Aires 1958, p. 116; J.A.C. GRANT, «El control jurisdiccional de la constitucionalidad de las Leyes: una contribución de las Américas a la ciencia política», *Revista de la Facultad de Derecho de México*, UNAM, T. XII, 45, 1962, p. 652; C.J. FRIEDRICH, *The Impact of American Constitutionalism Abroad*, Boston 1967, p. 83.

Due to the mixed character of the judicial review system, in all the countries that have adopted the mixed system of judicial review, except for Nicaragua, the amparo actions can be filed before a universe of courts, as happens in Brazil, Colombia, Dominican Republic, Ecuador, Guatemala, Perú, México and Venezuela. In Nicaragua, on the contrary, only the Supreme Court can hear actions of amparo.

I. THE AMPARO ACTION OR RECOURSE IN MIXED SYSTEMS OF JUDICIAL REVIEW, EXERCISED BEFORE ONE SINGLE TRIBUNAL: THE CASE OF THE SUPREME COURT OF NICARAGUA

In Nicaragua, the Supreme Court of Justice is the one called to hear and decide the recourse of amparo (Art. 164,3), which -according to Article 45 of the Constitution, corresponds to those «whose constitutional rights have been violated or are in danger of violation». Only two other Latin American countries assign to their Supreme Court the monopoly to decide amparo actions, Costa Rica and El Salvador, but with the difference that there, the judicial review system followed is an exclusively concentrated one, exercised by a Constitutional Chamber of the Supreme Court.

The recourse of amparo in Nicaragua is set forth against any provision, act or resolution, and in general against any action or omission of any official, authority or agent that violates or attempts to violate the rights and guarantees enshrined in the Constitution; and the recourse of *habeas corpus* in regulated in favor of those whose freedom, physical integrity and safety have been violated or are in danger of being violated (Articles 188 and 189 of the Constitution). Both recourses are of the exclusive competence of the Supreme Court of Justice to hear them (Article 164,3).

According to the 1988 Law of Amparo, the recourse of amparo proceeds against any disposition, act or resolution and in general, against any action or omission of any public official, authority or agent which violates or threatens to violate the rights and guaranties declared in the Constitution (Article 3). Thus, no amparo recourse can be filled against private individual's actions or omissions.

On the other hand, regarding the recourse of personal exhibition (habeas corpus), it proceeds in favor of those persons whose freedom, physical integrity and security are violated or in danger of being violated by any public official, authority, entity or public institution, autonomous or not, and acts restrictive of personal freedom of any inhabitant of the Republic performed by individuals (Art. 4).

As mentioned, the Supreme Court of Justice is the only competent tribunal to finally decide the recourse of amparo. According to Article 25 of the Amparo Law, the amparo recourse must be brought before the Courts of Appeals or its Civil Chambers, where the first path of the proceeding must be accomplished, including the suspension of the challenged act. The files must then be sent for the accomplishment of the final path of the procedure to the Supreme Court of Justice until the final decision. Even in cases in which the Courts of Appeals reject to hear the recourse, the plaintiff can bring the case by mean of an action de amparo before the Supreme Court, against the illegitimate act of fact (*vía de hecho*).

In cases of illegal detentions made by any authority, the recourse of personal exhibition must be filed before the Courts of Appeals or their Criminal Chambers. In cases of acts restrictive of freedom made by individuals, the habeas corpus must be filed before the Criminal District courts (Art. 54).

In Nicaragua, even though the Supreme Court is the only competent court to decide the amparo and personal exhibition recourses, as well as a recourse of unconstitutionality of statutes, the judicial review system is not a concentrated one but a mixed one, because all courts, in accordance with the principle of constitutional supremacy (Article 182 of the Constitution), can be considered as having the general power to decide upon the unconstitutionality of statutes when deciding concrete cases, with only *inter partes* effects.

The recourse of unconstitutionality is conceived as a direct action that can be brought before the Supreme Court by any citizen against any statute, decree or regulation (Article 2 of the Amparo Law). The decision is thus conceived as a popular action, and the Supreme Court's decision when declaring the unconstitutionality of the impugned act, has also general and formal *res judiciata* effects. The statute declared in contravention with the Constitution cannot be applied after the Court's decision has been adopted (Articles 18 and 19).

It must be highlighted that the question of the unconstitutionality of a statute, decree or regulation can also be raised in a particular case before the Supreme Court by the corresponding party in the proceeding of a recourse of cassation or of a recourse of amparo, in which cases, if the Supreme Court in its decision, in addition to the cassation of the judicial decision and to the constitutional protection to be granted to the party, must declare the unconstitutionality of the statute, decree or regulation, with the same general effects. Nonetheless, the decision cannot affect third party rights acquired from those statutes or regulations (Articles 20 and 22).

The Amparo Law also provides that in any judicial case in which a decision that cannot be challenged by mean of a cassation recourse has been adopted, resolving the matter with express declaration of the unconstitutionality or a statute, decree or regulation, the respective court must send its decision to the Supreme Court. The latter can ratify the unconstitutionality of the statute, decree or regulation and declare its inapplicability. In such case the decision cannot affect third party rights acquired from those statutes or regulations (Articles 21 and 22)

As mentioned, with the only exception of Nicaragua, in all other Latin American countries that follow the mixed system of judicial review combining the diffuse and concentrated method of judicial review of the constitutionality of statutes, the amparo recourse proceedings follows the diffuse trends, and can be filed before a universality of courts and not before one single court. It is the case of the systems of Brazil, Colombia, Dominican Republic, Ecuador, Guatemala, México, Perú and Venezuela.

II. THE AMPARO ACTION OR RECOURSE IN MIXED SYSTEMS OF JUDICIAL REVIEW EXERCISED BEFORE A UNIVERSALITY OF COURTS: THE CASE OF MÉXICO, VENEZUELA, BRAZIL, COLOMBIA, DOMINI-CAN REPUBLIC, ECUADOR, GUATEMALA AND PERÚ

As has been mentioned before, the supremacy of the Constitution in a democratic society, as the product of the people's will expressed by means of the constituent power, implies that the Constitution cannot be modified except only by means of the constitutional revision process enshrined by the people in the same Constitution. The people as creator of the Constitution have a right to its preservation and to its supremacy.

The consequence of such right to he supremacy of the Constitution is the set of guaranties the Constitution set forth in order to protect it, by means of the judicial review power attributed to the Judiciary or by means of the actions for protection of the Constitution that can be filed before the courts.

In both cases, if people have a constitutional right to the supremacy of the Constitution and its contents, it also has a constitutional right to the protection of such supremacy, referred not only to the organic part of the Constitution (State organization and division and separation of powers) but also regarding its dogmatic side, that is, the constitutional rights and freedoms declared in the Constitution as pertaining to the people. Thus, everyone has rights guarantied in the Constitution, and everyone has the constitutional right to be effectively protected by the Judiciary in the enjoyment and exercise of such constitutional rights.

The consequence of such approach is that there is a fundamental right that can be distinguished, above all, and it is the right to the judicial control for the enforcement of the Constitution, in order to assure the submission of the State organs to the latter.

Concerning the organic part of the Constitution, this right implies: first, the right to judicial review of legislation (statutes), by means of direct actions of unconstitutionality brought before a constitutional court in a concentrated method of judicial review or by mean of the diffuse method of judicial review where the constitutionality of statutes can be challenge before any court; second, the right to judicial review of administrative action, generally by special administrative courts, on ground of constitutionality and legality; and third, the right to judicial review of judicial decisions through ordinary (appeals) or extraordinary (cassation) means of review.

Moreover, regarding the dogmatic part of the Constitution, this fundamental right to effective judicial protection of constitutional supremacy is also manifest in a right to judicial protection of the constitutional rights and freedoms of the people, either by ordinary judicial effective actions or recourses, or by means of specific actions or recourses of «amparo» or other judicial means of immediate protection of such rights. These provisions of constitutional guarantees to the constitutional rights and freedoms are an essential characteristic of contemporary democratic constitutionalism, the basis of which continues to be the unequivocal statement of Article 16 of the 1789 Declaration of the Rights of Man and the Citizen:

Any society in which no provision is made for guaranteeing rights or for the separation of powers, has no Constitution.

The consequence of this fundamental right to constitutional supremacy and the right to its judicial protection undoubtedly implies the power/duty attributed to the courts for the purpose of guaranteeing constitutional supremacy, either by annulling State acts (statutes, administrative acts, judicial resolutions) that are contrary to the Constitution, or by re-establishing constitutional rights and freedoms impaired by illegitimate actions, both by State entities and by private individuals.

Such citizens' constitutional right, as all rights of the people guaranteed in the Constitution, can only be limited by the same Constitution. That is why statutory legal restrictions to this right to Constitutional supremacy and to «amparo» protection would be incompatible with their fundamental right character, whether manifested for instance in the exclusion of some State act to be challenged or of some constitutional rights whose violation cannot be immediately protected by the «amparo» action. Constitutional supremacy is an absolute notion that admits no exception, and therefore neither of the constitutional right could be excluded from the judicial protection guarantees, unless, of course, provided by the Constitution itself.

Anyway, as already mentioned, regarding the Latin American «amparo», the national constitutional and statutory regulations allow to distinguish two general systems according to whether the «amparo» of constitutional rights and freedoms is conceived to be *per se* a *constitutional right*, at the same time being a judicial guarantee in multiple ways; or as a specific judicial remedy for the protection of constitutional rights.

1. THE «AMPARO» AS A CONSTITUTIONAL RIGHT

Firstly, the «amparo» of constitutional rights and freedoms may be conceived in the constitutional system as a constitutional right of the citizens, derived from the right to the supremacy of the Constitution and to obtain judicial protection from all courts regarding such rights and freedoms. Such means of judicial protection may be ordinary judicial means, or a specific judicial means of immediate protection.

In these cases, therefore, the amparo has been regulated as a constitutional right, hence originating not just one judicial guarantee (action or recourse) of «amparo», but multiple judicial proceedings, both ordinary and specific, for the protection of constitutional rights and freedoms. Such is the case of México and Venezuela where, in addition, no distinction is made between an amparo action and an habeas corpus action, being the latter just an amparo directed to protect personal freedom and safety.

A. The Mexican suit of «amparo»

As has been mentioned before, under Article 25 of the 1847 Act of Constitutional Reforms, México introduced *the right of all inhabitants of the Republic to be legally protected by the courts* of the Federation regarding the rights and guarantees granted to them by the Constitution, against any attack by the Executive or Legislative Authorities, thereby establishing that the federal courts had the duty to provide protection only in concrete cases, without making general declarations concerning the act in question. This is how it arose the figure of constitutional «amparo», as a constitutional right of all people to the protection of their constitutional rights and freedoms, the subsequent development of which, has shaped the so-called «judgment or trail of amparo».

This amparo suit, according to Article 1,1 of the Amparo Law, is set forth in order to resolve any controversy arisen from statutes and authorities' acts which violate individual guaranties. But also, according to the same article, it also has the purpose of resolving any controversy produced by federal statutes or authorities acts harming or restricting the States sovereignty or by States statutes of authorities' acts invading the sphere of federal authority.

In this case of amparo, the judicial protection is granted by means of a quick and efficient procedure, characterized by the absence of formalisms, the intermediary role the judge has between the parties, the inquisitorial character of the procedure which grants the judge with wide and inclusive *ex officio* powers to conduct and direct the process and the concentration of the procedure in only one hearing[3].

This «trial of amparo», if it is true that is the only judicial means that can be used for the judicial protection of constitutional rights and guarantees and also for judicial review of the constitutionality of statutes, does not only have that purpose, being a very complex procedural institution which comprises at least five different judicial actions and proceedings which are generally differentiated processes in the other countries with a civil law tradition.

These five different aspects of the trial for *amparo*, have been systematized by Professor Héctor Fix-Zamudio[4], as follows:

The first aspect of the trial for *amparo* is the so called *«amparo de la libertad»* (protection of freedom) in which the *«amparo»* proceeding functions as a judicial means for the protection of fundamental rights established in the Constitution. In this respect the trial for *amparo* could be equivalent to the request for a writ of *habeas corpus* when it seeks the protection of personal liberty, but can also serve as the protection of all other fundamental rights established in Articles 1 to 29 when violated by an act of an authority[5].

The second aspect of the trial of *amparo* is that it also proceeds against judicial decisions (Art. 107, III, V Constitution) when it is alleged that they have incorrectly applied legal provisions, which results in the so called *«amparo judicial»* or *«amparo casación»*, that is to say, in a judicial recourse very similar to the recourse of cassation that exists in civil and criminal procedural law in the civil law countries, to seek control of the legality or constitutionality of judicial decisions by the Supreme Courts of Justice. The institution is called *recurso de casación* following the French word *casation*, being in general the attribution of the Court on cassation or of the Supreme Court in their Civil, Labor and Criminal Cassation Chambers. It is an extraordinary judicial recourse which proceeds against definitive and final judicial decisions issued after the exhaustion of all ordinary appeals, and that can only be founded on violations of the Constitution and statutes or of the judicial procedural formalities. By this judicial mean, the Supreme Court assures the uniformity of legal interpretation and judicial application of law. As mentioned, in all Latin American countries it is a specific extraordinary judicial recourse, except in México, where it is one of the modalities of the amparo trail.

The third aspect of the trial for *amparo* is the so-called *«amparo administrativo»* through which it is possible to impugn administrative acts that violate the

---

3 Héctor FIX-ZAMUDIO, *Ensayos sobre el derecho de amparo*, Universidad Nnacional Autónoma de México, Editorial Porrúa, México, 2003.

4 H. FIX-ZAMUDIO, *El juicio de amparo*, México 1964, pp. 243, 377; H. FIX-ZAMUDIO, «Reflexiones sobre la naturaleza procesal del amparo», *Revista de la Facultad de Derecho de México*, 56, 1964, p. 980. H. FIX-ZAMUDIO, «Algunos aspectos comparativos del derecho de amparo en México y Venezuela», *loc. cit.*, p. 345; H. FIX-ZAMUDIO, «Lineamientos fundamentales del proceso social agrario en el derecho mexicano» in *Atti della Seconda Assemblea. Istituto di Dirito Agrario Internazionale a Comparato*, Vol I, Milán, 1964, p. 402; Eduardo FERRER MAC-GREGOR, *La acción constitucional de* amparo *en México y España, Estudio de Derecho Comparado*, 2nd Edition, Edit. Porrúa, México D.F., 2000; Ignacio BURGOA O., *El juicio de amparo*, Twenty-eighth Edition, Editorial Porrúa S.A., México, 1991.

5 *Cf.* R.D. BAKER, *Judicial Review in México. A Study of the Amparo Suit*, Texas, 1971, p. 92.

Constitution or the statutes (Art. 107, IV Constitution . This aspect of the trial for *amparo* results in a mean for judicial review of administrative action, equivalent to the French born *contentieux administratif* extended to almost all civil law countries.

It must be also stressed that in the majority of Latin American countries, in some way influenced by the French administrative law doctrine, some kind of special courts and recourses have been created in order to control the legality and constitutionality of Public Administration's actions and in particular, of administrative acts, seeking their annulment. Even in some countries, such as Colombia, a *Consejo de Estado* has been created following the *Conceil d'État* French model, as the head of a Judicial Review of Administrative Action separate Jurisdiction. In the other countries, the head of the Jurisdiction has been located in the Supreme Court, and the main purpose of it, as mentioned, is to challenge administrative acts seeking their annulment, when being considered unconstitutional or illegal. The important trend of such Jurisdiction is that it is not only devoted to protect human or constitutional rights, but in general, the legality of the administrative actions.

Again in this regard, the Mexican system is also an exception in the sense that for controlling the legality of administrative action and for the protection of individual constitutional rights and guaranties, the administrative amparo has been developed. Consequently, in similar way to the Anglo-American tradition, the ordinary courts are in charge of controlling the Public Administration, but in the case of México, by means of the amparo suit.

The fourth aspect of the trial for *amparo* is the so called *amparo agrario* which is set up for the protection of peasants against acts of the agrarian authorities which could affect their agrarian rights, regulated by the agrarian reform provisions particularly referred to collective rural property (Art. 107, II).

Finally, the fifth aspect of the trial for *amparo*, is the so called *amparo contra leyes* (*amparo* against laws), which can be used to challenge statutes that violate the Constitution, which results in a means of judicial review of the constitutionality of legislation, exercised in a direct way in the absence of any administrative act of enforcement or judicial act of application of the statute considered unconstitutional. This aspect of the trial for *amparo* has been considered as the most specific in constitutional justice aspects.[6]

In all these five aspects of the trial for *amparo*, this particular means of constitutional judicial protection can be used as a means of judicial review of the constitutionality of legislative acts, in which cases they have the common trends of the diffuse system of judicial review, the fifth aspect of the *amparo* against laws, but have additional peculiarities.

In effect, all the four first mentioned aspects of the trial for *amparo* can be used as a means for judicial review of legislation when a constitutional question, having been raised in a particular proceeding, the courts decide the case, based on a statute considered to be unconstitutional. In such cases, the party which alleges being injured in his rights or interests by the decision, can exercise a recourse of *amparo*

[6] H. FIX-ZAMUDIO, «Algunos problemas que plantea el amparo contra leyes», *Boletín del Instituto de Derecho Comparado de México*, UNAM, 37, 1960, 15, 20.

against the judicial decision, seeking judicial review of legislation.[7] In these cases, the recourse of *amparo*, being a review of a judicial decision, must be brought before a Collegiate Circuit Court or the Supreme Court of Justice, according to their respective jurisdictions (Art. 107, V,VI).[8]

In cases of this direct *amparo* brought before the Collegiate Circuit Courts, the constitution confers the power of reviewing the decisions taken to the Supreme Court, only when constitutional issues are involved, In particular, the article 107, IX of Constitution sets forth:A

> Decisions in direct amparo rendered by a Collegiate Circuit Court are not revisable unless the decision involves the unconstitutionality of a law or establishes a direct interpretation of a provision of the constitution, in which case it may be taken to the Supreme Court of Justice, limited exclusively to the decision of actual constitutional questions.

Nevertheless, the same constitutional provision states that the Collegiate Circuit Courts decisions in direct *amparo* are not revisable if they are based «on a precedent established by the Supreme Court of Justice as to the constitutionality of a law or the direct interpretation of a provision of the constitution».

Anyway, in all these cases of *amparo*, judicial review of legislation has an incidental character regarding a concrete judicial proceeding in which the constitutional question is raised and which brings about the use of the «recourse» of *amparo*, against the judicial decision which applied the unconstitutional statute.

Judicial review of legislation through the trial for *amparo*, therefore, has the general trends of the diffuse systems of judicial review according to the North American model,[9] even though with a few very important particular features which result from this unique judicial proceeding.

First of all, as we mentioned, the jurisdiction for a trial for *amparo* is reserved to the federal courts. Judicial review of the constitutionality of legislation in México is not a power of all courts but attributed only to the federal courts.

Secondly, since the *amparo* trial is initiated either through a recourse of *amparo* in its first four aspects or through an action in the fifth aspect of the *amparo* against laws, it is always developed against a «public authority», whether it be the judge who has dictated the judicial decision or the administrative authority that has produced the administrative act which are both the object of the recourse of *amparo*; or the legislative authorities that have approved the statute which is the object of the *amparo* against laws action. This aspect reveals another substantial difference between the Mexican system and the general diffuse system, in which the parties in the process in where a constitutional question is raised, continue to be the same.[10]

---

7 H. FIX-ZAMUDIO, «Aspectos comparativos del derecho de amparo en México y venezuela...» *loc. cit.* pp. 358, 359; «Algunos problemas que plantea el amparo contra leyes...», *loc. cit.*, pp. 22, 23.

8 *Cf.* H. FIX-ZAMUDIO, «Algunos problemas que plantea el amparo contra leyes...», *loc. cit.*, p. 22

9 J.A.C. GRANT, «El control jurisdiccional de la constitucionalidad de las leyes: una contribución de las Américas a la ciencia política», *Revista de la Facultad de Derecho de México*, 45, México 1962, p. 657.

10 *Idem*, pp. 657-661.

As we have said, in the first four aspects of the trial for *amparo,* the proceedings are initiated through a recourse of *amparo* normally exercised against a judicial decision, the situation being different in the fifth aspect of the trial for *amparo,* so called *amparo* against laws, in which judicial review of constitutionality of legislation is sought through an «action of unconstitutionality», rather than through a recourse, where the action is exercised against the legislative bodies that approved the challenged statute.

In effect, as we have said, one of the five aspects of the trial for *amparo* is the so called «*amparo* against laws», whose peculiarity regarding the other aspects of the trial for *amparo* consists in the fact that in this case, it is a proceeding initiated through a direct action brought before a federal district court (Art. 107, XII) by a plaintiff, against a particular statute. The defendants being the supreme organs of «the state» which intervened in the process of formation of the statute, namely, the Congress of the Union, or the state Legislatures which produced it; the President of the Republic or the Governors of the states which enacted it, and the Secretaries of state which countersigned it and ordered its publication.[11] In these cases, the federal district courts decisions are revisable by the Supreme Court of Justice. (Art. 107, VIII,a).

The *amparo* against laws, therefore, is a direct action against a statute, and the existence of a concrete administrative act or judicial decision for its enactment or its application is not necessary to its exercise.[12] Nevertheless, the constitutional question involved in this action is not an abstract one, and that is why only the statutes that inflict a direct injury on the plaintiff, without the necessity of any other intermediate or subsequent state act, can be the object of this action.[13] Therefore, the object of this action is self-executing statutes, that is to say, statutes that with their sole enactment, cause personal and direct prejudice to the plaintiff. That is why, in principle, the action seeking the *amparo* against laws must be brought before the court within 30 days after their enactment. Nevertheless, the action can also be brought before the Court within 15 days after the first act of enactment of the said statute so as to protect the plaintiff's rights to sue (Art. 21. Amparo Law).[14]

Regarding the effects of the judicial decision on any of the aspects of the trial for *amparo,* in which judicial review of constitutionality is sought whether in a pure incidental way or through the action to request an «*amparo* against laws», the constitution has expressly established (since the institution of the trial for *amparo* in the middle of the last century) that the courts cannot «make any general declaration as to the law or act on which the complaint is based», the judgment affecting «only private individuals» and limited to affording them shelter and protection in a special case to which the complaint refers» (Art. 107, II).[15] Therefore,

---

11 H. FIX-ZAMUDIO, «Algunos problemas que plantea el amparo...», *loc. cit.*, p. 21.

12 *Cf.* R.D. BAKER, *op. cit.*, p. 164.

13 Self-executed Statutes (auto-aplicativas). *Cf.* R.D. BAKER, *op. cit.* p. 167, H. FIX-ZAMUDIO, «Algunos problemas que plantea el amparo...», *loc. cit.* p. 24.

14 *Cf.* H. FIX-ZAMUDIO, «Algunos problemas que plantea el amparo...», *loc. cit.*, p. 32. *Cf.* R.D. BAKER, *op. cit.* p. 171.

15 The principle is named the «Otero formula» due to its inclusion in the 1857 constitution under the influence of Mariano Otero. *Cf.* H, FIX-ZAMUDIO, «Algunos aspectos comparativos del derecho de amparo...» *loc. cit.,* p. 360; and H. FIX-ZAMUDIO, «Algunos problemas que plantea el amparo...», *loc. cit.*, pp. 33, 37.

a decision in a «trial for *amparo*» in which judicial review of legislation is accomplished, can only have *inter partes* effects, and can never consist of general declarations with *erga omnes* effects.

Therefore, the courts in their decisions regarding the unconstitutionality of a statute do not annul or repeal it; therefore, the statute remains in the books and can be applied by the courts, the only effect of the declaration of its unconstitutionality being directed to the parties in a concrete process.

On the other hand, it must be said that the decisions of the trials for *amparo*, whether or not referred to judicial review, do not have general binding effects even regarding other courts, and are only obligatory to other courts in cases of established *jurisprudencia*, that is to say, of obligatory precedent. The constitution does not expressly establish when an obligatory precedent exists and refers to the special Organic law of the Constitutional Trial to specify «the terms and cases in which the *jurisprudencia* of the courts of the federal judicial power is binding, as well as the requirements for modifying it»(Art. 107, XIII, 1). According to that Organic law *jurisprudencia* is established by the Supreme Court of Justice or by the Collegiate Circuit Courts when five consecutive decisions to the same effect, uninterrupted by any incompatible rulings are rendered (Art. 192, 193) but it can be modified when the respective Court pronounces a contradictory judgment with a qualified majority of votes of its members(Art. 194).[16]

Nevertheless, as *jurisprudencia* can be established by the federal Collegiate Circuit Courts and by the Supreme Court, contradictory interpretations of the constitution can exist, having binding effects upon the lower courts. In order to resolve these conflicts, the constitution establishes the power of the Supreme Court or of the Collegiate Circuit Court to resolve the conflict, when the contradiction is denounced by the Chambers of the Supreme Court or another Collegiate Circuit Court; by the Attorney General or by any of the parties to the cases in which the *jurisprudencia* was established (Art. 107, XIII).[17] Anyway the resolution of the contradiction between judicial doctrines, has the sole purpose of determining one single *jurisprudencia* on the matter, and does not affect concrete juridical situations, derived from the contradictory judicial decisions adopted in the respective trials (Art. 107, XIII).[18]

Finally, regarding the practical effects of the trial for *amparo*, it must be stressed that the constitution establishes a particular preliminary remedy during the trial for *amparo*, which consists of the possible suspension of the application of the contested state act, which in certain aspects is similar to the injunction in the North American system but reduced to an *injunction pendente litis*.[19] In this respect, Article 107 of the constitution established that:

Contested acts may be subject to suspension in those cases and under conditions and guaranties specified by law, with respect to which account shall be taken of the nature of the alleged violation, the difficulty of remedying the damages that might be incurred by the aggrieved party by its performance, and the damages that the suspension might cause to third parties and the public interest (Art. 107, X).

---

16 See the quotations in R.D. BAKER, *op. cit.* p. 263.

17 See the comments, in R.D. BAKER, *op. cit.*, p. 264.

18 See the comments in J.A.C. GRANT, *loc. cit.* p. 662.

19 J.A.C. GRANT, *loc. cit.*, p. 652, note 33.

The amparo suit, if against definitive judicial decisions of a District Court, must be filled before another District Court in the same District or before the Collegiate Circuit Courts when there is no other ordinary available recourse to modify it (Articles 40 and 158, Amparo Law). In all other cases, the action must be brought before the District judges with jurisdiction in the place where the challenged act is executed or is trying to be executed (Article 36 Amparo Law). In places where there is no District court, the First Instance courts can receive the complaint, being authorized to order the facts to be maintained as they are and to ask for the relevant reports on the case, before sending the files to the respective District Court (Article 38).

According to Article 114 the petition of amparo must be brought before the District Courts when they are filled: 1) against federal or local statutes, international treaties, national executive regulations or State's Governors regulations or any other administrative regulations which causes prejudices to the plaintiff by its enacting or due to their first applicatory act; 2) against acts issued by judicial, administrative or labor courts; 3) against acts issued by judicial, administrative or labor courts executed outside the trial or after its conclusion; 4) against execution of judicial acts regarding persons of assets which are of impossible to repair; 5) against acts issued within or outside the trial that affect persons not involved in it; 6). against federal statutes or authority acts; and 7) against the Public prosecutor resolutions confirming the not filling or desisting from criminal claims.

It must be also mentioned that according to a constitutional reform passed in 1983, based in the experience of the North American writ of certiorari, the Supreme Court was vested with a discretionary competency to select to review the cases of amparo of constitutional importance; and according to another constitutional reform on 1988, the Supreme Court was attributed the competency to decide in last instance all cases of amparo where the constitutionality of a statute were at stake. Both attributions allow the Supreme Court to give final interpretation of the Constitution in a uniform way[20].

As we can see, although having peculiarities that cannot be reproduced in any other legal system, the trial for *amparo* remains within its own particular trends, a means for judicial review that follows the features of the diffuse system of judicial review.

The above implies that in the case of México, the amparo is not reduced to one single guarantee (action or recourse) of the protection of constitutional rights, but is rather a varied range of judicial procedures that make it more of a constitutional right than a specific guarantee.

Finally, it must be mentioned that regarding judicial review of constitutionality of statutes, the 1994 Mexican constitutional reform, for the first time in México, introduced an abstract judicial review proceeding of statutes, by attributing to the Supreme Court the power to decide with general binding effect, actions regarding the constitutionality of statutes. In this respect, Article 105,II of the Constitution assigns to the Supreme Court of the nation the power to decide judicial actions raising contradictions between a general norm (regulation) and the Constitution, for instance, a federal statute, when filed within 30 days after its publishing, by a

[20] See Joaquín BRAGE CAMAZANO, *La jurisdicción constitucional de la libertad (Teoría general, Argentina, México, Corte Interamericana de Derechos Humanos)*, Editorial Porrúa, Instituto Mexicano de Derecho Procesal Constitucional, México, 2005, pp. 153-155.

number equivalent to the 33% of the members of the Chamber of Representatives or of the Senate; by the Attorney General of the Republic; or against electoral statutes by the national representatives of the political parties. In these cases, the Supreme Court resolution can declare the invalidity of the statute with *erga omnes* effects when approved by not less than 8 of the 11 votes[21].

B. The right to «amparo» in Venezuela

As Héctor Fix Zamudio himself pointed out in 1970, when Venezuela incorporated Article 49 regulating the *right to* amparo in its 1961 Constitution, «... it definitively enshrined the right to amparo as a procedural instrument to protect all the constitutionally enshrined fundamental rights of the human person», in what he described as «one of the most outstanding achievements of the very advanced Magna Carta of 1961»[22].

In fact, the great contribution of the Venezuelan constitutional text of 1961, a concept that is followed under Article 27 of the 1999 Constitution, in relation to fundamental rights, was the establishment of the amparo as one more fundamental right, and not just as a sole dependent guarantee of the rest of the constitutional rights[23]. Therefore, the Constitution of Venezuela not only established an «action of amparo» to protect constitutional rights, but what it provided was «a constitutional right to amparo» and the subsequent obligation of all Tribunals to provide amparo to the people of the Republic in the enjoyment of the rights and freedoms enshrined in the Constitution, or which, when not listed in the text, are inherent to the human person.

That is why Article 1 of the Organic Law of Amparo of Constitutional Rights and Guarantees states the following:

> Any individual living in the Republic or artificial person domiciled therein, may request from the competent courts the amparo provided in Article 49 of the Constitution, of the enjoyment and exercise of constitutional rights and guarantees, even of those fundamental rights of the human person that are not expressly provided in the Constitution, in order that the infringed juridical situation or the situation most resembling such situation be reestablished immediately.

The guarantee of personal freedom that regulates the constitutional habeas corpus, shall be governed by this Law[24].

---

21 See Joaquín BRAGE CAMAZANO, «El control abstracto de la constitucionalidad de las leyes en México» in Eduardo FERRER MAC GREGOR (Coordinador), *Derecho Procesal Constitucional*, Editorial Podrúa, MéxicoVol I, 2003, pp. 919 ff.

22 See Héctor FIX ZAMUDIO, «Algunos aspectos comparativos del derecho de amparo en México y Venezuela», *Libro Homenaje a la Memoria de Lorenzo Herrera Mendoza*, UCV, Caracas, 1970, Volumen II, pp. 333-390.

23 See Héctor FIX-ZAMUDIO, «La teoría de Allan R. BREWER-CARÍAS sobre el derecho de amparo latinoamericano y el juicio de amparo mexicano» in *El Derecho Público a comienzos del Siglo XXI. Libro Homenaje al profesor Allan R. Brewer-Carías*, Volumen I, Instituto de Derecho Público, Editorial Civitas, Madrid, 2003, pp. 1125 *et seq*.

24 On the action of amparo in Venezuela, in general, see: Gustavo BRICEÑO V., *Comentarios a la Ley de Amparo*, Editorial Kinesis, Caracas, 1991; José Luis CASTILLO MARCANO *et al.*, *El amparo constitucional y la tutela cautelar en la justicia administrativa*, Fundación Estudios de Derecho Administrativo (FUNEDA), Caracas, 2000; Rafael J. CHAVERO GAZDIK, *El nuevo régimen del*

By regulating and establishing the *action of* amparo of all constitutional rights and freedoms, even for the protection of personal freedom and safety (Article 38), the Organic Law of the Amparo of Constitutional Rights and Guarantees, in force since January 22, 1988[25], expressly recognized that the exercise of the right of amparo is not exhausted nor it is exclusively incurred by such procedural means, but that it can *also* be exercised through other actions or recourses established in the legal order.

This was definitively resolved by the Supreme Court decision of July 7, 1971 (Caso: *Tarjetas Banvenez*)[26] referred to by the same Supreme Court in decision dated June 1oth 1992, in which the Court stated:

> «The Amparo Law set forth two adjective mechanisms: the (autonomous) action for amparo and the jointly filing of such action with other actions or recourses, which differs in their nature and legal consequences. Regarding the latter, that is to say, the filing of such action of amparo jointly with other actions or recourses, the Amparo Law distinguishes tree mechanism: a) the action of amparo filed jointly with the popular action of unconstitutionality against statutes and State acts of the same rank and value (Article 3); b) The action of amparo filed jointly with the judicial review of administrative act recourse or against omissive conducts of Public Administration (article 5); and c) the amparo action filed jointly with ordinary judicial actions (article 6,5).

The Court has also sustained that the action for amparo in neither of these cases is an autonomous action of amparo, but a subordinate one, accessory to the action or recourse to which it has been joined, subject to its final decision. Being joined actions, the case must be heard by the competent court regarding the principal action»[27].

---

amparo *constitucional en Venezuela,* Editorial Sherwood, Caracas, 2001; Rafael J. CHAVERO GAZDIK, *La acción de* amparo *contra decisiones judiciales*, Fundaci6n Estudios de Derecho Administrativo (FUNEDA)-Editorial Jurídica Venezolana, Caracas, 1997; *El amparo constitucional en Venezuela (Doctrina, Jurisprudencia, Legislación)*, Volumen I, Instituto de Estudios Jurídicos del Estado Lara, Colegio de Abogados del Estado Lara, Diario de Tribunales 1987; *El amparo constitucional en Venezuela (Doctrina, Jurisprudencia, Legislación)*, Volumen II, Instituto de Estudios Jurídicos del Estado Lara, Colegio de Abogados del Estado Lara, Diario de Tribunales 1987; Gustavo José LINARES BENZO, *El proceso de amparo en Venezuela*, Editorial Jurídica Venezolana, Caracas, 1993; Gustavo José LINARES BENZO, *El Proceso de Amparo*, Universidad Central de Venezuela, Facultad de Ciencias Jurídicas y Políticas, Caracas, 1999; Otto MARÍN GÓMEZ, *La protección procesal de las garantías constitucionales de Venezuela. Amparo y Hábeas Corpus*, Universidad Central de Venezuela, Ediciones de la Biblioteca, Colección Ciencias Jurídicas y Políticas VI, Caracas, 1983; Nicolás VEGAS ROLANDO, *El amparo constitucional y jurisprudencias*, Ediciones Librerías Destino, Caracas, 1991; Francisco José Utrera and Luis A. ORTIZ ÁLVAREZ, *El amparo constitucional contra sentencias*, Editorial Torino, Caracas, 1997; Hildegard RONDÓN DE SANSÓ, *Amparo Constitucional*, Caracas, 1988; Hildegard RONDÓN DE SANSÓ, *La acción de amparo contra los poderes públicos*, Editorial Arte, Caracas, 1994.

25 See *Gaceta Oficial* N° 33.891 of January 22, 1988. See Allan R. BREWER-CARÍAS and Carlos M. AYALA CORAO, *Ley Orgánica de Amparo sobre Derechos y Garantías Constitucionales*, Caracas, 1988. See also Allan R. BREWER-CARÍAS, *El derecho y la acción de amparo*, Tomo V, *Instituciones Políticas y Constitucionales*, Editorial Jurídica Venezolana, Caracas, 1998, pp. 163 *et seq.*

26 See the text in *Revista de Derecho Público,* N° 47, EJV, Caracas, 1991, pp. 169-174.

27 See in *Revista de Derecho Público,* N° 50, Editorial Jurídica Venezolana, Caracas, 1992, pp. 183-184.

This decision, definitively clarified that the intention of the Amparo Law was to distinguish between the autonomous action for amparo and the amparo claim filed jointly with other existing actions, in which cases, the amparo is a claim dependant on the principal action, having the amparo decision a preliminary protective nature[28]

According to these provisions, Article 3 of the Amparo law provided the possibility for the claim of amparo to be filed jointly with the popular action of unconstitutionality of statutes, which is exercised before the Constitutional Chamber of the Supreme Tribunal of Justice. In these cases, when the popular action is founded on the violation of a constitutional right or guarantee, due to the nullity that such claim implies, the Organic Law authorizes the Supreme Tribunal to *suspend the effects of the disputed statute* in respect of the specific case, while the nullity popular action is decided.

On the other hand, Article 5 of the Amparo law expressly establishes that the claim of amparo against administrative acts and against Public Administration omissions may also be brought jointly with judicial review of administrative actions recourses. In such cases, when the cause of such recourse is the violation of a constitutional right by the challenged administrative act, the requirement of previously exhausting administrative procedures and the lapse for expiry that are common in judicial review of administrative actions recourses have been eliminated; and the courts are allowed to adopt immediate procedures for the abbreviation of lapses, as well as the power to suspend of the effects of the challenged act while the nullity judicial action is decided (Articles 5, and 6,5).

Finally, Article 6, Number 6, when establishing the causes of inadmissibility of the action of amparo, implicitly recognizes that the claim of amparo may also be brought jointly with other «ordinary judicial procedures» or «pre-existing judicial means», wherein the «violation or threat of violation of a constitutional right or guarantee may be alleged».. For instance, it can be filed jointly with the recourse of cassation, when the claim against the challenged judicial decision consists in its alleged violation of a constitutional right or guarantee. In such cases, the Cassation Chambers of the Supreme Tribunal shall follow the procedure and lapses established in the Organic Law of Amparo (Article 6,5), and the recourse will anyway have the effect of suspending the challenged decision.

In all these cases of amparo claims filed jointly with other judicial means, the Supreme Court of Justice has clearly set forth the proceeding rules, as follows:

> The amparo claims filed jointly with another action or recourse have all the inherent adjective character of the actions' joint proceedings, that is: it must be decided by only one court (the one competent regarding the principal action), and both claims (amparo and nullity or other) must be heard in only one proceeding that has two stages: the preliminary one regarding the amparo, and the contradictory one that necessarily include in its final decision, the preliminary one which ends in such time, as well as the decision on the requested nullity. In other words, if because the above analyzed characteristics

[28] See regarding the inadmisibility of the action, decision of First Court on Judicial Review of Administrative Action (CPCA: Corte Primera de lo Contenciosao Administrativo), December 14, 1992, en FUNEDA, *15 años de Jurisprudencia, Corte Primera de lo Contencioso-Administrativo 1977-1992. Amparo Constitucional*, Caracas, 1994, p. 121.

> the amparo order is reduced only and exclusively to the preliminary suspension of a challenged act, the decision which resolves the nullity requested leaves without effects the preventive preliminary measure, whether the challenged act is declared null or not.[29].

Of course, the action for amparo can also by brought before the first instance courts in an autonomous way, not being in such cases attached or dependent to any other proceeding. As the former Supreme Court of Justice pointed out in the already mentioned decision of July 10th, 1991 that undoubtedly:

> This action that is filed autonomously because of its re-establishing nature and its capability, sufficient and adequate nature to obtain the requested amparo mandamus, is a sufficient judicial mean in itself in order to return the things to the situation they had when the right was harmed and to make definitively disappear the offender act or fact, without the need to file any other judicial proceedings.
>
> That is why this Court has reiteratively sustained that in such cases, the plaintiff must invoke and demonstrate that it is a matter of flagrant, vulgar, direct and immediate constitutional harm, which must not be understood as saying that the constitutional rights and guaranties must not be regulated by statutes, but only that in order to decide, the courts must not base its ruling only on the violation of such statutes. On the contrary, it will not be a constitutional action for amparo but rather another type of recourse, for instance, the judicial review action against administrative acts, whose annulatory effects does not correspond with the restitutory effects of the amparo; and if such substitution be allowed, the amparo would arrive to substitute not only those actions but all the other procedural means set forth in the legal order, losing its extraordinary character[30].
>
> Even regarding administrative acts, Article 5 of the Organic Amparo law states that:
>
> The action for amparo proceeds against any administrative act, material actions, factual actions (vía de hecho), abstentions or omissions that violate or threaten to violate constitutional rights and guarantees, provided that no other brief, summary and efficient mean exist according to the constitutional protection.

And of course, a judicial mean of that sort is precisely to joint the amparo claim to the judicial review action to challenge the administrative act, provided that a competent court of the judicial review of administrative actions jurisdiction exists in the place where the administrative acts has been issued.

From all that has been mentioned above, it may be said that the Venezuelan right to amparo as a constitutional protection set forth in Article 27 of the 1999 Constitution, has certain peculiarities that distinguish it from the majority of similar institutions of protection of the constitutional rights and guarantees established nowadays, both in Europe and in Latin America[31].

Therefore, pursuant to this constitutional norm and the Organic Amparo Law regulations, it may be stated that in Venezuela, the amparo is enshrined as *a right* of

---

29 *Idem*. p. 171.

30 *Idem*. pp. 169-170. 95

31 See, in general, H. FIX ZAMUDIO, *La protección procesal de los derechos humanos ante las jurisdicciones nacionales*, Madrid, 1982, p. 366.

the inhabitants of the country to seek from courts that they protect and guarantee the enjoyment and exercise of all the rights and guarantees established by the Constitution or that are inherent to the human person, against any disruption, whether by public or private entities, by means of a procedure that shall be brief and summary, and that allows the judge to immediately reinstate the impaired juridical situation.

Therefore, the Constitution does not establish 'one' action or recourse of amparo as a particular means of judicial protection, but rather a right to amparo or «right to be subject to amparo», as a fundamental right that may materialize and which in fact materializes, through an «*autonomous action of* amparo»[32] which can, in principle, be exercised before any court or tribunal, irrespective of their hierarchy (Article 7); or by means of ordinary legal actions, when by means of brief and summary proceedings, the judge is empowered to immediately re-establish infringed legal situations. In all such cases, it is not that the ordinary means substitute the constitutional right of protection (or diminish it), but that they can serve as the judicial means for protection.

Thus, the «right to amparo» can be ensured by a variety of existing legal means (actions and recourses), in which case, the «right to protection» is not identified with any specific legal action. But in the case of the «action for amparo» -which, as it has been said, is of a subordinate nature in the sense that it is admissible only when there is no other judicial means of protection or relief formally provided for in the legal system-, this subordinate «action for amparo» does appear as differentiated from other means for the legal protection of rights and guarantees, and for the defense of the Constitution itself.

Indeed, this leads us to point out the substantial difference that exists between the Venezuelan «right to protection»- and even the subsidiary «action for amparo» contemplated in the Constitution, and the Mexican «trial for *amparo*», which is really a mixture, under one name, as we have seen, of five legal actions which in the Venezuelan legal system are completely different. These actions that in México are covered by the heading *juicio de amparo* are: firstly, the protection of personal liberty, which is basically the remedy of *habeas corpus*; secondly, what is known as the «*amparo* against laws», which complements the direct action for judicial review of unconstitutionality of laws; thirdly, the «*amparo* cassation», which is really the same as the recourse of cassation; fourthly, what is known as «administrative protection», which leads to judicial review of administrative actions; and fifthly, the Mexican system of protection also includes what is known as «agrarian *amparo*» for the protection of the rights of peasants.[33]

By contrast with the Mexican situation, the right to protection contemplated in the Venezuelan Constitution, as we have pointed out, firstly ensures the possibility of protection when fundamental rights are infringed by state acts by means of the action of unconstitutionality of statutes (popular action), or through the power attributed to any judge to not apply a statute when it is considered unconstitutional

[32] See Allan R. BREWER-CARÍAS, «El derecho de amparo y la acción de amparo», *Revista de Derecho Público*, N° 22, Editorial Jurídica Venezolana, Caracas, 1985, pp. 51 *et seq*.

[33] Héctor FIX-ZAMUDIO, «Algunos aspectos comparativos del derecho de *amparo* en México y Venezuela», *Libro Homenaje a la Memoria de Lorenzo Herrera Mendoza*, Universidad Central de Venezuela, Caracas, 1970, Vol. II, pp. 344-356.

(diffuse system of judicial review); by means of the recourse of cassation before the Cassation Chambers of the Supreme Tribunal with respect to judicial decisions; and by means of the administrative actions that can be exercised against administrative acts before the judicial review of administrative action Jurisdiction. Additionally, it ensures the possibility of protection of fundamental rights against infringement by other individuals through ordinary judicial means.

To ensure the effectiveness of all these ordinary judicial means to serve as means for protecting fundamental rights, the Amparo statute of 1988 has perfected them. For instance, in cases of the popular action seeking abstract judicial review of legislation, when its grounds are the infringement of a constitutional right or guarantee, an «amparo» joined petition can be filed, and due to the absolute nullity implied, seeking the Supreme Tribunal to decide the suspension of the effects of the challenged statute while the case is being decided.

In the procedure of the recourse of cassation, when the complaint against the challenged judicial decision is based on the violation of a fundamental right, the motives for the admissibility of the recourse could be widened, as well as the judicial decisions that could be impugned.

In the proceeding of judicial review of administrative action, when the grounds of the actions are the violation of fundamental rights, according to Article 5 of the Amparo Organic Statute, the expiry delay for the actions to be exercised is eliminated, due to the absolute nullity involved, and the judge is allowed to use his powers more freely to declare the emergency situation of the process, shortening delays, and to promptly suspend the effects of the challenged administrative act while the final decision of the case is produced.

However, as we have said, additional to all the ordinary means, the right to protection allows adequate protection to be achieved for constitutional rights and guarantees, by means of an «action for amparo» which has been regulated in the Amparo Organic Law, as a judicial means, completely different from the popular action for judicial review of unconstitutionality of statutes, the recourse of cassation, and from actions for judicial review of administrative actions, that can be brought before the first instance courts with jurisdiction in the site[34].

In this case, the «action for amparo» appears as a much broader action for protecting absolutely all constitutional rights and guarantees including the enjoyment and exercise of personal freedom.

Now, one of the features of this autonomous constitutional action, called the «action for amparo», is that it does not presuppose that other previous legal judicial or administrative means have to be exhausted before it can be exercised. This differentiates the institution of the «action for amparo» in Venezuela from the «recourse of *amparo* or the «constitutional complaint» developed in Europe, particularly in Germany and in Spain. In these countries, the protective remedy is really an authentic «recourse» that is brought, in principle, against judicial decisions. In Germany, for example, to bring a constitutional complaint for the protection of constitutional rights before the Federal Constitutional Tribunal, the available

[34] See: Allan R. BREWER-CARÍAS and Carlos M. AYALA CORAO, *Ley Orgánica de Amparo a los Derechos y Garantías Constitucionales*, Editorial Jurídica Venezolana, Caracas, 1988; Hildegard Rondón De Sansó, *Amparo Constitucional*, 1991.

ordinary judicial means need to be previously exhausted, which definitively entails a recourse against a final judicial decision, even though, in exceptional cases, a direct complaint for protection may be allowed in certain specific cases and with respect to a very limited number of constitutional rights.[35] In Spain, all legal recourses need to be exhausted in order to bring a «*recurso de amparo*» of constitutional rights before the Constitutional Tribunal, and, particularly when dealing with protection against administrative activities, the ordinary means for judicial review of administrative decisions must be definitively exhausted. For this reason, the recourse for protection in Spain is eventually a means for judicial review of decisions taken by the Administrative Judicial review courts.[36]

On the contrary, the «action for amparo» in Venezuela is not conditioned to previously exhausting other legal means, and thus it does not result as recourse against judicial decisions either. It is, as it has been pointed out, a judicial action that it is only admissible when no other legal action in the legal system exists to seek the protection of fundamental rights and their immediate reestablishment by means of brief, summary proceedings.

In this sense, in order to adequately understand the character of the «action for amparo», as an autonomous action, it must be borne in mind the protective character of other judicial means, among which are the actions for judicial review of administrative acts. It is not the case that the action for amparo requires the previous exhaustion of the actions for judicial review of administrative acts, when these violate fundamental rights, but that the action for judicial review can itself be considered as a means for protection of fundamental rights, in which case a petition in this regard can be joined to it. Thus, only when no judicial means for protection exists, and in the case of administrative acts, when actions for their judicial review are not effective as a means for protection due to the particular circumstances of the case, the «action for amparo» would be admissible.

On the other hand, it should be noted that according to the Constitution, the right to protection may be exercised according to the law, before «the Courts», and thus, as it has been said, the organization of the legal and procedural system does not provide for one single judicial action to guarantee the enjoyment and exercise of constitutional rights to be brought before one single Court.

The legal system may, and indeed does, regulate systems for the protection of constitutional rights and guarantees by means of ordinary actions, through brief and summary proceedings in which the judge has power to re-establish the infringed subjective legal situations immediately, which distinguishes the system from those in Europe, particularly from the action for protection in Germany or in Spain which is one, single action, to be brought before one, single Court, and which serves as a mechanism for the protection of certain constitutional rights and guarantees.[37]

---

35 K. SCHLAICH, «Procedures et techniques de protection des droits fondamentaux. Tribunal Constitutionnel Fédéral allemand», in L. Favoreu (ed.), *Cours constitutionnelles européenes et droits fondamentaux*, París, 1982, pp. 105-164.

36 See, J.L. GARCÍA RUÍZ, *Recurso de amparo en el derecho español*, Madrid, 1980. F. CASTEDO ÁLVAREZ, «El recurso de amparo constitucional» in Instituto de Estudios Fiscales, *El Tribunal Constitucional*, Madrid, 1981, Vol. I, pp. 179-208.

37 *Cf.* H. FIX-ZAMUDIO, «El derecho de amparo en México y en España. Su influencia recíproca», *Revista de estudios políticos*, N° 7, Madrid, 1979, pp. 254-255.

In Venezuela, according to Article 7 of the Organic Law on Amparo, the competent courts to decide amparo actions are the First Instance Courts with jurisdiction on matters related to the constitutional rights or guarantees violated, in the place where the facts, acts of omission have occurred. Regarding amparo of personal freedom and security the competent courts should be the Criminal First Instance courts (Article 40). Nonetheless, when the facts, acts or omissions harming or threatening to harm the constitutional right or guarantee occurs in a place where no First Instance court exists, the amparo action may be brought before and judge of the place, which must decide according to the law, and in a 24 hour delay it must send the files for consultation to the competent First Instance court (Article 9).

Only in cases in which facts, actions or omissions of the President of the Republic, his Cabinet members, the National Electoral Council, the Prosecutor General, the Attorney general and the General Comptroller of the Republic are involved, the power to decide the amparo actions correspond in only instance to the Constitutional Chamber of the Supreme Tribunal of Justice (Article 8).

Nonetheless, in all the other cases, the Constitutional Chamber of the Supreme Court has the power to review all «amparo» highest instance decisions by means of the extraordinary recourse of revision that the interested party can file before it, in which the Chamber can decide at its discretion, in a similar way as the North American writ of certiorari.

On the other hand, and independently of the autonomous action of amparo, the right to constitutional protection in Venezuela is expressed in several legal judicial means which may be brought before all the Courts, and which may serve as a protection by means of pre-existing actions and remedies, so long as provision is made for brief, summary proceedings with powers for the judge to restore the infringed subjective legal situations. For this reason, and given this all-inclusive characteristic, the «action for amparo» is not the only action or recourse admissible for protection but that, rather, it may also be obtained by other legal means regulated by the legal system.

However, whether by use of pre-established judicial means or through the autonomous action, the right to protection as expressed in the Venezuelan Constitution is to protect all the rights and guarantees that the Constitution establishes. This protection constitutes a fundamental guarantee of human rights, which in turn entails certain implications. Above all, the objective of the right to protection, according to the Constitution, is to protect the enjoyment and exercise of constitutional rights and guarantees, and thus, it applies not only to individuals as holders of such rights, but also to cases in which these rights are exercised by companies or corporations. There can be no doubt that, given the scope with which the Constitution declares the «right to amparo», the expression «all the inhabitants» cannot be understood to refer solely to human beings, rather, it also refers to all entities or organizations, since the rights established in the Constitution are moreover not only rights of individuals, but many of them are also rights of collective entities or artificial persons.

At the same time, however, the protection of the enjoyment and exercise of constitutional rights and guaranties is embodied in the Constitution not only regarding public actions, which may disrupt the enjoyment and exercise of such rights, but also regarding disruptions, which may originate from other private individuals. The Constitution makes no distinction in this respect, and thus the action for amparo is perfectly admissible against actions by individuals, the action for amparo has doubtlessly been conceived as a traditional means of protection against actions by the state and its authorities. However, despite this tradition of conceiving the action for protection as a means of protecting rights and guarantees against public actions, in Venezuela, the scope with which this is regulated by Article 27 of the Constitution allows the action for amparo to be brought against individual actions, that is to say, when the disruption of the enjoyment and exercise of rights originates from private individuals or organizations.

This also differentiates the Venezuelan system from that which exists in other systems such as México or Spain, in which the «action for amparo» is solely conceived against public actions.[38] For this reason, as we have said, in Spain the recourse of amparo is expressed as a review of decisions by the administrative judicial court when reviewing administrative acts.[39]

On the other hand, in the case of protection from disruption originating from public authorities, it should be affirmed, without doubt, that as regulated by Article 27 of the Constitution, this protection is admissible against all public actions, that is to say, against all state acts as well as against any other action by public officials. The right to protection has, of course, been regulated, in many cases in this field, by judicial means already established in the legal system. For example, as far as unconstitutional statutes, which affect constitutional rights and guarantees, are concerned, it is admissible to bring a popular action before the Supreme Tribunal of Justice, which can be considered a means for protection. Also, when a judge decides not to apply a law, under Article 334 of the Constitution or Article 20 of the Civil Procedural Code, because he decides that it infringes a constitutional right, he also ensures protection of that right.[40] The same occurs with actions brought before the administrative judicial Tribunals against administrative acts, which constitute a means for the protection of constitutional rights and guarantees when the basis for impugning the administrative act is the violation of the enjoyment and exercise of such rights and guarantees, and the judicial suspension of the effects of the challenged act may be obtained immediately, and is admissible against any type of administrative act, both express and implied.[41]

Additionally, it must be said that the subordinate action for amparo is admissible against any activity by the Public Administration, even when this does not constitute a formal administrative act and is thus not open to actions before the administrative jurisdiction. That is to say, it would be admissible, for example, against material acts by the administration; its *de facto proceedings*; its failure to act or to fulfill an obligation; in short, against any action or omission by the Administration, and even, of course, against specific acts which may not be contested before the administrative judicial courts.

---

[38] *Idem*, pp. 254-255. On the contrary in Argentina is accepted the recourse of «*amparo*» against individual actions. Kot case: *of 5.9.1958*. See G.R. CARRIO, *Algunos aspectos del recurso de amparo*, Buenos Aires, 1959, p. 13.

[39] *Cf.* J. González PÉREZ, *Derecho procesal constitucional*, Madrid, 1980, p. 278.

[40] See Allan R. BREWER-CARÍAS, *El control de la constitucionalidad de los actos estatales*, Caracas, 1978.

[41] Allan R. BREWER-CARÍAS, «Tipos de acciones y recursos contencioso-administrativos y el tema de la legitimación», in *Conferencia sobre la reforma de la justicia administrativa en Costa Rica*, Corte Suprema de Justicia, Marzo, 1986.

Indeed, the subordinate action for amparo may also be admissible against actions by the legislative body against which there are no legal means for objection, and may even be brought against judicial decisions against which no legal means of appeal exist or have been contemplated, or the recourse of cassation could not be exercised.

We have said, however, that the action for amparo also constitutes a means for the protection of the enjoyment and exercise of *all* rights and guarantees established in the Constitution: individual, social, cultural, economic, environmental and political rights.

By virtue of the Constitutional provision, there is nothing to suggest that the right to protection in Venezuela constitutes a means for the protection of only certain rights, but that rather, it relates, on the contrary, to all rights and guarantees established in the Constitution. This, of course, leads to the assertion that the right to protection and the subordinate «action for amparo» are means for protecting, not only those rights and guarantees listed in the Constitution, but also all the rights inherent to the human person, even when not specified in the Constitution. As abovementioned, this give substantial importance to the series of human rights listed in the Universal Declaration of the Rights of Man, and in the International Conventions that regulate human rights, such as those of the American Human Rights Convention, or the International Covenants on Civil and Political, and Economic and Social Rights, which are, moreover, laws of the Republic, because they have been approved in Congress by special laws.[42] But, though limiting our comments to the rights described in the Constitution, however, we must stress the fact that what is termed *amparo* is the right to a judicial means for protecting the enjoyment and exercise of absolutely all those constitutional rights, which means that a difference is established with respect to other *amparo* institutions particular to Latin America.

In fact, if the situation in Latin America is analyzed comparatively, the following criteria can, in general, be identified. In the first place, the system that identifies *amparo* with judicial protection from arbitrary detention (*habeas corpus*) always entails a writ requiring that the person detained be shown. This was the legal tradition, for example, in Chile. Secondly, there is the system that identifies *amparo* as a means for the protection of all rights, except that of personal liberty, which is granted a special means of protection, such as the remedy of *habeas corpus*. This system, in fact, distinguishes between the two types of actions, the action for protection and the writ of *habeas corpus*, and is for example, the tradition in the Argentinean, and Brazilian systems.

Thirdly, *amparo* is also seen as a means for the protection of all rights and guarantees enshrined in the Constitution, and it has been the tradition in Central America, particularly in Guatemala, Honduras and Nicaragua, in contrast to the situation in Europe, for example, in which the remedy is established for the protection of certain rights only.[43] This happens, for example, in Spain, where the recourse of protection is reserved for the protection of a limited group of constitutional rights only, equivalent to what the Venezuelan Constitution has characterized as «individual rights».[44]

42 See *Gaceta Oficial* N° 31.256 de 14-6-77 and N° 2.146 Extra. de 28-1-78.

43 Allan R. BREWER-CARÍAS, *Garantías constitucionales de los derechos del hombre*, Caracas, 1976, p. 69.

44 Art. 53, ord. 2. Spanish Constitution 1978.

We have pointed out that *amparo* is conceived in Venezuela as the right to a legal means (action or remedy) for the protection of absolutely all constitutional rights and guarantees, not only, of course, of individual rights, but also of the social, cultural, environmental, political and economic rights declared in the Constitution. Also, as *amparo* is intended for the protection of all the rights and guarantees enshrined in the Constitution, this implies that what is known as the right of *habeas corpus* is really a part of the right to protection, or if preferred, one manifestation of the *amparo*.

That is why the right to seek protection against any deprivation or restriction to personal freedom is regulated in the Organic Amparo Law, setting forth that the action must bring before the First Instance Criminal court with jurisdiction in the place where the aggrieving act is enforced or where the aggrieved person is, court that must issue an habeas corpus mandamus (Article 39).

From the terms of Article 27 of the Constitution, it can be said that the objective protected by the right to amparo is the enjoyment and exercise of constitutional rights and guarantees, and of course, protection for the enjoyment and exercise of such rights and guarantees is admissible, not only when some *direct* violation of a constitutional rule occurs, but also of course, when there is a violation of the legal rules that regulate the enjoyment and exercise of such rights. We consider that there is no foundation whatsoever in Venezuela for wishing to restrict the exercise of the subordinate action for protection only to cases in which a «direct violation» of the Constitution occurs[45].

In effect, we must bear in mind that the regulation of constitutional rights and guarantees in Venezuela is not uniform, and that the manner in which they are embodied in the Constitution gives rise to differing effects of such rights and guarantees.[46] In fact, we may identify, in the first place, the «absolute rights», among which are the right to life, the right not to be held incommunicado, not to be subjected to torture or other procedures that cause moral or physical suffering, which is the same thing as the right to personal integrity, and the right not to be condemned to prison for life, or to punishments that are defamatory or that restrict personal freedom for more than 30 years. These rights are expressed in the Constitution in such a way that it can be said that they are rights that can neither be limited nor regulated even by the legislator, and that are, moreover, the rights which may not be restricted by executive decision based on the powers attributed to the President of the Republic in cases of emergency or disturbances that may disrupt the peace of the Republic, or in serious circumstances which affect its economic or social life. With the exception of these absolute rights, all other rights and guarantees, by contrast, are liable to limitation or regulation by the Legislator, and may be subject to measures for their restriction or suspension (art. 241 Constitution).

---

[45] See the decision of the Supreme Court in Politico-Administrative Chamber of October 28, 1983, in *Revista de Derecho Público*, N° 16, Editorial Jurídica Venezolana, Caracas, 1983, p. 169. See the comments of René DE SOLA, «Vida y vicisitudes del recurso de amparo en Venezuela», *Revista del Instituto Venezolano de Derecho Social*, 47, Caracas, 1985, p. 58, (also published in *Revista SIC*; 472, Caracas, 1985, 74.

[46] Allan R. BREWER-CARÍAS, *Instituciones políticas y Constitucionales*, Vol IV, *Derechos y garantías Constitucionales*, Universidad Católica del Táchira, Editorial Jurídica venezolana, Caracas-San Cristóbal, 1996.

A second type of constitutional rights comprises those whose exercise may be restricted by the President of the Republic, even though, in principle, the legislator may not limit them. This stems from the manner in which the Constitution expresses the rights, for example, to protection of honor, reputation and privacy; the right not to take an oath or to make self-incriminating statements; not to remain imprisoned once officially released from jail; not to be punished twice for the same crime; the right to equality and freedom from discrimination; the right to religious freedom and to freedom of thought; the right to petition and to receive timely response; the right to be judged by one's ordinary judges; the right to defense; the right of association; the right to health protection; the rights to education and to work; and the right to vote.

A third category of rights, stemming from the Constitution, is that composed of those rights which may be limited by the legislator, although in a restricted way. This category contains, for instance, the prisoner's right, before being sentenced, to be heard «as indicated by the law»; the right to inviolability of the home, except in cases of search «according to the law and the decision of the courts»; the right to inviolability of correspondence, except in cases of inspection or fiscal supervision of accounting documents «according to the law»; the right to take public office, with the only restrictions being conditions of aptitude «required by law».

The fourth category comprises a series of constitutional rights that can be regulated and limited by the legislator in a wider form. Among such rights would be the right not to be detained unless caught *in fraganti*; «in the cases and with the formalities established in the law»; the freedom of movement «with the condition established by law»; the right to exercise a cult under the «supreme inspection of the State according to the law»; the right to carry on economic activities with no other limitations than those established by statute by reasons of security, health or other social interests; the right to property, submitted to the «contributions, restrictions and obligations established by law based on public or social interests»; the right to political association and to public demonstration «according to the formalities established by law». In all such cases, the exercise of rights is definitively subject to what the legislator stipulates, and within quite considerable margins.

The fifth and final category of constitutional rights and guarantees is formed by those established in such a manner that their exercise is definitively subject to legal regulation. Among such rights would be, for example, that of using the organs for the administration of justice «under the terms and conditions established by the law»; that of joining associations «according to the law»; and the right to strike «under the conditions set by the law». In all such cases, the manner in which the Constitution expresses the rights and guarantees requires that they be regulated by the Law so as to be exercised at all. From this classification of rights and guarantees into five groups, according to the Constitution, it is evident that there is no sense in holding that the right to protection, and in particular, the subsidiary «action for amparo», can only be admissible when the Constitution is «directly violated», since many rights are not only embodied in the Constitution, but rather, by virtue of the Constitution itself, their exercise is subject to provisions and regulations established by the Legislator. The right to protection is thus also admissible against violations of laws, which regulate the enjoyment, and exercise of rights.

We have pointed out that the right to protection, as regulated by the Constitution, has the definitive aim of ensuring the *enjoyment and exercise* of constitutional rights and guarantees. Precisely for this reason, the Constitution grants the competent judge the power to immediately «re-establish the infringed juridical situation», and precisely for this reason, also provides that «the procedure should be brief and summary».

This aim of the remedy of ensuring the enjoyment and exercise of constitutional rights and guarantees entails that the judge, of course, has power to adopt preventive and cautionary measures, but bearing in mind that the legal means of protection and even the subordinate action for amparo, are not necessarily exhausted thereby.

In other words, the protection for the enjoyment and exercise of constitutional rights and guarantees does not only entail, nor is it exhausted by the adoption of some immediate measure, by means of a brief and summary proceeding which re-establishes the infringed legal situation, but rather that the action or remedy for amparo by means of legal proceedings needs the judge in the case of *amparo* to decide on the substantive issue and give a verdict as to the legality and legitimacy of the «violation» of the right in question, without prejudice to the fact that, by means of brief and summary mechanisms, decisions may be adopted during the proceedings to immediately re-establish the infringed legal situation.

In our opinion and after analyzing the Venezuelan right for amparo, the following conclusions can be formed:

First, the Constitution consecrates a *right to amparo*, and not any particular «action» or «remedy» before a particular Court. This right is established as a fundamental right of individuals and collective persons.

Second, the right to protection implies an *obligation* of all Courts to protect according to the law, against disturbances of the enjoyment and exercise of rights and guarantees. Thus, the development the legislator has made regarding this right to amparo may take the form, as has happened, of pre-existing actions or remedies, or may consist of a subordinate action for protection, which is admissible when pre-existing actions and remedies cannot be effective by means of a brief and summary procedure with powers for the judge to protect fundamental rights and immediately re-establish the infringed legal situation.

Third, the right to protection may thus be guaranteed by means of *actions and recourse* contemplated in the legal order (the popular action of unconstitutionality; the power of all judges to decide not to apply a law considered unconstitutional; actions for judicial review of administrative actions; the provisional system of *habeas corpus*), or by means of the subordinate and autonomous action for protection[47] and that can be brought before any court according to its subject of attributions.

Fourth, the right of amparo is admissible to guarantee the enjoyment and exercise of *all* constitutional rights and guarantees. It may be put into effect with respect to disturbances of individual rights, as well as those of social, economic, cultural environmental and political rights.

Fifth, the right to amparo seeks to assure protection of constitutional rights and guarantees against *any disturbance* in their enjoyment and exercise, whether this is originated by *private* individuals or by *public* authorities. In the case of disturbance

47 Allan R. BREWER-CARÍAS, «La reciente evolución jurisprudencial en relación a la admisibilidad del recurso de amparo», *Revista de derecho público*, N° 19, Caracas, 1984, pp. 207-218.

by public authorities, the right of protection is admissible against legislative, administrative and judicial acts, by means of the actions and recourses contemplated in the legal order (the action of unconstitutionality, the recourse of cassation, or actions for judicial review of administrative actions) when they allow a legal situation which has been infringed, to be re-established by means of a brief and summary procedure, or by means of the subsidiary autonomous action for protection. Moreover, this action for protection is admissible against material acts or courses of action of the administration, thus it is not then admissible only against administrative acts.

Sixth, by virtue of the different ways in the Constitution for regulating fundamental rights, the right to amparo can be exercised to protect the enjoyment and exercise of constitutional rights and guarantees, *not only when there has been some direct violation of the Constitution*, but also when what has been violated are the legal developments which, by virtue of the Constitution, regulate, limit and even allow the exercise of such rights. Of course, protection must be exercised against an activity that directly violates a fundamental right established in the Constitution, whether it be regulated by statute or not, and whether or not the violation is contrary to what the law developing the right establishes.

Seventh, the decision of the judge as a consequence of the exercise of this right to amparo, whether this be pre-existing actions or recourses or by means of the subordinate and autonomous «action for protection», should not limit himself to precautionary or preventive measures, but should re-establish the infringed legal situation. To this end he should make a pronouncement on the substantive issue brought before him, namely the legality and legitimacy or otherwise the disturbance of the constitutional right or guarantee that has been reported as infringed.

Eighth, the Venezuelan system of judicial review, being a mixed one (can be exercised by all courts in whatever kind of judicial proceeding), where the diffuse system of judicial review has been fully developed, it is obvious that judicial review of legislation is a power that can be exercised by the courts when deciding action for amparo» of fundamental rights, when for instance, their violation is infringed by a public authority act based on a statute deemed unconstitutional. In such cases, if the judge gives the protection requested through an order similar to the writs of mandamus or to the injunctions, he must previously declare the statute based on which the challenged action was taken, inapplicable on the grounds of it being unconstitutional. Therefore, in such cases, judicial review of the constitutionality of legislation is also exercised when an action for amparo of fundamental rights is filed.

In this respect, some precisions must be made regarding the Venezuelan system of judicial review. Article 336 of the Constitution of 1999, following a constitutional tradition that can be traced back to the 1858 Constitution[48], sets forth the power of the Constitutional Chamber of the Supreme Tribunal, as Constitutional Jurisdiction, to review the constitutionality of statutes and other national, state or municipal normative acts and acts of government adopted by the President of the Republic, when requested by means of a popular action. That is to say, it provides for judicial review of the constitutionality of all state acts issued in direct application of the Constitution, and particularly of statutes.

[48] See J. G. ANDUEZA, *La jurisdicción constitucional en el derecho venezolano*, Universidad Central de Venezuela, Caracas, 1955 p. 46.

This judicial review power of the constitutionality of state acts allows the Supreme Tribunal of Justice to declare them null and void with *erga omnes* effects when they violate the Constitution. It thus constitutes a concentrated system of judicial review of the constitutionality of statutes and other state acts with similar rank or value.

Moreover, Article 334 of the same Constitution, also following a legal tradition that can be traced back to the 1897 Civil Procedure Code, sets forth the power of all courts to declare statutes or other normative state acts inapplicable in a given case, when they consider them unconstitutional and, hence, sets preference to constitutional rules, providing a diffuse system of judicial review.

Therefore, as also happens in the Portuguese system and in many Latin American countries, the Venezuelan system of judicial review of the constitutionality of statutes and other state acts, mixes the diffuse system of judicial review of the constitutionality of statutes with the concentrated systems.[49]

With respect to this mixed character of the Venezuelan system, the former Supreme Court has analyzed the scope of judicial review of the constitutionality of statutes, and has correctly pointed out that this is the responsibility:

> [N]ot only of the Supreme Tribunal of the Republic, but also of all the judges, whatever their rank and standing may be. It is sufficient that an official is part of the Judiciary for him to be a custodian of the Constitution and, consequently, to apply it's ruling preferentially over those of ordinary statutes. Nonetheless, the application of Constitution by the judges, only has effects in the concrete case at issue and, for that very reason, only affects the interested parties to the conflict. In contrast, when constitutional illegitimacy in a law is declared by the Supreme [Tribunal] when exercising its sovereign function, as the interpreter of the Constitution, and in response to the pertinent [popular] action, the effects of the decision extend *erga omnes* and have the force of law. In the first case, the review is incidental and special, and in the second, principal and general. When this happens -that is to say when the recourse is autonomous- the control is either formal or material, depending on whether the nullity has to do with an irregularity relating to the process of drafting the statute, or whether -despite the legislation having been correct from the formalist point of view- the intrinsic content of the statute suffers from substantial defects.[50]

Consequently, the Venezuelan system of judicial review is a mixed one, in which the diffuse system functions in parallel with the concentrated system of judicial review assigned to the Constitutional Chamber of the Supreme Tribunal of Justice.

As previously stated, Article 334 of the Constitution following what was set forth in Article 20 of the Civil Procedure Code since 1897, states:

---

49 See in general, Allan R. BREWER-CARÍAS, *El control de la constitucionalidad de los actos estatales*, Caracas, 1977; and also «Algunas consideraciones sobre el control jurisdiccional de la constitucionalidad de los actos estatales en el derecho venezolano», *Revista de Administración Pública*, 76, Madrid, 1975, pp. 419-446.

50 See decisión of Federal Court (which in 1961 was substituted by the Supreme Court of Justice), June 19, 1953 *Gaceta Forense*, 1, 1953, pp. 77-78.

Art. 334. [...] In case of incompatibility between this Constitution and a statute or other norm, the constitutional provisions will be apply, being the courts in any case, even ex officio, the ones to decide therein[51]

According to this norm, the diffuse system of judicial review allows any judge, from the lowest judicial rank to the Supreme Tribunal of Justice, to decide not to apply a statute in a concrete case that conflicts with any provision of the Constitution when the application of that statute is demanded by a party to litigation. This is, no doubt, the basic consequence of the principle of the supremacy of the Constitution, as considered since the beginning of the last century by all the commentators of the Civil Procedure Code.

According to this power attributed to all judges, the diffuse system of judicial review in Venezuela can be characterized by the following trends:

Firstly, as we have stated, the power attributed to all judges to control the constitutionality of legislation is the natural consequence of the principle of the supremacy of the Constitution. The judges are bound by the Constitution and have the duty to apply it; therefore, if a law is unconstitutional, they cannot apply it and must give preference to the Constitution, because an unconstitutional law can have no value.

It must be said that this was the basic principle established ever since the beginning of Venezuelan constitutionalism, in the 1811 Constitution where it has been considered that an implicit diffuse judicial review system was adopted.[52]

In effect, Article 227 of the 1811 Constitution set forth:

The present Constitution, the statutes to be adopted in its execution and the Treaties to be subscribed under the authority of the Union Government will be the supreme law of the state in the whole Confederation, and the authorities and inhabitants of the provinces are bound to religiously obey and observe them without excuse or pretext; but the statutes enacted against the text of the Constitution will have no value unless they fulfill all the required conditions for a just and legitimate revision and sanction.[53]

According to this norm, in the same sense as the North American model, unconstitutional laws were considered null and void, as they could have no effect whatsoever.

---

51 Article 334: En caso de incompatibilidad entre esta Constitución y una ley u otra norma jurídica, se aplicarán las disposiciones constitucionales, correspondiendo a los tribunales en cualquier causa, aún de oficio, decidir lo conducente». The text of article 20 of the Civil Procedure Code says: «Cuando la ley vigente, cuya aplicación se pida, colidiere con alguna disposición constitucional, los jueces aplicarán ésta con preferencia». The text was originally adopted in the 1897 Code (Art. 10), followed by the 1904 Code (Art. 10) and the 1916 Code (Art. 7). In the 1985 Code the only change introduced in relation to the previous text, is the word «judges» which substituted the word «Tribunals». See the text of the 1897, 1904 and 1916 Codes in *Leyes y Decretos Reglamentarios de los Estados Unidos de Venezuela*, Caracas, 1943, Vol. V.

52 H. J. LA ROCHE, *El control jurisdiccional de la constitucionalidad en Venezuela y Estados Unidos*, Maracaibo, 1971, p. 24; T. «El recurso de inconstitucionalidad en la Constitución venezolana de 1811», in *El pensamiento constitucional de Latinoamérica 1810-1830*, Congreso de Academias e Institutos Históricos, Actas y Ponencias, Caracas, 1962, Vol. 3, p. 208.

53 See in Allan R. BREWER-CARÍAS, *Las Constituciones de Venezuela*, Instituto de Estudios de Administración Local, Centro de Estudios Constitucionales, Madrid, 1985, p. 203.

The guarantee of the Constitution in that case was the nullity of the unconstitutional act, and not its annulability. Thus the judges were not bound to apply unconstitutional laws and acts; on the contrary, as established in the 1830 Constitution, all public officials had the duty not to «obey or execute orders evidently contrary to the Constitution or the laws».[54]

Now concerning fundamental rights and freedoms, ever since the 1893 Constitution the *nullity* of the statutes which violated or harmed them, as their basic guarantee has been expressly established.[55] That is why the 1999 Constitution expressly set forth that:

> **Art. 25**: Every act of the Public Power which violates or impairs the rights guaranteed by this Constitution is void, and the public officials and employees who order or execute it shall be held criminally, civilly or administratively liable, as the case may be, and orders of superiors manifestly contrary to the Constitution and the laws may not serve as an excuse.

Consequently, it can be said that since the 1811 Constitution, the diffuse system of judicial review of legislation, based on the principle of the supremacy of the Constitution and the nullity and infectivity of unconstitutional acts, has existed in Venezuela following the implicit North American constitutional trends, particularly until 1897, when it was expressly established as a power of all judges in the Civil Procedure Code.

It must be mentioned also that in the 1901 Constitution, following the approval of the 1897 Civil Procedure Code, the power of all judges to control the constitutionality of statutes was ratified. In that Constitution, competence to declare which disposition would prevail in a concrete case, when a lower judge *motu proprio* or at party instance, would have referred a constitutional question to the Supreme Court, was attributed to the Supreme Court. Nevertheless, it was expressly established that this referral did not have suspenssive effects on the procedure, and that the lower judge was empowered to decide the constitutional question if through the opportunity of adopting his own decision, the Supreme Court opinion was not received by the lower court.[56]

Anyway, historically and in the present constitutional system, Venezuela has always had, following the American model, a diffuse system of judicial review according to which all courts have the power to examine the constitutionality of statutes and not to apply them when considering them unconstitutional, giving preference to the Constitution. Of course, the expression «statute» (*ley*) used in the Constitution and in the Civil Procedure Code has always been interpreted in an extensive way, comprising not only formal statutes approved by Congress, but also all normative state acts, including executive regulations.

Following the general trends of all diffuse systems of judicial review, the Venezuelan system also has an incidental character, that is to say, the judge can only review the constitutionality of a statute and decide not to apply it, when

---

54 Art. 186. See in Allan R. BREWER-CARÍAS, *Las Constituciones ..., cit.*, p. 353.

55 Art. 17. See in Allan R. BREWER-CARÍAS, *Las Constituciones..., cit.*, p. 531.

56 Art. 106, 8 in Allan R. BREWER-CARÍAS, *Las Constituciones ..., cit.*, pp. 579-580. See the comments regarding this norm in R. FEO, *Estudios sobre el Código de procedimiento civil venezolano*, Caracas 1904, Vol. I, pp. 32-33.

deciding a concrete case brought before him by a party, in which the constitutional question is not, of course, the principal issue submitted for his decision, but only an incidental question regarding the law which the judge must apply for the resolution of the case as required by a party.

Therefore, the power of courts to control the constitutionality of legislation can only be exercised within a concrete adversary litigation (case and controversy), regarding the statute the application of which is demanded by a party, and when the constitutional issue is relevant to the case and necessary to be resolved in their decision. But in the Venezuelan system, the constitutional issue itself can be raised *ex officio* by the judge when deciding the concrete case so it is not necessarily required, as happens in the North American system, to be alleged by a party. Therefore, the Venezuelan diffuse system of judicial review although incidental, is not a control that is exclusively exercised through an «exception of unconstitutionality»[57] risen by a party. On the contrary, it can be exercised by the judge, *motu proprio* as stated since the 1901 Constitution (art. 106,8).

On the other hand, the nullity of unconstitutional laws, particularly those that violate fundamental rights; being the guarantee of the Constitution, the decision of the courts in the diffuse system of constitutional control has declarative effects. That is to say, the judge when deciding not to apply a statute in a concrete case declares it unconstitutional and, therefore, considers it unconstitutional ever since its enactment (*ab initio*), thus as never having been valid and as always having been null and void. Consequently, the decision of the court in the concrete case evidently has *ex-tunc* and *pro pretaerito* or retroactive effects, preventing the unconstitutional and inapplicable statute from having any effect in the case. Thus, the judge's decision is not a declaration «of nullity» of the statute he considered unconstitutional, but rather a declaration that the statute «is unconstitutional». In declaring the statute inapplicable to the concrete case, the court considers that the statute could never have produced effects in the particular case; as it has never existed. In other words, when the court declares that the statute is inapplicable to a particular case which was supposed to have been governed, in the past, by a statute whose applicability is demanded by one of the parties to the case, the judge is «ignoring» the -in his opinion- unconstitutional law, and thus considering it never having had effects on the particular case brought before him.

Of course, these declarative and *ex-tunc* effects of the decision, only refer to the concrete parties, in the concrete process in which the decision is adopted.

Thus, the decision only has *in casu et inter partes* effects,[58] as a consequence of the incidental character (*incidenter tantum*) control. Therefore, if a statute has been considered unconstitutional in a concrete judicial case decision, and the judge decided not to apply it to the case but gave preference to the Constitution, this does not mean that the law has been invalidated and is not enforceable and applicable elsewhere. According to the Civil Procedure Code, judges have no competence to make declarations of the nullity of the unconstitutional law, or to annul it, because these attributions are exclusively assigned in the Constitution to the Constitutional Chamber of the Supreme Tribunal. Thus, in the diffuse system of review, the decision

---

57 See a contrary opinion in H.J. LA ROCHE, *op. cit.*, pp. 137, 140, 150, 162; and in J.G. AN-DUEZA, *op. cit.*, pp. 37-38.

58 See the Federal Court decision of June 19, 1953, in *Gaceta Forense* N° 1, 1953, pp. 77-78.

in which the judge decides not to apply a statute in the concrete case only means that concerning that particular process and parties, the law must be considered unconstitutional, null and void, but with no effects regarding other cases, other judges or other individuals.

Therefore, the fact that a statute is declared inapplicable by reason of unconstitutionality by a judge in a particular case does not affect its validity nor is it equivalent to a declaration of nullity. The law as such continues to be valid, and will only lose its general effects if repealed by another law (art. 177, 1961 Constitution) or if annulled by the Supreme Tribunal of Justice (art. 215,3,4 1961 Constitution).

In this regard, it must be mentioned that the Organic law on the Supreme Tribunal of 2004 has incorporated a new provision imposing the Chambers of the Supreme Court, after ruling any statute as unconstitutional following the diffuse method of judicial review, to send the case to the Constitutional Camber to allow the latter to rule the matter, and if it proceeds, the statute can be annulled with *erga omnes* effects (article 5,1o, 22).

In any case, in the Venezuelan procedural system, the *stare decisis* doctrine has no application at all, the judges being sovereign in their decisions, only submitted to the Constitution and the law. Therefore, decisions regarding the inapplicability of a law considered unconstitutional do not have binding effects, neither regarding the same judge who may change his legal opinion in other cases, nor regarding other judges or courts, except in cases of decision issued by the Constitutional Chamber with obligatory effects.

On the other hand, like the American or Argentinean systems, in the Venezuelan system of constitutional judicial control, the 1999 Constitution has created an extraordinary means or review recourse that can be filed against judicial decisions in which constitutional questions are involved that can be brought before the Constitutional Chamber of the Supreme Tribunal.

Before 1999, judge's decisions on matters of unconstitutionality were only subject to the ordinary means of appeal and to the recourse of cassation, following the general rules established in the Civil Procedural Code. It was only in the 1901 Constitution that the Federal Court was assigned the power to establish general criterion in constitutional matters referred to by lower courts, when a constitutional issue was raised in concrete judicial cases, which power was eliminated in the subsequent constitutional reform of 1904.

Nevertheless, before 1999, the possible contradictions that could arise between different court decisions, with the consequent uncertainty in the legal order, were corrected ever since 1858, through the establishment, in parallel with the diffuse system of judicial review, of a concentrated system of constitutional control assigned now to the Constitutional Chamber of the Supreme Tribunal of Justice.

As mentioned, one of the important reforms introduced to the judicial review system by the 1999 Constitution was to give the Constitutional Chamber of the Supreme Tribunal, the power to «review the definitive decisions issued by the courts on amparo matters and on judicial review of statutes or other norms» (Article 336,10).

This power of the Constitutional Chamber was conceived as an extraordinary power to review, at its discretion, by means of an extraordinary recourse similar to the application to the writ of certiorari, highest instance courts decisions issued in matters of judicial review of legislation, and specifically on matters of amparo.

The essential trend of this attribution is its discretionary character[59], that allows the Constitutional Chamber to choose the cases to be reviewed. As the same Constitutional Chamber of the Supreme Tribunal pointed it out in its decision N° 727 of April 8th, 2003, «in the cases of the decisions subject to revision, the Constitution does not provide for the creation of a third instance. What has set forth the constitutional provision is an exceptional and discretional power of the Constitutional Chamber that as such, must be exercised with maxim prudence regarding the admission of recourses for review final judicial decisions»[60].

In absence of the statute that must regulate the Constitutional Jurisdiction assigned to the Constitutional Chamber, it has been the same Constitutional Chamber the one that has modeled the framework of this recourse for revision of judicial decisions on constitutional matters. By the end of 2000, as a consequence of the Chamber rulings N° 1, 2, 44 and 714, the Supreme Court doctrine regarding the conditions that a judicial decision must have in order to be the object of the review recourse was as follows:

1°) The decision must have been issued in second instance, by means of an appeal or consultation, so that the review cannot be understood as a new instance.

2°) The constitutional revision is only admissible in order to preserve the uniformity of interpretation of constitutional norms and principles, or when it exists a deliberate violation of constitutional prescription, which will be analyzed by the Constitutional Chamber, in a facultative way

3°) As a consequence, and different to consultations, the recourse for revision is not *ipso jure* admissible, because it depends on the party's initiative, and not on the initiative of the courts that issued the decision, unless the Constitutional Chamber ex officio decides to accepted it bearing always in mind its purpose[61].

After, in decision N° 93 of February 6th, 2001(Case: *Olimpia Tours and Travel vs. Corporación de Turismo de Venezuela*), the Constitutional Chamber began to extend its own review powers, adding to the recourse for revision other judicial decisions different to those issued in matters of amparo or on judicial review of constitutionality, as follows:

1. The last instance definitive judicial amparo decisions of any kind, issued by the other Chambers of the Supreme Tribunal of Justice and by any court or tribunal of the country.

---

59 As mentioned, in a certain way similar to the *writ of cerciorari* in the Nort American system. See Allan R. BREWER-CARÍAS, *Judicial Review in Comparative Law, op. cit.*, p. 141; See also the comments of Jesús María CASAL, *Constitución y Justicia Constitucional,* Caracas 2002, p. 92.

60 Case: *Revisión de la sentencia dictada por la Sala Electoral en fecha 21 de noviembre de 2002*, in *Revista de Derecho Público*, N° 93-96, Editorial Jurídica Venezolana, Caracas, 2003.

61 See decisión of November 2, 2000 (Case: *Roderick A. Muñoz P. vs. Juzgado de los Municipios Carache, Candelaria y José Felipe Márquez Cañizales de la Circunscripción Judicial del Estado Trujillo*) in *Revista de Derecho Público*, N° 84, (octubre-diciembre), Editorial Jurídica Venezolana, Caracas, 2000, p. 367.

2. The last instance definitive judicial decisions of courts and of the other Chambers of the Supreme Tribunal on judicial review of constitutionality of statutes or State regulations.
3. The last instance definitive judicial decisions issued by the other Chambers of the Supreme Tribunal or by the other courts and tribunals putting aside or expressly or tacitly by-passing the interpretations of the Constitution ruled in any Constitutional Chamber's decision issued before the impugned ruling, thus making an erroneous constitutional judicial review by erroneously applying the Constitution.
4. The last instance definitive judicial decisions issued by the other Chambers of the Supreme Tribunal of by the other courts and tribunals which, according to the Constitutional Chamber's criteria, would incur in a grotesque error regarding the interpretation of the Constitution or simply would disregard the interpretation of the constitutional provision; cases in which it would also be an erroneous judicial review of constitutionality[62].

According to this doctrine, the Constitutional Chamber has extended its review power regarding judicial decisions, that in the Constitution is reduced to «amparo» and judicial review decisions, including other judicial decisions, even those issued by the other Chambers of the Supreme Tribunal (Civil, Criminal and Social Chambers, Electoral Chamber and Administrative judicial review Chamber) which is not authorized in the Constitution, and constitutes a violation to the constitutional right to *res judicata*, affecting legal stability and security

The Constitutional Chamber, in effect, after analyzing the due process of law guarantees regarding the extraordinary revision of judicial decisions, in decision N° 93 of February 6th, 2001 (Case: *Olimpia Tours and Travel vs. Corporación de Turismo de Venezuela*), alter analyzing its constitutional role as guarantor of the supremacy or the Constitution and as the interpreter of the Constitution, concluded saying that «there are no doubts about the Constitution interpretative powers of the Chamber, whose decisions are obligatory for the other Chambers and the rest of the courts of the Republic. Thus, all the other Chambers of the Supreme Tribunal and the other courts and tribunal are obligated to decide accordingly to the interpretation of constitutional provisions issued by the Chamber...The Constitution gives the Constitutional Chamber the superior and unique power regarding the interpretation of the Constitution».

The conclusion from the argument developed by he Constitutional Chamber has been the affirmation of its powers to be «the maxim interpreter of the Constitution» with the power to issue obligatory interpretations, from which resulted its power to review, even ex officio, any judicial decision of any other Chamber of the Supreme Tribunal or of any court, when contrary to the constitutional interpretation set forth by the Chamber[63].

---

[62] See in *Revista de Derecho Público*, N° 85-88, Editorial Jurídica Venezolana, Caracas, 2001, pp. 414-415. See also decisión N° 727 of April 8th, 2003 (Caso: *Revisión de la sentencia dictada por la Sala Electoral en fecha 21 de noviembre de 2002)*, en *Revista de Derecho Público*, N° 93-96, Editorial Jurídica Venezolana, Caracas, 2003.

[63] *Idem*. pp. 412-414.

This doctrine, particularly regarding to the others Chamber of the Supreme Tribunal decisions, has been incorporated in the Organic Law of the Supreme Tribunal (art. 5,4).

But just regarding the «amparo» definitive last instance judicial decisions, the power of the Constitutional Chamber of the Supreme Court to hear the extraordinary review recourse, is a very important instrument in order to provide uniformity to the judicial constitutional interpretation and enforcement of human rights made by ordinary courts.

2. THE AMPARO ACTION OR RECOURSE AS A CONSTITUTIONAL GUARANTEE

A. The actions of constitutional protection in Brazil

Since 1934,[64] the Constitution of Brazil has expressly established the *mandado de segurança* as a special means for the protection of fundamental rights, other than personal liberty -which is protected through the recourse for *habeas corpus*. Thus, in the Brazilian constitutional system there are two main special actions for the constitutional protection of fundamental rights: the *mandado de segurança* and the *habeas corpus* actions. In particular, the *mandado de segurança* is intended to protect actual individual rights not protected through *habeas corpus,* whoever the authority responsible for the illegality or abuse of powers may be.[65]

But after the 1988 Constitution, additionally to the *mandado de segurança* and the *habeas corpus* recourses, other two specific recourses had been regulated: the *mandado de injunçao* and the *habeas data*[66].

Regarding the *habeas corpus,* it can be brought before the courts whenever anyone, suffers or feels threatened with suffering violence or duress in his or her freedom of movement because of illegal acts or abuses of power (Article 5, LXVIII of the Constitution). The right of movement (*ius ambuland)* is defined as the right of every person to enter, stay and leave national territory with his belongings (Article 5, XV). In principle, the action is brought before the Tribunals of First Criminal Instance, but actions may be heard by the Appeals Tribunals and even by the Supreme Federal Tribunal, if action is brought against the Tribunal of First Instance or against the Appeals Tribunal.

The second action of protection provided in the Constitution is the individual or collective *mandado de segurança,* regulated in Law N° 1533 of December 31 1951[67].

---

[64] Art. 113,33 Constitution 1934. A. RÍOS ESPINOZA, Presupuestos constitucionales del mandato de seguridad», *Boletín del Instituto de Derecho Comparado de México,* UNAM, 46, 1963, p. 71. (Also published in H. FIX-ZAMUDIO, A. RÍOS ESPINOSA and N. ALCALÁ ZAMORA, *Tres estudios sobre el mandato de seguridad brasileño,* México 1963, pp. 71-96.

[65] 153,21 Constitution.

[66] See (in general): José Alfonso DA SILVA, *Mandado de injunçao e habeas data,* Sao Paulo, 1989; Dimar ACKEL FILHO, *Writs Constitutionais,* Sao Paulo, 1988; Nagib Slaibi Filho, *Anotaçoes a Constituiçao de 1988,* Río de Janeiro, 1989; Celso AGRÍCOLA BARBI, *Do Mandado de Segurança,* 7th Edition, Revista, aumentada e actualizada de acordo com o Código de Processo Civil de 1973 e legislação posterior, Editora Forense, Río de Janeiro 1993; J. CRETELLA JÚNIOR, *Comentários à ley do mandado de segurança (de acordo com a constituição de 5 de outubro de 1988,* 5th Edition, Editora Forense, Río de Janeiro 1992.

[67] See J. CRETELLA JUNIOR, *Coméntarios à Lei do mandado de segurança. De acordo com a Constitução de 5 de Octubre de 1988,* Editora Forense, Rio de Janeiro, 1992.

This action is devoted to protect certain and determined rights that are not protected by *habeas corpus* or *habeas data,* when the party responsible for the illegal action or abuse of power is a public authority or an agent of an artificial person exercising attributions of the Authorities (Article 5, LXIX).

This recourse, which may be brought before any tribunal according to its competence, is not admissible when there are administrative recourses that can be brought against the act in question, or if the decisions are judicial, when there are recourses provided under procedural law by means of which the act may be corrected. Neither is the writ of *segurança* admitted against statutes, even those that are self-applicable.

The collective *mandado de segurança* is conceived as a means of protecting collective interests, which may be brought before the courts by political parties represented in the National Congress, trade union organizations, and legally organized entities or associations for the defense of the interests of their members or associates (Article 5, LXX).

Additionally, Brazil has a distinctive regulation which is the *mandado de injunçao* similar to the writ of injunction, directed to protect the exercise of constitutional rights and freedoms and of the prerogatives inherent to nationality, the sovereignty of the people or citizenship when the lack of a regulatory state on the matter can make such rights unviable (Article 5, LXXI), The purpose of this action against a legislative or regulatory omission is to obtain the order of a judge imposing the obligation to the legislative body to carry out or comply with a determined act, the violation of which constitutes an impairment of a right.

If the regulatory omission is attributable to the highest authorities of the Republic, the competent Tribunal is the Supreme Federal Tribunal; in other cases the High Courts of Justice are competent. Whatever the case, the respective judge cannot surrogate the legislative body in the sense that it cannot legislate by means of the writ of *injunçao,* but can simply order or instruct that the right established in the Constitution that is unviable because of lack of regulation be conceded,.

Lastly, the 1988 Constitution introduced the *habeas data,* provided to assure firstly, that the information relative to the plaintiff found in records or databanks of governmental or public sector entities be heard; and secondly, for the rectification of data, when not achievable through judicial or administrative proceedings (Article 5, LXXII). *Habeas data* may therefore be defined as a constitutional action used to guarantee three aspects: the right of access to official records; the right to rectify such records, and the right to correct them. The recourse can be brought before any competent court, and even before the Supreme Federal Tribunal.

In Brazil there also exists an extraordinary recourse of constitutionality that can be filed before the Federal Supreme Tribunal, against the judicial decision issued on matters of protection of constitutional rights by the Superior Federal Court or by the Regional Federal Courts, when it is considered that the courts have made the decisions in a way inconsistent with the Constitution, or in which the court has denied the validity of a treaty or federal statute, or when the decisions has declared the unconstitutionality of a treaty or of a Federal Law; and when they deem a local government law or act that has been challenged as unconstitutional or contrary to a valid federal law[68].

---

[68] Art. 199. III, b,c. Constitution.

In these cases the matter can reach the Federal Supreme Tribunal, which is the most important court on matters of judicial review (having Brazil a mixed system of judicial review) as happens with numerous Latin American that combine the diffuse system on judicial review with the concentrated one[69].

In effect, the Brazilian system of judicial review, in its origin, like the Argentinean, can be considered one of the Latin American systems that followed the North American model more closely[70]. It was after the 1934 Constitution, that a direct action of unconstitutionality was introduced. This action was conceived to be brought before the Federal Supreme Tribunal to impugned statutes. This is how the Brazilian system of judicial review began to be a mixed one.

In effect, the Federal Constitution of 1891 clearly influenced by the North American constitutional system[71] assigned the Supreme Federal Tribunal the power to review, through an extraordinary recourse, the decisions of the federal courts and of the courts of the Member States, in which the validity or the application of the treaties or Federal Laws was questioned, and the decisions were against; or in which the validity of laws or government acts of the states was questioned on the grounds of contravention to the Constitution or to federal laws; and the decisions considered the challenged laws or acts valid[72]. As a consequence of this express constitutional attribution, the Federal Law 221 of 1894[73] assigned the power to judge upon the validity of obviously unconstitutional laws and executive regulations, and to decide their inapplicability in concrete cases, to all federal judges. Thus, the diffuse system of judicial review of legislation was established in Brazil at the end of the last century, and was perfected through the subsequent constitutional reforms of 1926, 1934, 1937, 1946 and 1967[74]. Therefore, we can say that the main feature of the Brazilian system of judicial review is its diffuse character, with all its consequences according to the American model.

As mentioned, in addition to the diffuse system of judicial review, a concentrated system of review was established in the 1934 Constitution, by attributing power to the Supreme Federal Tribunal to declare the unconstitutionality

---

69 See in general Mantel GONCALVES FERREIRA FILHO, «O sistema constitucional brasileiro e as recentes inovacoes no controle de constitucionalidade» in *Anuario Iberoamericano de Justicia Constitucional*, N° 5, 2001, Centro de Estudios Políticos y Constitucionales, Madrid, España, 2001; José Carlos BARBOSA MOREIRA, «El control judicial de la constitucionalidad de las leyes en el Brasil: un bosquejo», in *Desafíos del control de constitucionalidad*, Ediciones Ciudad Argentina, Buenos Aires, Argentina, 1996; Paulo BONAVIDES, «Jurisdicao constitucional e legitimidade (algumas observacoes sobre o Brasil)» en *Anuario Iberoamerivanolberoamericano de Justicia Constitucional* N° 7, Centro de Estudios Políticos y Constitucionales, Madrid, 2003; Enrique Ricardo LEWANDOWSKI, «Notas sobre o controle da constitucionalidade no Brasil», en Edgar CORZO SOSA, y otros, *Justicia Constitucional Comparada*, Ed. Universidad Nacional Autónoma de México, México D.F. 1993; Zeno VELOSO, *Controle jurisdicional de constitucionalidade,* Ed. Cejup, Belém, Brasil, 1999.

70 H. FIX-ZAMUDIO and J. CARPIZO, «Amerique latine» in L. FAVOREU and J.A. JOLOWICZ (ed.), *Le contrôle juridictionnel des lois*, París 1986, p. 121.

71 O.A. BANDEIRA DE MELLO, *A teoria das Constituiçoes rigidas*, Sao Paulo 1980, p. 157; J. Alfonso DA SILVA, *Sistema de defensa da Constituiçao brasileira*, Congreso sobre la Constitución y su Defensa, UNAM, México 1982, p. 29. (mimeo).

72 Art. 59, III, 1. 1981 Constitution.

73 Art. 13,10. Law 221 of 20 November 1984

74 O.A. BANDEIRA DE MELLO, *op. cit.*, pp. 158-237

of member state Constitutions or laws (state laws) when required to do so by the Attorney General of the Republic.[75] Thus, a direct action of unconstitutionality was established as of 1934, to defend federal constitutional principles, against Member state acts,[76] later developed in subsequent Constitutions[77] up to its extension after the 1965 Constitutional Amendment, to control all normative acts of state, whether federal or of the Member States.[78]

Consequently, the Brazilian system can be considered a mixed one in which the diffuse system of judicial review operates in combination with a concentrated system.[79]

In the American model and in the Argentinean experience the powers of the courts to control the constitutionality of legislation were derived from the principle of constitutional supremacy as applied by the Supreme Court. Contrary to that, the diffuse system of judicial review arose in Brazil from express provisions in the 1891 Constitution,[80] and it is still based on constitutional norms. In this respect, as previously mentioned, the Constitution establishes the power of the Supreme Federal Tribunal to judge through extraordinary recourses, cases decided in the last resort by other courts or judges, first, when the challenged judicial decisions are against any disposition of the Constitution or denied the enforcement of a Treaty or federal law; second, when they declared the unconstitutionality of a Treaty or of a federal law; and third, when they deemed a law or other local government valid when such law challenges the Constitution or a federal law.[81]

According to this norm, not only is the diffuse system of judicial review established, but the power of the Supreme Tribunal to intervene in all proceedings in which constitutional questions have been resolved, is also established.

As we have mentioned, the diffuse system of judicial review in Brazil follows the general trends of the American model also developed in Argentina. Therefore, all the courts of first instance have the power not to apply laws (federal, state or Municipal laws) that they deem unconstitutional, when a party to the proceeding has raised the question of constitutionality. Thus, the judges have no *ex officio* power to judge the constitutionality of the laws, and can only exercise it when the question of constitutionality has been raised by the interested party as an exception or defense in the process.[82] The constitutional question, once raised, has a preliminary character regarding the final decision of the case, which the judge must decide beforehand.

Of course, the decision of the courts on constitutional matters has only *in casu et inter partes* effects, and the unapplied law is considered null and void *ab initio*. Thus, the decision has *ex tunc*, retroactive effects.[83]

---

75 Art. 12,2. 1934 Constitution.

76 J. Alfonso da Silva, *doc. cit.* p. 29.

77 Also in the Law N° 2271 of 22 July 1954.

78 *Cf.* J. Alfonso DA SILVA, *doc. cit.*, p. 31.

79 A. BUZAID, «La acción directa de inconstitucionalidad en el derecho brasileño», *Revista de la Facultad de Derecho*, UCAB, N° 19-22, Caracas 1964, p. 55; O.A. BANDEIRA DE MELLO, *op. cit.*, p. 157.

80 *Cf.*, J. Alfonso DA SILVA, *doc. cit.*, pp. 32, 34; J. Alfonso DA SILVA, *Curso de direito constitucional positivo*, Sao Paulo 1984, p. 17.

81 Art. 119, III b,c, Constitution. J. Alfonso DA SILVA, *Sistema... doc. cit.*, p. 43; O.A. BANDEIRA DE MELLO, *op. cit.*, p. 215.

82 J. Alfonso DA SILVA, *Curso...* p. 18; J. Alfonso da Silva, *Sistema... doc. cit.*, pp. 33, 37, 58.

83 J. Alfonso DA SILVA, *Sistema... doc. cit.*, pp. 41, 64; A. Buzaid, *loc. cit.*, p. 91.

The constitutional question can also be considered in a second instance, through the normal appeals process, in which case, when the court of second instance is a collegiate court, the decision upon matters of unconstitutionality of legislation must be adopted by a majority vote decision of its members.[84]

As already mentioned, the Brazilian Constitution, ever since the establishment of the constitutional review judicial system in 1891, has always expressly regulated the power of the Supreme Court to review lower courts decisions on matters of constitutionality, through an extraordinary recourse that can be brought before the Tribunal, by the party to the process who has lost the case.[85]

Finally it must be said that when deciding constitutional questions, the Supreme Federal Tribunal must adopt its decision with the vote of the majority of its members.[86] The decision, as the first instance one, when declaring the unconstitutionality of a law, has *inter partes* and *ex tunc* effects.[87] In such cases, the Tribunal in fact recognizes the *ab initio* unconstitutionality of the law, in a decision which has declarative effects, but does not annul or repeal the law, which continues in force and to be applicable.

In the Brazilian system, an additional feature can be distinguished: once adopted by the Tribunal, the decision must be sent to the Federal Senate which has the power, according to the Constitution, to «suspend the execution of all or part of a statute or decree when declared unconstitutional by the Supreme Federal Tribunal through a definitive decision,[88] in which case the effects of the Senate decisions have, of course, *erga omnes* and *ex nunc* effects.[89]

Anyway, it must be said that in Brazil, like in the North American system, a presumption of constitutionality also exists regarding laws and other state acts. Consequently, only when the unconstitutionality of a law appears to be without doubt, the Tribunal can declare its unconstitutionality. Thus, in case of doubt, it must reject the question and consider the law constitutional, and applicable in the concrete case.[90]

From the above mentioned, it can be deducted that additionally to the diffuse and concentrated systems of judicial review, an indirect means for judicial review, through the actions for protection of fundamental rights and liberties, can also be identified in the Brazilian constitutional system.

Nevertheless, it has been traditionally considered that laws or any other normative act of state, cannot be the object of an action requesting either *habeas corpus* or a *mandado de segurança*[91]. In this respect, as happened with the Argentinean

---

84 This qualified vote was first established in the 1934 Constitution (Art. 179), and is always required. See O.A. BANDEIRA DE MELLO, *op. cit.*, p. 159.

85 J. Alfonso DA SILVA, *Sistema... doc. cit.*, p. 44.

86 D.A. BANDEIRA DE MELLO, *op. cit.*, p. 218.

87 J. Alfonso DA SILVA, *Sistema... doc. cit.*, pp. 69, 71.

88 Art. 42, VII Federal Constitution.

89 J. Alfonso DA SILVA, *Sistema..., doc. cit.*, p. 73.

90 *Cf.* T.B. CAVALCANTI, *Do controle de constitutionalidade*, Rio do Janeiro, 1966, p. 69.

91 *Cf.* A. Alfonso DA SILVA, «*Sistema... doc. cit.*, p. 47; H. FIX-ZAMUDIO, «Mandato de seguridad y juicio de *amparo*», *Boletín del Instituto de Derecho Comparado de México*, UNAM; 46, 1963, pp. 11, 17. Also published in H. FIX-ZAMUDIO, A. Ríos Espinosa, N. ALCALÁ ZAMORA, *op. cit.*, pp. 3-69; A. RIOS ESPINOSA, *loc.cit.*, p. 88.

recourse for *amparo* until recent changes within the Supreme Court decisions, the abstract control of the constitutionality of laws is not possible through the exercise of the actions for a *mandado de segurança*, or *habeas corpus*. In other words, no direct action against laws can be exercised through the *mandado de segurança*, or *habeas corpus* actions, even if they are what the Mexican system calls auto-applicative or self executing laws.[92] Nevertheless, such actions can serve as an indirect means of judicial review, for the diffuse system, when they are exercised against an act of any authority when executed based on a law deemed unconstitutional. Thus, it is only the concrete situation that results from the execution or application of the law or normative act, the one that can be directly impugned by means of these actions for protection of fundamental rights, and only in an indirect way and in accordance with the diffuse method of review, that laws can be controlled by the courts on the grounds of their unconstitutionality.

B. The action of «tutela» in Colombia

During the constitution-making process of 1991, the intention of the drafters of the Colombian Constitution was to regulate the amparo as a constitutional right[93], in the same trend of the Mexican and Venezuelan systems of amparo.

Nonetheless, in the final version of the Constitution, the National Constituent Assembly abandoned the proposal to set forth the amparo as a constitutional right in itself, regulating the amparo action as a specific judicial mean for the protection of only some constitutional rights, changing its general Latin American denomination of «action of amparo» to «action of tutela»[94]. Thus, even though at the beginning of the application of the reform we identified the Colombian system more in the general category of the Mexican and Venezuela amparo[95], the statutory regulation and its very important application have molded the tutela as a specific mean for the protection of fundamental constitutional rights[96], which are not all the

---

92 H. FIX-ZAMUDIO, *loc. cit.*, p. 16; A. Alfonso DA SILVA, *Sistema... doc. cit.*, pp. 46,47.

93 See the draft in Jorge ARENAS SALAZAR, *La tutela. Una acción humaniaria*, Librería Doctrina y Ley, Bogotá 1992, pp. 47. See the comments in Allan R. BREWER-CARÍAS, «El amparo a los derechos y libertades constitucionales y la acción de tutela a los derechos fundamentales en Colombia: una aproximación comparativa» en Manuel José CEPEDA (editor), ***La Carta de Derechos. Su interpretación y sus implicaciones***, Editorial Temis, Bogotá 1993, pp. 21-81; y en la obra colectiva ***La protección jurídica del ciudadano. Estudios en Homenaje al Profesor Jesús González Pérez***, Tomo 3, Editorial Civitas, Madrid 1993, pp. 2.695-2.748.

94 Both words, «amparo»and «tutela» have the same meaning in Spanish. See the proposal in *Idem*, p. 49 ff.

95 See Allan R. BREWER-CARÍAS.

96 See, in general, in regard to the tutela in Colombia, Jorge ARENAS SALAZAR, *La Tutela Una acción humanitaria,* 1st Edition 1992, Ediciones Librería Doctrina y Ley, Santa Fe de Bogotá D.C., Colombia 1992; Manuel José CEPEDA, *La Tutela Materiales y Reflexiones sobre su significado,* Presidencia de la República, Consejería para el desarrollo de la Constitución, Imprenta Nacional de Colombia, Bogotá D.C. 1992; Oscar José DUEÑAS RUIZ, *Acción de Tutela, Su esencia en la práctica, 50 respuestas básicas,* Corte Suprema, Consejo de Estado, Legislación, Ediciones Librería del Profesional, Santa Fe de Bogotá D.C., Colombia 1992; Federico GONZÁLEZ CAMPOS, *La Tutela: Interpretación doctrinaria y jurisprudencial,* 2nd Edition, Ediciones Jurídicas Gustavo IBÁÑEZ, Santa Fe de Bogotá D.C., Colombia 1994; Manuel José CEPEDA, *Las Carta de Derechos. Su interpretación y sus implicaciones,* Temis Presidencia de la República Consejería para el Desarrollo de la Constitución, Santa Fe de Bogotá, Colombia 1993; Juan Manuel CHARRY U., *La acción de tutela,* Editorial Temis, Santa Fe de Bogotá 1992;

rights enshrined in the Constitution, regulating it in parallel to the habeas corpus recourse, regulated in the Criminal Code.

Additionally, the Constitution also regulated the popular actions in order to protect collective rights and interests related to public patrimony, public space, public safety and public health, administrative morals, the environment, free economic competition and others of like nature defined by statute.

The «action of *tutela*», has been regulated in Decree N° 2.591 of 1991, as an action that everybody has in order to claim before the courts, at all times and at in any place, through a preferential and summary procedure, by himself or by some one on his behalf, the immediate protection of their fundamental constitutional rights, whenever they are harmed by the action or the omission of any public authority or by individuals. In the latter case, the individuals are only those in charge of rendering a public service whose conduct seriously and directly affects collective interests, regarding which the aggrieved party finds himself in a position of subordination or defenselessness.

The Constitution does not exclude any State act from the tutela action, which includes judicial acts that harm fundamental rights. That is why Article 40 of the Decree 2591 provided for the action of tutela against judicial decisions. Nonetheless, this Article 40 of the Decree was annulled by the Constitutional Court in its October 1, 1992 decision, considering it unconstitutional[97]. Nonetheless, as abovementioned, the Constitutional Court has developed the doctrine of arbitrariness in order to admit the tutela against judicial decisions when it is thought that they are issued as a result of a judicial *voie de fact*[98].

The Decree set forth that the action of tutela can also be filed in states of exception, and when such exception measures refer to rights, the action of tutela can be exercised at least to defend its essential contents.

> According to Article 86 of the Constitution, such action shall only proceed when the affected party does not have another means of judicial defense, unless it is used as a temporary measure to avoid irreparable damage. This does not mean that the remedy can only be brought before the courts after exhausting the ordinary means; but that the action of tutela is only available for constitutional protection, when there are no other judicial preferred and brief means to achieve such purpose. That is why, as stated in Article 6,2 of the Decree N° 2591, the action of tutela is inadmissible when the recourse of *habeas corpus* can be filed for the protection of the particular right.

Herán Alejandro OLANO CORREA et al., *Acción de Tutela (Práctica Forense y Jurisprudencia)*, 2nd Edition 1994, Tunja-Boyacá-Colombia 1994; Carlos Augusto PATIÑO BELTRÁN, *Acciones de Tutela cumplimiento populares y de grupo. Guía Práctica*, Editorial Leyer, Bogotá D.C., Colombia 2000; *Pensamiento Jurídico. La Acción de Tutela, Revista de Teoría del Derecho y Análisis Jurídico* N° 7, Universidad Nacional de Colombia, Facultad de Derecho, Ciencias Políticas y Sociales, Santa Fe de Bogotá D.C. 1997.

97 See the decision N° C-543 of September 24, 1992 in *Derecho Colombiano*, Bogotá 1992, pp. 471 to 499; and in Manuel José CEPEDA, *Derecho Constitucional Jurisprudencial. Las grandes decisiones de la Corte Constitucional*, Legis, Bogotá 001, pp. 1009 ff.

98 See the decisión N° T-231 of May 13, 1994 in Manuel José CEPEDA, *Derecho Constitucional Jurisprudencial. Las grandes decisiones de la Corte Constitucional*, Legis, Bogotá 001, pp. 1022 ff.

For this reason, Decree Nº 2.591 of 1991 established, among the causes of inadmissibility of such protection, that it shall not proceed «when other recourses or judicial means of defense are available unless being used as a temporary measure to avoid irreparable damage», in the understanding that «irreparable damage is that which can only be wholly repaired by means of indemnification» (Article 6,1).

Therefore, pursuant to Decree Nº 2.591, Article 8, «even when the affected party has other means of judicial defense, the action of *tutela* shall proceed when used as a temporary mechanism to avoid irreparable harm». The statute also provides that «when used as a temporary mechanism to avoid irreparable harm, the action of *tutela* may be brought together with the action of annulment and others that are admitted before the judicial review of administrative action jurisdiction. In these cases, the judge may determine that the particular act be not applied to the specific judicial situation the protection of which is being sought, for as long as the trial lasts».

The Constitution set forth that the action of *tutela* for the protection of fundamental constitutional rights can be brought «before the judges»; and accordingly, Decree 2.591 of 1991 attributes the power «to hear the action of *tutela*, to the judges and tribunals with jurisdiction over the place where the violation or threat of violation takes place» (Article 37).

Decree 1380 of 2000, regarding the courts with jurisdiction in the place where the violation or threatens have taken place, before which the action must be filed, establishes the following rules, depending the defendant party. If it is 1) against any national public authority, before the Districts Superior Courts; 2) against any national or departmental decentralized entity for public utilities, before the Circuit courts; 3) against district or municipal authorities and against individuals, before the municipal courts; 4) against any general administrative act issued by a national authority, before the Cundinamarca Judicial review of administrative actions; 5) against any judicial entity, before the respective superior court; and 6) against the Supreme Court of Justice, the *Consejo de Estado* or the Superior Council of the Judiciary, or its Disciplinary Chamber before the same Corporation in the corresponding Chamber.

As mentioned above, in Colombia the action of *habeas corpus* also set forth in the Constitution (Article 30) is regulated in the Criminal Code as a right that proceeds in order to protect («amparo») personal freedom against any arbitrary act of any authority that tends to restrict it (Article 5). It can be filed when a person is captured violating its constitutional or legal guarantees, or its freedom deprivation is illicitly extended (Articles 430); before any criminal court in the place where the detainee is or where the person has been captured (Article 431).

Now, regarding the decisions on the actions of *tutela*, they are subject to appeal; and pursuant to Decree 2.591 of 1991, if no appeal has been filed, the decisions must be sent for their revision to the Constitutional Court (Article 31); the Court having discretionary power to determine which decisions of *tutela* will be reviewed (Article 33).

Since the 1991 Constitution, the Constitutional Court plays a very important role in matters of judicial review, being the Colombian system, like the Venezuelan and Brazilian ones, a mixed system[99], set forth as such since the 1910 Constitution.

---

99 See in general Eduardo CIFUENTES MUÑOZ, «La Jurisdicción constitucional en Colombia» en *La Jurisdicción constitucional en Iberoamérica,* Ed Dykinson, Madrid, España, 1997; Luis Carlos Sácchica, *La Corte Constitucional y su jurisdicción,* Ed. Temis, Bogotá, Colombia, 1993.

In it, the power attributed to all courts to declare the inapplicability of laws they deem contrary to the Constitution, was set forth in parallel with a concentrated system of judicial review attributed to the then Supreme Court, also through the exercise of a popular action.[100].

It was in the 1910 Constitution that the role of «guardian of the integrity of the Constitution» which is still today in the Fundamental text on the hands of the Constitutional Court, was attributed for the first time to the Supreme Court of Justice[101]. It was also in that same Constitution that the principle of the diffuse system of judicial review acquired constitutional rank, as established in Article 7 of the 1991Constitution, which states:

> **Art. 215.** The Constitution is the norm of norms. In all cases of incompatibility between the Constitution and a statute, the constitutional provisions shall be applied.

Anyway, since 1910, the Colombian constitutional system has mixed both the diffuse and the concentrated systems of judicial review, attributing now the concentrated power to annul, with *erga omnes* effects, to the Constitutional Court in a similar way to the Venezuelan system, by means of a popular action.

Regarding Article 7 of the Constitution, it provides the basis of the diffuse system of judicial review, according to which all judges have the power to decide not to apply a law in a concrete process, when they deem it contrary to the Constitution. The system, as it has been developed, functions entirely according to the North American model, particularly, because it has been conceived as an «exception of unconstitutionality».

Of course, in these cases of diffuse constitutional control, the judges cannot annul the law or declare its unconstitutionality, nor can the effects of their decision be extended or generalized. On the contrary, as happens in all other diffuse judicial review systems, the court must limit itself to deciding not to apply the unconstitutional law to the concrete case, of course only when it is pertinent to the resolution of the case. That decision has effects only concerning the parties to the case. Therefore, as with similar systems elsewhere, the law whose application has been denied in a concrete case, continues to be in force and other judges can moreover continue to apply it. Even the judge who chose not to apply it in a concrete case, can change his mind in a subsequent process.[102]

The creation of the Constitutional Court as the ultimate guardian of the Constitution originated the attribution of the Court to review all the judicial decisions resolving actions for *tutela.* As opposed to the Venezuelan or Argentinean cases, in Colombia there is not a specific matter for a recourse of revision, but an attribution that must be automatically accomplished in a discretionary way. In effect, the Decree regulating the procedure set forth that when a *tutela* decision is not appealed, it always must be automatically sent for revision to the Constitutional Court (Article 31). In cases in which the decisions are appealed, the superior court's

---

100 Concerning the mixed character of the system see: J. VIDAL PERDOMO, *Derecho constitucional general*, Bogotá 1985, p. 42; D.R. Salazar, *Constitución Política de Colombia*, Bogotá 1982, p. 305; E. SARRIA, *Guarda de la Constitución*, Bogotá, p. 78.

101 *Cf.* D.R. SALAZAR, *op. cit.*, p. 304.

102 *Cf.* L.C. SACHICA, *El control...cit.*, p. 65.

decision, whether confirming or revoking the appealed decision, must also be automatically sent to the Constitutional Court for its revision (Article 32). .

For that purpose, the Constitutional Court must appoint two of its Magistrates in order to select, without express motivation and according to their criteria, the *tutela* decisions which are to be reviewed. Nonetheless, any of the Magistrates of the Court and the Peoples' defendant can request the revision of the excluded decision, when they deem that the review can clarify the scope of a right or avoid a grave prejudice. Also, according to Decree 262 of February 2000, the General Attorney of the Nation can ask for the revision of *tutela* decisions when he deems necessary to defend the legal order, the public patrimony and the fundamental rights and guarantees (Art. 7,12).

All the decisions not excluded from review in a delay of 30 days, must be reviewed by the Court in a three month delay (Article 33). For that purpose, the Constitutional Court must appoint three magistrates who will integrate the Chamber called to decide (Article 34). All the review decisions that modify or revoke the *tutela* decision, that unify the constitutional judicial doctrine (*jurisprudencia*) or that clarify the scope of constitutional provisions must be motivated; the others must just be justified (Article 35). The Constitutional Court review decisions only produce effects regarding the concrete case. They must immediately be notified to the first instance court, which at his turn must notify it to the parties, and adopt the necessary decisions in order to adequate its own decision to the Court ruling.

C. The action of amparo in Dominican Republic

In the case of the Dominican Republic, as has been already mentioned, there are no constitutional or legal provisions regulating the amparo recourse as a specific judicial mean for protection of constitutional rights. The Constitution only refers to the recourse of habeas corpus for the protection of personal freedom, which has been regulated by the 1978 Habeas Corpus Law (*Ley de habeas corpus*), and based on such regulations, the Supreme Court traditionally limited the procedure of habeas data to the protection of the right to physical freedom and safety, excluding any possibility of using the habeas corpus recourse in order to protect other constitutional rights.

Nevertheless, as has been mentioned, the Supreme Court by means of a decision of February 24, 1999 (Case: *Productos Avon S.A.*) based in the American Convention on Human Rights, admitted the amparo recourse for the protection of constitutional rights and determined that the competent courts to decide on the matter of amparo are the courts of first instance in the place in which the challenged act or omission has been produced. A few months latter, by means of Resolution of June, 10 1999, the Supreme Court determined that the competent fist instance courts are those deciding civil matters.

The amparo action has been successfully used for the protection of constitutional rights. Among the multiple cases, the following can be mentioned: For instance, a 2002 case in which the Court of First Instance of the National District ordered the National Citizenship Registry to issue the Identification Card to two boys born in the Republic from Haitian illegally settled parents, arguing that the rejection of such documents constituted a violation of the boys identity and citizenship rights.

Other case decided by the same Court of First Instance of the National District originated in the order adopted by the Public prosecutor of the National District seizing of the Listin Diario Newspaper, which was considered contrary to the constitutional rights not to be applied statutes retroactively, to non discrimination, to freedom of press and to property rights[103].

It must be mentioned that in Dominican Republic, a mixed system of judicial review exists combining the diffuse method of judicial review with the concentrated one. Regarding the diffuse method, the 1844 Constitution, as well as the 2002 Constitution set forth that «all statutes, decrees, resolutions, regulations or acts contrary to the Constitution are null and void» (Article 46). From this express regulation of the consequences of the constitutional supremacy principle, all the Courts can declare an act unconstitutional and not applicable to the concrete case[104].

On the other hand, the Supreme Court of Justice has the exclusive power to hear the action of unconstitutionality of statutes that can be brought before the Court by the President of the Republic, the Presidents of the national Congress Chambers or by an interested party (Article 67,1).

D. The action of amparo in Ecuador

As it has been already analyzed, the 1988 Ecuadorian Constitution set forth the basic and extensive regulations not only regarding the action for amparo, but also regarding the action of habeas corpus and habeas data; which are statutorily developed in the 1997 Law on Constitutionality Control.

Regarding the amparo action, according to Article 46 of the Law, its purpose is to effectively protect the rights enshrined in the Constitution or in international declarations, covenants and instruments, in force in Ecuador, against any threat originated in an illegitimate act of public administration authorities that could have caused, have caused or can cause an imminent, grave and irreparable harm. It must be highlighted that in these cases, the amparo action can only be filed against actions from Public Administration, and not from other non executive entities of the State. The Constitution expressly excludes judicial decisions from the action of amparo.

The action can be filed in order to request the adoption of urgent measures directed to put an end to the harm or to avoid the danger of the protected rights. It can also be the object of an amparo action the omission in the issuing of an act or the absence of its enforcement.

The action may also be brought if the act or omission were carried out by persons that render public services or act by delegation or concession of a public authority. Only in such cases, an amparo can be filed against a private person.

As mentioned, according to Article 47 of the Law on Constitutional Control, the competent courts to hear the amparo action are the first instance courts where the challenged act has been in effect.

All decisions granting amparo adopted by the first instance courts by means of an advisory procedure must obligatorily be sent to the Constitutional Tribunal

---

103 See Samuel ARIAS ARZENO, «El Amparo en la República Dominicana: su Evolución Jurisprudencial», publicado en *Revista Estudios Jurídicos*, Vol. XI N° 3, Ediciones Capeldom, Septiembre-Diciembre 2002.

104 *Cf.* M. BERGES CHUPANI, «Report» in *Memoria de la Reunión de Cortes Superiores de Justicia de Ibero-America, El Caribe, España y Portugal*, Caracas, 1983, p. 380.

in order to be confirmed or revoked. When the first instance decision denies the amparo action (as well as the habeas corpus or habeas data actions), it can be appealed before the same Constitutional Tribunal (Articles 12,3; 31and 52).

The Constitutional Tribunal of Ecuador, in substitution of the former Constitutional Guarantees Tribunal, was vested in the 1998 Constitution with the power to declare the nullity on the grounds of unconstitutionality of any statute, decree, regulation or ordinance, when an action is brought before the Tribunal by the President of the Republic, the National Congress, the Supreme Court, one thousand citizens or by any person provided a previous favorable report from the Peoples' Defendant (Article 18).

But this power to annul statutes with *erga omnes* effects (Article 22) in a concentrated way, is combined in Ecuador with the diffuse method of judicial review which attributed to all courts the power to declare the unconstitutionality of statutes applying the Constitution with preference. The judicial review system in Ecuador, is thus a mixed one[105].

In this respect, Article 272 of the Constitution sets forth:

> «The Constitution prevails over any other legal norm. All the organic or ordinary statutes, decrees-law, ordinances, regulations or resolution dispositions, must conform to its provisions and in case they enter in contradiction with it or alters their provisions, they will have no value».

As a consequence of this supremacy principle, Article 274 of the Constitution sets forth the diffuse method of judicial review allowing any court at parties petitions or *ex officio*, to declare the inapplicability of any norm contrary to the Constitution, as follows:

> Any court or judge, in the cases they are hearing, at party's request or ex officio, may declare a legal provision contrary to the Constitution or to international treaties or covenants as inapplicable, notwithstanding its power to decide the controversy.

According to the same article, this declaration will not have obligatory force except in the case in which it is issued, that is to say, has only *inter partes* effects; and the court or tribunal must write a report on the declaration of unconstitutionality of the statute that must be sent to the Constitutional Tribunal in order for it to resolve the matter in a general and obligatory way, that is to say, with *erga omnes* effects.

---

105 See in general Hernán SALGADO PESANTES, *Manual de Justicia Constitucional Ecuatoriana*, Corporación Editora Nacional, Quito, Ecuador, 2004; Hernán SALGADO PESANTES, «El control de constitucionalidad en la Carta Política del Ecuador» en *Una mirada a los Tribunales Constitucionales. Las experiencias recientes. Lecturas Constitucionales Andinas* N° 4, Ed. Comisión Andina de Juristas, Lima, Perú; Ernesto LÓPEZ FREIRE, «Evolución del control de constitucionalidad en el Ecuador» en *Derecho Constitucional para fortalecer la democracia ecuatoriana*, Ed. Tribunal Constitucional - Kas, Quito, Ecuador, 1999; Marco MORALES TOBAR, «Actualidad de la Justicia Constitucional en el Ecuador» en Luis LÓPEZ GUERRA (Coordinador). *La Justicia Constitucional en la actualidad*, Corporación Editora Nacional, Quito, Ecuador, pp. 77-165; Oswaldo CEVALLOS BUENO, «El sistema de control concentrado y el constitucionalismo en el Ecuador» en *Anuario Iberoamericano de Justicia Constitucional*, N° 6, 2002, Madrid, España, 2002.

Thus, in matters of amparo, if when granting the constitutional protection the competent judges applying the diffuse method of judicial review has adopted decisions declaring the unconstitutionality of statutes[106], they must also write the report on the question of constitutionality to be sent to the Constitutional Tribunal by the advisory proceeding for its confirmation or revocation (Art. 12,6).

E. The «amparo» in Guatemala

In Guatemala the 1985 Constitution set forth the «amparo» as a specific judicial mean to protect people against the threat of violation of their rights, or to restore the rule of such rights when the violation has already occurred. According to the Constitution, «there is no scope that is not subject to amparo, and it shall be admitted provided that the acts, resolutions, provisions or statutes carry an implicit threat, restriction or violation of the rights guaranteed by the Constitution and the statutes» (Article 265).

In particular, according to Article 10 of the 1986 Amparo, personal exhibition and constitutionality Law, the amparo is due to protect all situations susceptible to risk, a threat, restriction or violation of the rights recognized in the Constitution and the statutes of the republic, whether the situation comes from public law persons or entities or private law entities. Article 9 of the Amparo Law specifies that amparo can be brought against the State, comprising decentralized or autonomous entities, against those entities sustained with public funds created by statute or by virtue of a concession, or those that act by delegation of the State, by virtue of a contract, concession or similar. Amparo can also be filed against entities to which persons must be integrated by law and other recognized by statute, like the political parties, associations, societies, trade unions, cooperatives and similar.

Article 10 of the Amparo Law enumerates as examples, the following cases in which everybody has the right to ask for amparo:

a) To ask to be maintained or to be restituted in the enjoyment of the rights and guarantees set forth in the Constitution or any other statute;

b) In order to seek a declaration in a concrete case, that a statute, regulation, resolution or authority act does not oblige the plaintiff because it contradicts or restricts any of the rights guaranteed in the Constitution or recognized by any other statute'

c) In order to seek a declaration in a concrete case that a non legislative disposition or resolution of Congress, is not applicable to the plaintiff because it violates a constitutional right;

d) When an authority of any jurisdiction issues a regulation, accord or resolution of any kind that abuses of power or exceeds its legal attributions, or when it has no attributions or they are exercised in a way that the harm caused or that can be caused would be irreparable through any other mean of defense.

e) When in administrative activities the affected party is compelled to accomplish unreasonable or illegal formalities, task or activities, or when no suppressive mean or recourse exists;

[106] See Hernán SALGADO PESANTES, *Manual de Justicia Constitucional Ecuatoriana,* Corporación Editora Nacional, Quito, Ecuador, 2004, p. 85.

f) When the petitions or formalities before administrative authorities are not resolved in the delay fixed by statutes, or in case that no delay exists, in a delay of 30 days once exhausted the procedure, or when the petitions are not admitted;

g) In political matters, when the rights recognized in the Constitution or statutes, are injured by political organizations;

h) In judicial and administrative matters, regarding which the statutes set forth procedures and recourses according to due process rules that can serve to adequately resolve them, if after the exhaustion of recourses by the interested party, the threat, restriction or violation to the rights recognized in the Constitution and guarantied by the statute, persist;

Article 263 of the Constitution and Article 82 of the Amparo Law also regulate the right to *habeas corpus* in favor of anyone who is illegally arrested, detained or in any other way prevented from enjoying personal freedom, threatened with losing such freedom, or suffering humiliation, even when their imprisonment or detention is legally founded. In such cases, the affected party has the right to request his immediate personal appearance (*habeas corpus*) before the court, either for his constitutional guarantee of freedom to be reinstated, for the humiliations to cease, or to terminate the duress to which was being subjected.

Pursuant to Articles 11 *et seq*. of the 1986 Law of Amparo, the competence to hear the amparo is attributed to all courts as follows:

1. To the *Constitutional Court*, as sole instance, in the cases of amparo brought against the Congress of the Republic, the Supreme Court of Justice, the President and the Vice President of the Republic (Article 11).

2. To the *Supreme Court of Justice*, in the cases of amparo brought against the Supreme Electoral Tribunal; Ministers or Vice Ministers of State when acting in the name of their Office; Chambers of the Courts of Appeal, Martial Courts, Courts of Second Instance of Accounts and Administrative judicial review Courts; the Attorney General; the Human Rights Commissioner; the Monetary Board; Ambassadors or Heads of Diplomatic Guatemalan Missions abroad; and the National Council of Urban and Rural Development.

3. To the ordinary Chambers of the *Court of Appeals*, in their respective jurisdictions, the amparos against: Vice Ministers of State and Director-Generals; judicial officials of any jurisdiction or branch of first instance; mayors and municipal corporations of departmental centers; the Head of the Comptroller General; the managers, heads or presidents of decentralized or autonomous State entities or their directors, councils or boards of directors of any kind; the Director-General of the Peoples' Registry; general assemblies and directors of professional associations; general assemblies and directors of political parties; consuls or heads of Guatemalan consulates overseas; regional or departmental councils of urban and rural development, and governors.

4. The *Judges of First Instance* in their respective jurisdictions, for amparos against: revenue administrators; minor judges; police chiefs and employees; mayors and municipal corporations not included in the previous article;

all other officials, authorities and employees of any jurisdiction or branch not specified in previous articles; and private law entities.

The competent courts in matters of habeas corpus are the same mentioned above, except regarding the attributions assigned to the Constitutional Court that corresponds to the Supreme Court of Justice (Article 83).

In all the cases, amparo decisions are subjected to appeal before the Constitutional Court (Art 60), recourse that can be filed by the parties, the Public prosecutor and the Human Rights Commissioner (Article 63).

The Constitutional Court in its decision can confirm, revoke or modify the lower court resolution (Art. 67); and can also annul the whole proceeding when it is proved that in the proceedings the legal prescription had not been observed.

The judicial review system of Guatemala is also a mixed system, in which the Constitutional Court plays a principal role.

The Constitutional Court by means of the concentrated method of judicial review is empowered to hear actions of unconstitutionality against statutes, regulations or general dispositions (Article 133), that can be brought before the Court by the board of directors of the Lawyer's (Bar) Association (Colegio de Abogados), the Public prosecutor; the Human Rights Commissioner; or by any person with the help of three lawyers members of the Bar (Article 134). The statutes, regulations or general dispositions declared unconstitutional, will cease in their effects from the following day after the publication of the Constitutional Court decisions in the Official Gazette (Article 140). Thus, the Constitutional Court's decision has *erga omnes* effects.

But besides the Constitutional Court powers following the concentrated method of judicial review, in Guatemala the diffuse method of judicial review of legislation has also been traditionally set forth, derived from the principle of the supremacy of the Constitution. That is why Article 115 of the Amparo Law declared that all «statutes, governmental dispositions or any order regulating the exercise of rights guaranteed in the Constitution, shall be null and void if they violate, diminish, restrict or distort them. No statute can contravene the Constitution's disposition. The statutes that violate or distort the constitutional norms are null and void.

The consequence of this principles is the possibility of the parties to raise in any concrete case (including cases of amparo and habeas corpus), before any court, at any instance or in cassation, before the decision is issued, as an action or as an exception or incident, the question of the unconstitutionality of the statute in order to its inapplicability to the concrete case be declared (Article 116). In such cases, once raised the constitutional question before any court, it assumes the character of constitutional tribunal (Art. 120).

In cases of action of unconstitutionality in concrete cases, it can be brought before the competent court by the Public prosecutor or by the parties in 9 days. The court must decide in three days, and the decision can be appealed before the Constitutional Courts (Article 121). If the question of unconstitutionality of a statute supporting the claim is raised has an exception or incident, the competent court must resolve the matter (Article 123). The decision can also be appealed before the Constitutional court (Article 130).

F. The recourse of amparo in Perú

Article 200 of the Perúvian Constitution sets forth the action of *habeas corpus* against any action or omission by any authority, official or person that impairs or threatens individual freedom; the action of amparo to protect all other rights recognized by the Constitution impaired or threatened by any authority, official or person; and the action of *habeas data*, against any act or omission by any authority, official or person that impairs or threatens the rights referred to in Article 2, Subsections 5 and 6 of the Constitution; that is, to request and receive information from any public office, except when they affect personal intimacy or were excluded for national security; to assure that public or private informatics services will not release information that affects personal and familiar intimacy.

In 2004 the first Constitutional Procedural Code in Latin America was sanctioned in Perú (Law 28.237)[107], which repealed the previous statutes regulating the amparo and the habeas corpus recourses (Law 23.506 of 1982, and Law 25.398 of 1991).

This Code highlights the purposes of the habeas corpus, habeas data and amparo guaranties, which is to protect the constitutional rights, in order to restore things to the state they had previous to the violation or threat of violation of constitutional rights, or dispose the accomplishment of a legal order or of an administrative act (Article 1).

According to Article 2 of the Code, the constitutional remedies of habeas corpus, amparo and habeas data are admissible when the constitutional rights are threatened or violated by actions or obligatory acts omissions from any authority, public official or person. In case of a threat being invoked, it must be of certain and imminent execution.

The competent courts to hear the amparo recourses are the Civil Courts with jurisdiction on the place where the right was affected, or of the plaintiff or defendant residence (Article 51). But if the harm has been caused by a judicial decision, the amparo must be filed before the Civil Chamber of the respective Superior Court of Justice.

According to the same Code, the amparo shall only be admitted when previous procedures have been exhausted (Articles 5,4; 45). However, in case of doubt over the exhausting of prior procedures, the Code requires that the amparo suit be given preference (Article 45).

Regarding the habeas corpus recourse, the competent judges are the Criminal ones (Article 28).

According to Article 202,2 of the Constitution, it is attributed to the Constitutional Tribunal the power to hear in last and definitive instance, the judicial decisions denying the habeas corpus, amparo and habeas data. Thus, all the habeas corpus, habeas data and amparo decisions can reach the Constitutional Tribunal of Perú, by means of a recourse of constitutional damage (*agravio*) that can be filed against the second instance judicial decision denying the claim (Article 18, Code). If this constitutional damage recourse is denied, the interested party can file

[107] See: Samuel B. ABAD YUPANQUI *et al.*, *Código Procesal Constitucional*, Ed. Palestra, Lima 2004. See (in general): Alberto BOREA ODRIA, *Las garantías constitucionales: Habeas Corpus y* Amparo, Libros Perúanos S.A., Lima 1992; Alberto BOREA ODRÍA, *El* amparo *y el Hábeas Corpus en el Perú de Hoy*, Lima, 1985.

before the Constitutional Tribunal a recourse of complaint (*queja*), in which case, if the Tribunal considered the complaint duly supported, it will the proceed to decide the constitutional damage recourse, asking from the superior court the envoy of the corresponding files (Article 19).

If the Constitutional Tribunal considers that the challenged judicial decision has been issued as a consequence of a defect or vice in the procedure that has affected its sense, will annul it and order the reposition of the procedure to the situation previous to when the defect happened. In cases in which the vice only affects the challenged decision, the Tribunal must repeal it and issue a substantive ruling (Article 20).

This Constitutional Tribunal of Perú, reinstalled in 1996, plays a very important role in the judicial review system, which nevertheless, is a mixed one, combining the diffuse system of judicial review with the concentrated one attributed to the Tribunal[108].

Article 138 of the 1993 Constitution sets forth the diffuse method of judicial review, providing:

> **Article 138.** The power to administer justice derives from the people and is exercised by the Judiciary, through its hierarchical organs according to the Constitution and the statutes. In any process, if an incompatibility exists between a constitutional norm and a legal norm, the courts must prefer the former. Likewise, must prefer the legal norm over the norms with inferior rank.

Thus, all courts can exercise judicial review of legislation in concrete cases, having their decisions in such cases *inter partes* effects[109].

Nonetheless, the Perúvian diffuse method of judicial review has a peculiarity that makes it unique in comparative law because the ordinary judges when deciding the inapplicability to a case of statutes based on constitutional arguments, according to Article 14 of the Organic Law on the Judiciary, must obligatorily send its decision to the Supreme Court of Justice. It is then the Supreme Court, through its

---

108 See in general Domingo GARCÍA BELAÚNDE, «La jurisdicción constitucional en Perú» en Domingo GARCÍA BELAÚNDE y Francisco FERNÁNDEZ SEGADO (Coord.), *La jurisdicción constitucional en Iberoamérica,* Ed. Dykinson, Madrid, España, 1977; Domingo GARCÍA BELAUNDE, «La jurisdicción constitucional y el modelo dual o paralelo» en *La Justicia Constitucional a fines del siglo XX, Revista del Instituto de Ciencias Políticas y Derecho Constitucional,* año VII, N° 6, Palestra editores, Huancayo, Perú; Domingo GARCÍA BELAUNDE (Coordinador) *La Constitución y su defensa,* Ed Jurídica Grijley, Lima, 2003, p. 96. César LANDA, *Teoría del Derecho procesal Constitucional,* Ed. Palestra, Lima, Perú, 2004; José PALOMINO MANCHEGO, «Control y magistratura constitucional en el Perú» in Juan VEGA GÓMEZ, and Edgar CORZO SOSA (Coordinadores.), *Instrumentos de tutela y justicia constitucional, Memoria del VII Congreso Iberoamericano de Derecho Constitucional,* Instituto de Investigaciones Jurídicas, UNAM, México. Aníbal QUIROGA LEÓN, «El derecho procesal constitucional Perúano» en Juan VEGA GÓMEZ y Edgar CORZO SOSA (Coord.) *Instrumentos de tutela y justicia constitucional, Memoria del VII Congreso Iberoamericano de Derecho Constitucional,* Instituto de Investigaciones Jurídicas, UNAM, México, pp. 471 y ss.

109 See Aníbal QUIROGA LEÓN, «Control difuso y control concentrado en el derecho procesal Perúano» en *Revista Derecho* N° 50, diciembre de 1996, Facultad de Derecho de la Pontificia Universidad Católica del Perú, Lima, Perú, 1996, pp. 207 ff.

Constitutional Law and Social Chamber, the one that eventually determines if the decision of the ordinary court was adequate or not, validating the non applicability of the statute to the concrete case.

But additional to the diffuse method of judicial review, in Perú a concentrated method is also set forth by attributing the Constitutional Tribunal the power to hear in unique instance the actions of unconstitutionality (Article 202,1) regarding norms of legal rank (statutes), legislative decrees, urgency decrees, treaties approved by Congress, Congress internal regulations, regional norms and municipal ordinances (Art. 77, Code).

This action can be brought before the Tribunal by: 1. The President of the Republic; 2. The Prosecutor General of the nation; 3. The Peoples defendant; 4. By a number equivalent to 25% of representatives to the Congress; 5. By 5.000 citizen whose signatures must be validated by the National Jury of Elections. If it is a local government regulation the action can be filed by 1% of the citizens of the corresponding; 6. The presidents of Regions with the vote of the Regional Coordinating Councils, or the provincial mayors with the vote of the local Councils, in matter of their jurisdiction; and 7. The professional associations (*Colegios)* in matters of their specialty (Article 203; Article 99 Code).

The decision of the Constitutional Tribunal, in these cases of the concentrated method of judicial review when declaring the unconstitutionality of a norm, must be published in the Official Gazzette. The day after such publication the statute will began to have no effects, and the decision of the Constitutional Tribunal will have no retroactive effects (Article 204). Thus, the decision has *erga omnes* and *ex nunc* effects, and the authority of *res judicata*, being obligatory to all public entities (Articles 81, 82 Code).

CHAPTER VII

THE JUSTICIABLE CONSTITUTIONAL RIGHTS BY MEANS OF THE «AMPARO» AND HABEAS CORPUS ACTIONS

I. CONSTITUTIONAL RIGHTS AND JUSTICIABILITY

Justiciability is the quality or state of being appropriate or suitable for review by a court[1]. Regarding specific Latin American actions for protection of constitutional rights, justiciability is the quality of a right of being suitable to be protected.

Amparo and habeas corpus recourses are specific constitutional means set forth in the Constitutions for the protection of constitutional rights. Consequently, not all individual rights are justiciable by means of the amparo and habeas corpus recourses; but only certain rights, those enshrined in the Constitution what places them out of reach from the Legislative branch of government. There lays the importance that in the Latin American systems of judicial protection constitutional declarations of human rights have; and also lays one of the main differences between the North American injunction remedies and the Latin American amparo.

Both are extraordinary remedies, but injunctions are equitable remedies that can be filed for the protection of any personal or property rights, even those of statutory origin, provided that they cannot be effectively protected by ordinary common law courts. Amparo, on the contrary, is an action that can only be filed for the protection of rights of constitutional origin and rank.

The consequence of the need of constitutional rank for a right to be justiciable by means of amparo and habeas corpus is that the rights that are only set in statutes and other lower rank norms cannot be protected by mean of amparo and habeas corpus, and it is thus compulsory to seek their judicial protection by means of the ordinary remedies.

In this regard, the system on the United States can be mentioned regarding the protection of social rights that are not declared in the Constitution and that their character of fundamental right have been denied by the Supreme Court, as it is the case of the right to education, or to have a dwelling. For instance, all were referred in the case *San Antonio Independent School District et al. v. Rodriguez et al.*, 411

---

1 Brian A. GARNER (Editor in Chief), *Black's Law Dictionary*, Wets Group, St. Paul, Minn. 2001, p. 391.

U.S. 1; 93 S. Ct. 1278; 36 L. Ed. 2d 16; (1973), decided by the Supreme Court on March 21, 1973, in which it was ruled that though education «is one of the most important services performed by the State (as was ruled in *Brown v. Bord of Education*), it is not within the limited category of rights recognized by this Court as guaranteed by the Constitution», thus denying such right the quality of «fundamental right». The decision was issued as a result of the attack to the Texas system of financing public education by Mexican-American parents whose children attend the elementary and secondary schools in an urban school district in San Antonio, Texas. They brought a class action on behalf of school children throughout the State who are members of minority groups or who are poor and reside in school districts having a low property tax base

The Court considered that:

> «[The] financing system did not impinge upon any fundamental right protected by the Constitution, so as to require application of the strict judicial scrutiny test under which a compelling state interest must be shown, since education, notwithstanding its undisputed importance, is not a right afforded explicit or implicit protection by the Constitution; even assuming that some identifiable quantum of education is a constitutionally protected prerequisite to the meaningful exercise of the right of free speech and the right to vote, nevertheless the strict judicial scrutiny rule is not applicable where the state's financing system does not occasion an absolute denial of educational opportunities to any of its children, and where there is no indication or charge that the system fails to provide each child with an opportunity to acquire the basic minimal skills necessary for the enjoyment of the rights of speech and of full participation in the political process».

In support of this decision, the Court referred to the case *Lindsaey v. Normet*, 405 U.S. 56 (1972) decided only the year before, in which it «firmly reiterates that social importance is not the critical determinant for subjecting state legislation to strict scrutiny» In that case, which denies constitutional rank to the right to have dwelling, the matter referred to the procedural limitations imposed on tenants in suits brought by landlords under Oregon's Forcible Entry and Wrongful Detainer Law. The tenants argued that the statutory limitations implied «fundamental interests which are particularly important to the poor», such as the «'need for decent shelter'» and the «'right to retain peaceful possession of one's home.'» The Supreme Court in the reference to this case, highlighted the following analysis made by Mr. Justice White, in his opinion for the Court, as instructive:

> «We do not denigrate the importance of decent, safe, and sanitary housing. But the Constitution does not provide judicial remedies for every social and economic ill. We are unable to perceive in that document any constitutional guarantee of access to dwellings of a particular quality or any recognition of the right of a tenant to occupy the real property of his landlord beyond the term of his lease, without the payment of rent... Absent constitutional mandate, the assurance of adequate housing and the definition of landlord-tenant relationships are legislative, not judicial, functions».

In a similar way, the court in its decision also referred to the case of *Dandridge v. Williams*, 397 U.S. 471 (1970), arguing that the Court's explicit recognition of the fact that the «administration of public welfare assistance . . . involves the most basic economic needs of impoverished human beings» provided no basis for departing from the settled mode of constitutional analysis of legislative classifications involving questions of economic and social policy. The Court then concluded that:

> «As in the case of housing, the central importance of welfare benefits to the poor was not an adequate foundation for requiring the State to justify its law by showing some compelling state interest. The Court refused to apply the strict-scrutiny test despite its contemporaneous recognition in *Goldberg v. Kelly*, 397 U.S. 354,364 (1970) that «welfare provides the means to obtain essential food, clothing, housing, and medical care».
>
> The lesson of these cases in addressing the question now before the Court is plain. It is not the province of this Court to create substantive constitutional rights in the name of guaranteeing equal protection of the laws. Thus, the key to discovering whether education is «fundamental» is not to be found in comparisons of the relative societal significance of education as opposed to subsistence or housing. Nor is it to be found by weighing whether education is as important as the right to travel. Rather, the answer lies in assessing whether there is a right to education explicitly or implicitly guaranteed by the Constitution.

Regarding the Latin American countries, there is no doubt regarding the constitutional rank of such rights, being the amparo the judicial mean for the protection of them, as rights declared in the Constitutions. Thus, when the Bolivian Amparo Law set forth that the amparo is devoted to protect rights and guaranties «recognized in the Constitution and the laws» (Article 94); the reference to «laws» must not be interpreted as an alternative (Constitution « or «laws), but in an accumulatively (Constitution and the laws). In the case of Guatemala, if it is true that Article 1 of the Amparo law refers to «rights inherent to persons protected by the Constitution, the laws and international agreements ratified by Guatemala», including «laws», it only refers to amparo as a «constitutional guaranty of defense»; thus, based on constitutional reasons.

II. AMPARO FOR THE JUSTICIABILITY OF CONSTITUTIONAL RIGHTS ONLY IN CASES OF CONSTITUTIONAL VIOLATIONS

Consequently, even in cases of rights enshrined in the Constitution, the amparo recourse is only admissible when the constitutional provision referred to the right has been violated.

Thus, it is not possible to file an action of amparo just basing it in the violation of the statutory provisions which regulate the right. It is, for instance, the case of property rights, widely regulated in the Civil Codes, regarding which all the conducts affecting those regulations in general terms had their own ordinary remedies. One example is the civil injunctions set forth in the Civil Code and the Civil Procedure Codes for the immediate protection of possession rights in cases of trespasses (*interdictos*) which are effective judicial remedies for the protection of a land owner or occupant rights. Thus, in cases of property trespass, the *interdicto of amparo* or of new construction are effective means for protection, and no amparo action can be filed in such cases.

As was decided by the Constitutional Chamber of the Supreme Tribunal of Justice of Venezuela,

> «The amparo action protects one aspect of the legal situations of persons referred to their fundamental rights, corresponding the defense of subjective rights -different to fundamental rights and public liberties- to the ordinary administrative and judicial recourses and actions. For instance, it is not the same to deny a citizen the condition to have property rights, than to discuss property rights between parties, the protection of which corresponds to a specific judicial action of recovery (*reivindicación*). But if the right to defend its property means the denial of a fundamental right, then the proprietor is denied of his right, and must be protected.
>
> This means that in the amparo proceedings the court judge the actions of public entities or Individuals that can harm fundamental rights; but in no case can it review, for instance, the applicability or interpretation or ordinary law by the Administration or the courts, unless than from them a direct violation of the Constitution can be deducted. The amparo is not a new judicial instance, nor the substitution of ordinary judicial means for the protection of rights and interest; it is the reaffirmation of constitutional values, by mean of which the court hearing an amparo can decide regarding the contents or the application of constitutional provisions regulating fundamental rights, can review the interpretation made by public administration or judicial bodies, or determine if the facts from which constitutional violations are deducted constitute a direct violation of the Constitution»[2].

This relates the subject, of course, to the general condition of the extraordinary character of the amparo action, in the sense that it can only be filed when no other appropriate and effective ordinary judicial means of protection are legally provided. This condition is set forth in a similar way to the «inadequacy» condition provided for the equitable injunction remedies in North America, in the sense that they are only admissible when there is no adequate remedy at law[3].

This inadequacy, of course, can result from the factual situations that impede granting the protection as was resolved since the well know case of *Wheelock v. Nooman* (NY 1888), in which an injunction was granted to require the defendant to remove great boulders which he had left on the plaintiff's property beyond the terms of the license to do so. The plaintiff in the case could not easily remove the boulders and sued the cost of removal of the trespassing rocks because of their size and weight[4]. On the contrary, the remedy at law is adequate if the defendant left litter on the property because the plaintiff can pay for someone to remove the trash and then sue the defendant for the cost incurred, as was decided in *Connor v. Grosso* (Cal. 1953)[5].

But in other cases in the United States, the extraordinary character of the injunctive remedies derives from the fact that the law cannot provide an adequate

---

2 Decision N° 828 of July, 27, 2000 (case: *Seguros Corporativos (SEGUCORP), C.A. et al. vs. Superintedencia* de *Seguros*), in *Revista de Derecho Público*, N° 83, Editorial Jurídica Venezolana, Caracas 2000, pp. 290 ff.

3 See Owen M. FISS and Doug RENDLEMAN, *Injunctions*, 2d Ed, The Foundation Press, Mineola, New Cork, 1984, p. 59.

4 See the reference in William M. TAB and Elaine W. SHOBEN, Remedies in a Nutshell, Thomson West, St. Paul, 2005, p. 24.

5 *Idem*.

remedy because of the nature of the right involved, which was the case of the constitutional claims in the case of school segregation which violated rights that require equitable intervention.

It is because of this nature of the rights that can be protected by means of amparo, as constitutional rights, that this specific action for protection can only be filed when the Constitution is directly infringed.

The Venezuelan First Court on Judicial Review of Administrative action Jurisdiction, in a decision of December 6, 1989, issued just after the Amparo Law was sanctioned (1988), fixed this doctrine, as follows:

> The amparo is admissible only in cases of violations of constitutional rights and guaranties. These rights and guaranties can be regulated in norms of inferior rank, but those are not the norms that can be alleged as violated, and reference must be made to the text that originates them. The extraordinary character of the amparo impedes that through it, the fulfillment or regulations and conditions set forth in statutory norms, those matters that can be discussed by other ordinary means be argued. If it were not conceived like this, the amparo jurisdiction would substitute any other, and the critics and fear would be raised by this new institution»[6].

Of course, and even if the constitutional right and guaranty can be regulated through statutory norms, the amparo action cannot be founded in the sole violation of such statutory provisions. As was subsequently ruled by the Supreme Court of Venezuela in decision of August 14, 1990, the amparo can only be filed because of direct and immediate contraventions of constitutional rights and guaranties; and for that purpose:

> It is necessary to demonstrate the sole harm to such norms and not to others of infra constitutional character. Thus, the action for amparo, is always of constitutional nature, it is justified in the measure that the rights or guaranties harmed or threatened are of such same rank. In conclusion, it is not enough to allege the violation of inferior rank norms, which are not the ones to be protected by amparo but for other means. Even if they apply constitutional provisions, it is indispensable, and also enough, to demonstrate the direct violation of a constitutional provision»[7] .

---

6 See in *Revista de Derecho Público,* N° 41, Editorial Jurídica Venezolana, Caracas, 1990, p. 99. This doctrine has been followed by the First Court on Judicial review of Adminsitrative action in the decisions of August 22, 1990 in FUNEDA *15 años de Jurisprudencia, op. cit., p.* 138; of September 16, 1992, in *Revista de Derecho Público,* N° 51, Editorial Jurídica Venezolana, Caracas, 1992, p. 151; ando f December 4, 1992, in *Revista de Derecho Público,* N° 52, Editorial Jurídica Venezolana, Caracas, p. 165 and in FUNEDA, *15 años de Jurisprudencia, op. cit.,* p. 140.

7 See in *Revista de Derecho Público,* N° 44, Editorial Jurídica Venezolana, Caracas, 1990 p. 143. See also, Supreme Court of Justice decisions (Politico Adminsitrative Chamber) of November 8, 1990, in *Revista de Derecho Público,* N° 44, Editorial Jurídica Venezolana, Caracas, 1990, p. 141; of April 4, 1990, in *Revista de Derecho Público,* N° 42, Editorial Jurídica Venezolana, Caracas, 1990; p. 112; of January 31, 1989, *Revista de Derecho Público* N° 37, Editorial Jurídica Venezolana, Caracas, 198, p; of August 14, 1989, in *Revista de Derecho Público,* N° 39, Editorial Jurídica Venezolana, Caracas, 1989, p. 144; of March 4, 1993, in *Revista de Derecho Público,* nos 53-54, Editorial Jurídica Venezolana, Caracas, 1993, p. 254; ando f the First Court on Judicial Reviwe of Administrative Action of September 7, 1992, in FUNEDA en *15 años de Jurisprudencia, op. cit.,* p. 127.

Consequently, as a matter of principle, all constitutional rights and guaranties are justiciable by mean of the amparo recourse, provided that the Constitution is directly infringed, notwithstanding the right to also be regulated by statutes. That is why, for instance, the Perúvian Code on Constitutional Jurisdiction is precise when it sets that the «amparo shall not be admitted in defense of a right that lacks direct constitutional founding or when it is does not directly refer to the protected constitutional aspects of such right». (Articles 5,1 and 38), which confirms the already mentioned principle of the amparo protection only regarding the violation of the Constitution provisions regarding the rights.

III. AMPARO AND HABEAS CORPUS FOR THE PROTECTION OF ALL CONSTITUTIONAL RIGHTS

Almost all Latin American countries set forth the habeas corpus recourse for the protection of personal freedom and safety, and the amparo recourse for the protection of all the other constitutional rights and guarantees. The only exception in this pattern, are México and Venezuela, where the personal freedom and safety are also protected through the general amparo suit or action, being thus the habeas corpus only a kind or a specie of the amparo. On the contrary, in all others Latin American Countries the habeas corpus is regulated as a separate action or recourse for the specific protection of personal freedom and safety.

The reason for the Mexican and Venezuelan exception is, precisely, the conception that those countries have of the amparo as a constitutional right and not exclusively as an adjective mean for protection of human rights.

But what is important regarding the amparo and habeas corpus recourses, is that in almost all the Latin American countries, by means of a general amparo suit or action or of both, amparo and habeas corpus recourses or actions, all constitutional rights are protected, without any exception. The exception in this regard are the countries where the amparo has been reduced to protect only certain constitutional rights, as is the case of the «tutela» action in Colombia and of the action for protection in Chile, conceived only for the protection of some constitutional rights qualified as «fundamental» or enumerated in the constitutional text. It is also the case of México, where the amparo suit is established for the protection of only the «individual guarantees».

Thus two general systems can be distinguish in Latin America regarding the amparo: those in which all constitutional rights and guaranties can be protected through the amparo and habeas corpus recourse; and those where the amparo recourse is directed to protect only some constitutional rights, those qualified as «fundamental rights» or « individual guarantees».

In the first system, the rights protected in principle are those enshrined in the Constitutions, thus the use of the expression «constitutional rights», in order, first, to comprise the rights enumerated in the constitutional texts; second, those that even not being enumerated in the Constitutions are inherent to human beings; and third, those enumerated in the international instruments on human rights ratified by the State. In the words of the Argentinean Amparo Law (Article 1) and in the Uruguayan 1988 Amparo Law (Article 72), the constitutional protection refers to the rights and freedoms «expressly or implicitly recognized by the Constitution».

Is the case of Venezuela, where the action of amparo is conceived as a means for the protection of the enjoyment and practice of absolutely all the constitutional rights and guarantees, as well as those inherent to human beings not enumerated in the Constitution or in the international instruments on human rights; the expression «instruments» comprising not only treaties, conventions and covenants but also declarations. This is what is expressly set forth in Article 27 of the Constitution.

Consequently, all constitutional rights listed in Title III (Human Rights, Guarantees and Duties) of the Constitution as the citizenship rights, the civil (individual) rights, the political rights, the social and family rights, the cultural and educational rights, the economic rights, the environmental rights and the indigenous people rights, can be protected by means of the amparo action (Articles 19-129). And additionally, other rights and guaranties derived from other constitutional provisions not included in Title III on «Human Rights, Guarantees and Duties», like the constitutional guarantee of the independence of the Judiciary[8], or the constitutional guarantee to the legality of taxation (that taxes can only by set forth by statute)[9], can also be protected by means of amparo.

But as aforementioned, the amparo action in Venezuela is also admissible for the protection of all «constitutional rights and guaranties, even those inherent to persons that are not expressly enumerated in the Constitution or in international instruments on human rights» (Art. 27, Constitution). This declaration leaves no loophole regarding right or guarantee to be constitutionally protected; particularly because of the open clause enshrined in Article 22 of the Constitution.

This clause, extensively used by the Latin American supreme courts to identity rights and guaranties not expressly listed in the Constitution, has its antecedent in the IX Amendment of the United States Constitution, even though, in contrast, in the United States the Supreme Court has had little occasion to interpret it. One of the few cases, though, is the case *Griswold v. Connecticut* decided on June 7, 1965, 381 U.S. 479; 85 S. Ct. 1678; 14 L. Ed. 2d 510; 1965[10], in which Justice Goldberg, delivering the opinion of the Court, held the unconstitutionality of the Connecticut's birth-control law because it intruded upon the right of marital privacy, which was considered as embraced by the concept of liberty, even if it was not explicitly mentioned in the Constitution. The Court based its ruling precisely on the **Ninth Amendment** to the Constitution, declaring that:

> To hold that a right so basic and fundamental and so deep-rooted in our society as the right of privacy in marriage may be infringed because that right is not guaranteed in so many words by the first eight amendments to the Constitution is to ignore the **Ninth Amendment** and to give it no effect whatsoever. Moreover, a judicial construction that this fundamental right is not protected by the Constitution because it is not mentioned in explicit terms by one of the first eight amendments or elsewhere in the Constitution would

---

8 Decision of the former Supreme Court of Justice, Political Administrative Chamber, dated march, 25, 1994 (Case *Arnoldo Echegaray*).

9 See Allan R. BREWER-CARÍAS, «Derecho y Acción de Amparo», *Instituciones Políticas y Constitucionales,* Vol. V., Caracas, 1998, pp. 209 y ss. See decision of the First Court on judicial review of Administrative Action, case *Fecadove*. See the reference in Rafael CHAVERO G, *El Nuevo régimen del amparo constitucional en Venezuela*, Caracas, 2001, p. 157.

10 U.S. LEXIS 2282.

violate the **Ninth Amendment,** which specifically states that «the enumeration in the Constitution, of certain rights, shall not be construed to deny or disparage others retained by the people

Rather, the **Ninth Amendment** shows a belief of the Constitution's authors that fundamental rights exist that are not expressly enumerated in the first eight amendments and an intent that the list of rights included there not be deemed exhaustive. As any student of this Court's opinions knows, this Court has held, often unanimously, that the Fifth and Fourteenth Amendments protect certain fundamental personal liberties from abridgment by the Federal Government or the States. See, e. g., Bolling v. Sharpe, 347 U.S. 497; Aptheker v. Secretary of State, 378 U.S. 500; Kent v. Dulles, 357 U.S. 116; Cantwell v. Connecticut, 310 U.S. 296; NAACP v. Alabama, 357 U.S. 449; Gideon v. Wainwright, 372 U.S. 335; New York Times Co. v. Sullivan, 376 U.S. 254. The **Ninth Amendment** simply shows the intent of the Constitution's authors that other fundamental personal rights should not be denied such protection or disparaged in any other way simply because they are not specifically listed in the first eight constitutional amendments...

In sum, the **Ninth Amendment** simply lends strong support to the view that the «liberty» protected by the Fifth and Fourteenth Amendments from infringement by the Federal Government or the States is not restricted to rights specifically mentioned in the first eight amendments. *Cf.* United Public Workers v. Mitchell, 330 U.S. 75, 94-95.

In determining which rights are fundamental, judges are not left at large to decide cases in light of their personal and private notions. Rather, they must look to the «traditions and [collective] conscience of our people» to determine whether a principle is «so rooted [there] . . . as to be ranked as fundamental». Snyder v. Massachusetts, 291 U.S. 97, 105. The inquiry is whether a right involved «is of such a character that it cannot be denied without violating those 'fundamental principles of liberty and justice which lie at the base of all our civil and political institutions' . . . .» Powell v. Alabama, 287 U.S. 45, 67. «Liberty» also «gains content from the emanations of . . . specific [constitutional] guarantees» and «from experience with the requirements of a free society». Poe v. Ullman, 367 U.S. 497, 517.

The Court thus concluded that:

«The entire fabric of the Constitution and the purposes that clearly underlie its specific guarantees demonstrate that the rights to marital privacy and to marry and raise a family are of similar order and magnitude as the fundamental rights specifically protected. Although the Constitution does not speak in so many words of the right of privacy in marriage, I cannot believe that it offers these fundamental rights no protection. The fact that no particular provision of the Constitution explicitly forbids the State from disrupting the traditional relation of the family -a relation as old and as fundamental as our entire civilization- surely does not show that the Government was meant to have the power to do so. Rather, as the **Ninth Amendment** expressly recognizes, there are fundamental personal rights such as this one, which are protected from abridgment by the Government though not specifically mentioned in the Constitution».

In sum, the Supreme Court concluded affirming that «the right of privacy in the marital relation is fundamental and basic a personal right retained by the people» within the meaning of the **Ninth Amendment», thus considering unconstitutional the Connecticut law that prohibits the use of contraceptives.**

The application of open clause on human rights in Venezuela, similar to the Ninth Amendment, has already been analyzed, expanding the scope of the constitutional rights protected by means of amparo. The same has happened in the other Latin American Countries, which had developed both the amparo and habeas corpus recourses for the protection of all human rights declared in the Constitutions and in the International Treaties.

Is the case of Costa Rica, where Article 48 of the Constitution is absolutely clear when it guarantees the right of every person to file the action of habeas corpus to guarantee their freedom and personal integrity and the action for amparo to maintain or reestablish the enjoyment of all other rights conferred by this Constitution as well as those of a fundamental nature established in international instruments on human rights, enforceable in the Republic. In the same sense it is regulated in the Ecuadorian Law where amparo is set for «the judicial effective protection of all rights enshrined in the Constitution and those contained in the declarations, covenants, conventions and other international instruments in force in Ecuador (Article 46).

Other legislations, in order to precise the extension of the constitutional amparo and habeas corpus protection, tend to be exhaustive in the listing of the constitutional rights to be protected, as is the case of Perú. For instance, when distinguishing the amparo and habeas corpus actions, the Constitutional Procedure Code (Law 28.237 of 2004) expressly lists and identifies the following rights as protected by mean of the *habeas corpus*:

1. Personal integrity and the right not to be submitted to torture or inhuman or humiliating treatment, nor coerced to obtain declarations.
2. The right not to be forced to render oaths nor be compelled to declare or recognize their own guilt, that of their spouse, or their family members up to the fourth level of consanguinity or second of affinity.
3. The right not to be exiled or banished or confined except by final judicial decision.
4. The right not to be expatriated nor kept away from one's residence except by legal order or by application of the Immigration Law.
5. The right of the foreigner to whom political asylum has been granted, not to be expelled from the country to the country that is persecuting him, or under no circumstance if his freedom or safety is in danger through being expelled.
6. The right of nationals or resident foreigners to enter, transit or leave national territory, except by legal order or application of the Immigration or Health Law.
7. The right not to be detained except by written and justified judicial order, or by the police forces for having committed a flagrant crime; or if he or she has been detained, to be brought before the corresponding Court within 24 hours or as soon as possible.

8. The right to voluntarily decide to render military service, pursuant to the law governing such matter.
9. The right not to be arrested for debt.
10. The right not to be deprived of the national identity document, or to obtain a passport or its renewal within the Republic or overseas.
11. The right not to be held incommunicado, except in those cases established under the Constitution (Article 2, 24, g).
12. The right to be assisted by a freely chosen defense lawyer at the moment of being summonsed or arrested by the police or other authority, without exception.
13. The right to have removed the surveillance of one's domicile or suspended police trailing, when arbitrary and unjustified.
14. The right of the person on trial or condemned to be released from jail, if his or her freedom has been decided by a judge.
15. The right to have the correct procedure observed in the case of the processing or detention of persons, pursuant to Article 99 of the Constitution.
16. The right not to be subject to a forced disappearance.
17. The right of the person under arrest or imprisoned not to be subject to treatment that is unreasonable or disproportional, in respect of the form and conditions in which the order of detention or imprisonment is carried out.

The article adds that «*habeas corpus* shall also be admitted in defense of constitutional rights associated with individual freedom, especially when due process and the inviolability of the home are concerned».

As far as the action of amparo is concerned, pursuant to the same Perúvian Code on Constitutional Procedure, such action shall be admitted in defense of the following rights expressly listed in article 37:

1. To equality and not to be discriminated because of origin, sex, race, sexual orientation, religion, opinion, economic or social condition, language or any other;
2. To publicly exercise any religious creed;
3. To information, opinion and expression;
4. To contract freely;
5. To the artistic, intellectual and scientific creation;
6. To the inviolability and secrecy of private documents and communications;
7. To assembly;
8. To honor, intimacy, voice, image and to the rectification of incorrect or harmful information;
9. To associate;
10. To work;
11. To unionize, collectively bargain and go on strike;
12. To property and to inherit;

13. To petition before the competent authority;
14. To participate individually and collectively in the political life of the country;
15. To citizenship;
16. To effective judicial protection;
17. To education and the right of the parents to choose the school and participate in the education of their children;
18. To teach according to constitutional principles;
19. To social security;
20. To compensation and a pension;
21. To the freedom to lecture;
22. To have access to the media, pursuant to Article 35 of the Constitution;
22. To enjoy an environment that is balanced and appropriate for developing one's life;
23. To health; and
24. To others recognized by the Constitution.

Fortunately, the last item referred to all «the other rights recognized in the Constitution» resolves the problems that normally have the practice to list in some statutes, specific situations with the risk of leaving thinks behind.

The Guatemalan Amparo Law also tends to exhaust the cases in which the amparo action can be filed[11], when setting in Article 10 that its admission extends to any situation that presents a risk, a threat, a restriction or a violation of the rights recognized by «the Constitution and the laws of the Republic of Guatemala», whether such situation is caused by public or private law entities or individuals. Therefore, as it is listed in the same Article 10, every person shall have the right to request amparo, in the following cases, among others:

a) To be maintained or reinstated in the enjoyment of the rights and guarantees established in «the Constitution or any other law».

b) To seek a decision to declare, in specific cases, that a law, regulation, resolution or act of the authorities shall not be enforced against the plaintiff because it contravenes or restricts a right that is guaranteed by «the Constitution or any other law».

c) To seek a decision to declare in specific cases, that a provision or resolution (not merely legislative) of the Congress of the Republic is not applicable to the plaintiff since it violates a constitutional right.

d) When an authority of any jurisdiction issues a regulation, decision or resolution of any kind, abusing its power or exceeding its legal powers, or when such powers are non-existent or exercised in such a way that the harm caused or likely to be caused «cannot be corrected by any other legal means of defense».

---

11 See: Jorge Mario GARCÍA LA GUARDIA, «La Constitución y su defensa en Guatemala», en el libro editado por la UNAM, *La Constitución y su defensa,* México, 1984, pp. 717-719; and *La Constitución Guatemalteca de 1985,* México, 1992.

e) When in administrative proceedings, the affected party is forced to comply with unreasonable or unlawful requirements, procedures or activities, or when «there is no means or recourse available to suspend their effect».

f) When petitions and procedures before administrative authorities are not resolved in the delay established by law, or, in absence of such delay, within thirty days following the exhaustion of the corresponding procedure; and also when petitions are not admitted for processing.

g) In political matters, when rights recognized by the law or by the by-laws of political organizations are infringed. Nevertheless, in purely electoral matters, the court analysis and examination shall be limited to legal aspects, accepting such questions of fact that are considered proven in the recourse of review.

h) In matters of judicial and administrative order, for which procedures and recourses are established by law, and by means of which such matters may be appropriately discussed in accordance with the legal principle of due process, if after the interested party has made use of the recourses established by law, there is still a threat, restriction or violation of the rights guaranteed by the Constitution and the law.

Even in the cases where this article of the Amparo law refers to rights protected in «the Constitution or the laws», the violation of the right must be a constitutional one. If it is just a legal one, the affected party has the ordinary means for protection, thus the amparo is not admitted when these ordinary means exists.

IV. AMPARO AND HABEAS CORPUS FOR THE PROTECTION OF ONLY SOME CONSTITUTIONAL RIGHTS

As already mentioned, in contrast with the general trend of the Latin American system of amparo and habeas corpus for the protection of all constitutional rights, in the case of Chile and Colombia, the specific action for protection of constitutional rights and freedoms is only established in the Constitution with respect to certain rights and guarantees which are listed as *fundamental*. These systems follow the general trend set by German and Spanish regulations on the amparo recourses.

1. The European antecedents

In Germany, in addition to the abstract judicial review of norms exercised by the Federal Constitutional Tribunal at the request of some State political organs, judicial review can also be exercised by the Constitutional Tribunal as a result of a constitutional complaint or «amparo» recourse that any person can bring before the Tribunal when he claims that one of his basic or fundamental rights has been directly violated by a normative state act. This «constitutional complaint», only constitutionalized in 1969 was originally established in the 1951 Federal Statute of the Constitutional Tribunal (Art. 90. Federal Constitutional Tribunal Law) and was conceived as a specific judicial means for the protection of fundamental rights and freedoms against any action of the state organs which violates them. Therefore, it is not a specific action only directed to obtain judicial review of legislation, but it can be used for that purpose, when exercised against a statute.

The constitutional complaint after the 1969 constitutional amendment is expressly established in Article 93, section 1, Nº 4ª of the Constitution when attributing the Federal Constitutional Tribunal power to decide:

On complaints of unconstitutionality, which may be entered by any person who claims that one of his basic (fundamental) rights or one of his rights under paragraph (4) of article 20, under articles 33, 38, 101, 103, or 104 has been violated by public authority.[12]

Therefore, the constitutional complaint can be brought before the Tribunal against any state act, whether legislative, executive or judicial, but in all cases, it can only be exercised once the ordinary judicial means for the protection of the fundamental rights that have been violated are exhausted (Art. 90, 2 Federal Constitutional Tribunal Law). Consequently, the constitutional complaint is a subordinate mean of judicial protection of fundamental rights,[13] and if there are other judicial recourses or actions that can serve the purpose of protecting fundamental rights, the constitutional complaint is not admissible, except when the Constitutional Tribunal considers the matter as being of general importance or when it considers that the claimant is threatened by a grave and irremediable prejudice if it is sent to the ordinary judicial means for protection (Art. 90, 2 Federal Constitutional Tribunal Law).

The most important feature of the German constitutional complaint, when comparing it with the Latin American amparo, is that it is set in the Constitution only for the protection of the rights listed in Article 93,1 of the Constitution, which are the following:

First, the fundamental rights (*Grundrechte*), enshrined in Articles 1 to 19 of the Constitution, which are the followings:

1. Man's dignity (Art. 1);
2. Freedom to develop its own personality (Art. 2-1);
3. Right to life and to physical integrity (Art. 2-2);
4. Equality (Art. 3);
5. Ideological and Religion freedom (Art. 4-1);
6. Freedom of cult (Art. 4-2);
7. Conscience objection (Art. 4-3 y Art. 12-a2);
8. Freedom of expression and to inform (Art. 5-1);
9. Freedom to teach and to research (Art. 5-3);
10. Marital freedom, family protection and non discrimination because of extra matrimonial birth (Art. 6);
11. Right to education (Art. 7);
12. Freedom of assembly (Art. 8);
13. Freedom of association (Art. 9);
14. Inviolability of communications secret (Art. 10);
15. Freedom of residence and of movement (Art. 11);

12 See also Arts. 90-96 FCT Law.

13 Art. 19.4 of the Constitution establishes in general that «Should any person's rights be violated by public authority resource to the courts shall be open to him. If jurisdiction is not specified, recourse shall be to the ordinary courts».

16. Freedom to freely choose a profession and the place of work (Art. 12);
17. Inviolability of domicile (Art. 13);
18. Private property rights and to inherit (Art. 14);
19. Right to German nationality (Art. 16-1);
20. Right to political asylum for aliens (Art. 16-2); and
21. Right to petition (Art. 17).

Additionally, it also can be protected by the constitutional complaint, the constitutional rights enshrined in Articles 20-4, 33, 38, 101, 103 and 104 of the same Constitution, which are the following:

21. Right to resist against who acts against the constitutional order (Art 20-4);
22. Equal rights and obligations of Germans in all Status of the Federation (Art. 33-1);
23. Right to have access in equal terms to public positions (Art. 33-2);
24. Right to vote and to be elected (Art. 38);
25. Prohibition of extraordinary courts and right to «natural judge» (Art. 101);
26. Right to be heard by courts (Art. 103-1);
27 Right to *non bis in ídem* principle (Art. 103-3); and
28 Judicial guarantees for deprivation of liberty (Art. 104).

In all these cases, the constitutional complaint can be exercised directly against a statute or any other normative state act on the grounds that it directly impairs the fundamental rights of the claimant. In that case, it leads directly to the exercise of a judicial review of normative state acts function by the Constitutional Tribunal. As a result of this constitutional complaint, if the statute is considered unconstitutional, it must be declared null (Art. 95, 3, B FCT Law).

The basic condition for the admissibility of constitutional complaints against laws is, of course, the fact that the challenged statute or normative state act, must personally affect the claimant's fundamental rights, in a direct and current way, without the need for any further administrative application of the norm. On the contrary, if this further administrative application is needed, he must wait for the administrative execution of the statute and complain against it. This direct prejudice caused by the normative act on the rights of the claimant, as a basic element for the admissibility of the complain, justifies the delay of one year after its publication established for the introduction of the action before the Tribunal (Art. 93, 1, B FCT Law).

It also explains the power of the Constitutional Tribunal to adopt provisional protective measures regarding the challenged statute, *pendente litis*, in the sense that the Tribunal can even theoretically, suspend the application of the challenged law (Art. 32 FCT Law).

Finally, regarding this constitutional complaint, Article 93, section 1, N° 4b of the Constitution, also empowers the constitutional tribunal to decide:

> On complaints of unconstitutionality, entered by communes (municipalities) or association of communes (municipalities) on the ground that their right to self-government under Article 28 has been violated by a law other than a Lander Law open to complaint to the respective land constitutional court.

Hence, the direct constitutional complaint against laws is not only attributed to individuals for the protection of their fundamental rights, but also to the local government entities, for the protection of their autonomy and right to self-government guaranteed in the Constitution, against federal statutes that could violate them. In these cases, it also results in a direct means of judicial review of statutes of legislation.

The 1978 Spanish Constitution, when setting forth the amparo recourse, in a certain way followed the features of the German constitutional complaint and also, of the amparo recourse originally established in the Republic in the thirties.

Thus, apart from the direct and incidental methods of judicial review, in the Spanish system a recourse of amparo has been created for constitutional protection also of fundamental rights, which can be brought before the Constitutional Tribunal by any person with direct interest in the matter, against state acts of a non legislative character (Art. 161,1,b, Constitution; and Art. 41,2 Organic Law 2/1979)

However, if the recourse for protection is based on the fact that the challenged state act is based on a statute that at the same time infringes fundamental rights or freedoms, the Tribunal must proceed to review its constitutionality through the procedural rules established for the direct action or recourse of unconstitutionality (Art. 52,2 Organic Law 2/1979).

The Spanish recourse of amparo, following the German constitutional complaint features, reduces the constitutional protection to only certain constitutional rights and freedoms also qualified as «fundamental», recognized in Article 14, in the first section of the Second Chapter (Arts. 15 a 20) and in the second paragraph of Article 30 of the Constitution, which are the following:

1. Equality before the law (Art. 14);
2. Right to life and physical and moral integrity (Art. 15);
3. Ideological, religious and freedoms and freedom of cult (Art. 16);
4. Right to personal freedom and safety (Art. 17);
5. Right to honor, personal and familiar intimacy and to one's image Arts. 18-1 and 18-4);
6. Inviolability of domicile (Art. 18-2);
7. Secrecy of communications (Art. 18-3);
8. Right to freely choose one's residence, to move within the territory and to freely leave Spain (Art. 19);
9. Right to freedom of expression and to freely propagate one's thought (Art. 20-1-a);
10. Right to produce and to literary, artistic, scientific and technical creations (Art. 20-1-b);
11. Freedom of teaching (chair) (Art. 20-1-c);
12. Right to communicate and to receive true information by any mean (Art. 20-1-d);
13. Right to meet and to demonstration (Art. 21);
14. Right to association (Art. 22);

15. Right to participate in public affairs (Art. 23-1);
16 Right to equal access to public functions or positions (Art. 23-2);
17. Right to obtain effective protection by courts and judges (Art. 24-1);
18. Right to have the ordinary and predetermined judge, to defense and to be assisted by a lawyer, to be inform of the accusation, to a public process without undue delays and with the guaranties of using the pertinent means of evidence for its defense, not to self incriminate, not to confess culpability and to the presumption of innocence (Art. 24-2;
19. Principle of criminal legality (*nullum crime sine legge*) (Art. 25-1);
20. Rights of the detainees to a pay work and to the benefits of social security, to have access to culture and to the integral development of one's personality (Art. 25-2);
21. Right to education and to the liberty to teach (Art. 27-1);
22. Freedom to create teaching centers, within the constitutional principles (Art. 27-6);
23. Freedom to freely unionized trade (Art. 28-1);
24. Right to strike (Art. 28-2);
25. Right to personal and collective petition (Art. 29); and
26. Right to conscience objection (Art. 30-2).

It must be said that notwithstanding the very ample enumeration of fundamental rights that can be protected by means of the amparo recourse before the Constitutional Tribunal, they are other constitutional rights not protected by the recourse which although constitutional, do not qualify as «fundamental rights».

This limitative approach to the justiciable rights by means of amparo is exceptionally followed in Latin America only in Chile and Colombia.

2. The Chilean «acción de protección» for the protection of some constitutional rights

In Chile, as in the majority of Latin American Countries, constitutional rights are protected by means of the action of habeas corpus, aimed at protecting any individual who is arrested, detained or imprisoned in breach of the Constitution; and by the recourse of protection, which is only aimed at guaranteeing the amparo of determined constitutional rights, in cases of arbitrary or illegal actions or omissions, or of privation, disturbance or threat in the legitimate exercise of the rights and guarantees established in Article 19, numbers 1, 2, 3 (paragraph 4), 4, 5, 6, 9 (final paragraph), 11, 12, 13, 15, 16 of the Constitution regarding to freedom to work and the right of freedom of choice and freedom of contract, and to what is established in the fourth paragraph and numbers 19, 21, 22, 23, 24 and 25. These rights are the following:

1. The right to life and to the physical and psychological integrity (19,1);
2. Equality before the law (19,2);
3. Right to be judged by one's natural judges (19,3);
4. Right to respect for private and public life and the honor of the individual and his family (19,4);

5. Right to the inviolability of home and all forms of private communication (19,5);
6. Freedom of conscience and of manifestation of all cults (19,6);
7. Right to choose the health system (19,9 fine);
8. Freedom of teaching (19,11);
9. Freedom to express opinions and to disseminate information (19,12);
10. Right to assemble (19,13).
11. Right to associate (19,15);
12. Freedom to work, and the right to free selection and contracting (19,16);
13. Right to affiliate to trade unions (19,19);
14. Economic freedom (19,21);
15. Right to a non-discriminatory treatment (19,22);
16. Freedom to acquire ownership (19,23);
17. Property right (19,24);
18. Right of authorship (19,25); and
19. Right to live in a contamination-free environment (20).

Apart from these constitutional rights and freedoms, the other rights enshrined in the Constitution have no specific means of protection, but rather their protection corresponds to the ordinary courts through ordinary judicial procedures.

3. The Colombian «action de tutela» for the protection of fundamental rights

In the case of Colombia, in similar way, the Constitution also sets forth two means of general protection of constitutional rights: the *habeas corpus* and the action of « tutela»; the latter designed in Article 86 of the Constitution for the immediate protection of «fundamental constitutional rights», which are not all the rights and guarantees enshrined in the Constitution.

In effect, Title II of the Constitution, on referring to «the rights, guarantees and duties», regulates them in several Chapters, as follows: Chapter 1, concerning «fundamental rights»; Chapter 2, concerning social, economic and cultural rights; and Chapter 3, concerning collective rights and the environment. From this it results that in principle, only the rights listed in Chapter I (Articles 11 to 41) as «fundamental rights» are the only constitutional rights that can be protected by the «action of tutela», being the other constitutional rights excluded from this means of protection, and thus, protected by the ordinary judicial mean.

On the other hand, Article 85 of the Constitution also defines which of the «fundamental rights» are of «immediate application», which, in principle, would imply that the action of tutela would only be admitted in these cases.

Such rights «of immediate application» and therefore susceptible of constitutional protection through the action of tutela, are the following:

1. Right to life (Article 11).
2. Right to not be disappeared, or be submitted to torture or inhuman or degrading treatment (Article 12).

3. Right to equality (Article 13).
4. Right to personality (Article 14)
5. Right to intimacy (Article 15).
6. Right to the free development of own personality (Article 16).
7. Prohibition of slavery, servitude, and human trade (Article 17).
8. Freedom of conscience (Article 18).
9. Freedom of cult (Article 19).
10. Freedom of expression (Article 20).
11. Right to honor (Article 21).
12. Right to petition (Article 23).
13. Freedom of movement (Article 24).
14. Right to exercise one's profession (Article 26).
15. Freedom to teach (Article 27).
16. Personal freedom (Article 28).
17. Right to due process and defense (Article 29)
18. Right to habeas corpus (Article 30).
19. Right to review judicial decisions (Article 31).
20. Right to not testify against oneself (Article 33).
21. Prohibition of deportation, life imprisonment, or confiscation penalties (Article 34).
22. Right to assemble (Article 37).
23. Right to political participation and to vote (Article 40).

Other rights enshrined in other articles of the Constitution can also be considered as fundamental rights, like the «fundamental rights» of children listed in Article 44 to life, physical integrity, health and social security

Apart from these constitutional expressly declared as fundamental rights and freedoms, other constitutional in principle, would not have constitutional protection under the «action of tutela», unless it is a right not expressly provided in the Constitution as being «fundamental», nature that the Constitutional Court can determine (Article 2, Decree of 1991). That is why, Decree N° 306 of 19-02-92 which regulates Decree 2.591 of 1991, expressly declares:

> **Article 2.** Pursuant to Article 1 of Decree 2.591 of 1991, the action of tutela only protects fundamental constitutional rights, and therefore, may not be used to enforce respect of rights that only have legal rank, or to enforce compliance with laws, decrees, regulations or any other regulation of an inferior level.

The Constitutional Court, in every case, has played a fundamental role in broadening protection by means of tutela to include rights not defined as «fundamental», such as the right to health, but interdependent of others such as the right to life. For that purpose in one of its first decisions, N° T-02 of May 8th, 1992, issued in a case regarding educational rights, the Constitutional Court fixed the following principal criteria to identify «fundamental rights»:

Being the human persons the subject, reason and purpose of the 1991 Constitution, the «first and most important criteria for the tutela judge to determine the fundamental constitutional rights, is to determine if it is or not an essential right to human beings». Thus, «in order to verify if a constitutional fundamental right derives from the concept of essential rights to human being, the tutela judge must rationally research from Articles 5 and 94 of the Constitution». The first article sets forth the recognition by the State, without any discrimination, of the primacy of the inalienable rights of persons and protects the family as a basic institution of society. The second sets forth the open clause regarding human rights, in the sense that the listing of rights and guaranties in the Constitution and international conventions, cannot be understood as denial of others that being inherent to human persons, are not expressly therein.

Both articles, being interpreted on the lights of the American Convention on Human Right, allow to infer what can be considered inalienable, inherent and essential, as the Constitutional Court ruled: «something is inalienable because it is inherent, and something is inherent because it is essential», being also another characteristic of the constitutional fundamental rights, the existence of correlative duties.

The Constitutional Court in the same decision also developed ancillary criteria to determine the fundamental rights, such as the concept of rights of immediate application, which do not require previous statutory regulation for its enforcement; and the location of the corresponding articles in the Titles of the Constitution, even though the latter cannot be considered as crucial. Thus, the list of «fundamental rights» of Chapter I of Title II of the Constitution does not exhaust the «fundamental rights» and does not exclude other rights for being considered fundamental and justiciable by means of tutela[14].

But, as abovementioned, the Constitutional Court has also developed its criteria of the connection of the rights seeking protection by means of amparo with other fundamental rights, particularly applying such criteria in cases of economic, cultural and social rights. The Constitutional Court thus has ruled that the acceptance of the tutela action regarding these (economic, social and cultural) rights is only possible in cases in which also a violation of a fundamental right exists. In the decision N° T-406 of June 5th, 1992, the Court heard a tutela brought before a court in a case of public drainage flooding, seeking the protection of the right to public health, the right to a healthy environment and to the population's health. The action was rejected by the lower court which considered that no fundamental rights were involved in the case, but the Constitutional Court admitted the action considering that the right to have sewage system, in circumstances in which it could evidently affect constitutional fundamental rights, as human dignity, right to life, rights of the disabled, it must be considered as justiciable by means of tutela[15].

4. The mexican amparo suit for the protection of only the «individual guarantees»

In México, as already mentioned, if it is true that the amparo suit has been regulated in the Constitution for the protection of all constitutional rights, these,

[14] See decision T-02 of May 8th, 1992, in Manuel José CEPEDA, *Derecho Constitucional Jurisprudencial. Las grandes decisiones de la Corte Constitucional,* Legis, Bogotá, 2001, pp. 49-54.

[15] See decision T-406 of June 5th, 1992 in Manuel José CEPEDA, *Derecho Constitucional Jurisprudencial. Las grandes decisiones de la Corte Constitucional,* Legis, Bogotá, 2001, pp. 55-63.

according to the wording of Article 103,1 are only the «individual guarantees» declared and enumerated in Section I, Articles 1 to 29 of the Constitution.

The *jurisprudencia* or judicial obligatory doctrine traditionally established by the Supreme Court, in effect, has been that «the amparo suit was established... not to safeguard the entire body of the Constitution but to protect the individual guarantees» enumerated in the first twenty nine articles of the Constitution[16]

This constitutional interpretation has in reduced the scope of the amparo protection, only to the following «individual guaranties»: prohibition of slavery and discrimination (Article 1); rights of the indigenous eoples (article 2); right to education, and right to educate; (Article 3); right to equal treatment; right to the protection of health; right to an adequate environment; right to dwelling; and minors rights (article 4); economic and occupation freedom and prohibition to render services without remuneration (Article 5); freedom of expression of ideas (Article 6); freedom of writing and publishing (Article 7); right to petition (Article 8); right to assemble and association (Article 9); right to bear arms (Article 10); right to movement and travel (Article 11); prohibition of nobility title (Article 12); right to natural judge (Article 13); guaranty of non retroactivity of laws, and due process of law rights (Article 14, 19, 20, 21, 23); rights regarding extradition (Article 15); personal freedom and detention and search guaranties (Article 16, 17, 18, 19, 22); right to justice and access to justice (Article 17, 21); freedom of religion (Article 24); right to privacy of correspondence, mail (Article 25); right to inviolability of home (Article 26); right to property and land ownership (Article 27); prohibition of monopolies (Article 28). Articles 1 and 29 regulate the suspension of guaranties.

This restricted scope of the amparo provoked multiple discussions and interpretations tending to extend it. In this regard, mention must be made of the opinion of Ignacio L. Vallarta, who served as President of the Supreme Court (1878–1882), and who sustained that the individual guaranties cannot be reduced to those enumerated in the first 29 articles of the Constitution, because they can also be declared in other articles of the Constitution, provided that they contain and contain an explanation, a regulation, a limitation of extension of the individual guarantees. He wrote that:

> «in the case of individual guarantees, it will frequently be necessary to refer to texts other that those that define them in order to decide with certainty whether one of them has been violated. Because of the intimate connection that exists between the articles containing guarantees and others that, although they de not mention them, nonetheless presuppose them, explain them or complement them; because of the undeniable correlation that exists between them, [the guarantee] cannot be considered in isolation without weakening them, without contradicting their spirit, without frequently rendering their application impossible...for instance, in order to know if persons may be deprived of the property guaranteed by Article 27, under the form of taxation, it would be necessary to consider Article 31, which provides that [such] contribution be proportional and equitable; similarly, to determine whether

---

16 See Suprema Corte de Justicia, *Jurisprudencia de la Suprema Corte*, Thesis 111, II, 246. See the referentes in Ignacio BURGOA, *El juicio de amparo*, Editorial Porrúa, México 191, p. 231, and Richard D. BAKER, *Judicial Review in México. A Study of the Amparo Suit*, University of Texas, Austin and London, 1971, p. 112.

the personal liberty defined in Article 5 is violated by requiring the performance of the public services, it would be necessary to [interpret] it in terms of the same article 31, which specifies certain limits on that liberty... [or] finally, in order to explain the competence to which Article 16 refers, it is necessary to examine Article 50, which established the constitutional distribution of powers between the three branches of government»[17].

According to this doctrine, as concluded by Vallarta, the amparo suit is admissible only in the cases defined in Article 103, «but it can be based on the concordance of the guaranties found in Section I of the Constitution with articles not included under that heading»[18]. This concordance doctrine has been the main tool for the extension of the constitutional protection of amparo, particularly regarding social guarantees referred to agrarian and labor matters included in Articles 27 and 123 of the Constitution, considered also as citizens' guarantees[19].

Nonetheless, constitutional rights not included in the firsts articles of the Constitution, according to the *jurisprudencia* of the Supreme Court, traditionally where not protected by means of amparo. In this regard, the Supreme Court maintained that «the violation of political rights does not give grounds for the admissibility of amparo because these [rights] are not individual guarantees»[20]. Nonetheless, also by means of the concordance doctrine in other cases the Supreme Court has given protection to political rights, by saying that «even when political rights are in question, if the act complained of may involve the violation of individual guarantees, a fact that cannot be judge *apriori*, the complaint... should be admitted»[21]; and that «although the Court has established that amparo is inadmissible against the violation of political rights, this jurisprudence refers to cases in which federal protection is sought against authorities exercising political functions and whose acts are directly and exclusively related to the exercise of rights of that nature. It cannot be applied to cases in which amparo is sought against judicial decisions, that although affecting political rights, may also violate individual guarantees».[22]

V. THE QUESTION OF THE PROTECTION OF RIGHTS IN SITUATIONS OF EMERGENCY

One last issue must be mentioned regarding the justiciability of rights, and it is the question of the admissibility of amparo actions in situations of emergency.

For instance, Article 6,7 of the 1988 Venezuelan Amparo Law used to provide that the amparo action was inadmissible «in case of suspensions of rights and guarantees» when referred to the protection of such. This decision of suspension,

---

17 See Ignacio L. VALLARTA, *Cuestiones constitucionales. Votos del C. Ignacio L. Vallarta, presidente de la Suprema Corte de Justicia en los negocios más notables*, III, pp. 145-149. See the references in Ignacio Burgoa, *op. cit*, p. 253; Richard D. BAKER, *op. cit*, p. 113t.

18 *Idem*.

19 See Ignacio BURGOA, *op. cit*, p. 263.

20 See Suprema Corte de la Nación, *Jurisprudencia de la Suprema Corte*, thesis 345, III, 645, *cit.*, by Richard D. BAKER, *op. cit.*, pp. 130, 156.

21 See Suprema Corte de la Nación, *Jurisprudencia de la Suprema Corte*, thesis 346, III, 656, *cit.*, by Richard D. BAKER, *op. cit.*, p. 157.

22 See Suprema Corte de la Nación, *Mendoza Eustaquio y otros, 10 S. J. (475) (1922), cit.* by Richard D. BAKER, *op. cit.*, pp. 130, 156.

according to Article 241 of the 1961 Constitution, could only be decided when in cases of interior or exterior conflict, a situation of emergency was declared. To the contrary, the American Convention on Human Rights provides that even in cases of emergency, the judicial guaranties of rights cannot be suspended. Thus, due to the prevalent rank that the American Convention on Human Rights has regarding internal law, as set forth in Article 23 of the 1999 Venezuelan Constitution, the abovementioned Venezuelan Amparo Law restriction was tacitly repealed. Thus, the prevalent regulation in Latin America is that the action for amparo can be filed even in states of emergency, as declared in Article 1st of the Decree regulating the action for tutela in Colombia. Also regarding the habeas corpus, in a similar sense, Article 62 of the Nicaraguan Law of Amparo sets forth that in case of suspension of the constitutional guaranties of personal freedom, the recourse of personal exhibition will remain in force.

The Perúvian Constitutional Procedure Code establishes the principle that during the emergency regimes, the amparo and habeas corpus as well as all the others constitutional proceedings, will not be suspended. According to Article 23 of the Code, when the recourses are filed in relation to the suspended rights, the court must examine the reasonability and the proportionality of the restrictive act, following these criteria:

1) If the claim refers to constitutional rights not suspended;
2) If referred to the suspended rights, the founding of the right's restrictive act does not have direct relation with the motives justifying the declaration of state of emergency;
3) If referred to the suspended rights, the right's restrictive act happens to be evidently unnecessary or unjustified bearing in mind the conduct of the aggrieved party or the factual situation briefly evaluated by the judge.

In particular, regarding the habeas corpus guarantee, the Argentinean Habeas Corpus Law provides that in case of state of siege when the personal freedom of a person is restricted, the habeas corpus proceeding is directed to prove, in the concrete case:

1) The legitimacy of the declaration of state of siege;
2) The relation between the freedom depriving order and the situation that originates the declaration of state of siege;
3) The illegitimate worsened detention way and conditions which in no case can be effective in prisons.

On October 1986, the Inter-American Commission on Human Rights submitted to the Inter American Court of Human Rights a request for advisory opinion seeking the interpretation of Articles 25,1 and 7,6 of the American Convention on Human Rights, in order to determine if the writ of habeas corpus is one of the judicial guarantees that, pursuant to the last clause of Article 27,2 of that Convention, may not be suspended by a State Party to the Convention.

Article 27 of the Convention authorizes States, in time of war, public danger, or other emergency that threatens the independence or security of a State Party, to take measures derogating its obligations under the Convention; but with the express declaration that such does not authorize any suspension of the following articles:

Article 3 (Right to Juridical Personality), Article 4 (Right to Life), Article 5 (Right to Humane Treatment), Article 6 (Freedom from Slavery), Article 9 (Freedom from Ex Post Facto Laws), Article 12 (Freedom of Conscience and Religion), Article 17 (Rights of the Family), Article 18 (Right to a Name), Article 19 (Rights of the Child), Article 20 (Right to Nationality), and Article 23 (Right to Participate in Government), or *of the judicial guarantees essential for the protection of such rights.*

The Inter American Court on Human Rights issued its *Advisory Opinion OC-8/87* of January 30, 1987 (Habeas Corpus in Emergency Situations), declaring that since «in serious emergency situations it is lawful to temporarily suspend certain rights and freedoms the free exercise of which must, under normal circumstances, be respected and guaranteed by the State...it is imperative that «the judicial guarantees essential for (their) protection» remain in force. Article 27(2)»[23]; adding that these «judicial remedies that must be considered to be essential within the meaning of Article 27(2) are those that ordinarily would effectively guarantee the full exercise of the rights and freedoms protected by that provision and the denial of which or restriction would endanger their full enjoyment»[24].

The Court also advises that the guaranties must not only be essential but also *judicial,* expression that «can only refer to those judicial remedies that are truly capable of protecting these rights» before independent and impartial judicial bodies[25]; concluding that:

42. From what has been said before, it follows that writs of habeas corpus and of «amparo» are among those judicial remedies that are essential for the protection of various rights the derogation of which is prohibited by Article 27(2) and that serve, moreover, to preserve legality in a democratic society.

43. The Court must also observe that the Constitutions and legal systems of the States Parties that authorize, expressly or by implication, the suspension of the legal remedies of habeas corpus or of «amparo» in emergency situations cannot be deemed to be compatible with the international obligations imposed on these States by the Convention.

In the same year 1986, the Government of Uruguay also submitted to the Inter-American Court a request for an advisory opinion on the scope of the prohibition of the suspension of the judicial guaranties essential for the protection of the rights mentioned in Article 27,2 of the American Convention; resulting in the issue of the *Advisory Opinion* OC-9/87 of October 6, 1987 (Judicial Guarantees in States Of Emergency), in which the Court, following its aforementioned Advisory Opinion OC-8/97, empathized that «the declaration of a state of emergency... cannot entail the suppression or ineffectiveness of the judicial guarantees that the Convention requires the States Parties to establish for the protection of the rights not subject to derogation or suspension by the state of emergency»; «therefore, any provision adopted by virtue of a state of emergency which results in the suspension of those guaranties is a violation of the Convention»[26]. The conclusion of the Court then was:

---

23 *Advisory Opinion OC-8/87* of January 30, 1987 (Habeas corpus in emergency situations), paragraph 27.

24 *Idem,* paragraph 29.

25 *Idem,* paragraph 30.

26 *Advisory Opinion* OC-9/87 of October 6, 1987 (Judicial Guarantees in States Of Emergency), paragraphs 25, 26.

1. That the «essential» judicial guarantees which are not subject to derogation, according to Article 27(2) of the Convention, include habeas corpus (Art. 7(6)), amparo, and any other effective remedy before judges or competent tribunals (Art. 25(1)), which is designed to guarantee the respect of the rights and freedoms the suspension of which is not authorized by the Convention[27].

The Inter American Court also concluded that the «essential» judicial guarantees which are not subject to suspension, «include those judicial procedures, inherent to representative democracy as a form of government (Art. 29©), provided for in the laws of the States Parties as suitable for guaranteeing the full exercise of the rights referred to in Article 27(2) of the Convention and the suppression of which or restriction entails the lack of protection of such rights»; and that «the above judicial guarantees should be exercised within the framework and the principles of due process of law, expressed in Article 8 of the Convention»[28].

This doctrine of Inter American Court is a very important one for the protection of human rights in Latin America, due to the unfortunate past experiences some countries have had in situations of emergency or of state of siege, particularly under military dictatorship or internal civil war cases; where there has been no effective judicial protection available to persons' life and physical integrity; where it has been impossible to prevent their disappearance or their whereabouts been kept secret; and other times no means have been effective to protect persons against torture or other cruel, inhumane, or degrading punishment or treatment.

Nonetheless, according to the Inter American Court on Human Rights doctrine following the provisions of the American Convention, the discussion that has been held in the United States regarding the possibility to exclude the habeas corpus protection to the so called «combatant enemies» which had been kept for years in custody without any judicial guaranty to protect their rights, cannot be held.

The matter was decided by the Supreme Court in *Rasul v.Bush,* 542 U.S. 466; 124 S. Ct. 2686; 159 L. Ed. 2d 548; 2004 in a case referred to aliens that had been captured abroad, from 2002 and onward, by United States authorities during hostilities with the Taliban regime in Afghanistan, and that were held in executive detention at the Guantanamo Bay Naval Base in Cuba. They filed various habeas corpus actions in the United States District Court for the District of Columbia against the United States and some federal and military officials, alleging that they were being held in federal custody in violation of the laws of the United States, that they had been imprisoned without having been charged with any wrongdoing, permitted to consult counsel, or provided access to courts or other tribunals. The District Court's jurisdiction was invoked under the federal habeas corpus provision (28 USCS § 2241©(3)) that authorized Federal District Courts to entertain habeas corpus applications by persons claiming to be held in custody «in violation of the Constitution or laws or treaties of the United States». The District Court dismissed the actions for jurisdiction, on the ground that aliens detained outside the sovereign territory of the United States could not invoke a habeas corpus petition; and the United States Court of Appeals for the District of Columbia Circuit, in affirming, concluded that the privilege of litigation in United States courts did not extend to aliens in military custody who had no presence in any territory over which the

---

[27] *Idem.* paragraph 41,1.

[28] *Idem,* paragraph 41,2 and 41,3.

United States was sovereign (355 US App DC 189,321 F3d 1134). On certiorari, the United States Supreme Court reversed and remanded, holding that the District Court had jurisdiction, under 28 USCS § 2241, to review the legality of the plaintiffs' detention.

Notwithstanding this Supreme Court decision, the Senate of the United States voted on November 2005 an amendment to a military budget bill, to strip captured «enemy combatants» at Guantánamo Bay, of the legal tool given to them by the Supreme Court when it allowed them to challenge their detentions in United States courts[29].

As mentioned before, a law banning the habeas corpus action could not even be proposed in Latin American Countries, due to its regulation in the Constitutions and in the Inter American Convention on Human Rights as a right that cannot be suspended even in situations of emergency. The same occurs, for instance, regarding personal freedom related to the length of administrative detention that in general is established in the Latin American Constitutions. Thus, no legal regulation or amendments can be approved extending that restrictive police custody, as for instance has occurred in Europe also due to the war against terrorism[30]. In Latin America, on the contrary, due to the constitutional rank of the regulation, the only way to extend police custody length restriction is through a constitutional amendment or reform.

29 See Eric SCHMITT, «Senate Approves Limiting Rights of U.S. Detainees», *The New York Times,* November 11, 2005.

30 As reported by Katrin BENNHOLD, in «Europe Takes Harder Line With Terror Suspects», *The New York Times,* April 17, 2006: «In December, France increased its period of detention without charge for terror suspects to six days from four; it retained rules that have allowed uncharged suspects to be denied access to a lawyer during the first three days.
Italy last year extended custody to 24 hours from 12 and authorized the police to interrogate detainees in the absence of their lawyers. In 2003, Spain extended the period in which suspected terrorists can be held effectively incommunicado to a maximum 13 days, according to the advocacy group Human Rights Watch.
Britain has gone furthest. The latest law doubles the period during which a terror suspect can be held in custody without charge to 28 days. It was just 48 hours in 2001, and Prime Minister Tony Blair fought for an extension to three months. The new law followed one filed soon after the attacks of Sept. 11, 2001, that allowed foreign terror suspects to be held indefinitely without charge. The House of Lords declared that measure unlawful in late 2004.

CHAPTER VIII

THE QUESTION OF THE JUSTICIABILITY OF SOCIAL CONSTITUTIONAL RIGHTS BY MEANS OF THE «AMPARO» ACTION

I. THE QUESTION OF THE JUSTICIABILITY OF SOCIAL RIGHTS

The most important question on the justiciability of constitutional rights in Latin America refers to those rights of economic, social and cultural character. As was argued by the Colombian Constitutional Court in the already mentioned decision N° T-406 of June 5th, 1992:

> The majority of the economic, social and cultural rights imply the rendering of an activity by the State and thus, an economic expenditure that in general terms depends on political decisions. It is based on these propositions that it is sustained that the provisions setting forth such rights cannot only be subject to the existence of a legislation issued by Congress in order to assure their enforcement. Nonetheless, the new principles of the Social State and the new relations deriving from the Welfare State impose the questioning of that solution...
>
> The *raison d'être* of these rights derives from the fact that its minimal satisfactions are an indispensable condition for the enjoyment of the civil and political rights. In other words, without the satisfaction of minimal conditions of existence, or in the sense of Article 1 of the Constitution, without respect to human dignity regarding the material conditions of existence, any aspiration of effectively ensuring the classical freedom and equalitarian rights enshrined in Chapter I of Title II of the Constitution, would be just simple and useless formalism...
>
> ...The judicial intervention in cases of economic, social and cultural rights is necessary when it is indispensable in order to assure the respect a constitutional principle or of a fundamental right.
>
> The Constitution is a present time legal (juridical) norm and has to be immediately applied and respected. From that, to sustain that the social, economic and cultural rights are reduced to a political responsibility link between the constituent and the legislator, is not only ingenuity regarding the existence of such link, but also an evident distortion regarding the sense and coherence that the Constitution must maintain. If the responsibility of the

> Constitution's efficiency would be in the hands of the legislator, the constitutional norm would not have any value and the validity of the constituent's will, would stay subject to the legislator's will[1].

Eventually the Constitutional Court of Colombia concluded its ruling saying that due to the fact that «the application of social, economic and cultural rights pose the political problem, not of generation of resources but of allocation of them, the admission of tutela regarding social, economic and cultural rights can only be accepted in cases where a violation of a fundamental right exists»[2].

Consequently, for instance, the Constitutional Court has protected the right to health of a military servicemen and to be treated in a military hospital, although he was not formally entitled to have such treatment because his military oath was yet to be given, considering that the right must be protected «when the health service is needed and is indispensable in order to preserve the right to life, in which cases the State is obligated to render it to persons in need»[3]. So when there are no such connections, the social right in itself cannot be protected by means of tutela, as for instance has been the case of the constitutional right to a dignified dwelling or housing, regarding which, the Constitutional Court has ruled that, «as happens with other rights of social, economic and cultural contents, no subjective right is given to persons to ask the State in a direct and immediate way, to plainly satisfy such right»[4].

For the same reason of the political character of the possible enforcement of social, economic and cultural rights, its justiciability has been widely discussed in contemporary constitutional law.

For instance, this has been the feature of the North American Supreme Court doctrine, even in the aftermath of the so called «The Rights Revolution» that shaped North America in the last decades of the XX Century. As Charles R. Repp has pointed out referring to the Supreme Court's scattered attention to individual rights in the thirties (when less than 10 percent of the Court's decisions involved individual rights other than property rights), and the revolutionary changes that occurred in the following decades:

> By the late sixties, almost 70 percent of its decisions involved individual rights, and the Court had, essentially, proclaimed it the guardian of the individual rights of ordinary citizen. In the process, the Court created and expanded a host of new constitutional rights, among them virtually all the rights now regarded as essential to the Constitution: freedom of speech and the press, rights against discrimination on the basis of race or sex, and the right to due process in criminal and administrative procedures[5]

This very important «Rights Revolution» in the United States led the Supreme Court to guarantee civil rights that were not effectively protected before, like the

---

1 See decision T-406 of June 5th, 1992 in Manuel José CEPEDA, *Derecho Constitucional Jurisprudencial. Las grandes decisiones de la Corte Constitucional,* Legis, Bogotá, 2001, p. 61.

2 *Idem*. p. 61.

3 See Decision T-534 of September 24, 1992, in pp. 461 ff.

4 See Decision T-251 of June 5, 1995, in p. 486.

5 See Charles R. REPP, *The Rights Revolution. Lawyers, Activists, and Supreme Courts in Comparative Perspective,* The University of Chicago Press, Chicago and London, 1998, p. 2. See also, pp. 26 ff.

non discrimination rights derived from the implementation of *Brown v. Board of Education* 347 U.S. 483 (1954) overturning the racial segregation in public schools; the extension of freedom of speech guaranteed in the First Amendment; restricting federal and state actions, from *Fiske v. Kansas* 274 U.S. 380 (1927); the due process of law rights of accused persons and prisoners, following *Mapp v. Ohio* 367 U.S 643 (1961) and *Gideon v. Wainwright* 372 U.S. 335 (1963); the women's rights regarding sex discrimination beginning in *Reed v. Reed* 404 U.S. 71 (1971 and in *Fontinero v. Richardson*, 411 U.S. 677 (1973).

But if it is true that in matters of judicial protection of civil and individual rights in the United States it is possible to talk about a Revolution, nothing similar can be said regarding social and cultural rights, many of them the Supreme Court had denied to even qualify them as fundamental rights, as happened with the right to education, to housing and to social welfare.

Nonetheless, in Latin America, the discussion is not whether social, economic and cultural rights like education, health, social welfare or housing are or are not fundamental constitutional rights, but even if they have such rank, the question is if they can be justiciable, that is to say, if they can be enforced by means of judicial actions against the State.

II. THE CASE OF THE RIGHT TO HEALTH IN LATIN AMERICAN CONSTITUTIONS AND THE STATE'S OBLIGATIONS

This is the main issue on the discussion in Latin America. Without doubts, the Constitutions of all Latin American countries recognized the constitutional and even the fundamental character and rank of social, economic and cultural rights, but not always the courts had decided actions for amparo of such rights, particularly when brought against the State.

One important constitutional right whose justiciability has been discussed in Latin America is the right to health, enshrined in all the Constitutions; justiciability that is conditioned, first, by the way the right is declared in the Constitutions; second regarding the scope given to the amparo action; and third by the concrete cases resolved by the Courts.

Not all the Latin American Constitutions set forth the right to health in the same way. Some refer to the matter as a public asset, as is the case of El Salvador, where the Constitution declares that «the health of the inhabitants of the republic is a public asset» (Art 65). In similar terms, it is set in the Constitution of Guatemala (Art. 95); and in both texts it is declared that the State and the individuals are obligated to take care of its preservation and reestablishment.

Nonetheless, in almost all Constitutions the «right to health» is listed as a constitutional right (Bolivia, Art. 7,a; Brazil, Art. 6 y 196; Ecuador Art. 46; Nicaragua, Art. 59); Venezuela, Art. 84), that corresponds to everybody in equal terms as it is expressed in the Constitution of Nicaragua (Art. 59); and is reaffirmed in the Constitution of Guatemala, by saying that «the enjoyment of health is a fundamental right of human beings, without any kind of discrimination» (Art. 93).

This constitutional formula of «right to health», though, in fact what reveals in a general declaration of principles regarding the commitment of the State and the society toward human beings, rather that a strict constitutional right, due to the absence of an *alter* party in the declaration. In fact nobody can be obligated to promise the health of a person, and conversely, nobody can have the «right» not become ill.

Nonetheless, it can be said that with this formula of the «right to health» in reality, what the Constitutions are setting forth is the constitutional right of everybody to the protection of health, or to be protected in their health, by the State. Thus, the State, as well as the whole society, has the obligation to watch for the maintenance and recuperation of people's health. That is why other Latin American Constitutions provide in a more precise way, the «right to the protection of health» (Honduras, Art. 145); or referrer to the right of everybody to the protection of their health» (Chile Art. 19,9; México, Art. 4; Perú, Art. 7); or the right «for their health to be taken care of or protected» (Cuba, Art. 50); or that everybody has to have the guarantee «to have access to the services for the promotion, protection and recovery of health» (Colombia, Art. 49). In Panama, Article 105 of the Constitution provides that:

> The individual, as part of the community, has the right to the promotion, protection, maintenance, restitution and rehabilitation of health, and the obligation to maintain it, understood as the complete physical, mental and social welfare».

In some cases, as it happens in the Venezuelan Constitution, both formulas have been put together, when Article 83 of the Constitution provides as follows: «Health is a fundamental social right... all persons have for their health to be protected». In similar sense, Article 68 of the Constitution of Paraguay referring to the «right to health», says: «In the interest of community, the State will protect and promote health as a fundamental right of persons».

But a right for health to be protected by the State, in fact, is a right to have access to the service that takes care of health. Nonetheless, only a few Constitutions assure the equalitarian right to have such access, in some cases without cost, regarding public health services. In the case of Chile, where the Constitution provides that «the State protects the free and equalitarian access to the actions for promotion, protection and recovery of health and of rehabilitation of the individuals» (Art. 19,9). The Cuban Constitution, in Article 50, sets forth that the State guarantees the rights of persons to have their health being taken care of and protected «with the rendering of free medical and hospital assistance».

In the case of Chile, in the same constitutional provision a distinction is made between the health public programs and services render, regarding which it is provided that «the public health programs and actions are free for all», but, «the public services of medical attention will be free for those who need them « (Art. 43). The Constitution also provides that «in no case the emergency attentions will be denied in public or private premises» (Art. 43). In similar sense the Constitution of Paraguay sets forth that «Nobody will be deprived of public assistance in order to prevent or treat diseases, pests or plague, or of help in cases of catastrophes or accidents» (Art. 68).

The Constitution of El Salvador provides that the State must «give free assistance to the sick who lacked resources, and in general to all inhabitants, when the treatment is an efficient mean to prevent the dissemination of a transmissible disease»; (Art. 66); and in Uruguay, the Constitution provides that «the State must freely provide the means for protection and of assistance only to those in need and to those without enough resources» (Art. 44). In other cases, the Constitutions refer to the statute to «define the terms through which the basis attention for all the inhabitants will be free and obligatory» (Colombia, Art. 49); or for the definition of «the rules and modes for the access to the health services» (México, Art. 4).

From all these constitutional regulations, additionally to the general duties imposed to everyone, the communities and society in general have the duty to preserve healthy conditions, in particular a series of constitutional duties are set forth regarding the State and public bodies, which in a certain way are the ones that can orient the scope of the justiciability of the right to health.

For instance, in the Panamanian Constitution it is set forth that «It is an essential State function to watch for the health of the population» (Art. 105); and the Constitution of Guatemala, provides as an «obligation of the State on health ad social assistance» that «The State must watch for the health and social assistance of all inhabitants. It will develop, through its institutions, actions for the prevention, promotion, recovery, rehabilitation, coordination and the complementary ones in order to seek the most complete physical, mental and social welfare» (Article 94).

The Venezuelan Constitution, after declaring health as a fundamental right, declares as an «obligation for the State, who must guarantee it as part of the right to life. The State must promote and develop policies devoted to raise the quality of life, the collective welfare and the access to the...» (Art. 83). In the Constitution of Honduras, Article 145 provides that «The state must maintain an adequate environment for the protection of people's helath».

And the Constitution of Cuba sets forth that the State guarantees the right of persons to have their health taken care of and protected» (Art. 50) «by means of rendering free medical and hospital assistance through the network of rural medical services, polyclinics, hospitals, prophylactic and special treatment facilities; by rendering free stomatology assistance; by means of the development of plans for sanitary and health education, periodical medical exams, general vaccination and other disease preventive measures».

In Ecuador, Article 42 of the Constitution prescribes that the State guarantees the right to health, and the promotion and protection of health, «by means of the development of the alimentary safety, the provision of drinking water and basic sanitation, the promotion of family, labor and community healthy environment and the possibility to have permanent an uninterrupted access to health services, according the equity, universality, solidarity, quality and efficiency principles».

Article 106 of the Panamanian Constitution provides that in matters of health; it is for the State basically to develop activities, integrating the prevention, restoration and rehabilitation, among other purposes for «the protection of the mother, the child and the adolescent by means of guaranteeing integral attention during the gestation, nursing, growth and development of youth and adolescence; the fighting of transmissible diseases by means of environmental sanitation, development of access to drinking water and to adopt measures for the immunization, prophylaxis and treatment, collectively and individually rendered to all the population; and to create, according to the needs of each region, facilities in which integral health services are rendered, and drugs are given to all the population. This health services and medication will be freely rendered to whom lacks economic resources».

In Bolivia the State has the «obligation to defend human persons by protecting the health of the population, to assure the continuity of subsistence and rehabilitation means of disabled persons; to commit the raise family group life conditions (Art. 158.I). The Constitution of Perú provides that «the State determines the health policy» (Art. 9); and in similar terms the Constitution of El Salvador prescribes that «The State will determine the national health policy and will control and supervise its application» (Art. 65). In Nicaragua, Article 59 of the Constitution provides that the State must establish basic conditions for health promotion, protection, recovery and rehabilitation, and that it must direct and organize health programs, services and actions and promote popular participation in its defense».

In Brazil, the State has the duty to guarantee health «through social and economic policies tending to reduce the risk of sickness and other risks and the universal and equalitarian access to actions and services for health promotion, protection and recovery» (Art. 196). In Ecuador, the State must promote «the culture for health and life, with emphasis on alimentary and nutrition education of mothers and children and in sexual and reproductive health, by means of society participation and the social media collaboration (Art. 43).

For such purpose, the State must formulate «a health national policy and will watch for its application; control the functioning of entities in the sector; recognize, respect and promote the development of traditional and alternative medicine, the exercise of which will be regulated by statute, and will promote the scientific and technological advancement in health are, subjected to bioethics principles. Will also adopt programs tending to eradicate alcoholism and other toxic manias» (Art. 44).

According to all these express constitutional provisions, in some case vaguely and in others very detailed and precise, the protection of health can be considered in general as a constitutional obligation of the State, which does not exclude the possibility for individual to render health care services. In this regard, for instance, the Chilean Constitution provides that «everyone has the right to choose the health care system to which want to belong, be it public or private» (Art. 19), which implies the right of individuals to render health care services. This is expressly set in the Brazilian Constitution by providing that «sanitary assistance is of free private initiative», but subjected to express constitutional restrictions such as the ones provided in Article 199, «private institutions may participate in a complementary way in the Unique Health System, according the rules set forth by it, by means of public law contract or agreement, favor being given the philanthropic institutions and non-profit entities»; that «it is forbidden that public funds be directed to help or subsidize profit-oriented private»; and that also «it is forbidden the direct or indirect participation of foreign companies or capital in the sanitary assistance in the country, except in cases provided by statute».

Anyway, except for this provision, in the other Latin American countries, it can be said that in general, no private initiative to render health care services is provided, and what is provided is the State's power to regulate all health care services. As it is provided in the Venezuelan Constitution: «The State shall regulate both public and private health care institutions» (Art. 85); or as is it provided in Article 19 of the Chilean Constitution, in which additionally to declaring that the coordination and control of the activities related to health corresponds to the State, it declares that «the State shall give preference to guarantee the execution of health assistance, whether undertaken by public or private institutions, in accordance with the form and conditions set by statute which may establish obligatory payments»

Article 44 of the Uruguayan Constitution provides that «The State must legislate on all questions related to public health and hygiene, tending to the physical, moral and social improvement of all inhabitants of the country». In Honduras, Article 149 assigns to the State the power to supervise all the private activities related to health. In Brazil, Article 197 of the Constitution, due to the public importance of health activities and services, empowers the public bodies directly or by third parties, to regulate, supervise and control them. Also, the Colombian Constitution provides in Article 49 that it is for the State to establish «the policies for the rendering of health care services by private entities, and to supervise and control them».

The general consequence of the Constitutions providing for State obligations to render health care services to answer individual's constitutional right to receive health care materializes in public utilities or public services. As provided expressly in the Colombian Constitution: «health care and environment sanitation are public services that the State has to meet (Article 49); and the Bolivian Constitution adds that «The social services and assistance are State functions» being the regulations related to public health of coactive and obligatory character (Art. 164).

In this regard, the majority of Latin American Constitutions contained the general principles regarding public and private health care services, integrated in a national or unique system (Chile, Art. 45: Paraguay, Art. 69; Venezuela, Art. 84; Brazil, Art. 198).

III. THE JUSTICIABILITY OF THE RIGHT TO HEALTH

The people's constitutional right to health -particularly due to the obligations imposed to the States to provide services for the maintenance and recovery of people's health- pose the question of its justiciability by means of the amparo recourses or actions. Being constitutional rights, in principle they can be enforced by courts through the specific means for the protection of human rights.

Nonetheless, this has only been expressly regulated in one Latin American country: Perú. The Perúvian Constitutional Procedure Code, which expressly provides that the amparo recourse can be filed for the defense of the right «to health» (Article 37,24). In the case of Chile, the Constitution refers to the recourse of protection only to protect the «right to choose the system of health» (Article 19,9). No other specific regulation exists regarding amparo and right to health, which does not exclude the judicial protection. On the contrary, as a matter of principle, amparo actions can be brought before the courts for the protection of the right to health.

Nonetheless, the decisions of the courts in this regard have not been as protective as the constitutional provisions can allow. In general terms, and taking into account judicial decisions of the Constitutional Courts or Constitutional Chambers of Supreme Courts, as well as other court decisions of Perú, Colombia, Costa Rica, Chile and Venezuela, it is possible to distinguish two general tendencies: First, of wide protection in three cases: in cases in which it exists a concrete legal relationship between the plaintiff and the public entity defendant party, like the one derived from the social security system paid by the individual; in cases in which the right to health is protected because of its connection with other fundamental rights as the right to life; and in cases in which the courts have denied the programmatic character to the right to health; and second, of limited protection in cases which impose the State obligations to render services of health care which surpass the resources originally set forth.

The first cases related to amparo decisions for protection of the rights to health in concrete legal situations usually derived from the social security obligations regarding insured persons. This is the case of the Constitutional Chamber of the Supreme Tribunal of Justice of Venezuela decision N° 487 of April 6th, 2001 (Case: *Glenda López y otros vs. Instituto Venezolano de los Seguros Sociales*), in which the Court started by pointing out that the right to health or to the protection of health is «an integral part of the right to life, set forth in the Constitution as a fundamental social right (and not simply as an assignments of State purposes), whose satisfaction mainly belongs to the State and its institutions, thorough activities intended to progressively raise the quality of life of citizens and the collective welfare». This implies, according to the Court's decision that «the right to health is not to be exhausted with the simple physical care of the illness of a person, but it must be extended to the appropriate care in order to safeguard the mental, social, environmental etc., integrity of persons, including the communities, as collective imperfect entities, in the sense that they do not have by-laws organizing them as artificial persons».

In the concrete case heard by the Court, the violation of the right to health (and also the threat regarding the right to life) was alleged by HIV/AIDS infected persons, as caused by the Venezuelan Institute for Social Security, which they considered was obligated to «give medical integral care to its affiliates». The Constitutional Chamber thus ruled that because the omission of the Institute «to provide the plaintiffs, in a regular and permanent way, the drugs for the treatment of HIV/SIDA prescribed by the specialist attached to the Hospital Domingo Luciani, and to practice the specialized medical exams directed to help the efficient treatment of HIV/AIDS»; the right to health and even the right to life of the plaintiff were put in danger[6].

The second cases are related to the protection of the right to health as a consequence of the protection of the right to life, as has been decided in Colombia and Costa Rica.

As mentioned before, the Colombian Constitution does not include, among the fundamental rights protected by means of the action of tutela, the right to health or to the protection of health, so that the Constitutional Court has constructed the possibility of its protection establishing its connection to the right to life. In the decision N° T-484/92 of August 11, 1992[7], when deciding a revision recourse of a tutela decision against the Institute of Social Security, the plaintiff in the case, also infected with HIV/AIDS, claimed that it was infected while being covered by the Social Security program and had a favorable decision of the first instance Court which ordered the Institute to continue to render the plaintiff the health care services that we had been receiving. The Constitutional Court, when deciding, affirmed that

---

6 Véase en *Revista de Derecho Público*, N° 85-88, Editorial Jurídica Venezolana, Caracas, 2001, pp. 139-141.

7 File N° 2130, Case: *Alonso Muñoz Ceballos.*

«health is one of those assets that because of its inherent character to the dignified existence of man, is protected and especially, regarding persons that because of its economic, physical or mental conditions are in a manifest weakness condition» (Article 13, Constitution); being it a right that «seeks the assurance the fundamental right to life (Article 11 Constitution). Thus, the assistance nature imposes a primordial and preferential treatment by public entities and the legislator, in order for its effective protection». The Court, moreover, when connecting the right to health with the right to life, pointed out that:

The right to health comprises in its legal nature a bunch of elements that can be classified in two great blocks: First, those that identify it as an immediate condition to the right of life, thus, attacking peoples health is equivalent to attacking life itself. Thus conducts that harass the safe environment (Article 49,1), are to be treated in a concurrent manner with the health problems. Additionally, the recognition of the right to health forbids personal conducts that can cause damage to others, originating criminal and civil liabilities. Because all of these aspects, the right to health comes out as a fundamental right. The second block of elements place the right to health within an assistance character derived from the Welfare State, due to the fact that its recognition imposes concrete actions, developed through legislation, in order to render a public service not only for medical assistance, but also regarding hospital, pharmaceutical and laboratory rights. The threshold between the right to health as fundamental and assistance is imprecise and above all subject to the circumstances of each case (Article 13 Constitution), but in principle it can be asserted that the right to health is fundamental when related to the protection of life».

Based on the foregoing, regarding the concrete case of the petitioner infected with HIV/AIDS who was been treated by the health care services from the Institute of Social Security, the Court ratified the inferior decision's on tutela, bearing in mind that in the particular circumstance, the prevention of the right to health, was the condition for the protection of the his fundamental right to life.

In a similar sense, the Constitutional Chamber of the Supreme Court of Justice of Costa Rica, in decision N° 2003-8377 of August 8th, 2003[8], deciding an amparo recourse filed by the People's Defendant on behalf of the aggrieved person against the Costa Rican Institute of Social security because of the denial of the requested treatment for the disease known as Gaucher type 1, arguing that such denial «harmed the right to life and to health of the minor» who required the prescribed drug for «maintaining his life», the Constitutional Chamber after referring to the doctrine of the right of life in previous Court's decisions, including the right to health, concluded that «the Constitution provides in its Article 21 that he human life is inviolable, from which it derives the right every citizen has to health, thus corresponding to the State to ensure public health... (N° 5130-94 of 17:33 hrs on 7 September 1994)».

The Chamber added that «the preeminence of life and health, as superior values of people, is present and is of obligatory protection by the State, not only in the Constitution, but also in the various international instruments ratified by the country», making reference to Article 3 of the Universal Declaration on Human Rights, Article 4 of the American Convention on Human Rights; Article 1 of the American Declaration on Rights and Duties of Man; Article 6 of the International

8 File. 03-007020-0007-CO, Case: *Tania González Valle.*

Covenant on Civil and Political Rights; Article 12 of the International Covenant on Economic, Social and Cultural Rights; and Articles 14 and 26 of the Convention on Chile Rights (Law 7184 of July 18, 1990).

Due to the responsibilities of the State derived from these norms, the Constitutional Chamber comes in to analyzing the mission and functions of the Costa Rican Institution of Social Security making reference to its previous decision n° 1997-05934 of September 23, 1997, in which «it was considered that the denial from the Costa Rican institutions on Social Security to provide patients infected with HIV/AIDS the adequate therapy harms their fundamental rights». Departing from this premise, the Chamber analyzes the concrete case of the protected Tania González Valle, being proved in the files that she was not receiving the prescript treatment. Regarding the arguments of the Institutions based on financial aspects, the Chamber pointed out that:

> «This Court is conscientious regarding the scattered financial resources of the social security system, nonetheless it considers that the principal challenge the Costa Rican Institution of Social Security faces in this stage of its institutional development, -where Costa Rica has achieved life standards qualities similar to those of developed countries-, is to optimize the management of available resources of the system of health insurance and reduce the administrative costs in order to efficiently invest these resources. The Chamber considers that the prescript drugs are undoubtfully onerous, nonetheless, due to the exceptional characteristics of the illness suffered, which is lethal, and due to the impossibility for her parents to contribute for the acquisition of the drugs, based on Articles 21 and 173 of the Constitution, and 24 and 26 of the Convention on the Child's Rights, it proceeds to confirm the recourse. The acceptance of the recourse implies that the Costa Rican Institution on Social Security must immediately provide Tania Gonzalez Valle with the drug «Cerezyme» (Imuglucerase) in the conditions prescribed by her doctor».

In Perú, the Constitutional Court in a decision of April 20, 2004[9], also ruled regarding the right to health when deciding an extraordinary revision recourse filed against an amparo decision issued by the Superior Court of Justice of Lima. The latter had partially adjudicated the amparo action brought against the Perúvian State (Ministery of Health), demanding for the plaintiff, an HIV/AIDS infected «integral health care by means of the constant provision of drugs needed to treat HIV/AIDS, as well as the performance of periodical exams and tests that the doctor orders».

The Constitutional Tribunal, referring to the rights that are protected by means of the action of amparo, admitted that «the right to health is not among the fundamental rights set forth in Article 2 of the Constitution, but is rather recognized in Articles 7 and 9 of the Constitution in the Chapter related to social and economic rights»; nonetheless, concluded in a «similar way decided by the Colombian Constitutional Court, that when the violation of the right to health compromises other fundamental rights, like the right to life, the right to physical integrity and the right to the free development of one's personality, such right acquires fundamental right character and, therefore, must be protected by means of amparo action *(STC N.° T- 499 Corte Constitucional de Colombia)*».

---

9 File N.° 2945-2003-AA/TC, Case: *Azanca Alhelí Meza García.*

The nature of the economic and social rights, as is the case of the right to health, originates State obligations directed to provide social assistance. The Tribunal argued that the right health, as all the so called *prestacionales* («rendering») rights, like social security, public health, housing, education and other public services, it represents «one of the social goals of the State through which individuals can achieve their complete auto determination». Individuals can then «demand» the accomplishment of State duties by «asking the State to adopt adequate measures in order to achieve the social goals». However, «not in all cases the social rights are by themselves legally enforceable, due to the need of a budget support for its accomplishment».

Notwithstanding the above mentioned, the Constitutional Tribunal pointed out that «there were not just programmatic provisions with mediate effects as has been traditionally considered when differentiating them from the so called civil and political rights of immediate efficacy, because the indispensable guarantee for the enjoyment of the civil and political rights is precisely its minimal satisfaction. Accordingly, without dignified education, health and life quality, it would be difficult to talk about freedom and social equality, which motivates both the Legislator and the Judiciary to think jointly and interdependently on the recognition of such rights. Their satisfaction also requires a minimum action from the State, by means of the establishment of public services to render health care in equal conditions for all the population.

In this regard, the Tribunal ruled that «the social rights must be interpreted as true citizen guaranties that bind the State within a vision that tends to reevaluate the legal validity of constitutional norms, thus of the enforcement of the Constitution». Thus, the enforcement of these rights implies the need to surpass the programmatic conception allowing the improvement of the social prescriptions of the Constitution, as well as the State obligation, to which it is necessary to impose quantified goals in order to guaranty the force of the right». According to the Tribunal criteria, «this new vision of the social rights allows to recognize in its essential content, principles like solidarity and human being dignity respect, which are the funding of the Welfare State based on the rule of Law».

After analyzing these principles, the Tribunal considered as «erroneous the argument of the State defendant when arguing that the right to health and the national policy of health are just programmatic norms that more that a concrete right only signify a plan of action for the State»; adding that it would be naïve «to sustain that the social rights are reduced to be just a link for political responsibility between the Constituent and the legislator, which would be «an evident distortion regarding the Constitution's sense and coherence».

Regarding the right to health and its inseparable relation to the right to life, the Tribunal ruled that according to the Constitution «the defense of human beings and the respect of their dignity... presupposes the unrestricted enforcement of the right to life»; because «the exercise of any right, privilege, faculty or power has no sense or turns out to be useless in cases of non existence of physical life of somebody in favor of which it can be recognized». The Tribunal continued its ruling saying:

> 28. Health is a fundamental right due to its inseparable relation with the right to life, which is irresoluble, due to the fact that an illness can provoke death or in any case, the deterioration of life conditions. Thus the need to materialize

actions tending to take care of life is evident, which supposed a health care oriented to attack the illness signs...

Since the right to the protection of health is recognized in Article 7 of the Constitution, persons have also a right to attain and preserve a plain physical and psychical condition; consequently, they have «the right to be assigned sanitary and social measures for nourishing, clothing, dwelling and medical assistance, according to the level allowed by public funds and social solidarity».

The Tribunal then considered the question of the justiciability of social rights, like the right to health, ruling that «they cannot be requested in the same way in all cases, due to the fact that it is not a matter of specific rendering, because its depend on budget allocations; on the contrary, that would suppose that each individual could judicially ask at any moment for an employment or for a specific dwelling or for health»; concluding that:

> 33. To judicially demand a social right will depend on various factors, such as seriousness and reasonability of the case, its relation to other rights and State's budget resources, provided that concrete actions can be proved for the accomplishment of social policies»...

The Tribunal then analyzed the State's actions in the case, due to the pleading of the plaintiff's rights which affects his own life, ruling that «if it is true that in developing countries it is difficult to demand immediate attention and satisfaction of social policies for the whole population, [this Tribunal] reaffirms that its justification is valid only when concrete State actions are observed for the achievement of the resulting effect; on the contrary, the lack of attention would result in an unconstitutional omission situation».

Regarding the public policies in matters of HIV/AIDS the Tribunal considered that «in general, regarding social rights such as the right to health, no rendering obligation results in it itself because it depends on the State's financial resources, which nevertheless, in no way can justify a prolonged inaction, because it would result in an unconstitutional omission». The conclusion in the case was «the granting of the legal protection to a social right as the right to health, due to the fact that in this particular case the conditions justifying it are fulfilled» not only «due to the potential damage to the right to life, but also because of the motives on which the legislation is based in the matter which has organized the means for maximum protection to the AIDS infected persons».

1. The right to health and the State's financial resources

In other cases, the justiciability of the right to health regarding HIV/AIDS treatment has been completely subordinated to the disposal of resources. This has been the sense of some 2000/2001 Chilean courts' decisions regarding action for protections suits. In one case, the action was filed against the Ministry of Health, for failing to provide medical treatment to a group of HIV patients, arguing violation to the right to life and the right to equal protection. The plaintiff asked to be treated with the same therapy that was been given to others HIV patients, which the Ministry had denied arguing that it lacked enough economic resources for providing it to all Chilean HIV patients. The Court of appeals of Santiago ruled that the obligation of the Ministry of Health, according to the Law regulating health care provisions (Law N° 2763/1979), was to provide health care in accordance with the resources that are available to it considering reasonable the explanation provided by the Ministry based on the lack of economic resources to provide the best available treatment to the plaintiffs. The decision was confirmed by the Supreme Court[10].

In another 2001 decision, the same Ministry of Health was sued for the same reasons by HIV patients on a more critical conditions, and even though the Court of appeals of Santiago ruled in favor of the petitioners, ordering the Ministry to provide them immediately with the best available treatment, the Supreme Court reversed the ruling, arguing that the Ministry had acted in accordance to the law[11].

2. The rejection to protect the right to health in an abstract way

Finally, it must be mentioned a recent ruling of the Venezuelan Constitutional Chamber of the Supreme Court, that while contradicting previous rulings, decided that the right to health was not able to be protected by means of amparo actions, but only through political mechanisms of control regarding public policies.

The Chamber in a decision N° 1002 of May 26, 2004 (Case: *Federación Médica Venezolana*), rejected an amparo action brought by the Venezuelan Medical Federation «defending diffuse society rights and interests, and in particular those of the physicians», seeking protection to health, against the «*omissive*» conduct of the Ministry of Health and Social Development and the Venezuelan Institute of Social Security, because it failed to «directly provide an efficient service of health to the population in all the national territory, by means of promptly providing the necessary equipment and resources».

The Constitutional Chamber, in order to reject the claim, began by establishing a distinction that is not reflected in the Constitution, «between the civil and political rights and those of third generation», pointing out that:

> The dichotomy between civil and political rights and the economic, social and cultural ones was establish since the preparatory works of the two United nations Covenants, and particularly, in the 1951 decision of the General Assembly not to frame on both instruments the regulation of the two category of rights as an expression of the idea that the civil and political rights where rights that can be immediately enforced -because of implied abstention duties form the State-; whereas the economic, social and cultural rights were implemented by means of rules of that ought to be progressively developed -due to the fact that they implied positive obligations. Such criterion was also followed in the European Social Charter- in which's negotiation process existed the conviction that it would be difficult to guaranty the application of economic, social and cultural rights by means of judicial control- and in the American Convention on Human Rights».

The Constitutional Chamber, after recognizing the indivisibility of human rights, in the sense that the full enjoyment of the civil and political rights is impossible without the enjoyment of economic, social and cultural rights -as declared in the Teheran Conference on Human Rights and accepted by the General Assembly

---

10 See the reference in Javier A. COURSO, «Judicialization pd Chilean Politics» in Rachel Sieder, Line Schjolden and Alan Angeli (Ed.), *The Judicializacion of Politics in Latin America*, Palgrave Macmillan, New York, 2005, pp. 119-120.

11 *Idem*. p. 120.

of United Nations in Resolution N° 32/130-; pointed out that such assertion did not vanish the incertitude regarding the role of States in economic, social and cultural rights and its obligations deriving form such rights. The doubt subsists, because as explained by the Constitutional Chamber, the implementation of economic, social and cultural rights «faces the debt crisis and the resulting impoverishment of Latin American countries, so the satisfaction of such rights depends on the availability of existing resources, the State being committed only to provide means in order to progressively achieve its goals».

But, as pointed out by the Chamber, due to the fact that the 1999 Venezuelan Constitution set forth not only the Welfare State based on the Rule but on the consideration of the economic, social and cultural rights as «fundamental rights», this situation imposes the need to do a theoretical effort to framework the protection of such rights, in order to not issue decisions that could be qualified as demagogic because of their impossibility to enforce.

The Constitutional Chamber began its argument by saying that the idea of the Welfare State based on the Rule of law refers to a State devoted to satisfying the basic needs of individuals, in order to the achievement of higher living standards in the population; but from that sole idea it is not possible to deduct rights, or consider that they are within the subjective sphere of citizens. From this idea what results is the aspiration to satisfy basic needs of individuals as a guiding principle of administrative activity. Regarding the justiciability of rights, the Constitutional Chamber added:

> In contrast, at least in the 1999 Constitution, the economic, social and cultural rights are declared as fundamental rights, which implies specific consequences, among them, -in principle- the applicability of the protection by means of amparo, because the Constitution, in contrast to what is establish in other legal orders, does not exclude certain rights from that guaranty, nor its immediate applicability, due to the fact that our constitutional order has a normative immediate value and application, rejecting what are known as programmatic rights.

Consequently, having such economic, social and cultural rights a fundamental rights character; they are undoubtedly judicially protected, because on the contrary, we will not be facing a right but a moral value aspiration».

But after affirming this, the Constitutional Chamber built the denial of such justiciability of social right, stating that «the point is to determine when one is asking for the enforcement of an economic, social or cultural right, and when one is asking that the Public Administration perform the Welfare State based on the Rule of Law State clause, given that the way s to ask in both cases differ». This distinction derives from the recognition of the political value of the State's activity devoted to satisfy the existence needs, and from the definition of the essential core of each of the rights that is stake». From this, the Chamber went to rule on the non justiciability of social rights, arguing that they were only submitted to political control, emphasizing that:

> In the first case we must begin affirming that the policy, is basically manifested itself, through acts, and also through application, design, planning, evaluation and follow-up regarding the government trends and public expenses, so that policy does not exhaust itself in the legal framework. In this context the acts

are subjected to judicial review, but only regarding its legal elements (conformity of the concrete action to the law, and not in a general or abstract way). The of participation set forth in the Constitution and the laws (during the accomplishment of governmental and administrative functions, and in case of evident incapacity of Public Administration to plan in an efficient way its activity to satisfy the existence needs, citizens will withdraw the confidence given to their representatives by mean of election, as a sign of a process of de legitimization of political actors».

....the point is to emphasize the impossibility for the judge to challenge the opportunity and convenience of the Administration, of the government or of the legislation, or the material or technical impossibility that in some occasions exists of enforcing the judicial decisions that order the accomplishment of certain duties...

...in the public activity, the State has freedom to organize itself, which cannot be legitimately substituted by the Judiciary. It has it as a consequence of the accomplishment of its constitutional duties resulting from the nature of such functions, that is, as a derivation of the principle of separation of powers that sets forth a scope reserved to each power and excludes the substitution of wills, and that the Government-Judiciary relation prevents for judicial review to be the measure for the sufficiency of the rendering burden».

The Constitutional Chamber then went to quote the doctrine of the Spanish Constitutional Tribunal and of the German federal Constitutional Tribunal, regarding the absence of judicial review in political acts or political order acts, generalizing as follows:

«Policies are in principle, outside the scope of judicial review, but not for that reason they escape control only that this applicable control is the political one also set forth in the Constitution. The State organs act under their own responsibility, which can be challenged in the political level, meaning that they cannot be unvested of the authorization in their political management. But that process of de-legitimating can not be qualified by the Judiciary, unless when determining an administrative liability for damages caused by the political activity and putting aside that a fundamental right be affected by the decision, in which case, eventually, the control will not be regarding the political elements of the act and turn to be a control regarding its juridical elements...»

From the abovementioned, the Constitutional Chamber then concluded that:

a) The economic, social and cultural rights have, as all rights, judicial protection; b) In order to know if one is facing one of such rights, it must exist a perfectly defined juridical relation where the harm to them comes from a change to the juridical sphere of a citizen or of collectivity; c) The State activity directed to satisfy the existence need is an activity with political contents; d) That such activity can manifest itself by acts or through policies; e) That such acts can be the object of judicial control in their juridical elements, not in the political; f) That the policies, in principle, can not be the object of judicial control but of political control; g) That such judicial impossibility cannot be understood as the rejection of the citizens right to action».

The Constitutional Chamber eventually ruled that «resulting from the principle of separation of powers, the Judiciary cannot substitute the Legislative or the Executive definition of social policies, the violation of which, could led to a government by judges», adding that «due to the fact that the economic, social and cultural policies depend on the existing resources, the Judiciary has the power to control in positive way, that bearing in mind the economic situation of the State, it has made a maximal use of the available resources -including legislative measures-; and in negative sense, the absolute absence of economic, social and cultural policies (which voided the essential core of the respective rights), as well as those policies openly directed to harm the juridical situation that protect the economic, social or cultural rights, cases that impose the State the burden of proof, also implying regarding the former, the analysis of the distribution of social spending».

Regarding the amparo action, the Constitutional Chamber concluded affirming that being «of a reestablish nature, the possibility to judicially control the economic, social and cultural policies are not comprised by this constitutional guaranty, but it is completely within the nature of the functions of the People's Defendant.

Finally, referring the right to health, and the claim of the *Federación Médica Venezolana* asking to the court to order the accomplishment of economic resources to the hospitals, and budget allocation for the acquisition of medical equipment and hospital materials, the Chamber rejected it considering that it is a very evident political activity, abstract in nature, which makes it «impossible to be the object of an amparo action directed to restore concrete juridical situations». In the proceedings of the public hearing on the case, the Chamber finally ruled that «social or third generation rights, contrary to those of first or second generation, have a specific structure» that originates certain differences which impose the precision on what can be referred the judicial protection regarding such rights, pointing out that:

> «Such rights, by themselves, are not in the subjective sphere of citizens due to the fact that, *ab initio*, they are guiding principles of the administrative activity; they are the basis of the Social and Justice State based on the Rule of law clause, and thus, they are elements defining the goals, in the sense that they qualified what must be considered of public interest.

Consequently, the enforcement of the third generations of rights is not possible, being the political control the only way to verify its accomplishment. Faced to the evident incapacity of Public Administration to efficiently plan its activities, the citizens will withdraw the confidence given to their representatives by means of suffrage, as demonstration of the de-legitimating of the actors»[12].

---

12 See in *Revista de Derecho Público*, N° 97-98, Editorial Jurídica Venezuela, Caracas 2004, p. 143 ff.

CHAPTER IX

THE EXTRAORDINARY CHARACTER OF THE AMPARO ACTION AND THE GENERAL PROCEDURAL RULES OF THE SUIT

I. THE EXTRAORDINARY CHARACTER OF THE AMPARO

The most common characteristic of the Latin American amparo action, is its extraordinary character, in the sense that in general terms it is granted when there are no other adequate judicial means to obtain the immediate protection of the constitutional right that has been violated.

This characteristic also applies in the United States to the injunctions and to all other equitable remedies like the mandamus and prohibitions, in the sense that they are considered available only «after the applicant shows that the legal remedies are inadequate»[1] since they are reserved for extraordinary cases[2].

This main characteristic of the injunction as an extraordinary remedy has been established since the XIX Century in *In re Debs* 158 U.S. 564, 15 S.Ct 900, 39 L. Ed. 1092 (1895), in which, in words of Justice Brewer, who delivered the opinion of the court, it was decided that:

> «As a rule, injunctions are denied to those who have adequate remedy at law. Where the choice is between the ordinary and the extraordinary processes of law, and the former are sufficient, the rule will not permit the use of the latter».[3]

In Latin America, even though the common law distinction between remedies at law and equitable remedies does not exist, regarding the amparo action, -which comprises in only one institution all the drastic remedies established in North American law (injunctions, mandamus and prohibitions), it has the same general characteristic of extraordinary remedy. This is provided not only in the Latin

---

1 See in Owen M. Fiss and Doug Rendleman, *Injunctions*, The Foundation Press, Mineola New York, 1984, p. 59.

2 Exparte Collet, 337 U.S. 55, 69 S. Ct 944, 93 L. Ed. 1207, 10 A.L.R. 2D 921 (1949). See in John Bourdeau et al, «Injunctions» in Kevin Schroder, John Glenn and Maureen Placilla, *Corpus Juris Secundum*, Volume 43A, Thomson West, 2004, p. 20.

3 See in Owen M. Fiss and Doug Rendleman, *Injunctions*, The Foundation Press, Mineola New York, 1984, p. 8.

American sense that it is only established for the protection of constitutional rights and guaranties, but also in the sense that it is admissible only when there are no other adequate judicial means for obtaining the constitutional protection.

This extraordinary character of the Latin American amparo action, equivalent to the so called «subordinate» character of the North American injunction, implies then that the amparo is only admissible when there are no other judicial means for granting the constitutional protection, or in case they exist, are not adequate means for the immediate protection of the harmed or threatened constitutional rights. The questions of the non availability and of the inadequacy are, thus, two key factors regarding the admissibility of the action.

Only in a very few Latin American countries, the filing of the amparo action requires the obligatory previous exhaustion of ordinary existing judicial means, as it is established in Spain regarding its amparo action.

1. The question of the previous exhaustion of the ordinary judicial means

Actually, the general principle in Spain is that since the protection of constitutional rights and liberties is a task attributed to the courts, the filing of an amparo action before the Constitutional Tribunal can only be admitted when the ordinary judicial means have been exhausted, so that the Tribunal can only be asked to decide an amparo action when filed against the final judicial decision. The amparo action in Spain can then be considered as *subsidiaria* («ancillary») in the sense that it can only be filed after a prior judgment has been issued[4].

In Latin America, this condition of the necessary prior exhaustion of the existing ordinary judicial or administrative means is only regulated in México, Guatemala and Perú.

In México, the condition of the previous exhaustion of the ordinary judicial means in order to file an amparo action, responds to the principle of the «definitive character of the challenged act» set forth in Article 103 of the Constitution and Article 73 of the Amparo Law, in the sense that when the amparo action is directed against a judicial act, it can only be filed against the definitive and final judicial rulings, regarding which there is no other judicial remedy available to obtain its modification or repeal (Art 73, XIII). The only exception to this condition is when the challenged act implies a danger of extinguishing life or deportation or any act forbidden in Article 20 of the Constitution. Regarding administrative acts the amparo action is inadmissible when they can be challenged by a recourse, suit or any other mean of defense, providing that the statutes allow for the suspension of the effects of the challenged acts without additional conditions to those set forth in the Amparo Law (Art. 73, XV). The general consequences of this «definitively» rule are the followings:

1. It is necessary that regarding the authority act challenged by means of amparo that all the recourses and means of defense that can modify or repeal it, be filled.

---

4 See Eduardo FERRER MAC GREGOR, *La acción constitucional de amparo en México y España. Estudio de derecho comparado*, Editorial Porrúa, México, 2002, pp. 292 ff.

2. The above mentioned judicial means must be exhausted, which means that it is not sufficient for them to be filed, but they must be pursued up to the final stage obtaining the definitive decision of the authority[5].

A similar principle is followed by the Guatemalan Amparo Law, by setting forth that «in order to file an amparo, except in the cases specified in this statute, it is necessary that the ordinary judicial and administrative recourses by mean of which the matters can be adequately resolved according to the due process principle, be exhausted»(Art. 19)[6]. It must be highlighted that in this case, the exhaustion rule refers not only to judicial recourses but also to administrative ones[7]. In the case of Brazil, Article 5,1 of the *mandado de segurança* Law also sets forth that it will not be admissible against acts against which administrative recourses with suppressive effects can be filed, independently of bail.

It must be said also regarding injunctions against administrative acts in the United States that they can only be filed after the available administrative remedy has been exhausted (*Zipp v. Geske & Sons, Inc*, 103 F. 3d 1379 (7th Cir. 1997)); the rule is not applied when the exhaustion of the remedy will cause imminent and irreparable harm (*State ex rel. Sheehan v. District Court of Minn. In and For Hennepin County*, 253 Minn. 462, 93 N.W.2d 1 (1958))[8].

In Perú, Articles 5 and 45 of the Constitutional Procedures Code also provide for the inadmissibility of the amparo action when the «previous means» were not exhausted beforehand; adding that in case of doubt regarding such exhaustion, the amparo will be preferred.

This «previous means» that must be exhausted are basically the administrative procedure challenging recourses, like the hierarchical one in order to obtain the decision of the peck of Public Administration hierarchy before filing the amparo. As was justified by the Constitutional Tribunal, «the need for the exhaustion of such [administrative] mean before filing the amparo, is founded in the need to give the Public Administration the possibility to review its own acts, in order to allow the possibility for the Administration to resolve the case, without the need to appear before the judicial organs»[9].

This condition for the admissibility of the amparo action, considered as a Public Administration «privilege» that could in itself harm the constitutional right to obtain judicial protection, has some exceptions provided in Article 45 of the same Constitutional Procedure Code, when establishing that the exhaustion of the previous means would not be required in the following cases:

---

5 See Eduardo FERRER MAC GREGOR, *La acción constitucional de amparo en México y España. Estudio de derecho comparado*, Editorial Porrúa, México, 2002, pp. 315, 392 ff.; Richard D. BAKER, *Judicial Review in México. A Study of the Amparo Suit*, University of Texas Press, Austin, 1971, p. 100.

6 See the courts' decision in this sense in Jorge Mario GARCÍA LAGUARDIA, *Jurisprudencia constitucional. Guatemala., Honduras, México, Una Muestra*, Guatemala 1986, pp. 43, 45.

7 In Honduras, for instance, regarding the habeas data action, article 40 of the Amparo law set forth that in only can be filed when exhausted the corresponding administrative procedure (art. 40).

8 See the reference in John BOURDEAU et al, «Injunctions» in Kevin SCHRODER, John GLENN and Maureen PLACILLA, *Corpus Juris Secundum*, Volume 43A, Thomson West, 2004, p. 225.

9 See Exp 1042-AA-TC, decision of December 6, 2002, F.J. N° 2). See the reference in Samuel B. ABAD YUPANQUI, *El proceso constitucional de amparo*, Gaceta Jurídica, Lima 2004, p. 234.

1) If a resolution, even if its not the last in the administrative procedure, has been executed before the exhaustion of the delay established in order to be considered as consented; 2) If because of the exhaustion of the previous mean the aggression could become irreparable; 3) If the previous mean is not regulated or has been unnecessarily initiated by the injured party; or 4) If the previous mean is not resolved within the delays fixed for its resolution.

The Constitutional Tribunal has extensively elaborated all these exceptions: regarding the first exception, it has considered that the amparo action is admissible in all cases in which the challenged resolution has been immediately executed by the Public Administration before any possibility for the affected party to challenge it in the administrative procedure[10]. Regarding the irreparability of the damage exception, it has been considered that that situation occurs when the exhaustion of the administrative means would impede the harmed right to be restored to the position exiting before the harm was caused[11]. This is the case, for instance, when a Municipal administrative decision to demolish a building, would be executed during the exhaustion of the administrative recourse. Regarding the last exception, it tends to avoid the perpetuation of undefined situations due to the lack of decision regarding administrative petitions[12].

Even though it is not expressly regulated, in cases of amparo actions filed against judicial decisions when the due process rights are being clearly and ostensibly harmed, the Constitutional Tribunal has also imposed the previous exhaustion of the ordinary judicial means in order to bring the amparo action before the competent court[13]; being consider the adequacy for the constitutional protection of the judicial ordinary means[14].

As aforementioned, only in México, Guatemala and Perú it is imposed as a general condition for the filing of the amparo action -although with important exceptions- the need to previously exhaust all the existing ordinary judicial and administrative means.

In the other Latin American countries such condition has not been imposed; and the admissibility condition discussion is referred to the effective existence of adequate means for the immediate protection of the harmed or threatened constitutional rights. In these cases, the questions to be discussed in order to determine the admission of the amparo action refer to the availability or non availability of judicial or administrative means for protection of the harmed right; and to the

---

10 See Samuel B. ABAD YUPANQUI, *El proceso constitucional de amparo*, Gaceta Jurídica, Lima 2004, pp. 246-250.

11 Exp. N° 1266-2001-AA/TC, decisión of September 9, 2002, El Perúano -Garantías Constitucionales- April 4, 2003, p. 6081. See the reference in Samuel B. ABAD YUPANQUI, *El proceso constitucional de amparo*, Gaceta Jurídica, Lima 2004, pp. 251-255.

12 See Samuel B. ABAD YUPANQUI, *El proceso constitucional de amparo*, Gaceta Jurídica, Lima 2004, pp. 258-260.

13 Exp. N° 1821-98, decision June 25, 1999, El Perúano -Jurispurdencia-, November 7, 2001, p. 4501. See the reference in Samuel B. ABAD YUPANQUI, *El proceso constitucional de amparo*, Gaceta Jurídica, Lima 2004, p. 242.

14 See Luis R. SÁENZ DÁVALOS, «Las innovaciones del Código Procesl Constitucional en el recurso constitucional de amparo», in Susana CASTAÑEDA et al, *Introducción a los procesos constitucionales. Comentarios al Código Procesal Constitucional*, Jurísta Editores, Lima 2005, p. 135.of.

adequacy or inadequacy of the existing judicial means for such protection, rather than to their imposed exhaustion.

2. The question of the non availability of other adequate judicial or administrative means for protection

In this regard, the general principles referred to the admissibility of the amparo action are very similar to the same question referred to the admission of the injunction remedy in North America, where one of its traditional and fundamental bases is the inadequacy of the existing legal remedies as the main prerequisite to granting an injunction (*Beacon Theatres, Inc. v. Westover*, 359 U.S. 500, 79 S.Ct. 948, 3L.Ed. 2d 988, 2 Fed. R. Serv. 2d 650 (1959))[15]. The North American judicial doctrine on the matter has been summarized as follows:

> «An injunction, like any other equitable remedy, will only be issued where there is no adequate remedy at law. Accordingly, except where the rule is changed by statute, an injunction ordinarily will not be granted where there is an adequate remedy at law for the injury complained of, which is full and complete. Conversely, a court of equitable jurisdiction may grant an injunction where an adequate and complete remedy cannot be had in the courts of law, despite the petitioner's efforts. Moreover, a court will not deny access to injunctive relief when procedures cannot effectively, conveniently and directly determine whether the petitioner is entitled to the relief claimed»[16].

This condition regarding injunctions has been also referred in the United States as to the «availability» or the «sufficiency» rule[17], and also to the «irreparable injury» rule, implying the admission of the injunction only when the harm «cannot be adequately repaired by the remedies available in the common law courts if the threatened harm is one that can be rectified by a legal remedy, then the judge will refuse to enjoin».[18]

This situation, as pointed out by Owen M. Fiss «makes the issuance of an injunction conditional upon a showing that the plaintiff has no alternative remedy that will adequately repair the injury. Operationally this means that as general proposition the plaintiff is remitted to some remedy other than an injunction unless he can show that his non injunctive remedies are inadequate»[19].

This term «inadequacy», according to Tabb and Shoben, «has a specific meaning in the law of equity because it is a shorthand expression for the policy that equitable remedies are subordinate to legal ones. They are subordinate in the sense that the damage remedy is preferred in any individual case if it is adequate»[20]. But in parti-

---

15 See in John BOURDEAU et al, «Injunctions» in Kevin Schroder, John Glenn and Maureen Placilla, *Corpus Juris Secundum*, Volume 43A, Thomson West, 2004, p. 89.

16 See in John BOURDEAU et al, «Injunctions» in Kevin Schroder, John Glenn and Maureen Placilla, *Corpus Juris Secundum*, Volume 43A, Thomson West, 2004, pp. 89-90; 119 ff.; 224 ff.

17 See in John BOURDEAU et al, «Injunctions» in Kevin Schroder, John Glenn and Maureen Placilla, *Corpus Juris Secundum*, Volume 43A, Thomson West, 2004, pp. 119 ff.

18 See Owen M. FISS and Doug RENDLEMAN, *Injunctions*, The Foundation Press, Mineola New York, 1984, p. 59.

19 Owen FISS, *The Civil Rights Injunction*, Indiana University Press, 1978, p. 38.

20 See William M. TABB and Elaine W. SHOBEN, *Remedies*, Thomson West 2005, p. 15.

cular, regarding constitutional claims involving constitutional rights such as those for school desegregation, it has been considered that their protection precisely requires of the extraordinary protection that can be obtained by equitable intervention, as was decided by the Supreme Court regarding school desegregation in its second opinion in *Brown v. Board of Education* (S. Ct. 1955) and regarding the unconstitutional cruel and unusual punishment in the prison system in *Hutto v. Finney (S.Ct. 1978)*.[21]

The same general principle of the availability and adequacy, even though with any relation whatsoever to the distinction between law and equitable remedies, is applied in some Latin American countries like Argentina, Uruguay, Colombia, Venezuela, Chile and Dominican Republic, where in general terms, the amparo action cannot be admissible if there exists another adequate judicial or administrative means for the immediate protection of the constitutional right.

This is the case of Argentina, where the amparo action is also considered as an extraordinary and residual judicial remedy reserved for the «delicate and extreme situations in which, because of the lack of other legal means, the safeguard of fundamental rights is in danger»[22]. The same expression regarding the «extraordinary or residual» character of the amparo action is used by the Uruguayan courts[23].

That is why, in Argentina, Article 43 of the Constitution provides that the amparo action is admissible «as long as it does not exist another more adequate judicial mean»; and Article 2,a of the Amparo Law provides that the amparo is inadmissible «when there exist other juridical or administrative recourses or remedies which allow to obtain the protection of the constitutional right or guaranty». Because in Argentina the amparo action is not admitted against judicial decisions, regarding the amparo against administrative acts, this article refers first, to the availability of judicial and administrative means for the protection, the latter (administrative recourses) to be exercised before the superior organs of Public Administration; and second, to the adequacy of those means, in the sense that they must be adequate, sufficient and effective in order to protect the plaintiff. Therefore, even when other remedies exist, the amparo action is admissible when their use could provoke grave and irreparable harm or they cannot be adequate for the immediate protection required for the harmed or threatened constitutional right[24]. Being a condition of admissibility, it is for the plaintiff to allege and proof that there are no other adequate means for the protection of his rights[25]. As was decided by the Supreme Court:

> «It is indispensable for the admission of the exceptional remedy of amparo that those claimant judicial protection to prove, in due form, the inexistence

---

21 See William M. TABB and Elaine W. SHOBEN, *Remedies*, Thomson West 2005, pp. 25-26.

22 CSJN, 7/3/85, LL, 1985-C-140; íd., Fallos, 303"422; 306; 1253. See in Néstor Pedro SAGÜÉS, *Derecho procesal Constitucional,* Vol 3, *Acción de amparo*, Editorial Astrea Buenos Aires 1988, p. 166.

23 J.L. Cont. Adm. 2º S. 194 del 9/9/92; tAC 7º S. 171 del 25/9/92; TAC 7º S. 27 del 28/2/90; J.L. Cont. Adm, 2º res. Del 10/10/91. See in Luis Alberto VIERA, *Ley de Amparo*, Ediciones Idea, Montevideo 1993, pp. 145, 148, 149.

24 See José Luis LAZZARINI, *El juicio de amparo*, Ed. La Ley, Buenos Aires1987, pp. 94-95, 122 ff., 139; Alí Joaquín SALGADO, *Juicio de amparo y acción de inconstitucionalidad*, Editorial Astrea, Buenos Aires, 1987, pp. 31 ff.

25 See Néstor Pedro SAGÜÉS, *Derecho Procesal Constitucional*, Vol 3, *Acción de Amparo*, Editorial Astrea, Buenos Aires, 1988, p. 170.

of other legal means for the protection of the harmed right or that the use of the existing could provoke an ulterior irreparable harm»[26].

In Uruguay, in a more or less similar way, Article 2 of the Amparo law also provides that «the amparo action will only be admissible when no other judicial or administrative means exist permitting to obtain the same result established in Article 9,B (the precise determination of what must or not must be done) or when if in existence, because of the circumstances they were ineffective for the protection to the right». Is his admissibility condition what gives the amparo action in Uruguay its «extraordinary, exceptional, residual character, in the sense that it is admissible when the normal means for protections will be powerless».[27]

Also in Colombia, Article 86 of the Constitution provides that the amparo action can only be filed when the affected party does not have another judicial mean available for his protection; and Article 6,1 of the Tutela Law prescribes that the amparo action is inadmissible «when other judicial recourses or means of defense exists, unless when they are used as a transitory mechanism to prevent irreparable harms». In the later case, the question of the efficacy of the existing judicial means must be judged in concrete, according to the circumstances of the plaintiff» (Art, 6, 1).

It must be highlighted that the residual character of the Colombian tutela only refers to the existence of other judicial means, and not to administrative means or recourses considered in Colombia as optional for the plaintiff (Art. 9 Tutela law). Also in Costa Rica it is expressly provided in the Amparo Law that it is not necessary to file any administrative recourse prior to the filling of the amparo action (Art. 31)[28].

The other judicial means of protection that in Colombia instead of the tutela action are considered as serving for effective protection of fundamental rights, are the public action of unconstitutionality, the exception of unconstitutionality, the habeas corpus action, the action for compliance, the popular actions, the judicial review of administrative acts actions, the exception of illegality and the provisional suspension of the effects of administrative acts[29]. In any case, it is for the tutela judge to determine if there are other judicial means for protection, as it has been ruled by the Constitutional Court, when deciding that:

> «When the tutela judge finds that other judicial defense mechanisms exists are applicable to the case, he must evaluate if according to the facts expressed in the claim and the scope of the harmed or threatened fundamental right, the available remedies include all the relevant aspects for the immediate, complete and efficient protection of the violated rights, in matters of proof and of the alternate defense decision mechanism»[30].

---

26 Case *Carlos Alfredo Villar v. Banco de la República Argentina*. See he reference in Samuel B. ABAD YUPANQUI, *El proceso constitucional de amparo*, Gaceta Jurídica, Lima, 2004, pp. 223-224.

27 See Luis Alberto VIERA, *Ley de Amparo*, Ediciones Idea, Montevideo 1993, p. 20. See the court decisions reference regarding the «residually» rule in pp. 57, 131 ff; 154 ff.; and 158 ff.

28 See Rubén HERNÁNDEZ, *Derecho Procesal Constitucional*, Editorial juricentro, San José, 2001, p. 242.

29 See Juan Carlos ESGUERRA PORTOCARRERO, *La protección constitucional del ciudadano*, Legis, Bogotá, 2004 p. 125.

30 See decisión &-100/94, march 9, 1994. See the reference in Samuel B. ABAD YUPANQUI, *El proceso constitucional de amparo, Gaceta Jurídica*, Lima, 2004, p. 229.

As mentioned, the only exception to the rule imposing the need to file the other judicial existing means for protection before bringing a tutela action, is the possibility to use the tutela as a transitory protective mean in order to avoid harms considered irreparable (Art. 8), that is, harms that because of their imminence and gravity impose the immediate adoption of protection[31].

The same principle also applies in Venezuela, event without an express legal provision as those existing in the Argentinean, Colombian and Uruguayan laws. As it has been decided by the former Supreme Court of Justice in a decision dated March 8, 1990,

> «the amparo is admissible even in cases where although ordinary means exist for the protection of the infringed juridical situation, they would not be suitable, adequate or effective for the immediate restoration of the said situation»[32].

In similar sense, the Supreme Court in a decision dated December 11, 1990, ruled that:

> «The criteria of this High Court as well as the authors opinions, has been reiterative in the sense that the amparo action is an extraordinary or special judicial remedy that is only admissible when the other procedural means that could repair the harm, are exhausted, do not exist or would be inoperative. Additionally, Article 5 of the Amparo Law provides that the amparo action is only admissible when no brief, summary and effective procedural means exist in accordance with the constitutional protection».
>
> This objective procedural condition for the admissibility of the action, turns the amparo into a judicial mean that can only be admissible by the court once it has verified that the other ordinary means are not effective or adequate in order to restore the infringed juridical situation. If other means exist, the court must not admit the proposed amparo action»[33].

The Supreme Court in another decision dated June 12, 1990, decided that the amparo action is admissible:

> «when there are no other means for the adequate and effective reestablishment of the infringed juridical situation. Consequently, one of the conditions for the admissibility of the amparo action is the non existence of other more effective means for the reestablishment of the harmed rights. If such means are adequate to resolve the situation, there is no need to file the special amparo action. But even if such means exists, if they are inadequate for the immediate reestablishment of the constitutional guaranty, it is also justifiable to use the constitutional protection mean of amparo»[34].

---

31 See Juan Carlos ESGUERRA PORTOCARRERO, *La protección constitucional del ciudadano*, Legis, Bogotá 2004 p. 127.

32 See in *Revista de Derecho Público,* N° 42, Editorial Jurídica Venezolana, Caracas, 1990, pp. 107-108. See also decision of First Court on Judicial Review of Administrative Actions dated September 5, 1991 in FUNEDA, *15 años de Jurisprudencia, op. cit.,* p. 130.

33 See in en *Revista de Derecho Público,* N° 45, Editorial Jurídica Venezolana, Caracas, 1991, p. 112.

34 See decision of the Politico Administrative Chamber of the Supreme Court of Justice of June 12, 1990, *Revista de Derecho Público* N° 43, Editorial Jurídica Venezolana, Caracas, 1990, p. 78. See also in *Revista de Derecho Público,* N° 55-56, Editorial Jurídica Venezolana, Caracas, 1993, pp. 311-313.

Of course, the question of the availability and of the adequacy of the existing judicial means for the admissibility or not of the amparo action, in the end is a matter of judicial interpretation and adjudication, decided always in the concrete case decision, when evaluating the adequacy question. For instance, in a decision of the First Court on administrative jurisdiction dated May 20, 1994 (case *Federación Venezolana de Deportes Equestres*) it was ruled that the judicial review of administrative acts actions were not adequate for the protection requested in the case, that seeks the participation of the Venezuelan Federation of Equestrian Sports in an international competition. The case required immediate decision, so the court ruled as follows:

> It is the opinion of this court that when the action was brought before it, the only mean that the claimant had in order to obtain the reestablishment of the infringed juridical situation was the amparo action, due to the fact that by means of the judicial review of administrative acts recourse seeking its nullity, they could never be able to obtain the said reestablishment of the infringed juridical situation that was to assist to the 1990 the international competitions».[35]

In contrary sense and after having established for years a judicial doctrine admitting the autonomous amparo action against administrative acts, in recent years, the Supreme Tribunal of Justice of Venezuela has been progressively imposing a restrictive interpretation on the matter, ruling on the adequacy of the judicial review action seeking the annulment of such acts before the Administrative Jurisdiction. This can be realized from the decision taken in a recent and polemic case referred to the expropriation of some premises of a corn agro-industry complex, which developed as follows:

In August 2005, officers from the Ministry of Agriculture and Land and military officers and soldiers from the Army and the National Guard, surrounded the installation of the company *Refinadora de Maíz Venezolana, C.A. (Remavenca)*, and announces were publicly made regarding the appointment of an Administrator Commission that would taking over the industry. These actions where challenged by the company as a de facto action alleging the violation of the company rights to equality, due process and defense, economic freedom, property rights and to the non confiscation guaranty of property. A few days latter, the Governor of the State of *Barinas* where the industry is located, issued a Decree ordering the expropriation of the premises, and consequently the Supreme Tribunal declared the inadmissibility of the amparo action that was filed, basing its ruling on the following arguments:

> The criteria established up to now by this Tribunal, by which it has concluded on the inadmissibility of the autonomous amparo action against administrative acts has been that the judicial review of administrative act actions -among which the recourse for nullity, the actions against the administrative abstentions and recourse filed by public servants- are the adequate means, that is, the brief, prompt and efficient means in order to obtain the reestablishment of the infringed juridical situation, in addition to the wide powers that are attributed to the administrative jurisdiction courts in Article 29 of the Constitution.

[35] See the reference in Rafael CHAVERO G. *El nuevo amparo constitucional en Venezuela,* Ed. Sherwood, Caracas 2001, p. 354.

Accordingly, the recourse for nullity or the expropriation suit, are the adequate means to resolve the claims referred to supposed controversies in the expropriation procedure; those are the preexisting judicial means in order to judicially decide conflicts in which previous legality studies are required, and which the constitutional judge cannot consider.

Thus, the Chamber considers that the claimants, if they think that the alleged claim persists, they can obtain the reestablishment of their allegedly infringed juridical situation, by means of the ordinary actions and to obtain satisfaction to their claims. So existing adequate means for the resolution of the controversy argued by the plaintiff, it is compulsory for the Chamber to declare the inadmissibility of the amparo action, according to what is set forth in Article 6,5 of the Organic Law[36].

Also even without statutory regulation, the same rule of admissibility has been adopted in Chile[37] and in Dominican Republic. In the latter country, the Supreme Court has ruled as follows:

«According to the Dominican legal doctrine, as well as to the international doctrine and jurisprudence, the amparo action has a subordinate character, which implies that it can only be filed when the interested person does not have any other mean to claim for the protection of the harmed or threatened right; the principle supposes that the amparo action cannot be filed when other procedures exists in parallel, in which the injured party has the possibility to claim for the protection of the same fundamental rights[38].

3. The question of the previous election of other remedies that are pending of decision, including amparo suits

The extraordinary character of the amparo suit not only implies that it can only be filed when the affected party does not have any other available ordinary judicial to obtain adequate protection for his harmed or threatened constitutional rights, but that the affected party in seeking protection when bringing an amparo suit, must not have a pending action or recourse brought before a court for the same purpose. This can be considered also as a general rule on the matter, similar to what is called in North American law, the «doctrine of the election of remedies» regarding the equitable defenses in the suit for injunctions. As Tabb and Shoben have pointed out: «The doctrine of elections of remedies provides that when an

---

36 See decision of the Constitucional Chamber of the Supreme Tribunal of Justice N° 3375 of November 4, 2005, Case: *Refinadora de Maíz Venezolana, C.A. (Remavenca), y Procesadora Venezolana de Cereales, S.A. (Provencesa) vs. Ministro de Agricultura y Tierras y efectivos de los componentes Ejército y Guardia Nacional de la Fuerza Armada Nacional.*

37 See Humberto NOGUEIRA ALCALÁ, «El derecho de amparo o protección de los derechos humanos, fundamentales o esenciales en Chile: evolución y perspectivas», in Humberto Nogueira Alcalá (Editor), *Acciones constitucionales de amparo y protección: realidad y perspectivas en Chile y América Latina*», Editorial Universidad de Talca, Talca 2000, p. 27. In contrary sense, see Emilio PFEFFER URQUIAGA, «Naturaleza, caracteristicas y fines del recurso de protección», in Humberto Nogueira Alcalá (Editor), *Acciones constitucionales de amparo y protección: realidad y perspectivas en Chile y América Latina*», Editorial Universidad de Talca, Talca 2000, p. 153.

38 Manuel A. VALERA MONTERO, *Hacia un nuevo concepto de Constitución. Selección y clasificación de decisiones de la Suprema Corte de Justicia de la República Dominicana en materia constitucional 1910-2004*, Santo Domingo, 2006, pp. 374-375.

injured party has two available but inconsistent remedies to redress a harm, the act of choosing one constitutes a binding election that forecloses the other»[39].

In similar sense, the general rule in Latin America, as it is set forth in Article 73, XIV of the Mexican Amparo Law, is that the amparo suit is inadmissible when the claimant has brought before an ordinary court any recourse or legal defense seeking to modify, repeal or nullify the challenged act». So pending the decision on a judicial process in which the claimant has asked the same protective remedies, the amparo suit cannot be admissible[40]. The Perúvian Code on Constitutional procedures also establishes that the amparo action is inadmissible «when the aggrieved party has previously chosen other judicial processes seeking protection of his constitutional right» (Art 5, 3). The same has been decided by the Chilean courts regarding the action for protection.[41]

In Venezuela, Article 6,5 of the Amparo Law also provides that the suit is inadmissible «when the injured party has chosen other ordinary judicial means or has used other preexisting judicial means». In such cases, when the violation or threat of constitutional rights and guarantees has been alleged, the court must follow the procedure set forth in the Amparo Law (Arts. 23, 24 and 25), in order to provisionally suspend the effects of the challenged act.

This inadmissibility clause is only applicable when in the other judicial action or recourse the constitutional violation has been alleged; so that the constitutional protection can be obtained. Thus, it is possible to obtain in an immediate way the effective protection of the constitutional rights, this justifies in such cases, the inadmissibility of the amparo action.

This inadmissibility clause has been applied in cases of the exercise of judicial review against administrative acts actions, when a protection of constitutional rights has been conjunctly requested, seeking the suspension of the effects of the challenged administrative acts. In these cases, the First Court on Administrative Jurisdiction in a decision dated May 11, 1992 (Case *Venalum*), ruled as follows:

> «It has been the criteria of this court that Article 6,5 of the Amparo law imposes the inadmissibility of the amparo action when the aggrieved party has chosen for the ordinary judicial means or has used the preexistent judicial means. The court has considered in previous cases that when the plaintiff is asking for the suspension of the challenged administrative act according to Article 136 of the Supreme Court Organic Law, that means the use of a parallel mean for protection that turns in inadmissible the amparo action, because such petition for a provisional remedy requested conjunctly with the nullity action, is in itself a cause of inadmissibility[42].

---

39 See William M. TABB and Elaine W. SHOBEN, *Remedies*, Thomson West 2005, p. 56.

40 See Eduardo FERRER MAC-GREGOR, *La acción constitucional de amparo en México y España. Estudio de derecho comparado*, Editorial Porrúa, México, 2002, pp. 393.; Richard D. BAKER, *Judicial Review in México. A Study of the Amparo Suit*, University of Texas Press, Austin, 1971, p. 100.

41 See Juan Manuel ERRAZURIZ G. and Jorge Miguel OTERO A., *Aspectos procesales del recurso de protección*, Editorial Jurídica de Chile, Santiago, 1989, p. 114.

42 See en *Revista de Derecho Público*, N° 50, Editorial Jurídica Venezolana, Caracas, 1992, pp. 187-188. See also the decisions of the First Court of February 21, 1991, *Revista de Derecho Público*, N° 45, Editorial Jurídica Venezolana, Caracas, p. 146, and of September 24, 1991,

On the other hand, it most be highlighted that the inadmissibility clause only applies when the plaintiff has used other judicial means for protection exercised before the courts; so if only administrative recourses have been used, the inadmissible clause is not applied, because the administrative recourses are not judicial ordinary means that can impede the filing of the amparo action[43].

Nonetheless, in Argentina, even thought the same general rule of inadmissibly has been developed through judicial interpretation, it has also comprised the cases in which the injured party has chosen to use administrative means for defense. As was decided in the Hughtes Tool Company SA. case, «the sole fact that the plaintiff has chosen to file a petition or recourse before the Administration, provokes the inadmissibility of the amparo action, because a claim of this nature cannot be used to take the case from the authority intervening in the case because so asked by the same plaintiff'[44]. In other cases, the decision has been that «it is not legal nor logic for a plaintiff in parallel and simultaneously to use two means of different procedural nature, one ordinary and the other extraordinary because it would be incompatible and it would place the claimant in a position of privileged or advantage contrary to the principle of equality in the exercise of procedural rules»[45].

Finally, in order to assure the effective protection of rights, the courts in Argentina have developed the doctrine that even in cases in which the interested party has chosen to use other judicial means for the protection of the harmed constitutional rights other than the amparo action, a subsequent amparo action could be admissible when there is an excessive delay in the resolution of the previous procedure to be issued; delay that can provoke the grave and irreparable harm that can justify the filing on the amparo action in order to obtain the immediate protection needed[46].

On the other hand, in the legislation of Bolivia, Ecuador, México and Venezuela the inadmissibility of the amparo action is specifically regulated in cases in which a previous amparo action has been previously filed. In this regard, in Bolivia

---

en FUNEDA, *15 años de Jurisprudencia... cit.*, p. 105; of December 5, 1991 and April 1, 1993 in *Revista de Derecho Público,* N° 53-54, Editorial Jurídica Venezolana, Caracas, 1994, p. 263. See also decisión of the Politico Administrative Chamber of the Supreme Court of July 13, 1992 (*Case Municipio Almirante Padilla*), *Revista de Derecho Público,* N° 51, Editorial Jurídica Venezolana; Caracas, 1992, pp. 215-216; and decisión of November 11, 1993, Caso *UNET*, in *Revista de Derecho Público,* N° 55-56, Editorial Jurídica Venezolana, Caracas, 1993, p. 489.

[43] See the decisión of the First Court on administrative jurisdiction has decided on a decision dated march 8, 1993 (Case: Federico Domingo) in *Revista de Derecho Público,* N° 53-54, Editorial Jurídica Venezolana, Caracas, 1994, p. 261. See also decision dated May 6, 1994 (Caso *Universidad Occidental Lisandro Alvarado*), en *Revista de Derecho Público,* N° 57-58, Editorial Jurídica Venezolana, Caracas, 1994. See Rafael CHAVERO G. *El nuevo amparo constitucional en venezuela,* Ed. Sherwood, Caracas 2001, pp. 250 ff.

[44] See in Alí Joaquín SALGADO, *Juicio de amparo y acción de inconstitucionalidad*, Editorial Astrea, Buenos Aires 1987, pp. 33.

[45] See ST La Rioja, 27/1/71, J.A., 10-1971-782. See the reference in Néstor Pedro SAGÜÉS, *Derecho procesal Constitucional,* Vol 3, *Acción de amparo,* Editorial Astrea, Buenos Aires 1988, p. 187.

[46] See Alí Joaquín SALGADO, *Juicio de amparo y acción de inconstitucionalidad*, Editorial Astrea, Buenos Aires 1987, p. 34; José Luis lazzarini, *El juicio de amparo*, Ed. La Ley, Buenos Aires1987, p. 143.

the Amparo Law provides that the amparo action is inadmissible when a previous constitutional amparo action has been filed with identity on the person, the object and the cause (Art. 96, 2); and in Ecuador, the Amparo Law forbids the filing of more that one amparo action regarding the same matter and with the same object, before more than one court. That is why, those filing an amparo action must declare under oath in the written request that he has not filed before other courts another amparo action with the same matter and object (Art 57).

In México, Article 73, III of the amparo law also provides the inadmissibility of the amparo action against statutes and acts that are the object of another amparo suit pending of resolution, filed by the same aggrieved party, against the same authorities and regarding the same challenged act, even if the constitutional violations are different.

Also in Venezuela, Article 6,8 of the Amparo law provides the inadmissibility of the action for amparo when a decision regarding another amparo suit has been brought before the courts regarding the same facts and is pending of decision[47].

II. THE CHARACTER OF THE AMPARO SUIT PROCEDURE

1. The brief character of the procedure

Being the amparo suit an extraordinary remedy for the immediate protection of constitutional rights, its main feature is the brief character of the procedure, which is justified because its purpose is to protect a person in cases of irreparable injuries or threats to his constitutional rights. Thus, this irreparable character of the harm or threat and the immediate need for protection are the key elements that conform the procedural rules of the amparo suit.

In this regard, the same principle applies to the North American injunctions, regarding which the judicial doctrine on the matter has established the following principles:

> «An injunction is granted only when required to avoid immediate and irreparable damage to a legally recognized rights, such as property rights, constitutional rights or contract rights. There must be some vital necessity for the injunction so that one of the parties will not be damaged and left without adequate remedy. This requirement cannot be met where there is no showing of any real or immediate threat that the petitioner will be wronged again. Except as is otherwise provided by statute, to warrant an injunction it ordinarily must be clearly shown that some act has been done, or is threatened, which will produce irreparable injury to the party asking for the injunction, regardless of whether the party may additionally prove that the activity sought to be enjoined is illegal per se...
>
> The very function of an injunction is to furnish preventive relief against irreparable mischief or injury, and the remedy will not be awarded where it appears to the satisfaction of the court that the injury complained of is not such a character. More specifically, a permanent, mandatory injunction, a

[47] See for instance decision of the Politico Administrative Chamber of the Supreme Court of Justice of October 13, 1993, in *Revista de Derecho Público*, N° 55-56, Editorial Jurídica Venezolana, Caracas, 1993, pp. 348-349.

preliminary, interlocutory or temporary injunction, a preliminary mandatory injunction, or a preliminary, interlocutory or temporary restraining order, will not, as a general rule, be grated where it is not shown that an irreparable injury is immediate impending and will be inflicted on the petitioner before the case can be brought to a final hearing, no matter how likely it may be that the moving party will prevail on the merits»[48].

In general terms, these same principles applies to the amparo suit, but with the particular feature that in Latin America they have given shape to specific and particular procedural rules that govern the judicial procedure of the amparo suit, characterized by being a brief judicial process that is justified because of its protective objective regarding constitutional rights against violations, that requires immediate protection.

Those rules are characterized by a few particular trends, mainly referred to the general brief configuration of the procedure and, in particular, to the rules governing the complaint to be filed; the proof activity of the parties; the defendant report needed because of the bilateral character of the process and the hearing of the case.

That is, even being the nature of the amparo suit procedure a brief an prompt one, the bilateral character of the procedure imposes the respect of the due process rules and the need to guarantee the right to self defense of the defendant. That is why no definitive amparo adjudication can be given without the participation of the defendant. That is why only in a very exceptional way, some legislation as the Colombian one, admits the possibility of granting the constitutional protection (tutela) *in limene litis*, that is, «without any formal consideration and without previous enquiry, if the decision is founded in an evidence that shows the grave and imminent violation of harm to the right» (Art. 18). In the Venezuelan Amparo Law, from which such provision was taken, also provided for the possibility for the amparo judge «to immediately restore the infringed juridical situation, without considerations of mere form and without any kind of brief enquiry», being required in such cases, that «the amparo protection be founded in an evidence which constitute a grave presumption of the violation of harm of violation» (Art. 22).

Nonetheless, this article of the Venezuelan Amparo Law was annulled by the former Supreme Court of Justice[49], considering that it violated in a flagrant way the constitutional right to defense, and denying to establish its constitutional interpretation as just as a provision which only established -although with incorrect wording- a provisional and not definitive judicial measure of protection[50].

2. The brief and prompt nature of the procedure

The Latin American statutes regulating the amparo suit not only provide for a specific judicial mean for the protection of constitutional rights, but also for

[48] See in John BOURDEAU et al, «Injunctions» in Kevin Schroder, John Glenn and Maureen Placilla, *Corpus Juris Secundum*, Volume 43A, Thomson West, 2004, pp. 76-78.

[49] Decision dated May 21, 1996. See in *Gaceta Oficial Extra* N° 5071 May 29, 1996. See the comments in Allan R. BREWER-CARÍAS, «Derecho y Acción de Amparo», Vol. V, *Instituciones Políticas y Constitucionales*, Editorial Jurídica venezolana, Caracas, 1998, pp. 388-396; Rafael CHAVERO GAZDIK, *El nuevo régimen del amparo constitucional en Venezuela*, Edit. Sherwood, Caracas 2001, pp. 212, 266 ff., 410 ff.

[50] See the comments in Allan R. BREWER-CARÍAS, «Derecho y Acción de Amparo», *Instituciones Políticas y Constitucionales*, Vol V, Editorial Jurídica venezolana, Caracas 1998, pp. 398.

specific rules of procedure particularly referred to the amparo suit, which differ from the general rules that govern the ordinary judicial procedure. These specific rules are conditioned by the brief and promptness nature of the amparo procedure, which is imposed by the need for the immediate protection of constitutional rights.

As it is provided in Article 27 of the Venezuelan Constitution: the procedure of the constitutional amparo action must be oral, public, brief, free of charge and not subject to formality». Regarding some of these principles, the First Court on Judicial review of administrative actions even before the enactment of the Amparo law in 1988 ruled that because of the brief character of the procedure, it must be understood as having «the condition of being urgent, thus it must be followed promptly and decided in the shorter possible time»; and additionally it must be summary, in the sense that «the procedure must be simple, uncomplicated, without incidences and complex formalities». In this sense, the procedure must not be converted in a procedural complex and confused situation, limited in time to resolve the multiple» and various challenges and questions opposed as previous stage»[51]. According to these principles, the Amparo Law of 1988 provided for the brief, prompt and summary procedure that governed the amparo suit up to the enactment of the 1999 Constitution, when the Constitutional Chamber interpreted the Statute provision according to the new Constitution having re-written its regulations by constitutional interpretation[52].

III. THE PRINCIPLES GOVERNING THE PREFERRED CHARACTER OF THE PROCEDURE

The general principles governing these specific rules are often expressly enumerated in the Amparo Laws, as guidelines for their general judicial interpretation. For instance, in Colombia, these are «the principles of publicity, prevalence of substantial law, economy, promptness and efficacy» (Art 3); in Ecuador, «the principles of procedural promptness and immediate [response]» (*inmediatez*) (Art 59); in Honduras, the «principles of independence, morality of the debate, informality, publicity, prevalence of substantial law, free of charge, promptness, procedural economy, effectiveness, and due process» (Art. 45); in Perú, «the principles of judicial direction of the process, free of charge regarding the plaintiff acts, procedural economy, immediate and socialization» (Art. III).

In particular, as a key principle for interpretation of procedural rules, it must be highlighted the one provided in the Honduras Law regarding the need for the prevalence of substantial rules over formal provisions, in the sense that because in the procedure «the merits on the matter must prevail», the «procedural defects must not prevent the quick development of the procedure». Consequently, it is provided that «the parties can correct their own mistakes, if remediable» being the

---

51 See decision of January 17, 1985, in *Revista de Derecho Publico,* N° 21, Editorial Jurídica Venezolana, Caracas, 1985, p. 140.

52 See the decisión of the Constitucional Chamber of the Supreme Tribunal of Justice N° 7 dated February 1, 2000 (Case *José Amando Mejía*), in *Revista de Derecho Público,* N° 81, Editorial Jurídica Venezolana, Caracas, 2000, pp. 245 ff. See the comments in Allan R. BREWER-CARÍAS, *El sistema de justicia constitucional en la constitución de 1999 (Comentarios sobre su desarrollo jurisprudencial y su explicación, a veces errada, en la Exposición de Motivos),* Editorial Jurídica Venezolana, Caracas, 2000 and in Rafael CHAVERO GAZDIK, *El nuevo régimen del amparo constitucional en Venezuela,* Edit. Sherwood, Caracas, 2001, pp. 203 ff.

courts also authorized to ex officio correct them (Honduras, Art. 4,5; Guatemala, Art. 6; Paraguay, Art. 20; El Salvador, Art. 80). That is why the Perúvian Code specifies that «the judge and the Constitutional Tribunal must adjust the formalities set forth in this Code, to the attainment of the purposes of the constitutional processes» (Art. III) which is the immediate protection of constitutional rights.

For such purposes, in the Venezuelan Constitution is provided that «any time will be workable time and the courts will give preference to the amparo regarding any other matter» (Art. 27). These principles are set forth in almost all the Amparo Laws in Latin America, by expressly providing that the amparo action can be filed at any time (Colombia, Arts. 1 and 15; Honduras, Art. 16; Guatemala, Art. 5), even on holidays and out of labor hours (Costa Rica Art. 5; Ecuador, Art. 47; El Salvador Art. 79; Paraguay, Art.19).

One of the abovementioned procedural principles is the preferred character of the amparo in the sense that the procedure must be followed with preference, which implies that when an amparo is filed, the courts must postpone all other matters of different nature (Guatemala, Art. 5; Honduras, Arts. 4,3; Perú; Venezuela, Art. 13), except the cases of habeas corpus» (Colombia, Art. 15; Brazil, Art. 17; Costa Rica, Art. 39; Honduras, Art 511).

The Amparo Laws also assigns the courts the task of directing the procedure, empowering them to act ex officio (El Salvador, Art. 5; Guatemala, Art. 6; Honduras, Art. 4,4; Perú, Art. III) even in matter of evidence; the inertia of the parties not being valid to justify any delay (Costa Rica, Art. 8; El Salvador, Art. 5). Additionally, the notifications made by the court can be done by any mean including technical, electronic or magnetic ones (El Salvador. Art. 79).

In the amparo procedure, as a general rule, the procedural terms cannot be extended, nor suspended nor interrupted, except in cases expressly set forth in the statute (Costa Rica, Arts. 8 and 39; El Salvador, Art. 5; Honduras 4; Perú, Art 33,8; Paraguay Art. 19). Any delay in the procedure is the responsibility of the courts (Costa Rica, Art. 8; Honduras, Art. 4,8; Perú, Art. 13).

Another general rule regarding the amparo suit procedure is that no incidents are allowed in it (Honduras, Art. 70; Uruguay, Art. 12; Panamá, Art. 2610; Paraguay, Art. 20; Uruguay, Art. 12); thus, neither excuse or recuse of judges are admitted or they are restricted (Argentina, Art.16; Colombia, Art. 39; Ecuador Art. 47, and 59; Honduras, Art. 18; Panamá, Art. 2610; Paraguay, Art. 20; Perú Art. 33, 1 and 2; Venezuela, Art. 11). Nonetheless, the Amparo law in some countries provides for specific and prompt procedure rules to resolve the situation regarding the cases of impeding situations of the competent judges to resolve the case (Costa Rica, Art. 6; Guatemala, Arts. 17, 111; México, Art. 66; Panama, Art. 2610; Perú, Art. 52; Venezuela, Art. 11).

1. General provisions regarding the filing of the petition

The general principle on judicial procedure in Latin America, is that the petitions that are to be brought before the courts must always be filed in writing. That is why, all the Amparo Laws specify with detail the necessary content of the petition in matters of amparo.

Nonetheless, some exceptions have been established allowing the oral presentation of the amparo in cases of urgency (Venezuela, Arts. 16, 18; Colombia,

Art. 14; Honduras, Art. 16; Perú, Art. 27), danger to life, deprivation of liberty without judicial process, deportation or exile (México, Art. 117) or if the plaintiff is short of means (Guatemala, Art. 26 Honduras, Art. 22 -habeas corpus-). Nonetheless, is such cases, the petitions must be subsequently ratified in writing.

In other cases, it is allowed for the plaintiff to bring the petition before the court by telegram or radiogram (Brazil, Art. 4; Costa Rica, Art. 38) or by electronic means (Perú, Art. 27).

Since the normal way to bring the amparo action before the competent court is through a written text -as it is also required for the petition for injunction in North America[53], the petitioner must express in it, in a clear and precise manner, all the necessary elements regarding the alleged right to relief and on the arguments for the admissibility of the action. Thus, according to what is established in the Amparo Laws in Latin America, in general terms, the petition or complaint must comprise the following:

1) The complete identification and information regarding the plaintiff (Argentina, Art 6,a; Bolivia, Art. 97,I; Colombia, Art. 14; El Salvador, Art. 14; México, 116,1 and 166, 1; Nicaragua, Art. 27,1; Perú, Art, 42,2; Paraguay, Art.; 6,a; Venezuela, Art. 18, 1 and 2). If someone is acting on behalf of the plaintiff, also his identification; and if the plaintiff is an artificial person, its identification as well as the representative's complete identification (El Salvador, Art. 14,1; Guatemala Arts. 21,b and c; Honduras, Art. 49,2)

2) The individuation of the injurer party (Argentina, Art 6,b; Bolivia, Art. 97, II; Honduras, Art. 49, 2; Paraguay, Art. 6,b; Venezuela, Art. 18,2), and regarding public entities, the harming public authority, and if possible, the organ provoking the harm or threat (Colombia, Art. 14; Costa Rica, Art. 38; El Salvador, Art. 14; Guatemala, Art. 21,d; panama, Art. 2619,2; México, Arts. 116,III and 166,III; Nicaragua, Art. 27,2 and 55).

3) The detailed narration of the circumstances in which the harm or the threat has been caused (Argentina, Art., 6,c; Bolivia, Art. 97,III; Colombia, Art. 14; Costa Rica, Art. 38; El Salvador, Art. 14,5; Guatemala, Art. 21,e; Panama, Art. 2619,3; Paraguay, Art. 6,d; Honduras, Art. 49,5; Nicaragua, Art. 55; Perú, Art. 42,4; Venezuela, Art. 18,5), and in particular, the act, action, omission or fact causing the harm or threat (El Salvador, Art. 14,3; Honduras, Art. 49,3; Nicaragua, Art. 27,3; Perú, Art. 42,5; México Arts. 116, IV and 166,IV).

4) The constitutional right or guaranty that has been violated, harmed or threatened (Bolivia, Art. 97,IV; Colombia, Art. 14; El Salvador, Art. 14,4; Panamá, Art. 2619,V; Honduras, Art. 49,6; Venezuela, Art. 18,4), with the precise indication of the articles of the Constitution containing the rights or guarantees (Guatemala, Art. 21,f; México, Arts. 116, V and 166,VI; Nicaragua, Art. 27,4). The Tutela Law in Colombia exempts the need of identifying the article of the constitution providing that the harmed or threatened right is identified with precision (Art. 14). A similar provision is set forth in the Costa Rican Constitutional Jurisdiction Law (Art. 38).

[53] See in John BOURDEAU et al, «Injunctions» in Kevin Schroder, John Glenn and Maureen Placilla, *Corpus Juris Secundum*, Volume 43A, Thomson West, 2004, pp. 346 ff.

5) The plaintiff must specify the concrete petition for the judicial order to be issue in protection of his rights that is requested from the court (Argentina, Art. 6,d; Bolivia, Art. 97,VI; Honduras, Art. 49,7; Perú. Art. 42,6; Paraguay, Art 6,d).

6) Finally, the plaintiff must base the conditions for the admissibility of the action, in particular, regarding the inadequacy of the other possible judicial remedies and the irreparable injury the plaintiff will suffer without the amparo suit protection[54].

In order to soften the consequences of not mentioning correctly all the abovementioned requirements that have to be complied with in the presentation of the petition, almost all the Latin American Amparo Laws, in protection of the injured party right to sue, provides that the courts are obliged to return to the plaintiff the petition that does not conform with those requirements in order for him to make the necessary corrections. That is to say, the petition will not be considered inadmissible because of the non compliance with the requirements of the Laws, and in order to have them corrected or mended the court must return it to the petitioner for him to correct it in a brief delay. And only if the petitioner does not make the corrections then the complaint will be rejected (Colombia, Art. 17; Costa Rica, Art. 42; El Salvador, Art. 18; Guatemala, Art. 22; Honduras, Art. 50; México, Art. 146; Nicaragua, Art. 28; Perú, Art. 48; Paraguay, Art. 7; Venezuela, Art. 19).

2. General principles regarding evidence and burden of proof

As has been studied in previous chapters, the amparo suit is a specific judicial mean regulated in Latin America in order to obtain the immediate protection of constitutional rights and guaranties, when the aggrieved or injured parties have no other adequate judicial means for such purpose.

In any case, the violation of a constitutional right that can found an amparo action, in general terms must be a flagrant, vulgar, direct and immediate, caused by a perfectly determined act or omission, and the harm or injury caused to the constitutional rights must be manifestly arbitrary, illegal or illegitimate, consequence of a violation of the Constitution; all of which, in principle must be clear and ostensible from what the plaintiff argues before the court in his petition.

This conditions, similar to what is established in the United States regarding the injunctions[55], imposes to the plaintiff the burden to proof the existence of the right, the alleged violations of threat, and the illegitimate character of the action causing it, with clear and convincing evidence. That is why, for instance, all the Amparo Laws in Latin America require that all the circumstances of the case must be explained in the text of the petition, with all the evidences supporting it. Also some statutes impose the need for the petition to be filed attaching all the documentary evidence (Argentina, Art. 7; Bolivia, Art. 97,V; Guatemala, Art. 21,g; Panama, Art. 2619; Uruguay, Art. 5), and specifying all the other evidences to be

---

54 In similar way as in the injunction petition in the United States. See in John BOURDEAU et al, «Injunctions» in Kevin Schroder, John Glenn and Maureen Placilla, *Corpus Juris Secundum*, Volume 43A, Thomson West, 2004, pp. 346, 352.

55 See Kevin Schroder, John Glenn and Maureen Placilla (Editors), *Corpus Juris Secundum*, Vol. 43A, Thomson West, 2004, p. 54.

presented (Argentina, Art. 7; Uruguay, Art. 5). In México the evidences must be shown in the hearing, except the documentary evidence that can be filed before (Art. 151).

In any case, the amparo suit is a brief and prompt procedure for the immediate protection of constitutional rights based in sufficient evidence, which cannot be involved in complex evidence activity. If the latter situation is the case, the Argentinean Amparo Law provides for the inadmissibility of the amparo action, by establishing it in cases «where in order to determine the invalidity of the [challenged] act, a mayor scope of debate or proof is required» (Art., 2d).

Accordingly, the courts have rejected amparo actions in complex cases where a mayor debate is needed, and in cases in which the evidences are difficult to be provided[56], which is considered incompatible with the brief and prompt character of the amparo suit that requires that the alleged violation be «manifestly» illegitimate and harming. Even though without the clear provision on the matter of the Argentinean Law, this same principle has been considered as applicable regarding the *mandado de seguranca* in Brazil, Uruguay[57] and Venezuela[58]

On the other hand, regarding the «evidence phase» in the process in the amparo suit, regulated in some Laws (El Salvador, Art, 29; Guatemala, Art. 35); some legislations, as is the case of Perú, discard its existence, providing that the evidences must be presented with the petition, and that they will be accepted if they do not require further procedural developments (Art. 9). The courts also have among their ex officio powers, the competence to obtain evidences (Costa Rica, Art. 47; Guatemala, Art. 36; Paraguay, Art. 11) if it does not cause an irreparable prejudice to the plaintiff (Venezuela Art. 17), or to do whatever they consider necessary without affecting the length of the procedure. In the latter case no previous notification to the parties is required (Perú, Art 9).

In principle, all evidences are admitted in the amparo suit, so the court can found its decision to grant or not the required protection in any evidence (Colombia, Art. 21). Nonetheless, some legislations forbid some evidences in the amparo suit, as is the case of confession (Argentina Art. 7; El Salvador, Arts. 29; México, Art. 150; Paraguay, Art 12), and those considered contrary to morality or good costumes (México, Art. 150).

3. The decision regarding the admissibility of the petition

It can be considered as a general feature of the procedure of the amparo suit, the power of the competent court to decide at the beginning of the procedure upon the admission of the petition, when it accomplishes with all the admissibility conditions set fort in the Amparo Laws. Consequently, the courts are empowered to decide *in limine litis* about the inadmissibility of the action when the petition does not accomplish in a manifest way with the conditions determined in the

---

56 See José Luis LAZZARINI, *El juicio de amparo*, Ed. La Ley, Buenos Aires1987, pp. 94-95, 173 ff.; Alí Joaquín SALGADO, *Juicio de amparo y acción de inconstitucionalidad*, Editorial Astrea, Buenos Aires, 1987, p. 52; Néstor Pedro SAGÜÉS, *Derecho procesal Constitucional*, Vol 3, *Acción de amparo*, Editorial Astrea, Buenos Aires, 1988, pp. 231-239.

57 See Luis Alberto VIERA, *Ley de Amparo*, Ediciones Idea, Montevideo 1993, p. 17.

58 See Rafael CHAVERO G., *El nuevo amparo constitucional en Venezuela*, Ed. Sherwood, Caracas, 2001, p. 340.

statute (Argentina, Art. 3; Bolivia, Art. 98; Costa Rica, Art. 9; México, Art. 145; Perú, Art. 47; Uruguay, Art. 2).

4. The defendant (the injurer or aggrieving party) pleading or answer

In almost all the Latin American Laws regulating the amparo suit, after the decision of the court to admit the action, one of the main phases of the procedure refers to the need for the court to notify the aggrieving party in order to request it, a formal answer regarding the alleged violations of constitutional rights of the plaintiff. Due to the bilateral character of the procedure, as happens in the injunctive relief procedure in the United States, an amparo ruling must not be issued until the pleadings by the defendant have been joined[59]. In the cases of Bolivia and Ecuador, the Amparo Laws do not require the filing of an answer, which can be nonetheless be presented before the court in the hearing of the case (Bolivia, Art. 100; Ecuador, Art. 49).

Thus, after admitting the claim, the first procedural step the court must take is the request from the defendant and the formal answer of the petition formulated by the injured party, in which, in addition the defendant must put forward his counter evidences. This is what was established in the Venezuelan Amparo Law (Art. 24); which nonetheless has been eliminated by the Constitutional Chamber in its decision of 2000, interpreting the Amparo law according to the new 1999 Constitution, reshaping the amparo suit procedure[60].

In the other Latin American countries, the defendant's answer or pleading regarding the harm or threat alleged by the plaintiff to be sent to the court, must be sent in a very brief term (Argentina, Art. 8; Bolivia, Art. 100; Panama, Art. 2591) of hours (24h: El Salvador, Art. 21; 48h: Venezuela, Art. 23) or three days (Colombia, Art. 19; Costa Rica, Arts. 19, 43, 61; Paraguay, Art. 9), five days (Honduras, Arts. 26, 52; México, Art. 147, 149; Perú, Art. 53) of ten days (Nicaragua, Art. 37). The omission by the court to request the defendant's answer produces the nullity of the process (Argentina, Art. 8).

The omission of the defendant to send his pleading answer to the court, implies that the facts alleged by the injured party facts and acts causing the harm or threat must be considered as certain (Colombia, Art. 19; Costa Rica, Art. 45[61]; El Salvador, Art. 22; Honduras (habeas corpus), Art. 26; México, Art 149; Nicaragua, Art. 39); or that the constitutional right or guarantee that is allegedly be violated, must in fact be considered violated (Honduras, Art. 53) or that the plaintiff alleged facts must be considered as accepted by the defendant (Venezuela, Art. 23). In those cases, the consequence of the omission by the defendant to send his answer to the court is that the amparo should be granted (Argentina, Art. 20; Costa Rica, Art. 45; Honduras, Art. 53). In some cases, the effect of such omission is to grant a preliminary relief, suspending the effects of the challenged act (Guatemala, Art. 33).

---

59 See in John BOURDEAU et al, «Injunctions» in Kevin Schroder, John Glenn and Maureen Placilla, *Corpus Juris Secundum*, Volume 43A, Thomson West, 2004, pp. 357 ff.

60 See Rafael CHAVERO G., *El nuevo amparo constitucional en Venezuela*, Ed. Sherwood, Caracas, 2001, pp. 264 ff.

61 In cases of habeas corpus article 23 of the Costa Rican Law set forth that the facts could be considered as certain.

Notwithstanding, in certain cases, the court can insist on the remittance of the answer or ask for new information (Argentina, Arts. 20, 21; Colombia, Art. 21; Costa Rica, Art. 45; Perú, Art. 53)

5. The hearing in the amparo suit

In all the Latin American Amparo Laws, one of the most important steps on the procedure is the hearing that the court must convene, also in a very prompt term of days, with the participation of the parties (Argentina, Art. 9; Bolivia, Art. 100; Ecuador, Art. 49; Uruguay, Art. 6; Paraguay, Art. 10; Venezuela, Art. 26) The absence of the defendant in general terms does not produce the suspension of the hearing (Bolivia, Art. 100).

According to some Amparo laws, if the plaintiff does not assist to the hearing it is understood that he desisted his action, with payment of the costs (Argentina, Art. 10; Ecuador, Art. 50); and if it is the defendant the one who does not assist, the hearing is not suspended (Ecuador, Art. 5), and the evidences presented by the plaintiff will be accepted and the court then must proceed to decide (Art. 10).

In some Latin American Laws, it is set forth that the court must take its decision in the same hearing or trial (Bolivia Art. 100; Uruguay, Art. 6; Venezuela, or in the following days (Venezuela, Art. 24).

CHAPTER X

THE PROTECTED PERSONS: THE INJURED PARTY IN THE AMPARO SUIT INDIVIDUAL AND COLLECTIVE ACTIONS AND THE GENERAL STANDING CONDITIONS

I. THE PARTIES IN THE AMPARO SUIT

The Latin American amparo is always conceived as a suit, that is, as a proceeding initiated by a party or parties, the injured or offended party, by mean of an action or a recourse brought before the competent court, against another party (the injurer or offender party) whose actions or omissions has violated or has caused harm to his constitutional rights.

The final outcome of the amparo suit is always a judicial order, similar to the North American writs of injunction, mandamus or error, directed to the injuring party ordering to do or to abstain from doing something or a decisions suspending the effects or annulling the damaging act causing the harm.

Thus, in general terms, it can be said that the amparo suit has similarities with the civil suit for an injunction that an injured party can bring before a court to seek for the enforcement or restoration of his violated rights or for the prevention of its violation. It also can be identified with a «suit for mandamus» brought by an injured party before a court against a public officer whose omission has caused harm to the plaintiff, in order to seek for a writ ordering the former to perform a duty which the law requires him to do but he refuses or neglects to perform. Also, the suit for amparo has similarities with some kind of «suit for writ of error» brought before the competent superior court by an injured party whose constitutional rights have been violated by a judicial decision, seeking the annulment or the correction of the judicial wrong or error.

What is clear in the Latin American amparo legislations, is that the amparo is not only the remedy, or the final court written order (writ) commanding the addressee to do or refrain from doing some specific act[1]. It is, above all, a suit that is specifically designed to protect constitutional rights following an adversary process according to the «cases or controversy» condition derived from Article III of the North American Constitution; which opposes one or multiple injured or

1 Bryan A. Garner (ed), *Black's Law Dictionary*, Secod Pocket Edition, St. Paul, Minn. P. 2001.

complaining parties acting as plaintiffs, against one or multiple injuring parties acting as defendants, ending with a judicial decision or judicial order directed to protect the constitutional rights of the injured party. Also being considered as parties the interested third parties that can be harmed or benefited by the action and its results, as well as the Public Prosecutor (Attorney General) or the People's Defendant.

That is why in the amparo suit the procedural adversary principle or principle of bilateralism[2] prevails, in the sense that the judicial proceeding of the suit, although it has to be brief and speedy, must always assure the presence of both parties and the respect of the constitutional guaranties of defense. Thus, a judicial guarantee of constitutional rights as is the amparo suit can in no way transform itself in a proceeding violating the other constitutional guarantees like the right to defense. Except regarding preliminary judicial orders, the principle of *audi alteram partem* (hear the other party or listen to both sides) must then always be respected. That is why, for instance, the Supreme Court of Justice of Venezuela in a 1996 judicial review procedure, annulled Article 22 of the 1988 Amparo Law, which allowed the courts to adopt final decisions on amparo in cases of grave violations of constitutional rights, reestablishing the constitutional harmed right without any formal or summary inquiry and without hearing the plaintiff or potential injurer. Even if the Article could be constitutionally interpreted as only directed to allow the adoption of *inaudita partem* preliminary decisions or injunctions in the proceeding[3], the Supreme Court considered the Article as a vulgar and flagrant violation of the constitutional right to self defense[4], and annulled it.

Accordingly, one of the most important aspects of the amparo suit legislations in Latin America, refers to the parties in the suit, which can only be initiated at the party's request. Thus, no case of *ex officio* amparo proceeding is possible or admissible.

The suit must the be initiates by mean of an action or recourse brought before a court by the injured party or parties, as the complainant or plaintiff, against the injurer party or parties, as defendants, called to the proceeding because they provoked the harm or violation to the constitutionals rights of the former. The initiation of the suit can be an action or recourse, the latter when exercised against an administrative act or a judicial decision which is to be challenged only after the exhaustion of the available administrative or judicial recourses. When through an action, the amparo can be brought directly before the courts against facts, acts or omissions, without the need to exhaust previous recourses.

This principle of bilateralism regarding the amparo, which always implies the existence of a controversy between two parties, always initiated by a complainant or injured party against an injurer party, can be considered as the common trend in Latin America. The only exception in this regard is Chile, where in the absence of

2 José Luis LAZZARINI, *El Juicio de Amparo*, Editorial La Ley, Buenos Aires, 1987, pp. 270 y ss.

3 As was asked to be decided by the Supreme Court. See Allan R. BREWER-CARÍAS, «Derecho y Acción de Amparo», *Instituciones Políticas y Constitucionales*, Vol V, Universidad Católica del Táchira, Editorial Jurídica Venezolana, Caracas, 1998, pp. 389 y ss.

4 Decision of the Supreme Court of Justice of May, 21 1996, in *Gaceta Oficial Extra*. N° 5071 of May, 29, 1996. See the comments in Allan R. BREWER-CARÍAS, «Derecho y Acción de Amparo», *Instituciones Políticas y Constitucionales*, Vol V, Universidad Católica del Táchira, Editorial Jurídica Venezolana, Caracas, 1998, pp. 389 y ss; and in Rafael CHAVERO, *El Nuevo Régimen del Amparo Constitucional en Venezuela*, Caracas, 2001, pp. 212, 266 y ss. and 410 y ss.

a statutorily regulated amparo, it has been considered that the proceeding of the recourse for protection is not based on a controversy between parties, but on a request raised by a party before a court, being the procedural relation the one established between a complainant and a court, and not between an injured and an injurer party[5].

Regarding the plaintiff, the Latin American amparo legislations have detailed regulations in relation to who can be the specific aggrieved or injured party, in the sense of who has standing to sue for constitutional judicial protection; in relation to how can the injured party act in the judicial proceeding; and in relation to the conditions the constitutional right harms or violations most have for the action to be brought before the courts.

In respect to the defendants or injurer party, the Latin American amparo laws also set forth extensive regulations regarding the authorities that can be sued before the courts for constitutional violations, as well as the individuals or private persons that can be sued before the competent courts when responsible for the harm or the violation of a constitutional rights; how can all the injurer or offender parties act in the judicial proceeding; and also, the specific public or private acts or omissions that have caused those harms or violations in the plaintiff's constitutional rights.

II. THE INJURED PARTY

In the amparo suit, the injured party, also named the claimant, the complainant or the petitioner, who in the proceeding is the plaintiff, is the person holder of a constitutional right that has suffered an actionable wrong, that is, whose constitutional right have been violated, thus having sufficient concrete interest in bringing the case before a court, and regarding the outcome of the controversy. Being the amparo action an action *in personam* for the protection of constitutional rights, the litigant must be the injured or aggrieved person. That is why, it is generally considered that the amparo action needs to be personalized, as attributed to the particular person enjoying the harmed right, that is, the person who has a justiciable interest in the subject matter of the litigation in his own right, or a personal interest in the outcome of the controversy. As ruled regarding injunctions in *Parkview Hospital v. Com., Dept. of Public Welfare*, 56 Pa. Commw. 218, 424 A. 2d 599 (1981): to bring an action «requires an aggrieved party to show a substantial, direct, and immediate interest is the subject matter of the litigation»[6]. Or as ruled in *Warth v. Seldin*, 422 U.S. 4909, 498-500 (1975): the plaintiff must «allege such a personal stake in the outcome of the controversy» as to justify the exercise of the court's remedial powers on his behalf, because he himself has suffered «some threatened or actual injury resulting from the putatively illegal action»[7].

---

5 See for example Sergio LIRA HERRERA, *El recurso de protección. Naturaleza jurídica, doctrina, jurisprudencial, derecho comparad*, Santiago de Chile 1990, pp. 157 y ss.; Juan Manuel ERRAZUZIZ G. y Jorge Miguel OTERO A, *Aspectos procesales del recurso de protección*, Editorial Jurídica de Chile, Santiago, 1989, pp. 39, 40 y 157. In contrary sense, Enrique PAILLAS considers that in the recourse for protection the principle of bilateralism applies. See Enrique PAILLAS, *El recurso de protección ante el derecho comparado*, Editorial Jurídica de Chile, Santiago, 1990, p. 105.

6 See the reference in Kevin SCHRODER et al, «Injunction», *Corpus Juris Secundum*, Thomson West, Volume 43A, 2004, p. 331, note 4.

7 M. Glenn ABERNATHY and Barbara A. PERRY, *Civil Liberties Under the Constitution*, University of South Carolina Press, 1993, p. 4

It is in this sense that Article 23 of the Nicaraguan Amparo law provides that only the aggrieved party can file the amparo, defining as such, «any natural or artificial person being harmed or in a situation of imminent danger of being harmed by any disposition, act or resolution, and in general, by any action or omission from any public officer, authority or its agent, that violates or threats to violate the rights and guaranties enshrined in the Constitution».

A few questions must be emphasized regarding the injured or aggrieved party: first, the matter of standing to sue; second, the quality of the persons entitled to sue, in the sense of it being a physical person or human being and also artificial persons or corporation, including public law entities; third, the possibility for the Public Prosecutors or Peoples' Public Defendants to sue in amparo; and forth, regarding the third parties that can intervene in the proceedings on the side of the claimant.

1. Injured persons and standing

In the amparo suit, having the action a personal character, the plaintiff or injured party can only be the holder of the violated right; thus, the aggrieved party can only be the person whose constitutional rights have been injured or threatened of being harmed[8]. Thus, nobody can sue in amparo alleging in his own name a right belonging to another[9].

As it was ruled by the former Supreme Court of Justice of Venezuela regarding the personal character of the amparo suit, which imposes for its admissibility:

> «A qualified interest of who is asking for the restitution or reestablishment of the harmed right or guaranty, that is, that the harm be directed to him and that, eventually, its effects affect directly and indisputably upon him, harming his scope of subjective rights guarantied in the Constitution. It is only the person that is specially and directly injured in his subjective fundamental rights by a specific act, fact or omission the one that can bring an action before the competent courts by mean of a brief and speedy proceeding, in order that the judge decides immediately the reestablishment of the infringed subjective legal situation»[10].

Thus the amparo action has been qualified as a «subjective action»[11], that can only be brought before the courts personally by the aggrieved party which having

---

[8] See decisions of the former Politico-Administrative Chamber of the Supreme Court of Justice of June 18, 1992, *Revista de Derecho Público* N° 50, Editorial Jurídica Venezolana, Caracas, 1992, p. 135; and of August 13, 1992, *Revista de Derecho Público,* N° 51, Editorial Jurídica Venezolana, Caracas, 1992 p. 160.

[9] See decision of the former Politico-Administrative Chamber of the Supreme Court of Justice of February 14, 1990, in *Revista de Derecho Público,* N° 41, Editorial Jurídica Venezolana, Caracas, 1990, p. 101.

[10] See decision of the former Politico-Administrative Chamber of the Supreme Court of Justice of August 27, 1993 (Case: *Kenet E. Leal*), in *Revista de Derecho Público,* N° 55-56, Editorial Jurídica Venezolana, Caracas, 1993, p. 322.

[11] See decision First Court on Judicial Review of Administrative Action, of November 18, 1993, in *Revista de Derecho Público,* nos. 55-56, Editorial Jurídica Venezolana, Caracas, 1993, pp. 325-327.

the personal, legitimate and direct interest[12], is the one that directly or through his duly appointed representative has the standing to sue[13].

Even though this is the general rule in Latin America, a few legislations authorized other persons different to the injured parties or their representatives, to file the amparo suit on their behalf. It is then possible to distinguish in matter of amparo, the *legitimatio* or standing *ad causam* from the *legitimatio* or standing *ad processum*[14].

The standing *ad causam* in the amparo suit refers to the person or entity that enjoys the particular constitutional right which has been violated. The standing *ad processum* refers to the particular capacity the persons has to act in the procedure (procedural capacity), that is, the ability to appear in court and to use the appropriate procedures in support of a claim, which can refer to his own rights or to the rights of others.

In conclusion, any person whose constitutional rights have been violated or threatened to be violated, has the right to seek protection form the courts by means of the action for amparo; whether being *natural persons* or human beings without distinction of being citizens, disabled or foreigners; or being *artificial* persons or entities. And the word persons is used in the sense of human beings or entities that are recognized by law as having rights and duties, including corporations or companies[15].

Exceptionally, though, in some countries the amparo suit has been admitted when filed by groups or communities without formal legal «personality» attributed by law, as has happened in Chile with the recourse for protection[16] in some cases filed by affected individual or collective entities without having personality (Case: RP, *Federación Chilena de Hockey y Patinaje*, C. de Santiago, 1984, RDJ, T, LXXXI, N° 3, 2da, P., Secc.5ta, p. 240).[17]

---

12 See decisios of the former Politico-Administrative Chamber of the Supreme Court of Justice of October 22, 1990 and October 22, 1992, in *Revista de Derecho Público,* N° 52, Editorial Jurídica Venezolana, Caracas, 1992, p. 140 and of November 18, 1993, in *Revista de Derecho Público,* N° 55-56, Editorial Jurídica Venezolana, Caracas, 1993, p. 327.

13 See decision of the First Court on Judicial Review of Administrative Action of August 21, 1992, in *Revista de Derecho Público,* N° 51, Editorial Jurídica Venezolana, Caracas, 1992, p. 161.

14 See in general, Alí Joaquín Salgado, *Juicio de amparo y acción de inconstitucionalidad*, Astrea Buenos Aires 1987, pp. 81 ff; Joaquín Brage Camazano, *La jurisdicción constitucional de la libertad*, Editorial Porrúa, México 2005, pp. 162 ff.; Sergio Lira Herrera, *El recurso de protección. Naturaleza jurídica. Doctrina. Jurisprudencia. Derecho Comparado*, Santiago 1990, pp.

15 Argentina (article 5: «any individual or juridical persons»), Colombia (Article 1: «any person»); Ecuador (article 48: «natural or juridical persons»); El Salvador (article «3 and 12: «any person»; (Guatemala (article 8: «persons»), Honduras (article 41: «any aggrieved person»; article 44: «any natural or juridical person»), México (article 39: affected person»); Panamá (article: 2615: «any person»); Perú (article 39: «the affected»); Uruguay (article 1: any physical or juridical person, public or private»); Venezuela (article 1: «natural or juridical persons»).

16 The Chilean Constitution in matter of standing refers to «el que» (who), not mentioning «persons» (art. 20) See, Juan Manuel ERRAZURIZ and Jorge Miguel OTERO A., *Aspectos procesales del recurso de protección*, Editorial Jurídica de Chile, Santiago 1989, pp. 15, 50; 9.

17 Nonetheless, in other judicial decisions the contrary criteria has been sustained. See the reference in Sergio LIRA HERRERA, *El recurso de protección. Naturaleza jurídica. Doctrina. Jurisprudencia. Derecho Comparado,* Santiago 1990, pp. 144-145.

2. Natural persons: Standing ad causam and ad processum

The general principle in Latin America, is that all natural persons, as human beings, when their constitutional rights are arbitrarily or illegitimately harmed or threatened with violation, have the necessary standing to file the action for protection, as is expressly set forth in all the Amparo Laws, when referring to «persons» in general, comprising human beings and juridical or artificial persons, without distinctions,

Regarding the natural persons, of course, the expression is not equivalent to «citizens», being the latter those persons who by birth or naturalization are members of the political community represented by the State. But if it is true that the amparo is a judicial guarantee granted to all persons, citizens or foreigners; regarding the protection of political rights, like the right to vote, being the citizens the only persons entitled to those rights, only they have the right to sue in amparo for their protection.

As natural persons, foreigners also have the same general rights as nationals, having the needed standing to exercise the right to amparo. Only in México an exception can be found regarding the decisions where the President of the Republic is constitutionally authorized to adopt measures expulsing foreigners, in which case it has been recognized that they cannot challenge such decisions vía amparo[18].

Except this particular case, the general trend in Latin America has been to apply an extensive interpretation regarding standing *ad causam*, allowing all affected persons to file the amparo suit. As an example of this trend, the interpretation of the Venezuelan Law of Amparo can be mentioned, regarding the expression of its Article 1 which entitles «all natural persons inhabitants of the Republic» (Art. 1) to file amparo suits. The main problem with this article resulted from the condition to be «inhabitant of the Republic», that is, to physically be in the territory of the Republic as resident, tourist or in any other situation, which was originally interpreted to deny the right to amparo to persons not living in the country. The Supreme Court of Justice, progressively widened the interpretation, admitting the amparo action filed by a person not inhabitant of the Republic, no matter his nationality or legal condition, providing, according to a decision of August 27, 1993, «that his constitutional rights and guaranties had been directly harmed or threatened by any act, fact or omission carried out, issued or produced in the Republic»[19].

The following year this same Supreme Court, by mean of the exercise of its diffuse judicial review powers, declared unconstitutional the limiting reference of Article 1 of the Law when stressing the character of «inhabitants of the Republic», ruling on the contrary, that any person whether or not living in the Republic whose rights are harmed in Venezuela, has enough standing to file an amparo action[20]

---

18 See Eduardo FERRER MAC-GREGOR, *La acción constitucional de amparo en México y España*, Editorial Porrúa, México 2002, p. 230.

19 See in *Jurisprudencia Ramírez & Garay*, Tomo CXXVI, p. 667. See the references in Allan R. BREWER-CARÍAS, «Derecho y Acción de Amparo», Vol V, *Instituciones Políticas y Constitucionales*, Editorial Jurídica Venezolana, Caracas, 1998, p. 319.

20 Decision of December 13, 1994 (Case: *Jackroo Marine Limited*). See the reference in Rafael CHAVERO, *El Nuevo Régimen del Amparo Constitucional en Venezuela*, Caracas, 2001, pp. 98-99.

Minors, of course, also have standing *ad causam*, and through their representatives (parents or tutors) can file amparo actions for the protection and defense of their constitutional rights, and only exceptionally they are allowed to act personally. Is the case of México, were the Amparo law provided that a minor «can ask for amparo without the intervention of his legitimate representative when he is absent or impaired»; adding that «in such case, the court, without being impeded to adopt urgent measures, must appoint a special representative in order to intervene in the suit»(Art. 6).

The standing *ad processum* regarding natural persons, that is, the possibility to appear before the court, in principle corresponds to the same injured persons for the defense of their own rights. Thus, as a matter of principle, no other person can judicially act on behalf of the injured person, except when legally prescribed, for instance in the case of minors or incapacitated that must act in court through their representatives.

A general exception for this principle refers to the action of habeas corpus, in which case, generally, being the injured person impeded to act personally because he is under detention or has his freedom restrained, normally the Law authorizes anybody to file the action on his behalf[21]. In México, the Law imposes the injured party the obligation to expressly ratify the filing of the amparo suit, to the point that if the complaint is not ratified it will be considered as not filed (Art. 17). In some cases, as is the case of Guatemala (art. 86) and Honduras (art. 20), the courts even have *ex officio* power and the obligation to initiate the habeas corpus suit, in cases where they happen to have knowledge of the facts.

But regarding the amparo suit, as mentioned, the principle of its personal character prevails, in the same sense as the rule of standing to seek injunctive relief in the United States, which only is attributed to the person affected[22]. Thus, the injured party is the one that in principle can file the action, as is expressly set forth for instance in Ecuador[23]. In Costa Rica, even though the Amparo Law provides that the action can be filed by anybody (Article 33), the Constitutional Chamber has interpreted that it refers to anybody that has been injured in his constitutional rights[24]; and in case of an amparo action filed by a person different form the injured party, in order for the proceeding to continue, the latter must approve the filing. Otherwise, there would be lack of standing[25].

Some Amparo Laws, in order to guarantee the constitutional protection, set forth the possibility for other persons to act on behalf of the injured party, and file the action in his name. It can be any lawyer or a relative as established in Guatema-

---

21 Argentina (article 5: anybody on his behalf»); Bolivia (article 89: anybody in his name); Guatemala (art 85: any other person); Honduras Art. 19: any person); México (article 17: any other person in his name); Nicaragua (article 52: any inhabitant of the republic); Perú: (article 26: anybody in his favor); Venezuela (article 39: anybody acting on his behalf).

22 See Kevin SCHRODER et al, «Injunctions» in *Corpus Juris Secundum*, Vol. 43A, West 2004, p. 229.

23 See Hernán SALGADO PESANTES, *Manual de Justicia Constitucional Ecuatoriana*, Corporación Editora Nacional, Quito 2004, p. 81.

24 Decisión 93-90. See the reference in Rubén HERNÁNDEZ VALLE, *Derecho Procesal Constitucional*, Editorial Juricentro, San José, 2001, p. 234.

25 Decisión 5086-94. See the reference in Rubén HERNÁNDEZ VALLE, *Derecho Procesal Constitucional*, Editorial Juricentro,San José, 2001, p. 235.

la (Article 23), it can be anybody, as for instance in Colombia, where anyone can act on behalf of the injured party when the latter is in a situation of inability to assume his own defense (Article 10)[26]. What the Legislator wanted to assure in this case, was the possibility for an effective protection of the rights, for instance, in cases of physical violence infringed by parents regarding their children, in which case a neighbor is the person that can intervene filing an action for tutela. Otherwise, in such cases, the action for protection could not be filed, particularly because the parents are the legal representatives of their children.[27]

Also, in Ecuador, any spontaneous agent justifying the impossibility of the affected party to do so can file the action in his name, which nonetheless must be ratified within the three subsequent days (Art. 48). In Honduras the Amparo Law authorizes anyone to act on behalf of the injured party, without needing a power of attorney, in which case Article 44 provides that the criteria of the affected party shall prevail (Art. 44). In Uruguay (Art. 3) and Paraguay (Art 4), the Amparo Laws provides that in cases where the affected party, by himself of through his representative, cannot file the action, then anybody can do it on his behalf, being subjected the acting person to liability if initiating the amparo with fraud malice or frivolity (Article 4). In similar sense the Perúvian Code also set forth a general rule on the matter, that:

> **Article 41**. Any person can appear in court in the name of another person without procedural representation, when it is impossible for the latter to file the action on his own behalf, whether because his freedom is being concurrently affected, has a founded fear or threat, there is a situation of imminent danger or any other analogous cause. Once the affected party is in the possibility of acting, he must ratify the claim and the procedural activity followed by the person acting in fact.

Another aspect to be pointed out is that being the amparo suit a judicial process, some Latin American Amparo Laws impose the need for the parties in the amparo suit to act personally or through formal representatives, and in any case to formally appoint an attorney to assist them, as set forth in the Panamanian Judicial Code (Art. 22618). In Venezuela, according to what is provided in the Attorneys Law (*Ley de Abogados*), in all judicial processes the parties must be assisted by lawyers, which was also considered to be applicable to the amparo suit»[28]. Nonetheless, in more recent decisions, the Constitutional Chamber of the Supreme Tribunal, due to the non formalistic character of the amparo proceeding, has ruled that even though the injured party does not need to be assisted by an attorney when filing the action, it must appointed one in the course of the proceeding or the court must appoint one to act on his behalf.[29]

---

26 See Carlos Augusto PATIÑO BELTRÁN, *Acciones de tutela, cumplimiento, populares y de grupo*, Editorial Leyer, Bogotá 2000, p. 10i.

27 See Juan Carlos ESGUERRA PORTOCARRERO, *La protección constitucional del ciudadano*, Lexis, Bogotá 2005, p. 122.

28 See for instantes decisions of the First Court on Judicial Review of Administrative Action of November 18, 1993 (*Caso: Carlos G. Pérez*), *Revista de Derecho Público*, N° 55-56, Editorial Jurídica Venezolana, Caracas, 1993, pp. 353-354; of September 14, 1989, *Revista de Derecho Publico* N° 40, Editorial Jurídica Venezolana, Caracas, 1989, p. 105; and of March 4, 1993 and March 25, 1993, *Revista de Derecho Público*, N° 53-54, Editorial Jurídica Venezolana, Caracas, 1993, p. 258 v.

29 See decision of July, 19 2000 (Case: *Rubén Guerra*). See the reference and comments in Rafael CHAVERO, *El Nuevo Régimen del Amparo Constitucional en Venezuela*, Caracas, 2001, pp. 129-135.

3. Artificial persons: Standing at causam and ad processum

As mentioned before, artificial persons also have the right to file amparo actions when their constitutional rights have been violated. If it is true that «human rights» are of the exclusivity of human beings, they are constitutional rights that are not only attributed to human beings but to all other persons, with rights and obligations, like associations, foundations, corporations or companies. These artificial persons, like human beings, also have constitutional rights such as the right to non discrimination, the due process of law guaranties, the right to defense or property rights.

The action of tutela in the Constitution of Colombia can only be used for the protection of immediately applicable «fundamental rights», which in principle are individual rights, artificial persons, however, may file the action of tutela for the protection of rights such as that of petition (Article 22), due process and defense (Article 29) and review of judicial decisions (Article 31).

Thus, in case of violations of those rights, the entities have the needed standing *ad causam* to file the action of amparo, as is accepted in almost all Latin American Amparo laws[30]. Even in the Dominican Republic, were the amparo suit was admitted by the Supreme Court, even without constitutional or legal provision, precisely in a suit brought before the Court by a commercial company (Productos Avon SA)[31]. Of course, like all artificial persons, they must act by means of their directors or representatives as regulated in their by-laws (México, Article 8).

The main question regarding the artificial persons as injured parties with standing to file amparo suits refers to the possibility for the public artificial persons or entities that are part of the State general organization to file amparo suits.

It is clear that historically, the amparo suit, being a specific judicial mean for the protection of constitutional rights, was originally conceived as a constitutional guarantee for individuals or private persons facing public officers or public entities; that is, as a guarantee for protection against the State. So initially, it was unconceivable that a public entity could file an amparo against other public or private entity; but currently it is accepted in most Latin American Countries that public entities can be holders of constitutional rights and file actions of amparo for their protection, as is the case, for instance, of Argentina[32], Uruguay (where it is expressly regulated in the Amparo Law when referring to «public or private artificial persons») or Venezuela. Among the amparo cases decided in Argentina as a consequence of the emergency economic measures adopted by the Government in 2001, freezing all deposits in saving and current accounts in all the Banks, and converting them from US dollars into Argentinean devaluated pesos, one that must be mentioned is the *Case San Luis*, decided by the Supreme Court on March 5, 2003, in which not only the Court declared the unconstitutionality of the Executive but in the case, «ordered the Central Bank of the Argentinean Nation the reimbursement to the Province of San Luis of the amounts

---

30 In Ecuador, the standing of artificial persons to file an amparo action has been denied by Marco MORALES TOBAR in «La acción de amparo y su procedimiento en el Ecuador», *Estudios Constitucionales. Revista del Centro de Estudios Constitucionales*, Año 1, N° 1, Universidad de Talca, Santiago, Chile 2003, pp. 281-282.

31 See for instante, Juan DE LA ROSA, *El recurso de amparo, Estudio Comparativo*, Santo Domingo, 2001, p. 69.

32 See José Luis LAZZARINI, *El juicio de Amparo*, Ed. La Ley, Buenotes 1987, pp. 238-240; 266.

of North American dollars deposited, or its equivalent in pesos at the value in the day of payments, according to the rate of selling of the free market of exchange». The interesting aspect of the suit was that it was filed by the Province of San Luis against the National State and the Central Bank of the Argentinean Nation, that is, a Federated State (Provincia de San Luis) against the National State for the protection of the constitutional rights to property of the former[33].

In other countries, on the contrary, as in the case of Perú, the Code of Constitutional Procedure expressly declares the inadmissibility of the amparo suit when referring to «conflicts between public law internal entities. The constitutional conflicts between those entities, whether public powers of the State, organs of constitutional level of importance, local or regional governments, will be settled through the corresponding constitutional procedures» (Article 5,9). The Code substituted the Law 25011 provision that declared inadmissible actions of amparo, but «when filed by the public offices, including public enterprises, against public powers of the State and the organs created in the Constitution, against acts accomplished in the regular exercise of their functions» (Article 5,4, Code)[34].

Thus, and particularly because of the assumption of economic activities by public entities in the same level of activities as private persons, the amparo also protect them, when their constitutional rights are illegitimately harmed. In some countries, as is the case of México, it is expressly admitted for public corporations to file amparo suits but only when their economic interests (*intereses patrimoniales*) are harmed (Article 9). In no other way can a public entity in México, for instance a State, a Municipality or a public corporation file an amparo suit, because it would otherwise result in a conflict between authorities that cannot be resolved through this judicial action[35]. The Supreme Court has decided that «it is absurd to pretend that a public dependency of the Executive could invoke the violation of individual guaranties seeking protection against acts of other public entities also acting within the Executive branch of government»[36]. In another decision the Supreme Court has ruled that: «it is not possible to concede the extraordinary remedy of amparo to organs of the state against acts of the state itself manifested through other of its agencies, since this would establish a conflict of sovereign powers, whereas the amparo suit is concerned only with the complaint of private individual directed against an abuse of power»[37]

In some countries, discussions have arisen regarding the possibility of the exercise of the amparo suit between public entities in a federal system in order to

---

33 See the comments in Antonio María HERNÁNDEZ, *Las emergencias y el orden constitucional*, Universidad Nacional Autónoma de México, Rubinzal-Culsoni Editores, México, 2003, pp. 119 y ss.

34 See the comments regarding this provision in the repealed Law 2501, in Victor Julio ORCHETO VILLENA, Jurisdicción y procesos constitucionales, Editorial Rhodas, Lima, p. 169.

35 See Eduardo FERRER MAC-GREGOR, *La acción constitucional de amparo en México y España*, Editorial Porrúa, México 2002, pp. 244-245; Richard D. BAKER, *Judicial Review in México. A Study of the Amparo Suit*, University Press of Texas, Austin 1971 pp. 107-109.

36 See Tesis jurisprudencial 916, *Apéndice al Semanario Judicial de la Federación*, 1917-1988, Segunda Parte, Salas y Tesis Comunes, p. 1500. See the reference in Eduardo FERRER MAC-GREGOR, *La acción constitucional de amparo en México y España*, Editorial Porrúa, México 2002, p. 245, note 427.

37 See Tesis 450, III, pp. 868-868. See the reference in Richard D. BAKER, *Judicial Review in México. A Study of the Amparo Suit*, University Press of Texas, Austin 1971 p. 108.

protect the constitutional guarantee of political autonomy and self government. In Germany, for example, a constitutional complaint may be brought before the Federal Constitutional Tribunal by municipalities or groups of municipalities when alleging that their right to constitutional autonomy or self government, recognized in the Constitution (Article 28-2) has been violated by a federal legal provision. In the case of violations by a law of the *Lander,* such recourse shall be brought before the Constitutional Tribunal of the respective *Lander* (Article 93,1,4 of the Constitution). A similar situation, albeit debatable, is to be found in Austria with regard to the constitutional recourse. Whatever the case, of course it would not be an amparo for the protection of fundamental rights, but rather of a specific constitutional guarantee of the autonomy of local entities.

In the case of México, Article 103, III and 107 of the Constitution set forth the amparo suit in case of controversies arisen «because laws or acts of federal authority infringe or restrict the States sovereignty»; provision that could be understood as establishing the action of amparo for the protection of the distribution of power between the federal and state level of the State, that is, for the protection of the federated States constitutional autonomy regarding the invasions from the federal State. Nonetheless, the Supreme Court has denied such possibility arguing that:

> «the amparo suit was established in Article 103 of the Constitution not for the protection of all the constitutional text, but for the protection of individual guarantees; and what is established in Section III must be understood in the sense that a federal law can only be challenged in the amparo suit when it invades or restricts the sovereignty of the States, when there is an affected individual which in a concrete case claims against the violation of his constitutional guarantees»[38].

The same discussion has been raised in Venezuela, also a federal state, regarding the guarantee of the political autonomy of the States and Municipalities, recognized and guaranteed in the Constitution, in order to determine if their violation could give rise to constitutional protection through an action of amparo. In this sense, in 1997 several Municipalities brought an action of unconstitutionality against a national statute limiting the income that higher-level state and municipal officials could have; action to which the claimants joined an action of amparo for the protection of the constitutional autonomy impaired by the Law. In the end the constitutional protection was denied by the then Supreme Court of Justice, in a decision of October 2, 1997 in which the Court ruled that if «it is undoubted that artificial persons, and consequently, political-territorial entities can be holders of the majority of rights enshrined in the Constitution, as for instance, the rights to defense, non discrimination of property» they are also «holders of public powers and prerogatives, public functions exclusively directed to obtain constitutional goals»; and that if it is true that those prerogatives are also guarantied in the Constitution, these institutional guaranty cannot be equivalent to the guaranty of constitutional rights; thus not admitting the amparo as a means for protection of such guaranties. Additionally, the Court ruled that being the amparo an extraordinary action that «can only be filed when no other efficient means for constitutional protection exists», due to the fact that in Venezuela the Constitution sets forth a series of recourses

---

38 See Tesis jurisprudencial 389, *Apéndice al Semanario Judicial de la Federación*, 1917-1995, Tribunal Pleno, p. 362. See the reference in Eduardo FERRER MAC-GREGOR, *La acción constitucional de amparo en México y España*, Editorial Porrúa, México 2002, p. 246, note 425.

directed to impede the miss knowledge or invasion of public prerogatives between territorial entities, the amparo cannot be used for those purpose. The Court concluded affirming that:

> «the territorial entities, as artificial persons, can have standing to sue in amparo; but only regarding the protection in strict sense of constitutional rights and guaranties, thus excluding from the amparo the protection of their prerogatives and powers, as well as to resolve the conflicts among those entities between themselves or regarding other Public Power entities».[39]

The Constitutional Chamber latter, in a decision N° 1595 of November 2000, confirmed the ruling rejecting an amparo action, this time filed by a State of the Federation against the Ministry of Finance which, it was alleged, affected their financial autonomy, arguing as follows:

> «The object of the amparo is the reinforced protection of constitutional rights and guaranties, which comprises the rights enumerated in the Constitution, some of which are outside of Title III (see for instance articles 143,260 and 317 of the Constitution), as well as those set forth in international treaties on human rights ratified by the Republic, and any other inherent to human persons.
>
> The aforementioned does not imply to restrict the notion of constitutional rights and guaranties only to the rights and guaranties of natural persons, because also artificial persons are holders of fundamental rights, Even the public law artificial persons can be holders of rights.
>
> But what has been said allows to conclude that the political-territorial entities as the States and the Municipalities, can only file amparo suits for the protection of the rights and liberties they can be holders of, as the right to due process, or the right to equality or to the retroactivity of the law. Conversely, they cannot file an amparo in order to protect the autonomy the Constitution recognized to them or the powers or competencies derived from the latter.
>
> The autonomy of a public entity only enjoys protection through amparo when the Constitution recognizes it as a concretion of one funded fundamental right, like the universities autonomy regarding the right to education (Article 109 of the Constitution).
>
> In the concrete case, the claimants have not invoked a constitutional right of the States which could have been violated, but the autonomy the Constitution assures, and in particular, «the guaranty of the financial autonomy regulated in Articles 159; 164, section 3; and 167, sections 4 and 6 of the Constitution».
>
> Nonetheless, under the concept of constitutional guaranty there cannot be submitted contents completely strange to the range of constitutionally protected public freedoms, as is pretended, due to the fact that the guarantee is closely related with the right. The guarantee can be understood as the constitutional reception of the rights or as the existing mechanisms for its protection. Whether in one or other sense the guarantee is consubstantial to the right, thus it is not adequate to use the concept of guarantee to expand the amparo's scope of protection, including in it any power or competency constitutionally

[39] See the reference and comments in Rafael CHAVERO, *El Nuevo Régimen del Amparo Constitucional en Venezuela*, Caracas, 2001, pp. 122- 123.

guaranteed. The latter would conduct to the denaturalization of the amparo, which would lose its specificity and convert it in a mean for the protection of all the Constitution»[40].

The restrictive criteria has been also followed by the Constitucional Chamber of Costa Rica, arguing that «the object and matter of the amparo is not to guarantee in an abstract way the enforcement of the Constitution, but the threats and violations of the enjoyment of fundamental rights of persons...and in the case examined that situation is not present». The case referred to an alleged violation of the official procedures followed to facilitate the operation of a cellular mobile network by a company, concluding the Chamber that «the violation of Constitutional norms cannot be demanded through an amparo action»[41].

On the other hand, in systems such as Brazil's, where the *mandado de segurança* can only be brought against the State and not against individuals, it is argued that the State itself or its agencies cannot file the suit[42].

III. STANDING AND THE PROTECTION OF COLLECTIVE AND IFFUSE CONSTITUTIONAL RIGHTS

Constitutional rights are commonly identified with individual or civil rights that corresponds to individuals who enjoy them in a personalized way. That is why the amparo action, as a judicial mean for the protection of constitutional rights, has also been traditionally characterized as a personal action that can only be brought before the competent courts by the particular person holder of the rights or his representatives. Some legislations like the Brazilian one, regarding the *mandado de securança* set forth that in case of rights threatened or violated covering a few persons, any of them can file the action (Article 1,2). In Costa Rica, also, regarding the constitutional right to rectification and response in cases of offenses, the Constitutional Jurisdiction Law provides that when the offended are more than one person, any of them can file the action; and in cases in which the offended could be identified with a group or an organized collectivity, the standing to sue must be exercised by their authorized representative (Article 67).

Nonetheless, some rights are collective by nature in the sense that they correspond to a group more or less defined of persons, in which case its violations affects not only the right of each of the individuals who enjoy them, but also the group of persons or collectivity to which the individuals belongs. In these cases, the amparo action can also be filed by the group or association of persons representing their associates, even if those associations do not have the formal character of an artificial person. That is why, for instance, the Amparo Law of Paraguay, when defining standing to sue in matters of amparo, additionally to physical or artificial persons, refers to political parties duly registered, entities with guild or professional identities and societies or associations that without being given the character of

---

40 Case *State Mérida and other v. Ministry of Finances*, in *Revista de Derecho Público*, N° 84, Editorial Jurídica venezolana, Caracas, pp 315 ff.

41 See Vote 285-90. See the reference in Rubén HERNÁNDEZ VALLE, *Derecho Procesal Constitucional*, Editorial Juricentro, San José 2001, p. 235.

42 See Celso AGRÍCOLA BARBI, *Do mandado de Seguranca*, Editora Forense, Río de Janeiro, 1993, pp. 68 ff; José Luis LAZZARINI, *El Juico de Amparo*, Editorial La Ley, Buenos Aires, 1987, pp. 267-268.

artificial persons, according to their by-laws their goals are not contrary to public good (*bien público*) (Art. 5). In Argentina, the Amparo Law also provides the standing to file amparo actions by these associations that without being formally artificial persons can justify, according to their by-laws that they are not against «public or collective interest» (*bien público*) (Article 5).

In Venezuela, the 1999 Constitution expressly sets forth the constitutional right of everybody to have access to justice, not only to seek for the enforcement of specific personal rights and interests, but even to enforce «collective or diffuse interests» (Art. 26); which opened the possibility of amparo actions that can be filed on behalf of collective or diffuse interest.

The Constitutional Chamber of the Supreme Tribunal of Justice in a decision N° 656 of May 5, 2001 (Case: *Defensor del Pueblo vs. Comisión Legislativa Nacional*, defined the diffuse and the collective interests or rights, as concepts established not for the protection of a number of individuals that can be considered as representing the entire or an important part of a society, which are affected on their constitutional rights and guarantees destined to protect the public welfare by an attack to their quality of life. The Constitutional Chamber defined the collective rights, when the «damage is specifically located in a groups that can be determined as such, even if it is not quantifiable or individualized, as would be that case of the inhabitants of an area of the country affected by an illegal construction that creates problems with the public services in the area». These focused specific interests are the collective ones, which «refer to a determined and identified sector of the population (even though not quantified), individually, within the group there exists or might exist a legal bond uniting them. This is the case of damages to professional groups, to groups of neighbors, to labor unions, to the inhabitants of a certain area, etc.»

In a different sense, regarding the diffuse rights, they affect the population as a whole because they are intended to assure the people, in a general way, an acceptable quality of life (basic conditions of existence). When they are affected, the quality of life of the entire community or society in its different scopes diminishes, and an interest arises in each member of that community and of the other components of society, in preventing that situation to occur, and that it be repaired if that situation already occurred. Thus, the Constitutional Chamber has ruled, in these cases:

> «it is a diffuse interest (that originates rights), since it spread among all the individuals of a society, even though from time to time the damage to the quality of life may be limited to groups that are able to be individualized as sectors that suffer as social entities. It can be the case of the inhabitants of a given sector or people pertaining to a same category, or the member of professional groups, etc. Nevertheless, those affected shall be no specified individuals, but a totality or groups of individuals or corporations, since the damaged goods are not susceptible of exclusive appropriation by one subject ...
>
> Despite the concept that rules the diffuse interest or right as part of the defense of the citizenship, it is aimed at satisfying social or collective needs, before the personal ones. Since the damage is general (to the population or broad parts of it), the diffuse right or interest unites individuals who do not know each other, who individually lack of connection or legal relations among them, who at the beginning are undetermined, but united only because of the

> same situation of damage or danger they are involved in as members of a society and due to the right that arises in everyone to the protection of their quality of life, set forth in the Constitution...
>
> The common damage to the quality of life, which concerns any component of population or society as such, despite the legal relations they may have with other of these undetermined members, is the content of the diffuse right or interest.

In this sense, damages to the environment or to the consumers, for example, even in the case that they occur in a certain place, have expansive effects that harm the inhabitants of large sectors of the country and even the world, and respond to the undetermined obligation of protecting the environment or the consumers. Thus according to the doctrine of the Constitutional Chamber,

> The diffuse interests are the wider ones, where the damaged good is the most general good, since it concerns the entire population and, contrary to the collective interests or rights, they arise from an obligation of uncertain object; while in the collective ones, the obligation may be concrete, yet not demandable by individualized persons.
>
> Consumers are all the inhabitants of the country. The damage to them as such responds to a *supra* individual or *supra* personal right, and to an uncertain obligation in favor of them, from those managing goods and services. Their quality of life diminishes, whether they realize it or not, since many massive communicational mechanisms shall annul or alter the conscience of the damage. Their interest, or the one of those affected, for example, due to the damages to the environment, is diffuse and so is the right raised to preventing or impeding the damage.
>
> The interest of the neighbors, whose neighborhood is worsened in its public services by a construction, for example, responds as well to a supra personal legal right, yet it can be determined, located in specific groups, and it is the interest that allows a collective action. That is the collective interest. It gives origin to collective rights and may refer to a certain legal object.
>
> The truth in both cases (diffuse and collective interest) is that the damage is suffered by the social group equally, even if some members do not consider themselves damaged, since they consent the damage. This concept differs from the personal damage directed to a personal legal right. This difference does not impede the existence of mixed damages, the same fact damaging a personal legal right and a supra individual one».[43]

Now, regarding the standing to bring before courts action for amparo seeking the protection of collective and diffuse constitutional rights, the same Constitutional Chamber of the Supreme Court, for instance, has admitted the filing of an action of *amparo* to protect political electoral rights filed by one voter exercising his own right, even having granted precautionary measures with *erga omnes* effects «to both individuals and corporations who have brought to suit the constitutional protection, and to all voters as a group»[44].

---

43 See decision of the Constitutional Chamber N° 656 of 06-05-01 (Case: *Defensor del Pueblo vs. Comisión Legislativa Nacional*.

44 Decision of the Constitutional Chamber N° 483 of 05-29-2000 (Case: «*Queremos Elegir*» *y otros*), *Revista de Derecho Público*, N° 82, 2000, Editorial Jurídica Venezolana, pp. 489-491. In the same sense, decision of the same Chamber N° 714 of 13-07-2000 (Case: *APRUM*).

The Constitutional Chamber, with this same orientation, has interpreted Article 26 of the Constitution in a wide way regarding the action of *amparo* of collective or diffuse interests by stating that:

> «Consequently, any individual with legal capacity to bring suit, who is going to impede a damage to the population or parts of it where he belongs to, is entitled to bring to suit grounded in diffuse or collective interests, and where he had suffered personal damages, he shall claim for himself (jointly) the compensation of such. This interpretation, grounded in Article 26, extends the standing to companies, corporations, foundations, chambers, unions and other collective entities, whose object is the defense of the society, as long as they act within the boundaries of their corporate object, aimed at protecting the interests of their members regarding their object. Article 102 of the Organic Law of Urban Planning follows this orientation.
>
> In the Venezuelan legislation, currently, an individual shall not bring to suit a compensation for the damaged collectivity, when claiming diffuse interests. Such claim corresponds to entities such as the Public Prosecutor or the Defender of the People.
>
> When the damages harm groups of individuals that are legally bound or pertain to the same activity, the action grounded in collective interests, whose purpose is the same as the one of the diffuse interests, shall be brought to suit by the corporations that gather the damaged sectors or groups and even by any member of that sector or group as long as he acts in defense of that social segment...
>
> Due to the foregoing, it is not necessary for whoever brings a suit grounded on diffuse or collective interests, if it is a diffuse one, to have a bond previously established with the offender. It is necessary that he acts as a member of the society, or its general categories (consumers, users, etc.), and invokes his right or interest shared with the citizenship, since he participates with them in the damaged factual situation because of the infringement or detriment of the fundamental rights concerning the collectivity, which generates a common subjective right that despite being indivisible, may be enforced by anyone in the infringed situation, since the legal order acknowledges those rights in Article 26 of the Constitution. It is a legal interest guaranteed in the Constitution. It cannot be appropriated individually and exclusively by any individual, since anyone damaged is able to enforce it, unless it is restricted by law, which can be claimed to whoever owes the obligation of certain object.
>
> Even though it is a general right or interest enjoyed by the plaintiff, which allows various plaintiffs, he himself shall be threatened, shall have suffered the damage or shall be suffering it as a part of the citizenship, whereby whoever is not residing in the country, or is not damaged shall lack of standing; this situation separates these actions from the popular ones.
>
> Whoever brings suit based on collective rights or interests, shall do it in his condition of member of the group or sector damaged, therefore, he suffers the damage jointly with others, whereby he assumes an interest of his own and gives him or her the right to claim the end of the damage for himself and the others, with whom shares the right or interest. It shall be a group or sector not individualized, otherwise, it would be a concrete party.

In both cases, if the action is admitted, a legal benefit will arise in favor of the plaintiff and his common interest with the society or collectivity of protecting it, maintaining the quality of life. The defense of society's interests is guaranteed.

The plaintiff is given the subjective right to react against the damaging act or concrete threat, caused by the offender's violation of the fundamental rights of the society in general.

Whoever is entitled to act shall always plea for an actual interest, which does not terminate for the society in one single process.

If an individual brings suit grounding his action in diffuse rights or interests, yet the judge considers that it is about them, he shall subpoena the Defender of the People or the entities established by law in particular subjects, and shall notify through an edict all the parties in interest, whether there are processes in which the law excludes and grants representation to other individuals. All these legitimate interested parties shall intervene as third party claimants, if the judge admits them as such taking into consideration the existence of diffuse rights and interests.[45]

The Constitutional Chamber has also determined the general conditions of standing in these cases of collective or diffuse rights, in a decision N° 1948 of February 17, 2000 (Case: *William O. Ojeda O. vs. Consejo Nacional Electoral*), in which it ruled that is necessary that the following elements be combined:

«1. That the plaintiff sues based not only on his personal right or interest, but also on a common or collective right or interest.

2. That the reason of the claim (or the action of amparo filed) be the general damage to the quality of life of all the inhabitants of the country or parts of it, since the legal situation of all the member of the society or its groups has been damaged when their common quality of life was worsened.

3. That the damaged goods not be susceptible of exclusive appropriation by one subject (as the plaintiff).

4. That it concern an indivisible right or interest that involves the entire population of the country or a group of it.

5. That a bond exists, even if it is not a legal one, between whoever demands in general interest of the society or a part of it (social common interest), raised from the damage or danger in which collectivity is (as such). This damage or danger and the possibility of it happening are known by the judge due to common knowledge.

6. That a necessity of satisfying social or collective interests exist, before the individual ones.

7. That a person is obliged to an undetermined obligation, the enforcement of which is general».[46]

---

45 See decision of the Constitutional Chamber N° 656 of 06-05-2001, Case: *Defensor del Pueblo vs. Comisión Legislativa Nacional.*

46 Decision N° 1.048 of the Constitutional Chamber dated 02-17-00, Case: *William Ojeda vs. Consejo Nacional Electoral.*

One of the most important issues regarding these collective and diffuse amparo actions relates to the standing of the «representative». The Constitutional Chamber, on the matter, has ruled the following criteria:

> «Any person capable in procedure that tends to impede harms to the population or sectors of it to which he appertains, can file actions in defense of diffuse or collective interest...This interpretation founded in Article 26 (of the Constitution), extend standing to the associations, societies, foundations, chambers, trade unions and other collective entities, devoted to defend society, provided they act within the limits of their societal goals referred to watch for the interest of their members».

> The Chamber added that:

> «Those who file actions regarding the defense of diffuse interest do not need to have any previously established relation with the offender, but has to act as a member of society, or of its general categories (consumers, users, etc.) and has to invoke his right or interest shared with the population's, because he participates with all regarding the harmed factual situation due to the noncompliance of the diminution of fundamental rights of everybody, which give birth to a communal subjective right, that although indivisible, is actionable by any one place within the infringed situation»[47].

But in spite of all the aforementioned progressive decisions regarding the protection of collective and diffuse rights, like the political ones, in a recent decision dated November 21, 2005, the Constitutional Chamber has set back, and in the case, originated by a claim filed by the director of a political association named «Un Solo Pueblo» against the threat of violations of the political rights of the aforesaid political party and of all the other supporters of the calling of a recall referendum regarding the President of the Republic, ruled that:

> «The action of amparo was filed for the protection of constitutional rights of an undetermined number of persons, whose identity was not indicated in the filing document, in which they are not included as claimants.

> It is the criteria of this Chamber, those that could result directly affected in their constitutional rights and guaranties by the alleged threat attributed to the Ministry of Defense and the General Commanders of the Army and the National Guard are, precisely, the persons that are members or supporters of «Un solo Pueblo», or those who prove they are part of one of the groups that promoted the recall referendum; in which case they would have standing to bring before the constitutional judge, by themselves or through representatives, seeking the reestablishment of the infringed juridical situation or impeding the realization of the threat, because the *legitimatio ad causam* exists in each one of them, not precisely as constitutionally harmed of aggrieved.

> Due to the foregoing, the Chamber considers that Mr. William Ojeda, who said he acted as Director of the political association called «Un Sólo Pueblo»,

---

47 Decisión of the Constitutional Chamber of June 30, 2000 (Case *Defensoría del Pueblo*). See the reference and comments in Rafael CHAVERO, *El Nuevo Régimen del Amparo Constitucional en Venezuela*, Caracas, 2001, pp. 110-114.

quality that he furthermore has not demonstrated, lacks of the necessary standing to seek for constitutional amparo of the constitutional rights set forth in Articles 19, 21 and 68 of the Constitution regarding the members, supporters and participants of the mentioned political association as well as the political coalition that proposed the recall referendum of the President of the Republic, and consequently, this Chamber declares the inadmissibility of the amparo action filed»[48].

Besides the foregoing inconsistencies in judicial doctrine, «Collective suits» of amparo for the protection of diffuse rights have been expressly constitutionalized in Argentina, where the Constitution provides in Article 43, that the amparo suit can be filed by «the affected party, the People's Defendant and the registered associations that tend to those goals»:

> Against any form of discrimination and regarding the rights for the protection of environment, the free competition, the user and the consumer, as well as the rights of collective general incidence, the affected party, the People's Defendant and the registered associations that tend to those goals, could file this action.

Regarding the associations that can file the collective amparo suits, the Supreme Court of Argentina has also considered that they do not require formal registration[49].

Three specific collective actions result from this article: amparo against any form of discrimination; amparo for the protection of the environment; and amparo for the protection of free competitions, the user and the consumer. That is why regarding discrimination, the object of this amparo is not a discrimination regarding a particular individual but a group of persons between which a nexus or common trend exists which originates the discrimination.[50]

On the other hand, regarding the protection of the environment, it was formalized the trend that began to be consolidated after a 1983 case in which an amparo was filed for the protection of the ecologic equilibrium regarding the protection of dolphins. The Supreme Court accepted in that case, the possibility for anybody individually or in representation of his family, to file an amparo action when pursuing the maintenance of the ecological equilibrium, due to the right any human being has to protect his habitat[51].

In Perú, Article 40 of the Constitutional Procedure Code authorizes any person to file the amparo suit «in cases referred to threats or violation of environmental rights or other diffuse rights that enjoy constitutional recognition, as well as the non lucrative entities whose goals are the defense of such rights».

---

48 See Case: *William Ojeda vs. Ministro de la Defensa y los Comandantes Generales del Ejercito y de la Guardia Nacional*, in *Revista de Derecho Público*, N° 104, Editorial Jurídica Venezolana, Caracas, 2005.

49 Decisions 320:690, Case: *Asociación Grandes Usuarios and Decision 323:1339*, Asociación Benghalensis. See the referentes in Joaquín Brage Camazano, *La jurisdicción constitucional de la libertad*, Editorial Porrúa, México 2005, pp. 92-93.

50 See Joaquín BRAGE CAMAZANO, *La jurisdicción constitucional de la libertad*, Editorial Po-rrúa, México 2005, p. 94.

51 See Alí Joaquín SALGADO, *Juicio de amparo y acción de inconstitucionalidad*, Astrea Buenos Aires 1987, pp. 81-89.

In Brazil, Article 5, LXIII of the Constitution sets forth the *mandado de securanca colectivo* , as a sort of *mandado de seguranca* for the protection of actual rights not protected by habeas-corpus or habeas-data, when the responsible of the illegality or abuse of power is a public authority or an agent of a artificial person acting in exercise of public power attributions, but that can be filed by: a) political parties with representation in national Congress, b) trade unions, class institutions or associations legally established and functioning at least for one year in defense of the interests of its members. This *mandado de securanca* is thus not intended to protect individual rights, but diffuse or collective rights.

It must also be mentioned, that since 1985 a «collective civil action» has been developed in Brazil, with similar trends as the Class Actions of the United States, very widely used for the protection of group rights, like consumers though limiting the standing to the public entities (national, state and municipal) and to associations[52].

In Ecuador, Article 48 of the Amparo Law also authorizes any person, natural or artificial to file the amparo action, «when it is a matter of protection of the environment». Thus, any person, including the indigenous communities through their representative, can file the amparo suit[53]

It also must be mentioned the case of Costa Rica, where the collective amparo has also been admitted in matters of environment by the Constitutional Chamber of the Supreme Court. Article 50 of the Constitution, in effect, provides that «any person has the right to a healthy and ecologically equilibrated environment»; thus, it has standing to denounce the acts which infringe that right and to claim the reparation of the harm caused». Even though not expressly referring to the amparo suit, the Constitutional Chamber did refer to a similar norm of the previous Constitution (Article 89) which gave standing to anybody «to file amparo actions for the defense of the right to the conservation of the natural resources of the country. Even tough it does not exist a direct and clear suit for the claimant as in the concrete case of the State against an individual, all inhabitants, regarding the violations of Article 89 of the Constitution, suffer a prejudice in the same proportion as if it where a direct harm, thus it is accepted that an interest exists in his favor that authorizes him to file an action for the protection of such right to maintain the natural equilibrium of the ecosystem»[54].

Even in the Dominican Republic, where no constitutional provision exists regarding the amparo suit, the Supreme Court not only has created it but, accordingly, the courts have admitted that any person legally capable and with interest in the general enforcement of collective human rights, as the right to education, can file an action for amparo due that the matter is not only and exclusively a private one[55].

---

[52] See Antonio GIDI, «Acciones de grupo y «amparo colectivo» en Brasil. La protección de derechos difusos, colectivos e individuales homogéneos», in Eduardo FERRER MAC-GREGOR (Coordinator), *Derecho Procesal Constitucional*, Colegio de Secretarios de la Suprema Corte de Justicia de la Nación, Editorial Porrúa, Tomo III, México 2003, pp. 2.538 ff.

[53] Hernán SALGADO PESANTES, *Manual de Justicia Constitucional Ecuatoriana,* Corporación Editora Nacional, Quito 2004, p. 76.

[54] Decision 1700-03. See the reference Rubén HERNÁNDEZ VALLE, *Derecho Procesal Constitucional,* Editorial Juricentro, San José, 2001, pp. 239-240.

[55] See decisión 406-2 of June 21, 2001, First Instante Court of San Pedro Macoris. See the reference in Miguel A. VALERA MONTERO, *Hacia un Nuevo concepto de constitucionalismo,* Santo Domingo, 2006, pp. 388-389.

In México, contrary to the current tendency of other countries, the amparo suit continues to have an essential individual character, based in the personal and direct interest[56]. The only cases in which the amparo in certain way protects collective interest are those related to the agrarian amparo, for the protection of peasants and of collective agrarian land owners[57].

In Colombia, the general principle is also that the action for tutela is a personal and private action, that can only be filed by the holder of the individual right protected by the constitutional norm. Thus it is not a public or popular action. The tutela action can only be exercised in person, seeking the protection of a personal, fundamental right, of constitutional rank of the person on whose behalf it is filed[58]. That is why, Article 6,3 of the Tutela Law expressly provides that the action of tutela is inadmissible when the rights seeking to be protected are «collective rights, as the right to peace and others referred to in Article 88 of the Constitution», particularly because for that purposes a special judicial means for protection is established called «popular actions». Article 6,3 of the Tutela Law added that the foregoing will not prevent that the holder of rights threatened to be violated or that have been violated can file a tutela action in situations compromising collective rights and interest and of his own threatened or violated rights, when it is a matter to prevent an irremediable harm».

According to Article 88 of the Constitution, the diffuse or «collective» rights are protected not by the tutela action, but by means of the «popular actions» or the group actions. The former are those established in the Constitution for the protection of rights and interests related to public property, public space, public security and health, administrative morale, environment, economic free competition and others of similar nature. All these are diffuse rights, and for its protections, the law 472 of 1998 has regulated these popular actions.

This statute also regulates other sort of actions, for the protection of rights in cases of harms suffered by a plural number of persons. These group actions are similar to the class actions of North American Law.

Regarding the popular actions, they can be filed by any person, the Non Governmental Organizations, the Popular or Civic Organizations, the public entities with control functions, when the harm or threat is not initiated by their activities, the General Prosecutor, the Peoples 'Defendant and the District and Municipal prosecutors, and the mayors and public officers that because of their functions they must defend and protect the abovementioned rights (Art. 12).

Regarding the group actions set forth for the protection of a plurality of persons in cases of suffering harm in their rights in a collective way, the Law 472 of 1998 establishes these actions basically with indemnizatory purposes, and they can only be filed by 20 individuals, acting all of them on their own behalf. Thus, these are not actions directed to protect the whole population or collectivity, but only a plurality of persons that have the same rights, and seek for its protection.

---

56 See Eduardo FERRER MAC-GREGOR, *Juicio de amparo e interés legítimo: la tutela de los derechos difusos y colectivos*, Editorial Porrúa, México 2003, p. 56.

57 See Eduardo FERRER MAC-GREGOR, *La acción constitucional de amparo en México y España*, Editorial Porrúa, México 2002, p. 233 ff.

58 Juan Carlos EZQUERRA PORTOCARRERO, *La protección constitucional del ciudadano*, Lexis, Bogotá, 2005, p. 121.

These group actions have some similarities with the class actions regulated in Rule 23 of the Federal Rules of Civil Procedure filed for the protection of civil rights, that is, the «civil rights class actions». According to that Rule, in cases of a class of persons who have question of law or fact common to the class, but have so numerous members that joining all of them would be an impracticable task, then the action can be filed by one or more of its members as representative plaintiff parties on behalf of all, provided that the claims of the representative parties are typical of the claims of the class and that such representatives parties will fairly and adequately protect the interests of the class. (Rule 23, Class Actions, a).

The class actions have been applied in cases of violation of civil rights, particularly regarding to the right of non discrimination. It was the case decided by the Supreme Court *Zablocki, Milwaukee County Clerk v. Redhail* case of January 18, 1978, 434 U.S. 374; 98 S. Ct. 673; 54 L. Ed. 2d 618, as a result of a class action brought before a federal court under 42 U.S.C.S. § 1983, by Wisconsin residents holding that the marriage prohibition set forth in Wisconsin State § 245.10 (1973) violated the equal protection clause, U.S. Const. amend. XIV. According to that statute, Wisconsin residents were prevented from marrying if they were behind in their child support obligations or if the children to whom they were obligated were likely to become public charges. The Court found that the statute violated equal protection in that it directly and substantially interfered with the fundamental right to marry without being closely tailored to effectuate the state's interests.

Another Supreme Court decision, *Lau et al. v. Nichols et al.*, dated January 21, 1974, 414 U.S. 563; 94 S. Ct. 786; 39 L. Ed. 2d 1; 1974 also decided in favor of a class, on discrimination violations. In the case, non-English speaking students of Chinese ancestry brought a class suit in a federal court of California against officials of the San Francisco Unified School District, seeking relief against alleged unequal educational opportunities resulting from the officials' failure to establish a program to rectify the students' language problem. The Supreme Court eventually held that the school district, which received federal financial assistance, violated dispositions that ban discrimination based on race, color, or national origin in any program or activity receiving federal financial assistance, and furthermore violated the implementing regulations of the Department of Health, Education, and Welfare, by failing to establish a program to deal with the complaining students' language problem.

IV. THE PEOPLES' DEFENDANT STANDING ON THE AMPARO SUIT

As the amparo suit has been instituted in Latin America as a specific judicial means for the protection of constitutional rights, another general tendency in Latin American constitutionalism is for the creation in the Constitution or Legislation (Costa Rica) of a specific autonomous State entity or body with the objective of protecting and seeking for the protection of constitutional rights, called the Defendant of the People (People's Defendant) or of Human Rights.

In some cases, the institution follows in general lines the classical Scandinavian Ombudsman, initially conceived as a parliamentary independent entity for the protection of citizens' rights regarding Public Administration. In other Latin American countries, it is more conceived as an autonomous institution, from both parliament and the Executive as well as from the Judicial Power.

In the first group, closer to the European model, the Argentinean Constitution in the chapter referred to the Legislative Power (Art. 86) establishes the Defendant of the People for the protection of human rights regarding Public Administration. It is conceived as an independent entity in the scope of the Congress, acting with functional autonomy and without receiving instructions from any authority. Its mission is the defense and protection of human rights guaranteed in the Constitutions and statues against Public Administration facts, acts or omissions, and to control the exercise of administrative functions. The Peoples defendant is nominated by the Congress, by 2/3 of the votes of the members present in the voting and can only be removed in the same way.

In the Constitution of Paraguay, the Peoples' Defendant is a parliamentary commissioner for the protection of human rights, for the channeling of popular claims and for the protection of communitarian interests, without having any judicial or executive functions (Art. 276). It is elected by the Chamber of Representatives, from a proposal by the Senate, with the vote of 2/3 of its members.

In Guatemala, the Constitution establishes a Procurator on Human Rights as a parliamentary commissioner, elected by Congress from a proposal made by a Commission on Human Rights integrated by representatives of the political parties in Congress. His mission is to defend human rights and to supervise Public Administration (Article 274). The Law on amparo in Guatemala gives the Public Prosecutor and the Procurator on Human Rights sufficient standing to file amparo actions «for the defense of the interests assigned to them» (Article 25).

In the majority of the Latin American Constitutions, the Peoples' defendant or the Procurator for the Defense of Human Rights are created without any specific reference to Public Administration, thus they face all State organs, for the protection of human rights. This is the case of Colombia, Ecuador and El Salvador, even though in the last two countries, it is regulated attached to the Public Prosecutor's Office (*Ministerio Público*).

In Colombia, the Peoples' Defendant, elected by the representative Chamber of Congress from a proposal formulated by the president of the Republic, is created as part of the Public Prosecutor Office (Article 281), with the specific mission of watching for the promotion, exercise and divulgation of human rights. Within its powers is to invoke the right to habeas corpus and to file actions for tutela, without prejudice of the interested party rights. The Tutela Law also authorizes the Peoples' Defendant to file these actions on behalf of anyone when asked to do so, in cases of the person being in a non protective situation (Articles 10 and 46), or regarding Colombians residing outside the country (Article 51). In such cases, the Peoples' Defendant will be considered party in the process together with the injured party (Article 47).

In El Salvador, the Procurator for the Defense of Human Rights in part of the Public Ministry, together with the Public Prosecutor and the Attorney General of the Republic (Art. 191), all elected by the Legislative Assembly by a 2/3 vote of its members. Within its functions are to watch for the respect and guarantee of human rights and to promote judicial actions for their protection (Article 194).

Other countries have a Peoples Defendant as a complete independent and autonomous institution regarding the classical branches of government, as is the case of Ecuador, with the Peoples' Defendant, also elected by the Congress with the vote of the 2/3 of its members (Article 96). Among its functions are to defend and encourage the respect of the fundamental constitutional rights, to watch for the quality of the public services and to promote and support the habeas corpus and amparo actions at the person's request. The Law regulating the matter in Ecuador also authorizes the Peoples' defendant to file habeas corpus and amparo actions (Articles 33 and 48).

In México, the Constitution has also established that Congress and the state legislatures must create entities for the protection on human rights, receiving grievances regarding administrative acts or omissions of any authority except the judicial power, that violate such rights. At the national level, the entity is named National Commission on Human Rights. Nonetheless, the Amparo Law authorizes the Federal Public Prosecutor to file action for amparo in criminal and family cases, but not in civil or commercial cases (Article 5, 1,IV),

In Bolivia, the Constitution also creates the Peoples' Defendant for the purpose of watching for the enforcement and respect of the persons' rights and guarantees regarding administrative activities on all the public sector, as for the defense, promotion and divulgation of human rights (Article 127). The Peoples defendant does not receive instructions from the public powers and is elected by Congress (Article 128). Among its functions are to file the actions of amparo and habeas corpus without needing any power of attorney (Article 129).

In Perú, the Constitution also creates the Peopels' Defendant Office as an autonomous organ, the head of which is elected by Congress also with 2/3 votes of its members (article 162), for the purpose of defending persons and community human and fundamental rights, to supervise for the accomplishment of public administration duties and the rendering of public services to the people. The Constitutional Procedure Code authorizes the People' Defendant, in exercising its competencies, to file amparo actions (Article 40).

In Nicaragua the Constitution only establishes that the National Assembly will appoint the Procurator for the defense of Human Rights (Article 138,30).

The tendency to create an independent and autonomous organ of the State for the protection of human rights has reached the extreme regulation in the 1999 Venezuelan Constitution, which establishes a *penta* separation of powers, between the Legislative, Executive, Judicial, Electoral and Citizens branches of government, creating within the Citizens Power the Peoples' Defendant. Also the Public Prosecutor Office and the General Comptroller Office form part of the Citizens Power (Article 134).

The Peoples' Defendant is created for the promotion, defense and supervision of the rights and guaranties set forth in the Constitution and in the international treaties on human rights, as well as for the citizens' legitimate, collective and diffuse interests (Article 281). In particular, according to Article 281 of the Constitution, it also has among its functions to watch for the functioning of public services power and to promote and protect the peoples' legitimate, collective and diffuse rights and interests against arbitrariness or deviation of power in the rendering of such services, being authorized to file the necessary actions to ask for the compensation of the damages caused from the malfunctioning of public services. It also has among its functions, the possibility of filing actions of amparo and habeas corpus.

In Venezuela, the Constitutional Chamber has admitted the standing of the Defender of the People to file actions for *amparo* on behalf of the citizens as a whole, as was the case of the action filed against the Congress'pretension to appoint the Electoral National Council members without fulfilling the constitutional requirements. In the case, decided on June, 6, 2001, the Constitutional Chamber, when analyzing Article 280 of the Constitution, pointed out that:

> «As a matter of law, the Defender has standing to bring to suit actions aimed at enforcing the diffuse and collective rights or interests; not being necessary the requirement of the acquiescence of the society it acts on behalf of for the exercise of the action. The Defender of the People is given legitimate interest to act in a process defending a right granted to it by the Constitution itself, consisting in protecting the society or groups in it, in the cases of Article 281 *eiusdem*.
>
> ...The forgoing, according to this Chamber criteria, makes clear that the issue of the protection of diffuse and collective rights and interests may be raised by the Defender of the People, through the action of amparo, and it is declared this way.
>
> As for the general provision of Article 280 *eiusdem*, regarding the general defense and protection of diffuse and collective interests, this Chamber considers that the Defender of the People is entitled to act to protect those rights and interests , when they correspond in general to the consumers and users (6, Article 281), or to protect the rights of Indian peoples (paragraph 8 of the same Article), since the defense and protection of such categories is one of the faculties granted to said entity by Article 281 of the Constitution in force. It is about a general protection and not a protection of individualities.
>
> Within this frame of action, and since the political rights are included in the human rights and guarantees of Title III of the Constitution in force, which have a general projection, among which the ones provided in Article 62 of the Constitution can be found, it must be concluded that the Defender of the People on behalf of the society, legitimated by law, is entitled to bring to suit an action of amparo tending to control the Electoral Power, to the citizen's benefit, in order to enforce Articles 62 and 70 of the Constitution, which were denounced to be breached by the National Legislative Assembly...» (right to citizen participation).
>
> Due to the difference between diffuse and collective interests, both the Defender of the People, within its attributions, and every individual residing in the country, except for the legal exceptions, are entitled to bring to suit the action (be it of amparo or an specific one) for the protection of the former ones; while the action of the collective interests is given to the Defender of the People and to any member of the group or sector identified as a component of that specific collectivity, and acting defending the collectivity. Both individuals and corporations whose object be the protection of such interests may raise the action, and the standing in all these actions varies according to the nature of the same, that is why law can limit the action in specific individuals or entities. However, in our Constitution, in the provisions of Article 281 the Defender of the People is objectively granted the procedural interest and the capacity to sue»[59].

---

[59] Decision of the Constitutional Chamber N° 656 of 06-05-2001, Case: *Defensor del Pueblo vs. Comisión Legislativa Nacional.*

V. THE QUESTION OF OTHER PUBLIC (STATE) INSTITUTIONS STANDING ON THE AMPARO SUIT

Another important issue regarding standing in filing amparo suits is to determine if other State entities can file amparo actions on behalf of the people, in defense of collective or diffuse rights. In contrast with what has occurred in the United States, it can be said that in general terms, beside the Peoples' Defendant standing, no other public entity can assume the defense of the rights of the peoples by means of filing amparo suits.

In the United States, in the Supreme Court decision *In Re Debs*, 158 U.S. 565, 15 S.Ct. 900,39 L.Ed. 1092 (1895), the standing of the Attorney General for the protection of the State's general interest as the property on the mail in injunctive proceedings, was admitted, even being a party against the members of a railway trade union which threatened the functioning of railways. A few years before, the Congress had approved the Sherman Antitrust Act which granted authority to the Attorney General to commence injunctive proceedings to prevent restraints to trade.

Half a century later, after the Supreme Court decision in *Brown v. Board of Education of Topeka,* 347 U.S. 483 (1954); 349 U.S. 294 (1955) declared the dual school system («separate but equal») unconstitutional, by means of the Civil Rights Act of 1957, the Congress authorized the Attorney General to bring injunctive suits to implement the Fifteenth Amendment referred to right to vote in a non discriminatory basis. As referred by Owen R. Fiss:

> «The very next congressional initiative, the Civil Rights Act of 1960, was in large part intended to perfect the Attorney General's injunctive weaponry on behalf of voting rights. In each of the subsequent civil rights acts, those of 1964 and 1968 the pattern was repeated; the Attorney General was authorized to initiate injunctive suits to enforce wide range of rights -public accommodations (e.g. restaurants), state facilities (e.g. parks), public schools, employments, and housing»[60].

Thus, after *Brown*, it can be said that the United States ceased to participate in civil rights proceedings just as *amicus curia*, and in his name the Attorney General began to play prominent role acting in civil rights proceedings even before having specific authorization from Congress. As mentioned by Fiss: «The civil rights era forced the Attorney General and the courts to re-examine the non-statutory powers of the United States to sue to enforce the Constitution»[61].

The standing of the Attorney General was finally generally admitted regarding the protection of human rights in the case *United States v. City of Philadelphia*, 644 F.2d. 187 (3d Cir. 1980), in which the United States authority to sue a city and its officials for an injunction against the violation of the XIV Amendment rights of individual because of police brutality, was admitted; the United States was considered as suing as class representative for the city of Philadelphia. The United States Court of Appeals, Third Circuits ruled in the matter, as follows:

---

[60] See Owen M. FISS, *The Civil Rights Injunction,* Indiana University Pres, Bloomington & London, 1978, p. 21.

[61] See Owen M. FISS and Doug RENDLEMAN, *Injunctions*, Second Edition, University Casebook Series, The Foundation Press, Mineola, New York, 1984, p. 35.

Article II section 3 of the Constitution charges the Executive to «take care that the Laws be faithfully executed». Independent of any explicit statutory grant of authority, provided Congress has not expressly limited its authority, the Executive has the inherent constitutional power and duty to enforce constitutional and statutory rights by resort to the courts. When Federal courts have upheld executive standing without explicit congressional authority, they have looked to other provisions of the Constitution, such as the commerce clause (See, e. g., Sanitary District of Chicago v. United States, 266 Us. 405,45 S. Ct. 176, 69 L. Ed. 352 (1925); In re debs, 158 U.S. 564 15 S. Ct. 900, 39 L. Ed. 1092 (1895) and cases cited infra, p 218. and the fourteenth amendment (See United States v. Brand Jewelers, 318 F. Supp. 1293 (S.D.N.Y. 1970) and to a general statutory scheme defining federal rights but lacking the specific remedy of executive suit (See, e. g., Wyandotte Transp. Co. v. United States, 389 U.S. 191, 88 S. Ct. 379, 19 L. Ed. 2d. 407 (1967); United States v. American Bell Telephone Co., 128 U.S. 315, 9 S. Ct. 90, 32 L. Ed. 450 (1888); United States v. San Jacinto Tin Co., 125 U.S. 273, 8 S. Ct. 850, 31 L. Ed. 747 (1888)). In addition, 28 U.S.C. § 518 (b) affords the Attorney General statutory authority to «conduct and argue any case in a court of the United States in which the United States is interested». The Supreme Court has held that this statute confers on the Executive general authority to initiate suits «to safeguard national interests». (United States v. California, 332 U.S. 19, 27, 67 S. Ct. 1658, 1662, 91 L. Ed. 1889 (1946)). Moreover, the Supreme Court has held that the Executive's general constitutional duty to protect the public welfare «is often of itself sufficient to give it standing in court». (In re Debs, 158 U.S. 564, 584, 15 S. Ct. 900, 906, 39 L. Ed. 1092 (1895).

Thus, the standing of the Attorney General in the United States as well as of other public agencies has been admitted to file injunctions seeking the protection of some constitutional rights of citizens. For example, the standing of the United States and of the Secretary of Education, has been recognized to seek an injunction against a university to stop the release of student records in violation of a federal statute (*United States v. Miami University*, 294 F. 3d 797, 166 Ed. Law Rep. 464 2002 FED App. 0213P (6th Cir. 2002)[62]. In general terms, the standing of the United States, the States and the Municipalities has been accepted in all cases in which they act in its capacity as protectors of the public interest, like public welfare, public safety or public health. That is why actions for injunction in cases of the illegal practice of medicine, and other allied professions had been brought by the attorney general, a State board of health or a county attorney[63],

Contrary to this North American tendency, in the Latin American countries except for the already mentioned standing assigned to the Peoples' Defendant, no other public officer or agency can claim the representation of collective or diffuse rights in order to file an amparo suit. This has even been expressly ruled in Venezuela, where the Constitutional Chamber of the Supreme Court deciding an amparo suit initiated by a Governor of one of the federated States, in a decision of November 21, 2000 ruled the following:

The States and Municipalities cannot file actions for diffuse and collective rights and interest, except if a statute expressly authorizes them.

---

62 See the reference in Kevin SCHRODER et al, «Injunction», *Corpus Juris Secundum*, Thomson West, Volume 43A, 2004, p. 252.

63 See the referentes to specific cases in Kevin Schroder et al, «Injunction», *Corpus Juris Secundum*, Thomson West, Volume 43A, 2004, p. 271 ff.

The collective and diffuse rights and interests pursue to maintain in all the population or sectors of it, an acceptable quality of life, in those matters related to the quality of life that must be rendered by the State of by individuals. They are rights and interest that can coincide with individual rights and interests, but that according to Article 26 of the Constitution and unless the statute denies the action, can be claimed by any person invoking a right or interest shared with the people in general or a sector of the population, and who fears or has suffered, being part of such collectivity, a harm in his quality of life.

Now, being for the State to maintain the acceptable quality of life conditions, its bodies or entities cannot ask from it to render an activity; thus, within the structure of the State, the only institution that can file such actions is the Peoples' Defendant due to the fact that it represents the people and not the State, as well as other public entities when a particular statute gives them such actions[64].

In this sense, the Venezuelan Constitutional Chamber has denied the standing to file collective actions for amparo to the governors or mayors. In an action for judicial review of a statute with a joint amparo claim, of May 6, 2001, the Chamber decided that:

> [The] actions in general grounded in diffuse or collective rights and interests may be filed by any Venezuelan person or legal entity, or by foreign persons residing in the country, who have access to the judicial system through the exercise of this action. The Venezuelan State, as such, lacks of it, since it has mechanisms and other means to cease the damage to those rights and interests, specially through administrative procedures; but the population in general is entitled to bring them in the way explained in this decision, and those ones can be brought by the Defender of the People, since as for Article 280 of the Constitution, the Defendant of the People is in charge of the promotion, defense and guardianship of the legitimate, collective and diffuse interest of the citizens. According to this Chamber, said provision does not exclude or prohibit the citizens the access to the judicial system in defense of the diffuse and collective rights and interests, since Article 26 of the Constitution in force sets forth the access to the judicial system to every person, whereby individuals are entitled to bring to suit as well, unless a law denies them the action. Within the structure of the State, since it does not have those attributions granted, the only one who is able to protect individuals in matters of collective or diffuse interest is the Defender of the People (in any of its scopes: national, state, county or special). The Public Prosecutor (except in the case that a law grants it), Mayors, or Municipal auditors lack both such attribution and the action, unless the law grants them both)».[65]

VI. THE INJURED THIRD PARTY

As in all suits, and particularly in matters of amparo and protection of constitutional rights, it is possible that third parties not originally connected with the suit, have some personal interest in the action filed because the omission, the

---

64 Case *William Dávila. Gobernación Estado Mérida*. See the comments in Rafael CHAVERO, *El Nuevo Régimen del Amparo Constitucional en Venezuela*, Caracas, 2001, p. 115.

65 Decision of the Constitutional Chamber N° 656 of June 5, 2001, Case: *Defensor del Pueblo vs. Comisión Legislativa Nacional*.

particular situation or the challenged act, also affects their constitutional rights, coinciding whether with the claimant or plaintiff or with the allegations of the defendants.

Injured third parties, thus, may be added in the proceedings so that their rights in the subject matter may be also determined and enforced by the corresponding court when coinciding with the plaintiff allegations. Of course the general rule is the same as in the injunctions proceeding in the United States: persons with a unity of interest in the subject matter of the suit and who are entitled to, and seek the same character of relief, may join the plaintiff claim[66]. Consequently, a person is allowed to intervene in an amparo proceeding adhering to the plaintiff claim and in defense of it because they have a direct interest in the matter that can be affected with the final decision; claim that cannot be modified nor expand by the third party.

Some Latin American Amparo Laws refer specifically to the intervention of third parties, as is the case of Guatemala where Article 34 of the Law establishes the obligation of

> «the authority, the person denounced or the claimant, if they arrive to know of any person with direct interest in the subject matter or the suspension of the challenged act, resolution or procedure, whether because they are party in the proceedings of because they have any other legal relation with the exposed situation; to tell the foregoing to the court, indicating name and address and in a brief way, the relation with such interest. In this case the court must hear the referred person, as well as the Public prosecutor, considered as a party».

In México, Article 5 of the Amparo Law, in addition to the aggrieved person or persons and to the challenged authority or authorities, are declared also as parties in the amparo suit, «the affected third party or parties», having the possibility to intervene in such character, the following:

a) The counterpart of the injured when the claimed act is issued in a non criminal trail or controversy, or any of the parties in the same trail when the amparo is filed by a person strange to the procedure:

b) The offended or the persons that according to the law, have right to have the damage repaired or to demand for civil liability derived from the commitment of the crime, in amparo suits filed against criminal judicial decisions, when the latter affects the reparation or the liability;

c) The person or persons that have argued in their own favor regarding the challenged act against which the amparo is filed, when being acts adopted by authorities other than judicial of labor; or that without arguing in their favor, they have direct interest in the subsistence of the challenged act.

In the case of Perú, the Constitutional Procedural Code following the universal procedural rules, provides that when in the suit for amparo, it appears for the court the need to incorporate third parties not initially summoned, the judge must incorporate them if from the suit or the answer it is evident that the final decision will affect other parties (Art. 43). Additionally, Article 54 of the Code provides the right to anybody having legal and relevant interest in the outcome of the trail to be

---

66 See the comments in reference in Kevin SCHRODER et al, «Injunction», *Corpus Juris Secundum*, Thomson West, Volume 43A, 2004, p. 332.

incorporated to the procedure and be declared as third interested party, being incorporated to the proceedings at the stage as it is.

Finally, regarding third parties, and without prejudice to what has being said about the intervention of the Peoples' Defendants in the amparo suits, before the extension of this public officer, it has been a legal tradition in Latin American regulations referred to habeas corpus and amparo, to consider the Public Prosecutor (Ministerio Público) in its character of general guarantor for the respects of constitutional rights in the judicial proceedings, as a *bona fide* third party that must be summoned to allow its participation in the proceedings.

In this respect, for instance, the Argentinean Habeas Corpus Law regulates the intervention of the Public Prosecutor, for which purpose the court once received the complaint, must notify its representatives, which will have in the proceedings the same rights given to all those that intervene in it, without any need to notify them for the accomplishment of any procedural act. The Public Prosecutor can file arguments and make the appeals considered necessary (Article 21).

The same occurs in México, where the Amparo Law guarantees the Public prosecutor its right to intervene in the procedure (Article 5, I, IV). In similar sense the Venezuelan Law of Amparo allows the intervention of the Public prosecutors in all amparo suits, but points out that its non intervention cannot affect the continuity or validity of the procedure (Article 14).

In similar sense regarding the participation of the Public Prosecutor as third party in good faith, in the United States, particularly in matters of judicial protection of civil rights, the participation of the Attorney General in injunctive proceedings as *amicus curiae* has been even encouraged by the courts. In the Texas prison case *Estelle v. Justice,* 426 U.S. 925; 96 S. Ct. 2637: 49 L. Ed. 2d 380 (1976) the matter was definitively resolved: the trial Judge in the case invited the Attorney general to participate as *«litigating amicus»*, with the same rights normally associated with the party, for instance to present evidence and to cross-examine witnesses. This participation was challenged by the State but finally was accepted.

However, since the expansion of injunctive process for the protection of civil rights, beginning with school desegregation cases following the Supreme Court's decisions in *Brown v. Board of Education of Topeka,* (1955), the Attorney General has had a very important role intervening in what has been called «structural injunctions». Through them, on civil rights massive violation matters, the courts have undertaken to judicially supervise the authorities' institutional policies and practices, in many cases with the active participation of the Attorney General in the litigation as *amicus curiae*. As defined by Tabb and Shoben:

Structural injunctions are modern phenomenon born of necessity from development in Constitutional law where the Supreme Court has identified substantive rights whose enforcement requires substantial judicial supervision. These rights concern the treatment of individuals by institutions, such as the right not to suffer inhumane treatment in prisons or public mental hospital. Enforcement of such rights by injunction has become an implicit part of the Constitutional guarantee of protecting individual liberties from inappropriate government action[67].

---

[67] See William M. TABB and Elaine W. SHOBEN, *Remedies,* Thomson West, 2005, pp. 87-88.

CHAPTER XI

THE DAMAGING OR INJURING PARTY IN THE AMPARO SUIT, AND THE ACTS OR OMISSIONS CAUSING THE HARM OR THE THREATS TO CONSTITUTIONAL RIGHTS

The amparo suit is governed by the principle of bilateralism, in the sense that not only the procedure must be initiated by a plaintiff that must in principle be the party whose constitutional rights and guaranties have been injured or threatened, but in principle, it must also always exist a defendant party, that is, the party whose actions or omissions are those precisely causing the harm or threats. This means that the judicial decision the plaintiff is seeking through the amparo suit, must always be directed to somebody that must be individuated[1].

This is similar to what occurs in the United States, regarding injunctions, referring to its individuated character, which implies that in general terms the resulting judicial order must be «addressed to some clearly identified individual, not just the general citizenry»[2]

I. THE QUESTION OF THE INDIVIDUATION OF THE DEFENDANT

The general principle regarding amparo, then, is that in the complaint, the plaintiff must clearly identify the authority, public officer, person or entity against whom the action is filed, that is the defendant, as is set forth in the Amparo Laws (Argentina, Art. 6,b; Bolivia, 97,II; Colombia, Art. 14; Costa Rica, Art. 38; El Salvador, Art. 14,2; Guatemala Art. 21,d; Honduras, Art. 21; 49,4; México 116, III; 166,III; Nicaragua, Art. 27,2; Panama, Art. 2619,2; Paraguay, Art. 6,c; Perú, Art. 42,3; Venezuela Art. 18,3).

Nonetheless, some legislations although establishing that the need for the identification of the defendant, provide that this condition only applies «when it is

---

[1] The only exception to the principle of bilateralism is the case of Chile, where the offender is not consider a defendant party but only a person whose activity is limited to inform the court and give it the documents it have. That is why in the Regulation set forth by the Supreme Court it is said that the affected state organ, person of public officer just «can» appear as party in the process. See Juan Manuel ERRAZURIZ G. and Jorge Miguel OTERO A, *Aspectos procesales del recurso de protección*, Editorial Jurídica de Chile 1989, p. 27.

[2] See Owen M. FISS, *The Civil Rights Injunction*, Indiana University Press, 1978, p. 12.

possible» (Argentina, Art. 6,b; Colombia 14; Nicaragua, Art. 25; 55; Venezuela Art. 18, 3); and some Laws as the Paraguayan one, even establish that when the identification of the defendant is not possible, it is for the judge to provide the necessary measures in order to establish the procedural bilateral relation.

Thus, from the beginning of the procedure when the action is filed, or latter in the proceeding, the bilateral character of the amparo suit implies that in principle, a procedural relation must be established between the injured party and the injurer one, which must participate in the process. This implies the individuation character of the suit, equivalent to its personal character.

In this regard, the former Supreme Court of Justice of Venezuela in a decision of December 15, 1992 pointed out that:

> «The amparo action set forth in the Constitution, and regulated in the Organic Amparo law, has among its fundamental characteristic its basic personal or subjective character, which implies that a direct, specific and undutiful relation must exist between the person claiming for the protection of his rights, and the person purported to have originated the disturbance, who is to be the one with standing to act as defendant or the person against whom the action is filed. In other words, it is necessary, for granting an amparo, that the person signaled as the injurer be in the end, the one originating the harm»[3].

But as mentioned, in some situations, it is not possible for the plaintiff or for the judge, to clearly identify the defendant. The important aspect to clearly determine is the fact or action causing the harm, in which case, even without the identification of the exact authority or public officer who had produced it, the constitutional protection must be given. In Argentina this question has been analyzed, and it has been considered as a general principle, that the individuation of the author of the challenged act or omission will only be requested, when possible, because «preferably the amparo tends to focus on the damaging act and only in an accessory way in its author»[4]. In other words, that once the injurer act has been proved, the sole fact that its author has not been determined, cannot impede the decision to repair the harm, «due to the fact that the amparo action tends to restore the aggrieved constitutional rights, more than to individualize its author»[5].

That is why, in the *Angel Siri* Argentinean leading case, in which and without statutory regulations, the Supreme Court in Argentina admitted the amparo action, the Court protected the owner of a newspaper that was shoot down by the government, notwithstanding that in the files there was no clear evidence regarding the authority that closed it, nor the motives of the decision[6].

Nonetheless, in case of absence of individuation of the author of the injuring action, the court must to adopt the necessary measures in order to determine it, and eventually, for the purpose of preserving the bilateral character of the process,

---

3 See decision of the Politico Administrative Chamber of the Supreme Court of Justice of December 16, 1992 (Caso *Haydée Casanova*), *Revista de Derecho Público,* N° 52, Editorial Jurídica Venezolana, Caracas, 1992, p. 139.

4 See Alí Joaquín SALGADO, *Juicio de amparo y acción de inconstitucionalidad*, Astrea, Buenos Aires, 1987, p. 92.

5 José Luis LAZZARINI, *El juicio de amparo*, La Ley, Buenos Aires, 1987, p. 274.

6 See José Luis LAZZARINI, *El juicio de amparo*, La Ley, Buenos Aires, 1987, pp. 275-276.

designate a public defendant in the case. The Uruguayan Amparo law in this regard expressly provides the possibility to file the action in urgent cases even without knowing with precision about the person responsible for the harm fact, in which case, the court must publish public notices to identify it, and in case of the responsible not showing, the court must appoint an ex officio defendant (Art. 7).

Nonetheless, in other cases of absence of individuation of the injurer party, the claim has been rejected when it is determined that what the plaintiff pretends is to force the court to do the job. It was the case decided by the Argentinean Supreme Court rejecting an amparo actions filed by the former President of the Republic *Juan D. Perón* case, asking for the return of the body of his dead wife. In that case, the Supreme Court ruled about the need for a «minimal individuation of the author of the act originating the claim», due to the fact that:

> «the general principles of procedural law do not suffer any exception due to the exceptional character of the amparo, and must be respected, in order to eventually assure the exercise of the right to defense, from which the counterpart must not be deprived... This is evident from the text of the suit in which it is affirmed that the act provoking the claim has been executed 'by disposition of the former Provisional Government' without adding any other reference or explanation regarding the pointed public officer or entity. It is evident that the minimal requirements of individuation of the defendant, referred above, have not been accomplished in the case. On the contrary what is revealed in the files of this case, is that in lieu of seeking protection to his constitutional guarantees harmed by a an illegal State act, the plaintiff has intended to use the amparo procedure with the purpose of obtaining from the judges the order to practice the necessary inquiries regarding the facts, which are not proved or specified with precision. And it is clear that the performance of the instruction phase can not be achieved by means of this amparo remedy, whose incorporation to Argentinean positive law has purposes different to the one pursued in this case»[7].

Anyway, with the aforementioned exceptions, the principle of the individuation of the defendant rules in amparo maters. If the aggrieving party is a natural person (human being), whether a public officer or an individual, it must be identified in the usual way, being necessary in any case, to be the person originating the harm or threat to the plaintiff's rights. Being the aggrieving party an artificial person which needs to act through its representatives, whether it be a public entity or a corporation, the action for amparo must be filed against it, identifying with precision the entity and its representative, when possible. In the latter case, the action can be filed against the entity or corporation itself, or personally against the representative itself (public officer or manager), if the harm or threat has been personally provoked by the latter, independently of the artificial person or entity for which he is acting.

That is, as it has been decided by the Venezuelan courts, the aggrieving party must always be directly responsible for the conduct violating the constitutional rights and guaranties of the aggrieved party[8]; consequently, if a

7 Fallos: 248-537, referred in José Luis LAZZARINI, *El juicio de amparo*, La Ley, Buenos Aires, 1987, p. 275.

8 See decisions of the First Court on Judicial Review of Administrative Action of May 12, 1988, *Revista de Derecho Público,* N° 34, Editorial Jurídica Venezolana, Caracas, 1988, p. 113; and of June 16, 1988, *Revista de Derecho Público,* N° 35, Editorial Jurídica Venezolana, Caracas, 1988, p. 138.

person is denounced as aggrieving without being so, the amparo action must be rejected[9] As decided by the Fist Court on Judicial review of Administrative Action in a decision of July 13, 1993:

> «Among the basic characteristics of the amparo action, it is its subjective character, which requires for its admissibility that the threat of violation of a constitutional right be immediate, possible and realizable by the person identify as aggrieving, which means that in the case of a once materialized violation, it must be executed directly by the accused, that is, a direct relation must exist between the person asking for the protection to his rights and the person identified as aggrieving who will be the one with standing, and this being the person against whom the action is filed. This leads to affirm that for the admissibility of the amparo action, it is necessary that the person identified as aggrieving eventually be the one causing the purported harm and the one which would be obliged to follow the amparo order in case of the granting of the protection petition.
>
> This essentially personal and subjective character of the amparo action results from the very reading of Article 18,3 of the Amparo Law which imposes on the plaintiff the burden of sufficiently identifying the aggrieving party, when possible. It is also evident from Article 32,a, where it is set forth the need for the decision to expressly mention «the authority, private body or person against whose acts or resolution the amparo is conceded; because on the contrary it could happen that processes could be filed against persons different to those that supposedly caused the harm, which will be contrary to the spirit, purpose and raison d'êter of the Amparo Law. Anyway, the problem of the precise identification of the aggrieving party has been raised regarding amparo actions against Public Administration activities, in order to avoid that the amparo actions be unnecessarily filed against the Republic as a legal person. The necessary identity between the 'aggrieved party and the person accused as being the aggrieving -which must be the one provoking the constitutional harm- has been repeatedly ruled by this Chamber, particularly in order to avoid the filing of amparo processes against the Republic, and to encourage the filing against the specific public officer who produced the purported harm act, fact or omission. In this sense it was decided in ruling of August 1°, 1991 (Case: *María Pérez, N° 391*) where it was said that «the constitutional amparo action, because of its special nature, is an action directly filed against the administrative authority which harms or threatens to harm the constitutional right»[10].

That is why Article 27 of the Venezuelan Amparo Law provides that in case of amparo against public officials, the court deciding on the merits must notify its decision to the competent authority «in order for it to decide the disciplinary sanctions against the public official responsible of the violation or the threat against a constitutional right or guarantee». This implies that in the filing of the action of

---

9 See decision of the Politico Administrative Chamber of the Supreme Court of Justice of November 22, 1993, *Revista de Derecho Público,* N° 55-56, Editorial Jurídica Venezolana, Caracas, 1993, pp. 487-489.

10 See decisiбn of the Politico-Administrative Chamber of the Supreme Court of Justice of December 15, 1992 (Caso *Haydee Casanova*), *Revista de Derecho Público,* N° 52, Editorial Jurídica Venezolana, Caracas, 1992, p. 139.

amparo in cases of Public Administration activities, «the person acting on behalf of (or representing) the entity who caused the harm or threat to the rights or guarantees must be identified, which is, the signaled person who has the exact and direct knowledge of the facts»[11].

But the requirement to identify the individual or natural person representative of the entity causing the harm, does not imply that the action must always be filed against such individual; it can be directly filed against the entity in itself. This has been for instance, the general trend in civil right injunctions in the United States, particularly when filed through class actions where the lost of individuation in the act and beneficiary has also provoked its address «to the office rather than the person»[12].

This is also the sense of aggrieving authority in the Mexican system where the responsible authority is conceived in institutional rather than personal terms, in the sense that the institution involved remains responsible regardless of the changes in personas[13]. In this sense it has been decided by the Supreme Court of México, ruling that the discharge, transfer, promotion, demotion, death, or other removal of the individual who has actually ordered or executed the act object of the complaint, or any transfer of jurisdiction over the matter in contest, is no bar to the suit[14].

Thus, the amparo suit against artificial persons can be filed against the organ or directly against the person in charge of it. In the former case, the person in charge can be changed, that is for instance the case of public entities, where the public official can be changed, but this circumstance does not change the bilateral relation between aggrieved and aggrieving parties. As it has been decided by the Venezuelan First Court on Judicial review of Administrative Action in a decision of September 28, 1993 regarding an amparo action filed against the dean of a Law Faculty, in which case the person in charge as Dean was changed:

> «the heading of the position does not change its organic unity. If the dean of the Faculty changes, it will always be a subjective figure that substitutes the preceding one. That is why in a decision of September 11, 1990 this Court ruled that the circumstance of the head of an organ mentioned as aggrieving being changed does not alter the procedural relation originated with the amparo action. To the latter it must in this case be added that it would have no sense to rule that the procedural relation be continued with the person that doesn't occupy anymore the position, because in case the constitutional amparo is granted, then the ex public official would not be in a position to reestablish the factual infringed situation. As much, the former public officer could be liable for the damages caused, but as it is known, the amparo action has the

---

11 See decision of the First Court on Judicial Review of Administrative Action of June 16, 1988, *Revista de Derecho Público,* N° 35, Editorial Jurídica Venezolana, Caracas, 1988, p. 138.

12 See Owen M. FISS, *The Civil Rights Injunction*, Indiana University Press 1978, p. 15.

13 See Richard D. BAKER, *Judicial Review in México. A Study of the Amparo Suit*, Texas University Press, Austin1971, p. 209.

14 Suprema Corte, *Jurisprudencia de la Suprema Corte*, Tesis 183, II, p. 365; also Suprema Corte, *Montufar Miguel*, 17 S.J. 798 (1925). See the references in Richard D. BAKER, *Judicial Review in México. A Study of the Amparo Suit*, Texas University Press, Austin1971, p. 208–109, note 36.

only purpose of reestablishing the harmed legal situation, and that can only be assured by the current public official»[15].

Consequently, according to the Venezuelan judicial doctrine on the matter, in cases in which the aggrieved party identifies with precision as aggrieving the public official responsible for the harm, it is this one and only him who must act in the procedure, in which case no notice must be made to its superior or to the Attorney general[16]. Conversely, if the action is for instance filed against a Ministerial entity as an organ of the Republic, the action must be understood to be filed against the latter, being in such cases the Attorney general the entity that must act as the judicial representative of it[17]. On the contrary, if the amparo suit is exercised against a perfectly identified and individuated organ of Ministerial entity and not against the Republic, the judicial representative of the latter has no procedural role to play[18]. That is, if the amparo action is directed against an individuated administrative authority, for instance, a Ministry, the representative of the Republic can not act on his behalf[19]. In such cases, it is the individuated person or public officer that must personally act as aggrieving party[20].

II. THE DEFENDANT IN THE AMPARO SUIT: AUTHORITIES AND INDIVIDUALS

One of the most important aspects regarding the damaging, aggrieving or injurer party in the amparo suit, that is, the defendant, is related to whether the amparo can only be filed against public authorities or can it also be filed against particulars or individuals. That is, whether the specific judicial means of amparo is only established for the protection of constitutional rights and guaranties against

---

15 See decision of the First Court on Judicial Review of Administrative Action of September 28, 1993, *Revista de Derecho Público*, N° 55-56, Editorial Jurídica Venezolana, Caracas, 1993, p. 330.

16 See decisions of the First Court on Judicial Review of Administrative Actions of May 12, 1988, *Revista de Derecho Público*, N° 34, Editorial Jurídica Venezolana, Caracas, 1988, p. 113; and of September 7, 1989, *Revista de Derecho Público* N° 40, Editorial Jurídica Venezolana, Caracas, 1989, p. 107. Also decision of the Politico Administrative Chamber of the Supreme Court of Justice of March 16, 1989, *Revista de Derecho Público*, N° 38, Editorial Jurídica Venezolana, Caracas, 1989, p. 110.

17 See decision of the First Court on Judicial Review of Administrative Actions of September 7, 1989, *Revista de Derecho Público*, N° 40, Editorial Jurídica Venezolana, Caracas, 1989, p. 107.

18 See decision of the First Court on Judicial Review of Administrative Actions of November 21, 1990, *Revista de Derecho Público*, N° 44, Editorial Jurídica Venezolana, Caracas, 1990, p. 148.

19 See decisions of the First Court on Judicial Review of Administrative Actions of October 10, 1990, *Revista de Derecho Público*, N° 44, Editorial Jurídica Venezolana, Caracas, 1990, p. 142; and of July 30, 1992, *Revista de Derecho Público*, N° 51, Editorial Jurídica Venezolana, Caracas, 1992, p. 164; and decisions of the Politico Administrative Chamber of the Supreme Court of Justice of August 1, 1991, *Revista de Derecho Público*, N° 47, Editorial Jurídica Venezolana, Caracas, 1991, p. 120, and of December 15, 1992, *Revista de Derecho Público*, N° 52, Editorial Jurídica Venezolana, Caracas, 1992, p. 139.

20 See decision of the Politico Administrative Chamber of the Supreme Court of Justice of March 8, 1990, *Revista de Derecho Público*, N° 42, Editorial Jurídica Venezolana, Caracas, 1990, p. 114; and of the First Court on Judicial Review of Administrative Actions of November 21, 1990, *Revista de Derecho Público*, N° 44, Editorial Jurídica Venezolana, Caracas, 1990, p. 148. Igualmente en FUNEDA, *15 años de Jurisprudencia, cit.*, p. 164; and of July, 14, 1988, FUNEDA, *15 años de Jurisprudencia, cit.*, p. 177.

public entities and authorities harms or threats, that is, in general terms, against the State, or it can also be used against private individuals' actions harming or threatening such rights.

The former position can be considered as the general trend in Latin America, following the historical fact that the amparo suit was originally created to protect individuals against the State. Nonetheless, nowadays, in the majority of the countries, this situation does not exclude the admission of the amparo suit for the protection of constitutional rights against individual's actions, as is the case in Argentina, Bolivia, Chile, Dominican Republic, Perú, Venezuela and Uruguay, as well as, although in a more restrictive way, in Colombia, Costa Rica Ecuador, and Guatemala.

III. THE AMPARO AGAINST PUBLIC AUTHORITIES: PUBLIC ENTITIES AND PUBLIC OFFICERS

In general terms, all Latin American countries establish that the amparo action shall be filed against public entities and public officials, following the original features of the amparo as a special judicial means for the protection of human rights, facing the State. But this situation, as mentioned before, has changed to the point that, nowadays, the countries that only admit the amparo suit against public entities or officers, excluding the suit against individuals or private persons, are the minority, as is the case in Brazil, El Salvador, Panama, México and Nicaragua. In all the other Latin American countries, additionally to the amparo suit against public entities and officers, the action for constitutional protection can be filed against private parties.

Regarding civil rights injunctions, the United States can also be included in the former group. If it is true that in this country, injunctions, as general judicial means for rights' protection can be filed against any person as «higher public officials or private persons»[21] causing the harm to a right, in matters of constitutional or civil rights guaranties, it has been considered that it is only admissible regarding public entities. As explained by, M. Glenn Abernathy and Barbara A. Perry:

> «Limited remedies for private interfere with free choice. Another problem in the citizen's search for freedom from restriction lies in that many types of interference stemming from private persons do not constitute actionable wrongs under the law. Private prejudice and private discrimination do not, in the absence of specific statutory provisions, offer grounds for judicial intervention on behalf of the sufferer. If one is denied admission to membership in a social club, for example, solely on the basis of his race or religion or political affiliation, he may understandably smart under the rejection, but the courts cannot help him (again assuming no statutory provision batting such distinctions). There are, then, many types of restraints on individual freedom of choice which are beyond the authority of courts to remove or ameliorate.
>
> It should be noted that the guarantees of rights in the United States Constitution only protect against governmental action and do not apply to

---

[21] See M. Glenn ABERNATHY and Barbara A. PERRY, *Civil Liberties under the Constitution*, Sixth Edition, University of South Carolina Press, 1993, p. 8.

purely private encroachments, except for the Thirteenth Amendment's prohibition of slavery. Remedies for private invasion must be found in statutes, the common law, or administrative agency regulations and adjudications»[22].

In Latin America, as mentioned before, only Brazil, El Salvador, Panama, México and Nicaragua leave the amparo action to be filed no more than against the State, that is, public entities and public officials. This was the situation at the origin of the amparo suit in México, as it currently remains when Article 103 of the Constitution provides that the amparo shall be filed against infraction to constitutional guarantees committed by an «authority», in the sense that it must always be a responsible authority. Accordingly, Article 11 of the Amparo Law points out that «The authority responsible is the one who edicts, promulgates, orders, executes or tries to execute the statute or the claimed act». This article has been interpreted in the sense that authorities are not only those superior ones which order the acts, but also those subordinate ones that execute or try to execute them; the amparo being admitted against any of them»[23].

This term «authority» could be interpreted in the wider sense of any public entity of public official regardless its powers of functions. This is the sense given, for instance, to the Amparo laws of Argentina, Perú or Venezuela. But in Argentina, the notion of «authority» regarding the amparo suit, even though apparently wider, has in fact a restrictive meaning, when it refers only to those public officers with power to decide. As was defined in the *case Campos Otero Julia* (1935), this term is understood as «an organ of the State legally vested with the powers of decision and command necessary for imposing upon individuals either its own determinations or those that emanate form some other State organs»[24]. This definition was expanded to include «all those persons who dispose of public power (*fuerza pública*) by virtue of either legal or *de facto* circumstances, and who, consequently find themselves in a position to perform acts of a public character, due to the fact that the power they have is public»[25].

Three aspects must be emphasized regarding the judicial doctrine on the notion of «authority» in México: First, the idea of the *de facto* public officer, in the sense that even if the offender is not the legitimate holder of the public office whose authority is exercised, the amparo must be admitted because the harm is caused by some one that pretends to be exercising public power, the citizens having the right to legitimate confidence in those who exercise public power.

---

22 See M. Glenn ABERNATHY and Barbara A. PERRY, *Civil Liberties under the Constitution*, Sixth Edition, University of South Carolina Press, 1993, p. 6.

23 See «Autoridades para efectos del juicio de amparo» (*Apéndice al Semanario Judicial de la federación, 1917-1988*, Segunda parte, tesis 300, p. 519. See the reference in Eduardo FERRER MAC-GREGOR, *La acción constitucional de amparo en México y España. Estudio de derecho comparado*, Editorial Porrúa, México, 2002, p. 254.

24 See Suprema Corte, *Campos Otero Julia*, 45, S.J. 5033 (1935). See the reference in Richard D. BAKER, *Judicial Review in México. A Study of the Amparo Suit*, Texas University Press, Austin, 1971, p. 94.

25 See «Autoridades para efectos del juicio de amparo» (*Apéndice al Semanario Judicial de la Federación*, 1917-1988, Segunda parte, tesis 300, p. 519. See the reference in EDUARDO FERRER MAC-GREGOR, *La acción constitucional de amparo en México y España. Estudio de derecho comparado*, Editorial porrúa, México 2002, p. 253. Also see Suprema Corte, *Jurisprudencia de la Suprema Corte*, thesis 179, II, 360. see the referente in Richard D. BAKER, *Judicial Review in México. A Study of the Amparo Suit*, Texas University Press, Austin, 1971, p. 94.

Second, that because the definition of «authority» refers to those public entities that are in a position to make a decision and to impose or execute them by a coactive use of public power, in many cases, the courts had rejected the amparo suit against public entities considering that they do not have the power to decide, like those with purely staff or consultative nature[26]. According to this interpretation, for instance, many decentralized public entities like *Petróleos Mexicanos,* the National Commission on Electricity, the Human Rights' Defendant of the UNAM and the Autonomous Universities were initially excluded from the category of «authorities»[27]. Nonetheless, progressively the amparo suit has been admitted against some of these entities based on the decision powers they have in concrete cases[28].

Third, that from a procedural point of view, all the authorities materially involved in the aggrieving action must be identified by the plaintiff in his action and be notified by the court; not only those who ordered the action, but those who have decided it and that have to execute or apply it. As decided by the Supreme Court: if in the amparo claim it is only mentioned the responsible authority adopting the act -the authority who orders- and the suspension of the act is requested, this cannot be granted because the situation will be of acts consented; on the contrary, if there are only mentioned as responsible authorities those who have executed the act, then the suspension can be granted, but the case must be discontinued because the facts resulted from a consented act[29].

In contrast with this restrictive interpretation on the concept of authority regarding the Mexican amparo suit, in Argentina, for instance, the amparo action can be filed against «any public authority act or omission» (Art. 1), being interpreted the term «public authority», in a wide sense including all sorts of public entity or officials of all branches of government. It must be said that the expression «public authority» in Article 1 of the the Amparo Law was incorporated because of the intention of the 1964 legislator to not regulate the amparo against individuals, which nonetheless was already admitted by the Supreme Court and later expressly regulated in the Civil Procedure Code. Even though the expression could also be interpreted in a restrictive way referring only to public officers with *imperium,* that is, those with power to command and to edict obligatory decisions and to require the use of public force to execute them, the general trend is to interpret it in a wide sense comprising any agent, employee, public official, magistrate of government agent acting in that condition, including individuals accomplishing public functions, like the public

---

26 Richard D. BAKER, *Judicial Review in México. A Study of the Amparo Suit,* Texas University Press, Austin, 1971, p. 95.

27 See the references to the judicial decisions in Eduardo FERRER MAC-GREGOR, *La acción constitucional de amparo en México y España. Estudio de derecho comparado,* Editorial Porrúa, México, 2002, pp. 255-256.

28 Se Eduardo Ferrer MAC GREGOR, *La acción constitucional de amparo en México y España. Estudio de derecho comparado,* Editorial Porrúa, México 2002, p. 257.

29 See the Supreme Court jurisprudencia on «Actos Consumados. Suspensión «improcedente» y actos derivados de actos consentidos» en Apéndice al Semanario Judicial de la federación, 1917-1995, Primera sala, tesis 1090, p. 756; y Tribunal Pleno, Tesis 17, p. 12. See the references in Eduardo FERRER MAC-GREGOR, *La acción constitucional de amparo en México y España. Estudio de derecho comparado,* Editorial Porrúa, México 2002, p. 255, notes 450 and 451.

services concessionaries[30]. In some cases it has even been considered that actions of a Provincial Constituent Assembly violating constitutional rights can be challenged via the amparo action[31]

In similarly wide sense, the term «public authorities» is also conceived for the purpose of the amparo protection, for instance, in Bolivia (Art. 94), Colombia (Art.1), El Salvador (Art. 12), Perú (Art. 2), Uruguay (Art. 2) and Venezuela (Art. 2). In Brazil, Article 1 of the statute regulating the *mandado de segurança* provides that this action can be filed against any violation provoked by «authorities, no matter its category and functions»; and in Nicaragua the expression refers to «any public official, authority of its agents» (Art. 3). Some legislations, in order to dissipate any doubts, are enumerative and include any act from any of the branches of government, including delegated, decentralized or autonomous entities, municipal corporations or those supported with public founds or that act by delegation of a State organ by means of a concession, contract or resolution (Guatemala Art. 9, Honduras Art. 41).

The only Latin American country where the amparo action regarding authorities is statutorily reduced expressly to those of the Executive branch of government is Ecuador, where Article 46 of the Amparo Law only admits the amparo against «public administration authorities»(Art. 46).

But besides this specific exception, in contrast, it can be said that in almost all other Latin American countries, the amparo action is established as a specific judicial means for the protection of constitutional rights and guaranties against any acts, facts or omissions of any public authority (public entities or public officials), which can be part of any of the branches of government, whether executive, legislative, judicial or control.

As set forth in the Guatemalan Amparo law, «*no sphere shall be excluded from amparo*» and the action will be admitted against acts, resolutions, dispositions and statutes of authority which could imply a threat, a restriction or a violation of the rights guarantied in the Constitution and in statutes» (Art. 8).

It is also the case in Venezuela, where Article 2 of the Amparo law provides that the action can be filed against «any fact, act or omission of any of the National, States, of Municipal Public Powers (branches of government); which means that the constitutional protection can be filed against any public action, that is, any formal state act, any material action and any factual activity (*vía de hecho*) (Art. 5); as well as against any omission from public entities.

This universality of the amparo suit has been developed by judicial decisions doctrine. For instance, in the case Aura Loreto Rangel, the First Court on Judicial review of Administrative Action of November 11, 1993, it was ruled that:

---

30 See Néstor Pedro SAGÜÉS, *Derecho procesal Constitucional, Vol 3, Acción de amparo*, Editorial Astrea Buenos Aires 1988, pp. 91-93; Joaquín BRAGUE CAMAZANO, *La Jurisdicción constitucional de la libertad (Teoría general, Argentina, México, Corte Interamericana de Derechos Humanos)*, Editorial Porrúa, México 2005, p. 97. José Luis LAZZARINI, *El juicio de amparo*, Editorial La Ley, Buenos Aires 1987, pp. 208-209.

31 See Alí Joaquín SALGADO, *Juicio de amparo y acción de inconstitucionalidad*, Editorial Astrea, Buenos Aires, 1987, pp. 24-25.

«From what Article 2 of the Amparo law sets forth, it results that there is no conduct type, regardless of its nature or character, or from their authors, which can be excluded per se from the amparo judge revision in order to determine if it harms or not constitutional rights or guarantees»[32].

The same criterion has been adopted by the Political Administrative Chamber of the Supreme Court of Justice in a decision of may 24, 1993 as follows:

The terms on which the amparo action is regulated in Article 49 of the Constitution (now Article 27) are very extensive. If the extended scope of the rights and guarantees that can be protected and restored through this judicial mean is undoubted; the harm cannot be limited to those produced only by some acts. So, in equal terms it must be permitted that any harming act -whether an act, a fact or an omission- with respect to any constitutional right and guarantee, can be challenged by means of this action, due to the fact that the amparo action is the protection of any norm regulating the so called subjective rights of constitutional rank, it cannot be sustained that such protection is only available in cases in which the injuring act has some precise characteristics, whether from a material or organic point of view. The *jurisprudencia* of this Court has been constant regarding both principles. In decision N° 22, dated January 31, 1991 (Case: *Anselmo Natale*), it was decided that 'there is no State act that could not be reviewed by amparo, the latter understood not as a mean for judicial review of constitutionality of State acts in order to annul them, but as a protective remedy regarding public freedoms whose purpose is to reestablish its enjoyment and exercise, when a natural or artificial person, or group or private organization, threaten to harm them or effectively harm them (See, regarding the extended scope of the protected rights, decision of December 4, 1990, Case *Mariela Morales de Jimenez*, N° 661)[33].

In another decision dated February 13, 1992, the First Court ruled:

«This Court observes that the essential characteristic of the amparo regime, in its constitutional regulation as well as in its statutory development, is its universality.., so the protection it assures is extended to all subjects (physical or artificial persons), as well as regarding all constitutionally guaranteed rights, including those that without being expressly regulated in the Constitution, are inherent to human beings. This the departing point in order to understand the scope of the constitutional amparo... Regarding Public Administration, the amparo against it is so extended that it can be filed against all acts, omissions and factual actions, without any kind of exclusion regarding some matters that always related to the public order and social interest»[34]

Notwithstanding this general principle of the universality of the amparo, a series of exceptions can be identified in various legislations, regarding some particular and specific State activities that are expressly excluded. In this regard, we will

[32] See in *Revista de Derecho Público,* N° 55-56, Editorial Jurídica Venezolana, Caracas, 1993, p. 284.

[33] See in *Revista de Derecho Público,* N° 55-56, Editorial Jurídica Venezolana, Caracas, 1993, pp. 284-285.

[34] See in *Revista de Derecho Público,* N° 49, Editorial Jurídica Venezolana, Caracas, 1992, pp. 120-121.

analyze the situation regarding the amparo against legislative, executive and judicial acts as well as the particular exceptions established in the statutory regulations of the amparo suit.

1. The Amparo against legislative actions

Congress and parliamentary commissions are public authorities, and by means of its actions they can harm constitutional rights and guaranties; that is, legislative bodies, from national Congress down to municipal councils, can be a source of interference with personal freedom[35]. Against such legislative actions or omissions that injure constitutional rights or guarantees, amparo suits can be brought before the competent courts.

A. *Amparo against parliamentary bodies' and their commissions' decisions*

Regarding parliamentary bodies (Chambers) and its commissions, in Argentina, Costa Rica[36] and Venezuela, for instance, the amparo action has been admitted against their acts when they harm constitutional rights.

In Argentina, it was the case of the parliamentary enquiries developed in 1984 regarding the facts occurred during the previous de facto government, in which the parliamentary commission ordered the breaking into law offices of various lawyers and the seizure of documents. In the court decisions, particularly in the Case *Klein* decided in 1984, without questioning the powers of the parliamentary commissions to make inquiries, it was ruled that they cannot, without formal statutory provisions, validly restrict individual rights, in particular, to break into the personal domicile of people and to seize their personal documents. It was thus decided that the order, could only be taken based on a statutory provision, not by the sole decision of the commissions, and eventually based in a judicial order[37]

In Venezuela, a similar situation can be identified regarding the privative attributions of legislative bodies. Although the 1961 Constitution (Art. 159) set forth that they were not to be reviewed by other branches of government, regarding the former Congress and their commissions, the Supreme Court admitted the amparo action against their acts, in a decision dated January 31, 1991 (Caso: *Anselmo Natale*), ruling as follows:

> «The exclusion of judicial review regarding certain parliamentary acts -except in cases of extra limitation of powers- set forth in Article 159 of the Constitution, as a way to prevent, due to the rules of separation of powers, that the executive and judicial branches could invade or interfere in the orbit

---

35 See *Stuab v. City of Baxley*, 355 U.S. 313 (1958). See the comments in M. Glenn ABERNATHY and Barbara A. PERRY, *Civil Liberties under the Constitution*, University of South Carolina Press, 1993, pp. 12-13.

36 See Rubén HERNÁNDEZ VALLE, *Derecho Procesal Constitucional*, Editorial Juricentro, San José 2001, pp. 211-214.

37 See the comments on the First Instance decision of 1984 (1ª *InstCrimCorrFed*, Juzg N° 3, 10-9-84, ED 110-653) in Néstor Pedro SAGÜÉS, *Derecho procesal Constitucional*, Vol 3, *Acción de amparo*, Editorial Astrea Buenos Aires 1988, pp. 95-97; Joaquín Brague Camazano, *La Jurisdicción constitucional de la libertad (Teoría general, Argentina, México, Corte Interamericana de Derechos Humanos)*, Editorial Porrúa, México 2005, p. 98. José Luis Lazzarini, *El juicio de amparo*, Editorial La Ley, Buenos Aires 1987, pp. 216-216.

of the legislative body which is the trustee of the popular sovereignty, is restricted to determine the intrinsic regularity of such acts regarding the Constitution, in order to annul them, but it does not apply when it is a matter of obtaining the immediate reestablishment of the enjoyment and exercise of harmed rights and guarantees set forth in the Constitution»[38].

Consequently, after ruling -as has been above mentioned- that «it cannot exist any State act excluded from revision by means of amparo, the purpose of which is not to annul State acts but to protect public freedoms and restore its enjoyment when violated or harmed», the Supreme Court decided as follows:

> The Chamber considers that the constitutional amparo, understood in this way, can be filed by any person, natural or artificial, even against acts excluded from judicial control as those set forth in Article 159 of the Constitution as established in that provision, alleging a harm or violation of constitutional rights or guarantees, or those that being inherent to human beings, are not listed expressly in it»[39].

In the case of México, Article 73, VIII of the Amparo Law expressly excludes from the amparo suit, the resolutions and declarations of the Federal Congress and its Chambers, as well as of the State Legislative bodies and heir Commissions, regarding the election, suspension or dismissal of public officers, in cases in which the corresponding Constitutions confer them the power to resolve the matter in a sovereign or discretionary way[40]. There are also excluded from the amparo suit, the decisions adopted by the Representative Chamber of by the Senate in cases of impeachments, which Article 110 of the Constitution declares as non challenging ones[41].

In the United States, the general rule is that injunctions may not be directed against Congress; and injunctions have been rejected for instance to suspend a congressional subpoena, where the complainant had an adequate remedy to protect his rights in connection with a hearing[42].

B. *Amparo against laws (statutes)*

One of the most important issues regarding the Latin American amparo refers to the possibility of filing the amparo action against statutes, which if it is true that it is accepted in some countries like México, Venezuela and Guatemala, is excluded -in some cases expressly- in others, like Argentina, Brazil, Colombia, Chile, Costa Rica, El Salvador, Panama, Perú and Uruguay. But regardless of the acceptance in

---

38 See in *Revista de Derecho Público,* N° 45, Editorial Jurídica Venezolana, Caracas, 1991, p. 118.

39 See in *Revista de Derecho Público,* N° 45, Editorial Jurídica Venezolana, Caracas, 1991, p. 118. See also decision of the First Court on Judicial review of Administrative action of June 18, 1992 See in *Revista de Derecho Público,* N° 46, Editorial Jurídica Venezolana, Caracas, 1991, p. 125.

40 See Richard D. BAKER, *Judicial Review in México. A Study of the Amparo Suit,* Texas University Press, Austin 1971, p. 98.

41 See Eduardo FERRER MAC-GREGOR, *La acción constitucional de amparo en México y España. Estudio de derecho comparado,* Editorial Porrúa, México 2002, p. 378.

42 See U.S. -Mins et al. V. MCCARTY, 209 F. 2d 307 (D.C. Cir. 1953), in John Bourdeau et al, «Injunctions» in Kevin Schroder, John Glenn and Maureen Placilla, *Corpus Juris Secundum,* Volume 43A, Thomson West, 2004, p. 230.

some countries, the admissibility of the amparo action against laws has been progressively restricted, allowing in some countries its filing only against self-executing statutes (México), or only regarding the acts which apply the particular statute, not being in general, admitted directly against the statute itself, except in Guatemala.

In effect, in México, Article 1,I of the Amparo Law establishes that the amparo can be filed against statutes that violate the constitutional guarantees. In such cases, the amparo action can be filed directly against self executing or self applicable statutes (laws) when considered contrary to the Constitution, giving rise in such cases, to a judicial means of judicial review of constitutionality of the statutes. In these cases, the action can be filed directly against the statute, without any need for an administrative or judicial act of application of the statute, because the statute in itself is the one that causes direct harm to the constitutional guarantees of the plaintiff[43]. In these cases, the action has to be filed within 30 days following their enforcement. In such cases, the defendants are the supreme institutions of the State that had intervened in the drafting of the statute, that is, the Congress of the Union or the legislatures of the States that passed the statute, the President of the Republic or State Governors that ordered its execution and the Executive Secretariats that approved it and ordered its enactment.

Consequently, the amparo against laws in México, is considered a judicial means for the direct control of the constitutionality of such statutes, even if it is not brought in an abstract manner, since the claimant must have been directly harmed by the legislation, without the need for another state act for the application of the statute. On the contrary, when the statute in itself does not cause direct and personal harm to the claimant, that is, the statute is not self executing, the amparo action is inadmissible, unless it is filed against the State acts that apply it to a specific person[44]. As it is expressly set forth in Article 73,VI, the amparo suit is inadmissible «against statutes, treaties or regulations that, by its sole passing, they do not cause harm to the plaintiff, but need a subsequent act of its application in order for the prejudice to initiate». In these cases, of statutes that are not self-executing, the amparo action must be filed within 15 days following the issuing of the first act of its execution or application.

The main aspect to be stressed on the matter, of course, is the distinction between the self executing and not self executing laws. Following the doctrine established in the case of *Villera de Orellana María de los Angeles y coags.*, the former are those immediately obligatory, in which provisions the persons to whom are applicable are clearly and unmistakably identified, being *ipso jure* subjected to an obligation which implies the accomplishment of acts not previously required, resulting a prejudicial modification of the person's rights[45].

---

[43] See Garza Flores Hnos., Sucs., 28 S.J. 1208 (1930). See the reference in Richard D. BAKER, *Judicial Review in México. A Study of the Amparo Suit*, Texas University Press, Austin1971, p. 167.

[44] See Eduardo FERRER MAC-GREGOR, *La acción constitucional de amparo en México y España. Estudio de derecho comparado*, Editorial Porrúa, México 2002, p. 387.

[45] Suprema Corte de Justicia, 123 S.J. 783 (1955). See the comments in Richard D. BAKER, *Judicial Review in México. A Study of the Amparo Suit*, Texas University Press, Austin, 1971, pp. 168-173e.

The Mexican solution is similar to the United States exceptions to the doctrine of non-interference, according to which injunctions, if not admitted in principle against legislative acts, are admitted against municipal ordinances and regulations, when by its mere passage they immediately produce some irreparable loss or injury to the plaintiff[46].

According to the universality character of the system set forth in the Venezuelan Constitution regarding the acts that can be challenged by means of amparo, one of the most distinguishable innovations of the 1988 Amparo Law was the regulation of the amparo against statutes and other normative acts, complementing the general mixed system of judicial review[47]. In this regard, Article 3 of the Amparo law establishes the following:

> **Artículo 3°** The amparo action is also admissible when the violation or the threats of violation derives from a norm contrary to the constitution. In this case, the resulting judicial decision resolving the filed action, must take notice of the inapplicability of the challenged norm and the court must inform its decision to the Supreme Court.
>
> The action of amparo may also be brought together with the popular action of unconstitutionality of laws and other state normative acts, in which case, if it deems it necessary for the constitutional protection, the Supreme Court of Justice may suspend the application of the norm in respect of the specific juridical situation whose violation is alleged, whilst the suit for its annulment lasts.

This article sets forth two ways through which an amparo pretension can be filed before the competent court: in an autonomous way, or exercised together with the popular action of unconstitutionality of statutes. In the latter case, the amparo pretension is subordinated to the principal action for judicial review, producing only the possibility for the court to suspend the application of the statute pending the unconstitutionality suit. In this case, the situation is similar to the one of the popular action of unconstitutionality in the Dominican Republic when the amparo pretension is filed together with it[48].

But in the former case, Article 3 of the Venezuelan Amparo Law sets forth a direct amparo action against statutes, different to the popular action of unconstitutionality whose nullity results have *erga omnes* effects, seeking only the inapplicability of the statute to a concrete case with *inter partes* effects[49]. But even thought the clear wording of the article, it can be said that the amparo action against laws has in fact been eliminated in Venezuela as a consequence of the

46 See. *Larkins v. City of Denison*, 683 S.W. 2d 754 (Tex. App. Dallas 1984). See the reference to this and other court decisions on the matter in John Bourdeau et al, «Injunctions» in Kevin Schroder, John Glenn and Maureen Placilla, *Corpus Juris Secundum*, Volume 43A, Thomson West, 2004, pp. 257-260.

47 See Allan R. BREWER-CARÍAS, «Derecho y Acción de Amparo», Vol V, *Instituciones Políticas y Constitucionales*, Editorial Jurídica Venezolana, Caracas, 1998, pp. 227 ff.

48 See Eduardo Jorge PRATS, *Derecho Constitucional*, Vol. II, *Gaceta Judicial*, Santo Domingo 2005, p. 399.

49 See Allan R. BREWER-CARÍAS, «Derecho y Acción de Amparo», Vol V, *Instituciones Políticas y Constitucionales*, Editorial Jurídica Venezolana, Caracas 1998, pp. 224 ff; Rafael Chavero, *El nuevo régimen del amparo constitucional en Venezuela*, Editorial Sherwood, Caracas, 2001, pp. 553 ff.

interpretation made by the former Supreme Court of Justice, imposing the need of the action to be always and only directed against the State acts applying the statute and not directly against it. In a decision dated May 24, 1993, the Politico Administrative Chamber of the Supreme Court issued a decision that has been the leading case on the matter, ruling that:

> Thus, it seem that there is no doubt that Article 3 of the Amparo law does not set forth the possibility of filing an amparo action directly against a normative act, but against the act, fact or omission that has its origin in a normative provision which is considered by the claimant as contrary to the Constitution and for which, due to the presumption of legitimacy and constitutionality of the former, the court must previously resolve its inapplicability to the concrete case argued. It is obvious, thus, that such article of the Amparo law does not allow the possibility of filing this action for constitutional protection against a statute or other normative act, but against the act which applies or executes it, which is definitively the one that in the concrete case can cause a particular harm to the constitutional rights and guaranties of a precise person»[50].

The Court, in its decision, admitted the distinction between the self executing and not self executing statutes, ruling that the former imposes an immediate obligation for the persons to whom it is issued, with its promulgation; and on the contrary, the latter requires an act for its later execution, in which case its sole promulgation cannot produce a constitutional violation»[51]. But even though it admits the distinction, the Supreme Court concluded its ruling declaring the impossibility for a real normative act to directly and by itself, harm the constitutional orbit of a concrete and particular situation of an individual.

But by rejecting the possibility of direct harms that a statute can cause to particular constitutional rights, the Court in principle admitted the possibility for the unconstitutional statute to cause threats to those same persons' rights, ruling that in such case the threats ought to be «imminent, possible and realizable» in order for an amparo action to be admitted. But in the same decision, such possibility was rejected with the following argument:

> «In case of an amparo action against a norm, the concretion of the possible harm would not be 'immediate', because it will always be the need for a competent authority to execute or apply it in order for the statute to effectively harm the claimant. It must be concluded that the probable harm produced by the norm will always be a mediate and indirect one, due to the need for the statute to be applied to the concrete case. So that the harm will be caused by mean of the act applying the illegal norm.
>
> The same occurs with the third condition, in the sense that the probable and imminent threat will never be made by the possible defendant. If it would be possible to sustain that the amparo could be admissible against a statute whose constitutionality is challenged, it would be necessary to accept as aggrieved party the legislative body issuing it, being the party to participate in the

---

50 See in *Revista de Derecho Público*, N° 55-56, Editorial Jurídica Venezolana, Caracas, 1993, pp. 287-288.

51 See in *Revista de Derecho Público*, N° 55-56, Editorial Jurídica Venezolana, Caracas, 1993, p. 285.

process as defendant. But it must be highlighted that in the case in which the possible harm could be realized, it would not be the legislative body the one called to execute it, but rather the public officer that must apply the norm in all the cases in which an individual is located in the situation regulated.

If it is understood that the object of the amparo action is the statute, then the conclusion would be that the possible defendant (the public entity enacting the norm whose unconstitutionality is alleged) could not be the one that could make the threat. The concrete harm would be definitively made by a different entity or person (the one applying the unconstitutional norm to a specific and concrete case)[52].

From the above mentioned, the Venezuelan Supreme Court concluded rejecting the amparo action against statutes and normative acts, not only because it considered that the Amparo laws does not set forth such possibility -bypassing its text-, but because even being possible to bring the extraordinary action against a normative act, it would not comply with the imminent, possible and realizable conditions of the threats set forth in Article 6,2 of the Amparo Law.

In Guatemala the amparo against laws is established in a direct form, being the Constitutional Courts empowered to «declare in specific cases that a statute, a regulation, resolution or act of the authorities does not bind the claimant, since it contravenes or restricts any of the rights guaranteed by the Constitution or recognized by any Law (Article 10,b Guatemala Law). This same judicial power, but only regarding to executive regulations, is established in Honduras (Article 41,b Law). In both cases, the judicial decisions on amparo suspend the application of the statute, the executive regulation, resolution or challenged act in respect of the claimant, and if applicable, the re-establishment of the juridical situation affected or the cessation of the measure (Article 49,a Guatemala)[53].

In other Latin American countries, the possibility of bringing an action of amparo against statutes is expressly excluded. This is the case of Costa Rica, where the Law on Constitutional Jurisdiction provides that the amparo action against statutes and other regulatory provisions is not admissible, except when challenged together with the acts individually applying it, or when dealing with automatically enforced regulations, in such a way that their prescriptions become automatically enforceable simply by their enactment, without the need for other regulations or acts that develop them or render them applicable to the claimant (Art 30,a Costa Rica Law). Nonetheless, in these cases, the amparo against the self executing statute is not directly decided by the Constitutional Chamber, and instead, it is converted into a direct action on judicial review of the constitutionality of the challenged statute[54]. In such cases, the President of the Constitutional Chamber must suspend the procedure and give the plaintiff 15 days in order for him to formalize a direct action on judicial review of constitutionality against the statute (Art. 48 Costa Rica Law). So, only after the statute is annulled by the Constitutional Chamber, the amparo action will be decided.

---

52 See in *Revista de Derecho Público,* N° 55-56, Editorial Jurídica Venezolana, Caracas, 1993, pp. 288 a 290.

53 See Edmundo ORELLANA, *La justicia constitucional en Honduras*, Universidad Nacional Autónoma de Honduras, Tegucigalpa, 1993, p. 102, note 26.

54 See Rubén HERNÁNDEZ, *Derecho Procesal Constitucional,* Editorial Juricentro, San José, 2001, pp. 45, 208-209, 245, 223.

In Uruguay, in similar sense, the amparo against statutes is excluded regarding statutes and State acts of similar rank (Art. 1,c Law 16011), being the only means to challenge the constitutionality of a statute, the judicial action file to obtain a declaration of its unconstitutionality in a concrete case by the Supreme Court. In such cases, the amparo pretension can only have a suppressive effect regarding the application of the statute to the plaintiff pending the Supreme Court decision on the unconstitutionality of the statute[55]

In Argentina, even with its longstanding tradition on judicial review of legislation by means of the diffuse method of judicial review, the amparo against statutes is not admitted[56]. Nonetheless, if in an amparo action against State acts, the statute in which the challenged act is based is considered unconstitutional, the amparo judge, by means of the diffuse method of judicial review can decide upon the inapplicability of the statute in the case. In this regard, Article 2,d of the Amparo Law when setting forth that the amparo action is not admissible «when for the purpose of determining the invalidity of the challenged act it is required the declaration of the unconstitutionality a the statute», has been considered as not being in force because it contradicts Article 31 of the Constitution (supremacy clause)[57]. Additionally, Article 43 of the 1994 Constitution, now regulating the amparo action, has expressly solved the discussion by setting forth that «In the case, the judge can declare the unconstitutionality of the norm in which the act or omission is based». After discussions based in previous legislation, regarding the admissibility in the judicial doctrine of the amparo against self executing statutes[58], in similar sense to the Argentinean solution, the Perúvian Constitutional Procedure Code has established as follows: «When it is argued that the acts causing threats or violation are based in the application of a norm not compatible with the Constitution, the decision declaring the claim founded must additionally decide on the inapplicability of such norm» (Article 43). In this case, also, the court in order to decide must use its judicial review powers through the diffuse method.

In other countries, the amparo action against statutes is just declared as inadmissible in the legislation or considered as such by the courts: as is the case in Chile[59], Uruguay (Art. 1,c Amparo Law), Panamá and El Salvador[60]. In Brazil, the *mandado de segurança* is also excluded against laws or legal provisions when they have not been applied through an administrative act[61]. In Colombia, the tutela action is also excluded regarding all «acts of a general, impersonal and abstract

---

55 See Luis Alberto VIERA, *Ley de Amparo*, Ediciones Idea, Montevideo 1993, pp. 23.

56 See José Luis LAZZARINI, *El juicio de amparo*, Editorial La Ley, Buenos Aires 1987, p. 214; Néstor Pedro SAGÜÉS, *Derecho procesal Constitucional*, Vol 3, *Acción de amparo*, Editorial Astrea Buenos Aires 1988, p. 97.

57 See Néstor Pedro SAGÜÉS, *Derecho procesal Constitucional*, Vol 3, *Acción de amparo*, Editorial Astrea Buenos Aires 1988, pp. 243-258.

58 See Samuel B. ABAD YUPANQUI, *El proceso constitucional de amparo*, Gaceta Jurídica, Lima 2004, pp. 352-374.

59 Humberto NOGUEIRA ALCALÁ, «El derecho de amparo o protección de los derechos humanos, fundamentales o esenciales en Chile: evolución y perspectivas», in Humberto Nogueira Alcalá (Editor), *Acciones constitucionales de amparo y protección: realidad y perspectivas en Chile y América Latina*», Editorial Universidad de Talca, Talca 2000, p. 45.

60 See Edmundo ORELLANA, *La Justicia Constitucional en Honduras*, Universidad Nacional Autónoma de Honduras, Editorial Universitaria, Tegucigalpa 1993, p 102, note 26.

61 See José Luis LAZZARINI, *El juicio de amparo*, La Ley, Buenos Aires, 1987, pp. 213-214.

nature» (Art 6,5); and in Nicaragua, the amparo action is not admissible «against the process of drafting the statute, its promulgation or publication or any other legislative act or resolution» (Article 51, Law).

2. Amparo against executive and administrative acts and actions

The general terms, it can be said that the amparo action was born seeking the protection from executive authorities, in particular, against administrative acts issued by public officers or facts or omissions accomplished by them; that is, against acts, facts or omissions from the entities or bodies forming Public Administration at all its levels (national, state, municipal). These acts, facts or omissions are always considered as produced by public authorities, particularly from the executive branch of government and its decentralized or deconcentrated bodies.

In general terms it can be said that in all Latin American countries the amparo actions are admitted against executive and administrative acts causing harms or threats to constitutional rights and guarantees, including acts issued by the Head of the Executive, that is, the President of the Republic, in contrary sense to what happens in the United States where in principle, the coercive remedy of an injunction cannot be directed against the President[62]. The only express exceptions on these matters are the Mexican amparo suit against executive acts of expulsion of foreigners from the territory (Art. 33)[63], and in Uruguay, the amparo action against executive regulations[64].

Regarding in particular the amparo against administrative acts, Article 5 of the Venezuelan Amparo Law[65] provides that:

> The action of amparo shall be admitted against any administrative act, material action, irreversible facts, abstentions or omissions that violate or threaten

[62] See Sloan v. Nixon, 60 F.R.D. 228 (S.D.N.Y. 1973), aff'd, 93 F.2d 1398 (2d Cir. 1974), judgment aff'd, 419 U.S. 958, 95 S. Ct. 218, 42 L. Ed. 2d 174 (1974). See the reference in John BOURDEAU et al, «Injunctions» in Kevin Schroder, John Glenn and Maureen Placilla, *Corpus Juris Secundum*, Volume 43A, Thomson West, 2004, p. 229.

[63] See Eduardo FERRER MAC-GREGOR, *La acción constitucional de amparo en México y España. Estudio de derecho comparado*, Editorial Porrúa, México 2002, p. 377.

[64] See Luis Alberto VIERA, *Ley de Amparo*, Ediciones Idea, Montevideo 1993, pp. 99.

[65] **Artículo 5.** *La acción de amparo contra actos administrativos, vías de y hecho y conductas omisivas de la Administración.* La acción de amparo procede contra todo acto administrativo, actuaciones materiales, vías de hecho, abstenciones u omisiones que violen o amenacen violar un derecho o una garantía constitucionales, cuando no exista un medio procesal breve, sumario y eficaz, acorde con la protección constitucional.
Cuando la acción de amparo se ejerza contra actos administrativos de efectos particulares o contra abstenciones o negativas de la Administración, podrá formularse ante el Juez Contencioso-Administrativo competente, si lo hubiere en la localidad, conjuntamente con el recurso contencioso administrativo de anulación de actos administrativos o contra las conductas omisivas, respectivamente, que se ejerza. En estos casos, el Juez, en forma breve, sumaria, efectiva y conforme a lo establecido en el artículo 22, si lo considera procedente para la protección constitucional, suspenderá los efectos del acto recurrido como garantía de dicho derecho constitucional violado, mientras dure el juicio.
Parágrafo Único. Cuando se ejerza la acción de amparo contra actos administrativos conjuntamente con el recurso contencioso-administrativo que se fundamente en la violación de un derecho constitucional, el ejercicio del recurso procederá en cualquier tiempo, aun después de transcurridos los lapsos de caducidad previstos en la Ley y no será necesario el agotamiento previo de la vía administrativa.

to violate a constitutional right or guarantee, when there is no brief, summary and efficient procedure available, in accordance with the constitutional protection.

When an action for amparo is brought against administrative acts of particular effects or against abstentions or denials of Public Administration, it can be filed before the Judicial review of administrative action jurisdiction, together with the judicial review recourse seeking the nullity of administrative acts or against the omission. In such cases, in a brief, summary and effective way, if it deems necessary for the constitutional protection, pending the suit, the court may suspend the effects of the challenged act, as guarantee of the violated constitutional right.

In such cases of exercising the amparo action together with the judicial review recourse against the administrative act based on violation of a constitutional right, there will be no delay for the exercise of the recourse, which can be brought even after those statutorily established lapses have elapsed, and it will not be necessary the exhaustion of the administrative recourses.

This regulation can be considered as one of the most comprehensive in all Latin American Amparo laws regarding amparo actions against administrative acts, regulating the possibility of exercising the amparo action in two ways: in an autonomous way or together with a nullity recourse for judicial review of the act. Regarding the latter, the former Supreme Court of Justice in the decision of July, 10, 1991 (Caso: *Tarjetas Banvenez*), clarified that in such case, the action is not a principal one, but subordinated and ancillary regarding the principal recourse to which it has been attached, and subjected to the final nullifying decision that has to be issued in it[66]. That is why, in such cases, the amparo pretension that must be founded in a grave presumption of the violation of the constitutional right, has a preventive and temporal character, pending the final decision of the nullity suit, consisting in the suspension of the effects of the challenged administrative act. This provisional character of the amparo protection pending the suit, is thus subjected to the final decision to be issued in the nullity judicial review procedure against the challenged administrative act[67].

The main difference between both procedures according to the Supreme Court doctrine is that:

In the first case of the autonomous amparo action against administrative acts, the plaintiff must allege a direct, immediate and flagrant violation to the constitutional right, which in its own demonstrates the need for the amparo order as a definitive means to restore the harmed juridical situation. In the second case, given the suspensive nature of the amparo order which only tends to provisionally stop the effects of the injuring act until the judicial review of administrative action confirming or nullifying it is decided, the alleged unconstitutional violations of constitutional provisions can be formulated together with violations of legal or statutory provisions developing the constitutional ones, because it is a judicial review action against administrative acts, seeking their nullity, they can also be founded on legal

66 See the text in *Revista de Derecho Público,* N° 47, Editorial Jurídica Venezolana, Caracas, 1991, pp. 169-174 See also the comments in *Revista de Derecho Público,* N° 50, Editorial Jurídica Venezolana, Caracas, 1992, pp. 183-184.

67 *Idem.* pp. 170-171.

texts. What the court cannot do in these cases of filing together the actions, in order to suspend the effects of the challenged administrative act, is to found its decision only in the legal violations alleged, because that would mean to anticipate the final decision on the principal nullity judicial review recourse[68].

The Supreme Court then concluded affirming that the final distinction between both lies, first, in their purpose: in the autonomous action of amparo against administrative acts it has a restorative character, and in the case of the amparo filed together with the judicial review action against the challenged act, it has a nullifying character. Second, in the first case the alleged and proved constitutional right violation must be a direct, immediate and flagrant one; in the second case, what has to be proved is the existence of a grave presumption of the constitutional violation. And third, in the first case, the judicial decision issued is a definitive constitutional protection one; in the second case, it has only preventive character of suspension of the effects of the challenged act pending the principal judicial review process[69].

In some way similar to the Venezuelan solution, in Article 8 of the Colombian Tutela Law[70] it can also be found a regulation regarding the «tutela as a transitory mean» of protection, as follows:

First, it is provided that even in case the injured party would have another judicial means of protection, the action for tutela will be admitted when used as a transitory means in order to prevent an irreparable damage. In such cases, the court will expressly rule in its decision that the protection [order] will be in force only during the term the competent judicial court will use in order to decide on the merits of the action brought by the injured party. In any case, the affected party must file such action in the maximum delay of 4 month from the tutela decision. In case that the action is not filed, the tutela decision will cease in its effects.

Second, in cases in which the tutela is used as a transitory means in order to prevent an irreparable injury, the action for tutela can also be filed together with the nullifying action before the judicial review of administrative action (contencioso-administrativo) jurisdiction. In these cases, if the court deems it justified, it could order, pending the process, the non application of the particular act regarding the concrete juridical situation whose protection is being demanded.

---

68 *Idem.*, pp. 171-172.

69 *Idem.*, p. 172. See also regarding the nullity of article 22 of the Organic Amparo law the Supreme Court decisión dated May 21, 1996, in Allan R. BREWER-CARÍAS, *Acción y Derecho de* Amparo, Tomo V, *Instituciones Políticas y Constitucionales*, Editorial Jurídica Venezolana, Caracas, 1996, pp. 392 y ss.

70 **Artículo 8° La tutela como mecanismo transitorio.** Aún cuando el afectado disponga de otro medio de defensa judicial, la acción de tutela procederá cuando se utilice como mecanismo transitorio para evitar un perjuicio irremediable.
En el caso del inciso anterior, el juez señalará expresamente en la sentencia que su orden permanecerá vigente sólo durante el término que la autoridad judicial competente utilice para decidir de fondo sobre la acción instaurada por el afectado.
En todo caso el afectado deberá ejercer dicha acción en un término máximo de cuatro (4) meses a partir del fallo de tutela.
Si no se instaura, cesarán los efectos de éste.
Cuando se utilice como mecanismo transitorio para evitar un daño irreparable, la acción de tutela también podrá ejercerse conjuntamente con la acción de nulidad y de las demás precedentes ante la jurisdicción de lo contencioso administrativo. En estos casos, el juez si lo estima procedente podrá ordenar que no se aplique el acto particular respecto de la situación jurídica concreta cuya protección se solicita, mientras dure el proceso.

Finally, regarding executive and administrative acts and actions, mention must be made of the Argentinean restriction regarding the possible filing of the amparo action, in matters related to national defense and to public services (public utilities).

Article 2,b of the Amparo Law declares inadmissible the amparo action against «acts issued in express application of the Law 16.970», which is the so called Law of National Defense. For this exception to be applied, it has been considered that the challenged act must in a clear and exact way rely on the provisions of such law[71].

On the other hand, also in Argentina, the Amparo Law sets forth the inadmissibility of the amparo action in cases in which «the judicial intervention could directly or indirectly place in a compromising situation the regularity, continuity and efficacy of rendering a public service for the development of the essential activities of the State» (Article 2,c). Due to the general expressions used in the article (compromising, directly, indirectly, regularity, continuity, efficacy, rendering, public service), this provision has been highly criticized, being considered that with it «it is difficult to see an amparo against the State to be granted»[72], particularly, due to the fact that any administrative activity of the State can always be related to a public service[73]. Nonetheless, the final decision corresponds to the court, and if it is true that in practice the exception has hardly been used[74], in some important matters it was alleged. It happened for instance in the amparo actions filed in 1985 against the Central Bank of the Republic decision suspending for a few months delay the payments of the deposits in foreign currency. Even though some courts rejected amparo actions in the matter[75], in the «Peso» Case the Federal National Chamber on judicial review of administrative actions of Buenos Aires decided to reject the arguments asking for the rejection of the amparo action based in the consideration of the matter as related to a «public service», considering that the Central bank activities have not the elements to be considered as a public service in the sense of public utility[76]. A few years latter, regarding similar decisions of the Central Bank on the non payments of deposit in foreign currencies, in the cases referred to as the «Corralito», there was no allegation whatsoever considering those Central Bank decisions, which were adopted on situation of state of economic emergency, as public service activities. In such cases, the amparo actions were admitted and granted, but with multiple judicial incidents[77].

---

71 See Case *Diario El Mundo c/ Gobierno nacional*, CNFed, Sala 1 ContAdm, 30/4/74, JA, 23-1974-195. See the comments in Néstor Pedro SAGÜÉS, *Derecho procesal Constitucional*, Vol 3, *Acción de amparo*, Editorial Astrea Buenos Aires 1988, pp. 212-214.

72 José Luis LAZZARINI, *El juicio de amparo*, La Ley, Buenos Aires, 1987, p. 231.

73 Néstor Pedro SAGÜÉS, *Derecho procesal Constitucional*, Vol 3, *Acción de amparo*, Editorial Astrea Buenos Aires 1988, pp. 226 ff.

74 See José Luis LAZZARINI, *El juicio de amparo*, La Ley, Buenos Aires, 1987, p. 233; Néstor Pedro SAGÜÉS, *Derecho procesal Constitucional, Vol 3, Acción de amparo*, Editorial Astrea Buenos Aires 1988, p. 228.

75 See Cfed B. Blanca, 13/8/85, ED, 116-116. See the comments in Alí Joaquín SALGADO, *Juicio de amparo y acción de inconstitucionalidad*, Editorial Astrea 1987, p. 51, note 59.

76 See CNFedConAdm, Sala IV, 13/6/85, ED, 114-231. See the comments in Alí Joaquín SALGADO, *Juicio de amparo y acción de inconstitucionalidad*, Editorial Astrea, 1987, p. 50, note 56.

77 See for instance the *Smith* and the *San Luis* cases, 2002, in Antonio María HERNÁNDEZ, *Las emergencias y el orden constitucional*, Universidad Nacional Autónoma de México, México 2003, pp. 71 ff. And 119 ff. In Duch cases, the Laws and Decrees of Economic Emergency were declared unconstitutional.

3. Amparo against judicial acts and decisions

There is a general acceptance of the amparo action as a specific judicial means for constitutional rights protection against administrative acts (including those administrative acts issued by courts and tribunals), but the same cannot be said regarding judicial decisions on jurisdictional matters. In some countries, their Amparo Laws expressly reject and consider inadmissible the filing of amparo actions against judicial decisions, issued applying jurisdictional power[78]. This is the case of Argentina (Art. 2,b)[79], Bolivia (Art. 96,3), Costa Rica (Art. 30,b)[80], Chile[81], Dominican Republic[82], Ecuador[83], Nicaragua (Art. 51,b), Paraguay (Art. 2,a) and Uruguay (Art. 2,a)[84]. In El Salvador and Honduras, the exclusion is in particular referred to judicial acts issued «in judicial matters that are purely civil, commercial or labor-related, and in respect of definitive decisions in criminal matters» (El Salvador, Art. 13; Honduras Art. 45,6). In Brazil, the *mandado de seguranca* Statute excludes it against judicial decisions when according to the procedure statutes it exists a judicial recourse against them, or when they can be modified by means of correction (Art. 5,II).

On the contrary, in other Latin American countries, the amparo action can be filed against judicial decisions, as is the case in México, where the direct amparo suit finds its broadest application (amparo cassation)[85], and is also the case in Guatemala (Art. 10,h), Honduras (Arts. 9,3 and,10,2,*a*), Panama (Art. 2615)[86], Perú and Venezuela.

The general principle in this cases, as set forth in the Perúvian Code on Constitutional Procedures, is that the amparo is admitted against definitive judicial resolutions when «they manifestly impair the effective procedural protection,

---

78 Administrative acts issued by courts can be challenged by means of amparo. See for exaple, regarding Argentina, Néstor Pedro SAGÜÉS, *Derecho procesal Constitucional, Vol 3, Acción de amparo,* Editorial Astrea Buenos Aires 1988, pp. 197 ff.

79 See Joaquin BRAGUE CAMAZANO, *La Jurisdicción constitucional de la libertad (Teoría general, Argentina, México, Corte Interamericana de Derechos Humanos),* Editorial Porrúa, México 2005, p. 98. José Luis LAZZARINI, *El juicio de amparo,* Editorial La Ley, Buenos Aires 1987, pp. 218–223; Alí Joaquín SALGADO, *Juicio de amparo y acción de inconstitucionalidad,* Astrea, Buenos Aires, 1987, p. 46.

80 See Rubén HERNÁNDEZ VALLE, *Derecho Procesal Constitucional,* Editorial Juricentro, San José 2001, pp. 45, 206, 223, 226.

81 See Juan Manuel ERRAZURIZ G. and Jorge Miguel OTERO A., *Aspectos procesales del recurso de protección,* Editorial Jurídica de Chile, Santiago 1989, p. 103. Nonetheless, some authors considers that sthe recourse for protection is admisible against judicial decisions when issued in an arbitrary way and in violation of due process rights.See Humberto NOGUEIRA ALCALÁ, «El derecho de amparo o protección de los derechos humanos, fundamentales o esenciales en Chile: evolución y perspectivas», in Humberto Nogueira Alcalá (Editor), *Acciones constitucionales de amparo y protección: realidad y perspectivas en Chile y América Latina»,* Editorial Universidad de Talca, Talca 2000, p. 45.

82 See Eduardo Jorge PRATS, *Derecho Constitucional,* Vol. II, Gaceta Judicial, Santo Domingo 2005, p. 391.

83 Hernán SALGADO PESANTES, *Manual de Justicia Constitucional Ecuatoriana,* Corporación Editora nacional, Quito 2004, p. 84.

84 See Luis Alberto VIERA, *Ley de Amparo,* Ediciones Idea, Montevideo 1993, pp. 50, 97.

85 See Richard D. BAKER, *Judicial Review in México. A Study of the Amparo Suit,* Texas University Press, Austin 1971, p. 98.

86 With no suspensive effects. See Boris BARRIOS GONZÁLEZ, *Derecho Procesal Constitucional,* Editorial Portobelo, Panama 2002, p. 159.

including access to justice and due process» (Art. 4)[87]. In the case of Venezuela, in a similar way to what it was established in the Perúvian legislation prior to the Code, Article 4 of the Amparo law provides that «the action of amparo shall also be admitted when a Tribunal of the Republic, acting outside its competence, pronounces a resolution or decision or orders an action that impairs a constitutional right». Since no court has power to unlawfully cause harm to constitutional rights or guarantees, the amparo against judicial decisions is admitted when a court decision directly harms the constitutional rights of the plaintiff, normally related to the due process of law rights. As was decided by the Cassation Chamber of the former Supreme Court of Justice in a decision of December 5, 1990, the amparo against judicial decisions is admitted «when the decision in itself injures the juridical conscience, when harming in a flagrant way individual rights that cannot be renounced or when the decision violates the principle of juridical security (judicial stability), deciding against *res judicata*, or when issued in a process where the plaintiff's right to defense has not been guaranteed, or in any way the due process guarantee has been violated»[88].

In Colombia, Article 40 of the the Decree N° 2.591 of 1991, due to the fact that the Constitution did not exclude it, also established the possibility of bringing an action of amparo against judicial actions, when the impairment of the right is a direct consequence of them, adding that «when the right invoked is that of due process, the tutela shall be brought together with the appropriate recourse», that is, together with the recourse of appeal». Notwithstanding the statutory admissibility of tutela against judicial decisions, the Constitutional Court in ruling C-543 of October 1, 1992, declared the aforementioned Article 40 of Decree 2.591 unconstitutional, and hence null and void, considering it contrary to the principle of intangibility of the *res judicata*.[89] Nonetheless, one year later, and after numerous judicial decisions on the matter, the same Constitutional Court admitted the tutela action against judicial decisions when they constitute a *vía de hecho* (voi de fait) or factual action[90], being considering as such:

> The ostensible and grave violation of the rules governing the process in which the challenged decision was issued, up to the point that because the flagrant disregard of the due process and other constitutional, the plaintiff's constitutional rights had been directly violated by the challenged act.
>
> This means that the via de hecho is in fact the arbitrary exercise of the judicial function, in such terms that the deciding court has decided not according to law -which thus has been violated- but only according to its personal will»[91]

---

87 See Samuel B. ABAD YUPANQUI, *El proceso constitucional de amparo*, Gaceta Jurídica, Lima, 2004, p. 326

88 *Case José Díaz Aquino*, also refered to in decisión dated December 14, 1994 of the same cassation Chamber. See the reference in Alan R. BREWER-CARÍAS, «Derecho y Acción de Amparo», *Instituciones Políticas y Constitucionales* Vol V, Editorial Jurídica Venezolana, Caracas, 1998, pp. 261 ff; Rafael CHAVERO, *El nuevo régimen del amparo constitucional en Venezuela*, Editorial Sherwood, Caracas, 2001, pp. 483 ff.

89 See in Manuel José CEPEDA ESPINOSA, *Derecho Constitucional jurisprudencial. Las grandes decisiones de la Corte Constitucional*, Legis, Bogotá 2001, pp. 1009 ff.

90 See decision S-231 dated May 13, 1994, in Manuel José CEPEDA ESPINOSA, *Derecho Constitucional jurisprudencial. Las grandes decisiones de la Corte Constitucional*, Legis, Bogotá, 2001, pp. 1022 ff.

91 See SU-1218 decision of November 21, 2001. See in Juan Carlos ESGUERRA, *La protección constitucional del ciudadano,* Legis, Bogotá 2004, p. 164. See Eduardo CIFUENTES MUÑOZ, «Tutela contra sentencias (El caso colombiano)», in Humberto Nogueira Alcalá (Editor), *Acciones constitucionales de amparo y protección: realidad y perspectivas en Chile y América Latina*», Editorial Universidad de Talca, Talca 2000, pp. 307 ff.

According to this doctrine, applicable to almost all the other cases in which the amparo action is admissible against judicial decisions, it can be said that for granting the amparo, the challenged judicial decision must have been issued in grave and flagrant violation of the due process of law guaranties, thus constituting not a lawful decision but an unlawful one or *vía de hecho*, that is, an action with no legal support whatsoever.

In a certain way regarding injunctions on judicial matters, it can be said that in the United States, injunction can also be granted when for instance, it clearly appears that the prosecution of law actions will result in fraud, gross wrong or oppression, and that justice clearly requires equitable interference. As has been decided by the courts:

> «The power of a court of equity to interfere with the general right of a person to sue and to restrain the person from prosecuting the action will be exercised only where it appears clearly that the prosecution of the law action will result in a fraud, gross wrong, or oppression, and that conscience and justice clearly require equitable interference. Accordingly, an action at law may be restrained under these restrictive rules where a person is attempting to, or would, through the instrumentality of an action at law, obtain an unconscionable advantage of another».[92]

On the other hand, some restrictions have been established in the Amparo law admitting the amparo actions against judicial decisions. Besides the need to the exhaustion of the available ordinary judicial recourses against the challenged decision, the decisions of the Supreme Court (México, Panama, Art 2.615; Venezuela, Art 6,6) or the Constitutional Tribunal (Perú) had been expressly excluded form the amparo action. In some cases, the judicial amparo decision itself cannot be the object of another amparo suit (Honduras, Art 45,2; México, Art. 73,II[93]); in the same sense that in the United States, an injunction against an injunction, sometimes referred to as a counter injunction, should not be issued[94]. In other countries, on the contrary, the amparo actions are admitted even against amparo judicial decisions (Colombia[95], Perú[96], Venezuela[97] because those decisions, in their selves, can also additionally violate constitutional rights, different to those claimed in the initial suit.

4. Amparo against acts of other constitutional entities

In contemporary Latin American constitutional law, additionally to the three classic branches of government, the separation of powers principle has given origin

---

92 See Miles v. Illinois Cent. R. Co. 315 U.S. 698, 62 S. Ct. 827, 86 L. Ed. 1129, 146 A.L.R 1104 (1942); Langenau Mfg. Co. v. City of Cleveland, 159 Ohio St. 525, 50 Ohio *Op*. 435, 112 N.E. 2d 658 (1953); Kardy v. Shook, 237 Md. 524, 207 A2d 83 (1965). See in John BOURDEAU et al, «Injunctions» in Kevin Schroder, John Glenn and Maureen Placilla, *Corpus Juris Secundum*, Volume 43A, Thomson West, 2004, pp. 114-115.

93 See Eduardo FERRER MAC-GREGOR, *La acción constitucional de amparo en México y España. Estudio de derecho comparado*, Editorial Porrúa, México 2002, p. 379.

94 See Sellers v. Valenzuela, 249 Ala. 620, 32 So. 2d 520 (1947). See in John BOURDEAU et al, «Injunctions» in Kevin Schroder, John Glenn and Maureen Placilla, *Corpus Juris Secundum*, Volume 43A, Thomson West, 2004, pp. 87.

95 See Juan Carlos ESGUERRA, *La protección constitucional del ciudadano*, Legis, Bogotá 2004, p. 164.

96 See Samuel B. ABAD YUPANQUI, *El proceso constitucional de amparo*, Gaceta Jurídica, Lima 2004, pp. 327, 330.

97 See Allan R. BREWER-CARÍAS, «Derecho y Acción de Amparo», Vol. V, *Instituciones Políticas y Constitucionales*, Editorial Jurídica Venezolana, Caracas, 1998, pp. 263 ff.

to other State organs, not dependent on the Legislative, Executive or Judicial branches, with certain types of autonomy and independence. It is the case, for instance of the Electoral bodies, in charge of governing the electoral processes, the Peoples' Defendant or Human Rights Defendants Office, the Public Prosecutor Offices, the General Audit entities (Contraloría General) and the Council of the Judiciary for the government and administration of courts and tribunals. Being State organs, their acts, facts and omissions can also be challenged by means of amparo actions when violating constitutional rights.

Nonetheless, regarding these State entities, some exceptions have been established regarding the justicablility of their actions by means of amparo actions. For instance, in Costa Rica (Art. 30,d)[98], México (Art. 73,VII)[99], Nicaragua (Art. 51,5), Panamá (Art. 2.615)[100], Perú (Art. 5,8)[101] and Uruguay (Art. 1,b), the amparo suit is excluded regarding acts of the electoral bodies, in similar sense as the injunctions are excluded in the United States regarding actions of the election officers in the performance of their duties[102].

On the other hand, regarding the Council of the Judiciary (Consejo de la Magistratura), the Perúvian Amparo Law excludes the acts of that entity from being challenged through the amparo action, when referred to the dismissal or ratification of judges, when the decisions are duly motivated and issued after the interested party being heard (Art. 5,7)[103].

5. The amparo action and the political questions

In has been a traditional judicial doctrine in the United States to consider as non justifiable the so called «political questions» mainly related to the «separation of powers» and particularly with «the relationship between the judiciary and the co-ordinate branches of the Federal Government».[104] It is considered that the

---

98 See Rubén HERNÁNDEZ VALLE, *Derecho Procesal Constitucional*, Editorial Juricentro, San José 2001, pp. 228-229. Other matters decided by the Tribunal Supremo de Elecciones like citizenship, personal capacity or personal status matters, are justiciables by means of amparo. See José Miguel VILLALOBOS, «El recurso de amparo en Costa Rica» in», in Humberto Nogueira Alcalá (Editor), *Acciones constitucionales de amparo y protección: realidad y perspectivas en Chile y América Latina»*, Editorial Universidad de Talca, Talca 2000, pp 222-223.

99 See Eduardo FERRER MAC-GREGOR, *La acción constitucional de amparo en México y España. Estudio de derecho comparado*, Editorial Porrúa, México 2002, p. 378; See Richard D. BAKER, *Judicial Review in México. A Study of the Amparo Suit*, Texas University Press, Austin, 1971, pp. 98, 152.

100 See Boris BARRIOS GONZÁLEZ, *Derecho Procesal Constitucional*, Editorial Portobelo, Panama 2002, p. 161.

101 Nonetheless, the amparo action can be admitted if the decision of the Jurado Nacional de Elecciones does not have jurisdiccional nature or if jurisdiccional, it violates the effective judicial protection (due process). See Samuel B. ABAD YUPANQUI, *El proceso constitucional de amparo*, Gaceta Jurídica, Lima 2004, pp. 128, 421, 447.

102 See Boyd v. Story, 350 Ark. 56, 84 S.W.3d 444 (2002). See in in John BOURDEAU et al, «Injunctions» in Kevin Schroder, John Glenn and Maureen Placilla, *Corpus Juris Secundum*, Volume 43A, Thomson West, 2004, pp. 238-239.

103 See Samuel B. ABAD YUPANQUI, *El proceso constitucional de amparo*, Gaceta Jurídica, Lima 2004, p. 126.

104 Baker v. Carr, 369 U.S. 186 (1962). See in See M. Glenn ABERNATHY and Barbara A. PERRY, *Civil Liberties under the Constitution*, Sixth Edition, University of South Carolina Press, 1993, pp. 6-7.

preemptive political nature of these questions imposes their solution in the political branches of government rather than in the courts. That is why, the exemption not only applies to judicial review in general, but also to injunctions.

The main source of questions considered as political and thus non justiciable by the Supreme Court are related to foreign affairs which involves -as the Supreme Court stated in *Ware* v. *Hylton* (1796)- «considerations of policy, considerations of extreme magnitude, and certainly entirely incompetent to the examination and decision of a Court of Justice».[105] Decisions concerning foreign relations therefore, as stated by Justice Jackson in *Chicago and Southern Air Lines v. Waterman Stamship Co.* (1948):

> Are wholly confined by our constitution to the political departments of the government. ... They are decisions of a kind for which the Judiciary has neither aptitude, facilities nor responsibility and which has long been held to belong in the domain of political power not subject to judicial intrusion or inquiry.[106]

Even though developed mainly in the foreign affairs sphere, the Supreme Court has also considered certain matters relating to the government of internal affairs, a political question, and thus non justiciable; like the decision as to whether a state must have a republican form of government, which in *Luther* v. *Borden* (1849) was considered a «decision binding on every other department of the government, and could not be questioned in a judicial tribunal».[107]

Any way and even though that through the decisions of the Supreme Court, a list of «political questions» that the Court has considered as non-justifiable can be elaborated, the ultimate responsibility in determining them corresponds to the Supreme Court.

As the Court said in *Baker* v. *Carr* (1962):

> Deciding whether a matter has in any measure been committed by the constitution to another branch of government, or whether the action of that branch exceeds whatever authority has been committed, -said the Court- is itself a delicate exercise in constitutional interpretation, and is a responsibility of this Court as ultimate interpreter of the constitution...[108].

Following the United States tradition, in Argentina, the Supreme Court of Justice has developed the same exception to judicial review and to the amparo action, concerning political questions, even though the Constitution does not expressly establish anything on the matter. These political questions are related to the «acts of government» of «political acts» doctrine developed in continental European law, and within which it can be mentioned the following: the declaration of state of siege; the declaration of federal intervention in the provinces; the declaration of «public use» for means of expropriation; the declaration of war; the declaration of emergency to approve certain direct tax contributions; acts concerning

---

105 *Ware v. Hylton*, 3 Dallas, 199 (1796).

106 Chicago *and Southern Air Lines v. Waterman Steamship Co.*, 333 US 103 (1948) p. 111.

107 Luther v. Borden 48 U.S. (7 Howard), 1,(1849). See in M. Glenn ABERNATHY and Barbara A. PERRY, *Civil Liberties under the Constitution*, Sixth Edition, University of South Carolina Press, 1993, pp. 6-7.

108 Baker v. Carr, 369 U.S. 186 (1962).

foreign relations; the recognition of new foreign states or new foreign state governments; the expulsion of aliens, etc.[109] In general, within these political questions there are acts exercised by the political powers of the state in accordance with powers exclusively and directly attributed to them in the constitution, which can be considered the key element for their identification.

Apart from Argentina, only in Perú the issue of the political questions as non justiciable matter by means of amparo has been considered by the Constitutional Tribunal[110].

6. The amparo against executive and administrative omissions

In general terms, the amparo action can be filed in all Latin American countries, not only against positive acts or actions from public officers or authorities (and also from individuals) that cause harm or threat upon constitutional rights and guarantees, but also against the omissions of such entities or persons when they do not comply with their general obligations to decide petitions, which can also cause such harms of threats. In particular, the amparo action has been frequently used to challenge Public Administration omissions or abstentions to act; but in the countries where amparo is admissible against individual, it also can be filed against their omissions harming or threatening constitutional rights.

Regarding public officers omissions, the amparo action in Latin America is generally filed in order to obtain from the court an order directed against a public officer in order for him to act in a matter with respect to which he has authority or jurisdiction. The amparo action against omissions in these cases is similar to the North American mandamus or mandatory injunction[111], defined as «a writ commanding a public officer to perform some duty which the laws require him to do but he refuses or neglects to perform». Thus mandamus cannot be used if the public officer has any discretion in the matter; «but if the law is clear in requiring the performance of some ministerial (nondiscretionary) function, then mandamus may properly be sought to nudge the reluctant or negligent official along in the performance of his or her duties»[112]. As it was decided by the Supreme Court in Wilbur v. United States, 281 U.S. 206, 218 (1930):

---

109 See José Luis LAZZARINI, *El juicio de amparo*, La Ley, Buenos Aires, 1987, p. 190 ff.; Néstor Pedro SAGÜÉS, *Derecho procesal Constitucional*, Vol 3, *Acción de amparo*, Editorial Astrea, Buenos Aires, 1988, pp. 270 ff.; Alí Joaquín SALGADO, *Juicio de amparo y acción de inconstitucionalidad*, Astrea, Buenos Aires, 1987, p. 23.

110 See Samuel B. ABAD YUPANQUI, *El proceso constitucional de amparo*, Gaceta Jurídica, Lima 2004, pp. 128 ff.

111 In the United Status, it has been considered that while as a general rule courts will not compel by injunction the performance by public officers of their official duties (Bellamy v. gates, 214 Va. 314, 200 S.E. 2d 533, (1973)), a court may compel public officers or boards to act in a matter with respect to which they have jurisdiction or authority (Erie v. State By and Through State Highway Commission, 154 Mont. 150, 461 P 2d 207 (1969)). See in in John BOURDEAU et al, «Injunctions» in Kevin Schroder, John Glenn and Maureen Placilla, *Corpus Juris Secundum*, Volume 43A, Thomson West, 2004, pp. 221, 222, 244.

112 See M. Glenn Abernathy and Barbara A. Perry, *Civil Liberties under the Constitution*, Sixth Edition, University of South Carolina Press, 1993, p. 8. One of the important features of the writ of mandamus in North America y that the writ does not issue to purely private persons, but can only be directed to public officials or persons performing some quasi-public functions. Idem, p. 8.

«Where the duty in a particular situation is so plainly prescribed as to be free from doubt and equivalent to a positive command it is regarded as being so far ministerial that its performance may be compelled by mandamus, unless there be provision or implication to the contrary, But where the duty is not thus plainly prescribed but depends upon a statute the construction or application of which is not free from doubt, it is regarded as involving the character of judgment or discretion which cannot be controlled by mandamus»[113].

In Latin America, for an omission to be the object of an amparo action, it must produce a direct violation of a constitutional right of the plaintiff, who in cases of illegalities in some countries like Venezuela, will only be allowed to use other judicial remedies, as the judicial review of administrative omission action before the special courts of the matter (contencioso-administrativo).

According to the judicial doctrine established by the former Supreme Court of Justice of Venezuela, the amparo action against omissive conducts of Public Administration, must comply with the following two conditions:

«a) That the alleged omissive conduct be absolute, which means that Public Administration has not accomplished in any moment the due function; and b) that the omission be regarding a generic duty, that is, the duty a public officer has to act in compliance with the powers attributed to him, which is different to the specific duty that is the condition for the judicial review of administrative omissive action. Thus, only when it is a matter of a generic duty, of procedure, of providing in a matter which is inherent to the public officer position, he incurs in the omissive conduct regarding which the amparo action is admissible[114].

From this Venezuelan judicial doctrine results that the important condition for the admissibility of the amparo action against public officer omissions, is the one related to the nature of his duties, being only admissible when the matters refer to generic duties and not to specific ones. As defined by the same former Supreme Court in a decision dated February, 11, 1992:

«In cases of Public Administration abstentions or omissions a distinction can be observed regarding the constitutional provisions violated when they provide for generic or specific duties. In the first case, when a public entity does not comply with its generic obligation to respond [a petition] of continuing the procedure or recourse filed by an individual, it violates the constitutional right to obtain prompt answer [to petitions] set forth in Article 67 of the Constitution; whereas when the inactivity is produced regarding a specific duty imposed by a statute in a concrete and ineludible way, no direct constitutional violation occurs. Condition in the latter case that the Court has been imposing for the filing of the judicial review of administrative omissions recourse...

---

113 See the reference in See M. Glenn ABERNATHY and Barbara A. PERRY, *Civil Liberties under the Constitution*, Sixth Edition, University of South Carolina Press, 1993, p. 8.

114 See thye decisions of the former Supreme Court of Justice, Politico Adminsitrative Chamber, dated November 5, 1992 (Caso *Jorge E. Alvarado*), in *Revista de Derecho Público*, N° 52, Editorial Jurídica Venezolana, Caracas, 1992, p. 187; and November 18, 1993, in *Revista de Derecho Público*, N° 55-56, Editorial Jurídica Venezolana, Caracas, 1993, p. 295.

From the aforementioned reasons the Court deems conclusive that the inactivity of Public Administration to accomplish a specific legal duty precisely infringes in a direct and immediate way the legal (statutory) text regulating the matter, in which case the Constitution is only violated in a mediate and indirect way. For the amparo judge, in order to detect if an abstention of the aggrieved entity effectively harms a constitutional right or guarantee, it must first, rely himself on the supposedly unaccomplished statute in order to verify if the abstention is regarding an specific obligation. In which case it must deny the amparo action and give to the plaintiff another remedy, as the judicial review action against Public Administration omissions[115].

In these cases, the judicial order of mandamus eventually consists in commanding the public officer to perform the duty the Constitution requires him to do which he refuses or neglects to perform, that is, to promptly decide the petitions individuals had filed before him[116]. In general terms, then, the court order cannot substitute the public officer decision[117]; and only in cases when a specific statute provides what is called the «positive silence» (the presumption that after the exhaustion of a particular delay, it is considered that Public Administration has decided accordingly to what has been asked in the particular petition), then the judicial order impliedly gives positive effects to the official abstention or omission[118]

IV. THE Amparo against individuals or private persons

If it is true that the amparo action, as a specific means for the protection of constitutional rights and guarantees was originally conceived for the protection of individuals against the State and its public officials, it has been progressively admitted against private persons, corporations or institutions whose actions can also cause harm or threats regarding constitutional rights of others. As was ruled in the Argentinean *Samuel Kot Case,* in which the Supreme Court of the Nation began to admit the amparo against acts of individuals, by saying that:

> «There is nothing in the letter and spirit of the Constitution that allows for the assertion that the protection of constitutional rights is circumscribed only to attacks of the State, since, sustained the High Court, what is to be kept in mind is not only the origin of the impairment of constitutional rights but the rights themselves, because the same attention is not paid to the aggressors as to the rights aggrieved»[119].

---

[115] See in *Revista de Derecho Público,* N° 53-54, Editorial Jurídica Venezolana, Caracas, 1993, pp. 272-273.

[116] See the former venezuelan Supreme Court decisión dated August 26, 1993 (*Caso Inversiones Klanki*), *Revista de Derecho Público,* N° 55-56, Editorial Jurídica Venezolana, Caracas, 1993, p. 294.

[117] See for instante in Argentina, Néstor Pedro SAGÜÉS, *Derecho procesal Constitucional, Vol 3, Acción de amparo,* Editorial Astrea Buenos Aires 1988, pp. 73 ff.

[118] See the venezuelan former Supreme Court decision dated December 20, 1991 (Caso *BHO, C.A.*), en *Revista de Derecho Público,* N° 48, Editorial Jurídica Venezolana, Caracas, 1991, pp. 141-143.

[119] See José Luis LAZZARINI, *El juicio de amparo,* La Ley, Buenos Aires, 1987, p. 228; Joaquín BRAGE CAMAZO, La jurisdicción constitucional de la libertad (Teoría general, Argentina, México, Corte Interamericana de derechos humanos), Editorial Porrúa, México, 2005, p. 99; Néstor Pedro SAGÜÉS, *Derecho procesal Constitucional,* Vol 3, *Acción de amparo,* Editorial Astrea Buenos Aires 1988, pp. 13, 512, 527 ff.

Nonetheless, not in all Latin American countries amparo actions against individuals are admitted. In México, for instance, the amparo suit is not admitted against violations caused by acts of private individuals, so the constitutional protection through the amparo suit is established exclusively against the authorities[120]. Similarly, when regulating the *mandado de segurança*, the Constitution of Brazil provides for its admission to protect constitutional rights and freedoms «when the party responsible for the illegality or abuse of power is a public authority or an agent of a legal entity exercising attributions of the Authorities», thus excluding this recourse of protection against the actions of private individuals[121]. Similar provisions are set forth in the Amparo law regulations in Panamá (Art. 50 Constitution; Art 2608 Judicial Code), El Salvador (Art. 12) and Nicaragua (Art. 23).

As mentioned above, in other Latin American countries, after the Argentinean *Kot Case*, the amparo against individual's actions or omissions causing harm or threats to constitutional rights of other individuals has been admitted, although in some countries in a restrictive way. In general terms it is admitted in Argentina, even though the 1966 Law 16.986 only refers to the amparo action against the State, that is «against every act or omission of the authorities» (Article 1); the amparo against individuals being regulated in articles 321,2 and 498 of the Code of Civil and Commercial Procedure.

In Venezuela, the amparo action against acts of individuals, is expressly provided in the 1988 Organic Law of Amparo[122], where Article 2 provides:.

> [The amparo action] shall be admitted against any fact, act or omission originated by citizens, legal entities, private groups or organizations that have violated, violate or threaten to violate any of the guarantees or rights that are entitled to the amparo of this Law.

In a similar manner, Uruguay's 1988 Law 16.011 of Amparo admits, in general, the action of amparo «against any act, omission or fact of the state or public sector authorities, as well as individuals, that is deemed to currently or imminently, manifestly and unlawfully impair, restrict, alter or threaten any of the rights and freedoms expressly or implicitly recognized by the Constitution» (Art. 1)[123]. A similar provision is set forth in Article 2 of the Perúvian Code of Constitutional procedures[124] and in the Bolivian Constitution (Art. 19).

Also in Chile, it has been interpreted that the action for protection of constitutional rights and freedoms against arbitrary or unlawful acts or omissions that perturb or threaten when legally exercised (Article 20), being established without making any distinction as to the origin of such acts or omissions, can also be

---

120 See Eduardo FERRER MAC-GREGOR, *La acción constitucional de amparo en México y España. Estudio de derecho comparado*, Editorial Porrúa, México 2002, p. 251; Joaquín Brage Camazo, La jurisdicción constitucional de la libertad (Teoría general, Argentina, México, Corte Interamericana de derechos humanos), Editorial Porrúa, México, 2005, 181.

121 See Celso AGRÍCOLA BARBI, *Do mandado de segurança*, Editora Forense, Rio de Janeiro 1993, p. 92.

122 Allan R. BREWER-CARÍAS, *Instituciones Políticas y Constitucionales*, Vol V, *Derecho y Acción de Amparo*, Editorial Jurídica Venezolana, Caracas 1998, pp. 96, 128.

123 See Luis Alberto VIERA, *Ley de Amparo*, Ediciones Idea, Montevideo 1993, pp. 63, 157.

124 See Samuel B. ABAD YUPANQUI, *El proceso constitucional de amparo*, Gaceta Jurídica, Lima 2004, pp. 389 ff.

brought against acts or omissions of individuals[125]. Similar interpretation was adopted by the Supreme Court of the Dominican Republic regarding the admissibility of the amparo against individuals[126].

Other Latin American countries, such as Colombia, Costa Rica Ecuador and Guatemala admit the amparo action when filed against individuals, but in a restricted way, only regarding the individuals that are in a position of superiority regarding citizens or in some way exercises public functions or activities or are rendering public services or public utilities[127]. In this regard, the Costa Rican Law of Constitutional Jurisdiction restricts the amparo against individual[128] as follows:

> **Article 57.** The recourse of amparo shall also be admitted against actions or omissions of individual subjects of the law when they act or should act in exercise of public functions or authority, or are by right or in fact in a position of power before which ordinary jurisdictional remedies are clearly insufficient or belated for guaranteeing the rights and freedoms referred to in Article 2,a of this Law.

In similar terms it is provided in the Guatemalan Law on Amparo (Art. 9) and in Colombia where the Constitution expressly refers to the law for the establishment of «the cases in which the action of tutela may be filed against private individuals entrusted with providing a public service or whose conduct may affect seriously and directly the collective interest or in respect of whom the applicant may find himself/herself in a state of subordination or vulnerability» (Art. 86). Was in compliance with this constitutional mandating that the Decree 2.591 of 1991 (Article 42) establishes that the action of tutela shall be admitted against acts or omissions of private individuals[129] in the following cases:

1. When the person against whom action is brought is in charge of the public service of education, in protection of the rights enshrined in Articles 13, 15, 16, 18, 19, 20, 23, 27, 29, 37 and 38 of the Constitution.

2. When the person against whom action is brought is in charge of rendering a public health service, to protect the rights to life, intimacy, equality and autonomy.

3. When the person against whom action is brought is in charge of rendering public services.

---

[125] See Humberto NOGUEIRA ALCALÁ, «El derecho de amparo o protección de los derechos humanos, fundamentales o esenciales en Chile: evolución y perspectivas», in Humberto Nogueira Alcalá (Editor), *Acciones constitucionales de amparo y protección: realidad y perspectivas en Chile y América Latina»*, Editorial Universidad de Talca, Talca 2000, p. 41.

[126] See Eduardo Jorge PRATS, *Derecho Constitucional*, Vol. II, Gaceta Judicial, Santo Domingo 2005, p. 390.

[127] In a similar way to the injunctions admitted in the United Status against public services corporations. See in John BOURDEAU et al, «Injunctions» in Kevin Schroder, John Glenn and Maureen Placilla, *Corpus Juris Secundum*, Volume 43A, Thomson West, 2004, p. 182 ff.

[128] See Rubén HERNÁNDEZ VALLE, *Derecho Procesal Constitucional*, Editorial Juricentro, San José 2001, pp. 275, 281 ff.

[129] See Juan Carlos ESGUERRA, *La protección constitucional del ciudadano*, Legis, Bogotá 2004, p. 151.

4. When the request is directed against a private organization, against who effectively controls such organization or is the real beneficiary of the situation that caused the action, provided the claimant is in a position of subordination or defenselessness before such organization.
5. When the person against whom action is brought violates or threatens to violate Article 17 of the Constitution.
6. When the private entity is the one against which the request for habeas data would have been brought, pursuant to Article 15 of the Constitution.
7. When requesting the rectification of incorrect or erroneous information. In this case it is necessary to attach the transcription of the information or copy of the publication and of the rectification requested that was not published in such a way that its effectiveness be assured.
8. When the individual acts or should act in exercise of his or her public functions, in which case the same régime that regulates public authorities shall be applied.

When the request is for the tutela of the life or safety of the person who is in a position of subordination or defenselessness with respect to the matter against which action was brought. The minor who brings an action of tutela shall be presumed defenseless.

Finally, also in Ecuador, the amparo actions is admitted against entities that though not public authorities, they render public services by delegation or concession and in general against individuals but only when their actions or omissions cause harm or threats to constitutional rights and affect in a grave and direct way common, collective or diffuse interests (Art. 95,3)[130]. In this regard, for instance, amparo actions can be filed against political parties or their officials when their conduct violates the rights of other persons, as it has also being admitted in the United States[131].

V. THE PARTICIPATION OF THIRD PARTIES FOR THE DEFENDANT IN THE AMPARO SUIT

In the amparo suit, the injurer or damaging parties are those authorities, public officials, private persons, entities or corporations duly individuated whose actions or omissions are those precisely causing the harm or threats to the constitutional rights and guaranties of the plaintiff. Nonetheless, third parties can also act in the process, defending the injurer party position. It happens with those persons that, for instance, are beneficiaries of the authority act challenge. In this sense the Mexican Amparo Law provides that besides the injured and the injurer, are also considered party in the amparo suit, the persons that have obtained challenged act in their favor or those that could have direct interest in the act's endurance (Art. 5, III, c)[132]. In similar sense in the Norte American procedure on

[130] Hernán Salgado Pesantes, *Manual de Justicia Constitucional Ecuatoriana*, Corporación Editora Nacional, Quito, 2004, p. 77.

[131] *Maxey v. Washington State Democratic Committee*, 319 F. Supp. 673 (W.D. Wash. 1970), in John BOURDEAU et al, «Injunctions» in Kevin Schroder, John Glenn and Maureen Placilla, *Corpus Juris Secundum*, Volume 43A, Thomson West, 2004, p. 240.

[132] See Eduardo FERRER MAC-GREGOR, *La acción constitucional de amparo en México y España. Estudio de derecho comparado*, Editorial Porrúa, México 2002, pp. 249-250.

injunctions, it is considered that all persons whose interest will necessarily be affected by the decree in a suit for injunction are properly joined as defendants[133].

Due to the general bilateral procedural rule, the principle applies in all Latin American countries, except in Chile, where, as mentioned, the bilateralism of the procedure is not admitted[134]. In some cases even the need for the participation of third parties for the defendant is necessary, as is the case in Venezuela on the amparo actions against judicial decisions, in which the party beneficiary of the challenged ruling must obligatorily be notified to participate in the procedure as defendant of the challenged decision.[135]

---

133 Silva V. ROMNEY, 473 F. 2d 287 (1st Cir. 1973); Greenhouse v. Greco, 368 F. Supp. 736 (W.D. La. 1973). See the reference in John BOURDEAU et al, «Injunctions» in Kevin Schroder, John Glenn and Maureen Placilla, *Corpus Juris Secundum*, Volume 43A, Thomson West, 2004, pp. 332-333.

134 See Juan Manuel ERRAZURIZ G. and Jorge Miguel OTERO A., *Aspectos procesales del recurso de protección*, Editorial Jurídica de Chile 1989, p. 149.

135 See Rafael CHAVERO, *El nuevo régimen del amparo constitucional en Venezuela*, Editorial Sherwood, Caracas 2001, pp. 489.

CHAPTER XII

THE MOTIVES FOR THE AMPARO SUIT: THE INJURY OR THE THREAT OF VIOLATION TO THE PLAINTIFF'S CONSTITUTIONAL RIGHTS

The amparo action, as a specific judicial means for the protection of constitutional rights and guaranties, can be filed by the plaintiff when he is personally affected in his own rights, in a direct and present way; or when he is threatened to be harmed in those rights in an imminent way.

The personal character of the amparo suit is then related to the direct harm caused to the plaintiff or to the threat that affects such rights (which must be an imminent one).

I. THE GENERAL PERSONAL AND DIRECT CHARACTER OF THE INJURY

The claimant or plaintiff in the amparo suit must have suffered a direct, personal and present injury in his constitutional rights or must have been threatened in them.

That is, in cases of injury it must personally affect the claimant, in a direct and present way regarding his constitutional rights. If it harms only statutory established rights, or another person's rights or only affects the plaintiff in an indirect way, the action is inadmissible.

The Mexican Constitution, in this regard, refers to the need for the plaintiff to have «a personal and direct» harm (Art. 107,I), in the sense that his personal constitutional rights must have been directly affected. That is why the claimant must be the 'affected» person (Argentina: Article 5; Perú: Article 39), the «aggrieved» person (Nicaragua, Article 23) or the one who «suffers» the harm (Brazil: Article 1). Consequently if the harm does not affect the plaintiff in his constitutional rights, in a personal and direct way, the action is considered inadmissible[1].

The foregoing means, first, that the rights that must be directly affected or harmed for the amparo action to be admissible must be of constitutional order, and second, that the harm must directly and personally affect the plaintiff. Consequently, rights just recognized in statutes without constitutional rank, cannot be protected

1 See Eduardo FERRER MAC-GREGOR, *La acción constitucional de amparo en México y España*, Editorial Porrúa, México 2002, pp. 386-387.

by means of amparo actions, and this is one of the main distinctions between the North American injunctions and the amparo.

In this sense, in Venezuela the courts have ruled that the harm caused must always be the result of a violation of a constitutional right that must be «flagrant, vulgar, direct and immediate, which does not mean that the right or guarantee are not due to be regulated in statutes, but it in not necessary for the court to base its decision in the latter to determine if the of the violation of the constitutional right has effectively occurred»[2].

In other words, only direct and evident constitutional violations can be protected by means of amparo; thus, for instance, as ruled in 1991 by the Venezuelan courts, the internal electoral regime of political parties or of professional associations could not be the object of an amparo action funded in the right to vote set forth in the Constitution, «which only applies to the national electoral process [not being applied] to the internal electoral process of the political parties», concluding that the amparo only protects constitutional rights and guaranties and not legal (statutory) ones, and much less the ones contained in association's by-laws»[3]. In other decisions, the courts declared inadmissible amparo actions for the protection of rights when the allegations were only founded «in legal (statutory) considerations», as the right to work commonly conditioned by statutes regarding dismissals. Thus, the amparo is not the judicial mean for the protection of such right if the violation is only referred to the labor Law provisions»[4].

As mentioned, the violation of the constitutional right must be a direct violation caused by a concrete action or omission which the claimant must allege and must proof. The courts in Venezuela have ruled in this regard that

> «the amparo action can only be directed against a perfectly and determined act or omission, and not against a generic conduct; against an objective and real activity and not against a supposition regarding the intention of the presumed injurer, and against the direct and immediate consequences of the activities of the public body or officer. It is necessary, though, that the denounced actions directly affect the subjective sphere of the claimant, consequently excluding the generic conducts, even if they can affect in a tangential way on the matter.

That is why the amparo action is not a popular action for denouncing against the illegitimacy of the public entities of control over convenience or opportunity,

---

2 See Supreme Court of Justice, Case *Tarjetas Banvenez*, July 10, 1991, in *Revista de Derecho Público*, N° 47, Editorial Jurídica Venezolana, Caracas, 1991, pp. 169-170. See also deci-sión of may 20, 1994, Corte Primera de lo Contencioso Administrativa (Case *Federación Venezolana de Deportes Ecuestres*); in *Revista de Derecho Público*, N° 57-58, Editorial Jurídica Venezolana, Caracas, 1994, p.

3 See decision of August, 8, 1991, *Revista de Derecho Público*, N° 47, Editorial Jurídica Venezolana, Caracas, 1991, p. 129.

4 See decision of October 8, 1990, *Revista de Derecho Público*, N° 44, Editorial Jurídica Venezolana, Caracas, 1990, pp. 139-140. In similar sense, the violation of the right to self defense because the right to cross examination of a witness was denied according to article 349 of the Procedural Civil Code, cannot be founded in article 68 of the Constitution because that would signify to analyze the violation of norms of statutary rank and not of constitutional rank. See decision of the Politico Administrative Chamber of the Supreme Court of Justice of November 8, 1990, *Revista de Derecho Público*, N° 44, Editorial Jurídica Venezolana, Caracas, 1990, pp. 140-141.

but a protector remedy of the claimant sphere when it is demonstrated that it has been directly affected»[5].

In another decision, the Supreme Court of Justice ruled abut the need that:

> The violation of the constitutional rights and guaranties be a direct and immediate consequence of the act, fact or omission, not being possible to attribute or assign to the injurer agent different results to those produced or to be produced. The right's violation must be the product of the harming act»[6].

The main consequence of being the injury a direct and immediate one regarding the claimant is that he has to prove his assertions, that is to say, in the amparo action the injured party has the burden to proof the personal and direct harm. Similar to the rules on injunctions, as resolved by the North American courts, according to which, «the party seeking an injunction, whether permanent or temporary, must establish some verifiable injury»[7]. That is why, regarding documental proofs, the claimant must always present them with the filling of the action (Amparo Laws: Argentina, Article 7; Uruguay, Article 5).

II. THE ARBITRARY, ILLEGAL AND ILLEGITIMATE MANIFEST INJURY

On the other hand, the harm or injury caused to a constitutional right in order for an amparo action to be admitted, must be manifestly arbitrary, illegal or illegitimate, and consequence of a violation of the Constitution.

In this regard, for instance, the Argentinean Amparo Law, is precise in indicating that for an amparo action to be admissible it must be filed against any «manifestly arbitrary or illegal» act or omission of a public authority, that «harms, restricts, alters or threatens the constitutional rights and guaranties» (Art. 1). This feature of the challenged official action or omission to be manifestly illegal or arbitrary, is a consequence of the presumption of validity that as a general principle of public law, all official acts have. The Uruguayan Amparo law refers to acts issued with «manifest illegitimacy» (Art. 1); and the Brazilian Law, in similar sense, also set forth expressly that the *mandado de segurança* is established for the protection of constitutional rights when being violated «*ilegalmente ou com abuso do poder*» (Art 1)[8].

The challenged act or omission, thus, must be manifestly contrary to the legal order (*legalidad*), that is, the rules of law contained not only in the Constitution, but also in statutes and regulations; or it must be manifestly illegitimate, because it lacks of any legal support; or because it is manifestly arbitrary, that is, an act not reasonable or unjust; in other words, contrary to justice or to reason[9]. The same

---

5 See decisión of December 2, 1993, *Revista de Derecho Público,* N° 55-56, Editorial Jurídica Venezolana, Caracas, 1993, pp. 302-303.

6 See decisión of August 14, 1992, *Revista de Derecho Público,* N° 51, Editorial Jurídica Venezolana, Caracas, 1992, p. 145.

7 See Kevin Schroder, John Glenn and Maureen Placilla (Editors), *Corpus Juris Secundum,* Vol. 43A, Thomson West, 2004, p 54.

8 The principle is also referred to in Chile and Ecuador. Juan Manuel ERRAZURIZ G. and Jorge Miguel OTERO A., *Aspectos procesales del recurso de protección,* Editorial Jurídica de Chile, Santiago, 1989, pp. 51-55; Hernán SALGADO PESANTES, *Manual de Justicia Constitucional Ecuatoriana,* Corporación Editora Nacional, Quito 2004, p. 79.

9 See Alí Joaquín SALGADO, *Juicio de amparo y acción de inconstitucionalidad,* Astrea, Buenos Aires 1987, pp. 28-29.

principle applies in the United States imposing to the plaintiff in civil right injunctions the burden to prove the alleged violations in order to destroy the presumption that the official acts are valid, which has been considered a limitation on judicial power to protect rights. As M. Glenn Abernathy and Perry have commented:

> «The courts do not automatically presume that all restraints on free choice are improper. The burden is thrown on the person attacking acts to prove that they are improper. This is most readily seen in cases involving the claim that an act of the legislature is unconstitutional...Judges also argue that acts of administrative officials should be accorded some presumption of validity. Thus a health officer who destroys food alleged by him to be unfit for consumption is presumed to have good reason for his action. The person whose property is so destroyed must bear the burden of proving bad faith on part of the official, if an action is brought as a consequence»[10].

Consequently, when expressly established in the statutes or not, the same principle applies in Latin America, in the sense that in the amparo action, the act or omission challenged by the plaintiff because it harms his rights, must be manifestly illegal, illegitimate, arbitrary or issued with abuse of power, which implies the need for the claimant on the contrary, to build his arguments upon reasonable basis, and to prove that the challenged act or omission of the public official is an unreasonable one.

III. The actual and real character of the injury

Another general condition of the injury in order to be protected by the amparo action is its actual character, as is expressly provided in the Argentinean (Article 1) and Uruguayan (Amparo, Art 1) Laws, in the sense that the harm must be presently occurring and must not have ceased. In similar sense as it is the rule regarding the injunctions in the United States:

> «A petitioner is not entitled to an injunction where no injury to the petitioner is shown from the action sought to be prevented. Ordinarily, a person, in order to be entitled to injunctive relief, whether prohibitory or mandatory in its nature, must establish an actual and substantial, serious, injury, or an affirmative prospect of such an injury»[11].

The actual character of the injury regarding the amparo suit, as argued by the Venezuelan courts, signifies that the injury «must be alive, must be present in all its intensity», in other words, the actual character of the harm «refers to the present character, not to the past, nor to facts already happened, which appertain to the past, but to the present situation which can be prolonged in an in definitive length of time»[12].

In this regard, Article 6,1 of the Amparo law of Venezuela establishes as a cause of inadmissibility of the amparo action, that the violation would have not

---

10 See M. Glenn ABERNATHY and Barbara A. PERRY, *Civil Liberties under the Constitution*, University of South Carolina Press, 1993, p. 5

11 See Kevin Schroder, John Glenn and Maureen Placilla (Editors), *Corpus Juris Secundum*, Vol. 43A, Thomson West, 2004, p 66.

12 See decision of the First Court on Judicial Review of Administrative Action of May 7, 1987 (Caso: *Desarrollo 77 C.A.*), in FUNEDA *15 años de Jurisprudencia cit.*, p. 78.

ceased, that is, «it must be actual, recent, alive»[13]. The principle is the same in Argentina, where if the harm has ceased, the claim by mean of amparo must be declared inadmissible[14]. In Honduras (Art. 46,6 Constitutional Justice Law) and Nicaragua (Art. 51,3, Amparo Law) prescribes that the recourse for amparo is inadmissible when the effects of the challenged act have ceased, in which case the court could reject *in limene* (*de plano*) the claim. Also in México, Article 73,XVI of the Amparo law declares inadmissible the amparo action when the challenged acts have ceased in their effects, or when even those acts subsist, they cannot produce material or legal effects whatsoever, because they have lost their object or substance. In Perú, the Constitutional procedure Code also prescribes the inadmissibility of the amparo action when at the moment of its filing the threat or the violation of the constitutional rights has ceased (Art. 5,5).

In this regard, the First Court on Judicial Review of administrative actions of Venezuela resolved the inadmissibility of an action for amparo because, during the proceedings, the challenged act was repealed[15]. The Supreme Court also decided that in the proceedings of an amparo suit the harm must not have ceased before the judge decision; on the contrary, if the harm has ceased, the judge must declare *in limine litis*, the inadmissibility of the action[16]. For instance, in the case of an amparo against the omission of a court to decide a case, which as alleged harms the rights of somebody, if before the filing of the action or during the proceeding the challenged court has decided, from that moment on the harm can be considered to have ceased[17]

In similar sense, the Constitutional Chamber of Costa Rica has determined that it has not jurisdictional present interest to examine the circumstances for the suspension [of the effects on an act], when [the act has been repealed], and thus, when the affected party has been reestablished in the enjoyment of his rights before filing the recourse[18]. But regarding the actual character of the harm, it is possible to consider that when new a fact modifies to such an extreme an already known and declared situation as not being present at the moment the harm occurred, then the new argument could provoke different or contradictory results regarding the previous ones. This could occur, for instance, when the amparo judge, that must know regarding an specific, actual and determined situation, could determine the

---

13 See decision of the First Court on Judicial Review of Administrative Action of November 13, 1988, in FUNEDA, *15 años de la Jurisprudencia, cit.*, p. 134

14 Alí Joaquín SALGADO, *Juicio de amparo y acción de inconstitucionalidad,* Astrea, Buenos Aires 1987, p. 27.

15 See decision of the First Court on Judicial Review of Administrative Action of August 14, 1992 in *Revista de Derecho Público,* N° 51, Editorial Jurídica Venezolana, Caracas, 1992, p. 154.

16 See decisions of the Politico Administrative Chamber of the former Supreme Court of Justice of December 15, 1992, *Revista de Derecho Público* N° 52, Editorial Jurídica Venezolana, Caracas, 1992, p. 164; and of May 27, 1993, *Revista de Derecho Público,* nos 53-54, Editorial Jurídica Venezolana, Caracas, 1993, p. 264. *Cfr.* Decision of the First Court on Judicial Review of Administrative Actions of December 12, 1992 (Caso *Allan R. Brewer-Carías*), *Revista de Derecho Público,* N° 49, Editorial Jurídica Venezolana, Caracas, 1992, pp. 131-132.

17 See Rafael CHAVERO G., *El nuevo régimen del amparo constitucional en Venezuela,* Editorial Sherwood, caracas 2001, pp. 237-238.

18 Decision N° 1051-97, in Rubén HERNÁNDEZ VALLE, *Derecho Procesal Constitucional,* Editorial Juricentro, San José 2001, pp. 244-245.

existence of a new fact that had not occurred at the moment of the filing, and that could alter or modify that situation, in which case, the action can be admitted and decided protecting the plaintiff, even if it had been beforehand rejected[19].

Regarding the actual character of the harm for granting the amparo or constitutional protection, the rule in federal cases in the United States is that an actual controversy must exist not only at the time the action was initiated, but at all stages of the proceeding, even at appellate or certiorari review. Nonetheless, in the important case *Roe v. Wade,* 410 U.S. 113 (1973), in which the Supreme Court expanded the women's right to privacy, striking down states laws banning abortion. The Court recognized that even if this right of privacy was not explicitly mentioned in the Constitution, it was guaranteed as a constitutional right for protecting «a woman's decision whether or not to terminate her pregnancy», even though admitting that the states legislation could regulate the factors governing the abortion decision at some point in pregnancy based on «safeguarding health, maintaining medical standards and in protecting potential life».

But the point in the case was that, pending the procedure, the pregnancy period of the claimant came to term, so the injury claimed lost its present character. Nonetheless, the Supreme Court ruled in the case that

> «[When], as here, pregnancy is a significant fact in the litigation, the normal 266-day human generation period is so short that pregnancy will come to term before the usual appellate process is complete. If that termination makes a case moot, pregnancy litigation seldom will survive much beyond the trial stage, and appellate review will be effectively denied. Our law should not be that rigid. Pregnancy comes more than once to the same woman, and in the general population, if man is to survive, it will always be with us. Pregnancy provides a classic justification for a conclusion of non mootness. It truly could be 'capable of repetition, yet evading review'»[20].

In Perú, even though the same general rule is established regarding the inadmissibility «when at the filing of the action the harm or threat to a constitutional rights has ceased», it has been considered that when the harm or threat ceases after the action has been filed, the Constitutional Procedure Code allows the continuation of the proceedings, taking into account the harm produced, and that the amparo be granted[21].

On the other hand, as established in the Amparo laws of México (Art. 73, IX) and Honduras (Art. 46,5), in cases of injuries or harms produced to constitutional rights, the amparo action can only be filed when the injury is a reparable one or the harm is reversible; thus, the amparo action is inadmissible when the challenged act provoking the harm has already been accomplished or has already been completed (*consumado*) in an irreparable way. That is, amparo actions cannot be the adequate remedy regarding fait accompli.

---

[19] *Cfr.* decision of the Politico Administrative Chamber of the former Supreme Court of Justice of August 5, 1992, *Revista de Derecho Público,* N° 51, Editorial Jurídica Venezolana, Caracas, 1992, p. 145.

[20] See M. Glenn ABERNATHY and Barbara A. PERRY, *Civil Liberties under the Constitution,* University of Scout carolina Press, 1993, pp. 4-5.

[21] See Luis SANZ DÁVALOS, «Las innovaciones del Código Procesal constitucional en el proceso constitucional de amparo», in Susana CASTAÑEDA et al, *Introducción a los procesos constitucionales. Comentarios al Código Procesal Constitucional,* Jurista Editores, Lima 1005, p 126.

In México, the classical example regarding this condition of admissibility of the amparo suit, has been the situation of an executed death sentence[22], in which case it will be wholly irrelevant to file an amparo action. The non admissibility condition applies to all cases «when it is materially or juridically impossible to return the injured party to the position occupied prior to the violation»[23]; or when in general terms the challenged act is in fact irreparable because it is «physically impossible to turn back the things to the stage they had before the violation»[24].

This is also the general condition for the admissibility of the injunctions in the United States, as has been decided by the courts, constructing the following judicial doctrine:

> The purpose of an injunction is to restrain actions that have not yet been taken and, therefore, an injunction will not lie to restrain an act already completed at the time the action is instituted, since the injury has already been done. There is no cause for the issuance of an injunction unless the alleged wrong is actually occurring or is actually threatened or apprehended with reasonable probability and a court cannot enjoin an act after it has been completed. An act which has been completed, such that it no longer presents a justiciable controversy, does not give grounds for the issuance of an injunction[25].

IV. THE RESTORATIVE NATURE OF AMPARO SUIT AND THE REPARABLE CHARACTER OF THE INJURY

In general terms, regarding violations of constitutional rights, the amparo action in Latin America has a restorative character, tending to restitute the affected right to the situations existing when the right was harmed, eliminating the detrimental act or fact, or to restore the personal situation of the plaintiff to one closer to the existing before the injury. Regarding threats to rights, the amparo action has a preventive character, in the sense that it seeks to impede the injury to be produced or completed.

In this sense, regarding constitutional rights that has been violated, the amparo action has similarities with the so called reparative injunctions in the United States, which seeks to eliminate the effects of a past wrong or to compel the defendant to engage in a course of action that seeks to correct those effects[26]. As has been explained by Owen M. Fiss:

> To see how it works, let us assume that a wrong has occurred (such as an act of discrimination). Then the missions of an injunction -classically conceived

---

[22] Tesis 32, II, 90. Supreme Corte, Jurisprudencia de la Suprema Corte. See the reference in Richard D. BAKER, *Judicial Review in México. A Study of the Amparo Suit*, University of Austin Press, Austin 1971, p. 95, note 11.

[23] See Robert D. BAKER, *Judicial Review in México. A Study of the Amparo Suit*, University of Austin Press, Austin 1971, p. 96.

[24] Tesis «Actos consumados de modo irreparable», Apéndice al Semanario Judicial de la federación 1917-1988, Segunda Parte, salas y Tesis Comunes, pp. 106-107. See the referente in Eduardo FERRER MAC-GREGOR, *La acción constitucional de amparo en México y España*, Edit. Porrúa, México 2002, p. 388, notes 232 and 233.

[25] See Kevin Schroder, John Glenn, Maureen Placilla (Editors), *Corpus Juris Secundum*, Vol 43A, Thomson West, 2004, p. 73.

[26] Seen Owen M. FISS, *The Civil Rights Injunction*, Indiana University Press 1978, p. 7.

> as a preventive instrument- would be to prevent the recurrence of the wrongful conduct in the future (stop discriminating and do not discriminate again). But in *United States v. Louisiana* (380 U.S. 145, (1965)), a voting discrimination case, Justice Black identified still another mission for the injunction -the elimination of the effects of the past wrong the past discrimination). The reparative injunction -long thought by the nineteenth-century textbook writers, such as High (*A Treatise on the Law of Injunction* 3, 1873) to be an analytical impossibility- was thereby legitimated. And in the same vein, election officials have been ordered not only to stop discriminating in the future elections, but also to set aside a past election and to run a new election as a means of removing the taint of discrimination that infected the first one (*Bell v. Southwell*, 376 F.2de 659 (5th Cir. 1976)). Similarly, public housing officials have been ordered both to cease discriminating on the basis of race in their future choices of sites and to build units in the white areas as a means of eliminating the effects of the past segregative policy (placing public housing projects only in the black areas of the city)(*Hills v. Gautreaux*, 425 U.S. 284 (1976)).[27]

Accordingly, as also decided by the former Supreme Court of Justice of Venezuela, in 1996:

> One of the principal characteristics of the amparo action is to be a restorative (restablecedor) judicial means, the mission of which is to restore the infringed situation or, what is the same, to put the claimant again in the enjoyment of his constitutional rights which has been infringed. The abovementioned characteristic of this judicial means, besides been recognized by court decisions doctrine and by legal writers, is set forth in the Amparo Law, when establishing in Article 6,3, as a motive for the inadmissibility of the action, «when the violation of the constitutional rights and guarantees, turns on in an evident irreparable situation, being impossible to restore the infringed legal situation. It is understood that the acts that by means of the amparo can not be turn up thinks to the stage they had before the violation are irreparable»[28].

Due to this restorative character of the amparo, no new juridical situations can be created by means of this judicial action, nor is it possible to modify those in existence[29]. The Constitutional Chamber of the Supreme Tribunal of Justice, in a decision of January 20, 2000 ruled in this sense that a claimant cannot pretend to obtain the claimed asylum right by means of an amparo action, which through he pretended to obtain the Venezuelan citizenship but without following the established procedure. The Court ruled in the case, that:

> «This amparo action has been filed in order to seek a decision from this court, consisting in the legalization of the situation of the claimant, which would consist in the constitution or creation of a civil and juridical status the petitioner did not have before filing the complaint for amparo».

---

27 Seen Owen M. FISS, *The Civil Rights Injunction*, Indiana University Press 1978, pp. 7-10.

28 See decisión of February 6, 1996, case: Asamblea legislativa del Estado Bolívar. See in Rafael CHAVERO, *El nuevo régimen del amparo constitucional en Venezuela*, Ed. Sherwood, Caracas 2001, pp. 185, 242-243.

29 See decisions of the Politico Administrative Chamber of the former Supreme Court of Justice, of October 27, 1993 (Case *Ana Drossos*), and November 4, 1993 (Case *Partido Convergencia*), in *Revista de Derecho Público,* nos 55-56, Editorial Jurídica Venezolana, Caracas, 1993, p. 340.

Thus this petition was considered «contrary to the restorative nature of the amparo»[30].

In another decision issued on April 4, 1999, the former Supreme Court in a similar sense, declared inadmissible an amparo action in a case in which the claimant was asking to be appointed as judge in a specific court or to be put in a juridical situation that he did not have before the challenged act was issued. The Court decided that in the case, it was impossible for such purpose to file an amparo action, declaring it inadmissible, thus ruling as follows:

> «This Court must highlight that one of the essential characteristics of the amparo action is it reestablishing effects, that is, literally, to put one thing in the stage it possessed beforehand, in its natural stage, which for the claimant means to be put in the situation he had before the production of the claimed violation. The foregoing means that the plaintiff claim must be directed to seek 'the reestablishment of the infringed juridical situation'; the amparo actions are inadmissible when the reestablishment of the infringed situation is not possible; when through them the claimant seeks a compensation of damages, because the latter cannot be a substitution of the harmed right; nor when the plaintiff pretends the court to create a right or a situation that did not exist before the challenged act, fact or omission. All this is the exclusion for the possibility for the amparo to have constitutive effects»[31].

What in the suit for amparo can certainly be done is to restore things to the stage they had at the moment of the injury, making the challenged and proved infringing fact or act regarding a constitutional right or guarantee, to disappear. Thus when the violation to a constitutional right turns up to be an irreparable situation, the amparo actions is inadmissible. This is congruent with what Article 29 of the Venezuelan Constitution and Article 1 of Amparo Law provide in that the amparo action seeks to «the immediate restoring of the infringed juridical situation or to the situation more similar to it»[32].

In this regard, the former Supreme Court of Justice declared inadmissible an amparo action against a undue tax collecting act, once paid, considering that in such case it was not possible to restore the infringed juridical situation[33]; and the First Court on Judicial review of administrative action on a decision of September 7, 1989, declared inadmissible an amparo action referred to maternity protection rights (pre and post natal leave) filed after the childbirth, ruling that:

> «It is impossible for the plaintiff to be restored in her presumed violated rights to enjoy a pre and post natal leave during 6 month before and after the

---

[30] See Case *Domingo Ramírez Monja*. See the reference in Rafael CHAVERO, *El nuevo régimen del amparo constitucional en Venezuela*, Ed. Sherwood, Caracas 2001, p. 244.

[31] Decision of April 21, 1999, Case *J. C. Marín*. See the reference in Rafael CHAVERO, *El nuevo régimen del amparo constitucional en Venezuela*, Ed. Sherwood, Caracas, 2001, pp. 244-245

[32] See First Court on Judicial review of Administrative Action, decision of January 14, 1992, in *Revista de Derecho Público*, N° 49, Editorial Jurídica Venezolana, Caracas, 1992, p. 130; and decision of the former Supreme Court of Justice, Politico Administrative Chamber, of March 4, 1993, in *Revista de Derecho Público*, N° 53-54, Editorial Jurídica Venezolana, Caracas, 1993, p. 260.

[33] CSJ-CP 21-3-88- *Revista de Derecho Público*, N° 34, Editorial Jurídica Venezolana, Caracas, 1988, p. 114.

childbirth, because we are now facing an irremediable situation that can not be restored, due that it is impossible to date back the elapsed time»[34].

In similar sense, the former Supreme Court of Justice in a decision of November 1, 1990, considered inadmissible an amparo action, when the only way to restore the infringed juridical situation was declaring the nullity of an administrative act, which the amparo judge cannot do in its decision[35].

The abovementioned can be considered the general trend regarding the amparo regulations in Latin America. In México, Article 73,X of the Amparo Law prescribes that the amparo in inadmissible against acts adopted in a judicial or administrative proceeding, when due to the change of the juridical situation, the violations claimed in the proceeding must be considered as completed in an irreparable way. It is also the general trend regarding the tutela in Colombia where the Law provides that the action is inadmissible «when it is evident that the violation originated a completed harm, unless the action or omissions harming the rights continues».

In conclusion, in general terms, the amparo suit imposes the need for the harm to possibly be amended, or if it has not been initiated, to be restored by a judicial order impeding its execution, or if it has continuous effects, for its suspension in case it has not been initiated; and regarding those effects already accomplished, the possibility to date back things to the stage before the harm commenced. What the amparo judge cannot do is create situations that were inexistent at the moment of the action's filing; or to correct harms to rights when it is too late to do so. As resolved by the First Court on Judicial Review of administrative action of Venezuela, regarding a municipal order for the demolition of a building, in the sense that if the demolition was already executed, the amparo judge cannot decide the matter, because of the irreparable character of the harm[36].

The First Court also ruled in a case decided in February 4, 1999 regarding a public university position contest that, «the pretended aggrieved party is seeking to be allowed to be registered itself in the public contest for the Chair of Pharmacology in the School of Medicine José María Vargas, but at the present time, the registration was impossible due to the fact that the delay had elapsed the previous year, and consequently the harm produced must be considered as irreparable, declaring the inadmissible the action for amparo»[37].

Another example that can also be mentioned refers to the right to the protection of health, different to a possible right to have one's health restored. The former Supreme Court of Justice, in a decision of March 3, 1990, ruled as following:

---

34 See decision of First Court on Judicial Review of Administrative Actions of September 17, 1989, *Revista de Derecho Público* N° 40, Editorial Jurídica Venezolana, Caracas, 1989, p. 111.

35 See decisions of the Politico Administrative Chamber of the former Supreme Court of Justice of November 1, 1990, *Revista de Derecho Publico,* N° 44, Editorial Jurídica Venezolana, Caracas, 1990, pp. 152-153; *Cfr.* decision of the First Court on Judicial Review of Administrative Actions of September 10, 1992, *Revista de Derecho Público,* N° 51, Editorial Jurídica Venezolana, Caracas, 1992, p. 155.

36 See the January 1st, 1999 decision (Case: *B. Gómez*). See the reference in Rafael Chavero, *El nuevo régimen del amparo constitucional en Venezuela*, Ed. Sherwood, Caracas, 2001, p. 242.

37 See Case *C. Negrín*. See the reference in Rafael CHAVERO, *El nuevo régimen del amparo constitucional en Venezuela*, Ed. Sherwood, Caracas, 2001, p. 243.

«The Court considers that the infringed juridical situation is reparable by means of amparo, due to the fact that the plaintiff can be satisfied in his claims through such judicial means. From the judicial procedure point of view, it is possible for the protection of health the possibility for the judge to order the competent authority to assume precise conduct for the medical protection of the claimant conduct. The claim of the petitioner is to have a particular and adequate health care, which can be obtained via the amparo action, seeking the reestablishment of a harmed right, and this can be obtained by means of amparo. In this case, the claimant is not seeking her health to be restored to the stage it had before, but to have a particular health care, which is perfectly valid»[38].

In Perú, the Constitutional Procedure Code also prescribes that the amparo action, as well as all constitutional proceedings, are inadmissible when at the moment of its filing, the violation of the constitutional rights has become irreparable (Art. 5,5). Nonetheless, being the purpose of the constitutional processes to protect constitutional rights, reestablishing the thighs to the stage they had before the constitutional rights violation or threat or prescribing the accomplishment of a legal mandate or an administrative act, the Code establishes that if after the filing of the claim, the aggression or threat has ceased because of a voluntary decision of the aggressor, or if the harm turns up to be irreparable, the court, taking into account the injury, will grant the claim indicating the scope of its decision and ordering the defendant to refrain from performing again the actions or omissions that provoked the filing of the suit.

V. THE PREVENTIVE NATURE OF AMPARO SUIT AND THE IMMINENT CHARACTER OF THE THREAT

The amparo suit is not only the effective judicial means for the restoration of the injured constitutional rights that has been harmed, similar to the reparative or restorative civil rights injunctions, but it is also the effective judicial means for the protection of such rights and guaranties when threatened to be violated or harmed. This latter amparo suit is then similar to the preventive civil rights injunctions which, in this case, «seeks to prohibit some discrete act or series of acts from occurring in the future»[39], and is designed «to avoid future harm to a party by prohibiting or mandating certain behavior ay another party. The injunction is 'preventive' in the sense of avoiding harm»[40].

All the amparo laws on Latin America expressly refers to the possibility of filing the amparo suit not only against actual violation of constitutional rights but

---

38 See in *Revista de Derecho Público,* N° 42, Editorial Jurídica Venezolana, Caracas, 1990, p. 107.

39 See Owen M. FISS, *The Civil Rights Injunction*, Indiana University Press, 1978, p. 7.

40 See William M. TABB and Eliane W. SHOBEN, *Remedies*, Thomson West, 2005, p. 22. The last sentence is very important from the terminological point of view when comparing the injunctions with the amparo suits: in Spanish the word «*preventivo*» is used in procedural law (*medidas preventivas o cautelares*) to refers to the «temporary»: or «preliminary» orders or restraints that in North America the judge can issue during the proceeding. So the preventive character of the amparo and of the injunctions cannot be confused with the «*medidas preventivas*» or temporary or preliminary measures that the courts can issue during the trial for the immediate protection of rights, facing the prospect of an irremediable harm that can be caused.

also and basically against threats (*amenaza*) of harming or injuring constitutional rights and guaranties; threats that in general terms must also be real and certain, but additionally, must be immediate, imminent, possible and realizable (Nicaragua, Articles 51, 57, 79; Perú, Article 2; Venezuela, Articles 2; 6,2).

As decided by the Venezuelan courts: to threaten means to provoke fear to others or to make others feel in danger regarding their rights; conversely, a violation is a situation in which a fact has already been accomplished, so no threat is possible[41]. In this regard, the Colombian Constitutional Court has drawn the distinction between harm and threat, as follows:

> «The harm has implicit the concept of injury or prejudice. A right is harmed when its object is damaged. A right is threatened when that same object, without being destroyed, is put in a situation of suffering a decrease»[42].

> «Harm and threat of fundamental rights are two different concepts clearly distinguishable: the former needs an objective verification that the tutela judges must do, by proving its empirical occurrence and their constitutional repercussions; the latter, conversely, adds subjective and objective criteria, conforming itself not by the intention of the public officer or the individual, but by the result the action or omission can have regarding the spirit of the affected person. Thus, in order to determine the constitutional hypothesis of the threat, the confluence of subjective and objectives elements are needed: the fear of the plaintiff that feels his fundamental rights are in danger of perish and the validation of such perception by means of external objective elements, the significance of which is the one offered by the temporal and historical circumstances in which the facts are developing»[43].

A threat is then, a potential harm or violation, that is imminent and to occur soon, regarding which the same Constitutional Court of Colombia has said:

> «A threat to a fundamental constitutional right has multiple expressions: it can be referred to the specific circumstances of a person regarding the exercise of the right; to the existence of positive and unequivocal signs regarding the intention of a person capable to execute acts that can violate the right; or be represented in the challenge of someone (attempt), with direct repercussion on the right; also it can be constituted by non deliberated acts that, according to its characteristics, can lead the amparo court to be convinced that if no order is issued, impeding the conduct to continue, the violation of the right will be produced; also it can correspond to an authority omission whose extension in time allows the risk to appear or to increase; its configuration is also feasible in case of the existence of a norm -authorization or mandate- contrary to the Constitution, the application of which in the concrete case would be in itself an attack or a disregard of the fundamental»[44].

---

41 Decision First Court on Judicial Review of Administrative Actions of July 16, 1092, *Revista de Derecho Público*, N° 51, Editorial Jurídica Venezolana, Caracas, 1992, p. 155.

42 Decision T-412 of June 17, 1992. See he references in Juan Carlos ESGUERRA PORTOCARRERO, *La protección constitucional del ciudadano*, Legis, Bogotá 2005, p. 147; and in Federico GONZÁLEZ CAMPOS, *La tutela. Interpretación doctrinaria y jurisprudencial*, Ediciones Jurídicas Gustavo IBÁÑEZ, Bogotá, 1994, pp. 46-47.

43 Decision T-439 of July 2, 1992. See he references in Juan Carlos ESGUERRA PORTOCARRERO, *La protección constitucional del ciudadano*, Legis, Bogotá, 2005, p. 148.

44 See decision T- 349 of August 27, 1993. See the references in Rafael CHAVERO, *El nuevo régimen del amparo constitucional en Venezuela*, Ed. Sherwood, Caracas, 2001, pp. 238-239.

Of course there are some constitutional rights that if they are not protected against threats, they could lose all sense in their selves. It happens with the right to life, in the sense that if someone has received imminent death threats, the only way to guarantee the right to life is by avoiding the concretion of the threats, for instance, providing the person with due police protection.

According to Article 2 of the Venezuelan Amparo Law, the threats that can be protected by the amparo suits, must be imminent, adding Article 6,1 of the same Law that the action for amparo will not be admitted when the threat of violation of a constitutional right has ceased, or when the threat against a constitutional right or guarantee is not «immediate, possible and feasible (Art. 6,2)[45]. Regarding these general conditions, the Venezuelan former Supreme Court of Justice, ruled that they must be concurrent conditions when referred to the constitutional protection against harms that will soon be done by someone to the rights of others[46].

In similar sense, the Constitutional Chamber of the Supreme Court of Costa Rica has ruled that «according to Article 29 (of the Constitutional Jurisdiction Law), the amparo against a threat regarding a fundamental right can only be granted if the threat is certain, real, effective and imminent; thus, those probable prejudices not capable of being objectively apprehended cannot be protected by amparo»[47].

In this regard, the *jurisprudencia* of the Supreme Court of México has developed as a non admissibility cause for the amparo suit, when the action refers to «future and probable acts»[48]. This refers to acts that have not yet occurred, thus referring to injuries that not only do not presently exist but may never be inflicted; in other words, «simple futurity is not in itself a sufficient bar to the suit. If the execution of the act is imminent and certain, although not formally completed or in process, the amparo suit is admissible»[49]. In the same sense in Ecuador, regarding the «imminent» character of the harm prescribed in Article 95 of the Constitution must be to occur in the near future, as a true potential injury that is not a mere conjecture. Additionally, the harm must be concrete and real and the claimant must prove how it affects his rights[50].

---

45 *Cfr.* See decisions of the Politico Administrative Chamber of the former Supreme Court of Justice of June 9, 1988, *Revista de Derecho Público,* N° 35, Editorial Jurídica Venezolana, Caracas, 1988, p. 114; and of August 14, 1992, *Revista de Derecho Público,* N° 51, Editorial Jurídica Venezolana, Caracas, 1992, pp. 158-159; and of the First Court on Judicial Review of Administrative Actions of June 30, 1988, *Revista de Derecho Público,* N° 35, Editorial Jurídica Venezolana, Caracas, 1988, p. 115.

46 See decisions of the Politico Administrative Chamber of the Supreme Court of Justice of June 24, 1993, *Revista de Derecho Público,* N° 55-56, Editorial Jurídica Venezolana, Caracas, 1993, p. 289; and of March 22, 1995 (Case: *La Reintegradora*), in Rafael CHAVERO, *El nuevo régimen del amparo constitucional en Venezuela,* Ed. Sherwod, Caracas 2001, p. 239.

47 See Vote 295-93. See the references in Rubén HERNÁNDEZ VALLE, *Derecho Procesal constitucional,* Editorial Juricentro, 2001, p. 222.

48 Tesis jurisprudencial 74, *Apéndice al Semanario Judicial de la Federación*, 1917-1988, Segunda parte, salas y tesis Comunes, p. 123. See the reference in Eduardo FERRER MAC-GREGOR, *La acción constitucional de amparo en México y España,* Edit. Porrúa, México, 2002, p. 395.

49 Tesis 44 and 45. *Jurisprudencia de la Suprema Corte*, pp. 110, 113. See the referencie in Richard D. BAKER, *Judicial Review in México. A study of the Amparo Suit*, University of Texas Press, Austin, 1971, p. 96, note 12.

50 See Hernán SALGADO PESANTES, *Manual de Justicia Constitucional Ecuatoriana*, Corporación Editora nacional, Quito 2004, p. 80.

In the same sense, in México the courts have ruled regarding the imminent character of the harm that they are those that have been sufficiently proved that they will occur, because for instance, previous actions had been taken or they will ineludible be consequence of past facts also proved[51]. This distinguishes the imminent actions from those already existing or from those just to be occurring in the future. What is certain is that if the amparo action were only to be admitted against existing facts, the affected party, even though having complete knowledge of the near occurrence of a harm, in order to file the amparo action, would have to patiently wait for the act to be issued, with all its harming consequences.

But what is basically needed for the amparo against threats regarding constitutional rights is its imminent character. This rule has also been developed in the United States as an essential requirement for preventive injunctions, in the sense that courts will order them only when the threatened harm is imminent, in order to prohibit future conduct; and not when the harm is considered remote, potential or speculative. *In Reserve Mining Co. v. Environmetal Protection Agency* 513 F.2d, 492 (8th Cir 1975), the Circuit Court did not grant the requested injunction ordering Reserve Mining Company to cease discharging wastes from its iron ore processing plant in Silver Bay, Minnesota, into the ambient air of Silver bay and the waters of lake Superior, because even though the plaintiff has established that the discharges give rise to a «potential threat to the public health...no harm to the public health has been shown to have occurred to this date and the danger to health is not imminent. The evidence calls for preventive and precautionary steps. No reason exists which requires that Reserve terminate its operations at once»[52]. In other classically cited case, *Fletcher v. Bealey*, 28 Ch. 688 (1885), referred to waste deposits in the plaintiff land by the defendant, the judge ruled that being the action brought to prevent continuing damages, for a *quia timet* action, two ingredients are necessary:

> «There must, if no actual damage is proved, be proof of imminent danger, and there must also be proof that the apprehended damage will, if it comes, be very substantial. I should almost say it must be proved that it will be irreparable, because, if the danger is not proved to be so imminent that no one can doubt that, if the remedy is delayed, the damage will be suffered, I think it must be shown that, if the damage does occur at any time, it will come in such a way and under such circumstances that it will be impossible for the Plaintiff to protect himself against it if relief is denied to him in a *quia timet* action»[53].

As happens also regarding injunctions in the United States, the amparo in Latin American Countries cannot be granted «merely to allay the fears and apprehensions or to soothe the anxieties of individuals, since such fears and apprehensions may exist without substantial reasons and be absolutely groundless or speculative»[54]. The amparo, as the injunction, is an extraordinary remedy

---

51 Joaquin BRAGE CAMAZANO, *La Jurisdicción Constitucional de la Libertad. Teoría general, Argentina, México, Corte Interamericana de Derechos Humanos*, Ed. Porrúa, México, 2005, pp. 171-173.

52 See the comments in Owen M. FISS and Doug RENDELMAN, *Injunctions*, The Foundation Press, Mineola New York, 1984, pp. 116 ff.

53 See the reference in Owen M. FISS and Doug RENDELMAN, *Injunctions*, The Foundation Press, Mineola New York, 1984, pp. 110-111.

54 See Kevin Schroder, John Glenn and Maureen Placilla (Editors), *Corpus Juris Secundum*, Vol. 43A, Thomson West, 2004, p. 57.

«designed to prevent serious harm, is not to be used to protect a person from mere inconvenience or speculative and insubstantial injury»[55].

As mentioned, the imminence of the harm must be certain, so that for example, the Mexican courts have ruled that mere possibility for the authorities to exercise their powers of investigation and control, cannot be sufficient for the filing of an amparo action[56]. In this same sense it is regulated, regarding the tutela action, in Article 3 of Decree 306-92 of Colombia».

> **Article 3:** *When it does not exist threat to a fundamental constitutional right*: It will be understood that a fundamental constitutional right will not be threaten by the only fact of the opening of an administrative enquiry by the competent authority, subjected to the procedure regulated by law.

In the same sense, the Supreme Court of Justice of Venezuela ruled in 1989 that

> «the opening of a disciplinary administrative inquiry is not enough to justify the protection of a party by means of the judicial remedy of amparo, moreover if the said proceeding, in which all needed defenses can be exercised, may conclude in a decision discarding the incriminations against the party with the definitive closing of the disciplinary process, without any sanction to the party»[57].

On the other hand, the threats regarding which constitutional rights can be protected by the amparo suit must be proven by the claimant, as threats against his rights that are precisely made by the defendant. That is why, the Argentinean courts for instance, have rejected an amparo action against non proved threats, for instance, when a mother filed a complaint asking the police protection to avoid an order of seizure of a minor, issued by a foreign court, because the existence of the order was not proved, nor sufficient elements for judging the case were alleged in order to prove that the local authorities were going to fail to apply the legal dispositions that apply to the execution in the country of foreign judicial decisions, which prescribes enough guarantees for the defense of rights and to protect internal public order[58].

The proof of the harm can also be based on previous acts or conducts of the defendant, or on his past pattern of conduct. One example, in the United States, as resumed by Tabb and Shoben, is the case *Galella v. Onassis* (S.D.N.Y. 1972) originated in the claim of the wife of J. F. Kennedy, the former President of the United States, seeking for an injunction against a professional free-lance photographer to restrain him from violating her rights of privacy. «The evidence showed that the photographer had repeatedly engaged in harassing behavior of the Onassis family

---

55 Kevin Schroder, John Glenn and Maureen Placilla (Editors), *Corpus Juris Secundum*, Vol. 43A, Thomson West, 2004, pp. 57-58.

56 See *Semanario Judicial de la Federación*, Tomo I, Segunda parte-2, p. 697. See the reference in Joaquín BRAGE CAMAZANO, *La Jurisdicción Constitucional de la Libertad. Teoría general, Argentina, México, Corte Interamericana de Derechos Humanos*, Ed. Porrúa, México 2005, p. 173, note 269.

57 See decision of the Politico Administrative Chamber of October 26, 1989 (Case *Gisela Parra Mejía*). See the reference in Rafael CHAVERO, *El nuevo régimen del amparo constitucional en Venezuela*, Ed. Sherwood, Caracas 2001, pp. 191, 241.

58 See the references in Néstor Pedro SAGÜES, *Derecho Procesal Constitucional, Acción de Amparo*, Vol 3, Astrea, Buenos Aires, 1988, pp. 117; and in Rafael Chavero, *El nuevo régimen del amparo constitucional en Venezuela*, Ed. Sherwood, Caracas 2001, pp. 190 and 239.

in order to obtain pictures, but each time the invasive behavior was different. Based upon the pattern of past conduct, the court concluded that the photographer's behavior would continue indefinitely in the future. The evidence on imminency was very strong because the photographer had even sent an advertisement to customers announcing future anticipated pictures of Onassis. Even though the pattern of behavior was varied in the types of invasive conduct, the overall nature of it was harassing. With sufficient evidence, even an unpredictable pattern can establish imminency»[59].

The threat must also be attributed to the defendant; on the contrary, the amparo action must be rejected. It was the case of an amparo action brought before the former Venezuelan Supreme Court of Justice in 1999, against the President of the Republic, denouncing as injuring acts possible measures to be adopted by the National Constituent Assembly convened by the President, once it were installed. The Court rejected the action not only because «the reasons alleged by the plaintiff were of eventual and hypothetical nature, which contradicts the need of an objective and real harm or threat to constitutional rights or guarantees» in order for the amparo to be admissible; but said, regarding the alleged defendant in the case, the following:

> «This court must say, that the action for constitutional amparo serves to give protection against situations that in a direct way could produce harms regarding the plaintiff's constitutional rights or guarantees, seeking the restoration of its infringed juridical situation. In this case, the person identified as plaintiff (President of the Republic) could not be by himself the one to produce the eventual harm which would condition the voting rights of the plaintiff, and the fear that the organization of the constituted braches of government could be modified, would be attributed to the members of those that could be elected to the National Constituent Assembly not yet elected. Thus in the case there does not exist the immediate relation between the plaintiff and the defendants needed in he amparo suit»[60].

Another aspect to be mentioned is the possibility to file an amparo action against the legislator based on the threat to constitutional rights provoked by statutes or legislative acts, which is related to the main subject of the amparo against laws. In this regard, the former Supreme Court of Justice of Venezuela, in a restrictive, has ruled that a statute or a legal norm, in itself, cannot originate a valid possible, imminent and feasible threat, to allow the filing of an amparo action. In a decision of May 24, 1993, the Politico-Administrative Chamber of the Supreme Court ruled:

> It is indisputable that a legal norm violating the Constitution can also harm persons situated in the juridical situation it regulates, so in such case, the harm could be considered 'possible', according to Article 6,2 of the Amparo law.
>
> Nonetheless, when an amparo action is filed against a norm, -that is, when the object of the action is the norm in itself-, the concretion of the possible alleged harm would not be «immediate», due to the fact that there would be

[59] See William M. TABB and Eliane W. SHOBEN, *Remedies*, Thomson West, 2005, p. 29.

[60] See decision of April 23, 1999 (Case: *A. Albornoz*). See the reference in Rafael CHAVERO, *El nuevo régimen del amparo constitucional en Venezuela*, Ed. Sherwood, Caracas, 2001, p. 240.

always necessary for the competent authority to proceed to the execution or application of the norm, in order to harm the plaintiff. One must conclude that the probable harm caused by a norm will always be mediate and indirect, needing to be apply to the concrete case. Thus, the injury will be caused through and by means of an act applying the disposition that is contrary to the rule of law.

The same occurs with the third condition set forth in the Law; the threat, that is, the probable and imminent harm, will never be feasible -that is, concreted- by the defendant. If it could be sustained that the amparo could be filed against a disposition the constitutionality of which is challenged, then it would be necessary to accept as defendant the legislative body or the public officer which had sanctioned it, being the latter the one that would act in court defending the act. It can be observed that in case the possible harm would effectively arrive to be materialized, it would not be the legislative body or the sate organ which issued it, the one that will execute it, but the public official for whom the application of the norm will be imposing in all the cases in which an individual would be in the factual situation established in the norm.

If it is understood that that the norm can be the object or an amparo action, the conclusion would be that the defendant (the public entity sanctioning the norm the unconstitutionality of which is alleged) could not be the one entity conducting the threat; but that the harm would be in the end concretized or provoked by a different entity (the one applying to the specific and concrete case the unconstitutional provision).

Thus the amparo against law and other normative acts must be discarded, not only because the Amparo law does not establish such possibility, but also because even though being possible to file the extraordinary action against a normative act of general effects, the court must declare its inadmissibility because the conditions set fort in Article 6,2 of the Amparo law are not covered»[61].

Accordingly, the former Supreme Court rejected the possibility to fill amparo actions against laws, restricting the scope of the Amparo Law in our opinion without major basic arguments, and facing the possibility for the constitutional protection to be needed, ruled as follows:

«Nonetheless, this High Court considers necessary to point out that the previous conclusion does not signify the impossibility to prevent the concretion of the harm -objection that could be drawn from the thesis that the amparo can only proceed if the unconstitutional norm is applied-, due to he fact that the imminently aggrieved person, must not necessarily wait for the effective execution of the illegal norm, because since he faces the threat having the conditions established in the Law, he could seek for amparo for his constitutional rights. In such case, thou, the amparo would not be directed against the norm, but against the public officer that has to apply it. In effect, being imminent the application to an individual of a normative disposition

[61] See decision of the Politico Administrative Chamber of May 25, 1993 in *Revista de Derecho Público,* N° 55-56, Editorial Jurídica Venezolana, Caracas, 1993, pp. 289-290.

contrary to any of the constitutional rights or guaranties, the potentially affected person could seek from the court a prohibition directed to the said public officer plaintiff, compelling not to apply the challenged norm, once evaluated by the court as being unconstitutional»[62].

VI. THE NON CONSENTED CHARACTER OF THE INJURY

The injury to a constitutional right or guarantee that can permit an individual to seek constitutional judicial protection by means of an amparo action, must not only be actual, possible, real and imminent, and not provoked by the plaintiff himself[63], but must not be a consented harm or injury; that is, the complainant must not have expressly or tacitly consented to the challenged act or the harm caused to his right.

Regarding the express consent, it exists, as ruled in the Venezuelan Amparo Law, when there are «unequivocal signs of acceptance» (Art. 6,4)[64] of the act, the facts or the omissions causing the injury, in which case the amparo action is inadmissible.

This case of inadmissibility of the amparo action is also expressly regulated in the Amparo Laws of México, against expressly consented acts or acts consented as consequence of «expression of will that implies such consent» (article 73, XI); in Nicaragua, against «acts that have been consented by the claimant in an express way» (Article 51,4); and in Costa Rica, «when the action or omission would be legitimately consented by the aggrieved person»(Article 30,ch).

In certain aspects, this inadmissibility clause for the amparo suit referred to the express consent of the plaintiff, has some equivalence with the equitable defense in the United Stated injunctions called *estopell*, which refers to actions of the plaintiff prior to the filing of the suit, that are inconsistent with the rights it asserts in his claim.

The classic example of *estopell*, as referred to by Tabb and Shoben, «is that a plaintiff cannot ask equity for an order to remove a neighbor's fence built over the lot line if the plaintiff stood by and watched the fence construction in full knowledge of the location of the lot line. The plaintiff silence with knowledge of the facts is an action inconsistent with the right asserted in court»[65].

The other clause of inadmissibility in the amparo suit refers to the tacit consent of the plaintiff regarding the act, fact or omission causing the injury to his rights, which happens when a precise delay of time has elapsed without the claim being brought before the courts.

This clause for the inadmissibility of the amparo suit is also equivalent to what in North American procedure for injunction is called laches, which as resumed by Tabb and Shoben, «bars a suitor in equity who has not acted promptly in bringing the action; it is reflected in the maxim: 'Equity aids the vigilant, not those who slumber in their rights'»[66].

---

62 *Idem.*, p. 290.

63 See Hernán SALGADO PESANTES, *Manual de Justicia Constitucional Ecuatoriana*, Corporación Editora Nacional, Quito 2004, p. 80.

64 The Venezuelan Law qualifies this express consent as «tacit».

65 See William M. TABB and Eliane W. SHOBEN, *Remedies*, Thomson West, 2005, pp. 50-51.

66 See William M. TABB and Eliane W. SHOBEN, *Remedies*, Thomson West, 2005, p. 48.

As argued in *Lake Development Enterprises, Inc. v. Kojetinsky*, 410 S.W. 2d 361, 367-68 (Mo. App. 1966):

> '«Laches» is the neglect, for an unreasonable and unexplained length of time under circumstances permitting diligence, to do what in law, should have been done. There is no fixed period within which a person must assert his claim or be barred by laches. The length of time depends upon the circumstances of the particular case. Mere delay in asserting a right does not of itself constitute laches; the delay involved must work to the disadvantage and prejudice of the defendant. Laches is a question of fact to be determined from all the evidence and circumstances adduced at trial»[67].

The difference between the doctrine of laches regarding injunctions and the Latin American concept of tacit consent referred to amparo suits, basically lays in the fact that the delay to file the action for amparo in Lain America, is in general expressly established in the Amparo Laws, so the exhaustion of the delay without the filing of the action, is what is considered to be a tacit consent regarding the act, the fact or the omission causing the injury.

In this regard, and only with few exceptions, as Ecuador[68] and Colombia (where for instance, the tutela law establishes that the action for tutela can be filed in any moment, Art. 11), the Amparo Laws in Latin America set forth a delay, considering that it is tacitly understood that the injured party has consented the acts, when the recourses or actions are not filed within the delays set forth in the statutes. The established delay varies in the legislation in a number of days counted from the date of the challenged act or from the day the injured party has known about the violation: Argentina, 15 days (Art. 2,e); Brazil, 120 days (Art. 18); Guatemala, 30 days (Art. 20); Honduras, 2 months; México, 15 days as a general rule, but with many other delays with different length of time (Arts. 21, 22 and 73,XII); Nicaragua, 30 days (Art. 26; 51,4); Perú, 60 days (Arts. 5,10; 44); Uruguay, 30 days (Art 4); Venezuela, 6 months (Art. 6,4). In the cases of Dominican Republic and Chile, where the delay (15 days) has been regulated by Supreme Court, discussions have arisen regarding the constitutionality of such norms, due to the criteria that a delay of such type must be only established by the Legislator[69].

In Costa Rica, the Constitutional Jurisdiction Law establishes that the amparo recourse can be filed at any time while the violation, threat, injury or restriction endures, and up to 2 months after the direct effects regarding the injured party, have ceased (Arts. 35, 60). This delay can also be suspended if the interested party decides to file an administrative recourse against the particular act (Art. 31). Regarding this clause of inadmissibility of the amparo action, the former Supreme Court of Justice of Venezuela ruled in a decision of October 24, 1990, that:

> «Being the amparo action a special, brief, summary and effective judicial remedy for the protection of constitutional rights...it is logic for the Legislator to

---

67 See the reference Owen M. FISS and Doug RENDELMAN, *Injunctions*, The Foundation Press, Mineola New York, 1984, pp. 102-103.

68 See Hernán SALGADO PESANTES, *Manual de Justicia Constitucional Ecuatoriana*, Corporación Editora Nacional, Quito 2004, p. 81.

69 See Juan Manuel ERRAZURIZ and Jorge Miguel OTERO A., *Aspectos procesales del recurso de protección*, Editorial Jurídica de Chile, Santiago 1989, p. 130; Miguel A. VALERA MONTERO, *Hacia un nuevo concepto de Constitución*, Santo Domingo, 2006, p. 404.

prescribe a correct proportion of time between the moment in which the harm is produced and the moment the aggrieved party is to file the action. To let pass more that 6 months from the moment in which the injuring act is issued for the exercise of the action is the demonstration of the acceptance of the harm from the side of the aggrieved party; the indolence must be sanctioned, impeding the use of the judicial remedy that has its justification on the urgent need to reestablish a legal situation»[70].

Of course, as a general rule in this matter, the exhaustion of the delay without filing the amparo action, although considered as a tacit consent regarding the injury, does not prevent the interested person from filing any other recourse or action against the act provoking the harm, as it is expressly regulated in the Costa Rican Law (Art. 36)[71].

A particular aspect can be mentioned, regarding the situation in cases of wrongs that are continuous in nature. In the United States, it is considered that laches cannot be urged as a defense to a suit to enjoin a wrong which is continuing in its nature (Pacific Greyhound Lines v. Sun Valley Bus Lines, 70 Ariz. 65, 216 P. 2d 404, 1950; Goldstein v. Beal, 317 Mass. 750, 59 N.E. 2d 712, 1945)[72]. A similar rule has been applied for instance, in Venezuela, where the Fist Court on Administrative Judicial review actions in a decision of October 22, 1990 (Case: *María Cambra de Pulgar*) in which when deciding on a defense on inadmissibility of an action, ruled:

> «In spite that a number of the facts indicated had been produced more that 6 months ago, they have been described in order to reveal a supposed chain of events that, due to their constancy and re incidence, allows presuming that the plaintiff is threatened with those facts being repeated. This character of the threat is what the amparo intends to stop. According to what the plaintiff point out, no tacit consent can be produced from his part ... Consequently, there are no grounds for the application to any of the inadmissibility clauses set forth in the Amparo Law»[73].

VII. EXCEPTIONS TO THE TACIT CONSENT RULE

On the other hand, since there are constitutional question involved, the Laws establish various exceptions regarding the caducity or lapsing of the action. For instance, in Honduras, it is expressly regulated that the action can be filed after the exhaustion of the delay, when the impossibility to bring the action before the court is duly proved (Art. 46,3). In similar sense it is regulated in Article 4 of the Uruguayan Law when the plaintiff has been impeded by «just cause» to file the action.

In México, in particular, regarding the amparo against laws, the action can be filed not only against the statute, but also after the exhaustion of the delay, against the first concrete act that applies it; so the tacit consent rule applies in this case, only

---

70 See in *Revista de Derecho Público,* N° 44, Editorial Jurídica Venezolana, Caracas, 1990, p. 144.

71 See the comments in Ruben HERNÁNDEZ VALLE, *Derecho procesal Constitucional,* Editorial Juricentro, 2001, pp. 226-229, 243.

72 See the references in Kevin Schroder, John Glenn and Maureen Placilla (Editors), *Corpus Juris Secundum,* Vol. 43A, Thomson West, 2004, p. 329.

73 See decision of October 22, 1990, in *Revista de Derecho Público,* N° 44, Editorial Jurídica Venezolana, Caracas, 1990, pp. 143-144.

when the latter is not challenged in the delay set forth in the Amparo Law (Art. 73,XII)[74]. But additionally to this particular exception, Article 22 of the Amparo Law of México establishes other general exception to the tacit consent rule, in cases of authority acts endangering the life, the personal freedom, deportation, any other acts prohibited in Article 22 of the Constitution, or the forced incorporation to the army[75]. In these cases the amparo action can be brought before the courts at any time. Also the amparo action can be filed at any time, in cases of the protection of peasants rights related to communal land (Art. 217).

In Costa Rica, Article 20 of the Constitutional Jurisdiction Law also establishes as an exception regarding the delay, in cases in which the amparo action is filed against the risk of an unconstitutional law or regulation to be applied in concrete cases, as well as in cases of a manifest possibility of acts harming the plaintiff rights could be issued or occur.

In Venezuela, the Amparo Law also provides a few exceptions regarding the tacit consent rule, when the amparo action is filed together or jointly with another nullity action, in which cases the general 6 month delay established for the filing of the action does not apply. This is the rule in cases of harms or threats originated in statutes or regulations, and in administrative acts or public administration omissions, when the amparo action is filed jointly with the popular action for judicial review of unconstitutionality of statutes, or with the judicial review action against administrative actions or omissions.

Regarding the judicial review popular action against statutes, it is conceived in the Organic Law of the Supreme Tribunal as an action that can be filed at any time, so if a petition for amparo is filed together with the popular action, no delay is applicable. This is why, no tacit consent can be understood when the harm is provoked by a statute.

Similarly, the tacit consent rule does not apply either in cases of administrative acts or omissions, when the amparo action is filed together with the judicial review action against administrative acts or omissions, in which case, due to the constitutional complaint, the latter can be filed at any moment, as is expressly provided in the Amparo Law (Art. 5).

Finally, mention must be done to the exception regarding the tacit consent rule regarding actions or omissions established in Article 6,4 of the Venezuelan Amparo Law, in cases when the violations of constitutional rights infringes «public order and good conduct», an exceptional situation that must derive from a rule of law[76].

This concept of «public order» in the Venezuelan legal system refers to situations where the application of a state concerns the general and indispensable legal order for the existence of the community, which cannot be bequeathed; and

---

74 See Eduardo FERRER MAC-GREGOR, *La acción constitucional de amparo en México y España*, Editorial Porrúa, México 2002, p. 391; Richard D. BAKER, *Judicial Review in México. A Study of the Amparo Suit*, University of Austin Press, Austin 1971, p. 172.

75 Eduardo FERRER MAC-GREGOR, *La acción constitucional de amparo en México y España*, Editorial Porrúa, México 2002, p. 331.

76 See decision of the Politico Administrative Chamber of March 22, 1988, in *Revista de Derecho Público,* N° 34, Editorial Jurídica Venezolana, Caracas, 1988, p. 114.

it does not apply in cases that only concern the parties in a contractual or private controversy. As ruled by the Cassation Chamber of the Supreme Court in Venezuela, in a decision of April 3, 1985, «the concept of public order tend to make the general interest of the Society and of the State to win over the individual particular interest, in order to assure the enforcement and purpose of some institutions»[77].

For instance, as a matter of general principle, public order provisions in public law are those establishing competencies or attributions to the public entities[78], including the Judiciary, and those concerning the taxation powers of public entities. In private law, for instance, all the provisions referring to the status of persons (for instance: *patria potestas*, divorce, adoption) are norms in which public order and good customs are involved[79].

But in many cases it is the lawmaker itself that has expressly declared in a particular statute that its provisions are of «public order» character, in the sense that its norms cannot be modified through contracts. That is the case for instance, of the 2004 Consumers and Users Protection Law[80], where Article 2 sets forth that its provisions are of public order and may not be renounced by the parties.

Regarding the amparo action and the exception to the tacit consent rule, the First Court of Administrative Judicial Review, has ruled as follows:

> «It is true that the tacit or express consent does not extinguish the action when the violation infringes the public order or the good customs, and that Article 14 of the Amparo Law qualifies the action, whether in its principal or incidental aspects up to the judicial decision execution, as «eminent public order». A textual interpretation could lead to the absurd of considering that, because all matters of amparo are of public order, the express consent (configured by the delay exhaustion) does not extinguish the action; but such interpretation contradicts the logic of the system and the nature of amparo, which is a brief and speedy mean regarding actual harms. Thus, it must be interpreted that the extinction of the amparo action due to the elapse of the delay (express consent, according to the legislator), is produced in all cases, except when the way through which the harm has been produced, is of such gravity that it constitutes an injury to the juridical conscience. It would be the case, for instance, of flagrant violations to individual rights that cannot be denounced by the affected party; deprivation of freedom; submission to physical or psychological torture; maltreatment; harms to human dignity and other extreme cases»[81].

---

77 See the reference in decisión of the Politico Administrative Chamber of February 1, 1990 (*Case Tuna Atlántica C.A.*) and of June 30, 1992, in *Revista de Derecho Público,* N° 60, Editorial Jurídica Venezolana, Caracas, 1992, p. 157.

78 See for instante, decisión of the Constitucional Chamber of the Supreme Tribunal of March 1, 2001 (Case: *Alcalde del Municipio Baruta, Bingos*). See the reference in Rafael CHAVERO G., *El nuevo régimen del amparo constitucional en Venezuela*, Editorial Sherwood, Caracas 2001, 187.

79 Allan R. BREWER-CARÍAS, *Contratos Administrativos*, Editorial Jurídica Venezolana, Caracas, 1992, pp. 265-268.

80 *Official Gazette*, N° 37.930, May 4th 2004.

81 See the decision of the First Court on Judicial Review of Administrative Actions of October 13, 1988, in *Revista de Derecho Público,* N° 36, Editorial Jurídica Venezolana, Caracas, 1988,

Consequently not all violations of constitutional rights and guarantees are considered in their selves as having public order concern, but only those where the juridical or legal conscience of society is harmed, like when human dignity is injured in a flagrant and grave way, as happens with freedom deprivation and infringement of tortures. In such cases, no tacit consent can be admitted, and the amparo judicial protection must be admitted even tough the delay for filing the action would have been exhausted.

p. 95. This opinion was followed exactly by the Politico Administrative Chamber of the Supreme Court of Justice, decision of November 1, 1989, in *Revista de Derecho Público,* N° 40, Editorial Jurídica Venezolana, Caracas, 1989, p. 111; and by the Cassation Chamber of the same Supreme Court of Justice, in decision of June 28, 1995, (Exp. N°. 94-172). See the reference in Rafael CHAVERO G., *El nuevo régimen del amparo constitucional en Venezuela,* Editorial Sherwood, Caracas, 2001, p. 188, note 178. See other judicial decision on the matter in pp. 214 and 246.

CHAPTER XIII

JUDICIAL ADJUDICATIONS IN THE «AMPARO» SUIT: PRELIMINARY MEASURES AND DEFINITIVE RULINGS: PREVENTIVE AND RESTORATIVE DECISIONS

The final purpose of filing an amparo action is for the plaintiff to obtain a judicial adjudication from the competent court, seeking for the immediate protection of his harmed or threatened constitutional right or guarantee, which in general terms, using the same wording used for the North American injunctions, can consist on:

> «Restrain action or interference of some kind; to furnish preventive relief against irreparable mischief or injury; or to preserve the status quo. It is a remedy designed to prevent irreparable injury by prohibiting or commanding certain acts. The function of injunctive relief is to restrain motion and to enforce inaction. An injunction is designed to prevent harm, not redress harm; it is not compensatory. The remedy grants prospective, as opposed to retrospective, relief; it is preventative, protective or restorative, but not addressed to past wrongs»[1].

Thus, if it is true that the general purpose of both institutions can be considered the same, and that both have an extraordinary character in procedural law, there is a basic distinction between them, regarding their protective object: the North American injunction is a judicial equity remedy that can serve for the protection of any kind of personal or property right that in a particular circumstance cannot be adequately protected by remedies at law. In contrast, the Latin American Amparo is conceived as a specific judicial means for the exclusive protection of constitutional rights and guarantees. That is why the general rules governing the injunctions in North America are set forth in the general procedural statutes. Instead, in Latin America, the general rules for the amparo suit are set forth in the Constitutions.

As in the injunctive procedure, two general sort of judicial adjudications can also be issued in the amparo suit for the protection of the claimed constitutional rights or guaranties: preliminary measures that can be issued since the beginning of the procedure and that are in general subject to the final court ruling; and definitive preventive or restorative adjudications ending the process.

---

1 See the reference to the corresponding judicial decisions in John BOURDEAU et al, «Injunctions» in Kevin Schroder, John Glenn and Maureen Placilla, *Corpus Juris Secundum*, Volume 43A, Thompson West, 2004, p. 20.

I. PRELIMINARY MEASURES IN THE AMPARO SUIT

The preliminary, interlocutory and temporal judicial measures that a Latin American court can adopt in any judicial process before full trial on the merits, generally regulated in the Procedural Codes and applicable to the amparo processes are what in Spanish are called «*medidas preventivas*» or «*medidas cautelares*» issued in an interlocutory way, the expressions «*preventiva*» or «*cautelar*» being used in to describe «preliminary» procedural decisions in contrast to definitive or final adjudications. Thus, the Spanish expression «*preventiva*», is not used exclusively in the English sense of «preventive» as to prevent or to avoiding harm. In the North American system, the «preventive injunction» is a definitive injunction and not a «preliminary» one. In other words, as explained by Tabb and Shoben:

> «The classic form of injunctions in private litigation is the preventive injunction. By definition, a preventive injunction is a court order designed to avoid future harm to a party by prohibiting or mandating certain behavior by another party. The injunction is «preventive» in the sense of avoiding harm. The wording may be either prohibitory («Do not trespass») or mandatory («Remove the obstruction»)[2].

The preliminary judicial measures, of course, can also have «preventive» effects in the sense of preserving the *status quo*, but only in a temporary or preliminary basis, pending the procedure. As the same authors Tabb and Shoben have said:

> «Upon a compelling showing by the plaintiff, the court may issue a coercive order even before full trial on the merits. A preliminary injunction gives the plaintiff temporary relief pending trial on the merit. A temporary restraining order affords immediate relief pending the hearing on the preliminary injunction. Both of these types of interlocutory relief are designed to preserve the status quo to prevent irreparable harm before a court can decide the substantive merits of the dispute. Such orders are available only upon a strong showing of the necessity for such relief and may be conditioned upon the claimant posting a bond or sufficient security to protect the interests of the defendant in the event that the injunction is later determined to have been wrongfully issued»[3].

So, in order to avoid confusions, we are going to use the English expression «preliminary» measures to identify what in Spanish is called «*medidas preventivas o cautelares*» as interlocutory and temporal judicial protective measures that are issued pending the suit, which are similar to the North American «preliminary injunctions» also issued as interlocutory and temporal relief pending the trial. In both cases, the preliminary measures are different from the final judicial protective (permanent injunction) decisions consisting in preventive or restorative adjudication[4].

That is why, in general terms, the amparo suit in Latin America does not have a «cautelar» in the sense of preliminary nature, but tends to protect in a definitive way the constitutional right or guarantee alleged as harmed or threatened. Nonetheless, some terminological confusion can be identified in some countries in

---

2 See William M. TABB and Elaine W. SHOBEN, *Remedies*, Thomson West, 2005, p. 22.

3 See William M. TABB and Elaine W. SHOBEN, *Remedies*, Thomson West, 2005, p. 4.

4 See John BOURDEAU et al, «Injunctions» in Kevin Schroder, John Glenn and Maureen Placilla, *Corpus Juris Secundum*, Volume 43A, Thompson West, 2004, pp. 24 ff.

which it has been given to the amparo action a «cautelar» nature, based on the distinction between «cautelar» measures and «cautelar actions». Nonetheless, in those cases, the leveling of the amparo action as «cautelar» is not in the sense of just having a «preliminary» nature, but in the sense of deciding only about the immediate protection of a constitutional right without resolving the other matters of a controversy. This can be seen in Ecuador and Chile, where the amparo suit has been considered to have «cautelar» nature, but in a sense not equivalent to a «preliminary» nature. The Constitutional Court of Ecuador, for instance, has decided as followed:

> «That the amparo action set forth in Article 95 of the Constitution is in essence, preliminary (*cautelar*) regarding the constitutional rights, not allowing [the court] to decide on the merits or to substitute the proceedings set forth in the legal order for the resolution of a controversy, but only to suspend the effects of an authority act which harms those rights; and the decisions issued in the amparo suit do not produce *res judicata*, so the authority, once corrected the incurred defects, may go back to the matter and issue a new act, providing it is adjusted to the constitutional and legal provisions»[5]

In similar way, in Chile the action for protection has been considered to have a *«cautelar»* nature, not in the sense of «preliminary» measures, but as tending to obtain a definitive protective adjudication regarding constitutional rights[6].

But putting aside these terminological clarifications, in the amparo procedure, preliminary measures can be adopted by the courts pending the final adjudication, in order to preserve the *status quo*, avoiding harms or restoring the plaintiff situation to the original situation, during the development of the procedure. The Latin American Laws vary in the regulatory scope of the preliminary measures, in the sense that in some cases they are enumerated in a restrictive way, and in others, the range of power for preliminary protective measures is unlimited.

1. The suspension of the effects of the challenged act

The preliminary judicial measures can consist in the suspension of the effects of the challenged acts. This is considered to be the most traditional preliminary measure, having its origin in the traditional conception of the amparo as a judicial mean for the protection of constitutional rights against State acts.

Two legal regulations can be distinguished in this matter of the suspension of the effects of the challenged acts, regarding the automatic suspension or the need for a court decision on the matter.

In the specific case of Costa Rica, the suspension of the effect of the challenged act can be considered an automatic preliminary effect of the filing of the amparo action, but in the other cases, it is properly a preliminary protective decision that the court must take.

In effect, in Costa Rica, when the amparo action is filed against a statute or other normative act, the application of them to the plaintiff is automatically sus-

---

5 See the text and comments in Hernán SALGADO PESANTES, *Manual de Justicia Constitucional Ecuatoriana,* Corporación Editora Nacional, Quito, 2004, p. 78.

6 See Eduardo Soto KLOSS, *El recurso de protección. Orígenes, doctrina y jurisprudencia,* Editorial Jurídica de Chile, Santiago 1982, p. 248; Juan Manuel ERRAZURIZ and Jorge Miguel OTERO A., *Aspectos procesales del recurso de protección,* Editorial Jurídica de Chile, Santiago, 1989, pp. 34-38.

pended. In concrete challenged acts, their effects are also automatically suspended (Art. 41). The court can also adopt any other adequate conservatory or security measure in order to prevent material risks or avoid the production of other harms consequence of the facts occurred, (Art. 41). Being the suspension of the challenged act an automatic consequence of the filing of the amparo petition, it is for Public Administration to ask the court to order the execution of the challenged act. For such purpose, the same Article 41 of the Amparo Law provides that in grave exceptional cases the court can order the execution or the continuation of the execution of the challenged act, at the request of Public Administration. This power that can be exercised ex officio, in cases when the suspension of the effects of the act may cause or threaten to cause effective and imminent damages and prejudices to the public interest, bigger that those that could be caused to the aggrieved party. The court can issue the preliminary measures that it considers adequate for the protection of rights and liberties of the aggrieved party and to prevent that the effects of an eventual resolution granting the amparo in his favor become illusory (Art. 41)[7].

Except in this exceptional case, the suspension of the effects of the challenged act is set forth as a preliminary protective measure that the competent court can issue.

The initial regulations on the matter began with the amparo suit Laws in México, where the suspension of the challenged act is the classic preliminary measure on matters of amparo, which can be decided ex officio or at the request of the party (Art. 122). The decision to suspend the effect of the challenged act can be granted when it means a danger of deprivation of life, deportation, expulsion or other conducts prohibited in Article 22 of the Constitutions; or an act that if executed would make physically impossible for the plaintiff to enjoy the individual guarantee claimed. The suspension will consist 1) In ordering the end of the acts that are endangering the life, or that allows the deportation or the expulsion of the plaintiff, or the execution of any of those forbidden in Article 22 of the Constitution; or 2) in ordering that things be maintained in the stage they are, the court having to adopt the adequate measures in order to avoid the consummation of the challenged acts (Art. 123).

Additionally, the suspension can only be decided, when requested by the party; when the harm caused to the aggrieved would be difficult to repair if the act is executed; or when because of the suspension no prejudice is provoked to the social interest, nor the public order norms are contravened. It is understood that the latter is produced when the suspension for instance, implies the continuation of vicious or criminal activities or related to drug production or trafficking, alcoholism or that prevent the adoption of measures to fight grave diseases (Arts. 124, 130)[8].

In a more precise way, the suspension of the effects of the challenged act has been regulated as a preliminary measure in Articles 31 ff. of the Nicaraguan Amparo Law, as follows:

---

7 See Rubén HERNÁNDEZ VALLE, *Derecho Procesal Constitucional*, Editorial Juricentro, San José 2001, pp. 248-254.

8 See Richard D. BAKER, *Judicial Review in México. A Study of the Amparo Suit*, University of Texas Press, Austin 1971, p. 233 ff.; Joaquín BRAGE CAMAZANO, *La jurisdicción constitucional de la libertad (Teoría general, Argentina, México, Corte Interamericana de derechos humanos)*, Editorial Porrúa, México 2005, p. 197.

1) Three days after the filing of the petition, the court ex officio or at the party's request can suspend the effects of the challenged act (Art. 31).

2) The suspension will be ex officio decided when the challenged act if executed would make physically impossible to restore the plaintiff in the enjoyment of his right, or when a notorious lack of jurisdiction of the authority or public officer against the action is filed, or when the challenged act is one of those that no authority can legally execute (Art. 32).

3) If the suspension is requested by the party, it will be granted when the following circumstances concur: a) That the suspension not cause harm to the general interests nor be contrary to public order provisions; b) That the damages and prejudices that could be caused to the aggrieved party with the execution of the act be deemed by the court as difficult to repair; c) That the petitioner post sufficient bond or guarantee in order to repair the damages or compensate the prejudices that the suspension could cause to third parties, in case the amparo action is rejected (Art. 33).

4) Once the suspension order is issued, the court must establish the situation according to which things must remain, and adopt the adequate measures for the conservation up to the end of the procedure, of the matter object of the amparo, (Art. 34).

5) The suspension will lose its effects if a third interested party gives sufficient bond in order to restore things to the stage it was before the challenged act and to pay the damages and prejudices that occur to the plaintiff in case the amparo is granted (Art. 35).

In similar sense to the Nicaraguan regulations, the Guatemalan Amparo Law also sets forth the provisions for what is called the «provisional amparo» decision, consisting in the suspension of the challenged acts (Art. 23 ff). The same principles can be found in the Honduran Amparo Law (arts. 57 ff).

In other Amparo Laws such as in El Salvador, the general provision is the possibility for the court to decide on «the immediate provisional suspension of the challenged act when its execution could cause irreparable harm or damages of difficult reparation by the definitive ruling»(Art. 20). The Law also sets forth that the provisional suspension can only refer to acts with positive effects (Art. 19), thus no suspension is admitted regarding acts with negative effects, that is, for instance, acts denying a petition, because the suspension would be equivalent to provisionally granting the original petition.

Also in Brazil, in the mandado de segurança regulations it is set forth as a provisional measure the possibility for the court to suspend the challenged act when from the evidences filed it could result the inefficacy of the definitive measure in case it is granted (Art. 7,2)[9].

In Colombia, Article 7 of the Tutela Law provides for the «provisional measures for the protection of a right», as follows:

> **Art. 7.** From the filing of the petition, when the court considers it expressly necessary and urgent for the protection of a right, it will suspend the application of the concrete act that threatens or harms it.

[9] See José Luis LAZZARINI, *El juicio de amparo*, Ed. La Ley, Buenos Aires 1987, p. 319.

Nonetheless, at party's request or *ex offico*, the execution or the continuation of the execution can be decided in order to avoid certain and imminent prejudices to public interest. In any case, the court must order what it considers necessary to protect the rights and to prevent that the effects of an eventual decision in favor of the plaintiff become illusory».

The court, *ex officio* and at the request of a party, according to the circumstances of the case, can also issue any conservatory or security measure tending to protect the right or to avoid further damages produced by the facts.

In Venezuela, when the amparo action is filed jointly with the judicial review popular action for nullity against statutes or with the judicial review of administrative actions recourse, the amparo petition has always a preliminary (*cautelar*) character, and consequently, the decision granting the amparo pending the principal suit is always of a preliminary character of suspension of the effects of the challenged act. Thus, in the case of statutes it is the Constitutional Chamber the competent one for deciding the suspension of the application of the statute, in such cases, with *erga omnes* effects[10]; and regarding administrative acts, the courts of the Administrative Jurisdiction are the ones that can decide the matter of suspension of the effects of the administrative challenged act pending the judicial review suit[11].

2. The order not to adopt innovative actions

In Argentina Amparo law refers to the preliminary measures in an indirect way in Article 15, referring to non innovative measures and to the suspension of the effects of the challenged act; the former tending to the maintenance of the *status quo*, thus, paralyzing the facts that even with the filing of the action, pending the brief procedure of the amparo action, could continue to prejudice the integral repairing of the harmed constitutional right. The measure, as all the preliminary measures, tends to assure the result of the definitive decision ending the amparo suit, and to ensure that it will have the same efficacy as if it would have been issued at the moment of the filing of the action[12].

In similar way the Amparo Law of Paraguay also authorizes the competent court, ex officio or at the party's request, to order non innovation orders at any moment, in case that the execution has begin or of imminent grave harm. In such cases, when the violation of the rights and guarantees appears in an evident way and the harm could result irreparable, the court must order the suspension of the challenged act, order the accomplishment of the omitted act, or order the preliminary convenient measures (Art. 8).

---

10 See Rafael CHAVERO G. *El nuevo amparo constitucional en Venezuela*, Ed. Sherwood, Caracas 2001, pp. 468 ff. 327 ff.; Allan R. BREWER-CARÍAS, «Derecho y Acción de Amparo, Vol V, *Instituciones Políticas y Constitucionales*, Editorial Jurídica venezolana, Caracas, 1998, pp. 277 ff.

11 See Allan R. BREWER-CARÍAS, «Derecho y Acción de Amparo, Vol V, *Instituciones Políticas y Constitucionales* Editorial Jurídica venezolana, Caracas, 1998, pp. 281 ff.

12 See José Luis LAZZARINI, *El juicio de amparo*, Ed. La Ley, Buenos Aires 1987, pp. 314-315; Alí Joaquín SALGADO, *Juicio de amparo y acción de inconstitucionalidad*, Editorial Astrea, Buenos Aires 1987, pp. 109; Néstor Pedro SAGÜÉS, *Derecho procesal Constitucional, Vol 3, Acción de amparo*, Editorial Astrea Buenos Aires 1988, p. 460.

3. The other preliminary protective measures

In other Latin American countries, the preliminary measures that the court can issue in the amparo suit, are referred in a wider sense, in that the judge can order at any moment the «preliminary measures» for the protection of the rights (Costa Rica, Art. 21[13]; Uruguay, Art. 7[14]); as is the case in the Bolivian Law, which authorizes the court to issue «the necessary preliminary decisions» in order to avoid the completion of the threat, to restrict or suspend a constitutional right or guarantee in which the petition is founded and that at the court's criteria could create an irreparable situation by means of the amparo» (Art. 99).

4. The conditions for the issuing of preliminary protective measures

In the Peruvian Code on Constitutional Procedures, which is the most recent of all the Latin American legislation referred to the amparo suit, the preliminary protective measures have found a precise regulation, particularly regarding the conditions that need to be accomplished for its issuing, as follows:

> **Article 15.** Preliminary measures. In the constitutional processes, preliminary measures can be adopted as well as the suspension of the harming act. In order for it issuance, the appearance of good right, the danger in the delay and the adequacy of the petition to guarantee the efficacy of the claim, must be required. They can be issued without the knowledge of the other party and the appeal is only granted without suspensive effects. Its justification, formality and execution will depend on the content of the constitutional claim and the final decision securing...».

> This article is the only one that can be found in the Latin Amparo Laws expressly establishing the conditions for the issuance of preliminary measures, which in the other countries have been constructed through judicial doctrine[15]. The main conditions refer, first, to what is called the *fumus boni juris* or the need for the petitioner to prove the existence of his right or guarantee set forth in the Constitution that can be violated or threatened. And second, to what is called the *periculum in mora* or the need to prove that the delay in granting the preliminary protection will make the harm irreparable. Additionally it also exists a condition called *periculum in dammi*, referred to the need to prove the imminence of the harm that can be caused; and the need to balance the collective and particular interest involved in the case[16].

As was ruled by the Supreme Tribunal of Justice of Venezuela, in a decision N° 488 dated March 3, 2000:

> «In order for an anticipated protective measure to be granted it is necessary to examine the existence of three essential elements due to its preliminary content, and always balancing the collective or individual interest; such conditions are:

---

13 See Rubén HERNÁNDEZ, *Derecho Procesal Constitucional*, Editorial Juricentro, San José, 2001, pp. 248, 252.

14 See Luis Alberto VIERA, *Ley de Amparo*, Ediciones Idea, Montevideo, 1993, pp. 41, 206.

15 See Samuel B. ABAD YUPANQUI, *El proceso constitucional de amparo*, Gaceta Jurídica, Lima, 2004, pp. 491, 422 ff. 501 ff.

16 As for instante has been decided by the Venezuelan First Court on Adminsitrative Jurisdiction, Case: *Video & Juegos Costa Verde, C.A. vs. Prefecto del Municipio Maracaibo del Estado Zulia*, in *Revista de Derecho Público*, N° 85-98, Editorial Jurídica Venezolana, Caracas 2001, p. 291.

1. *Fumus Boni Iuris*, that is, the reasonable appearance of the existence of good right in hands of the petitioner alleging its violation, appearance that must derive from the documents attached to the petition.
2. *Periculum in mora*, that is, the danger that the definitive ruling could result illusory, due to the necessary delay in resolving the incident of the suspension.
3. *Periculum in Damni*, that is, the imminence of the harm caused by the presumptive violation of the fundamental rights of the petitioner and its irreparability. These elements are those that basically allow seeking for the necessary anticipatory protection of the constitutional rights and guarantees».[17]

In general terms, these conditions for the issuance of the preliminary protective measures in the amparo suit are the same as those expected to be tested when issuing the preliminary injunctions in the United States. As has been summarized by Tabb and Shoben:

> «Most circuits follow the traditional test for a preliminary injunction. That test has four prerequisites for the issuance of a preliminary injunction. They are: 1) a probability of prevailing on the merits; 2) an irreparable injury if the relief is delayed; 3) a balance of hardship favoring the plaintiff; 4) a showing that the injunction would not adverse to the public interest. The burden of proof on each of these four elements rests with the movant»[18].

5. The inaudita pars issuing of the preliminary protective measures

Due to the extraordinary character of the amparo action, the preliminary protective measures requested by the plaintiff, if the abovementioned prerequisites are fulfilled, can be decided and issued by the court in an immediate way, without a previous hearing of the potential defendants, that is, *inadi alteram parte* or *inaudita pars*, as it is expressly provided in the Perúvian Constitutional Procedures Code (Art. 15)[19]. Nonetheless, many Amparo laws provide for the need of an immediate notification of the corresponding authority when the suspension of effects of his acts is decided as a preliminary protective measure (Colombia, Art. 7; México, Art. 123,II; El Salvador, Art. 24; Honduras, Art. 6o).

In a similar sense, in the United States, the preliminary injunctions and restraining orders can be issued in cases of great urgency and when an immediate threat of irreparable injury exists which forecloses the opportunity to give reasonable notice to the plaintiff, in which the court must balance the harm sought to be preserved against the rights of notice and hearing.[20]

Due to this character of being decided without previous hearing the potential defendant, the preliminary decision is adopted at the responsibility and risk of the

---

[17] Case *Constructora Pedeca, C.A. vs. Gobernación del Estado Anzoátegui*, in *Revista de Derecho Público*, N° 81, Editorial Jurídica Venezolana, Caracas, 2000, p. 459.

[18] See William M. TABB and Elaine W. SHOBEN, *Remedies*, Thomson West, 2005, p. 63.

[19] See Samuel B. ABAD YUPANQUI, *El proceso constitucional de amparo*, Gaceta Jurídica, Lima, 2004, pp. 508.

[20] See the reference to the corresponding judicial decisions in John BOURDEAU et al, «Injunctions» in Kevin Schroder, John Glenn and Maureen Placilla, *Corpus Juris Secundum*, Volume 43A, Thompson West, 2004, pp. 339 ff.

plaintiff, as is provided in the Honduras Law (Art. 58); the court being empowered to ask for the posting of a bond in order to guarantee the damages that can be caused by the measure, in particular, regarding third parties (México, Art. 124 ff.; Honduras, Art. 58; Paraguay, Art. 8).

The preliminary measures in the amparo process, as happens with the injunctions[21], are essentially modifiable or revocable by the court, particularly at the request of the defendant or of third parties (Colombia, Art. 7; Honduras, Art. 61; Guatemala, Art. 30). In México, even third parties can place a bond requesting the revocation of the preliminary measure of suspension of challenged acts effects, in order to restore things to how they were before the guarantee was violated an to pay the damages and prejudices that could be caused to the petitioner, in case the amparo is granted (Art. 126).

II. THE DEFINITIVE JUDICIAL ADJUDICATION IN THE AMPARO SUIT

The purpose of the amparo suit is for the injured or aggrieved party (the plaintiff), to obtain a judicial protection (*amparo, tutela, protección*) of his constitutional rights or guarantees that have been harmed or threatened by an aggrieving or injurer party (the defendant). The final result of the process, characterized by its bilateral frame which imposes the need for the defendants to have the right to participate and to be heard[22], is thus a formal judicial decision or order issued by the court in order to protect threatened rights or to restore the harmed one. This order, like the North American injunction:

> «Is a court order commanding or preventing virtually any type of action, or commanding someone to undo some wrong or injury. It is a judicial order requiring a person to do or refrain from doing certain acts, for any period of time, no matter its purpose. This is to say, an injunction is a writ framed according to the circumstances or the case commanding an act which the court regards as essential in justice, or restraining an act which it deems contrary to equity and good conscience»[23].

In similar sense, the function of the amparo court's decision is, on the one hand, to prevent the defendant from inflicting further injury on the plaintiff, similarly the «preventive injunction» in the United States, that can be prohibitory or mandatory; or on the other hand, to correct the present by undoing the effects of a past wrong, similarly the «restorative or reparative injunction» in the United States[24].

---

21 See the reference to the corresponding judicial decisions in John BOURDEAU et al, «Injunctions» in Kevin Schroder, John Glenn and Maureen Placilla, *Corpus Juris Secundum*, Volume 43A, Thomson West, 2004, pp. 406 ff; 421.

22 Similarly, regarding definitive injunctions, they only can be granted if process issues and service is made on the defendant. See the reference to the corresponding judicial decisions in John Bourdeau et al, «Injunctions» in Kevin Schroder, John Glenn and Maureen Placilla, *Corpus Juris Secundum*, Volume 43A, Thomson West, 2004, p. 339.

23 See the reference to the corresponding judicial decisions in John BOURDEAU et al, «Injunctions» in Kevin Schroder, John Glenn and Maureen Placilla, *Corpus Juris Secundum*, Volume 43A, Thomson West, 2004, p. 19.

24 See William M. TABB and Elaine W. SHOBEN, *Remedies*, Thomson West, 2005, pp. 86-89; John BOURDEAU et al, «Injunctions» in Kevin Schroder, John Glenn and Maureen Placilla, *Corpus Juris Secundum*, Volume 43A, Thomson West, 2004, pp. 28 ff.

But the amparo judicial order in Latin America, where the distinction between equitable and law extraordinary remedies does not exist, is not only similar in its purposes and effects to the North American injunction, but also to the other non equitable extraordinary remedies, like the mandamus and prohibition legal remedies. That is, the amparo order can not only be prohibitory, that is, issued to restrain an action or that certain acts be forbidden (to command a person to refrain from doing a specific act), but also mandatory, that is, to compel an action; that is, like the writ of mandamus, it can compel the execution of some act (command a person to do a specific act), and likewise, the mandatory injunction can also require undoing an act, restoring the statu quo. The amparo judicial order can also be similar to the writ of prohibition, when the order is directed to a court, what normally happens in the cases of amparo actions filed against judicial decisions[25].

Regarding for instance the Venezuelan amparo process, where the courts have very extensive powers that allow them, in similar way to the North American and British judges[26], to provide for remedies in order to effectively protect constitutional rights, in that they can issue orders to do, to refrain from doing, or to undo; or prohibitions[27].

1. The preventive and restorative nature of the amparo

The contents of the final adjudication in the amparo suit is a very extensive one, and in general consists, as is set forth in Article 86 of the Colombian Constitution, in an order directed to the person or persons «against whom the tutela is filed, in order to act or to refrain from act»; or as it is set forth in a more generic way in the Amparo Law, the decision must establish «the order and precise definition of the conduct to be accomplished in order to make effective the tutela» (Colombia, Art. 29,4[28]); the «precise conduct to be accomplished» (Argentina, Art. 12,b[29]; Honduras, Art. 63,3[30]; México, Art. 77,III; Nicaragua, Art. 45; Paraguay, Art. 16,b; Perú, Art. 17,5; Uruguay, Art. 9,b[31]; Venezuela, Art. 32,b[32]). That is why in general terms the Honduran Law states that the court, when issuing its decision,

---

25 See for the reference to the North American remedies, William M. TABB and Elaine W. SHOBEN, *Remedies*, Thomson West, 2005, pp. 86 ff; and in John BOURDEAU et al, «Injunctions» in Kevin Schroder, John Glenn and Maureen Placilla, *Corpus Juris Secundum*, Volume 43A, Thompson West, 2004, pp. 21 ff.; 28 ff.

26 Véase F. H. LAWSON, *Remedies of English Law*, Londres, 1980, p. 175; B. SCHWARTZ y H.W. R. WADE, *Legal control of government*, Oxford, 1978, p. 205.

27 See Allan R. BREWER-CARÍAS, «Derecho y Acción de Amparo, Vol V, *Instituciones Políticas y Constitucionales* Editorial Jurídica Venezolana, Caracas 1998, pp. 143 ff.

28 Juan Carlos ESGUERRA PORTOCARRERO, *La protección constitucional del ciudadano*, Legis, Bogotá, 2004 p. 153.

29 See Néstor Pedro SAGÜÉS, *Derecho procesal Constitucional*, Vol 3, *Acción de amparo*, Editorial Astrea Buenos Aires, 1988, p. 434; Alí Joaquín SALGADO, *Juicio de amparo y acción de inconstitucionalidad*, Editorial Astrea, Buenos Aires, 1987, p. 100; José Luis LAZZARINI, *El juicio de amparo*, Ed. La Ley, Buenos Aires, 1987, pp. 345, 359.

30 Edmundo ORELLANA, *La justicia constitucional en Honduras*, Universidad Nacional Autónoma de Honduras, Tegucigalpa, 1993, pp. 181, 208, 216.

31 See Luis Alberto VIERA, *Ley de Amparo*, Ediciones Idea, Montevideo, 1993, p. 52, 207 ff.

32 Rafael CHAVERO G. *El nuevo amparo constitucional en Venezuela*, Ed. Sherwood, Caracas, 2001, p. 185 ff., 327 ff.; Allan R. BREWER-CARÍAS, «Derecho y Acción de Amparo, Vol V, *Instituciones Políticas y Constitucionales* Editorial Jurídica Venezolana, Caracas, 1998, pp. 399 ff.

must always bear in mind that its «purpose is to guarantee the aggrieved party the complete enjoyment of his fundamental rights and to return things, when possible, to the stage they had previous to the violation» (Art. 63).

That is, the order can be of a restorative nature, consisting in seeking for the reestablishment of the juridical situation of the plaintiff to the stage it had before the violation or to the most similar one; and can be of a preventive nature, compelling the defendant to do or refrain from doing acts in order to maintain the plaintiff in the situation of enjoyments of is rights. As it is expressly provided in Article 80 of the Mexican Amparo Law:

> **Article 80.** When the claimed act is of a positive character, the decision granting the amparo will have the purpose to restore the aggrieved party in the complete enjoyment of the harmed constitutional guarantee, reestablishing things to the stage they had before the violation; when the claimed act is of negative character, the effect of the amparo will be to compel the responsible authority to act in the sense to respect the guarantee and to accomplish what the same guarantee implies.

The same provision is set forth in Article 49 of the Costa Rican Constitutional Jurisdiction Law; as well as in Article 46 of the Nicaraguan Amparo Law. Its content has been explained by Baker as follows:

> «When the act complained of is of a positive character, the writ of amparo has the form of a prohibitory injunction plus whatever additional elements that may be necessary to repair damages already inflicted. The latter is to be accomplished by reproducing the situation that existed before the Constitution was violated. When the act is negative in character, the writ takes the form of an order directing the responsible authority to actively comply with the provisions of the violated constitutional guarantee. In both cases, the purpose of the judgment is to restore to the complaint the full and unimpaired enjoyment of his constitutional rights. Consistent with this purpose, monetary damages are not appropriate remedies in amparo»[33].

Accordingly, it can be said that one of the main characteristic of the amparo in all Latin American countries is its restorative or reestablishing purpose. In this regard, for example, the Colombian Tutela Law provided that «when the claim is directed against an authority action, the tutela decision has the purpose of guaranteeing the aggrieved party the complete enjoyment of his right and when possible, to return the situation to the stage previous to the violation» (Art. 23). A similar provision is established in El Salvador (Art. 35), Costa Rica (Art. 49) and in Perú (Art. 1), where Article 55,3 of the Constitutional Procedures Code provides as one of the contents of the amparo decision «the restitution or reestablishment of the aggrieved party in the complete enjoyment of his constitutional rights ordering that things will revert to the stage they had before the violation», as well as the order for the conduct to be accomplished for the effective compliance with the decision (Art. 55,4).

In other perspective, in Guatemala, the Amparo law regarding the effects of the amparo decision states that it will suspend, regarding the claimant, the

[33] See Richard D. BAKER, *Judicial Review in México. A Study of the Amparo Suit*, University of Texas Press, Austin, 1971, p. 238.

application of the challenged statute, regulation, resolution or act, and being the case, the reestablishment of the affected juridical situation or the ending of the measure» (Art. 49,a; Ecuador, Art. 51). Also in Colombia, according to Article 29,6 of the Tutela Law, «when the violation or threat of harming derives form the application of a norm incompatible with the fundamental rights, the resulting judicial decision resolving the action must also order the inapplicability of the challenged norm in the concrete case». In a similar sense it is stated in the Honduran Constitutional Justice Law (Art. 63,2)

But the amparo decision also can have protective character when issued against omissions or actions. In cases in which the harm to the constitutional right is caused by a negative of action or an omission from a public authority, in which cases, as set forth in the Colombian Tutela Law, «the decision will order the issuance of the act or the accomplishment of the adequate actions, for which purpose it must establish a prompt delay» (Art. 23). A similar provision is established in the El Salvador Amparo Law (Art. 35) and in the Ecuatorian Amparo law (Art. 51). Also, the Guatemalan Amparo Law sets forth that in such cases the amparo decision will establish a term for the delay to be ended, if the case is only a matter of delay in resolving» (Art. 49,b; Costa Rica, Art 49); and in cases where the amparo is filed against an omission of the authority to issue a regulation of a statute, the court will decide determining the basis and elements to be apply in the case according to the general principles of law (Art. 49,c). Additionally, in Costa Rica, in such cases, the judicial order must establish a term of two months for the authority to issue the regulation (Art. 49).

In cases referred to mere conduct or material activity or threats, according to the Costa Rican Constitutional Jurisdiction Law (Art. 49) and Colombian Tutela Law (Art. 23), the amparo or tutela decision will «order its immediate ending, as well as measures to prevent any new violation or threat, disturbance or restriction». Also, in cases where if by the moment where the tutela protection is granted, the challenged act has ceased in its effects or has produced them, making impossible to restore the plaintiff in the enjoyment of his rights, the court will warn the public authority not to cause again in any way, the actions or omissions which originated the tutela suit (Colombia, Art. 24). In a similar way it is stated in the Perúvian Constitutional Procedures Code (Art. 1).

2. The question of the annulling content of the amparo decision

In general terms it can be said that the amparo suit in Latin America does not have annulling purposes regarding the State acts that can cause or provoke the harm or threats to constitutional rights, corresponding the decisions to annul statutes to the Constitutional Jurisdiction and to the Administrative Jurisdictions when administrative acts are targeted.

In effect, if the amparo action is filed directly against statutes, as in some countries it is possible in cases of self executing laws (México[34], Guatemala[35], Hon-

[34] See Eduardo FERRER MAC-GREGOR, *La acción constitucional de amparo en México y España. Estudio de derecho comparado*, Editorial Porrúa, México, 2002, pp. 262-263; Richard D. BAKER, *Judicial Review in México. A Study of the Amparo Suit,* University of Texas Press, Austin, 1971, p. 270.

[35] See in Jorge Mario GARCÍA LAGUARDIA, *Jurisprudencia constitucional. Guatemala., Honduras. México, Una Muestra*, Guatemala, 1986, pp. 23, 24, 92, 93.

duras[36]), the amparo judge, when granting the amparo has no power to annul the statute, and in order to protect the harmed or threatened right it only declares its inapplicability to the plaintiff, as is also the case in Venezuela[37]. In countries where the concentrated method of judicial review exists, the annulment of statutes with general or *erga omnes* effects, is a judicial power reserved to the Constitutional Jurisdictions (Constitutional Courts or Tribunal); and in countries with the diffuse method of judicial review, if it is true that there is not such judicial power to annul statutes, the courts are only empowered to declare their unconstitutionality regarding the concrete case. Thus, in countries with the diffuse method of judicial review, in general terms when the competent courts in an amparo suit grants the constitutional protection, they have the power to declare the unconstitutionality of the applicable statute in the concrete case.

Nonetheless, the case of Costa Rica must be mentioned because the Constitutional Chamber of the Supreme Court is the competent court to decide the amparo suits and the nullity actions against statutes, Article 48 of the Constitutional Jurisdiction Law provides that when the amparo is filed against a statute norm or when the Constitutional Chambers determines that the challenged acts are founded in a statute, it will decide to suspend the procedure and ask for the petitioner to file a petition in a term of 15 days, for judicial review of the unconstitutionality of the statute (Art. 48).

In Venezuela, regarding the possibility for the Chambers of the Supreme Tribunal to exercise the diffuse control of the constitutionality of legislation when deciding in a concrete case, the Law regulating the Tribunal provides that the other Chambers must notify the Constitucional Chamber for it to proceed to examine in an abstract way the constitutionality of the statute and eventually declare its nullity (Articles 5, 1,22; and 5,5)[38].

In cases where the amparo action is filed against administrative acts, again, in general terms the amparo decision cannot annul the corresponding administrative act, but only suspend its application to the plaintiff, corresponding to the Administrative Jurisdiction the exclusive power to annul such acts, as is the case in Venezuela[39]. In this regard, the case of Perú must be highlighted because its Constitutional Procedures Code expressly provides that the amparo decision must contain «the declaration of the nullity of the decision, act or resolution that has impeded the complete exercise of the constitutional rights protected with the ruling, and in the case, the extension of its effects» (Art. 55)[40]. Also in Costa Rica, according to Article 49 of the Constitutional Jurisdiction Law, it is considered that in case of amparo actions against administrative acts, the granting of the amparo implies the annulling effects of the decision.

36 See Edmundo ORELLANA, *La justicia constitucional en Honduras*, Universidad Nacional Autónoma de Honduras, Tegucigalpa, 1993, pp. 208, 221.

37 Rafael CHAVERO G. *El nuevo amparo constitucional en Venezuela*, Ed. Sherwood, Caracas 2001, pp. 468 ff.

38 See Allan R. BREWER-CARÍAS, *Ley Orgánica del Tribunal Supremo de Justicia*, Editorial Jurídica Venezolana, Caracas, 2004, p. 40.

39 Rafael CHAVERO G. *El nuevo amparo constitucional en Venezuela*, Ed. Sherwood, Caracas 2001, pp. 358 ff.; Allan R. BREWER-CARÍAS, «Derecho y Acción de Amparo, Vol V, *Instituciones Políticas y Constitucionales*, Editorial Jurídica Venezolana, Caracas, 1998, pp. 144; 400.

40 See Samuel B. ABAD YUPANQUI, *El proceso constitucional de amparo*, Gaceta Jurídica, Lima, 2004, p. 186.

Finally, regarding the amparo action when filed against judicial decisions, the effects of the ruling granting the amparo protection are also the annulment of the challenged judicial act or decision, as happens in Venezuela[41].

3. The non compensatory character of the amparo decision

Similarly to the North American injunction[42], in general terms, the Latin American amparo suit and decision have not a compensatory character in the sense that the function of the courts in such suit is not to condemn the defendant to pay the plaintiff any sort of compensation for damages caused. For instance in the case of an illegitimate administrative order to demolish a building issued by a municipal authority, if executed, even if it violates the constitutional right to property, it cannot be the object of an amparo action due to the irreparable character of the harm. Consequently, the amparo judge is not competent to condemn the public entity to pay damages. The amparo judge, in such cases, could only have the possibility to prevent the harm, for instance by suspending the demolition before its execution, but never to condemn the entity to the payment of compensation. The amparo suit, as mentioned, is in general terms a preventive and restorative process, but not a compensatory one[43].

Nonetheless, if it is true that this is the general principle, some Latin American Amparo Laws give compensatory character to the amparo suit a. This is the case of Bolivia, Colombia and Costa Rica.

In Bolivia, Article 102,II of the Law, regarding the content of the amparo decision, states that when granting the amparo the court will determine the existence of civil and criminal liability, fixing the amount of the damages and prejudices to be paid. Also, in Guatemala, Article 59 of the Law refers to the damages and prejudices, stating that when the court in its decision condemns to the payment of damages and prejudices, it must fix its amount or at least establish the basis for its determination (Art. 59).

Bolivia and Guatemala are the only Latin American Amparo Laws that provide for a direct compensatory character of the amparo decision. In other legislations, such as Colombia and Costa Rica the compensation in the amparo decision is only established in an abstract way.

In effect, in Costa Rica, Article 51 of the Constitutional Jurisdiction Law provides that «always when an amparo is granted the court, in abstract, will condemn for the compensation of damages and prejudices», and the settlement belongs in the stage of the execution of the decision. When the amparo action is

---

41 See Rafael CHAVERO G. *El nuevo amparo constitucional en Venezuela*, Ed. Sherwood, Caracas, 2001, p. 511; Allan R. BREWER-CARÍAS, «Derecho y Acción de Amparo, Vol V, *Instituciones Políticas y Constitucionales* Editorial Jurídica Venezolana, Caracas, 1998, p. 297.

42 See John BOURDEAU et al, «Injunctions» in Kevin Schroder, John Glenn and Maureen Placilla, *Corpus Juris Secundum*, Volume 43A, Thomson West, 2004, p. 20.

43 See José Luis LAZZARINI, *El juicio de amparo*, Ed. La Ley, Buenos Aires1987, pp. 346-347; Néstor Pedro SAGÜÉS, *Derecho procesal Constitucional*, Vol. 3, *Acción de amparo*, Editorial Astrea Buenos Aires, 1988, p. 437; Rafael CHAVERO G. *El nuevo amparo constitucional en Venezuela*, Ed. Sherwood, Caracas 2001, pp. 185, 242, 262, 326, 328; Allan R. BREWER-CARÍAS, «Derecho y Acción de Amparo, Vol V, *Instituciones Políticas y Constitucionales*, Editorial Jurídica Venezolana, Caracas, 1998, p. 143.

filed against authorities, the condemnation will be issued against the State or against the entity where the defendant works, and jointly with the latter if he has acted with dolus or guilt, without excluding all other administrative, civil or criminal liabilities. Also, in case when the amparo process is pending and the challenged State act is revoked, stopped or suspended, the amparo will be granted only to the effects of the corresponding decision awarding compensation (Art. 52). In these cases the settlement will be made by the Administrative Jurisdiction courts[44].

In cases where the amparo action is filed against individuals, Article 53 of the same Law provides that when granting the amparo, the court must also condemn the person or responsible entity to compensate for the damages and prejudices, the settlement of which will be made in the civil judicial execution of the decision mean.

Also in Colombia, Article 25 of the Tutela Law provides that when the affected party has not other means, and the violation of his rights is manifest and a clear and indisputable consequence of an arbitrariness, in the decision granting the tutela the court can, ex officio, order in an abstract way the compensation of the damages caused, provided it is needed in order to assure the effective enjoyment for the right. Similarly to what is provided in the Costa Rican Law, Article 23 of the Colombian Law establishes that the condemn will be issued against the entity where the defendant works, and jointly with the latter if he has acted with dolus or guilt, without excluding all other administrative, civil or criminal liabilities. The settlement of the compensation corresponds to the Administrative Jurisdiction courts in an incidental procedure that must take place within the following six months[45].

Also, in case where the tutela process is pending and the challenged State act is revoked, stopped or suspended, the tutela will be granted only to the effects of the corresponding decision awarding the compensation (Art. 26).

Except in these cases of Bolivia, Colombia and Costa Rica, in all other Latin American countries, the judicial actions tending to seek for compensation from the defendant, because of its liability as a consequence of the constitutional right harm or threat, must be filed before the civil or administrative judicial jurisdiction by means of the ordinary judicial remedies established for that purpose. This is provided in some Latin American Amparo Laws (El Salvador, Art. 35; Panama, Art. 2627). The Venezuelan Amparo Law also expressly provides that in cases of granting an amparo, the court must send copy of the decision to the competent authority where the public officer causing the harm works, in order to impose the corresponding disciplinary measures (Art. 27).

Finally, regarding the economic consequences of the amparo suit, in general terms in the Latin American Laws it is provided that the party against whom the decision is directed is due to pay the costs of the process (Argentina, Art. 14; Bolivia, Art. 102,III; Colombia, Art. 25; Costa Rica, Arts. 51, 53; El Salvador, Art. 35; Guatemala, Arts. 44, 45, 100; Honduras, Art. 105; Paraguay, Art. 22; Perú, Art. 56).

---

[44] See Rubén HERNÁNDEZ, *Derecho Procesal Constitucional*, Editorial Juricentro, San José, 2001, p. 268; José Luis VILLALOBOS, El recurso de amparo en Costa Rica», in Humberto Nogueira Alcalá (Editor), *Acciones constitucionales de amparo y protección: realidad y perspectivas en Chile y América Latina*», Editorial Universidad de Talca, Talca, 2000, p. 229.

[45] See Juan Carlos ESGUERRA PORTOCARRERO, *La protección constitucional del ciudadano*, Legis, Bogotá, 2004, p. 155.

Only in Venezuela the order to pay the costs is provided regarding the amparo suits only against individuals and not against public authorities (Art. 33).

4. The effects of the definitive judicial ruling on the amparo suit

The question of the effects of the amparo ruling refers to various aspects: first, to the scope of the effects of the judicial decision granting the amparo, whether *inter partes* or general effects; second, to the *res judicata* effects of the decision; and finally, to the extent of the compulsory effects of the ruling, regarding the consequences of the disobedience of the judicial orders.

A. *The* inter partes *effects and its exceptions*

The general rule regarding the amparo judicial decisions effects, is that it only has *inter partes* effects, that is, between the parties that have been involved in the suit, that is, the plaintiff or plaintiffs, the defendant or defendants and the third parties that have participated in the process on the side or any the aforementioned.. As it is established in the Mexican Amparo Law: «the decisions in the amparo suits only refers to the individuals or corporations, private or public which filed the actions, limiting their scope to protect them in the case, without making general declarations regarding the statute or act causing the suit» (Art. 76). In the same sense it is set forth in Article 44 of the Nicaraguan Law.

Thus, and as in the case of the injunctions in North America[46], the decision rendered binds only the parties to the suit, and only regarding the controversy. This is the most important consequence of the personal character of the amparo, which is an action mainly devoted for the protection of personal constitutional rights or guarantees. Other aspects refer to the general content of the ruling on constitutional questions, which in North America implies that in cases decided by the United States Supreme Court, because of the doctrine of precedent (*stare decisis*), all courts are obliged to apply the same constitutional rule in cases with a similar controversy[47]. The same rule exists in Latin America, in cases where the Supreme Courts or Constitutional Courts rulings, regarding the constitutional interpretation, have been entrusted with obligatory general effects, as is the case in Venezuela with the Constitutional Chamber rulings (Art. 336 of the Constitution) and of Perú, with the Constitutional Tribunal decisions (precedents, Art. VII of the Code on Constitutional procedures).

Thus, as a general rule, regarding the particular ruling in the amparo suit, the decision is only binding on the parties to the suit, including third parties. Those are the beneficiaries and the obliged parties.

But of course, progressively, the amparo suit in many cases has acquired a collective nature, for instance, in cases of violation of environmental rights and other diffuse and collective rights[48], in which cases, as happens in the class actions

---

[46] See the reference to the corresponding judicial decisions in John BOURDEAU et al, «Injunctions» in Kevin Schroder, John Glenn and Maureen Placilla, *Corpus Juris Secundum*, Volume 43A, Thomson West, 2004, pp. 414; 417.

[47] See M. Glenn ABERNATHY and Barbara A. PERRY, Civil Liberties under the Constitution, University of South Carolina Press, 1993, p. 5.

[48] See Rafael CHAVERO G. *El nuevo amparo constitucional en Venezuela*, Ed. Sherwood, Caracas, 2001, pp. 333 ff.

in the United States[49], the definitive ruling can benefit other persons different to those that have actively participated in the procedure as plaintiff.

The Venezuelan regulations can be highlighted in this regard. In principle, the court decisions have been constant in granting the action of *amparo* a personal character where the standing belongs firstly to «the individual directly affected by the infringement of constitutional rights and guarantees».[50]

Nonetheless, by virtue of the constitutional acknowledgment of the legal protection of diffuse or collective interests, the Constitutional Chamber of the Supreme Tribunal has also admitted the possibility of employing the action of *amparo* to assure the enforcment of those collective interests, including for instance, that of voters in their political rights. In such cases, the Chamber has granted precautionary measures with *erga omnes* effects «for both individuals and corporations who have instituted an action for constitutional protection and to all voters as a group».[51]

The Constitutional Chamber, has decided that «any individual is entitled to bring suit based on diffuse or collective interests» and has extended «standing to companies, corporations, foundations, chambers, unions and other collective entities, whose object is the defense of society, as long as they act within the boundaries of their corporate objects, aimed at protecting the interests of their members regarding those objects».[52]

In addition, the Peoples' Defendant has the authority to promote, defend, and guard constitutional rights and guarantees «as well as the legitimate, collective or diffuse interests of the citizens» (Art. 280 and 281,2 of the Constitution); consequently, the Constitutional Chamber has admitted the standing of the Peoples' Defendant to bring to suit in an action of *amparo* on behalf of the citizens as a whole group. In one case the Defender of the People acted against a threat by the National Legislative Commission to appoint Electoral National Council members without fulfilling constitutional requirements.

In that case, the Constitutional Chamber, decided that «the Defender has standing to bring actions aimed at enforcing diffuse and collective rights or interests» without requiring the acquiescence of the society on whose behalf he acts, but this provision does not exclude or prevent citizens' access to the judicial system in defense of diffuse and collective rights and interests, since Article 26 of the Constitution in force provides access to the judicial system to every person, whereby individuals are entitled to bring suit as well, unless a law denies them that action.[53] In all those cases, consequently, the judicial ruling benefits all the persons enjoying the collective rights or interest involved.

---

[49] See M. Glenn ABERNATHY and Barbara A. PERRY, Civil Liberties under the Constitution, University of South Carolina Press, 1993, p. 6.

[50] See for example, decision of the Constitutional Chamber dated 03-15-2000, *Revista de Derecho Público*, N° 81, Editorial Jurídica Venezolana, 2000, pp. 322-323.

[51] Decision of the Constitutional Chamber N° 483 of 05-29-2000 (Case: *«Queremos Elegir» y otros*), *Revista de Derecho Público*, N° 82, Editorial Jurídica Venezolana, 2000, pp 489-491. In the same sense, decision of the same Chamber N° 714 of 13-07-2000 (Case: *APRUM*).

[52] See decision of the Constitutional Chamber N° 656 of 06-05-2001 (Case: *Defensor del Pueblo vs. Comisión Legislativa Nacional*).

[53] Decision of the Constitutional Chamber N° 656 of 06-05-2001, (Case: *Defensor del Pueblo vs. Comisión Legislativa Nacional*).

B. *The question of the scope of the* res judicata *effects*

As all definitive judicial decisions, the amparo decision in Latin America has in general *res judicata* effects, which provides stability, and is binding not only for the parties in the suit or its beneficiaries, but regarding the court itself which cannot modify its ruling (immutability). *Res judicata* implies then, the impossibility for a new suit to take place regarding the same matter already decided, or that a decision be taken in different sense than the one already decided in a previous process.

In contrast, as a general rule, the injunction ruling in North America does not have, in general, this *res judicata* effect since the injunction orders can be modified by the court. As it has been summarized regarding the judicial doctrine on the matter:

> «Injunctions are different from other judgments in the context of *res judicata* because the parties are often subject to the court's continuing jurisdiction, and the court must strike a balance between the policies of *res judicata* and the right of the court to apply modified measures to changed circumstances»[54].

But in Latin America, although the *res judicata* effects have been admitted regarding the amparo decisions, discussions have developed in many countries following a traditional distinction established between the «material» and the «formal» *res judicata*, in order to determine which one applies to the amparo ruling.

In general terms, the concept of «formal res judicata» applies to judicial decisions that even when enforced, they do not impede for a new process between the same parties to be developed, due to the fact that in such cases the matter has not been decided on the merits and on the defenses; while «material *res judicata*» exists when the judicial decision has decided on the merits, not being allowed for other processes to develop regarding the same matter.

The matter in the amparo suit is the illegitimate and manifest harm or threat caused by an identified aggrieving party to the constitutional right or guarantees of the plaintiff; matter that is to be resolved in a brief and prompt procedure. Thus, the merits on the matters are reduced to determining the existence of such illegitimate and manifest violation of the right, regardless of other matters that can be resolved or in some cases must be resolved between the parties in other processes.

As it is set forth in the Argentina Amparo Law:

> **Article 13**. The definitive decision declaring the existence or nonexistence of an arbitrary or manifestly illegal harm, restriction, alteration or threat regarding a constitutional right and guarantee, produces res judicata regarding the amparo, and the exercise of the actions or recourses that could correspond to the parties subsist, in spite of the amparo.

A similar provision is set forth in Article 17 of the Paraguayan Law; and in Article 11 of the Uruguayan Law[55].

---

54 See the reference to the corresponding judicial decisions in John BOURDEAU et al, «Injunctions» in Kevin Schroder, John Glenn and Maureen Placilla, *Corpus Juris Secundum*, Volume 43A, Thomson West, 2004, p. 416. See also Owen M. FISS and Doug RENDLEMAN, Injunctions, The Foundation Press, 1984, pp. 497-498, 526.

55 See Luis Alberto VIERA, *Ley de Amparo*, Ediciones Idea, Montevideo, 1993, p. 40.

This provision, regarding the effects of the *res judicata*, has been considered interpreted in two ways: On the one hand, Lazzarini has considered it establishes the «material res judicata» effects regarding the protective amparo decision, arguing that the allusion the article makes regarding other actions or recourses, are referred to criminal actions tending to punish the offenses causing the harm, or to civil actions tending to obtain compensation, but not to other actions in which the amparo could be again reargued[56]. On the other hand, Sagües has considered that even being the amparo suit a bilateral process, due to its brief and prompt character with the consequent restrictions regarding proofs and formalities, there can not be a decision on the merits of the matter, so no material *res judicata* can be produced, but only a formal one, being possible for the merits to be resolved through the ordinary judicial means, only if the parties allege a violation to their due process rights occurred (for instance, regarding evidences) in the amparo process[57].

In the Venezuelan Amparo Law, in a similar way to the Argentinean provision, and with the same different approach regarding the material or formal *res judicata* effects[58], Article 36 establishes:

> **Article 36.** The definitive amparo decision will produce legal effects regarding the right or guarantee that has been the object of the process, without prejudice of the actions or recourses that legally correspond to the parties.

In this regard, the First Court on Administrative Jurisdiction, in a decision dated October 16, 1986 (*Case Pedro J. Montilva*), decided that if in a case «the action of amparo is filed with the same object, denouncing the same violations, based on the same motives and with identical object as the previous one and directed against the same person, then it is evident that in such case, the res judicata force applies in order to avoid the rearguing of the case, due to the fact that the controversy to be resolved has the same subjective and objective identity than the one already decided»[59].

According to this doctrine, and according to Article 36 of the Law, the *res judicata* in the amparo suit only refers to what has been argued and decided in the case regarding the violation of harm produced to a constitutional right or guarantee. Thus, the amparo decision in general terms does not resolve all the possible merits of the matter but only the aspect of the violation or harm of the rights or guarantees, which is the only aspect regarding which the decision can produce res judicata effects. That is why the decision only has restorative effects, due to the fact that by means of the amparo suit, as it has been resolved by the Supreme Court of Venezuela, «non of the three types of judicial declarative, constitutive or to condemn decision can be obtained, nor, of course, the interpretative decision»[60]. For example, if an amparo decision is issued against an administrative act because it causes harm to constitutional rights, it only has restorative or reestablishing effects suspending

[56] See José Luis LAZZARINI, *El juicio de amparo*, Ed. La Ley, Buenos Aires, 1987, pp. 356 ff.
[57] See Néstor Pedro SAGÜÉS, *Derecho procesal Constitucional*, Vol 3, *Acción de amparo*, Editorial Astrea Buenos Aires, 1988, pp. 449 ff.
[58] See Rafael CHAVERO G. *El nuevo amparo constitucional en Venezuela*, Ed. Sherwood, Caracas, 2001, pp. 338 ff.; Gustavo LINARES BENZO, *El proceso de amparo en Venezuela*, Caracas, 1999, p. 121 f.
[59] See in *Revista de Derecho Público*, N° 28, EJV, Caracas, 1986, p. 106.
[60] See decisión of the Politico-Administrative Chamber of July 15, 1992, in *Revista de Derecho Público*, N° 51, EJV, Caracas, 1992, p. 171.

the application of the challenged act, but it does not have annulling effects. Consequently, the amparo decision in such cases, does not have res judicata effects regarding the judicial review action that can be filed against the administrative act before the Administrative Jurisdiction courts.[61]

That is, in matters of amparo suit, in many cases the amparo decision regarding the violation of the right by the illegitimate action of omissions, resolves definitively the matter, not being necessary to discuss any other legal matter through any other process. In such cases, it can be said that the amparo ruling has material res judicata effects. But in other cases, after the amparo decision has been issued, other legal questions can remain pending to be resolved in other processes, and that is why the amparo decision is issued «without prejudice of the actions or recourses that could legally correspond to the parties». Is has been said that the amparo decision has formal res judicata effects, which do not refer to the matter of the right's violation ruling[62].

These effects of the amparo decision also exists regarding the amparo suit against individuals, and a case can illustrate the matter: in 1987 a controversy arose in a private Caracas University (Santa María), regarding the position for the Head of the institution (Rector), a position that was disputed by two professors that argued they where appointed by the University bodies. The First Court on Administrative Jurisdiction in a decision dated December 17, 1987, issued an amparo decision on the matter filed by one of the *Rectores* in order to assure legal security to the university community, due to the fact that the matter regarding who was the Head of the University could not remain indefinitely unresolved, ruled considering legitimate the designation of one of the Rectores, «until the controversy regarding the legitimacy of the bodies that made the appointments be resolved by the judicial competent court»[63]. According to this decision, a civil action was needed to be resolved in order to resolve the merits.

The different approaches to the *res judicata* regarding amparo decisions have been expressly resolved, for instance, in the El Salvador Amparo Law, which prescribes the following:

> **Article 81**. The definitive amparo decision produces *res judicata* effects against any person of public officer, had he intervened or not in the process, only regarding the matter of the challenged act being or not constitutional or contrary to the constitutional provisions. With all, the content of the decision does not constitute in itself a declaration, recognition or constitution of private rights of individuals or of the state; consequently the decision can not be opposed as a *res judicata* defense regarding any action that could be afterward filed before the courts of the Republic».

In similar terms it is set forth in the Honduran Law (Art. 72), and in the Guatemalan Law, which provides that «the decisions issued in the amparo suits have declarative effects and do not originate the res judicata defense, without prejudice of the provisions derived from the *jurisprudencia* on the matter (Art. 190).

---

[61] See Allan R. BREWER-CARÍAS, «Derecho y Acción de Amparo, Vol V, *Instituciones Políticas y Constitucionales* Editorial Jurídica Venezolana, Caracas, 1998, pp. 346 ff.

[62] See in this respect, Juan Manuel ERRAZURIZ and Jorge Miguel OTERO A., *Aspectos procesales del recurso de protección*, Editorial Jurídica de Chile, Santiago 1989, pp. 195 ff, 202.

[63] See in *El Universal*, Caracas, December 27, 1987, pp. 2-5.

Finally, in Perú, the Code of Constitutional Procedures does not resolve the discussion, just declaring that «In the constitutional processes, only the final decision deciding the merits acquire the *res judicata* authority» (Art. 6)[64]. But the Perúvian Code is one of the few that expressly regulates the effects of the *res judicata* authority regarding the preliminary orders or measures issued during the procedure, in the sense that they will be automatically extinguished. Nonetheless, if the final decision grants the amparo, the effects of the preliminary measures will be kept being converted if definitive (Art. 16).

III. THE OBLIGATORY CHARACTER OF THE AMPARO RULINGS AND THE PUNISHMENT FOR CONTEMPT

The amparo ruling, as all judicial decisions, is binding upon the parties and all other public officers that must apply them, and the defendant must immediately obey by it as it is expressed in the Amparo Laws (Bolivia, Art. 102; Colombia, Arts. 27, 30; Costa Rica, Art. 53; Ecuador, Art, 58; Honduras, Art. 65; Nicaragua, Art. 48; Perú, Arts. 22, 24; Venezuela, Arts. 29, 30).

In order to execute the decision, the courts, ex officio or at the party's request, must adopt all the measures directed to its accomplishment, being empowered in the Guatemalan Law to issue orders and mandamus to the authorities and public officers of Public Administration or obligated persons (Art. 55). The amparo courts are also empowered to use public enforcement units to assure the accomplishment of its decisions (Guatemala, Art. 105; Ecuador, Art. 61; El Salvador, Art. 61; Nicaragua, Art. 77).

But the amparo judges in Latin America do not have direct power to punish for disobedience, in other words, they do not have contempt power, which in contrast is one of the most important futures of the injunctive relief system in the United States. This is particularly important regarding criminal contempt, which was established since the *In Re Debs* case (158 U.S. 564, 15 S.Ct. 900, 39 L.Ed. 1092 (1895), where according to Justice Brewer who delivered the court's opinion, it was ruled:

> «But the power of a court to make an order carries with it the equal power to punish for a disobedience of that order, and the inquiry as to the question of disobedience has been, from time immemorial, the special function of the court. And this is no technical rule. In order that a court may compel obedience to its order it must have the right to inquire whether there has been any disobedience thereof. To submit the question of disobedience to another tribunal, be it a jury or another court, would operate to deprive the proceedings of half its efficiency...In Watson v. Williams, 36 Miss. 331, 341, it was said: «The power to fine and imprison for contempt, from the earliest history of jurisprudence, has been regarded as the necessary incident and attribute of a court, without which it could no more exist than without a judge. It is a power inherent in all courts of record, and coexisting with them by the wise provisions of the common law. A court without the power effectually to protect itself against the assaults of the lawless, or to

[64] See Samuel B. ABAD YUPANQUI, *El proceso constitucional de amparo*, Gaceta Jurídica, Lima 2004, pp. 194 ff.

enforce its orders, judgments, or decrees against the recusant parties before it, would be a disgrace to the legislation, and a stigma upon the age which invented it».[65]

These contempt powers are precisely what gave to the injunction in the United States its effectiveness regarding any disobedience, being empowered the same court to vindicate their own power by imposing criminal or economic sanctions by means of imprisonment and fines. The Latin American courts, in contrast do not have such powers, or they are very weak.

In effect, even though the disobedience of the amparo ruling is punishable in the Amparo Latin American Laws, it is not the power of the same amparo court to apply the sanctions. In general terms, the sanctioning powers are attributed to Public Administration of to criminal court. So, in case of disobedience, the court must seek for the initiation of an administrative disciplinary procedure against the disobedient public officer that must be developed by the corresponding superior organ in Public Administration (Colombia, Art. 27; Perú, Art. 59; Nicaragua, Art. 48). Regarding the application of criminal sanctions, the amparo court in cases of disobedience, must seek for the initiation of a criminal procedure against the disobedient to be brought before the competent criminal courts (Bolivia, Art. 104; Colombia, Arts. 27, 52, 53; Costa Rica, Art. 71; Ecuador, Art. 58; El Salvador, Art. 37, 61; Guatemala, Arts. 32, 54, 92; Honduras, Art. 62; Panama, Art. 2632; México, Arts. 202, 209; Nicaragua, Art. 77; Venezuela, Art. 31). Therefore, the amparo judge in Latin America does not have the power to impose directly to those that disobey their orders, disciplinary or criminal sanctions, and only in some countries there have been improvements in the legislations, granting the same amparo courts the powers to impose successive fines (*astreintes*) up to the accomplishing of the order to those disobeying them (Colombia, Art. 27; Guatemala, Art. 53; Nicaragua, Art. 66; Perú, Art. 22[66]) and in some cases, to impose administrative arrests (Colombia, Art. 27).

IV. THE REVISION OF THE AMPARO DECISIONS BY A CONSTITUTIONAL COURT OR THE SUPREME COURT

The amparo decisions, except in the cases where the competent court that issued them is the highest court in the country, as happens in Costa Rica (Constitutional Chamber of the Supreme Court of Justice), Nicaragua (Constitutional Chamber of the Supreme Court of Justice) and El Salvador (Constitutional Chamber of the Supreme Court of Justice), can be appealed according the general rules established in the procedural codes. Due to the general rule of double instance, the decisions cannot normally arrive to their revision by the Supreme Court of the Constitutional Court, except when an extraordinary means for revision is established, in some cases similar to the writ for certiorari in the United States.

In effects, whether or not they involve constitutional issues, the United States Supreme Court is authorized to review all the decisions of the federal courts of appeals, and of the specialized federal courts, and all the decisions of the supreme

---

[65] See Owen M. FISS and Doug RENDLEMAN, «Injunctions», The Foundation Press, 1984, p. 13. See also William M. TABB and Elaine W. SHOBEN, *Remedies*, Thomson West, 2005, pp. 72 ff.

[66] See Samuel B. ABAD YUPANQUI, *El proceso constitucional de amparo*, Gaceta Jurídica, Lima, 2004, p. 136.

courts of the states involving issues of federal law, but on a discretionary basis, when considering a petition for a writ of certiorari.

In effect, in all such cases where there is no right of appeal established and where the mandatory appellate jurisdiction of the Supreme Court is not established, they can reach the Supreme Court as petitions for certiorari, where a litigant who has lost in a lower court, petitions a review in the Supreme Court, setting out the reasons why review should be granted.[67] This method of seeking review by the Supreme Court is expressly established in the cases set forth in the 28 US Code, according to the Supreme Court's Rule N° 17,1 establishing that the rules governing review on certiorari are, «not a matter of right, but of judicial discretion, and will be granted only when there are special and important reasons therefore».

According to this Rule, consequently, in order to promote uniformity and consistency in federal law, the following factors might prompt the Supreme Court to grant certiorari: 1. Important questions of federal law on which the court has not previously ruled; 2. Conflicting interpretations of federal law by lower courts; 3. Lower courts decisions that conflict with previous Supreme Court decisions; and 4. Lower court departures from the accepted and usual course of judicial proceedings.[68]

Of course, review may be granted on the basis of other factors, or denied even if one or more of the above mentioned factors is present. The discretion of the Supreme Court is not limited, and it is the importance of the issue and the public interest considered by the Court in a particular case, which leads the Court to grant certiorari and to review some cases.

Although in different ways in Argentina, Bolivia, Brazil, Colombia, Honduras, México and Venezuela, the Constitutional Courts, the Constitutional Chambers of the Supreme Courts or the latter, can finally review the amparo decisions.

In effect, in Argentina, even thought the actions of amparo are in general exercised before the judges of first instance, the cases can reach the Supreme Court of the Nation, by means of an extraordinary recourse when in the judicial decision a matter of judicial review of constitutionality is resolved[69]. This is, undoubtedly, the judicial mean through which the Supreme Court normally decides upon the final interpretation of the Constitution when reviewing the constitutionality of state acts, and consequently it is the most important mean for judicial review.

But of course, the «extraordinary recourse» is quite different to the American request for writ of *certiorari*, in the sense that the Supreme Court of the Nation does not have discretionary powers in accepting extraordinary recourses. On the contrary, in such cases it is a mandatory jurisdiction, exercised as a consequence of a right the parties have to introduce the extraordinary recourse. In these cases the Supreme Court does not act as a mere third instance court, particularly because the Court does not review the motives of the judicial decision under consideration, regarding the facts. Its power of review is concentrated only in aspects of law regarding constitutional questions.

---

67 See L. BAUM, *The Supreme Court*, Washington, 1981, p. 81.

68 See. R.A. ROSSUM and G.A. TARR, *American Constitutional Law*, New York, 1983, p. 28.

69 See Elias GUASTAVINO, *Recurso extraordinario de inconstitucionalidad*, Ed. La Roca, Buenos Aires, Argentina, 1992.

In Brazil there also exists an extraordinary recourse of constitutionality that can be filed before the Federal Supreme Tribunal, which is the most important court on matters of judicial review[70], against the judicial decision issued on matters of protection of constitutional rights by the Superior Federal Court or by the Regional Federal Courts, when it is considered that the courts have made the decisions in a way inconsistent with the Constitution, or in which the court has denied the validity of a treaty or federal statute, or when the decisions has declared the unconstitutionality of a treaty or of a Federal Law; and when they deem a local government law or act that has been challenged as unconstitutional or contrary to a valid federal law (Art. 199,III,b,c) .

The general judicial procedural system in Venezuela is also governed by the by-instance principle, so that judicial decisions resolving cases on judicial review are subject to the ordinary appeal. The cases could only reach the Cassation Chambers of the Supreme Tribunal through cassation recourses (Art. 312 and ff. CCP). Because this situation could lead to possible dispersion of the judicial decision on constitutional matters, the 1999 Constitution, also provided a corrective procedure by granting the Constitutional Chamber of the Supreme Tribunal of Justice, the power to:

> «Review final judicial decisions issued by the courts of the Republic on amparo suits and when deciding judicial review of statutes, in the terms established by the respective organic law». (Art. 336,10 C)

Regarding this provision, it must be pointed out that it is neither an appeal nor a general second or third procedural instance. It is an exceptional faculty of the Constitutional Chamber to review, upon its judgment and discretion, through an extraordinary recourse (in similar sense as the *writ of certiorary*) exercised against *last instance* decisions in which constitutional issues are decided by means of judicial review or in *amparo* suits.

It is a reviewing non obligatory power that can be exercised in an optional way[71]. The Chamber has the power to choose the cases in which it considers convenient to decide because of the constitutional relevance of the matter.

In Colombia, the creation of the Constitutional Court as the ultimate guardian of the Constitution originated the attribution of the Court to review all the judicial decisions resolving actions for tutela. As opposed to the Venezuelan or Argentinean cases, in Colombia there is not a specific recourse for revision, but an attribution

70 See in general Manoel Goncalves FERREIRA FILHO, «O sistema constitucional brasileiro e as recentes inovacoes no controle de constitucionalidade» in *Anuario Iberoamericano de Justicia Constitucional*, N° 5, 2001, Centro de Estudios Políticos y Constitucionales, Madrid, España, 2001; José Carlos BARBOSA MOREIRA, «El control judicial de la constitucionalidad de las leyes en el Brasil: un bosquejo», in *Desafíos del control de constitucionalidad*, Ediciones Ciudad Argentina, Buenos Aires, Argentina, 1996; Paulo BONAVIDES, «Jurisdicao constitucional e legitimidade (algumas observacoes sobre o Brasil)» en *Anuario Iberoamerivano de Justicia Constitucional* N° 7, Centro de Estudios Políticos y Constitucionales, Madrid, 2003; Enrique Ricardo LEWANDOWSKI, «Notas sobre o controle da constitucionalidade no Brasil», en Edgar CORZO SOSA, y otros, *Justicia Constitucional Comparada*, Ed. Universidad Nacional Autónoma de México, México D.F. 1993; Zeno VELOSO, *Controle jurisdicional de constitucionalidade*, Ed. Cejup, Belém, Brasil, 1999.

71 See Allan R. BREWER-CARÍAS, *Judicial Review in Comparative Law*, *op. cit*. p. 141; See the comments of Jesús María CASAL, *Constitución y Justicia Constitucional*, Caracas 2003, p. 92.

that must be automatically accomplished in a discretionary way. In effect, the Decree regulating the procedure sets forth that when a tutela decision is not appealed, it must be automatically sent for revision to the Constitutional Court (Article 31). In cases where the decisions are appealed, the superior court's decision, whether confirming or revoking the appealed decision, must also be automatically sent to the Constitutional Court for its revision (Article 32). .

In Bolivia, according to the Constitution (Article 120,7), and to the Law of the Constitutional Tribunal (Articles 7,8; 93; 102,V), all judicial decisions issued on amparo or habeas corpus suits must be sent ex officio to the Constitutional Tribunal in order to be reviewed. The revision, in the case of Bolivia, is also different to the Argentinean, Brazilian, and Venezuelan extraordinary recourses for revision, and more similar to the situation in Colombia where it is not a recourse, but an obligatory revision that the Constitutional Tribunal must do, to which the decisions must be sent by the courts.

In Honduras, a procedure of two instances is also established and in all cases an obligatory consultation of the amparo decisions is provided. Regarding the decisions issued by the department courts, they must be sent in consultation before the Appellate Courts; and regarding these decision issued by the Appellate Courts, they can be subject to review by the Constitutional Chamber of the Supreme Court by means of the parties' request for study.

In such cases the Constitutional Chamber has also discretionary power to resolve the admissibility of the request (Article 68). Regarding the decisions adopted in first instance by the Appeals Courts in questions of amparo, they must also be sent for consultation before the Constitutional Chamber of the Supreme Court (Article 69).

Finally, the case of México must be also mentioned. Through the constitutional reform of 1983, the Supreme Court was vested with a discretionary competency to select to decide, requesting them from the Circuit courts, ex officio or at the request of the General Prosecutor of the Republic, the cases of amparo of constitutional relevance; Later, by means of another constitutional reform in 1988, power was attributed to the Supreme Court to decide in last instance all cases of amparo suits where the constitutionality of a statute is at stake. Both attributions allow the Supreme Court to give final interpretation of the Constitution in a uniform way[72].

---

72 See Joaquín BRAGE CAMAZANO, *La jurisdicción constitucional de la libertad (Teoría general, Argentina, México, Corte Interamericana de Derechos Humanos)*, Editorial Porrúa, Instituto Mexicano de Derecho Procesal Constitucional, México 2005, pp. 153-155.

THE CIVIL RIGHTS INJUNCTION FOR
THE PROTECTIONOF FUNDAMENTAL RIGHTS
THE LATIN AMERICAN «AMPARO» PROCEEDING
COURSE OF LECTURES 2006-2008,
de Allan R. Brewer-Carias
se imprimió en la República Argentina en febrero de 2021.

www.ingramcontent.com/pod-product-compliance
Lightning Source LLC
Chambersburg PA
CBHW031319230926
51848CB00001B/11
* 9 7 8 9 5 6 3 9 2 9 7 2 0 *